REVISITING THE VIETNAM WAR AND INTERNATIONAL LAW

This collection of scholarly and critical essays about the legal aspects of the Vietnam War explores various crimes committed by the United States against North Vietnam: war of aggression; war crimes in bombing civilian targets such as schools and hospitals and using napalm, cluster bombs, and Agent Orange; crimes against humanity in moving large parts of the population to so-called strategic hamlets; and alleged genocide and ecocide.

International lawyer Richard Falk, who observed these acts personally in North Vietnam in 1968, uses international law to show how they came about. This book brings together essays he has written on the Vietnam War and on its relationship to international law, American foreign policy, and the global world order. Falk argues that only a stronger adherence to international law can save the world from future such tragedies and create a sustainable world order.

STEFAN ANDERSSON studied religion and philosophy at Lund University, Harvard Divinity School, the University of California at Berkeley, the University of Toronto, and McMaster University, where the Bertrand Russell Archives are located. In 1994, he defended his doctoral thesis in the philosophy of religion at Lund University; it was published as *In Quest of Certainty: Bertrand Russell's Search for Certainty in Religion and Mathematics up to "The Principles of Mathematics"* (1903). Andersson then turned to Russell's political activism and started a project about student protests against the Vietnam War and the Russell–Sartre Tribunal on the United States War Crimes in Viet Nam.

Revisiting the Vietnam War and International Law

VIEWS AND INTERPRETATIONS OF RICHARD FALK

Edited by

STEFAN ANDERSSON
University of Lund

CAMBRIDGE
UNIVERSITY PRESS

University Printing House, Cambridge CB2 8BS, United Kingdom

One Liberty Plaza, 20th Floor, New York, NY 10006, USA

477 Williamstown Road, Port Melbourne, VIC 3207, Australia

314–321, 3rd Floor, Plot 3, Splendor Forum, Jasola District Centre, New Delhi – 110025, India

79 Anson Road, #06-04/06, Singapore 079906

Cambridge University Press is part of the University of Cambridge.

It furthers the University's mission by disseminating knowledge in the pursuit of education, learning, and research at the highest international levels of excellence.

www.cambridge.org
Information on this title: www.cambridge.org/9781108419154
DOI: 10.1017/9781108297011

© Richard Falk and Stefan Andersson 2018

First published 2018

Printed in the United States of America by Sheridan Books, Inc.

A catalogue record for this publication is available from the British Library.

Library of Congress Cataloging-in-Publication Data

Names: Falk, Richard A., author. | Andersson, Stefan, editor.
Title: Revisiting the Vietnam war and international law / views and interpretations of Richard Falk ; edited by Stefan Andersson.
Description: Cambridge, United Kingdom ; New York, NY, USA : Cambridge University Press, 2017. | Includes bibliographical references and index.
Identifiers: LCCN 2017035935 | ISBN 9781108419154 (hardback)
Subjects: LCSH: Vietnam War, 1961-1975—Law and legislation.
Classification: LCC KZ6795.V54 F35 2017 | DDC 341.6/909597—dc23 LC record available at https://lccn.loc.gov/2017035935

ISBN 978-1-108-41915-4 Hardback

ISBN 978-1-108-40996-4 Paperback

All Members shall refrain in their international relations from the threat or use of force against the territorial integrity or political independence of any state, or in any other manner inconsistent with the Purposes of the United Nations.

Charter of the United Nations
Chapter I: Purposes and Principles, Article 2(4), 26 June 1945
(http://www.un.org/en/sections/un-charter/chapter-i/index.html)

Contents

Foreword

The Harmful Legacy of Lawlessness in Vietnam

Richard Falk

Forty years after the defeat of the United States in Vietnam, the central lessons of that war remain unlearned. Even worse, the mistakes made and crimes committed in Vietnam have been repeated at great human, material, and strategic cost in a variety of subsequent national settings. The central unlearned lesson in Vietnam is that the collapse of the European colonial order fundamentally changed the *effective* balance of power in a variety of North/South conflict situations that reduce the agency of military superiority in a variety of ways.

What makes this change elusive is that it reflected developments that fall outside the policy parameters influential in the leadership circles of most governments for a cluster of reasons. Most fundamentally, governmental geopolitical calculations relating to world order continue to be based on attributing a decisive causal influence to relative military capabilities, an understanding at the core of "realist" thinking and behavior. Within this paradigm, military superiority is regarded as the main driver of conflict resolution, and the winners in wars are thought to reflect the advantages of hard-power differentials. The efficiency and rewards of military conquest in the colonial era vindicated this kind of realist thinking. Europe with its dominant military technology was able to control the political life and exploit the resources of populous countries throughout Asia, Africa, and Latin America with a minimum of expenditure and casualties, encountering manageable resistance, while reaping the rewards of empire. The outcomes of World War I and II further vindicated the wider orbit of the realist way of thinking and acting, with military superiority based on technological innovation, quantitative measures, and doctrinal adaptation to new circumstances of conflict receiving most of the credit for achieving political victories.

The Vietnam War was a dramatic and radical challenge to the realist consensus on how the world works, continuing a pattern already evident in nationalist victories in several earlier colonial wars, which were won – against expectations – by anti-colonial forces. Despite these illuminating results of colonial wars after World War II, the American defeat in Vietnam came as a shock. The candid acknowledgment of this defeat has been twisted out of recognition to this day by the interpretive spins placed upon the Vietnam experience by the American political establishment. The main motive of such partisan thinking was to avoid discrediting reliance on military power in the conduct of American foreign policy and to overcome political reluctance in the American public to fund high levels of military spending. Until the deceptive military victory in the First Gulf War of 1991, the policy community in the United States bemoaned what it described as "the Vietnam Syndrome," which was a shorthand designation for the supposedly unfortunate antipathy among the American citizenry to uses of hard power by the United States to uphold American geopolitical primacy throughout the world.

The quick and decisive desert victory against the imprudently exposed Iraqi armed forces massed on the desert frontier compelled Iraq to withdraw from Kuwait, which it had recently conquered and annexed. This result of war making was construed to vindicate and thus restore realist confidence in American war making as a crucial instrument of world order. On closer examination, this enthusiasm for war generated by the almost costless victory in the desert terrain of the First Gulf War involved a category mistake on the part of American leaders, or so it seems. It confused the continuing relevance of military capabilities in conventional war encounters between sovereign states with the declining utility of military supremacy in wars of intervention or counterinsurgency wars, that is, violent conflicts between a foreign adversary and a national resistance movement. It should have been clear to expert commentators that the Vietnam War was an example of a massive foreign intervention being defeated by a skillfully mobilized and efficiently led national movement, and in this respect totally different from the First Gulf War with respect to terrain of battle and what was at stake politically for the two sides.

Comprehending why the United States not only mishandled the war in Vietnam but also misconstrued its result is associated with earlier unlearned lessons that involved a misinterpretation of the lost colonial wars, most relevantly, the French defeat in the Indochina War despite the long and deep French presence. In retrospect it was evident to all that the French had failed to grasp the extraordinary resolve that informed the nationalist motivations of the Vietnamese that more than compensated for their military weaknesses, empowering Vietnamese society to endure severe and prolonged suffering to achieve eventual political independence and national sovereignty, and the accompanying collective sense of national pride. Under the inspirational leadership of Mohandas Gandhi, India achieved independence and recovered sovereignty through a militant nonviolent struggle that by heroic perseverance overcame the grim and unscrupulous determination of 10 Downing Street to retain "the jewel" in the crown of the British Empire whatever the costs of doing so might turn out to be. Whether articulated as the rise of "soft power" or explained by reference to the imbalance between imperial commitments and nationalist perseverance plus local knowledge, the storyline is the same. The intervening foreign or alien power has lower stakes in such struggles than does an indigenous population effectively mobilized as a movement of national resistance. Colonial powers were slow to recognize that moral and political resistance to their presence was growing more formidable as the ideology of nationalism spread around the world. Resistance became more credible and withstood a series of prodigious colonial efforts to retain control over colonized peoples, but as these struggles proceeded the former colonial overlords were at varying stages forced to recalculate their interests, and mostly decided that it was better to give up their colonial claims and withdraw militarily than further commit to what had become a lost cause.

We can also interpret this historical turn as reflecting the disparities between the political will of a people fighting for self-determination and a foreign government linked to private-sector interests that are trying to retain the benefits of control over a distant country for the sake of resources, prestige, settler pressures, geopolitical rivalry, or a combination of these factors. From the end of World War II onward, this imbalance of political wills seems to offer the best explanation of the outcome of colonial wars or military interventions in counterinsurgency struggles. In this regard, the French defeat in Indochina should have delivered a cautionary message to the Americans. In fairness, it should be pointed out that the French themselves did not learn much from their Indochina defeat, going on to wage and lose an even more damaging colonial war in Algeria eight years later. The noted French journalist Bernard Fall tried hard to warn the Americans of the great difficulty of achieving a reversal of the French experience in its Indochina War.[1] The French had higher-than-normal stakes in Indochina. It was to a significant extent "a settler colonial" state, meaning that the French human and cultural presence had sunk deep roots that raised the stakes of withdrawal for France, an experience repeated on a larger scale in Algeria, but producing the same outcome but

---

[1] See Bernard Fall, *Street Without Joy: The French Debacle in Indochina* (Mechanicsburg, PA: Stackpole Books, 1961).

only after inflicting massive suffering on the native population. The American intervention in Vietnam was primarily motivated by the ideological rivalry of the Cold War, and did not have the high level of material and human interests that led the French to fight so hard to crush the Vietnamese and Algerian challenges to their colonial rule.

The "settler colonial" situation of Algeria and, even more so, South Africa and Israel complicate the overall analysis. In the event of settler control of the colonial state, the issue of foreign or alien rule becomes blurred, and the question of the identity of "the nation" is itself contested in ways that are very different from the situation of a colonial administration governing on behalf of a European home country or metropole without any pretension of belonging to the occupied nation as if it was one's own. Each situation has its own originality. Jews in Israel who claim a biblical and ancestral mandate, and lack a default homeland option in a distinct territory, possess an intense political will to preserve their control of Palestine. The indigenous Arab population of Palestine also has a near-absolute will to resist dispossession from their native lands, and are unwelcome elsewhere in the region, having experienced vulnerability to changes in local circumstances and discrimination in neighboring Arab countries. For this reason, as reinforced by the special relationship of Israel with the United States, the Palestinians are waging an uphill battle in which their supposedly inalienable rights of self-determination have been for decades squeezed almost beyond recognition.[2]

Against this background, American reasoning about the Vietnam War displayed what later would be called "the arrogance of power," that is, the blind faith in the efficacy of its hard-power superiority in conflict situations, whether nuclear, conventional, or counterinsurgent.[3] The United States emerged from World War II as the dominant geopolitical actor in the world, having turned the tide of battle against Germany and Japan, as well as developing and using its monopoly over the ultimate weapon against Japan at the end of the Pacific war by dropping atomic bombs on Japanese cities. If Germany and Japan could not resist the American juggernaut, who could expect a country that Lyndon Johnson and Henry Kissinger called "a fourth-rate Asian power" to

---

[2] For a range of views, see Jeremy R. Hammond, *Obstacle to Peace: The US Role in the Israeli–Palestinian Conflict* (Cross Village, MI: Worldview Publications, 2016); Rashid Khalidi, *Brokers of Deceit: How the US Has Undermined Peace in the Middle East* (Boston: Beacon Press, 2013); Peter Bauck and Mohammed Omer, eds., *The Oslo Accords, 1993–2013* (Cairo: American University in Cairo Press, 2013). For the US/Israeli spin on the peace process, see Dennis Ross, *The Missing Peace: The Inside Story of the Fight for Middle East Peace* (New York: Farrar, Strauss & Giroux, 2004).

[3] J. William Fulbright, *The Arrogance of Power* (New York: Random House, 1966).

resist and repel the American military machine? In the end, it was the greater Vietnamese will to persevere and their cultural resilience that overcame American firepower, as well as the unsurpassed anti-colonial *legitimacy* of the Vietnamese struggle, which contributed to the rise of a robust worldwide anti-war movement of solidarity, including within the United States. By the mid-1960s it had become increasingly evident that the side that won the legitimacy war would prevail politically, even if compelled to endure devastating losses on the battlefield and throughout the country.[4]

The most serious blind spot of the realist paradigm is its inability to take account of its weaknesses with respect to legitimacy as a dimension of political life. This became manifest in the Vietnam setting. The American claims with respect to its presence in Vietnam were essentially ideological and geopolitical: the importance of avoiding the spread of communism and thus containing the expansionist challenge being allegedly mounted by the Soviet Union and China. In opposition to such reasoning were the historically more influential claims in support of nationalism and the right of self-determination, especially in contexts involving struggles of a colonized people against their colonial masters. Vietnamese legitimacy claims with respect to the United States were further validated by the flagrant disregard of international law constraints and the impact of this disregard on world public opinion, which contributed to mounting American domestic opposition to continuing the war.[5]

This collection of essays, written in support of the relevance of international law to the shaping of American foreign policy during the Vietnam era, remains instructive as the twenty-first century unfolds. The United States has continued to pursue a dubious diplomacy punctuated by military interventions in distant countries, fighting a series of losing counterinsurgency wars after Vietnam, remaining unresponsive to the constraints on recourse to war and war fighting embodied in international law and the UN Charter. The realist consensus, regarding law and morality as dispensable and marginal impediments to sustaining geopolitical effectiveness in world politics, continues to govern the policymaking entourage that shapes war/peace decisions, and has produced a string of costly defeats (especially, Afghanistan and Iraq) as well as badly damaging the United States' reputation as a global leader, which in the end depends far more on its legitimacy credentials than on its battlefield

---

[4]   As argued in Richard Falk, *Palestine: The Legitimacy of Hope* (Washington, DC: Just World Books, 2014).

[5]   Clergy and Laymen Concerned About Vietnam, *In the Name of America: The Conduct of the War in Vietnam by the Armed Forces of the United States as Shown by Published Reports: Compared with the Laws of War Binding on the United States Government and on Its Citizens*, director of research, Seymour Melman (Annandale, VA: Turnpike Press, 1968).

prowess, but suffers most when it both loses on the battlefield and should further lose if law and morality are taken into account. It is the contention of these essays that adherence to international law is vital for world peace and in the national interest of all countries on all occasions, and this includes the United States.

So-called American exceptionalism operates as a free pass in Washington to disregard the rules applicable to other sovereign states but, as the recent history of international conflicts reveals, it does no favors to the United States or its people, although it may further the careers of diplomats and enhance the profits of special interests. Further, it seems evident that the continuing exercise of discretion to ignore legal constraints on the use of international force will be accompanied by repeated disappointments in the conduct of foreign policy for this most mighty country in all of world history and will also continue to erode its legitimacy credentials.

The 9/11 attacks gave the United States a chance to start over, undertaking a response to mega-terrorism within the framework of the rule of law that would have been a great contribution to building up the global rule of law and charting a new path toward sustainable global governance. Instead, a "war on terror" was immediately launched, which amounted to a declaration of permanent warfare, undermining the authority of international law and the UN, and perversely leading to the spread and intensification of terrorist activities. The defaming scandals of Guantanamo, Abu Ghraib, and "enhanced interrogation" together with the failure to prosecute those responsible for authorizing and perpetrating "torture" during the presidency of George W. Bush confirm the deeply entrenched refusal of the US government to self-enforce minimum standards of international criminal accountability, and its obvious endorsement of a flawed international criminal law regime that currently rests on the major premise of *geopolitical impunity* as interpreted by way of American exceptionalism. The emergence of ISIS, as had been prefigured in Afghanistan by the rise of Al Qaeda and occasioned by American occupation policies in Iraq, is the ultimate blowback experience betokening an erroneous hard-power opportunism in Washington misleadingly chosen as the best approach to national and global security.

The essays in the volume also explore the failure to abide by the experience after World War II, which included imposing criminal accountability on those surviving German and Japanese military and political leaders responsible for the commission of state crime centering on the recourse to and prosecution of aggressive warfare, as well as the mass atrocities epitomized by the death camps. By now it is confirmed that the Nuremberg and Tokyo Judgments, although respectful of defendants' rights and substantively justified, were in a larger sense "victors' justice" by exempting the crimes of the winners from legal scrutiny.[6] The principles of law applied to the losers at Nuremberg and Tokyo were never intended to be applied to the winners, or to those who would after 1945 control the geopolitical dimensions of world politics and dominate its various episodes of warfare.[7] Criminal accountability in relation to warfare was cynically applied to the losers and those in subordinate positions of state power throughout the world, and still is.

Into this normative vacuum stepped the rising activism of civil society, and this became initially disclosed as part of the rising opposition to the Vietnam War. The great British philosopher and political activist, Bertrand Russell, convened a tribunal of conscience composed of moral and cultural author-ity figures with international stature to gather the best evidence available of American criminality in the ongoing Vietnam War. This bold initiative filled the institutional vacuum created by the lack of political will among governments or at the UN to carry forward the Nuremberg impulse with respect to accountability of individuals.[8] In effect, the project of imposing criminal accountability on the strong has become an exclusive undertaking of global civil society, although with some collaboration from moderate gov-ernments that do not enjoy the status of being geopolitical actors. It was this transnational collaboration between governments and civil society actors that generated the momentum leading to the unexpected establishment of the International Criminal Court in 2002, but as yet this institution has given little indication that it possesses the capacity or even the mandate to extend the logic of accountability to geopolitical actors, above all the United States and its closest friends.

Reviewing the international law debates that took place during the Vietnam War remains critically relevant to any reform of American foreign policy relat-ing to these war/peace issues. As in Vietnam, adherence to international law would have been consistently beneficial normatively (upholding law, protect-ing the vulnerable, avoiding casualties), geopolitically (respecting support for

[6] An important early account along these lines in the Japanese context is Richard H. Minear, *Victors' Justice: The Tokyo War Crimes Tribunal* (Princeton: Princeton University Press, 1971).

[7] Justice Robert Jackson, the American prosecutor, did argue to the tribunal in Nuremberg that the legitimacy of the judgment against the German defendants depended upon the victors in the future accepting the same framework of accountability, but such words fell on deaf ears in the capitals of the world powers.

[8] The proceedings of the Russell Tribunal can be found in John Duffett, ed., *Against the Crime of Silence: Proceedings of the Russell International War Crimes Tribunal, Stockholm–Copenhagen*, introduction by Bertrand Russell, foreword by Ralph Schoenman (New York: Bertrand Russell Peace Foundation and O'Hare Books, 1968).

the ethos of self-determination and human rights as evidenced by the flow of history since 1945), and ideologically (recognizing that "terrorism" is a law enforcement issue, not an occasion for war making; realizing that nationalist ideology does not translate into neighbors becoming "falling dominos").

The lesson that most needed to be learned in the Vietnam era, and remains unlearned forty years after the ending of war, is the practical and principled desirability of adherence to international law in war/peace situations. Systemic violations of international law lead to geopolitical disappointment, human suffering, societal devastation, and a nihilistic atmosphere of international lawlessness. In contrast, habits and policies of adherence to international law, especially with respect to war/peace issues and matters of national and global security, privilege an emphasis on diplomacy, international cooperation, law enforcement, and UN authority, as well as generating the self-confidence of political communities to be respectful of prudent restraint and develop greater reliance in pursuit of national goals on international procedures, norms, and institutions. Such a shift away from lawlessness is, of course, by no means a guaranty of peace and justice, but it provides the crucial foundation for creating better prospects for human wellbeing in the twenty-first century.

In my preoccupation during the years between 1963 and 1975 I became obsessed with the Vietnam War, and how I might act as a scholar and citizen to bring this imprudent, unlawful, and immoral war to an end. My writing in this period reflects a process of deepening engagement, and an evolving shift of focus and orientation. In my initial articles on the war I was seeking to demonstrate the unlawfulness of the underlying intervention in Vietnam, with a special emphasis on the American expansion of the war from a struggle for control of the state in what was then treated as "South Vietnam" to a conflict that included then "North Vietnam," which altered the nature of the war from an internal war in the South to a war between the two political communities that comprised Vietnam after the French defeat in 1954, and persisted until the American defeat in 1975. In the early selections represented here, the international law arguments were underpinned by a realist assessment that rested on the informed belief that this was an ill-considered commitment of US military forces for the sake of a very dubious conception of national interests, which centered on an imprudent opposition to the anti-colonial and pro-nationalist flow of history.

My attitudes toward the war, while never losing the central conviction that the United States was engaged in Vietnam in a manner that violated the most fundamental norms of international law, shifted in the direction of viewing the tactical conduct of the war as increasingly raising questions of international criminal accountability. This shift is reflected in the later selections from my writing that emphasize the relevance of the Nuremberg Principles to the American involvement in Vietnam.[9] I became convinced that a one-sided war in which high-technology weaponry was deployed against a totally vulnerable peasant society was an intrinsically criminal enterprise, and additionally almost inevitably gave rise to battlefield atrocities as mythified through treating the My Lai massacre as a singular event.[10] I was also struck by the degree to which the geopolitical status of the United States marginalized the United Nations and limited the relevance of international law to a domestic debate within the United States between the government and its critics in Congress and throughout American society.

One enduring effect of this debate was to give the American anti-war movement the confidence to challenge government policy despite the inhibitions of the Cold War that made any seeming sympathy for the communist side in the Vietnamese struggle grounds for suspicion and media hostility, particularly in the early years of the war. It is only toward the end of the Vietnam War when the government had lost the trust of a large portion of the citizenry and split the foreign policy establishment, as well as its becoming clear that the sacrifice of young American lives was not going to end in a military victory, that the prudential arguments against continuing the war began to outweigh the ideological case for its prosecution. This development also had the effect of pushing public opinion in an anti-war direction.[11]

---

[9] These issues were fully explored in Richard Falk, Gabriel Kolko, and Robert Jay Lifton, eds., *Crimes of War: A Legal, Political-Documentary, and Psychological Inquiry into the Responsibility of Leaders, Citizens, and Soldiers* (New York: Random House, 1971).

[10] For the initial exposé, see Seymour M. Hersh, *My Lai 4: A Report on the Massacre and Its Aftermath* (New York: Random House, 1970). See also Kendrick Oliver, *The My Lai Massacre in American History and Memory* (Manchester, UK: Manchester University Press, 2006).

[11] The release of the Pentagon Papers was a milestone along the path that led from a pro-war consensus to a rising tide of opposition. See interpretation by Daniel Ellsberg, *Secrets: A Memoir of Vietnam and the Pentagon Papers* (New York: Penguin Books, 2002).

Preface

When I contacted Richard Falk six years ago regarding a collection of his writings on the Vietnam War and international law, I did not know that he had a special relationship to Sweden. He had been invited by Peter Wallensteen who – from 1985 to 2012 – was Dag Hammarskjöld Professor of Peace and Conflict Research at Uppsala University to be Visiting Olof Palme Professor[12] for the academic year 1990–91, which, according to Professor Wallensteen, turned out to be a very successful appointment, not least for the doctoral students and the young researchers.[13]

According to Said Mahmoudi, who is now Professor of International Law at Stockholm University, Falk became a good friend and participated in the academic as well as the general cultural and political discussion in Sweden. Professor Mahmoudi responded to an e-mail regarding Falk's status as an international law scholar in Sweden and wrote that Falk

> held several important seminars and lectures during his stay in Stockholm. His time here coincided with the American invasion of Kuwait to push back Saddam Hussein. He gave a talk on the subject, which was very well received. I don't think he is unknown in Sweden. He published several important articles in DN [*Dagens Nyheter*] at that time. Among those Swedes who deal with international law, international relations and political science, he is a very well-known scholar. Even internationally, he is respected as one of the

---

[12] Regarding the Olof Palme Visiting Professorship: The *Swedish Research Council* visiting professor grant aims to allow universities the possibility of recruiting an internationally distinguished professor for a shorter period to develop a specific research area. The Olof Palme Visiting Professorship gives an internationally prominent foreign researcher the opportunity to spend one year at a university, higher education institute or research institute in Sweden. The Olof Palme Visiting Professorship was established in honour of Olof Palme (1927–86), Sweden's prime minister in 1969–76 and 1982–86.

[13] Personal communication (e-mail), December 22, 2016.

most leading living American international lawyers. He was a student and friend of the famous Yale international law professor Myers S. McDougal, but one of the very few who took a critical approach to the dominant power-inspired American policy in the world.[14]

A testimony of the appreciation of Falk's merits is that he was awarded an honorary doctorate from the Faculty of Law at Stockholm University in 2006.

However, Falk's contacts with Sweden go further back. Already in 1985 he had been consulted and thanked by Ann-Sofie Nilsson, who spent that year as a Visiting Fellow at the Center of International Studies at Princeton University, for his "valuable suggestions" to her doctoral thesis "Political Uses of International Law" in political science at the University of Lund in 1987.

The year after, in 1986, Falk attended a conference in Ronneby, Sweden. It was a so-called Yes-conference to follow up on the positive answers of the Great Peace Journey 1985–87, where Elisabeth Gerle was one of the main organizers. Elisabeth became Visting Scholar at the Center of International Studies at Princeton University and a life companion to Richard Falk for many years. Elisabeth Gerle presented her doctoral thesis in ethics at the Theological Faculty in Lund in 1995. The title is "In Search of a Global Ethics: Theological, Political, and Feminist Perspectives Based on a Critical Analysis of JPIC and WOMP." The second acronym stands for World Order Models Project, which has engaged Professor Falk since its beginning in the 1960s; he has published a number of important books in what Gerle calls a "transnational, humanistic, scholarly project to study 'preferred worlds' with a basically academic framework."[15] In her Preface, she writes, "His involvement with the Great Peace Journey built the bridge to Princeton and New York and to many other parts of the world. His encouragement of new visions in relation to politics and his continuous inspiration during classes in World Order Studies, seminars and endless discussions and shared explorations about the prospects for global ethics and its relationship to spiritual and religious imagery [have] been invaluable."[16]

The motivating force behind Falk's activities both as an academic and as a political activist is the deep conviction that a just world order can be achieved only if nation-states respect international laws. This includes environmental laws, and he never tires of pointing out that the use of nuclear weapons, which he considers unlawful, threatens life on this planet and must

---

[14] Personal communication (e-mail), December 17, 2016.
[15] See chapter III of Gerle's thesis, 128–97.
[16] *Ibid.*, 8.

be prevented. This warning has gained extra relevance since both Vladimir Putin and Donald Trump have announced their plans to update their nuclear capabilities.

There is a strong normative and philosophical dimension to all of Falk's writings, which is pointed out in the Introduction to *The Philosophy of International Law* by its editors Samantha Besson and John Tasioulas, who write: "it is possible to adopt a self-critical normative approach to international law without drawing on anything recognizable as a tradition of *philosophical* thought. The writings of the New Haven School, and especially those of its most influential contemporary representative, Richard Falk, offer ample testimony of the potential value of such an approach."[17]

Richard Falk is primarily known as an international law scholar and lawyer, particularly in the field of humanitarian law, but his writings are relevant to several other topics in the social sciences, such as international relations, human rights and – not least – peace and conflict studies. His wide range of knowledge and interests reflects his broad educational and professional background. He obtained a Bachelor of Science in Economics from the Wharton School, University of Pennsylvania, in 1952 before completing a Bachelor of Laws degree at Yale University. He received his Doctorate in Law (SJD) from Harvard University in 1962. His early thinking was influenced by readings of Albert Camus, Jean-Paul Sartre and C. Wright Mills, and he developed an overriding concern with projects to abolish war and aggression as social institutions, but also, in coordination, to address problems of social injustice, and later ecological sustainability. Falk began his teaching career at Ohio State University, during which time he completed his doctoral studies in law and philosophy at Harvard, providing occasion for the expression of his progressive beliefs in the late 1950s. He moved to Princeton University in 1961, which became his academic home. He is the Albert G. Milbank Professor of International Law and Practice Emeritus at Princeton University where he taught for forty years.[18] He is the Senior Vice President of the Nuclear Age Peace Foundation and a member of the board of the Just World Education Foundation. Since 2002 he has been a research professor at the Orfalea Center for Global International Studies at the University of California, Santa Barbara.

---

[17] (Oxford: Oxford University Press, 2010), 4.
[18] See Martin Griffiths, *Fifty Key Thinkers in International Relations* (London: Routledge, 1999), 119–24. For some hard-to-understand reason the entry on Richard Falk was removed by the editors of the second edition, published ten years later. This is surprising given the relevance of international law to the study of international relations, the volume and quality of Falk's writings and the importance of his message regarding respect for international law and the establishment of a stable world order.

He has been an influential international law expert since the late 1950s. As editor and one of the main contributors (twelve articles) to the four volumes of *The Vietnam War and International Law* (Princeton: Princeton University Press, 1968, 1969, 1972, 1976), he became a principal advocate of applying international law to American foreign policy. Much of his scholarly career was devoted to the promotion of a just and peaceful world order. He was among the most influential critics of United States warfare in Indochina. He has written extensively about the Vietnam War from legal, moral and political points of view.

The four volumes of *The Vietnam War and International Law* mainly consist of articles by and for specialists in the international law of war and international humanitarian law, the branch of international law that governs armed conflict between nation-states (law of armed conflict, LOAC). The purpose of LOAC is to prohibit and punish certain categories of conduct commonly viewed as gross and systematic violations and to make perpetrators of such conduct criminally accountable for their perpetration. The core crimes in international law are war crimes, crimes against humanity, genocide, and the crime of aggression, which still has not produced a legal definition acceptable to the International Criminal Court, which is situated in The Hague and began operation in July 2002.

Another book, *Crimes of War: A Legal, Political-Documentary, and Psychological Inquiry into the Responsibility of Leaders, Citizens, and Soldiers for Criminal Acts in Wars* (New York: Random House, 1971), which Falk edited with Gabriel Kolko and Robert Jay Lifton, had a broader audience in mind, but it contains most of the relevant legal documents.

Falk recognized from an early stage the importance of the Russell Tribunal as an attempt to uphold the Nuremberg Principles,[19] when very few international law experts were willing to give such a juridical innovation any credibility, and when international institutions had turned their backs on the criminality of the war.[20] He worked closely with a member of the Italian

[19] The Nuremberg Principles are a set of guidelines for determining what constitutes a war crime. The document was created by the International Law Commission of the United Nations to codify the legal principles underlying the Nuremberg Trials (1945–46) of Nazi Party members following World War II.
[20] There were other Commissions of Inquiry with which Falk cooperated. See the Prefaces to the first and second editions of Consultative Council Lawyers Committee on American Policy Towards Vietnam, John H. E. Fried, rapporteur, *Vietnam and International Law: The Illegality of United States Military Involvement* (Flanders, NJ: O'Hare Books, 1967), 7–9, 11–13. Falk wrote the preface to the 1990 edition: "Vietnam and International Law: The Past Recalled and the Future Challenged" (ix–xvii); and for Clergy and Laymen Concerned About Vietnam, *In the Name of America: The Conduct of the War in Vietnam by the Armed Forces of the United States as Shown by Published Reports Compared with the Laws of War Binding on the United*

parliament and leading lawyer, Lelio Basso, who himself was a member of the International War Crimes Tribunal and the principal founder of the Permanent Peoples' Tribunal.[21] Falk also had an important role in the War Crimes Tribunal on Iraq (2005).[22] He recently completed a six-year term as UN Special Rapporteur on Human Rights in Occupied Palestine.

The idea for a book with Professor Falk's writings on the Vietnam War grew naturally out of my work on the Russell Tribunal.[23] I found the four volumes of *The Vietnam War and International Law* in Mills Memorial Library at McMaster University in Hamilton in Canada, where the Bertrand Russell Archives are located, on one of my first searches for references to the Russell Tribunal. I looked in the index of volume I and found one. I looked up the page and read:

> Also for the first time since World War II there has been proposed a war crime tribunal to pass judgment on the United States role in Viet Nam and on the criminal responsibility of its President. Of course, Bertrand Russell's tribunal is a juridical farce, but the fact that it is plausible to contemplate such a proceeding and to obtain for its tribunal several celebrated individuals bears witness to the general perception of the war.[24]

States Government and on Its Citizens (Annandale, VA: Turnpike Press, 1968), he supplied an essay, "International Law and the Conduct of the Vietnam War" (22–27). He also wrote the introduction to *The Wasted Nations*, report of the International Commission of Enquiry into United States Crimes in Indochina, June 20–25, 1971, edited by Frank Browning [and] Dorothy Forman (New York: Harper Colophon Books, 1972), xi–xx. As a major critic of the United States war in Indochina, he became the target of those who supported it and thought it was conducted according to the rules of international law. See e.g. Telford Taylor, *Nuremberg and Vietnam: An American Tragedy* (New York: Bantam Books, 1971), Guenter Lewy, *America in Vietnam* (New York: Oxford University Press, 1978), and Norman Podhoretz, *Why We Were in Vietnam* (New York: Simon & Schuster, 1982).

[21] See Richard Falk, "Keeping Nuremberg Alive," in Giuliano Amato, et al., eds., *Homage to Lelio Basso* (Milan: Franco Angeli Editore, 1979), 811–20 (reprinted in *Human Rights and State Sovereignty* [New York: Holmes & Meier, 1981], ch. 8, 195–201, and in Richard Falk, Friedrich Kratochwil and Saul H. Mendlovitz, eds., *International Law: A Contemporary Perspective* [Boulder and London: Westview Press, 1985], 494–501).

[22] See Richard Falk, "The Role of Global Civil Society Tribunals, in Richard Falk, Irene Gendzier, and Robert Jay Lifton, eds., *Crimes of War – Iraq* (New York: Nation Books, 2006), 153–54.

[23] See Stefan Andersson, "A Secondary Bibliography of the International War Crimes Tribunal," *russell: The Journal of Bertrand Russell Studies*, NS 31, 2 (Winter 2011–12), 167–87, and Review Essay, "Behind the Scenes at the BRPF (Bertrand Russell Peace Foundation), the Vietnam Solidarity Campaign, and the Russell Tribunal" (a review of Ernest Tate, *Revolutionary Activism in the 1950s and 60s: A Memoir*), *russell: The Journal of Bertrand Russell Studies*, NS 34, 2 (Winter 2014–15), 75–83.

[24] Richard Falk, *The Vietnam War and International Law*, Vol. I (Princeton: Princeton University Press, 1968), 451, n. 12.

What especially caught my attention was that Falk referred to the Russell Tribunal as "a juridical farce," although the passage as a whole is quite positive. The article was written in 1966 and I later realized that Falk could have read some of the rumors that the Tribunal would condemn President Lyndon Johnson, Secretary of Defense Robert McNamara, Secretary of State Dean Rusk and General William Westmoreland as war criminals. These rumors were based on statements emanating from Russell himself, his secretary Ralph Schoenman and some individuals who had been asked to be members of the Tribunal.

By the time the Tribunal held its founding session in London from November 13 to 16, 1966, it had officially dropped the idea of prosecuting individuals and preferred to be treated as a Commission of Inquiry investigating possible war crimes committed by the United States in Vietnam. This shift of emphasis was mainly the result of ideas by the French branch of the Tribunal with Jean-Paul Sartre, Simone de Beauvoir, Vladimir Dedijer and Laurent Schwarz as the dominant figures. It could, of course, still be considered a "juridical farce" for several formal reasons, not least because it lacked the power and authority to punish anyone. Such enforcement was never a major goal of the undertaking; the most important purpose of the Tribunal was to "prevent the crime of silence" by showing the world what the United States was doing in Vietnam and letting its citizens respond as the ultimate judges of right and wrong in world politics.

In 2002 Arthur and Judith Klinghoffer published *International Citizens' Tribunals: Mobilizing Public Opinion to Advance Human Rights*[25] in which they quoted Falk's phrase "a juridical farce" out of context. This was disturbing as it gave a distorted picture of Falk's opinion. The Klinghoffers say:

> Richard Falk was at the time the chairman of the Consultative Council of the Lawyers' Committee on American Policy Toward Vietnam, an organization that denounced the United States for legal violations. However, his two-volume study of International Law and the Vietnam War labelled the hearings "a juridical farce."[26]

The Klinghoffers should have referred to Falk's views in their proper context, which would have given a quite different impression of his views.

I contacted Professor Falk and suggested my idea of publishing a book of his writings on the Vietnam War and international law. He reacted very positively.

---

[25] See my review in *russell: The Journal of Bertrand Russell Studies*, NS 22, 1 (Summer 2002), 83–89.
[26] (New York: Palgrave, 2002), 134.

Not long after that I met him, when he came to McMaster University to deliver the 2011 Gandhi Lecture, and we found out that we had more in common than just a great respect for Russell's commitment to peace and a just world order.

In one of his articles from 1975 Falk puts the Russell Tribunal into its historical context:

> In the years since the Nuremberg judgment of 1945, no official attempt has been made to apply the Nuremberg Principles to the concrete circumstances of violent conflict. An unofficial and symbolic application of the Nuremberg idea underlay the proceedings of the Bertrand Russell War Crimes Tribunal held in 1967 in two Scandinavian countries. The proceedings of the tribunal depict accurately the basic pattern of combat violations of the laws of war characteristic of the early years of heavy American involvement in Vietnam. Aside from this single controversial incident, there has been no effort by governments, international institutions, or public opinion to take seriously the justly celebrated American pledge at Nuremberg of the chief prosecutor for the United States, Justice Robert H. Jackson: "If certain acts in violation of treaties are crimes, they are crimes whether the United States does them or whether Germany does them, and we are not prepared to lay down a rule of criminal conduct against others which we would not be willing to have invoked against us."[27]

Falk was also one of the first to depict the crime of "ecocide." He says that he was influenced by the research of Arthur Westing and E. W. Pfeiffer, published in *Scientific American*, which described the tactics and effects of this highly destructive recourse to environmental warfare. The extensive use of Agent Orange by the United States caused much human suffering, and Vietnamese children continue to be born with genetic defects that can be traced back to this toxic herbicide. In spite of the promises given by President Nixon and the US government in the Paris Peace Accords of January 27, 1973, to compensate the Vietnamese for the suffering caused by the poison, not a penny was delivered during Nixon's administration or by subsequent US governments.[28]

---

[27] See Richard Falk, "A Nuremberg Perspective on the Trial of Karl Armstrong," in Richard Falk, *A Global Approach to National Policy* (Cambridge, MA: Harvard University Press, 1975), 133. The whole article is republished in this book as Chapter 10.

[28] See VAORRC (Vietnam Agent Orange Relief & Responsibility Campaign), Vietnam, www.vn-agentorange.org. Strangely enough, Vietnam Veterans have been more successful in receiving financial compensation for their suffering caused by Agent Orange. See www.benefits.va.gov/compensation/claims-postservice-agent_orange-settlement-settlementFund.asp.

It was at the Russell Tribunal that the crime of genocide[29] was brought up for the first time and its commission alleged and controversially documented. In 1946, the first session of the United Nations General Assembly adopted a resolution that "affirmed" that genocide was a crime under international law, but did not provide a legal definition of the crime. In 1948, the UN General Assembly adopted the Convention on the Prevention and Punishment of the Crime of Genocide (CPPCG), which defined the crime of genocide for the first time. Jean-Paul Sartre brought up the question of genocide at the second session of the Russell Tribunal: "Is the United States Government guilty of genocide against the people of Vietnam?" The question was unanimously answered with a "Yes" by the Russell Tribunal members.[30]

But why a book now with Falk's writings about the Vietnam War, more than forty years after the end of the war and despite the occurrence of several other similar counterinsurgency wars in between in which the United States has participated? One reason is that the American government in 2012 launched the commemoration of the fiftieth anniversary of the Vietnam War (the war started in 1965 according to the US government), the purpose of which is to try to control the historical narrative of the war and portray this failed military undertaking as a noble cause. President Barack Obama's inaugural speech in 2012, delivered at the Memorial Wall in Washington on Memorial Day to a small gathering of war veterans and their families, was an attempt to engage in such unfortunate revisionism, which needs to be revealed as deceitful rhetoric that distorts a historical and human tragedy, as well as a geopolitical disaster.

[29] The Bosnian International Court of Justice case addresses the genocide issue more authoritatively than other tribunals. The ad hoc international criminal tribunals for both the former Yugoslavia and Rwanda have extended discussions of genocide.

[30] John Duffett, ed., *Against the Crime of Silence: Proceedings of the Russell International War Crimes Tribunal, Stockholm–Copenhagen*, introduction by Bertrand Russell, foreword by Ralph Schoenman (New York: Bertrand Russell Peace Foundation and O'Hare Books, 1968); John Duffett, ed., *Against the Crime of Silence: Proceedings of the International War Crimes Tribunal, Stockholm, Copenhagen*, introduction by Bertrand Russell, preface by Noam Chomsky, expanded foreword by Ralph Schoenman (New York: Simon & Schuster, 1970); and *Prevent the Crime of Silence: Reports from the Sessions of the International War Crimes Tribunal founded by Bertrand Russell*, selected and edited by Peter Limqueco and Peter Weiss (London: Allen Lane, Penguin Press, 1971), with a Foreword and essay "After Pinkville" by Noam Chomsky. See also Anthony D'Amato, *International Law and Political Reality* (The Hague: Kluwer Law International, 1995), ch. 1, "The War-Crimes Defense," where he brings up both Falk's views and the Russell Tribunal.

It was not a lengthy speech, but it reveals the president's attempts to hide the truth about the first major war that the United States has lost. Here is only one example:[31]

> one of the most painful chapters in our history was Vietnam – most particularly, how we treated our troops who served there. You were often blamed for a war you didn't start, when you should have been commended for serving your country with valor. (Applause.) You were sometimes blamed for misdeeds of a few, when the honorable service of the many should have been praised. You came home and sometimes were denigrated, when you should have been celebrated. It was a national shame, a disgrace that should have never happened. And that's why here today we resolve that it will not happen again. (Applause.)

In the light of this misleading reconstruction of our sense of the Vietnam War by President Obama, it is important that we consider the views of others who were more in touch with the reality of what took place in Vietnam. President Obama says nothing about the criminal character of the American aggression and all the unjustified suffering it caused the Vietnamese people both in the North as well as in the South, and the peoples of Cambodia and Laos.

Falk, however, was prepared to speak truth to power at the time of the war. The wars in Afghanistan and Iraq indicate that the United States government has failed to heed the lessons of the Vietnam War; that its current behavior in the Middle East and elsewhere has produced several tragic repetitions of Vietnam; and that its militarist policies seem likely to lead to further disastrous wars, imposing terrible burdens on the victim societies and gravely damaging the United States' reputation as a constitutional democracy.

Falk argues in these selections that the only safe and reliable way to avoid future foreign policy disasters is through a consistent and principled adherence to international law in the conduct of American foreign policy. Such a

---

[31] The whole speech is available at www.whitehouse.gov/the-press-office/2012/05/28/remarks-president-commemoration-ceremony-50th-anniversary-vietnam-war. For a critical assessment of the project, see Bernard L. Stein, "How Pentagon Plans to Whitewash 50th Anniversary of Vietnam," forward.com/opinion/307223/how-pentagon-plans-to-whitewash-. See also Marvin Kalb and Deborah Kalb, *Haunting Legacy: Vietnam and the American Presidency from Ford to Obama* (Washington, DC: Brookings Institution Press, 2011), and Tom Hayden, *Hell No: The Forgotten Power of the Vietnam Peace Movement* (New Haven and London: Yale University Press, 2017), in which he talks about the "celebration" and particularly the content of the timeline that the organizers presented, which did not reflect what really happened particularly not with regard to all the different expressions of protests against the war. See Introduction, *ibid.*, pp. 1–17.

framework of legality is what the UN Charter tried to impose on the sovereign states of the world in 1945, but that framework has often been evaded and ignored and, if it is ever to be implemented, needs the strong support of public opinion.

The thirteen previously published writings included in this selection have been chosen from more than seventy published articles and chapters of books about the Vietnam War by Professor Falk from overlapping legal, moral and political perspectives.[32] The book's four parts parallel Falk's preoccupations with the Vietnam experience: first, the relevance of international law to foreign military intervention; secondly, examples of war crimes; thirdly, the bearing of the Nuremberg precedent on accountability for crimes of war; and, fourthly, the legacy and unlearned lessons of the Vietnam War. This final section bears most on current concerns of world order.

Considering the present situation in the world, the need for compassionate public intellectuals such as Bertrand Russell, Noam Chomsky and Richard Falk, who dare and care to speak truth to power, and not to be guilty of the crime of silence, is greater than ever. All three of them have been deeply involved in protesting American war crimes committed in Southeast Asia. As long as there are people like them, who care about the importance and upholding of international law and international morality, there is hope for establishing a more just world order and for bringing the war criminals to justice.

---

[32] The writings have been reproduced in a form as close as possible to their original publication, including language conventions that would be avoided today. Exceptions have been made to correct the small handful of minor errors that crept into the originals, and to provide full details for works in the footnotes, to enable readers to seek out sources should they choose to.

Acknowledgments

No man is an island and all scholars, regardless of which field of research they are devoted to, depend on the support of colleagues, librarians of different kinds and – in my case – the financial support of my parents Maj and Artur Andersson as long as they were alive; Dr. Margareta Norlin (a medical doctor) in whose beautiful apartment in Lund I've been living for the past few years; a very generous friend without whose financial support this book would not exist; two other friends with smaller contributions; and the Erik and Gurli Hultengren Foundation for Philosophy.

Most of the research for this collection of Richard Falk's writings on international law and the Vietnam War was done at the Bertrand Russell Research Centre and the Bertrand Russell Archives located in Mills Memorial Library at McMaster University in Hamilton, Canada,[33] which I visited for the first time forty-one years ago, when I was working on my doctoral thesis in the philosophy of religion about the British philosopher Bertrand Russell. This resulted in *In Quest of Certainty: Bertrand Russell's Search for Certainty in Religion and Mathematics up to "The Principles of Mathematics"* 1903 published by Almqvist & Wiksell International in 1994.

After that I changed focus of my studies and started to do research on Russell's International War Crimes Tribunal, which investigated the United States' warfare in Indochina in light of the Nuremberg principles and

---

[33] The student newspaper, *The Silhouette*, published an article about my part in the student occupation of McMaster University Student Center in the fall of 2011 and spring of 2012. See www.thesil.ca/talking-with-occupys-resident-russell-scholar. Among fellow occupiers I would particularly like to thank Ahmad, Alvand and Dorian for sharing the good feeling of being part of a student protest movement experiencing a breeze of the emotions that swept through the 1960s and early 1970s, when the main target of protest was the United States' warfare in Vietnam.

international law. That's how I very soon came across Professor Falk's writings on the Vietnam War and international law, but it wasn't until 2011 that I contacted him and suggested publishing a selection of his writings on the Vietnam War and international law, which you now hold in your hand.

I want to thank all the staff at the Bertrand Russell Research Centre: Nicholas Griffin, Andrew Bone, Arlene Duncan, Sheila Turcon and most of all Kenneth Blackwell, who is also the Honorary Archivist of the Bertrand Russell Archives. He has been of invaluable help for more than forty years and has also read and commented on the Introduction to this book.

Among the very helpful staff at the Ready Division of Archives and Research Collections, where the Bertrand Russell Archives are located, I would particularly like to mention Archivist Renu Barrett, whose friendship I've enjoyed since my first visit forty-one years ago, and Archives and Research Collections Librarian Rick Stapleton for his kindness and professionalism.

I would also like to thank the staff of the Lending Section at Mills Memorial Library who did everything they could to locate all of Richard Falk's published articles relating to the Vietnam War and international law in general.

In order to get a broad view of Falk's contributions to the fields of international law, international relations, human rights, peace and conflict studies and the social sciences in general, I have relied on the services of many libraries at Lund University and I would particularly like to extend my thanks to Librarian Per Carleheden at the LUX Library (handling books in the humanities and theology), who has dealt with my requests for Interlibrary loans, which are still free as long as the books can be found in one of the Nordic countries.

When this project was at the stage of looking for possible publishers, Richard Falk gave me a list of publishers and editors I could try. I first turned to a new publisher who was willing to publish the book if we could supply a substantial subsidy, which we couldn't. Mark Selden at Cornell University was, however, optimistic about finding a publisher and passed the suggestion on to John Berger at Cambridge University Press, the best publisher possible for a book like this. This turned out to be a stroke of good luck, and I would like to thank him and everyone else at the Press who has had a part in the production of the book: Claudia Bona-Cohen, Yamir Ashraf, the staff in the design department and particularly copy-editor Karen Anderson, whose professionalism has turned a far from perfect typescript into something almost platonic and with whom it has been a great pleasure to work. Finally I would like to thank Matt Sweeney, who took over as the content manager at the final stage of production.

I would also like to thank Noam Chomsky, who still gives lectures and interviews, teaches and – not least – responds to emails as part of his responsibilities as a "public intellectual,"[34] and Fredrik Logevall, who was born in Sweden, moved to Canada at the age of twelve and is now the Laurence D. Belfer Professor of International Affairs at the John F. Kennedy School of Government and Professor of History at Harvard, for having read and commented on my Introduction.

My final thanks go to Richard Falk himself, who has wholeheartedly supported this project ever since I first contacted him in 2011. He has inspired me to speed up the finishing of my own project about the International War Crimes Tribunal on American War Crimes in Vietnam, a.k.a. "the Russell Tribunal" or, in Europe, "the Russell–Sartre Tribunal," on which I've been working on and off for the last twenty years, and to start a new book project with his writings on nuclear war and international law.

My very final thanks go to my friend and colleague for many years, Curt Dahlgren, who was a professor in the Sociology of Religion at Lund University and a computer wizard. I don't know what I would have done without his help with turning scanned images into perfect Word documents. Thank you so much, Curt!

It is also my pleasure to acknowledge the permission to republish Richard Falk's articles and chapters from books: Princeton University, Center of International Studies, *Dissent, Yale Law Journal, Massachusetts Review, Toledo Law Review, American Journal of International Law, Columbia Journal of Transnational Law*, Harvard University Press and Howard Friel for letting us use a chapter from his and Richard Falk's book *The Record of the Paper: How the* New York Times *Misreports US Foreign Policy*, published by Verso, London.

---

[34] See the recently published Tim Madigan and Peter Stone, eds., *Bertrand Russell: Public Intellectual* (Rochester, NY: Tiger Bark Press, 2016), particularly the contributions by John Lenz, "How Bertrand Russell Became a New Kind of Intellectual During World War I"; Peter Stone, "Russell the Political Activist"; and David Blitz, "A Public Intellectual on War and Peace: Russell's 'Little Books' During the Great War and the Cold War." See also Noam Chomsky's now classic article, "The Responsibility of Intellectuals." It was first published as a special supplement by the *New York Review of Books* on February 23, 1967. Chomsky supplied a Foreword and an essay, "After Pinkville," to *Prevent the Crime of Silence: Reports from the Sessions of the International War Crimes Tribunal Founded by Bertrand Russell*, selected and edited by Peter Limqueco and Peter Weiss (London: Allen Lane, 1971). "After Pinkville" is about the My Lai (Son My) Massacre and was originally published in the *New York Review of Books*, 13, 12 (January 1, 1970), www.nybooks.com/articles/1970/01/01/after-pinkville/.

PART I

THE US ROLE IN VIETNAM
AND INTERNATIONAL LAW

"A Vietnam Settlement: The View from Hanoi," Princeton University, Center of International Studies, Policy Memorandum No. 34 (1968).

"US in Vietnam: Rationale and Law," *Dissent*, May–Jun. 1966, 275–84.

"International Law and the United States Role in the Viet Nam War," *Yale Law Journal*, 75, 7 (Jun. 1966), 1122–60.

"International Law and the United States Role in Viet Nam: A Response to Professor Moore," *Yale Law Journal*, 76, 6 (May 1967), 1095–1158.

"The Six Legal Dimensions of the Vietnam War," Princeton University, Center of International Studies, Research Monograph No. 34 (1968).

1

A Vietnam Settlement: The View from Hanoi

There are several reasons why I think it useful to circulate this memorandum concerning my visit to North Vietnam in June of 1968:

(1) To describe conversations with leaders of the North Vietnamese government and the National Liberation Front that shed some light on the distinction between "hard" and "soft" negotiating issues;

(2) To convey my central impression that the cumulative attitude of the North Vietnamese government toward the outcome of negotiations accords more closely with official American conditions for peace in Vietnam than has been generally understood in this country;

(3) To call attention to the fact that the North Vietnamese government thinks that it has already backed down from earlier negotiating demands, and seems prepared to take an especially conciliatory position on the central question of the reunification of Vietnam;

(4) To convey a sense of why I think the formation of the Alliance of National, Democratic, and Peace Forces is an important political development whether or not it is a front of the Front;

(5) To convey some impression of the human quality of the political leadership in Hanoi and of the destructive impact that American war policies have had upon North Vietnam;

(6) To report upon the degree to which there remains in North Vietnam an awareness and appreciation of America's own revolutionary tradition and an eventual hope for the establishment of normal diplomatic, economic, and cultural relations;

(7) To give some report on why the leaders of North Vietnam now feel that they were deceived by President Johnson's offer of peace negotiations on March 31, 1968.

This memorandum summarizes my impressions bearing on settling the Vietnam War. Although I have been convinced for some years that the American role in the Vietnam War has been misconceived and improper, I have tried to keep my opinions from shading my report of attitudes and conditions in North Vietnam. One can never be sure that preconceptions have not shaped perceptions, but I have certainly tried to adhere to the canons of objective reportage. The fact that what I report is at variance with what many Americans believe merely confirms my strong sense that it is important for as many of our citizens as possible to go to North Vietnam and see for themselves.

During the latter part of June I spent a week in North Vietnam, mostly in Hanoi, as the guest of the Vietnamese Association of Lawyers, the President of which is the Minister of Foreign Trade, Mr. Phan Arm. On the visit I was accompanied by Malcolm Burnstein, a lawyer in Oakland and a professor at San Francisco State College. In Hanoi we met with several leaders of the North Vietnamese government, including the Prime Minister, Mr. Pham Van Dong. In addition we had extended discussions with several prominent members of the National Liberation Front. The visit also provided an occasion to tour the bombed area around Phat Diem, a large village 100 miles or so south of Hanoi, and to meet with intellectuals, jurists, journalists, and other representative figures in North Vietnam. After leaving North Vietnam we came to Paris, where we had contact with the North Vietnamese delegation at the peace talks, including Xuan Thuy, and the DRV Ambassador to France, Mai Van Bo.

As an American in the "enemy" capital in time of war, many contradictory feelings of empathy and loyalty emerge. It is, perhaps, a unique feature of this war that American citizens can feel that they promote the national interest by better understanding the position and thinking of the North Vietnamese "adversary." I conceived of my visit in these terms, finding such a conception reciprocated in North Vietnam where we were both welcomed as guests and respected as Americans. Such a reception was a profoundly moving personal experience. It was moving partly because the suffering and devastation caused in North Vietnam by the United States is so pervasive and appalling. Almost every Vietnamese whom we met had sustained some very immediate family loss owing to the war, if not a death or maiming, then at least a prolonged separation from loved ones. A basic human reality in North Vietnam is separation, families torn asunder; at minimum, wives and children distributed over the countryside, quite often some part of a family living in complete isolation on the other side of the Seventeenth Parallel. The initial impression a visitor receives in North Vietnam is the human concreteness of the war's significance; even for the politically eminent in Hanoi, the war is not conceived primarily in abstract terms of ideology or geopolitics. A visitor to Hanoi finds no images of falling dominos.

Another impression – one that cannot be easily sensed at this distance – is the character and impact of warfare that follow from the awesome technological gap between the United States and North Vietnam. American air power is virtually unchallenged in North Vietnam except around the major cities. We spent a day in the town of Phat Diem, reported to us as having been bombed 406 times, and defended only by defense militia armed with single-bolt rifles. It is a difficult experience for an American to walk through the rubble of churches and convents at Phat Diem. To find a comparable example of a modern technological state waging war against a predominantly agricultural, virtually defenseless society, it is necessary to go back to the war of Italy against Ethiopia in the 1930s. The Vietnam war, of course, is on a far vaster scale. One must go through the village countryside to experience the brutal impact of the war on North Vietnam, and of course the devastation of South Vietnam is far worse. How does one explain bombing patterns directed against village communities? How are we to comprehend the use of anti-personnel bombs, napalm, and delayed-action bombs against rural areas that are far from supply lines and remote from battlefields? Who gave the orders to bomb Phat Diem? And what was the rationale? Americans will need to confront these questions sooner or later. It will not long assuage our moral conscience to purport ignorance or impotence. For the documentary record is building toward an overwhelming case. Let the skeptical consult John Gerassi's carefully evidenced book *North Vietnam: A Documentary.*[1]

A conversation in Hanoi hardly ever begins in the twentieth century. The Vietnamese are extraordinarily conscious of their history, especially of their many struggles through the centuries to beat off foreign invaders, beginning with the heroic exploits of the thirteenth century against three waves of Mongol invaders. The current war with the United States is placed in a historical setting created by the long dark night of French colonialism that lasted from the 1860s to the 1950s, and included the interim experience of Japanese occupation during World War II and Chinese Nationalist and British postwar reoccupation. The Vietnamese date their current struggle from the August Revolution of 1945, when Ho Chi Minh issued the Vietnamese Declaration of Independence, modeled in tone and language upon our earlier American

[1] New York, Bobbs-Merrill, 1968; for an anthology of newspaper accounts of "war crimes" committed in South Vietnam, see *In the Name of America* (study commissioned by Clergy and Laymen Concerned About Vietnam), Annandale, Virginia, Turnpike Press, 1968.

document of the same name which is explicitly invoked as a precedent.[2] The French restoration of colonial dominion was looked upon by Vietnamese nationalists as a deceitful repudiation of the Fontainebleau Agreements of 1946 that had gone a long way toward confirming Vietnam's right to be an independent nation. The war of independence against the French was an immediate, inevitable sequel. The North Vietnamese defeated the French finally and dramatically at Dien Bien Phu after eight long years of hardship and warfare against overwhelming military odds.[3] By that time, in 1954, the United States was heavily involved on the French side of the war, paying 80 percent of the bills and exerting an increasing influence on the politics of the struggle. American presidential leadership never accepted the defeat of French colonialism. As the peace talks in Geneva were proceeding (the conference itself being held in opposition to American wishes), United States diplomacy was seeking support from the British for Operation Vulture, a proposed heavy air strike against the Vietminh. The United States government refused the political ratification of the French military defeat that occurred at Geneva in 1954. By placing Ngo Dinh Diem in control of the Saigon regime, by rushing in funds and advice, and by organizing SEATO, the United States evolved "its commitment," and gave evidence of its intention to deny the Vietminh the fruits of their victory against the French (just as the Seventh Fleet has denied the Peking regime the natural outcome of victory in the Chinese civil war). The point is that the leadership in Hanoi is very conscious of the fact that their struggle for national independence has been a continuous one since the end of World War II. They believe that Americans have assumed the colonial role of the French, and that the Vietnamese on the American side are mainly the same people and interest groups that were on the French side before 1954.

Perhaps the strongest feeling that I had on boarding the International Control Commission plane to leave Hanoi on June 28 was that peace in Vietnam could be (and could have been) rapidly and "honorably" attained if the United States government could be (or could have been) induced to make a reasonable effort. The question that follows from such a feeling is how to induce that reasonable effort. This piece tries to make clear, on the basis of my trip, some of the grounds of this belief in the attainability of peace.

[2] For text of the Vietnamese Declaration of Independence of September 2, 1945, see George McT. Kahin and John W. Lewis, *The United States in Vietnam*, New York, Delta, 1967, Appendix I, pp. 345–47.

[3] On this period up until 1954, see Ellen Hammer, *The Struggle for Indochina, 1940–1955*, Stanford, Stanford University Press, rev. ed., 1966; Jean Lacouture and Philippe Devillers, *La fin d'une guerre, Indochine 1954*, Paris, Editions du Seuil, 1960; and Joseph Buttinger, *Vietnam: A Dragon Embattled*, New York, Praeger, 1967, Vol. I.

Each day Vietnamese and Americans die; each day the political passions loosed by this war in both societies are further inflamed; and daily countless more wounds are inflicted.

In thinking about peace in Vietnam, it is necessary to begin by reporting on the reaction in Hanoi to President Johnson's speech of March 31, 1968. The good faith of the United States government is held in serious doubt. North Vietnamese point out that, as soon as Hanoi indicated its willingness to negotiate, the United States backed away from its oft-repeated pledge to meet "at any forum, at any time." They mention that early in April a widely proclaimed military sweep was organized in South Vietnam under the peace-defying rubric Operation Certain Victory. Far more serious to the leadership in Hanoi, however, has been the contrast between the bombing patterns against North Vietnam and President Johnson's continuing claim that the geographical limitation of bombing to the area below the Twentieth Parallel constituted a major act of unilateral restraint on the part of the United States. They stress the fact that the number of missions flown against North Vietnamese territory and the per month tonnage of delivered bombs have actually *increased* since March 31. This circumstance is acutely aggravated by the fact that the panhandle region north of the DMZ is a heavily populated area that has been subjected to saturation bombing, some villages having been bombed by now between 2,000 and 3,000 times. Reports and films of the bombed zone reveal the enormity of the suffering caused to civilian village communities by these air attacks.

Miss Ta Anh Hoa, a pediatrician who had just returned from a visit to the bombed area south of the Twentieth Parallel, told of the conditions that she found. Her account left a deep impression upon us; she is a non-political young woman of warmth and simplicity. To give some suggestion, I include a short excerpt from my transcription of her words: "We conducted a medical examination of children living there. We reached conclusions that if published would increase the hatred of mothers all over the world against the United States government. If there is anything in the world that strikes against our humanity, it is to commit crimes against children . . . Through our investigation we found injuries so horrible that one can't believe it – children living year after year in darkness beneath the ground in tunnels, some nearsighted, others with twisted spines . . . children who have never seen the sun although we have much sun in Vietnam."

The special military justification for heavy bombing north of the DMZ was mainly removed, certainly by the end of June, as a result of the US withdrawal from Khe Sanh. It is not a convincing response to say, as the American military has said, that the bombing weather has improved since March 31; certainly the avowed intention to deescalate is feeble if it yields to favorable flying conditions. North Vietnamese officials say with vehemence that the United States is trying to fool public opinion by pretending a peace initiative without taking any of the steps that would bring the war to a negotiated end.

When one moves beyond this attitude of skepticism about United States good faith, several points that bear on settlement emerge rather clearly. As has been said so often, the first step to peace in Vietnam entails the halt of all bombing of North Vietnam. The Prime Minister of North Vietnam, Mr. Pham Van Dong, amply confirmed this precondition to substantive negotiations in the course of our long discussion: "It is for us a test of whether the United States wants to deescalate. It is not possible to give reciprocity. There is nothing for us to give." More significantly, the Prime Minister went on to say that "the United States government must recognize the principle of stopping the war. From this all problems can be solved in the wisest and most intelligent way. If the United States wants to make war we are resolved to fight for as much time as required. But we also know how to talk if that is desired."

The demand that bombing stop before peace talks begin is closely connected, I think, with the Prime Minister's emphasis on "the principle of stopping the war." A halt to the bombing of North Vietnam would be taken as evidence of a real intention by the United States to bring the war to an end; without that intention the North Vietnamese look upon negotiations as concerned primarily with dampening public opposition to the war without abandoning the pursuit of a military solution. Once the United States makes evident its intention to end the war, then the North Vietnamese appear disposed to be very flexible about working out a plan, and granting concessions in return. Both Hanoi and Front officials emphasized to underscore their own flexibility that they were prepared to be "realistic" and "reasonable" about the outcome of peace talks, and I think they have already conceded to the United States certain central aspects of a viable settlement. Part of my purpose here is to call attention to these concessions that have so far been glossed over even by critics of the war.

How is reasonableness to be measured? What is the United States entitled to expect from the peace settlement? North Vietnam imposes some hard negotiating conditions in exchange for giving ground on other principal objectives. The most important condition that will not be waived by North Vietnam is an insistence on the removal from South Vietnam of the present Saigon rulers; there was no hint of a willingness to consider a coalition that includes the Thieu–Ky group, nor was there evident any willingness to allow these leaders to remain at large in Vietnam after peace does come. The leaders in Saigon are looked upon as either residues of the old colonial–feudal social order of reactionary Vietnam or merely as "agents" of United States control. Such an image is reinforced by the recollection that many prominent members of the military junta fought for the French and against the Vietminh in the war of national independence between 1946 and 1954. Only the top echelon of Saigonese leadership must leave South Vietnam after peace to avoid punishment. Beyond this group, said to number under 100, both the Program and leaders of the Front and those of North Vietnam emphasize a broad willingness to work with the diverse elements of Vietnamese society, including people who have fought or worked for the various regimes in the South. As Pham Van Dong emphasized, "the Front is trying its best to win over its opponents and it shows great concern because these men are also Vietnamese." On no issue did the Prime Minister appear more insistent than on the prospect of reprisals: "It is unthinkable to use reprisals against those who remain. Why? Such a policy is unwise and inhuman. I assure you of this. You may tell this to the American people." Mr. Pham Van Dong is a strong and convincing presence; his words had a ring of authenticity. He also pointed out that, when the victorious Vietminh assumed control of North Vietnam, no reprisals were taken against those who sided with the French, despite the bitterness of that long war.

If we assume that an anti-Thieu–Ky coalition government emerges in postwar South Vietnam, then it would be unrealistic to expect that no reprisals would be carried out, especially at the district and local level. There has been too much bitterness and hostility on all sides to expect a pacific transition from present circumstances of strife to a condition of stable government without some accompanying bloodshed. A postwar atmosphere of continuing struggle is almost inevitable for South Vietnam, and should enter into realistic calculations for ending the war. Such a prospect of limited reprisal has to be compared with the burdens of an indefinite continuation of warfare at high levels of intensity. Also, it should be appreciated that this sequel to the war would happen whenever a settlement was reached and regardless of which side prevailed. The assurances of Pham Van Dong on the issue of reprisals, especially if such a commitment could be embodied in the final instrument of settlement, might help ensure that whatever reprisals did take place were a result of local conditions rather than an official expression of revenge and retaliation. Although accounts differ, it is apparently true that most of the bloodshed in North Vietnam after 1954 was a by-product of forced collectivization of agriculture rather than part of a program of reprisal directed against those Vietnamese who had collaborated with the French.[4] Some political purges did take place, however, and were directed especially at the leadership

---

[4] For a short account of this period, see Kahin and Lewis, *The United States in Vietnam*, pp. 87–92, n. 2.

of strongly anti-communist nationalist groups, the main rivals of the Vietminh in the competition for political dominance in North Vietnam.

An attitude of reconciliation was also expressed by Nguyen Van Hieu, head of the NLF Mission on Cambodia, a former professor of mathematics and a keen, articulate spokesman. As evidence that the climate for reconciliation was improving, Professor Hieu cited the fact that people siding with the Saigon regime have been muting their criticism of the Front. He observed that since the Tet offensive in February of 1968, "not one general [in the South Vietnam army] has publicly taken a position against the NLF; not even one divisional commander has said a word against the Front." Hieu felt that there was now a "great possibility to enlarge the Front" by including elements representing additional forces in South Vietnam. Finally, Hieu, portrayed as the leading Front spokesman in the French film on the NLF by Roger Pic, said, "Anyone who opposes the presence of United States troops can participate in government."

The minimum role of the Front in the settlement process is difficult to specify precisely. Pham Van Dong said that Hanoi "can discuss the general principles of peace, but on concrete questions the Front must have its say. The Front is doing the fighting and it will have a decisive voice as to the future of South Vietnam." A similar position was taken by Nguyen Van Tien, head of the NLF Mission in Hanoi, a prematurely white-haired man of subtle mind and impressive knowledge. Mr. Tien described the military situation in South Vietnam as one in which the Front substantially controls the countryside and also claims large portions of the cities as "liberated areas." These areas cannot yet be specifically claimed, Tien says, because they would in that event be quickly destroyed by US firepower. Independent French correspondents with whom I talked in Paris tended to accept these NLF claims as accurate.

Both Mr. Tien and Professor Hieu argued that the Saigon regime is presently very isolated, lacking any social or political base in Vietnamese society. It is in this context that they regard the formation of the Alliance of National, Democratic, and Peace Forces as an important new political development. The importance of the Alliance for these Front officials lay in the fact that leading personalities drawn from professional, religious, business, intellectual, and student sectors of urban society made a political commitment that reflected their judgment as to the domestic balance of forces in South Vietnam. Unlike North Vietnamese government officials, the representatives of the Front did not seem to look upon the Alliance with unmixed enthusiasm, nor did they mention its possible participation in a coalition government. It seemed clear that Mr. Tien, for instance, partly regarded the leaders of the Alliance as latecomers leaping aboard a bandwagon when compared to the leaders of the Front who had been in the jungle fighting and dying for almost a decade. I felt, also, that there may be some difference in socioeconomic outlook that would make the Front wary of working too closely with the Alliance. The Chairman of the Alliance, a lawyer named Trinh Dinh Thao, is from one of the richest landowning families in South Vietnam, as is one of its two Vice Chairmen, Lam Van Tot.

In the aftermath of the Second Honolulu Conference, it is more important than ever that Americans gain a proper appreciation of the importance of the Alliance of National, Democratic, and Peace Forces.[5] The formation of the Alliance was officially announced in April of 1968 as a direct consequence of the Tet offensive. Its leadership is drawn mainly from Saigon and Hue, and consists of respected and widely known non-Communist personalities; the Alliance is led by individuals who must be regarded as members of the South Vietnamese "establishment." The Thieu–Ky government has itself hinted at the importance of the Alliance by taking the extraordinary step of condemning ten of its leaders to death *in absentia* in a summary trial conducted before a military tribunal in Saigon on July 12, 1968.

Official American reactions have discounted the Alliance as a front of the Front, as a trick and delusion. Washington's reaction has been given some support by such influential journalists as Gene Roberts and Hedrick Smith (*New York Times*, July 9, 12, and 14, 1968), and Robert Shaplen (the *New Yorker*, June 29, 1968). Their reports have discounted the Alliance because it adopts a political line that resembles the Program of the NLF, and because the radio and press transmissions of the Alliance have been carried and endorsed by the official media of the Front and of North Vietnam. It would be a serious mistake to undervalue the Alliance because the evidence suggests that it might provide the leadership for a substantial third force in South Vietnam. It would also be a mistake because the North Vietnamese endorsement of the program of the Alliance may itself be an important political signal.

---

[5]   It is important because Presidents Johnson and Thieu issued a joint communiqué at Honolulu on July 20, 1968, in which it was said that "the United States will not support the imposition of a 'Coalition Government' or any other form of Government on the people of South Vietnam." For text of the Honolulu Communiqué, see the *New York Times*, July 21, 1968, p. 2. Such a statement, if it only refers to the "imposition" of a coalition government, is certainly not objectionable. It is objectionable, however, if the criterion for what is imposition is to be determined by the Saigon regime. Given the criminal prosecution of political moderates in South Vietnam shortly after the Honolulu meeting (see p. 16 for reference to conviction of Truong Dinh Dzu), it appears evident that the Thieu regime is seeking to eliminate from view any major candidates for participation in a coalition. In fact, in South Vietnam, as of July 1968, it is a crime to advocate a coalition government that includes NLF participation.

The first question that needs to be asked is why the admittedly non-Communist leadership of the Alliance, drawn from the urban upper classes, would put in jeopardy their lives, families, reputations, and properties by forming an underground political group that takes a position similar to that of the National Liberation Front. There are really only two plausible responses. First, that the domestic balance of forces in South Vietnam is so unfavorable to the Saigon–United States alignment that it has become expedient for non-Communist elements to identify themselves with the prevailing side in the latter stages of the struggle. This was the explanation that seemed to appeal to Mr. Tien. The second explanation is that the Tet offensive of February 1968 demonstrated clearly that urban groups could not safely remain aloof from the war any longer. The destructive impact of Tet on the cities provided urban leaders with a dramatic occasion on which to take sides in the struggle raging for the control of Vietnam.

The persuasiveness of this explanation of the Alliance rests on the assumption that the war in Vietnam has so polarized the domestic politics of South Vietnam that the only political choices are to side either with the US–Saigon position or with the DRV–NLF position. By spring 1968, all middle positions had been rendered irrelevant. It has long been evident that moderate anti-war leaders who, like Truong Dinh Dzu, participate openly in politics will be put into jail sooner or later.[6] Mr. Dzu, the opposition candidate who was the runner-up in the 1967 elections, has been sentenced to five years of hard labor in prison. His crime? Advocating direct peace talks with the NLF, and favoring a coalition government as part of a peace settlement.

Given this domestic setting, the formation of the Alliance was necessarily both clandestine and anti-regime. Pham Van Dong emphasized in our discussions that "it is a great victory for us that the leaders of the Alliance chose our side." He went on to say that "the Alliance is just the sort of civilian grouping of influential citizens that the United States has been trying to form for years." The Prime Minister felt that the emergence of the Alliance was an important political indicator of the domestic balance of forces in South Vietnam. It misses most of this point to worry about how distinct the Alliance is from the Front. Given the severity of war conditions in South Vietnam, it is to be expected that active entry into the arena would be in terms of an affiliation rather than as a completely distinct entity. As such, there would be no

---

[6]   For an account of the three-hour military trial of Mr. Dzu, see the *New York Times*, July 27, 1968, p. 6. See also the report of the trial and conviction of a student editor, Nguyen Truong Con, who, like Mr. Dzu, was "charged" with urging a coalition government (*New York Times*, July 26, 1968, p. 6).

reason to stress – except for the benefit of American sensitivities – differences between the orientation and purpose of the Front and the Alliance. Both groups are united by the common objective of ending the war in a manner that assures the withdrawal of United States military forces and the collapse of the Thieu–Ky government.

Despite this overriding present incentive to subordinate whatever differences do exist between the Front and the Alliance, there are embodied in the April Manifesto of the Alliance two substantive points that seem to be important for either the process of negotiations or the shape of settlement. Unlike either the NLF Program of 1967 or the Geneva Accords of 1954, the April Manifesto describes South Vietnam as *"a sovereign state."* The Manifesto says that the second objective of the Alliance is "to build in South Vietnam an independent, free, peaceful, neutral and prosperous *state.*" Later in the paragraph the following language is used: "South Vietnam will be a state, *independent, fully sovereign,* following a foreign policy of non-alignment, entering into good relations with all foreign countries without distinction as to their political regime." Recalling that South Vietnam was only a temporary regroupment zone in the Geneva Accords of 1954,[7] the language of the Alliance more closely parallels the hopes of Washington, not Hanoi, on this central matter of the future of South Vietnam. A North Vietnamese official told me that it was significant, given the reference to the sovereignty of South Vietnam, that both the DRV and the NLF had transmitted the Alliance Manifesto on their official broadcast facilities; he conveyed the impression that such media transmission was tantamount to an official endorsement. Given the almost obsessional concern of Vietnamese officials with precise political language, it seems that whatever the Alliance is as a political grouping, its Manifesto is worthy of attention. It is ironic that the ascription of sovereignty to South Vietnam would be more significant as a political signal if the Alliance were a front of the Front than if it were not.

The second point involves the availability of the Alliance for participation in negotiations. The Manifesto, in the section devoted to bringing the war to an end, affirms the readiness of the Alliance to enter into substantive discussions

---

[7] See especially the language used in Articles 1, 2, 3, and 4 of the Agreement on the Cessation of Hostilities in Vietnam, July 20, 1954; and Articles 6 and 12 of the Final Declaration of the Geneva Conference. Article 6 affirms "that the military demarcation line is provisional and should not in any way be interpreted as constituting a political or territorial boundary." Article 12 pledges members of the Geneva Conference in their relations with Cambodia, Laos, and Vietnam "to respect the sovereignty, the independence, the unity, and the territorial independence of the above-mentioned States." For convenient text of the Geneva Accords, see Richard Falk, ed., *The Vietnam War and International Law*, Princeton, Princeton University Press, 1968, Vol. I, pp. 543–60.

with the government of the United States. Would not the existence of the Alliance give the United States a means of negotiating with an anti-regime political grouping in South Vietnam without abandoning its long-standing refusal to negotiate peace with the NLF? The Alliance constitutes a political actor that is neither the Saigon regime nor the NLF, and very likely an actor with clear differences in social, political, and economic position from that of either Hanoi or the NLF. Is it not, at least, worth exploring this possibility of widening the negotiations without taking in either the NLF or the Saigon regime? Just as the United States has steadfastly refused to negotiate with the NLF, so the North Vietnamese have refused to negotiate with the Saigon regime. The Alliance, perhaps more broadly constituted, might offer some way out of this procedural impasse.

This appraisal of the Alliance adds to a single conclusion: Whether or not the Alliance is regarded as a fully autonomous political grouping, its existence and Manifesto deserve serious attention.

The Front appears presently to be seeking to unite all opposition to the American presence, thereby further isolating the Thieu–Ky regime. To the extent that such isolation is successfully taking place, it facilitates the necessary process of American disassociation from the Saigon government. The North Vietnamese and the Front officials make a very convincing case that the preeminent issue of the war is the application of the principle of national self-determination.

The present war against the United States is portrayed as the most recent and harrowing chapter in the continuing Vietnamese struggle to achieve and sustain the reality of national independence.[8] The gravest charge against the various Saigon regimes is that they have relied upon foreign military power to sustain themselves in power. By so doing, these "puppet" leaders have surrendered real political authority to a foreign power, thereby sacrificing any claim to political legitimacy in Vietnam. In this light, one appreciates better the determination of the Hanoi government to persevere in the war, despite the great military pressure that North Vietnam is under, without calling in the Soviet Union or China. Ideological affinity seems to be a secondary consideration in the thinking of North Vietnamese national autonomy. I found present a passionate pride in all that was distinctively Vietnamese, whether pertaining to politics or music or cuisine. This emphasis lends support to the intimations of North Vietnamese leaders that they are willing to compromise with

[8]   For an account of Vietnamese history, see Joseph Buttinger, *The Smaller Dragon: A Political History of Vietnam*, New York, Praeger, 1956.

regard to the political orientation of a future government for South Vietnam in exchange for real assurance as to its national autonomy.

Professor Hieu emphasized the degree to which the Program of the Front is reasonable, even if it is compared to the Geneva settlement of 1954. At Geneva, Vietnam was temporarily divided into two regroupment zones that were to be united by elections two years later, in July 1956. The language of the Geneva Accords was emphatic in its rejection of the idea that "two Vietnams" were being created. In the NLF Program of 1967 there is no timetable for reunification, but merely the recognition of the goal as "the sacred aspiration of our entire people," and the promise to work for an eventual reunification on a "step-by-step" basis. Reunification will be pursued by "peaceful means on the principle of negotiation between the two zones without either side using pressure against the other and without foreign interference." Such an approach was fully confirmed by Pham Van Dong: "I tell you frankly we will talk together – and starting from the interests of the South. We have no haste. We will not act in a negligent way. We will not disrupt things." At this point Pham Van Dong paused, then resumed his statement with dramatic emphasis: "I would add one point – we respect our compatriots in the South. We will comply with the wishes of our Southern countrymen." The implication was evident that reunification would not be imposed on the South by the North and that, even if favorable circumstances were present, it would be deferred for a considerable number of years. Other officials in North Vietnam indicated their opinion that the differing social, economic, and political experiences of the two parts of Vietnam over the last fourteen years made it desirable, quite independent of the terms of a peace settlement, to proceed slowly toward reunification.

At the same time, I heard often of the desire for a renewal of normal contact between all parts of Vietnam. Hardly anyone whom I met in North Vietnam did not have some relative in the South, but unless a relative was actually fighting in the Front all contact had been lost since 1954 when the Saigon government sealed the border, even against exchanges of mail. Vietnamese families normally unite over the Tet holidays at the home of the eldest living member, but many have been out of touch with relatives now since before World War II. The identity and importance of the family seemed so clear, even for leading political figures in Hanoi, that I think it correct to take seriously these reports of anguish. It is part of the incalculable atmosphere in Hanoi that seems to be inclining the political leadership to search for some sort of peace. But one needs to be guarded in this assertion, at least to the extent of understanding that, after all the sacrifices imposed on Vietnamese people by the long duration and ravaging impact of the war, it is essential that negotiations achieve an "honorable peace" from Hanoi's point of view.

The 1967 Program of the NLF conceives of a foreign policy for South Vietnam based on neutrality and non-alignment. It also pledges "to establish diplomatic relations with all countries regardless of their social and political system." Front officials emphasize that their Program is a very careful document that is meant to reflect major policy positions. After the inflammatory language is removed from the document, the Program of the Front appears to be a rather moderate and reasonable proposal for the future of South Vietnam.[9]

Why, then, does the NLF Program rely on so much inflammatory language to castigate the United States repeatedly as an "aggressor" and "imperialist"? Why does it insist on describing the leaders of the Saigon regime as "die-hard thugs" and "lackeys"? There are, I think, two main explanations for this immoderateness of language that contrasts so sharply with the moderateness of position. First, the Vietnamese feel that they have been victims of a cruel and brutal foreign intervention, disguised by reliance on puppet groups drawn from their own population. Their emotional need to castigate that experience is certainly very strong.

Second, and I think more significant, there is an almost incomprehensible insistence everywhere in North Vietnam upon distinguishing between the war policies of the United States government and the benevolent character of the American people. The North Vietnamese leaders appear sincere and literal when they talk of giving bouquets of flowers to departing American soldiers. There is an unexpected residual feeling of attraction for the United States evident everywhere in Hanoi. It is unexpected because it is accompanied by a sense of outrage directed at the use of cruel weapons and bombing tactics by American military authorities. Officials in Hanoi talk with conviction and compassion about the loss of American prestige in the world as a result of the Vietnam war. For instance, Hoang Quoc Viet, the Attorney General, and one of the founders of the Lao Dong Party, said that "intellectuals in Vietnam have a deep love for American culture," and emphasized, as had happened so often during my discussions in North Vietnam, the similarity between the aims of the United States Revolutionary War and the continuing Vietnamese struggle against colonialism. Vietnam has been engaged since 1945 in a continuous effort to achieve its full rights of national independence and to secure dignity and happiness for its peoples.

---

[9]   For text of the 1967 NLF Program, see "Political Program of the South Viet Nam National Front for Liberation," South Vietnam, Giai Phong Publishing House, 1967, pp. 5–39; for the 1961 NLF Program, see "Background Information Relating to Southeast Asia and Vietnam," Senate Foreign Relations Committee, 3rd rev. ed., 1967, pp. 269–74.

Pham Van Dong made the similar point in fervent fashion: "To us the American people are the first people to rise up and fight for their national independence. We know the United States Declaration of Independence almost by heart. The people of America are freedom-loving for themselves and for others. How can we make this truth clear to the American people? When the American people know that this is the truth of our struggle then we will be good friends. It is better that the time comes soon. More than anyone else we need it soon. If not soon, then it will be later. We love life, what is beautiful in the world, we love all people. It is for this reason that we will fight no matter what sacrifices are involved." Only the most hardened visitor to North Vietnam cannot be impressed by an openness remarkable in the midst of war to all things good in the American tradition.

Mr. Le Van Giang, the Minister of Higher Education, also spoke eloquently about the North Vietnamese effort at all levels of its educational system to emphasize the good things about the United States. Mr. Giang pointed out that the same attitude was taken toward the French. One notes that the present preliminary negotiations are being held in Paris, despite the long subjugation of the Vietnamese by the French and the bitter war of independence. There appears to be a very unusual compulsion embedded in the Vietnamese character to find pathways to reconciliation with former enemies. After the Vietnam war ends, I predict that Americans will begin to discover these bonds of friendship and affirmation, at first suspecting them, but finally coming to learn from them. I think back to World War II and the monolithic repudiation of Germany and Japan by Americans, although the war situation then was of far less gravity to American survival interests than the Vietnam war is to Vietnamese survival interests.

It is in this setting that North Vietnamese emphasis on the peace movement in the United States needs to be grasped. Top leaders in Hanoi rarely exaggerated the political influence of the United States peace movement, although I noted some glimmers of wishful thinking about its eventual rise to predominant power. The more central role of the peace movement in North Vietnamese thinking is to sharpen the distinction between what is good and bad in the United States. To underscore the role of the peace movement provides the Vietnamese with a patriotic way of affirming the American people in the midst of a most awful occasion of national suffering and destruction. Outside Hanoi, virtually every concrete structure that I saw, whether hospital, church, factory, or bridge, had been bombed, and much destruction was evident all along the 100 miles of road from Hanoi to Phat Diem. And yet, even when faced with the prospect of a resumption of attacks on Hanoi, there is no trace of generalized bitterness against the United States. I think that this

non-recriminatory attitude would be persuasive to most Americans who had
an experience of direct contact similar to mine. Such attitudes of receptivity and openness are sharply at variance with the rigid ideological mindset
I expected to find in Hanoi.

My discussions in Hanoi suggest a fairly coherent set of conclusions. First,
the DRV is not prepared to concede much explicitly in exchange for a complete bombing halt. Second, the Front and, indirectly, the DRV have already
conceded the outline of a political settlement that should be acceptable to the
US government: sovereign status for South Vietnam, gradual reunification
not tied to a timetable, and a foreign policy based on neutrality. Third, the
Prime Minister of North Vietnam has made strong reassurances on the issue
of reprisals and on the prospects for friendly relations between the United
States and Vietnam. Fourth, the way toward a coalition government admin-
istering South Vietnam from a mixed capitalist–socialist perspective seems
assured by the existence of the Alliance and by the Front's own program of
socioeconomic compromise.[10] Fifth, the defense of national autonomy against
any external encroachment is likely to remain the first order of business

---

[10] I would think that a negotiated rather than elected coalition government is called for at the
outset. The composition of this coalition needs to correspond as closely as possible with
the domestic balance of forces prevailing in South Vietnam, and give adequate representation
to the various political, religious, and ethnic groups that have substantial following in this
much-divided country. The incohesiveness of South Vietnam would bring torment to any
effort at centralized government even in the absence of ideological and socioeconomic struggle. A coalition should also be constituted to take account of the urban–rural balance in South
Vietnam and of the position of various social classes in the country. Government at the local
level, perhaps even at the district and province level, should be based on the *de facto* administrative realities as of the time of cease-fire. Many considerations bearing on political sub-
structure below the national level are imaginatively considered in a recent article by Samuel
P. Huntington, "Vietnam: The Bases of Accommodation," *Foreign Affairs*, 46 (July 1968),
pp. 642–56.

   In my judgment, given the divisive realities in South Vietnam under present conditions of
devastation and dislocation, it would be a dangerous error to select the initial coalition government through an electoral process. There has never been a fair and free election in Vietnam,
and the struggle to manipulate the electoral machinery might well imperil other aspects of
a negotiated peace settlement. No international force could do much to improve the prospects for meaningful elections unless it was both very large (over 100,000), and familiar with
Vietnamese traditions and the language; it is not realistic to envisage such supervision. An
insistence on elections as the basis for government at this point in South Vietnam could be justified only by relying on a mode of selection that Americans might regard as consistent with the
principle of self-determination. This is not an adequate justification. Given the circumstances
of South Vietnam and the delicate base of any peace settlement, the cause of Vietnamese
self-determination would be better served, in my judgment, by seeking a coalition government
by *negotiations* rather than by *elections*.

for Vietnamese foreign policy for a long time both north and south of the Seventeenth Parallel.

To reach a settlement, the United States would have to (1) stop all bombing of North Vietnam; (2) gradually withdraw support from the present Saigon regime and plan for the negotiation of a coalition government; and (3) plan, after a cease-fire, to withdraw US and other foreign military forces rather rapidly. Such actions seem a small price to pay for peace in Vietnam. Of course, many complicated questions of implementation, guaranty, and transition remain, but a minimum of trust and an acceptance of the shape of final settlement could create favorable opportunities for solving other questions such as the timetable and mode of mutual withdrawal of foreign forces, interim government for South Vietnam, and supervised elections.

After returning from North Vietnam and Paris, I am convinced that a diligent search for a reasonable peace settlement of the Vietnam War would yield results. If I am correct, then it is imperative to begin the effort to find peace at once. The daily horror of the Vietnam war is too great to put off this effort until a time of convenience emerges in the domestic politics of the United States.

2

US in Vietnam: Rationale and Law

I

A peaceful settlement of the Vietnam War requires some initial conception of a reasonable bargaining position for both sides. In my judgment, the United States has not sufficiently shown that it understands or is prepared to negotiate on such a basis.

Our continuing refusal to recognize the Vietcong as a formal participant in a peace settlement underscores our unreasonableness. It implies that the Saigon regime is the only legitimate political elite in South Vietnam, whereas the claims of the NLF to both autonomy and legitimacy are at least as good as, and probably considerably better than, those of Saigon. To say that Hanoi alone represents "the other side" is to insist upon the fiction that there is no genuine civil war in South Vietnam and that the war has from beginning to end been a consequence of aggression by North Vietnam. Such a premise for negotiations is obviously unacceptable to the NLF, but even Hanoi – however much it might like to control the future of South Vietnam – is naturally reluctant to concede this American interpretation of the war. Neither the actual political relationships nor the stated objectives of Hanoi bear out the American contention. As a preliminary adaptation to political reality, it is important for the United States to acknowledge the war for what it *primarily* is – a civil war in which both sides have received extensive military support and political guidance from outside states.

This interpretation leads to the conclusion that in any settlement Saigon and the NLF must participate and negotiate on the basis of *formal* equality. And if the negotiations are to succeed, once formal equality is established, it will also be necessary to recognize the factual inequality of the two sides. That is, it will be necessary to recognize that the NLF commands more military power and political stability than Saigon.

Our policy in Vietnam is an outcome of the crusade against Communism and typifies the pitfalls of accepting an over-generalized commitment to fight whenever and wherever there may otherwise result an extension of Communist influence. This anti-Communist crusade has led to the use of military power by the United States throughout the world. It has also led the United States to repudiate increasingly the procedures of the UN that it did so much to create.

The commitment to defend societies against Communist aggression had as its premises, first, the existence of a monolithic Stalinism active in world affairs and, second, the vulnerability of Western Europe to subversion after World War II. In 1947 the Truman Doctrine was formulated specifically to help the government of Greece defeat a Communist-led insurgency and to bolster the internal security of Turkey. The US commitment took explicit account of the inability of Great Britain to continue giving support to Greece. President Truman's central rationale appeared in a speech to Congress: "Greece must have assistance if it is to become a self-supporting and self-respecting democracy. The United States must supply that assistance. We have already extended to Greece certain types of relief and economic aid, but these are inadequate. There is no other country to which democratic Greece can turn. No other nation is willing and able to provide the necessary support for a democratic Greek Government." The civil war was won by the Greek government, the situation in Turkey was stabilized, and elsewhere in Western Europe the advance of Communism was halted, in part as a result of large-scale American aid made possible by the Marshall plan.

Our special responsibility in the struggle against Communism was reasserted in Korea, with our military power committed nominally as a peace-keeping operation under the auspices of the United Nations, but largely financed and handled under the independent authority of the United States. The American use of military power, however, rested upon the wider justification that North Korea was engaged in a war of conquest initiated by a massive armed attack across an internationally recognized frontier. Such recourse to aggression violated in blatant form the fundamental obligation of the United Nations Charter, and the action of the United States in defense of South Korea gave powerful evidence of a national commitment to back up this obligation. The reality of this commitment was further established by US opposition to the use of military force by Israel, France, and the United Kingdom in the Suez campaign of 1956. In retrospect the American stand is especially impressive because the attack on Egypt was partly in response to Egyptian "indirect aggression" in the form of *fedayeen* raids upon Israel from protected sanctuaries. Yet the United States took a strong stand in the UN against our closest allies, suggesting the precedence of collective security over the vagaries of alliance politics. Such a stand also tended to vindicate the American claims that it was not using the United Nations solely as a weapon in the cold war.

II

Then came a major change. The Eisenhower Doctrine of 1957 crucially expanded American responsibility for the containment of Communism. A joint resolution of Congress, at the request of Eisenhower, authorized the President "to use armed force to assist" nations in the Middle East resisting "armed aggression from any country controlled by international communism." In the summer of 1958 the Eisenhower Doctrine was invoked when several detachments of US marines were sent to Lebanon to help the shaky Chamoun regime survive internal crises allegedly provoked by external "intervention."

The Eisenhower Doctrine is very important because (1) it envisions the active use of military force by the United States in foreign countries, as distinct from the military aid given European countries; (2) it extends the US commitment beyond Europe to embrace the far less stable nation-states of the Middle East; (3) it was formulated in ideological rather than world-order terms; and (4) it anticipates US military involvement in conflicts that are in part, at least, civil wars. This new role for US military power was advanced without any serious consideration as to how it might affect our obligations to the United Nations, especially the commitment to renounce the use of force in international affairs except in case of self-defense against an armed attack from an external source. Furthermore, no criteria were offered to distinguish aggression from revolution or civil strife. The Eisenhower Doctrine implied a broad discretion by the United States government, a discretion that has come increasingly to mean US military intervention *anywhere*, if necessary to defend a government from a Communist takeover. Thus, the recent use of American military power in the Dominican Republic is an extreme instance of the claims originated in the Eisenhower Doctrine. The struggle in the Dominican Republic in 1965 was as purely internal as any political struggle can be in the contemporary world, and US intervention in it assumes an imperial prerogative to control the outcome of civil wars in which victory might otherwise be won by a regime with leftist sympathies or personnel. We label the war in whatever manner justifies our action and then refuse to allow international institutions to pass judgment upon what we do.

The Communist powers have their own symmetrical doctrine to justify interventions in civil wars, based upon rendering support for "wars of national liberation." But even the most militant Communist conception of support, the Chinese, falls far short of *overt* military intervention – except perhaps to offset overt military intervention on the other side. In 1965 Mao Tse-tung accurately pointed out in an interview with Edgar Snow that "China gave support to revolutionary movements but not by sending troops." Mao went on to say, "Of course, whenever a liberation struggle existed China would publish statements and call demonstrations to support it." Mao might have also added a willingness to send relatively low-level financial and military aid.

What is important here is the extreme militancy of US doctrine and practice with respect to using military power – even in comparison to China, the state alleged to be most destructive of minimum conceptions of world order. Both in word and deed, it is the United States that is using armies in flagrant disregard of the fundamental rules of world order and adopting the role of an imperial power accountable only to itself.

Even Vietnam has not led to a softening of this general commitment to a global crusade against Communism. Dean Rusk's opening statement to the Senate Foreign Relations Committee in February 1966 reiterated claims of unilateral prerogatives. Mr. Rusk relied heavily upon a strained construction of Article IV of the SEATO treaty – namely, "each party recognized that aggression by means of armed attack would endanger its own peace and safety, and agrees that it will in that event act to meet the common danger in accordance with its constitutional processes." Rusk went on to say that "it is this fundamental SEATO obligation that has from the outset guided our actions in South Vietnam." Such a conclusion seems to overlook the discrepancy between the unilateral quality of the United States' presence in Vietnam and the collective and consultative nature of the SEATO arrangement.

And, what is more, Mr. Rusk insisted that unilateral military action was authorized by the SEATO treaty without any obligation for accountability at either the regional or global level: "If the United States determines that an armed attack has occurred against any nation to whom the protection of the treaty applies, then it is obligated 'to act to meet the common danger' without regard to the views or actions of any other treaty member." The regional framework, then, operates as a legitimizing umbrella for decisions by single nations to use military power.

When applied to Vietnam, the notion that this SEATO framework imposes "an obligation" upon the United States is especially far-fetched. It would imply, for instance, that France is violating the treaty because it has refused to support our intervention. Also, given the Rusk view that each member of SEATO determines its own military response, it is possible to imagine two members of SEATO coming to opposite conclusions about who is the wrongful faction in a civil war and then engage in a war against one another, each acting to carry out its so-called fundamental SEATO obligation. All of which suggests how absurd it is to find justification in the SEATO treaty for an essentially unilateral operation. It is radical enough for the United States to consider itself a regional power in every part of the non-Communist world except Africa; but it is dramatically more so to consider that it has a unilateral prerogative, even an obligation, to use its military power to uphold regional security independent of the wishes of the countries that actually comprise the region, and to do all this under the banner of regionalism. The artificiality of this posture reinforces the widespread impression that the United States is using its great power to intervene brutally – and futilely – in a war that was and should have remained essentially Asian in character, that is, truly subject to regional control.

Vice President Humphrey's tour of Southeast Asia at the start of 1966 adds further to this picture of the United States acting on its own to guarantee governments of the area unlimited support in the event they are confronted with an internal or external enemy that we and they identify with Communism. The policy seems designed to pledge us to go on fighting wars of the Vietnam variety wherever and whenever they break out. One would have hoped that the minimum lesson of the war would be to convince the Administration that new procedures for collective responsibility and action must be devised to avoid a repetition of the Vietnamese nightmare.

Underlying this expectation that alternative means of promoting security might be developed is the strong belief that there exists a general interest among all countries in preventing aggression against themselves. The United States has neither a special insight into nor a special vulnerability to such aggression. Quite the contrary. The security of the United States in traditional terms of national independence is greater than that of any country in the world. Why are not other countries joining us more vigorously in our Vietnamese effort? Why is the United States alone willing to sacrifice the lives of its men and pay the enormous costs of waging this unsuccessful and protracted war? Part of the true explanation is the degree to which our perceptions have been shaped by a self-created myth of American responsibility. Over and over again President Johnson and his chief lieutenants have emphasized that we are in Vietnam "because we have a promise to keep." When examined, this promise turns out to be nothing more substantial than the SEATO obligation stressed by Secretary Rusk. The political underpinning of our continued commitment is the belief voiced by President Johnson in his Johns Hopkins speech of April 1965 that "Around the globe from Berlin to Thailand are people whose well-being rests in part on the belief that they can count on us if they are attacked." Thus, "to leave Vietnam to its fate would shake the confidence of all these people in the value of an American commitment and in the value of America's word." The result is a self-professed test of will, the outcome of which is made relevant to the whole future of collective self-defense. One wonders, also, whether a face-saving settlement in Vietnam attained after many years of protracted violence will reassure countries about the benefit of US support to an extent greater than would non-participation from the outset.

III

US spokesmen contend that we are fighting in Vietnam to uphold the principles of collective self-defense. This explanation presupposes an armed attack from North Vietnam and a legitimately vested political authority in South Vietnam competent to claim self-defense. Neither of these presuppositions seems to exist and, therefore, what is being tested by our military presence is not a commitment to collective self-defense.

There is no evidence that countries dependent upon our support would object to a settlement of the war in Vietnam even if it meant a partial or total Vietcong victory. And, if these countries did object, what could they do, in any event, except seek alternate means to uphold their security? Suppose the worst fears of Washington are realized and the American commitment is not taken as seriously as before – is this necessarily detrimental to national or global interests? Why? It is precisely my argument that the United States commitment is excessive – because it is both too unilateral and too extensive. Suppose our friends from Berlin to Thailand grow more self-reliant or search for alternative allies. Certainly these states are not likely to forgo their independence by seeking from Moscow or Peking what they no longer can obtain fully from Washington. For presumably it is the danger posed by the Soviet Union and China that has led them to seek (or accept) our support.

Not only is there no prospect that dishonoring the pledge, even if we take the leap of imagination needed to believe that it exists, would radiate detrimental consequences. The war in South Vietnam is not even a good test if the pledge is identified with obligations of collective self-defense. The notion of collective self-defense had been generally assumed to apply to the Korea-type war waged by one political entity against another. It was not previously thought to cover interventions in civil wars. In fact, if South Vietnam witnesses the expansion of the concept of collective self-defense to cover responses to interventions on the side of insurgents in a civil war, then the United States is promising a great deal indeed to countries around the globe. No one argued during the Spanish Civil War that the massive interventions by the Germans and the Italians on the side of Franco would have entitled the Soviet Union, as an ally of the incumbent, to bomb Germany and Italy in "self-defense" of Spain. The general conception had been that third powers owed a duty of neutrality to both sides in a civil war, but that if intervention did take place on one side it legitimized proportional counter-intervention, but did not create the basis for "action in self-defense."

This distinction between collective self-defense and counter-intervention is fundamental. The rule against armed attack of the kind present in Korea or Suez is a basic norm of world order which the United Nations, and its membership, is committed to uphold. Reinforcing this norm through bilateral and collective arrangements of collective self-defense probably serves a constructive role so long as international institutions cannot be relied upon to take effective action in support of a victim of armed attack. If the concept of armed attack is restricted to direct border-crossing forms of aggression, then it is relatively easy to identify the situations in which resort to self-defense outside the UN, whether individual or collective, is appropriate; some world-wide consensus can usually be mobilized under such circumstances.

At what point does external support for an insurgency become equivalent to an armed attack? It is this question that highlights the ambiguity of the American presence, and makes the war in South Vietnam such a poor demonstration of the effectiveness of collective self-defense as a security device. It is a poor demonstration because of the apparent facts and background of the conflict. For one thing, the French lost in 1954 a war fought to control the *entire* territory of Vietnam. Recently Jean Lacouture has correctly pointed out that, at Geneva, "The West succeeded in wresting from the victors half the territory and the larger part of the material wealth of Vietnam. Ho agreed to fall back to the north in exchange for a promise that elections preparing the way for unification would be held in 1956 – elections that he had no doubt of winning." The support given by the United States, then, to the regime of South Vietnam immediately and decisively undermined the expectations of all the principal participants at Geneva in 1954 – that is, that the Geneva Agreements, if carried out, would lead eventually to the control of all of Vietnam by the Hanoi government. This earlier expectation cannot be overlooked in trying to determine the terms for a fair settlement of the present war in Vietnam.

IV

Furthermore, the object of "defense" in Saigon is a regime of remarkably little viability. It would appear to be rather widely conceded that the regime of Ngo Dinh Diem, which first repudiated the Geneva concept, was instituted through the United States intervention. Successive regimes have also been brought into being, in part at least, by US intervention. The victim of attack, then, is an artificial entity that would not exist to be defended, nor would it request defense, if it had not been created and sustained by US military and economic power. To justify defending such a government is to pervert the notion of self-defense – as the United States correctly felt the Russians perverted the same notion when they militarily intervened in Hungary to suppress the Nagy uprising in 1956.

The Saigon regime can be sustained only by a spiraling of US commitments on a scale that seems out of all proportion to the matching North Vietnamese interventions on the side of the Vietcong. Despite the great military power of the United States, the Vietcong is said to control over 80 percent of the country, and to have the ability to bring terror to the cities. The Vietnam story on escalation is agonizingly familiar. From military aid to military advisers to ever-increasing military forces – without in any way turning the tide of the war. In a sense, then, the war arising out of the 1954 arrangements at Geneva, if its outcome is measured by the original parameters of conflict, has long since been lost; in fact, several successive such "wars" have been "lost." The appearance of defeat has been somewhat avoided by changing the parameters of conflict through a series of very critical escalations of the US military commitment, especially in terms of the numbers of American troops and the extension of violence to North Vietnam through bombing. If this is the way the United States deals with collective self-defense, it is not very comforting to those countries truly counting on us. From the viewpoint of the victim of attack it is better to be defended effectively from the outset or not at all; the worst possible reassurance is to be defended ineffectively but at ever-increasing magnitudes in a protracted conflict, the only function of the defense being to avoid the formal acknowledgment of defeat on the part of one's ally.

At some point, long since passed, the proxy quality of such a war becomes manifest to all. In Vietnam the Saigon regime functions as a puppet government without a real will of its own. It is the United States that seeks to end the war by negotiations undertaken in accord with its wishes, and appears on the international scene as the belligerent opposing the Vietcong. In effect, this combination of massive military intervention and political domination suggests that the original war in which the United States came to the defense of an embattled Saigon government has been lost and that a new one has begun in which the United States pits its own military might against the challenge of the Vietcong. Under such circumstances external aid to the Vietcong has, of course, also increased, though in a far less flamboyant manner. In fact, the relative invisibility of North Vietnamese military presence reinforces the impression that this second war is still being waged by a relatively autonomous South Vietnamese insurgency, receiving help on such a scale and on such terms as to leave political control, as nearly as we can tell, largely in the hands of the insurgents themselves. It is this realization that has prompted so many experts to commend formal and informal contacts directly with the leadership of the NLF, as against acting as if Hanoi asserts complete control over the insurgents in South Vietnam.

The war has significant asymmetries both in respect to the scale and visibility of military intervention by outside powers and in terms of the relative independence of the internal faction on whose behalf the intervention is taking place. A further asymmetry unfavorable to the US is that the Vietcong is the beneficiary mainly of help from North Vietnam, a small state and a member of the region, whereas the Saigon regime receives help from a great power with neither a physical nor traditional presence in Southeast Asia. More than any other, this asymmetry intensifies the perception of the war as a Western effort to frustrate the realization of Asian ambitions in the post-colonial period.

V

From the American point of view, even if one were to grant the validity of the extravagant role assumed by the United States in world affairs, fighting in Vietnam appears to be the wrong war in the wrong place waged for the wrong reasons. In general, a deviation from the basic legal restraints governing the use of military force in international affairs has led the United States to undertake action that is both ineffective and unpopular. The American role at the Bay of Pigs is the most prominent recent precedent. The United States is not able to altogether cast aside the restraints of international law. Instead, it tempers its use of force to moderate the illegal quality of the action and cut down the level of opposition in its own society. The result is a sort of compromise between pragmatics and law that leads to a failure of achievement and erodes the most basic limitations imposed by international law upon the discretion of states – rules governing the use of military force.

Bombing of North Vietnam is a dramatic illustration of this process. Bombing is clearly an illegal extension of the civil war to the territory of an external political entity, and not even an extension limited to the destruction of privileged sanctuary given to guerrillas. However, the non-military policy-makers have moderated the use of bombing in such a fashion as to assure that it will not be effective militarily. The consequence is an image of impotent unrestraint. Such an image seems frequently fostered when the United States casts aside respect for the rules and procedures of international law and embarks on military adventure. For the United States is not the sort of country that can mobilize a consensus within its own society for the effective use of military power when that use is in flagrant disregard of international law. This fortunate fact, if properly integrated into decision-making, suggests a beneficial set of limits upon American foreign policy.

The United States is, however, a country in which a consensus evidently can be mobilized in support of action that is at once moderately illegal and ineffective, but may nevertheless be very costly. In fact, the protracted quality of the war in Vietnam may cause more ultimate damage of every sort than if the United States would either conform altogether to governing rules of international law or ignore altogether legal and moral counsels of restraint in its recourse to military power. The dangers of the nuclear age and the values of the American policy make the imperialistic alternative highly unpalatable, although increasingly plausible to the extent that the realistic planners of military policy are frustrated by the incompatibility between the American mission in Vietnam and the military means needed to accomplish it.

The point is that the war in Vietnam has reached a level of intensity at which a fundamental orientation becomes essential. Accommodation of the two attitudes toward foreign policy is obviously unsatisfactory. Either the hawkish outlook must totally prevail with all its attendant risks and policies, including possibly the atomic mining of Haiphong and the nuclear bombing of Hanoi and China, or there must be a rather awkward retreat from the present position of military crusade, including possibly a concession of defeat in Vietnam, unilateral withdrawal, and a fundamental repudiation of the American option to use military power for purposes other than for the genuine instances of self-defense against armed attack. The immediate consequence of such a reorientation of policy would be to rehabilitate the distinction between civil war and international war, and a recognition that the phenomena of civil war must be handled either locally or by community action under the auspices of a regional or international institution, but not conducted as an American operation. I would identify this reorientation of policy as cosmopolitan isolationism. It is a necessary part of the rethinking that might lead to an understanding of what would, under the circumstances in Vietnam, constitute a reasonable set of expectations for a peace settlement.

3

International Law and the United States Role in the Viet Nam War

I

No contemporary problem of world order is more troublesome for an international lawyer than the analysis of the international law of "internal war."[1] A war is usefully classified as internal when violence takes place primarily within a single political entity, regardless of foreign support for the contending factions.[2] The insurgents who won the American Revolution were heavily supported by French arms. Wars of national liberation are not new, nor is external support for an incumbent regime. But considerable historical experience with foreign intervention in internal wars has not been adequately incorporated into prevailing doctrines of international law. In an age of civil turbulence and nuclear risk, the requirements of world order make imperative the effort to overcome the consequent confusion.[3]

The central issue is whether an externally abetted internal war belongs in either traditional legal category of war – "civil" or "international." Four

[1] See generally H. Eckstein, ed., *Internal War* (New York: Free Press, 1964); J. Rosenau, ed., *International Aspects of Civil Strife* (Princeton: Princeton University Press, 1964).

[2] The "internalness" of an internal war is a consequence of the objectives and arena of the violence. There is, of course, a range of different types of internal war. See Rosenau, "Internal War as an International Event," in Rosenau, ed., *International Aspects of Civil Strife*, 63–64. Rosenau usefully differentiates between internal wars, in terms of whether they are fought primarily to achieve changes in the personnel of the leadership, the nature of political authority, or the socio-political structure of the society.

[3] For helpful exposition, see Samuel P. Huntington, "Patterns of Violence in World Politics," in Samuel P. Huntington, ed., *Changing Patterns of Military Politics* (New York: Free Press of Glencoe, 1962), 17–50; see also L. Bloomfield, *International Military Forces* (Boston: Little, Brown, 1964), 24–46. See the table classifying examples of internal war in terms of "basically internal," "externally abetted internal instability," and "externally created or controlled internal instability" (*ibid.*, 28–30). Incidentally, Professor Bloomfield located the war in Viet Nam in the middle category as of 1964.

sub-inquiries are relevant. What are the legal restraints, if any, upon national discretion to treat a particular internal war as an international war? What rules and procedures are available to determine whether foreign participation in an internal war constitutes "military assistance," "intervention," "aggression," or "an armed attack"? What responses are permissible by the victim of "aggression" or "an armed attack"? Finally, what should be the roles of national, regional, and global actors in interpreting and applying the relevant rules?

If the internal war is regarded as a "civil" war, then the legally permitted response to intervention is restricted to counter-intervention;[4] an intervening nation whose own territory is not the scene of conflict may not attack the territory of a state intervening on the other side.[5] If foreign intervention were held to convert an "internal" war into an "international" war, the intervention could be regarded as an armed attack that would justify action in self-defense proportionate to the aggression. The victim of aggression is entitled, if necessary, to attack the territory of the aggressor, expanding the arena of violence to more than a single political entity.[6] Given the commitment of international law to limiting the scope, duration, and intensity of warfare, it would appear desirable severely to restrict, or perhaps to deny altogether, the discretion of nations to convert an internal war into an international war by characterizing external participation as "aggression" rather than as "intervention."[7]

The American outlook on these issues has dramatically changed in recent years. John Foster Dulles is properly associated with the expansion of American undertakings to defend foreign nations everywhere against Communist takeovers by either direct or indirect aggression. But even Dulles did not propose treating indirect aggression as the equivalent of an armed attack by one country on another. In fact, during the Congressional hearings on the Eisenhower

---

[4] I have developed this position in a paper given at the 1966 Annual Meeting of the American Society of International Law under the title "The International Regulation of Internal Violence in the Developing Countries,"*Proceedings of the American Society of International Law at Its Annual Meeting (1921–1969)*, 60 (1966), 58–67.

[5] The assertion in the text must be qualified to the extent that the United States decision to bomb North Viet Nam is treated as a law-creating precedent (rather than as a violation).

[6] If the conceptions of "aggression" and "armed attack" are so vague that nations can themselves determine their content, a self-serving legal description of the desired course of state action can be given and is not subject to criticism in a strict sense. A critic would be required to stress that an expansive definition of "armed attack," although not forbidden by prior rules of law, was an unwise legal claim because of its status as a precedent available to others and because of its tendency to expand the scope and magnify the scale of a particular conflict.

[7] It is important to distinguish between the factual processes of coercion and the legal labels used to justify or protest various positions taken by the participants. Aggression is a legal conclusion about the nature of a particular pattern of coercion.

Doctrine in 1957[8] Dulles declared, "if you open the door to saying that any country which feels it is being threatened by subversive activities in another country is free to use armed force against that country, you are opening the door to a series of wars over the world, and I am confident that it would lead to a third world war."[9] In my judgment, by bombing North Viet Nam the United States is opening such a door and is setting a dramatic precedent of precisely the sort that Dulles had in mind. Our pride as a nation is now so deeply dependent upon a successful outcome in Viet Nam that our Government seems insufficiently sensitive to the serious negative consequences of the Viet Nam precedent for the future of world order.[10]

The appraisal of a claim by a national government that an act of intervention is "aggression" is a complex task even if performed with utter impartiality. It depends on assessing very confused facts as to the extent and phasing of external participation, as well as upon interpreting the intentions of the participating nations. For instance, one must distinguish in the behavior of an international rival between a program of unlimited expansion through violence and intervention to assure the fair play of political forces in a particular domestic society. In the context of contemporary international politics, a crucial assessment is whether Communism or specific Communist states propose unlimited expansion by using unlawful force or whether they rely upon persuasion and permissible levels of coercion.[11] It is difficult to obtain adequate evidence

---

[8]   The critical section in the Eisenhower Doctrine (1957) is Section 2:

> The President is authorized to undertake, in the general area of the Middle East, military assistance programs with any nation or group of nations of that area desiring such assistance. Furthermore, the United States regards as vital to the national interest and world peace the preservation of the independence and integrity of the nations of the Middle East. To this end, if the President determines the necessity thereof, the United States is prepared to use armed force to assist any such nation or group of nations requesting assistance against armed aggression from any country controlled by international communism: *Provided,* That such employment shall be consonant with the treaty obligations of the United States and with the Constitution of the United States.

> *Department of State Bulletin*, 36 (1957), 481

[9]   The President's Proposal on the Middle East, Hearings before Senate Committees on Foreign Relations and Armed Services, 85th Cong., 1st Sess., pt. 1, 28 (1957).

[10] The role of national claims of a unilateral nature in the development of international law is examined in Richard Falk, "Toward a Responsible Procedure for the National Assertion of Protested Claims to Use Space," in H. Taubenfeld, ed., *Space and Society* (Dobbs Ferry, NY: Oceana Publications, 1964).

[11] This is the main theme of a speech by the Secretary of State. See Dean Rusk, "Address," *Proceedings of the American Society of International Law* (1965), 249–51.

on the limits of permissible political and paramilitary coercion.[12] Arguably, even a program of maximum expansion should be countered by self-limiting responses aimed at neutralizing Communist influence on internal wars and at building a world order that minimizes the role of military force.[13] We must also not overlook the welfare of the society torn by internal war. The great powers tend to wage their struggles for global dominance largely at the expense of the ex-colonial peoples.[14] These considerations support a conservative approach to internal wars, an approach treating them as civil wars, and permitting a neutralizing response as a maximum counteraction. And, specifically, if efforts to neutralize Communist expansion[15] in Viet Nam can be justified at all, the appropriate role of the United States is to counter "intervention" rather than to respond to an "armed attack."

The issue of self-determination is also relevant in the setting of internal war. If Communists or Communist-oriented elites can obtain political control without significant external support, it becomes difficult to vindicate Western intervention in terms of neutralizing Communist expansion. Castro's revolution represents a Communist success that was achieved without significant external support until after political control of Cuba was fully established. Part of the objection to American intervention in the Dominican Republic in 1965 arises from the absence of prior foreign intervention. The policies of preventing war, minimizing violence, and localizing conflict seem in these contexts to outweigh the objectives of anti-Communism; the United States serves both its own interests and those of the world community by respecting the outcome of internal political struggles. Unless we respect domestic political autonomy,

---

[12] I have discussed these issues in Richard Falk, "On Minimizing the Use of Nuclear Weapons: A Comparison of Revolutionary and Reformist Perspectives," in R. Falk, R. Tucker, and O. Young, *On Minimizing the Use of Nuclear Weapons* (Research Monograph No. 23, Center of International Studies, Princeton University, March 1, 1966).

[13] Everyone would agree in the abstract that it is important to reconcile policies directed at limiting the expansion of adversaries with those aimed at avoiding warfare, particularly nuclear warfare. See Richard Falk, *Law, Morality, and War* (New York: Praeger, 1963), 32–65.

[14] Relative peace is obtained through mutual deterrence at "the center" of the international system. Struggles for expansion are confined to "the periphery" where the risks of nuclear war can be minimized and where the costs of conflict can be shifted from the great powers to the ex-colonial nations.

[15] My own judgment, based on the analysis of the Geneva settlement in 1954, is that the war in South Viet Nam represents more an American attempt at "rollback" than a Communist attempt at "expansion." The Geneva Conference looked toward the reunification of the whole of Viet Nam under the leadership of Ho Chi Minh. The introduction into South Viet Nam of an American military presence thus appears as an effort to reverse these expectations and to deny Hanoi the full extent of its victory against the French. See also J. Lacouture, *Vietnam: Between Two Truces* (New York: Vintage, 1966), 17–68.

our adversaries have no incentive to refrain from participating on the side of their faction. The primary objective in relation to internal warfare is to establish rules of the game that allow domestic processes of political conflict to proceed without creating undue risks of a major war. In addition, human welfare and democratic ideals are best served by allowing the struggle between Communist and Western approaches to development to be waged by domestic factions. Recent events in Indonesia, Algeria, and Ghana demonstrate that these internal struggles for ascendancy are not inevitably won by Communists.

Civil strife can be analyzed in terms of three different types of violent conflict.[16] A Type I conflict involves the direct and massive use of military force by one political entity across a frontier of another – Korea, or Suez.[17] To neutralize the invasion it may be necessary to act promptly and unilaterally, and it is appropriate either to use force in self-defense or to organize collective action under the auspices of a regional or global institution. A Type II conflict involves substantial military participation by one or more foreign nations in an internal struggle for control, e.g., the Spanish Civil War. To neutralize this use of military power it may be necessary, and it is appropriate, to take offsetting military action confined to the internal arena, although only after seeking unsuccessful recourse to available procedures for peaceful settlement and machinery for collective security. A third type of conflict, Type III, is an internal struggle for control of a national society, the outcome of which is virtually independent of external participation. Of course, the outcome of a Type III conflict may affect the relative power of many other countries. Hungary prior to Soviet intervention, Cuba (1958–59), and the Dominican Republic prior to United States intervention typify this class of struggle. It is inappropriate for a foreign nation to use military power to influence the outcome. The degree of inappropriateness will vary with the extent and duration of the military power used, and also with the explicitness of the foreign nation's role.[18] Thus, the reliance on Cuban exiles to carry out the anti-Castro mission at the Bay of Pigs (1961) is somewhat less inappropriate than the use of United States Marines.

---

[16] These "types" are analytical rather than empirical in character. In actual experience a particular occasion of violence is a mixture of types, although the nature of the mixture is what makes one classification more appropriate than another.

[17] Border disputes generating limited, but overt, violence by one entity against another are a special sub-type under Type I that may or may not support a finding of "armed attack" or a defensive claim of "self-defense."

[18] See the emphasis on the *covertness* of the United States role in sponsoring the Bay of Pigs invasion of 1961 as an influential factor in the decision to proceed in Arthur Schlesinger, Jr., *A Thousand Days* (Boston: Houghton Mifflin, 1965), 233–97. And note that Schlesinger's opposition to the invasion was based in large part on his belief that it would be impossible to disguise the United States role (*ibid.*, 253–54).

Perhaps appreciating this distinction, North Viet Nam relied almost exclusively on South Vietnamese exiles during the early years of the anti-Diem war.[19]

These three models are analytical tools designed to clarify the nature and consequences of policy choices. Reasonable men may disagree on the proper classification of a particular war, especially if they cannot agree on the facts. An understanding of the controversy over the legality of United States participation in the war in Viet Nam seems aided by keeping in mind these distinct models.

The United States is treating the war as a Type I conflict. I would argue, for reasons set out in the next section, that the war belongs in Class III. But if this position entailing non-participation is rejected, then the maximum American response is counter-intervention as is permissible in a Type II situation.

Two general issues bear on an interpretation of the rights and duties of states in regard to internal wars of either Type II or III. First, to what extent does the constituted elite – the incumbent regime – enjoy a privileged position to request outside help in suppressing internal challenges directed at its control?[20] Traditional international law permits military assistance to the incumbent regime during early stages of an internal challenge. However, once the challenging faction demonstrates its capacity to gain control and administer a substantial portion of the society, most authorities hold that a duty of neutrality or non-discrimination governs the relations of both factions to outside states.[21] A state may act in favor of the incumbent to neutralize a Type III conflict only until the challenge is validated as substantial. A crucial question is whether outside states can themselves determine the point at which the challenge is validated, or whether validation is controlled, or at least influenced, by international procedures and by objective criteria of validation. The United States legal position stresses its continuing right to discriminate in favor of the incumbent regime and to deny even the political existence of the National Liberation Front (NLF), despite the *de facto* existence of the NLF over a long period and its effective control of a large portion of the disputed territory.[22]

[19]   See, e.g., D. Warner, *The Last Confucian* (London: Angus & Robertson, 1964), 155; Bernard B. Fall, *The Two Viet-Nams* (rev. ed.; New York: Praeger, 1964), 316–84.
[20]   See, e.g., J. Garner, "Questions of International Law in the Spanish Civil War," *American Journal of International Law*, 31 (1937), 66–73.
[21]   See generally A. Thomas and A. J. Thomas, Jr., *Non-Intervention: The Law and Its Impact in the Americas* (Dallas: Southern Methodist University Press, 1956), 215–21; see also H. Lauterpacht, *Recognition in International Law* (Cambridge: Cambridge University Press, 1957), 199–201, 227–33; Richard Falk, "Janus Tormented: The International Law of Internal War," in Rosenau, ed., *International Aspects of Civil Strife*, 197–209.
[22]   For a description of the extent of the NLF's governmental control, see W. Burchett, *Vietnam: Inside Story of the Guerilla War* (New York: International Publishers, 1965), 223–26; for legal argument, see Lauterpacht, *Recognition in International Law*, 175–238.

A second question partially applicable to Viet Nam is whether it is ever permissible to discriminate in favor of the counter-elite. The Communist states and the ex-colonial states of Asia and Africa assume that there are occasions warranting external participation in support of the insurgent faction. The Afro-Asian states argue that political legitimacy is established by an international consensus expressed through the formal acts of international institutions, rather than by the mere control of the constituted government.[23] This theory of legitimacy sanctions foreign military assistance to an "anti-colonialist" struggle. The extent to which this new attitude alters traditional international law is at present unclear, as is its full relevance to the conflict in Viet Nam. The argument for applicability to Viet Nam would emphasize the continuity between the 1946–54 anti-colonial war in Viet Nam and the present conflict. It would presuppose that the diplomatic recognition of South Viet Nam by some sixty countries conferred only nominal sovereignty, and that the Saigon regime is a client government of the United States, which has succeeded to the imperialistic role of the French. This approach implies that external states such as North Viet Nam, China, and the Soviet Union have "the right" to render support to the NLF.

These notions of permissible discrimination in favor of the constituted elite or the challenging counter-elite complicate considerably the legal analysis of participation in a Type III conflict and blur the boundaries between Types II and III. Any adequate statement of the international law of internal war must acknowledge this complexity, and admit along with it a certain degree of legal indeterminacy.[24]

II

The vast and competent literature on the war in South Viet Nam provides an essential factual background for an impartial approach to the legal issues presented in the Memorandum of Law prepared by the State Department.[25] It is

---

[23]   The legal status of a counter-elite in a colony is certainly improved by the repeated condemnations of colonialism in the United Nations and the recent passage of formal resolutions calling for decolonialization. Factors other than claims to be the constituted government are regularly taken into account in assessing claims of legitimacy in international relations.

[24]   For the theoretical background on legal indeterminacy in international law, see H. Lauterpacht, "Some Observations on the Prohibition of 'Non Liquet' and the Completeness of the Law," in *Symbolae Verzijl* (The Hague: Martinus Nijhoff, 1958), 196–221; J. Stone, "Non Liquet and the Function of Law in the International Community," *British Yearbook of International Law*, 35 (1959), 124–61.

[25]   Among those most helpful, see Lacouture, *Vietnam: Between Two Truces*; Fall, *The Two Viet-Nams*; Bernard B. Fall, *Viet-Nam Witness 1953–1966* (New York: Praeger, 1966); R. Shaplen, *The Lost Revolution* (rev. ed.; London: Deutsch, 1966); D. Lancaster, *The Emancipation of French Indo-China* (New York: Oxford University Press, 1961); Warner, *The Last Confucian*.

impossible to summarize all of the relevant facts, but it may be useful to indicate certain lines of reasoning that account for part of my disagreement with the official legal analysis. This disagreement reflects my interpretation of the internal war as primarily a consequence of indigenous forces. Even more, it stems from my concern for taking into account certain facts entirely excluded from the Memorandum, such as the pre-1954 war against the French and the repression of political opposition by the Diem regime.

It must be kept in mind that the present conflict in Viet Nam originated in the war fought between the French and the Vietminh for control of the whole of Viet Nam, which was "settled" at Geneva in 1954.[26] Although the intentions of the participants at Geneva were somewhat ambiguous, the general view at the time was that the Geneva agreements anticipated reunification under the leadership of Ho Chi Minh by 1956 to coincide with the French departure. France came to Geneva a defeated nation; the Vietminh held two-thirds or more of the country.[27] Had elections been held, it is generally agreed that reunification under Ho Chi Minh would have resulted, however one interprets the suppression of political opposition in the North or intimidation in the South.[28] Independent observers also agree that the anticipation of the prospect of peaceful reunification led Hanoi to observe the Geneva arrangements during the two years immediately following 1954. The undoubted disappointment caused by the refusal of the French and the Americans to make Saigon go through with the elections helps explain the resumption of insurrectionary violence after 1956.[29]

The Vietminh did leave a cadre of 5,000 or so elite guerrillas in the South, withdrawing others, as agreed, north of the Seventeenth Parallel.[30] Those

[26] The settlement was not very realistic. It failed to take into account Saigon's exclusion or the American opposition to the Geneva solution. No responsibility was imposed upon the French to assure compliance with the terms of settlement prior to their withdrawal. See Warner, *The Last Confucian*, 142–43.

[27] For a general account, see Lancaster, *The Emancipation of French Indo-China*, 290–358; Fall, *Viet-Nam Witness*, 69–83; for the fullest account of the Geneva negotiations, see J. Lacouture and P. Devillers, *La fin d'une guerre: Indochine 1954* (Paris: Éditions du Seuil, 1960). And see Dwight D. Eisenhower, *Mandate for Change* (New York: Doubleday, 1963), 332–75, for official American thinking during this period.

[28] There is agreement that an election held within the prescribed period would have been won by Ho Chi Minh. See, e.g., Shaplen, *The Lost Revolution*, xi; Warner, *The Last Confucian*, 142–43; Lacouture, *Vietnam: Between Two Truces*, 32: "The final declaration of the Geneva Conference foresaw, of course, that general election would permit the reunification of Vietnam two years later. And none doubted at the time that this would be to the benefit of the North."

[29] See Lacouture, *Vietnam: Between Two Truces*, 32–50.

[30] *Ibid.*, 32–68; *cf.* Fall, *Viet-Nam Witness*, 169–89.

left in the South apparently went "underground," hiding weapons for possible future use. This action seems no more than a reasonable precaution on the part of Hanoi in light of Saigon's continuing objection to the Geneva terms, and in view of Washington's evident willingness from 1954 onward to give Saigon political and military support. Given the terms of conflict and the balance of forces in Viet Nam prior to the Geneva Conference, French acceptance of a Viet Nam-wide defeat, American reluctance to affirm the results of Geneva, and Saigon's repudiation of the settlement, it seems quite reasonable for Hanoi to regard a resumption of the civil war as a distinct contingency. Although a decade of *de facto* independence (affirmed by diplomatic recognition) now gives South Viet Nam a strong claim to existence as a political entity, Hanoi certainly had no obligation in 1954 to respect claims of an independent political status for Saigon.[31] To clarify the diplomatic context in Geneva, it is well to recall that the Vietminh was the sole negotiator on behalf of Vietnamese interests at Geneva in 1954.

Later in 1954 the Saigon regime under Premier Diem ruthlessly suppressed all political opposition.[32] Observers agree that organization of an underground was an inevitable reaction to this suppression, and that the NLF at its inception included many non-Communist elements.[33] It also appears that Saigon was unwilling to negotiate, or even consult, on questions affecting reunification, and was unwilling to normalize economic relations with Hanoi. The great economic strain imposed on North Viet Nam forced it to use scarce foreign exchange to obtain part of its food supply from other countries.[34]

Furthermore, the French military presence soon was replaced by an American military presence prior to the scheduled elections on reunification.[35] The evolution of an American "commitment" to Saigon's permanence and legitimacy contrasts radically with both the expectations created at Geneva in 1954 and the subsequent attitudes of the French. United States involvement in the politics of South Viet Nam increased constantly; it was no secret

---

[31] Hanoi was "entitled" to prevent Saigon from establishing itself as a political entity with independent claims to diplomatic status as a sovereign state. A separation of Viet Nam into two states was not contemplated by the participants at Geneva.

[32] See Warner, *The Last Confucian,* 107–24; Lacouture, *Vietnam: Between Two Truces,* 17–31.

[33] Bernard B. Fall, "Viet-Cong – The Unseen Enemy in Viet-Nam," in Marcus G. Raskin and Bernard B. Fall, eds., *The Viet-Nam Reader* (New York: Vintage, 1965), pp. 252–61.

[34] Lacouture, *Vietnam: Between Two Truces,* 34–35, 68.

[35] This is the major thesis of Lacouture, "Vietnam: The Lessons of War," reprinted from *New York Review of Books,* March 3, 1966, 1, in *Hearings on S.2793 Before the Senate Committee on Foreign Relations,* 89th Cong., 2d Sess. 655–61 (1966) (hereinafter cited as *Viet Nam Hearings*).

that the Diem government largely was constituted and sustained in its early months by the United States.[36]

Despite the escalating American political, military, and economic assistance, the Saigon regime proved incapable of achieving political stability. Numerous regimes have come and gone. None has commanded the respect and allegiance of any significant segment of the population. Often in situations of civil war diverse factions are able to establish an expedient working unity during the period of common national emergency. The NLF seems to maintain substantial control over its heterogeneous followers while one Saigon regime after another collapses or totters on the brink. The United States recognized at an early stage that the Saigon regime had to transform its own feudal social structure before it could provide the basis for viable government in South Viet Nam.[37] This is a most unusual demand by an external ally; it bears witness to the fragile and dubious claim of each successive Saigon regime to govern even the parts of South Viet Nam not held by the Vietcong.

In addition, Saigon and the United States seem to have neglected repeated opportunities for negotiations with Hanoi during earlier stages of the war.[38] As late as February 1965, the United States Government rebuked U Thant for engaging in unauthorized negotiations. Until the prospects for a military solution favorable to Saigon diminished to the vanishing point, the United States made no attempt to negotiate a peaceful settlement or to entrust responsibility for settlement to either the Security Council or the Co-Chairmen of the Geneva Conference.[39] This reluctance, when added to the political losses

---

[36] For an account of the covert dimension of the United States role in the domestic affairs of South Viet Nam, see D. Wise and T. Ross, *The Invisible Government* (New York: Random House, 1964), 155–64. There are also references to the exercise of covert influence by the United States in Lacouture, *Vietnam: Between Two Truces*; Shaplen, *The Lost Revolution*; and Warner, *The Last Confucian*. American strategies of covert influence in foreign countries are analyzed and described in P. Blackstock, *The Strategy of Subversion* (Chicago: Quadrangle Books, 1964).

[37] *Cf.* letter of President Eisenhower to Premier Diem on October 23, 1954, Senate Committee on Foreign Relations, 89th Cong., 1st Sess., *Background Information Relating to Southeast Asia and Viet Nam* (Comm. Print 1965) (hereinafter cited as *Background Information*). For a recent reiteration, see "US and South Vietnamese Leaders Meet at Honolulu," *Department of State Bulletin*, 54 (Feb. 28, 1966), 302–07.

[38] The American approach to a negotiated settlement is recounted and criticized in American Friends Service Committee, *Peace in Viet Nam* (New York: Hill & Wang, 1966), 50–67. Among other observations, this report points out that "a careful reading of the *New York Times* shows that the United States has rejected no fewer than seven efforts to negotiate an end to the war" (*ibid.*, 51). See also the article by Flora Lewis, in *Viet Nam Hearings*, 323–34.

[39] For predictions of an American victory in South Viet Nam, see M. Raskin and B. Fall, "Chronology of Events in Viet-Nam and Southeast Asia," in *Background Information*, 377, 388–89, 390–92. As late as October 2, 1963, Secretary McNamara and General Taylor issued an official statement reporting their conclusion that "the major part of the United States

suffered by Hanoi at Geneva in 1954, makes it easier to comprehend Hanoi's reluctance to negotiate now.[40]

All of these considerations lead me to regard the war in South Vietnam primarily as a Type III conflict, in which the United States ought not to have participated. Because of Hanoi's increasing participation on behalf of the Vietcong, it is arguable, although rather unpersuasive, that this war is properly categorized as an example of Type II, so that the United States could legitimately give military assistance to Saigon, but is obligated to limit the arena of violence to the territory of South Viet Nam. The weakness of the Saigon regime compared to the NLF renders necessary a disproportionately large military commitment by the United States to neutralize the indigenous advantages of the Vietcong and the support of Hanoi.[41] Our disproportionate commitment makes it appear that the United States rather than Hanoi is escalating the war. And this appearance undercuts any defense of our participation as necessary to offset participation on the other side, and thereby give "the true" balance of domestic forces a chance to control the outcome.[42] The State

---

military task can be completed by the end of 1965"; and on November 1, 1963, General Paul D. Harkins, US military commander, wrote in *Stars & Stripes* (Tokyo) that, "Victory in the sense it would apply to this kind of war is just months away and the reduction of American advisers can begin any time now." The point of quoting these statements is to suggest that as long as a favorable military solution seemed forthcoming at a tolerable cost the United States was not interested in a negotiated settlement.

[40] An important element in the background of Vietnamese history was the successful resistance movement led by Ho Chi Minh against the Japanese in the closing years of World War II. When the Japanese left French Indo-China, Ho Chi Minh was in control of the entire territory, and was induced to accept the return to power of the French colonial administration in exchange for promises of political independence that were never fulfilled. The recollection of this first phase of the Vietnamese war, when added to the post-1954 experience, may deepen Hanoi's impression that its political success depends upon military effort. On negotiating with Hanoi, see also the *Report of the Ad Hoc Congressional Conference on Viet Nam*, 89th Cong., 2d Sess. 4-5 (Comm. Print 1966) (hereinafter cited as *Ad Hoc Congressional Conference*).

[41] Bernard Fall, writing on the sort of military superiority that is required to achieve victory over an insurgency, says:

in the past it [victory] has required a ratio of pacification forces versus insurgents that is simply not available in Viet-Nam today [Jan. 1965]. In Malaya, British and Malayan forces have achieved a ratio of 50 to 1; in Cyprus, British forces had achieved a 110 to 1 ratio, and in Algeria the French had reached 10 to 1. The present ratio in South Viet-Nam is 4.5 to 1, and the French ratio in the First Indochina War was an incredibly low 1.2 to 1, which (all other matters being equal) would suffice to explain France's ultimate defeat.

Fall, *Viet-Nam Witness*, 291

[42] Official United States Government statements frequently imply that the United States must render help to the Saigon regime equivalent to the help given by Hanoi to the NLF. If "equivalent" is measured by the needs of the ratio, then it may be as much as 110 times as great as the aid given to the insurgents whereas, if equivalent means arithmetically equal, it will be completely ineffectual.

Department Memorandum assumes that the war is a Type I conflict, and argues that American participation is really collective self-defense in response to an armed attack by North Viet Nam upon South Viet Nam. But to characterize North Viet Nam's participation in the struggle in the South as "an armed attack" is unwise as well as incorrect. Such a contention, if accepted as an authoritative precedent, goes a long way toward abolishing the distinction between international and civil war. The war in South Viet Nam should be viewed as primarily between factions contending for control of the southern zone, whether or not the zone is considered a nation.[43] A claim of self-defense by Saigon seems misplaced, and the exercise of rights of self-defense by committing violent acts against the territory of North Viet Nam tends toward the establishment of an unfortunate precedent.[44]

III

The Memorandum of the State Department was submitted by the Legal Adviser to the Senate Committee on Foreign Relations on March 8, 1966.[45] In assessing it, we should keep in mind several considerations. First, the United States Government is the client of the Legal Adviser, and the Memorandum, as is entirely appropriate, is an adversary document. A legal adviser in Hanoi could prepare a comparable document. Adversary discourse in legal analysis should be sharply distinguished from an impartial determination of the merits of opposed positions.[46]

Second, the Legal Memorandum was evidently framed as a response to the Memorandum of Law prepared by the Lawyers Committee on American

[43] Hanoi itself takes a conflict-confining position that the war in Viet Nam is a civil war being waged to determine control of South Viet Nam rather than a civil or international war to determine control of the whole of Viet Nam. See, e.g., "Policy Declaration of Premier Pham Van Dong of North Viet-Nam, April 14, 1965," in Raskin and Fall, eds., *Viet-Nam Reader*, 342–43 ("Hanoi's Four Points"). See also "Program of the National Liberation Front of South Viet-Nam," *ibid.*, 216–21 (on Dec. 20, 1960).

[44] But, as of July 1966, the United States has not attacked North Vietnamese centers of population and has made only limited attacks on industrial complexes (oil depots). The unjustified claim of self-defense has been noted, but it is well to appreciate the as yet restrained form of the claim.

[45] An earlier, somewhat skimpy, memorandum, "The Legal Basis for US Actions Against North Viet Nam," was issued by the Department of State on March 8, 1965; for the text, see *Background Information*, 191–94.

[46] I have tried to urge a non-adversary role for the international lawyer on several occasions: see Richard Falk, "The Adequacy of Contemporary Theories of International Law – Gaps in Legal Thinking," *Virginia Law Review*, 50 (1964), 233–43; and a recent paper delivered at the Harris Conference on New Approaches to International Relations, at the University of Chicago, June 1966, with the title "New Approaches to the Study of International Law," published in *American Journal of International Law*, 61 (1967), 477–95.

Policy Toward Viet Nam.[47] The argument of the Lawyers Committee fails to
raise sharply the crucial issue – namely, the discretion of the United States to
delimit its legal rights and duties by treating the conflict in South Viet Nam as
an international war of aggression rather than as a civil war.[48]

Third, the Legal Adviser's Memorandum implies that both the facts of
aggression and the legal rules governing self-defense are clear. This is misleading. Except in instances of overt, massive aggression across an international
frontier, international law offers very *indefinite* guidance about the permissible occasions for or extent of recourse to force in self-defense. Doctrinal
ambiguity is greatest with respect to internal wars with significant external
participation.[49] International law offers very little authoritative guidance on
the central issue of permissible assistance to the contending factions.[50] To conclude that international law is indefinite is not to suggest that it is irrelevant.
On the contrary, if rules are indefinite and procedures for their interpretation
unavailable, prevailing national practice sets precedents for the future. In this
light, American activity in Viet Nam is particularly unfortunate for the future
of doctrines aimed at limiting international violence.[51]

In this section I propose to criticize the legal argument of the Memorandum,
taking some issue with both inferences of fact and conclusions of law. I will
analyze the consequences of characterizing international participation in
Viet Nam as intervention and counter-intervention in an ongoing civil war.
Although I will call attention to the shortcomings in the legal position of the
United States, my main intention is to approach this inquiry in the spirit of

[47] See Lawyers Committee on American Policy Toward Viet Nam, "American Policy Vis-à-Vis
      Viet Nam, Memorandum of Law," in *Viet Nam Hearings*, 687–713.
[48] The Spanish Civil War is a useful historical precedent for the legal treatment of large-scale
      foreign interventions on both sides of an internal war. For a full analysis see N. Padelford,
      International Law and Diplomacy in the Spanish Civil Strife (New York: Macmillan, 1939).
      Another way of posing the issue would be to ask whether Cuba, after the Bay of Pigs invasion,
      might have been entitled to ask the Soviet Union for military assistance, including air strikes
      against staging areas in the United States. For a critical account of the legal status of American
      participation in the Bay of Pigs invasion, see Richard Falk, "American Intervention in Cuba
      and the Rule of Law," *Ohio State Law Journal*, 22 (1961), 546–85.
[49] I have argued to this effect, in Falk, "Janus Tormented," 210–40.
[50] By "authoritative guidance" I mean guidance of action by clear, applicable rules of inter-
      national law that are congruent with community expectations about permissible behavior;
      the rules must be clear enough to permit identification of a violation without independent
      fact-finding procedures.
[51] International customary law evolves as a consequence of national claims and counter-claims
      acquiring through time an authoritative status. States assert these claims and counter-claims
      to maximize policy considerations in various contexts. For a major exposition of this process
      see M. McDougal and W. Burke, *The Public Order of the Oceans* (New Haven: Yale University
      Press, 1962).

scholarly detachment rather than as an adversary critic.[52] Such detachment is not value-free. I try to appraise the claims of national actors in light of the requirements of world order. My appraisal presupposes the desirability of narrowing the discretion of nations to determine for themselves the occasions on which violence is permissible or that an increase of the scale and scope of ongoing violence is appropriate. I am convinced that it is important for any country (including my own) to reconcile its foreign policy with the rules regulating the use of force in international affairs, and that, therefore, it does not serve *even* the national interest to accept a legal justification for our own recourse to violence that we would not be prepared to have invoked against us by other states similarly situated.[53] The international legal order, predominantly decentralized, depends for effectiveness on the acceptance by principal states of the fundamental ordering notions of symmetry, reciprocity, and national precedent-setting.[54]

In analyzing the Memorandum I will adhere to its outline of issues, concentrating on the most significant.

Collective Self-Defense. The Memorandum argues that the United States may, at Saigon's request, participate in the collective self-defense of South Viet Nam because North Viet Nam has made a prior armed attack. But may indirect aggression be treated as an armed attack without the approval of an appropriate international institution? The United States rests its case on the role of Hanoi in the period between 1954 and 1959 in setting up "a covert political-military organization" and by its infiltration of "over 40,000 armed and unarmed guerrillas into South Viet Nam" during the subsequent five years. The Memorandum concludes that "the external aggression from the North is the critical military element of the insurgency," that "the infiltration of thousands of armed men clearly constitutes an 'armed attack' under any reasonable definition," and that, although there may be doubt as to "the exact date at which North Viet Nam's aggression grew into an 'armed attack,' [it certainly] had occurred before February 1965."

---

[52] An adversary debate may be useful to clarify the legal issues, but an impartial perspective is also needed to help in the process of choosing among the adversary presentations.

[53] America's relative inability to make effective legal protests against further nuclear testing on the high seas and in the atmosphere is partly a result of America's earlier legal defense of its own similar behavior. A legal precedent is created by the effective assertion of a claim to act, and this precedent may be difficult to repudiate, even if the precedent-setter has greater power than does the actor relying upon the precedent.

[54] See Richard Falk, *The Role of Domestic Courts in the International Legal Order* (Syracuse, NY: Syracuse University Press, 1964), 21–52.

This argument is questionable on its face, that is, without even criticizing its most selective presentation of the facts. Consider first the highly ideological character of prevailing attitudes toward the just use of force. The Communist countries favor support for wars of national liberation; the West – in particular, the United States – favors support for anti-Communist wars; and the Afro-Asian states favor support for anti-colonialist and anti-racist wars.[55] Consider also the importance, acknowledged by the United States in other settings,[56] of circumscribing the right of self-defense. The use of force on some other basis – for example, defensive intervention or regional security – moderates rather than escalates a conflict. But the invocation of self-defense as a rationale during a conflict previously contained within a single state tends to enlarge the arena of conflict to include states that are claiming and counter-claiming that each other's intervention in the civil strife is an armed attack. If the infiltration constitutes an armed attack, the bombing of North Viet Nam may be justified. But if North Viet Nam had operative collective defense arrangements with China and the Soviet Union it is easy to project a scenario of escalation ending in global catastrophe. If, on the other hand, infiltration is merely intervention, and appropriate responses are limited to counter-intervention, the area of violence is restricted to the territory of South Viet Nam and its magnitude is kept within more manageable limits.[57]

The argument in the Memorandum also assumes that armed help to the insurgent faction is under all circumstances a violation of international law. As mentioned earlier, at some stage in civil strife it is permissible for outside states to regard the insurgent elite as the equal of the incumbent regime and to render it equivalent assistance.[58] Since no collective procedures are available to determine when an insurgency has proceeded far enough to warrant this status, outside states enjoy virtually unlimited discretion to determine the

---

[55] Compare with these claims the prohibitions upon the use of force expressed in absolute terms in Article 2(4) of the United Nations Charter. Self-defense against a prior armed attack appears to be the only permissible national basis for the use of force (without authorization from the United Nations).

[56] See, e.g., avoidance of a self-defense rationale by government officials offering legal justification for the United States claims to interdict on the high seas Soviet intermediate range ballistics bound for Cuba in 1962: L. Meeker, "Defensive Quarantine and the Law," *American Journal of International Law*, 57 (1963), 515–24; A. Chayes, "The Legal Case for US Action on Cuba," *Department of State Bulletin*, 47 (1962), 763–65.

[57] For a fuller rationale see Falk, "The International Regulation of Internal Violence in the Developing Countries."

[58] *Cf.* the study of the international relations of the insurgent groups during the Algerian War of Independence by M. Bedjaoui, *Law and the Algerian Revolution* (Brussels: International Association of Democratic Lawyers, 1961).

comparative legitimacy of competing elites.[59] In effect, then, no rules of international law exist to distinguish clearly between permissible and impermissible intervention in civil strife.[60] To call hostile intervention not only impermissible but an instance of the most serious illegality – an armed attack – seems very unfortunate. In addition to a tendency to escalate any particular conflict, the position that interventions are armed attacks so broadens the notion of armed attack that all nations will be able to make plausible claims of self-defense in almost every situation of protracted internal war. It therefore seems desirable to confine the armed attack/self-defense rationale to the Korea-type conflict (Type I) and to deny its applicability in Viet Nam, whether the war in Viet Nam is denominated Type II or Type III. The Memorandum's argument on self-defense is also deficient in that it relies upon a very selective presentation of the facts. It ignores Saigon's consistent opposition to the terms of the Geneva settlement, thereby casting in very different light Hanoi's motives for the steps it took in South Viet Nam to assert its claims.[61] It is essential to recall that the pre-1954 conflict was waged for control of *all* of Viet Nam and that the settlement at Geneva was no more than "a cease-fire." President Diem's ruthless suppression of political opposition in South Viet Nam from 1954 onward, in violation of the ban on political reprisals included in the Geneva Agreements, is also relevant.[62]

Furthermore, the injection of an American political and military presence was, from the perspective of Hanoi, inconsistent with the whole spirit of Geneva.[63] The United States decision to commit itself to maintaining a

[59] If "the will of the international community" operates as the true basis of international law, the criteria of legitimacy shift to correspond to the values of the expanded membership in international society.

[60] See Lauterpacht, *Recognition in International Law*, 253–55.

[61] If mutuality is the basic condition for the existence of a legal obligation, it is essential that both disputants accept the terms of settlement. If there is non-acceptance on one side, the other side is in a position to protect its position *as if* the settlement did not exist. In the setting of Viet Nam this would suggest that Hanoi was free to pursue its war aims on a pre-1954 basis and ignore the division of the country into two zones. It is ironic that South Viet Nam owes its original political identity entirely to the Geneva Agreements.

[62] *Cf.* Article 15, "Agreement on the Cessation of Hostilities": "Each party undertakes to refrain from any reprisals or discrimination against persons or organizations for their activities during the hostilities and also undertakes to guarantee their democratic freedoms" (*Background Information*, 50, 53). See Lacouture, *Vietnam: Between Two Truces*, 28–31; Burchett, *Vietnam: Inside Story of the Guerilla War*, 109–28.

[63] The operative great power in the area was France. It was not in Hanoi's interest to give up a favorable battle position so that the United States could replace the French military presence. The worsening of their position in the area as a result of the negotiations at Geneva may explain, in part, their reluctance to negotiate a "settlement" and give up a favorable military position once again.

Western-oriented regime in South Viet Nam upset the expectations regarding
the Southeast Asian balance of power; in that respect, it was similar to the
Soviet attempt to upset the Caribbean balance of power by installing interme-
diate-range missiles in Cuba in 1962.[64]

The Memorandum seems to concede that until 1964 the bulk of infiltrated
men were South Vietnamese who had come north after the cease-fire in 1954.
The use of exiles to bolster an insurgent cause appears to be on the border-
line between permissible and impermissible behavior in contemporary international politics. The role of the United States Government in sponsoring
the unsuccessful invasion at the Bay of Pigs in 1961 was a far more flagrant
example of the use of exiles to overthrow a constituted government in a neighboring country than the early role of Hanoi in fostering an uprising in the
South.[65] The claim by the United States to control political events in Cuba is
far more tenuous than the claim by North Viet Nam to exercise control (or at
least remove the influence of a hostile superpower) over political life in the
South.[66] And Castro's regime was domestically viable in a manner that Saigon
regimes have never been – suggesting that South Viet Nam presents a more
genuine revolutionary situation than does contemporary Cuba. It seems more
destructive of world order to help overthrow a firmly established government
than to assist an ongoing revolution against a regime incapable of governing.

African countries admit helping exiles overthrow governments under white
control.[67] American support for Captive Nations Week is still another form
of support outside of the Communist bloc for exile aspirations.[68] In short,

[64] One influential view of the basis of international order stresses maintaining current balances
and expectations. Any attempt to rely upon military means to upset these balances and expectations is perceived and treated as "aggression." The intrusion of Soviet military influence
into the Western hemisphere by attempting to emplace missiles constituted the provocative element. The same military result could have been achieved by increasing the Atlantic
deployment of missile-carrying submarines. This sense of "provocative" might also describe
the perception of the escalating American military commitment in Southeast Asia.

[65] For an authoritative account of the United States role, see Schlesinger, *A Thousand Days*,
206–97.

[66] The strength of Hanoi's claim arises from the prior struggle to control the entire country, the
military victory by the Vietminh in that struggle, the expectations created at Geneva that the
elections would confirm that military victory, the delimitation of South Viet Nam as "a temporary zone," and, finally, the refusal by South Viet Nam to consult on elections or to refrain
from reprisals.

[67] In the Final Act of the Conference of Heads of States or Governments at Cairo in 1964
the following declaration was made by the forty-seven non-aligned powers assembled:
"Colonized people may legitimately resort to arms to secure the full exercise of their right to
self-determination."

[68] For perceptive discussion of the status of "Captive Nations Week" in international law, see Q.
Wright, "Subversive Intervention," *American Journal of International Law*, 54 (1960), 521–35.

international law neither attempts nor is able to regulate support given exile groups. The activities of Hanoi between 1954 and 1964 conform to patterns of tolerable conflict in contemporary international politics.

The Memorandum contends that, subsequent to 1964, Hanoi has increasingly infiltrated regular elements of the North Vietnamese army until at present "there is evidence that nine regiments of regular North Vietnamese forces are fighting in the South." Arguably, the NLF was not eligible to receive external support in the early years of strife after 1954, as its challenge to the government amounted to no more than "a rebellion." But certainly after the Vietcong gained effective control over large portions of the countryside it was *permissible* for North Viet Nam to treat the NLF as a "belligerent" with a right to conduct external relations.[69] This area of international law is exceedingly vague; states have a wide range of discretion in establishing their relations with contending factions in a foreign country.[70]

The remainder of the first section of the Memorandum responds to the Lawyers Committee Memorandum of Law, but is not relevant to the solution of the critical legal questions. It is persuasive but trivial for the State Department to demonstrate that international law recognizes the right of individual and collective self-defense against an armed attack; that non-members of the United Nations enjoy the same rights of self-defense as do members;[71] that South Viet Nam is a political entity entitled to claim the right of self-defense despite its origin as a "temporary zone";[72] and that the right of collective self-defense may be exercised independent of a regional arrangement organized under Chapter VIII of the United Nations Charter.[73] South

[69] See the extent of international recognition accorded the FLN in Algeria during their war against the French: Bedjaoui, *Law and the Algerian Revolution*, 110–38.

[70] No clear rules of prohibition nor any required procedures exist which subject national discretion to international review. National discretion consequently governs practice. For useful discussions stressing the survival under the United Nations Charter of a wider right of self-defense than the interpretation offered here, see D. W. Bowett, *Self-Defense in International Law* (New York: Praeger, 1958), 182–99; M. McDougal and F. Feliciano, *Law and Minimum World Public Order* (New Haven: Yale University Press, 1961), 121–260; for a position similar to the one taken in the text, see Louis Henkin, "Force, Intervention and Neutrality in Contemporary International Law," *Proceedings of the American Society of International Law* (1963), 147–62.

[71] For consideration of this question, see Bowett, *Self-Defense in International Law*, 193–95.

[72] See the first sentence of Article 6 of the Final Declaration: "The Conference recognizes that the essential purpose of the agreement relating to Viet-Nam is to settle military questions with a view to ending hostilities and that the military demarcation line is provisional and *should not in any way be interpreted as constituting a political or territorial boundary*" (*Background Information*, 58, 59; emphasis added). For Saigon's relevant conduct, see Lacouture, *Vietnam: Between Two Truces*, 24–31.

[73] For a useful analysis, see Bowett, *Self-Defense in International Law*, 200–48; McDougal and Feliciano, *Law and Minimum World Public Order*, 244–53.

Viet Nam would have had the right to act in self-defense *if an armed attack had occurred*, and the United States would then have had the right to act in collective self-defense.[74]

It is also important to determine whether the United States has complied with the reporting requirement contained in Article 51 of the United Nations Charter.[75] The United States did encourage a limited Security Council debate during August 1964 of the Gulf of Tonkin "incidents."[76] Furthermore, the United States submitted two reports to the Security Council during February 1965 concerning its recourse to bombing North Viet Nam and the general character of the war. And in January 1966 the United States submitted the Viet Nam question to the Security Council.[77] It seems reasonable to conclude that the Security Council (or, for that matter, the General Assembly) is unwilling and unable to intervene in any *overt* manner in the conflict in Viet Nam. This conclusion is reinforced by the hostility of the Communist states toward American proposals for a settlement.[78] On the other hand, there is no evidence of formal initiative by the members of the United Nations to question the propriety of the United States policies. The very serious *procedural* question posed is whether the failure of the United Nations to act relieves the United States of its burden to submit claims of self-defense to review by the organized international community.[79] A further question is whether any international

[74] That is, it would conform to expectations about what constitutes a permissible claim to use force in self-defense. Despite considerable controversy about the wisdom of the United States' involvement in the defense of Korea, there was no debate whatsoever (outside of Communist countries) about the legality of a defensive claim. There was some legal discussion about the propriety of United Nations involvement. For an argument in favor of legality, see M. McDougal and R. Gardner, "The Veto and the Charter: An Interpretation for Survival," in M. McDougal and associates, *Studies in World Public Order* (New Haven: Yale University Press, 1960), 718–60. In retrospect, however, Korea exemplifies "an armed attack" for which force in response is appropriate, even if used on the territory of the attacking state.

[75] For communications sent by the United States to the United Nations and relied upon to show compliance with the reporting requirements of Article 51, see *Viet Nam Hearings*, 634–40.

[76] For a description of official United States views, see "Promoting the Maintenance of International Peace and Security in Southeast Asia," HR Rep. No. 1708, 88th Cong., 2d Sess. (1964); see Ambassador Stevenson's statement to the Security Council on August 5, 1964, in *Background Information*, 124–28.

[77] No action was taken by the United Nations and the debate was inconclusive and insignificant.

[78] Neither China nor North Viet Nam indicates any willingness to acknowledge a role for the United Nations. Of course, the exclusion of China from representation in the United Nations may account for Chinese opposition to a UN solution. See also *Ad Hoc Congressional Conference*, 5.

[79] To what extent, that is, do states have residual discretion to determine the legality of claims to use force in the event of United Nations inability to reach a clear decision?

legal limitations upon national discretion apply when the United Nations refrains from passing judgment on claims to use force in self-defense.[80]

The Security Council failed to endorse American claims in Viet Nam, and this failure was not merely a consequence of Soviet or Communist opposition. Therefore, if the burden of justification for recourse to self-defense is upon the claimant, inaction by the United Nations provides no legal comfort on the *substantive issue* – that is, the legality of proportional self-defense given "the facts" in Viet Nam. As to the *procedural issue* – that is, compliance with the reporting requirement of Article 51 – the United States may be considered to have complied *pro forma*, but not in terms of the spirit of the Charter of the United Nations.

The overriding purpose of the Charter is to commit states to use force only as a last resort after the exhaustion of all other alternatives. In the early period after 1954 the United States relied heavily on its unilateral economic and military capability to protect the Saigon regime against the Vietcong. No *prior* attempt was made, in accordance with Article 33, to settle the dispute by peaceful means.[81] Yet the spirit of the Charter requires that a nation claiming to undertake military action in collective self-defense must first invoke the collective review and responsibility of the United Nations. The United States did not call for United Nations review until January 1966, that is, until a time when the prospects for a favorable military solution at tolerable costs seemed dismal, many months subsequent to bombing North Vietnamese territory. As long as a military victory was anticipated, the United States resented any attempt to question its discretion to use force or to share its responsibility for obtaining a settlement.[82] American recourse to procedures for peaceful settlement came as a last rather than a first resort. The United States had made no serious effort to complain about alleged North Vietnamese violations of the Geneva Agreements, nor to recommend a reconvening of a new Geneva Conference in the decade of escalating commitment after 1954.

---

[80] The nature of these restraints may be of two varieties: first, the considerations entering into the creation of a precedent; second, the restraints of customary international law requiring that minimum necessary force be used to attain belligerent objectives and requiring the maintenance of the distinction between military and non-military targets and between combatants and non-combatants. One wonders whether these latter distinctions can be maintained in a guerrilla war such as that in Viet Nam.

[81] UN Charter Art. 33(1):

The parties to any dispute, the continuance of which is likely to endanger the maintenance of international peace and security, shall, first of all, seek a solution by negotiation, enquiry, mediation, conciliation, arbitration, judicial settlement, resort to regional agencies or arrangements, or other peaceful means of their own choice.

[82] *Cf.* n. 39 above.

Saigon submitted complaints to the International Control Commission, but that body was neither constituted nor intended to deal with the resumption of a war for control of South Viet Nam that was apparently provoked by Saigon's refusal to hold elections.

Further, not until 1965 did the United States welcome the independent efforts of the Secretary-General to act as a negotiating intermediary between Washington and Hanoi.[83] Until it became evident that a military victory over the Vietcong was not forthcoming, the United States Government was hostile to suggestions emanating from either U Thant (or De Gaulle) that a negotiated settlement was both *appropriate* and *attainable*. The State Department's belated offer to negotiate must be discounted in light of its public relations overtones and our effort over the last decade to reverse the expectations of Geneva. The United States negotiating position is also made less credible by our failure to accord the NLF diplomatic status as a party in conflict.[84] This failure is especially dramatic in light of the NLF's ability effectively to govern territory under its possession and Saigon's relative inability to do so.

The American approach to negotiations lends support to the conclusion that our sporadic attempts at a peaceful settlement are belated gestures, and that we seek "victory" at the negotiating table only when it becomes unattainable on the battlefield. The United States showed no willingness to subordinate national discretion to the collective will of the organized international community. In fact, Viet Nam exemplifies the American global strategy of using military power whenever necessary to prevent Communist expansion and to determine these necessary occasions by national decisions. This militant anti-Communism represents the essence of unilateralism.[85]

One must conclude that the United States was determined to use its military power as it saw fit in Viet Nam in the long period from 1954 to January 1966. In 1966 at last a belated, if halfhearted, attempt to collectivize responsibility was made by appealing to the Security Council to obtain, in the words of the Memorandum, "discussions looking toward a peaceful settlement on the basis of the Geneva accords." The Memorandum goes on to observe that, "Indeed,

---

[83]   *Cf.* n. 38 above.

[84]   See the recommendations to this effect in *Ad Hoc Congressional Conference*, 5.

[85]   That is, it represents the claim to use force for purposes determined by the United States. The ideological quality of this unilateralism – its quality as an anti-communist crusade – is suggested by "the understanding" attached by the United States to its ratification of the SEATO treaty limiting "its recognition of the effect of aggression and armed attack . . . to communist aggression." It is very unusual to restrict the applicability of a security arrangement in terms of the ideological identity of the aggressor, rather than in terms of national identity or with reference to the character of the aggression.

since the United States submission on January 1966, members of the Council have been notably reluctant to proceed with any consideration of the Viet-Nam question." Should this reluctance come as a surprise? Given the timing and magnitude of the American request, it was inevitable that the United Nations would find itself unable to do anything constructive at that stage. United Nations inaction has deepened the awareness of the Organization's limited ability to safeguard world peace, whenever the nuclear superpowers take opposite sides of a violent conflict.[86] Disputes must be submitted *prior* to deep involvement if the United Nations is to play a significant role.[87] The war in Viet Nam presented many appropriate opportunities – the various steps up the escalation ladder – for earlier, more effective, American recourse to the United Nations. But during the entire war in Viet Nam, the United States has shown no significant disposition to limit discretionary control over its national military power by making constructive use of collective procedures of peaceful settlement.

Proportionality. Even if we grant the Memorandum's contention that North Viet Nam is guilty of aggression amounting to an armed attack and that the United States is entitled to join in the collective self-defense of South Viet Nam, important questions remain concerning the quantum, ratio, and modalities of force employed. Elementary principles both of criminal and of international law require that force legitimately used must be reasonably calculated to attain the objective pursued and be somewhat proportional to the provocation. As McDougal and Feliciano observe, "[U]nderlying the processes of coercion is a fundamental principle of economy."[88] This fundamental principle deriving from the restraints on violence found in the earliest version of the just war doctrine has two attributes: the effectiveness of the force employed and the avoidance of excessive force.[89]

The United States effort in Viet Nam combines ineffectual with excessive force. The level of military commitment to date seems designed to avert defeat rather than to attain victory. All observers agree that, if the other side persists

---

[86] For a generalized approach to the problems of international conflict given the structure of international society, see F. Gross, *World Politics and Tension Areas* (New York: New York University Press, 1966).

[87] In the Congo Operation the outer limits of United Nations capacity were tested, perhaps exceeded.

[88] McDougal and Feliciano, *Law and Minimum World Public Order*, 35.

[89] Implicit in the notion of economy of force is the idea that an unjust and illegal use of force is a futile use. The idea of futility is related to the attainability of a permissible belligerent objective and is difficult to measure. If a negotiated settlement rather than victory is the objective, the amount of force required can only be assessed in terms of the probable intentions of the other side, and these shift in response to many factors, including their assessment of intentions.

in its commitment, the search for a favorable military solution will be exceedingly prolonged. Since the United States has far greater military resources potentially available, our use of insufficient force violates general norms of international law.⁹⁰ At the same time, however, weapons and strategy are being employed to cause destruction and incidental civilian damage without making a proportional contribution to the military effort. This is particularly true of our reliance upon strategic area bombing against dispersed targets of small military value.⁹¹

The United States has at each juncture also claimed the legal right to engage in disproportionate responses to specific provocations. In August 1964 the Gulf of Tonkin incidents consisted of allegations that North Viet Namese torpedo boats had "attacked" some American warships on the high seas. Although no damage was reported, the United States responded by destroying several villages in which the boats were based.⁹² This was the first occasion on which force was used directly against North Viet Namese territory and the justifications rested upon a reprisal theory that was largely disassociated from the war in South Viet Nam. Such a disproportionate ratio between action and reaction is typical of great power politics in which superior force is used to discipline a minor adversary. But this exaggerated response violates the legal requisites of equivalency and symmetry between the injury sustained and the response undertaken. Acceptance of mutuality and symmetry is basic to the whole conception of law in a sovereignty-centered social order.⁹³

The bombing of North Viet Nam in February 1965 was also originally justified as a "reprisal" for a successful attack by the Vietcong upon two United States

⁹⁰ Here again a reinterpretation of traditional thinking on war is needed to satisfy the requirements of the nuclear age. American restraint in Viet Nam is explained in part by concern with generating a nuclear war or, at least, provoking a wider war in Southeast Asia. But what legal consequences follow if this inhibition leads to prolonged violence in Viet Nam of an indecisive but devastating form?

⁹¹

The Conference participants were in agreement that the bombings in the north were of little military value, while the diplomatic disadvantages were very serious. Further escalation of the bombings, it was felt, could not be expected to improve the situation.

Ad Hoc Congressional Conference, 4.

⁹² For a rather effective presentation of the North Viet Namese version of the Tonkin Incidents, see Nguyen Nghe, "Facing the Skyhawks" (pamphlet printed in Hanoi, 1964). For an attack on the legality of the United States response, see I. F. Stone, "International Law and the Tonkin Bay Incidents," in Raskin and Fall, eds., *Viet-Nam Reader*, 307–15. For the US position, see references cited in n. 94 below.

⁹³ *Cf.* J. Kunz, "The Distinctiveness of the International Legal System," *Ohio State Law Journal*, 22 (1961), 447–71.

air bases, principally the one at Pleiku. Only in retrospect was the justification for attacking North Viet Nam generalized to collective self-defense of South Viet Nam.[94]

No clear legal guidelines exist to measure the proportionality of force used in self-defense. There is also some doubt whether proportionality applies to the belligerent objective pursued or the size and character of the aggression. If we assume that the appropriate quantum of military force is that needed to neutralize the Vietcong (the mere agent, in the American view, of Hanoi), then our military response (given our capability) appears to be disproportionately low. A guerrilla war can be won only by a minimum manpower ratio of 10:1, whereas the present ratio is no better than 5:1. Our present level of commitment of military forces merely prolongs the war; it does not aim to restore peace by means of victory.[95]

If, on the other hand, North Viet Nam and the United States are considered as foreign nations intervening on opposite sides of an armed conflict, then in terms of money, materiel, manpower, and overtness the United States has intervened to a degree disproportionately greater than has North Viet Nam.[96] In the early period of the war the Vietcong captured most of its equipment from the Saigon regime and the level of material support from the North was low.

The objective of American military strategy is apparently to destroy enough that is important to Hanoi and the NLF to bring about an eventual *de facto* reduction of belligerent action or to force Hanoi to make a satisfactory offer of negotiations. Are there any legal rules that restrict such a strategy in terms of duration, intensity, or destruction? This question seems so central to the future of international law that it is regrettable, to say the least, that the Memorandum does not discuss it. That formalistic document implies that, if a state claims to use force in self-defense, and supports its claim with a legal argument, and if the United Nations does not explicitly overrule that claim, international law has nothing further to contribute.[97] I would argue, in

---

[94] *Cf.* the White House Statement of February 7, 1965, in *Background Information*, 146–47; see also 148–52 for the context used to justify extending the war to North Viet Nam. No charge is made that the attacks on United States military installations were ordered or performed by North Viet Nam personnel.

[95] *Cf.* n. 41 above; see also General Gavin's testimony before the Senate Foreign Relations Committee, in *Viet Nam Hearings*, 270–71.

[96] For an account of some features of the escalation, see M. Mansfield et al., Report to Senate Foreign Relations Comm., 89th Cong., 2d Sess., *The Viet Nam Conflict: The Substance and the Shadow* (Comm. Print Jan. 6, 1966). See also Shaplen, *The Lost Revolution*, xii, xxii; Fall, *Viet-Nam Witness*, 307–49.

[97] A state, in effect, satisfies the requirements of international law merely by filing a brief on its own behalf.

contrast, that it is crucial to determine what limiting considerations come into play at this point. It is certainly a regressive approach to international law to assume that if a state alleges "self-defense," it may in its untrammeled discretion determine what military action is reasonably necessary and proportional. The opposing belligerent strategies in Viet Nam seem to call for legal explanation, especially in view of the inability of either side to "win" or "settle" the war; the present standoff causes great destruction of life and property without progressing toward "a resolution" of the conflict.

The Relevance of Commitments to Defend South Viet Nam. The second main section of the Legal Adviser's Memorandum is devoted to establishing that the United States "has made commitments and given assurances, in various forms and at different times, to assist in the defense of South Viet-Nam." Much confusion is generated by a very misleading play on the word commitment. In one sense, commitment means a pledge to act in a specified manner. In another sense, commitment means an obligation of law to act in a specified manner.

During 1965–66 the United States clearly came to regard itself as having made a commitment qua pledge to assist in the defense of South Viet Nam. President Johnson expressed this pledge on many occasions. Two examples are illustrative:

> We are in Viet Nam to fulfill one of the most solemn pledges of the American nation. Three Presidents – President Eisenhower, President Kennedy, and your present President – over 11 years have committed themselves and have promised to help defend this small and valiant nation.[98]
>
> We are there because we have a promise to keep. Since 1954 every American President has offered support to the people of South Viet Nam. We have helped to build, and we have helped to defend. Thus, over many years, we have made a national pledge to help South Viet Nam defend its independence.[99]

The present commitment entailing a major military effort is of a very different order than the early conditional offers of economic and military assistance made by President Eisenhower.[100] American involvement in Viet Nam is usually traced to a letter from President Eisenhower to Diem on October 23, 1954, in which the spirit of the undertaking was expressed in the following sentence: "The purpose of this offer is to assist the Government of Viet-Nam in developing and maintaining a strong, viable state, capable of resisting

[98] *New York Times*, July 29, 1965.
[99] *New York Times*, April 8, 1965.
[100] D. Larson and A. Larson, *Vietnam and Beyond* (Rule of Law Research Center, Duke University, 1965), 17–29.

attempted subversion or aggression through military means." The letter contains no hint of a pledge. In fact, the United States conditions its offer to assist with a reciprocal expectation: "The Government of the United States expects that this aid will be met by performance on the part of the Government of Viet-Nam in undertaking needed reforms."[101] It is important to note that the letter contained no reference to SEATO despite the formation of the organization a few weeks before it was written, and that the role of the United States was premised upon satisfactory domestic progress in South Viet Nam.

As late as September 1963, President Kennedy said in a TV interview: "In the final analysis, it is their war. They are the ones who have to win it or lose it. We can help them, we can give them equipment, we can send our men out there as advisers, but they have to win it – the people of Viet Nam – against the Communists. We are prepared to continue to assist them, but I don't think that the war can be won unless the people support the effort."[102] This expression of American involvement emphasizes its discretionary and reversible character, and again implies that the continuation of American assistance is conditional upon certain steps being taken by the Saigon regime. Even in 1965 Secretary Rusk, in an address to the Annual Meeting of the American Society of International Law, provided a legal defense of the United States position in Viet Nam that stopped short of averring a commitment qua legal obligation. Mr. Rusk did not once refer to SEATO in his rather complete coverage of the subject. The crucial explanation of the American presence is contained in the following passage:

> In resisting the aggression against it, the Republic of Viet-Nam is exercising its right of self-defense. It called upon us and other states for assistance. And in the exercise of the right of collective self-defense under the United Nations Charter, we and other nations are providing such assistance. The American policy of assisting South Viet-Nam to maintain its freedom was inaugurated under President Eisenhower and continued under Presidents Kennedy and Johnson.[103]

Each successive increase in the level of American military involvement has been accompanied by an intensification of rhetoric supporting our presence in Viet Nam. By 1965 President Johnson was, as we observed, referring to Viet Nam as "one of the most solemn national pledges." It is disconcerting to realize that the United States has at each stage offset a deteriorating situation

---

[101] *Background Information*, 67–68.
[102] *Ibid.*, 99.
[103] Rusk, "Address," 251–52.

in South Viet Nam by increasing both its military and its rhetorical commitment. This process discloses a gathering momentum; at a certain point, policy becomes virtually irreversible. President Johnson's use of the rhetoric of commitment communicates the irreversibility of this policy and conveys a sense of the futility and irrelevance of criticism. If we have a commitment of honor, contrary considerations of prudence and cost are of no concern.[104]

But no commitment qua pledge has the capacity to generate a commitment qua legal obligation. The Administration seems to want simultaneously to invoke both senses of the notion of commitment in order to blunt and confuse criticism. A commitment qua legal obligation is, by definition, illegal to renounce. To speak of commitment in a legal memorandum is particularly misleading. To the extent that we have *any* commitment it is a *pledge of policy*.

Secretary Rusk has injected a further confusion into the debate by his stress on "the SEATO commitment" in the course of his testimony before the Senate Foreign Relations Committee in the early months of 1966.[105] He said, for instance, in his prepared statement: "It is this fundamental SEATO obligation that has from the outset guided our actions in Viet Nam."[106] The notion of the obligation is derived from Article IV (1) of the SEATO treaty which says that "each party recognizes that aggression by means of armed attack . . . would endanger its own peace and safety, and agrees that it will in that event act to meet the common danger in accordance with its constitutional processes." It is somewhat doubtful that Article IV (1) can be properly invoked at all in Viet Nam because of the difficulty of establishing "an armed attack."[107]

---

[104] For this reason the Administration is hostile to domestic criticism. It is, above all, unresponsive to this qualitative aspect of our presence in Viet Nam. *Cf.* President Johnson's speech at Johns Hopkins University on April 7, 1965, in *Viet Nam Hearings*, 640–44.

[105] *Ibid.*, 567. Secretary Rusk explains to the Senate Foreign Relations Committee that

> the language of this treaty is worth careful attention. The obligation it imposes is not only joint but several. That is not only collective but individual.
>
> The finding that an armed attack has occurred does not have to be made by a collective determination before the obligation of each member becomes operative.
>
> *Cf.* the shifting views of SEATO obligation recounted in K. Young, "The Southeast Asia Crisis," *Hammarskjold Forum* (1963), 54. Even Mr. Young, a staunch defender of administration policy, notes that, "Until the crisis in Laos in 1961, the United States looked upon SEATO as a collective organization which would take military action, with all eight members participating in the actions as well as the decision" (*ibid.*, 59).

[106] *Viet Nam Hearings*, 567; note the absence of reference to SEATO in Rusk, "Address," and in the 1965 legal memorandum, n. 45 above.

[107] See generally G. Modelski, ed., *SEATO: Six Studies* (Melbourne: F. W. Cheshire for the Australian National University, 1962), 3–45, 87–163.

Secretary Rusk contends, however, that this provision not only *authorizes* but *obliges* the United States to act in the defense of South Viet Nam.[108]

Ambiguity again abounds. If the commitment to act in Viet Nam is incorporated in a treaty, the United States is legally bound. Such an interpretation of Article IV (1) would apply equally to other states that have ratified the SEATO treaty. None of the other SEATO signatories acknowledge such "a commitment" to fulfill a duty of collective self-defense, nor does the United States contend they have one. France and Pakistan oppose altogether any military effort on behalf of the Saigon regime undertaken by outside states.

Secretary Rusk later softened his insistence that Article IV (1) imposed a legal commitment qua obligation upon the United States. In an exchange with Senator Fulbright during Senate hearings on Viet Nam, Mr. Rusk offered the following explanation:

> The Chairman. . . . do you maintain that we had an obligation under the Southeastern Asian Treaty to come to the assistance, all-out assistance of South Viet Nam? Is that very clear?
> Secretary Rusk. It seems clear to me, sir, that this was an obligation –
> The Chairman. Unilateral.
> Secretary Rusk. An obligation of policy. It is rooted in the policy of the treaty. I am not now saying if we had decided we would not lift a finger about Southeast Asia that we could be sued in a court and be convicted of breaking a treaty.[109]

It seems evident if an armed attack has been established, the treaty imposes a legal obligation to engage in collective self-defense of the victim. But in the absence of a collective determination by the SEATO membership that an armed attack has taken place, it is difficult to maintain that Article IV (1) does more than authorize discretionary action in appropriate circumstances.

The Memorandum argues that "the treaty does not require a collective determination that an armed attack has occurred in order that the obligation of Article IV (1) become operative. Nor does the provision require collective decision on actions to be taken to meet the common danger."[110] This interpretation of Article IV (1) is a blatant endorsement of extreme unilateralism, made more insidious by its pretense of "obligation" and its invocation of the multilateral or regional scaffolding of SEATO. Here the legal position of the State Department displays maximum cynicism, resorting to international law to

---

[108] *Viet Nam Hearings*, 567.
[109] *Ibid.*, 45; see also *ibid.*, 7–8.
[110] *Ibid.*, 567.

obscure the national character of military action. In essence, the United States claims that it is under an obligation to determine for itself when an armed attack has occurred, and that once this determination is made there arises a further obligation to act in response. This justification for recourse to force is reminiscent of the international law of war prior to World War I, when states were free to decide for themselves when to go to war.[111] The regressive tendency of this position is further intensified by applying it in a situation where there was a background of civil war and where the alleged aggression was low-scale, extended over time, and covert. Under "the Rusk Doctrine" a country alleging "armed attack" seems free to act in self-defense whenever it wishes. The rhetoric of commitment seems connected with the effort to make the policy of support for Saigon irreversible in domestic arenas and credible in external arenas, especially in Saigon and Hanoi, but it has little to do with an appreciation of the relevance of international law to United States action in Viet Nam.

The important underlying question is whether it is permissible to construe an occurrence of "an armed attack" in the circumstances of the internal war in South Viet Nam. If an armed attack can be held to have occurred, then both self-defense and collective self-defense are permissible. The legal status of a claim of collective self-defense is not improved by embedding the claim in a collective defense arrangement. In fact, the collective nature of an arrangement such as SEATO might imply some obligation to attempt recourse to consultative and collective procedures before acting, at least to determine whether an armed attack has occurred and by whom. Under Secretary Rusk's interpretation of the treaty, SEATO members with opposing views on the issue of which side committed an armed attack could become "obligated" to act in "collective self-defense" against one another.[112] Surely this is the *reductio ad absurdum* of collective self-defense.

In terms of both world order and the original understanding of SEATO, the conflict in Viet Nam calls for action, if at all, under Article IV (2).[113] To categorize the conflict under Article IV (1) would seem to require a unanimous collective determination that the assistance given by Hanoi to the Vietcong amounted to an armed attack. Once that determination had been made, it might seem plausible to maintain that the obligation to act in collective

---

[111] For a general survey of progressive attempts to regulate recourse to war, see Quincy Wright, *The Role of International Law in the Elimination of War* (Dobbs Ferry, NY: Oceana, 1961).

[112] E.g., suppose Laos and Thailand became involved in a conflict in which each state accused the other of being an aggressor – and this is not impossible.

[113] *Cf.* Modelski, ed., *SEATO*, xiv. It is made clear both that internal conflicts abetted by subversion were to be treated under Article IV (2) and that this provision required consultation as a prerequisite to action and had become "a dead letter."

self-defense exists on a joint and several basis, and that the United States might join in the defense of the victim of the armed attack without further collective authorization. Unlike the State Department position, the approach outlined in this paragraph requires that a multilateral determination of the facts precede acts of commitment. The United States might help build a more peaceful world by taking seriously the collective procedures governing the use of force which it has taken such an active role in creating.

The Geneva Accords of 1954. The agreements at Geneva were cast in the form of a cease-fire arrangement and a declaration of an agreed procedure for achieving a post-war settlement. The parties to the first war in Viet Nam were the French and the Vietminh, and the agreements were between their respective military commanders. The other powers at Geneva were mere sureties. At Ho Chi Minh's insistence the Saigon regime did not participate; Saigon was evidently dissatisfied from the outset with the terms of settlement.[114] The United States Government was also reluctant to regard the Geneva settlement as binding.[115]

The Final Declaration required elections to be held in July of 1956 "under the supervision of an international commission composed of representatives of the Member States of the International Supervisory Commission."[116] The Memorandum points out that South Viet Nam "did not sign the cease-fire agreement of 1954, nor did it adhere to the Final Declaration of the Geneva Conference" and adds that "the South Viet Namese Government at that time gave notice of its objection in particular to the election provisions of the accords." At the time of the Geneva proceedings, the Saigon regime exerted control over certain areas in the South, and this awkward fact made it unrealistic to suppose that the Geneva terms of settlement would ever be voluntarily carried out. When Diem came to power and the United States moved in to fill the place left vacant by the departure of the French, it became clear, especially in view of the nation-wide popularity of Ho Chi Minh, that the contemplated elections would never be held.[117] In a sense it was naive of Hanoi to accept the Geneva arrangement or to rely upon its implementation.[118]

---

[114] See Fall, *Viet-Nam Witness*, 74–83. Jean Lacouture has written recently that France bears a heavy responsibility for its failure to secure full implementation of the Geneva "solution" before withdrawing from Viet Nam; in Lacouture's view France's premature withdrawal created a political vacuum immediately filled by the United States. See Lacouture, *Vietnam: Between Two Truces*, 657.

[115] Fall, *Viet-Nam Witness*, 69–83; see Lancaster, *The Emancipation of French Indo-China*, 313–58, for a general account of the Geneva settlement.

[116] See Article 7, Final Declaration of Geneva Conference, July 21, 1954, in *Background Information*, 58, 59.

[117] Lancaster, *The Emancipation of French Indo-China*, 315–16.

[118] *Ibid.*, 313–37.

Saigon objected to the election provisions from the outset because it hoped for a permanent partition of Viet Nam. But permanent partition was so deeply incompatible with the objective sought by the Vietminh in the war against the French that it is hardly reasonable to expect Hanoi to acquiesce. In a sense, Hanoi's willingness to cooperate with the Geneva arrangement until 1956 is more surprising than is its later effort to revive the war in Viet Nam.

The Memorandum says that, even assuming the election provisions were binding on South Viet Nam, there was no breach of obligation arising from Saigon's failure "to engage in consultations in 1955, with a view to holding elections in 1956." The justification offered for Saigon's action is that "the conditions in North Viet Nam during that period were such as to make impossible any free and meaningful expression of popular will." But the election provision in the Final Declaration stated no preconditions about the form of interim government in the two zones, and the type of governmental control existing in the North could have been and presumably was anticipated by those who drew up the Final Declaration. The meaning of "free elections" in Communist countries was well known to all countries including the United States, and the conditions prevailing in South Viet Nam were no more conducive to popular expressions of will.[119] The real objection to the elections was a simple one – namely, the assurance that Ho Chi Minh would win.[120] The Memorandum offers only a self-serving endorsement of Saigon's refusal to go along with the terms of settlement, although they had been endorsed by the United States representative, Bedell Smith.[121]

The Memorandum suggests, in footnote 10, that North Viet Nam's remedies, had there been "a breach of obligation by the South, lay in discussion with Saigon, perhaps in an appeal to the co-chairmen of the Geneva conference, or in a reconvening of the conference to consider the situation." In light of the failure of the United States to make use of international remedies which it argues are obligatory for Hanoi, this statement is a shocking instance of legal doubletalk. Footnote 10 ends by saying that, "Under international law, North Viet Nam had no right to use force outside its own zone in order to secure its political objectives." This again is misleading. No authoritative rules govern the action of the parties in the event that a settlement of internal war breaks down. Certainly if the settlement is not binding on *all* the parties, no one of

[119] On the conduct of elections in Viet Nam, see Bernard Fall, "Viet Nam's Twelve Elections," *New Republic*, May 14, 1966, 12–15.

[120] Warner, *The Last Confucian*, 84–106, 142–43; *cf.* M. Gettleman, ed., *Vietnam* (Greenwich, CT: Fawcett, 1965), 191–94, 210–35.

[121] For text of Smith's statement, see *Background Information*, 61.

them is bound by its constraints. In the absence of the Geneva Accords, Saigon would not exist as a political entity. If Saigon repudiates the Accords, Hanoi would seem to be legally free to resume the pursuit of its political objectives and to ignore the creation of a temporary zone in the South. The principle of mutuality of obligation makes it inappropriate to argue that Saigon is free to ignore the Geneva machinery but that Hanoi is bound to observe it.

Furthermore, international law does not forbid the use of force within a single state. If Hanoi may regard Viet Nam as a single country between 1954 and 1956, its recourse to force in pursuit of political objectives is not prohibited even assuming that its "guidance" and "direction" of the Vietcong constitute "a use" of force by North Viet Nam.

The Memorandum misleadingly implies that the International Control Commission (ICC) endorsed the action of the United States and Saigon and condemned the action of North Viet Nam. Both sides were criticized severely by the ICC for violating provisions of the Geneva Accords.[122] It would appear that the massive military aid given to Saigon by the United States was the most overt and disrupting violation, directly contravening the prohibition on the entry of foreign military forces and new military equipment.[123] According to the reasoning of footnote 10, North Viet Nam's remedy lay in discussion and the Geneva machinery. But a quite different line of legal reasoning is taken to justify American activity:[124] Action otherwise prohibited by the Geneva Accords is "justified by the international law principle that a material breach of an agreement by one party entitles the other at least to withhold compliance with an equivalent, corresponding, or related provision until the defaulting party is prepared to honor its obligations." One wonders why this "international law principle" is not equally available to North Viet Nam after Saigon's refusal even to consult about holding elections. Why is Hanoi bound by the reasoning of footnote 10 and Washington entitled to the reasoning of reciprocal breach? The self-serving argument of the Memorandum confers competence upon the United States and Saigon to find that a breach has taken place and to select a suitable remedy, but permits Hanoi only to *allege* a breach, and forbids it to take countervailing action until the breach has been impartially verified.

[122] For a representative sample, see Gettleman, ed., *Vietnam*, 160–90.

[123] *Cf.* Articles 17 and 18 of "Agreement on the Cessation of Hostilities in Vietnam," in *Background Information*, 28, 34–35.

[124] *Cf.* Department of State White Paper, "Aggression from the North," in Raskin and Fall, eds., *Viet-Nam Reader*, 143–55; for criticism, see Stone, "A Reply to White Paper," *ibid.*, 155–62.

The Authority of the President Under the Constitution. I agree with the Legal Adviser's analysis that the President possesses the constitutional authority to use American military forces in Viet Nam without a declaration of war. Past practice and present policy support this conclusion. To declare war against North Viet Nam would further rigidify our own expectations about an acceptable outcome and it would almost certainly escalate the conflict. It might activate dormant collective defense arrangements between North Viet Nam and its allies.

But the Constitution is relevant in another way not discussed by the Memorandum. The President is bound to act in accordance with governing law, including international law. The customary and treaty norms of international law enjoy the status of "the law of the land" and the President has no discretion to violate these norms in the course of pursuing objectives of foreign policy. An impartial determination of the compatibility of our action in Viet Nam with international law is highly relevant to the constitutionality of the exercise of Presidential authority in Viet Nam.

The President has the constitutional authority to commit our armed services to the defense of South Viet Nam without a declaration of war *provided* that such "a commitment" is otherwise in accord with international law. Whether all or part of the United States action violates international law is also a constitutional question. International law offers no authoritative guidance as to the use of force *within* South Viet Nam, but the bombing of North Viet Nam appears to be an unconstitutional use of Presidential authority as well as a violation of international law.

IV

It is appropriate to reflect on the role of the international lawyer in a legal controversy of the sort generated by our role in Viet Nam. The rather keen interest in this controversy about international law results mostly from intense disagreement about the overall wisdom of our foreign policy rather than curiosity about the content of the law on the subject. International law has therefore been used as an instrument of persuasion by those who oppose or favor our Viet Nam policy on political grounds. In such a debate we assume that the United States strives to be law-abiding and that, therefore, it is important for partisans of existing policy to demonstrate the compatibility between law and policy and for opponents of the policy to demonstrate the opposite.

This use of international law to bolster or bludgeon foreign policy positions is unfortunate. It creates the impression that international law serves to inflame debate rather than to guide or shape public policy – an impression fostered by the State Department Memorandum. After a decade of fighting in Viet Nam, the Memorandum was issued in response to legal criticisms made by private groups and echoed by a few dissident members of Congress. It blandly white-washed the existing government position. The tone is self-assured, the method legalistic, and the contribution to an informed understanding of the issues minimal. None of the difficult questions of legal analysis are considered. In this intellectual context international lawyers with an independent voice need to be heard.

An international lawyer writing about an ongoing war cannot hope to reach clear conclusions about all the legal issues involved. It is virtually impossible to unravel conflicting facts underlying conflicting legal claims. Of course, we can hope that a legal commentator will acknowledge the uncertainties about the facts and that he will offer explicit reasons for resolving ambiguities in the way and to the extent that he does.[125]

Would it not be better, one is tempted to insist, for international lawyers to avoid so controversial and indeterminate a subject as the legal status of American participation in the war in Viet Nam? I think it important openly to raise this question of propriety, but clearly to answer it in the negative. The scholar has the crucial task of demonstrating the intractability of many, although not of all, the legal issues. Such an undertaking defeats, or calls into serious question, the dogmatic over-clarification of legal issues that arises in the more popular discussions of foreign policy questions. The international lawyer writing in the spirit of scholarly inquiry may have more to contrib-ute by raising the appropriate questions than by purporting to give authorita-tive answers. He may enable public debate to adopt a more constructive and sophisticated approach to the legal issues.

And, finally, an international lawyer not employed by a government can help modify a distorted nationalistic perspective. An international lawyer is, of course, a citizen with strong views on national policy, but his outlook is univer-salized by the realization that the function of law in world affairs is to reconcile inconsistent national goals. The international lawyer seeks a legal solution that is based upon an appreciation, although not always an acceptance, of the posi-tion of "the other side" in an international dispute. His goal is a system of world

---

[125] *Cf.* the inscription attributed to "An Old Jew of Galicia," in C. Milosz, *The Captive Mind*, Vol. II (New York: A. Knopf, 1953):

> When someone is honestly 55% right, that's very good and there's no use wrangling. And if someone is 60% right, it's wonderful, and let him thank God. But what's to be said about 75% right? Wise people say this is suspicious. Well, and what about 100% right? Whoever says he's 100% right is a fanatic, a thug, and the worst kind of rascal.

order in which all nations are constrained for the common good by rules and by procedures for their interpretation and enforcement. This implies a new kind of patriotism, one that is convinced that, to succeed, the nation must act within the law in its foreign as well as its domestic undertakings.

But are there occasions upon which it would be proper for a nation to violate international law? It may be contended that the United States must act as it does in Viet Nam because the international procedures of Geneva, the United Nations, and SEATO offer no protection to a victim of aggression such as South Viet Nam. The United States is acting, in this view, to fill a vacuum created by the failures of international regulatory machinery. In fact, it is often suggested, the refusal of the United States to act would tempt potential aggressors. Those who emphasize the obligations and ambiguities of power often talk in this vein and warn of the sterility of legalism in foreign affairs.[126] In general terms, this warning is sound, but its very generality is no guide to specific action, especially in the nuclear age. It remains essential to vindicate as explicitly as possible the reasons that might justify violating legal expectations about the use of military power in each instance by documented reference to overriding policies; slogans about peace, security, and freedom are not enough. The analysis must be so conditioned by the specific circumstances that it will not always justify the use of force. I do not believe that such an argument can convincingly be made with respect to Viet Nam, and therefore I affirm the relevance of legal criteria of limitation. If an argument in favor of military intervention is offered, then it should stress the limits and weaknesses of law or the priority of national over international concerns.[127] We would then gain a better understanding of what law can and cannot do than is acquired by the manipulative straining of legal rules into contrived coincidence with national policies.[128]

V

The foregoing analysis points to the following set of conclusions:

(1) The United States insistence upon treating North Viet Namese assistance to the Vietcong as "an armed attack" justifying recourse to "self-defense"

---

[126] See generally the writings of the critical legalists, e.g., George Kennan, *American Diplomacy 1900–1950* (Chicago: University of Chicago Press, 1951), 95, 96, 100; Hans Morgenthau, *In Defense of the National Interest* (London: Methuen, 1951).

[127] Little systematic attention has been given to the rationale and logic for rejecting the claims of law under certain circumstances in human affairs. The consequence is to lead perceptions into naive over-assertions or cynical denials of the relevance of law to behavior.

[128] There is a role for adversary presentation, but there is a more important need to seek bases upon which to appraise adversary claims.

goes a long way toward abolishing the legal significance of the distinction between civil war and international war. Without this distinction, we weaken a principal constraint upon the scope and scale of violence in international affairs – the confinement of violence associated with internal wars to the territory of a single political unit.[129] Another adverse consequence of permitting "self-defense" in response to covert aggression is to entrust nations with very wide discretion to determine for themselves the occasions upon which recourse to *overt* violence across international boundaries is permissible.[130] An extension of the doctrine of self-defense would defeat a principal purpose of the United Nations Charter – the delineation of fixed, narrow limits upon the use of overt violence by states in dispute with one another.

(2) The United States made no serious attempt to exhaust international remedies prior to recourse to unilateral military power. The gradual unfolding of the conflict provided a long period during which attempts at negotiated settlement could have taken place. Only belatedly and in a *pro forma* fashion did the United States refer the dispute to the United Nations. The United States made no attempt to comply with "the international law principle" alleged by footnote 10 of the Memorandum to govern the action of North Viet Nam. Nor did it attempt during the early phases of the war to subordinate its discretion to the Geneva machinery. No use was made even of the consultative framework of SEATO, an organization inspired by United States initiative for the specific purpose of inhibiting Communist aggression in Southeast Asia.[131] Policies of force were unilaterally adopted and put into execution; no account was taken of the procedural devices created to give a collective quality to decisions about the use of force. Yet the prospect for controlling violence in world affairs depends upon the growth of limiting procedural rules and principles.

(3) By extending the scope of violence beyond the territory of South Viet Nam, the United States has created an unfortunate precedent in international affairs. Where international institutions fail to provide clear guidance as to the character of permissible action, national actions create quasi-legislative precedents. In view of the background of the conflict in Viet Nam (including the expectation that South Viet Nam

---

[129] One can emphasize the refusal to permit external sanctuary for actors supporting an internal war as a constructive precedent, but its reciprocal operation creates dangers of unrestrained violence. See generally M. Halpern, *Limited War in the Nuclear Age* (New York: Wiley, 1963).

[130] Cf. Henkin, *Force, Intervention and Neutrality*.

[131] On the creation of SEATO, see Modelski, ed., *SEATO*, introduction, xiii–xix.

would be incorporated into a unified Viet Nam under the control of Hanoi after the French departure), the American decision to bomb North Viet Nam sets an unfortunate precedent. If North Viet Nam and its allies had the will and capability to employ equivalent military force, the precedent would even allow them to claim the right to bomb United States territory in reprisal.

(4) The widespread domestic instability in the Afro-Asian world points up the need for an approach to internal war that aims above all to insulate this class of conflict from intervention by the great powers. The early use of peace observation forces, border control machinery, restraints on the introduction of foreign military personnel, and standby mediation appears possible and beneficial. Responses to allegations of "aggression" should be verified prior to the unilateral use of defensive force, especially when time is available. Claims of covert aggression might then be verified with sufficient authority and speed to mobilize support for community security actions.

(5) In the last analysis, powerful nations have a responsibility to use defensive force to frustrate aggression when international machinery is paralyzed. Viet Nam, however, does not provide a good illustration of the proper discharge of this responsibility. North Viet Nam's action does not seem to constitute "aggression." Available international machinery was not used in a proper fashion. The domestic conditions prevailing in South Viet Nam were themselves so inconsistent with prevailing ideals of welfare, progress, and freedom that it is difficult to claim that the society would be better off as a result of a Saigon victory. The massive American presence has proved to be a net detriment, greatly escalating the war, tearing apart the fabric of Viet Namese society, and yet not likely to alter significantly the political outcome. The balance of domestic and area forces seems so favorable to the Vietcong that it is unlikely that the NLF can be kept forever from political control. The sacrifice of lives and property merely postpones what appears to be an inevitable result. The United States voluntarily assumed a political responsibility for the defense of South Viet Nam that has been gradually converted into a political commitment and a self-proclaimed test of our devotion to the concept of collective self-defense. This responsibility is inconsistent with the requirements of world order to the extent that it depends upon unilateral prerogatives to use military power. The national interest of the United States would be better served by the embrace of *cosmopolitan isolationism* – either we act in conjunction with others or we withdraw. We are the most powerful nation in world history. It is hubris

to suppose, however, that we are the policemen of the world.[132] Our wasted efforts in Viet Nam suggest the futility and frustration of the politics of over-commitment. We are not the only country in the world concerned with containing Communism. If we cannot find cooperative bases for action we will dissipate our moral and material energies in a series of Viet Nams. The tragedy of Viet Nam provides an occasion for rethinking the complex problems of use of military power in world affairs and calls for an examination of the increasingly imperial role of the United States in international society. Perhaps we will discover the relevance of international law to the *planning* and *execution* of foreign policy as well as to its *justification*. Certainly the talents of the State Department's Legal Adviser are wasted if he is to be merely an official apologist summoned long after our President has proclaimed "a solemn national commitment."

---

[132] Even Secretary Rusk has pointed out the limitations upon American power in emphatic terms: "We do not regard ourselves as the policeman of the universe . . . If other governments, other institutions, or other regional organizations can find solutions to the quarrels which disturb this present scene, we are anxious to have this occur" (*Vietnam Hearings*, 563); and Secretary McNamara stated in an address to the American Society of Newspaper Editors delivered at Montreal on May 18, 1966: "neither conscience nor sanity itself suggests that the United States is, should, or could be the global gendarme" (*New York Times*, May 19, 1966, 11).

4

International Law and the United States Role in Viet Nam: A Response to Professor Moore

In the best traditions of scholarly debate Professor John Norton Moore has taken sharp and fundamental issue with the legal analysis of the United States' role in the Viet Nam war that I outlined in a previous issue of the *Yale Law Journal*.[1] Professor Moore has not persuaded me either that my approach is "simplistic" or that its application to Viet Nam is "unsound," but he has identified weaknesses and incompletenesses in my earlier formulation.[2] In addition, he has developed an alternative legal framework for assessing foreign intervention in violent struggles for the control of a national society. My objective in responding is to clarify the contending world order positions that each of us espouses. Although Professor Moore affirms and I deny the legality of the United States' military role in Viet Nam, the main center of intellectual gravity in this debate is less passing judgment on the grand legal issue of American presence (at this stage, a legalistic exercise) than it is assessing the policy implications of the Viet Nam precedent for the future of international legal order.

Professor Moore and I agree that international law can serve as a significant source of guidance to the national policy-maker in the area of war and peace. International law implies a process of decision incorporating perspectives that tend to be left out of account when government officials develop national policies solely by considering capabilities, strategies, and current foreign policy goals that are designed to maximize the short-run "national advantage." International law contains rules and standards rooted in the cosmopolitan tradition of a community of nations, whereas foreign policy tends to be rooted

---

[1] Richard Falk, "International Law and the United States Role in the Viet Nam War," *Yale Law Journal*, 75 (1966), 1122–60.
[2] Pages in parentheses in this article refer to Professor Moore's article, "International Law and the United States Role in the Viet Nam War: A Reply," *Yale Law Journal*, 76 (1967), 1051–94.

in the more particularistic traditions of each state. The future of world legal order may depend to a great degree on the extent to which the decision process relied upon in principal states to form foreign policy can come increasingly to incorporate more cosmopolitan perspectives.

International law has itself evolved through a process of decision in which national policies governing the appropriate uses of military power have been clarified by the assertion of adverse national claims buttressed by supporting explanations and rationale. This process is especially germane whenever the relevance of the rules to the claims of states is challenged on a legal basis, as it has been since the outset of major United States involvement in Viet Nam. The claims of governments to use or resist coercion serve as precedents for future claims and imply commitments to develop a certain kind of international legal system deemed beneficial both to the countries directly concerned and to the wider community of all states. My disagreement with Professor Moore centers upon the degree of discretion that international law presently accords to states with respect to the use of force in an international conflict resembling the one that has unfolded in Viet Nam in the years since 1954 and extends to the sorts of considerations (and their relative weight) that should have been taken into account in the decisions that led to the American military involvement at the various stages of its increasing magnitude. I would contend that the American military involvement resulted from a series of geo-political miscalculations, as well as from a process of decision insensitive to world order considerations.

The Viet Nam conflict demonstrates the harmful consequences for the control of international violence that can arise from contradictory national interpretations of what constitutes "aggression" and what constitutes permissible acts of "defense." Given the decentralized character of international society, it becomes more important than ever, in my view, to inhibit unilateral recourse to violence arising from contradictory and subjective national interpretations of a conflict situation. The war in Viet Nam illustrates a situation in which it is "reasonable" for each side to perceive its adversary as guilty of unprovoked aggression.[3]

---

[3] For a persuasive account by a psychologist as to why the North Vietnamese perceive the United States' role in Viet Nam as aggression, see R. White, "Misperception of Aggression in Viet Nam," *Journal of International Affairs*, 21 (1967), 123–40; for a more fully documented presentation of the same position by the same author, see White, "Misperception and the Viet Nam War," *Journal of Social Issues*, 22 (1966), 1–164. The prospect of mutually contradictory perceptions of aggression held in good faith is central to my argument against Professor Moore's approach to world order problems. He takes no account of the reality or hazard of such misperception.

The potential for military escalation that follows from each side doing whatever it deems necessary to uphold its vital interests is an alarming freedom
to grant governments in the nuclear age. My approach to these world order
issues presupposes the central importance of establishing binding quasi-objective limits upon state discretion in international situations in which such
contradictory inferences of "aggression" are characteristic. I would argue, also,
that the whole effort of international law in the area of war and peace since
the end of World War I has been to deny sovereign states the kind of unilateral
discretion to employ force in foreign affairs that the United States has exercised in Viet Nam.[4]

Professor Moore appears content to endorse virtually unfettered sovereign
discretion. In the role of a disinterested observer, he purports to pass judgment
on the legal status of a contested claim to use force. Professor Moore sets forth
a certain conception of world order that he posits as crucial for human welfare,
and then proceeds to examine whether the claim to use force in the particular
situation of Viet Nam is compatible with it. Every national decision-maker is
expected to engage in the same process of assessment. But no account is taken
of the serious problems of auto-interpretation that arise when recourse to force
is contemplated or carried out in inflamed international settings. These problems arise because each side tends toward a self-righteous vindication of its own
contentions and an equally dogmatic inattention to the merits of the adversary's position. Professor Moore's approach recalls the natural law tradition in
which the purported deference to the normative restraints operative upon the
behavior of a Christian prince turned out in practice to be little more than a
technique of *post hoc* rationalization on the part of a government and its supporters. Surely, his analysis fails to accord reciprocal empathy to the adversary's
reasonable perceptions as to who is responsible for what in Viet Nam. In fact,
Professor Moore's endorsement of America's military role is neither widely nor
wholeheartedly shared among states normally allied with the United States.[5]

---

[4] For a concise history of these efforts, see Q. Wright, *The Role of International Law in the
    Elimination of War* (Dobbs Ferry, NY: Oceana, 1961).
[5] Anthony Lewis has summarized the situation in concise and moderate terms: "To go into the
    reasons for West European attitudes toward Viet Nam would require rehearsing all the argu-
    ments about America's role there. Suffice it to say that only the British Government has had
    much favorable to say about American policy in Viet Nam. No European country has a single
    soldier there. Much of the public on the Continent, rightly or not, see the situation as that
    of a huge power over-reacting" (Lewis, "Why Humphrey Got That Abuse in Europe," *New
    York Times*, April 16, 1967, §4, 4, col. 4). Even the British Government has disassociated itself
    through a formal statement by her Prime Minister from United States bombing in June of
    1966 of oil installations in Hanoi and Haiphong. For text of Mr. Wilson's statement, see *British
    Record*, No. 12, July 14, 1966, Supp.

It seems plain enough that Communist-oriented observers would regard the air strikes by the United States against North Viet Nam as unprovoked "aggression." Suggestions have even been made by more militant opponents of the United States' war actions that the passive role of the Soviet Union amounts to "appeasement" of the United States and that it is the Soviet Union, not the United States, that should heed the lesson of Munich.[6] Professor Moore's emphasis on the discretion of the United States to furnish military assistance to Saigon needs to be supplemented by a consideration of what military assistance it would be reasonable for the Soviet Union and China to give to Hanoi; would not North Viet Nam be entitled to act in collective self-defense in response to sustained, large-scale bombing of its territory? And what limits could be legally placed on its exercise of self-defense other than those self-imposed by prudence and incapacity?

If we examine the war in Viet Nam from the perspective of North Viet Nam and with the same deference to self-determined reasonableness that Professor Moore confers upon the United States Government then it seems clear that the failure of the war to reach global proportions has been a consequence of Soviet and Chinese restraint (or incapacity); that is, Moore's world order position seems to legalize almost unlimited escalation by adversaries that perceive an ally as a victim of "aggression," even though that perception is not vindicated by any wider community determination and even though disinterested and reasonable men disagree as to who did what to whom. My earlier classification of international conflict into three broad categories is based on the need to avoid the anarchic consequences of adversary perception by fixing arbitrary but definite legal limits upon divergent interpretations of the rights and duties of national governments that find themselves involved in Viet Nam-type situations.[7]

---

[6]   See, e.g., a passage from an editorial appearing in the French intellectual journal *Les Temps Moderne*:

> The lack of clarity, the prudent policy of 'wait and see' are the tombs of the Socialist and revolutionary movement; they pave the way for other disasters just as surely as nonintervention against Spanish Fascism in 1936 set the stage for 1940 and what followed. But the parallel extends beyond the Spanish Civil War; it includes the capitulations that preceded and followed the Munich Agreements.
>
> The United States is convinced that the Soviet Union will desist from any test of strength until the end.
>
> The editorial goes on to call for "Socialist counter-escalation" by means of Soviet rocket strikes at United States air and naval installations in the Pacific area. See "Affirmative: A Deliberate Risk," translated and reprinted in *Atlas*, 12, Nov. 1966, 19, 20.

[7]   The basic rationale is set forth in Falk, "International Law and the United States Role in the Viet Nam War," 1122–28. E.g., the United States is reported to have criticized the United Arab Republic for its attacks on Saudi Arabian border towns in the course of the struggle waged between the rival Yemeni factions for control of the Yemen. See *New York Times*, May 17, 1967, 1, col. 7.

Perhaps my position can be clarified by showing in a preliminary way why I reject the analogy between Viet Nam and Korea, an analogy that Professor Moore invokes to argue that similar defensive measures are appropriate in the two settings.[8] If the facts in Viet Nam are as Professor Moore and the United States Government contend, then it might be true that North Viet Nam is guilty of a *covert* equivalent of the aggression that was attempted *overtly* in 1950 by North Korea.[9] But the assessment of the facts in Viet Nam is subject to multiple interpretations by reasonable observers in a way that the facts in Korea were not. Only the Communist states argued seriously against the conclusion that North Korea was an aggressor.

[8] There are other significant differences, including a war ending in 1954 for control of the entire country, election provisions to translate this military outcome into political control at a certain time (1956), and a central government in Saigon that did not offer much prospect of governing South Viet Nam in any stable fashion even apart from Communist harassment. Part of the relevant background is the demonstrated competence of Ho Chi Minh to govern Viet Nam in an effective manner, a competence evident even in the writings of those who are hostile to Communism and opposed to reunification under Hanoi's control. The capacity to govern territorial units effectively in the areas of the world most vulnerable to domestic trauma is itself a valuable constituent of the sort of international stability that the United States aspires to achieve for the Afro-Asian world. The background of Vietnamese social and cultural history also supports strongly the inference of an autonomous Vietnamese spirit, one that above all would resist any effort at domination by the Chinese. Ho Chi Minh's reasonableness was demonstrated in the period after World War II when he cooperated successfully with non-Communist factions in Viet Nam and made notable concessions to the French in exchange for an acknowledgment of his leadership of an independent Republic of Viet Nam; the French later repudiated these negotiations and the First Indochina War was born. For the sense of background see E. Hammer, *The Struggle for Indo-China 1940–1955* (Stanford: Stanford University Press, 1955); L. Bodard, *The Quicksand War* (Boston: Atlantic Monthly Press, 1967); J. Buttinger, *Vietnam: A Dragon Embattled* (New York: Praeger, 1967). Recently these points have also been made effectively in T. Farer, "The Enemy – Exploring the Sources of a Foreign Policy," *Columbia University Forum*, Spring 1967, 13; see especially his quotation of the remark of Walter Robertson, Assistant Secretary of State for Far Eastern Affairs (an anti-Communist of such extreme character as to antagonize Anthony Eden because of his "emotional" approach): "If only Ho Chi Minh were on our side we could do something about the situation. But unfortunately he is the enemy" (*ibid.*).

[9] It is important, however, to appreciate the degree of ambiguity that necessarily inheres in the context of covert coercion unless the foreign state proclaims its aggressive design, as has the United Arab Republic in relation to Israel. Without such a proclamation, one never made by North Viet Nam, the attribution of motives is speculative and unconvincing, especially if the assumed motives are relied upon to justify major responsive violence. In Korea, it was North Korea that justified its recourse to overt coercion by vague and unsupportable allegations that South Korea was planning to attack North Korea.

   Bernard Fall, commenting on the assertion "that North Vietnamese infiltration into South Viet Nam is the equivalent of the North Korean invasion of the ROK," writes that the comparison "omits the embarrassing fact that anti-Diem guerrillas were active long before infiltrated North Vietnamese elements joined the fray": B. Fall, *The Two Viet-Nams* (2d rev. ed.; New York: Praeger, 1967), 345.

Her overt military attack was sufficiently clear to permit a global consensus to form in support of defensive action by South Korea. In contrast, the obscurity of the conflict in Viet Nam generates widespread disagreement outside the Communist world as to whether either side can be termed "the aggressor," and impartial observers as august as the Secretary General of the United Nations[10] and the Pope[11] have repudiated any interpretation of the war in Viet Nam that identifies North Viet Nam as the aggressor. France has openly repudiated the United States' conception of the war, and neutral public opinion at home and abroad is, to say the least, sharply split.[12]

---

[10]   There are many indications of Thant's position on the matter, e.g., *New York Times*, June 21, 1966, 1, col. 5.

[11]   Cf. Pope Paul's Encyclical on Peace of Sep. 19, 1966, text in *New York Times*, Sep. 20. 1966, 18, col. 2. For example, taking account of the tradition of indirect rhetoric, the following passage was written with obvious application to war in Viet Nam: "We cry to them in God's name to stop. Men must come together and offer concrete plans and terms in all sincerity. A settlement should be reached now, even at the expense of some inconvenience or loss, for it may have to be made later in the train of bitter slaughter and involve great loss." The following sentence also confirms the emphasis upon the non-condemnation of either side as aggressor: "Now again, therefore, we lift up our voice, 'with piercing cry and with tears' (Hebrews, v, 7), very earnestly beseeching those who have charge of the public welfare to strive with every means available to prevent the further spread of the conflagration, and even to extinguish it entirely." More recently, Pope Paul VI has specifically urged the cessation of all forms of violence throughout Viet Nam: *New York Times*, May 25, 1967, 4, col. 4.

[12]   I regard the unprecedented intensity, range, and character of the protest movement directed at the American military involvement in Viet Nam to be significantly relevant to an appraisal of the status of United States claims under international law. The standards governing the use of force in world affairs reflect moral attitudes toward those occasions upon which it is appropriate to rely upon military power. This widespread protest phenomenon reflects the moral conviction of people throughout the world that the United States is guilty of aggressive war in Viet Nam; such a moral conviction is not inconsistent with the democratically based support for the war given by the American public, according priority to winning a war that should not have been fought rather than to accepting the need to acknowledge error. Edwin O. Reischauer, the former American Ambassador to Japan, has well stated this orientation toward the war taken by those who continue to give their support, however, grudgingly, to the American effort in Viet Nam:

> There is not much agreement in this country about the war in Viet Nam, except that it is something we should have avoided. We are paying a heavy price for it – in lives, in national wealth and unity, and in international prestige and influence. The best we can hope for from the war is sufficient peace and stability to allow that small and weak country to get painfully to its feet at last; the worst is a nuclear conflict too horrible to contemplate.

> Reischauer, "What We Should do Next in Asia," *Look*, April 4, 1967, 21

It may also be well to ponder the following paragraph from the editorial columns of *The New Republic*:

> Simultaneously [with other beneficial international policies of the United States] Mr. Johnson is pushing the Viet Nam war – which is a disastrous thing. It is all very well to say the country backs him, Governor Romney being the latest "me too" recruit. Yes,

This situation of dissensus sharply distinguishes Viet Nam from Korea and strongly suggests that the discretion to act "defensively" requires some source of restraint more dependable than the wisdom of the belligerent states.[13]

---

the polls show the public supports continued bombing, 67 percent. But a second series of polls shows only 37 percent backing Mr. Johnson's handling of the war. Reconciling these two views isn't really very difficult. The public loathes the war. It doesn't want defeat, but it wants out. The two moods conflict. It backs the bombing on the simplistic ground that that will end the war quickly. And it is taking out its resentment for the war dilemma consciously or unconsciously by making Mr. Johnson the scapegoat.

New Republic, April 22, 1967, 2

Among those aspects of the protest against participation in the war that are most legally notable have been the efforts, never made in the Korean context to nearly the same extent, to obtain a determination by domestic courts that participation in the Viet Nam war is tantamount to the commission of a war crime; the reasoning being that the German and Japanese war crimes trials conducted after World War II concluded that an individual is criminally accountable for participation in a war of aggression (i.e., an illegal war) regardless of whether or not he is carrying out the orders of his government. There are also many cases now arising for the first time of "selective conscientious objection" in which individuals subject to the draft are claiming exemption not because they are opposed to war *in general* but because they oppose the Viet Nam war *in particular* on grounds of conscience. A dramatic instance of litigation to test whether there is a legal right of conscientious objection to a particular war has been filed: Capt. Dale E. Noyd of the Air Force Academy in the Federal District Court of Colorado in Denver (*New York Times*, April 20, 1967, 5, col. 3); for a description of the litigation, see *Civil Liberties*, 245, April 1967, 1, 5. For a continuing description of evidence supporting the invocation of selective conscientious objection in the Viet Nam context, see the responsible reporting of the weekly British newspaper *Peace News*, the bi-monthly American magazine *Viet Report*, or almost any French organ of opinion (left, right, or center). For one (among many) vivid account of the horrors inflicted on Vietnamese society, see M. McCarthy, "Report from Viet Nam II: The Problems of Success," *New York Review of Books*, May 4, 1967, 4.

Furthermore, for the first time during a period of war a group of international lawyers have gone on record against their own government to contend that the United States military involvement in Viet Nam is "illegal," and constitutes a violation of both international law and the US Constitution: Consultative Council of the Lawyers Committee on American Policy Towards Vietnam, John H. E. Fried, rapporteur, *Vietnam and International Law* (Flanders, NJ: O'Hare Books, 1967). The members of the Consultative Council are R. J. Barnet, R. A. Falk (Chairman), John H. E. Fried (Rapporteur), John H. Herz, Stanley Hoffmann, Wallace McClure, Saul H. Mendlovitz, Richard S. Miller, Hans J. Morgenthau, William G. Rice, and Quincy Wright.

Also for the first time since World War II there has been proposed a war crime tribunal to pass judgment on the United States role in Viet Nam and on the criminal responsibility of its President. Of course, Bertrand Russell's tribunal is a juridical farce, but the fact that it is plausible to contemplate such a proceeding and to obtain for its tribunal several celebrated individuals bears witness to the general perception of the war. For Jean-Paul Sartre's explanation of why he has agreed to serve as a judge on the Russell tribunal, see Sartre, "Imperialist Morality," *New Left Review*, 41 (1967), 3–10.

See also Senate Republican Policy Committee, *Blue Book on Viet Nam* (May 1, 1967); for the text of its principal conclusions questioning the entire basis of the war see excerpts from GOP Paper on War, *New York Times*, May 2, 1967, 10, col. 3.

[13] The vagueness of the justification is accentuated in consequence by the gradual evolution of "the commitment." What started off in Viet Nam as a reluctant and indirect involvement that

The presence or absence of a consensus has considerable bearing on the legal status of a contested claim to use force in international society.[14] The Charter of the United Nations purports to restrict the unilateral discretion of states to use force to resolve international conflicts.[15] In cases where a claim of self-defense is made and challenged, the burden of justification is upon the claimant. It is always possible to argue that a use of force is "defensive" and that it promotes world order by inhibiting "aggression." Therefore, fairly clear community standards would be needed to assure that what is called "defensive" is defensive; in the absence of clear community standards it becomes important to allow international institutions to determine whether recourse to "defensive force" is justified by a prior "armed attack." Where there are no generally accepted objective standards and where rivals put forward contradictory factual interpretations it becomes difficult or impossible to mobilize a consensus in the international institutions entrusted with the maintenance of peace and security.[16] Viet Nam

---

needed no special justification was successively widened and deepened until the involvement itself became the principal justification. With over 400,000 Americans fighting in Viet Nam and with casualties continuing to mount, there is a sense that the American effort must not be in vain; the consequence is an apparently irreversible government commitment to use military means to accomplish a political objective – namely, to defeat the Vietcong insurrection, without according any governmental legitimacy to the NLF.

[14] The relevance of an international consensus to the legality of contested national action is considered in Richard Falk, "On the Quasi-Legislative Competence of the General Assembly," *American Journal of International Law*, 60 (1966), 782–91. And see the dissenting opinion of Judge Tanaka in the South West Africa Cases for an analysis in the setting of human rights of the shift from an emphasis upon sovereign autonomy to community solidarity in determining the character of international legal obligations: Judgment in the South West Africa Cases, July 18, 1966, [1966] I.C.J. 248, 292–94.

[15] For a helpful exposition of restrictive intention of the relevant Charter provisions, see L. Henkin, "Force, Intervention, and Neutrality in Contemporary International Law," *Proceedings of the American Society of International Law* (1963), 147–62; P. Jessup, *A Modern Law of Nations* (New York: Macmillan, 1948), 165–67; in this context it is not necessary to contend that Article 51 restricts traditional self-defense in terms of some rigid conception of "armed attack," but only that the discretion of states to have recourse to force in self-defense is subject to justification and review. See, e.g., D. Bowett, *Self-Defense In International Law* (New York: Praeger, 1958), 216–18, 241, 244–45, 261, emphasizing the importance of restricting discretionary recourse to self-defense, especially on a collective basis, in the Viet Nam-type situation.

[16] Even a defensive alliance such as SEATO has been unable to maintain its solidarity in the face of the disputed facts and policies generated by the Viet Nam conflict. France and Pakistan, both Members, refuse to give their assent to SEATO's endorsement of the American "interpretation" of the war in Viet Nam. It should be recalled that SEATO was a pact among anti-Communist states determined to resist the coercive spread of Asian Communism, including explicitly its spread to South Viet Nam; the non-Communist neutralist states of Asia are, without exception, even more dubious about the American "interpretation." The relevant point is that a claim to be acting in a "defensive" way when force is used against a foreign society has no legal status unless it is supported by some kind of international authorization that

presents such a situation of uncertainty and institutional paralysis. What restraints upon sovereign discretion to use force remain relevant? The appraisals of disinterested international civil servants, especially the Secretary General of the United Nations, are distinctly relevant in this setting. The Secretary General contributes an impartial perspective and can, as U Thant has chosen to do with respect to Viet Nam, delineate the character of reasonable behavior by the adversary parties.[17] Normally such an official will refrain from judging the behavior of the participants in a conflict that cannot be handled by agreement in the political organs. The persistent refusal of the United States to comply with U Thant's proposals is indicative of its unilateral approach to the determination of the

---

commands respect; otherwise it is merely a contention by an adversary determined to make unilateral use of military power against a foreign society.

A study of South Viet Nam attitudes suggest that even in the late phases of the war in Viet Nam the people of the country reject the official United States version of "defensive" action. The poll was conducted for Columbia Broadcasting Company by Opinion Research Corporation, a respected professional polling outfit, consisted of an interview of 1,545 persons living in five major cities, 55 hamlets, and was limited to civilians of voting age living in "secured areas," those not under Vietcong control. The poll took place between November 24, 1966, and February 1, 1967. When asked who was responsible for continuing the war, 31 percent blamed the Vietcong and only 12 percent blamed the Government of North Viet Nam; when asked whether bombing should be continued against villages suspected of containing the Vietcong, 46 percent favored an end to bombing while 37 percent wanted it continued; when asked whether to stress negotiations with North Viet Nam or to extend military operations to North Viet Nam, 60 percent favored more emphasis on negotiations whereas only about 14 percent favored increased military action; and finally when asked whether they favored reunification after the end of the war 83 percent were reported in favor and only 5 percent opposed. See *New York Times*, March 22, 1967, 10, col. 7. The remarkable thing about this poll is that among strong anti-Communist South Vietnamese (65 percent blamed the Communist side for the continuation of the war and only 5 percent blamed the anti-Communist side) exposed primarily to government propaganda there still appears to be a rejection of the American idea that the war is a consequence of "aggression from the North." The attitudes on reunification also sharply question the Saigon–Washington insistence on separate sovereignty for the North and the South. See the similar character of an anti-Communist, anti-American interpretation of the war by a distinguished Buddhist in South Viet Nam, T. Hanh, *Vietnam: Lotus in a Sea of Fire* (New York: Hill & Wang, 1967).

[17] The essential aspect of a legal settlement is the search for impartial sources of decision. It is the impartial decision-maker that is in the best position to assess the relative merits of adversary positions. This does not assure correct or just decisions in any particular instance, but merely that there will be a legal quality for the decision. The Secretary General of the United Nations is the most authoritative impartial decision-maker in the international system, especially in relation to Members of the United Nations. To deny his role or to ignore his recommendation is to subordinate the process of impartial decision to the process of unilateral decision, tending thereby to rely on power rather than law to shape the outcome of controversy.

legitimacy of a contested use of international force.[18] The essence of a law-oriented approach to the use of force is to submit claims to the best available procedures for community review and to restrict force to the levels authorized.[19]

---

[18] The opposition of the United States to the efforts of U Thant to work for a settlement are summarized in American Friends Service Commitiee, *Peace in Viet Nam* (New York: Hill & Wang, 1966), 50–52; F. Schurmann, P. Scott, and R. Zelnik, *The Politics of Escalation in Vietnam* (Boston: Beacon Press, 1966), 135–38. On June 20, 1966, U Thant made a three-point proposal for ending the war in Viet Nam:

(1) Unconditional cessation of bombing in North Viet Nam;
(2) Scaling down of military operations in South Viet Nam;
(3) Inclusion of the National Liberation Front in any proposed negotiations.

New York Times, June 21, 1966, 1, col. 5

The failure of the United States to accept this proposal, consisting according to U Thant of those steps that "alone can create the conditions" leading to a peaceful settlement, is indicative of its unilateral approach to the use of military power in Viet Nam. U Thant, as Secretary General, represents the voice of the international community, a voice that deserves to be heeded especially by a Great Power using its military power to overwhelm a small state. The role of the Secretary General in identifying reasonable conduct for parties in conflict is especially great when the political organs have failed to discharge their responsibility to maintain international peace and security. As in other dealings with the United Nations during the Viet Nam war, the United States has made *pro forma* gestures indicating its acceptance of the Secretary General's role. See, e.g., Arthur J. Goldberg's letter to U Thant in which it is said that "the United States Government will cooperate fully with you in getting such discussion started promptly [on ending the war] and in bringing them to a successful completion" (Text, *New York Times*, Dec. 20, 1966, 6, col. 4). The United States will cooperate fully provided that it does not have to alter its belligerent and political posture. U Thant is setting forth his conception of reasonable preconditions for peace talks. What does our cooperation entail if it does not lead to an acceptance of these precondi-tions? Our non-cooperation with U Thant is heightened by the fact that the preconditions he describes are those that seem calculated to bring the war to an end and to initiate negotiations on a reasonable basis that corresponds to the domestic balance of forces. Negotiations would proceed on an unnatural basis if either the suspension of bombing was conditional – it would be a club of death suspended by a powerful state over the destinies of a weak one – or the NLF was not accorded some degree of legitimacy as a political force in South Viet Nam of a character equal to that of the Saigon regime. The insistence on non-recognition is part of the effort to negotiate as if the NLF were a creature of North Viet Nam rather than a political entity with a reality of its own. President Johnson has often repeated the idea that during the negotiations "the Vietcong will have no difficulty having their views heard," but this is not a very satisfactory assurance for an insurgent faction that has fought for over a decade to control South Viet Nam: Transcript of President's News Conference on the Guam Parley, *New York Times*, March 22, 1967, 11, col. 3. It does not make the consent of the NLF an ingredient of settlement, nor does it give to the NLF any of the formal prerogatives of the Saigon regime. In effect, the civil war is ended not as a stalemate, but as a victory for the government side as it remains the sole constituted political elite.

[19] We associate the intervention of law in human affairs with the role of the third party deci-sion-maker who is entrusted with the task of sorting out adversary contentions. International society as decentralized often successfully works out the content of reasonableness through

A second kind of restraint in a situation of ambiguity is to confine violence within existing international boundaries. The decision by the United States to bomb North Viet Nam and to take military action in the territory of Laos and Cambodia is further disregard for available limits upon the self-interpretation of legal rights.[20] It is true that the United States is *not* yet using all the military power at its disposal against North Viet Nam, but such restraint is itself based on the exercise of discretion rather than upon deference to community procedures or to quasi-objective standards of limitation.[21]

---

action and interaction of adversary parties, provided the issues at stake are not vital to national security or national honor. In the context of force, however, the differential of power between adversaries of unequal strength influences their degree of flexibility in responding to counter-claims; the differences between the results of adversary interaction and of impartial third-party judgment are likely to be pronounced. The substitution of law for force in any social order involves, then, the gradual replacement of the ideology of self-help by that of third-party judgment. Perhaps the clearest jurisprudential discussion of the limits of law in a decentralized political system is contained in H. Kelsen, *Principles of International Law*, ed. R. Tucker (2d rev, ed.; New York: Holt, Rinehart and Winston, 1966), 3–87.

[20]　Both sides have violated "the sovereignty" of Laos and Cambodia, but the United States has frequently bombed infiltrators and supply lines within the territory of both states, thereby expanding further the extra-national scope of violence beyond South Viet Nam. See Mansfield, et al., Report to Senate Foreign Relations Comm., 89th Cong., 2d Sess., *The Viet Nam Conflict: The Substance and the Shadow* (Comm. Print 1966) (hereinafter cited as Mansfield Report), 8–10. An equivalent action by North Viet Nam or the Soviet Union would be to attack the United States air bases in Thailand. Such an expansion of the arena of combat would move the conflict dramatically closer to the threshold of general warfare. It is important to emphasize that the limited scope of the war in Viet Nam is a consequence of the failure of the Soviet Union and China to take *equivalent action* on behalf of Hanoi; such a failure is especially important in view of the United States demand that Hanoi take equivalent action in exchange for an end to bombing. See n. 27 below.

[21]　The United States reserves the discretion to decide for itself the degree of military force that it requires to secure North Viet Nam's acquiescence. In this David and Goliath situation, David is on a rack of death that has been slowly tightened over the years by a process we describe as "escalation." Goliath has had and continues to have the capacity at any point to kill David, but has sought instead to inflict pain and to threaten increasing pain until David gives in to the demands of Goliath. There is no reciprocity in such a situation of inequality. To claim restraint for Goliath is to ignore the rationale for this way of proceeding by stages. Among other factors to bear in mind is that Goliath knows that David has powerful, Goliath-like friends that may enter the scene more actively. See, e.g., the report of Harry Ashmore's visit to Hanoi on behalf of the Center for the Study of Democratic Institutions in which he quotes "a Colonel of the North Vietnamese General Staff" who "answered very solemnly" a question about his estimate "of North Viet Nam's capacity to resist the American troops":

> We've thought about this a great deal. We think we can handle up to 2,000,000 Americans. This assumes that you do not increase your bombing beyond its present level. I think your combat troops will concede that we are masters of guerilla war. We should be – we've been at it for twenty-five years. We are far less dependent on heavy supplies than your army. We are accustomed to fighting in this terrain of jungle and mountains and this advantage offsets the undoubted superiority of your sophisticated weapons

In this respect, the mode of Type I conflict (Korea) allows proportionate defense responses including unilateral action against the attacking state,[22] whereas in a Type II or III conflict (Viet Nam) third-party military action is either prohibited altogether or its scope confined to the political entity wherein the struggle is going on. In either event, the tendency to escalate is curtailed. My categorization of international conflict is intended to guide decision-makers and observers toward a sense of what is reasonable in a particular situation. A strong element of national discretion remains. The limits on international violence are only quasi-objective restrictions upon sovereign prerogatives.[23]

---

and planes. This is why we think we can handle up to 2,000,000 of your troops, and stay here the rest of the century if necessary. Of course, if you put in more than 2,000,000 soldiers, or if you escalate the bombing to the point where you completely destroy our communications, then we have to accept volunteers from China, from Russia, and it would be a new war. It would no longer be our war. It would be World War III.

Mr. Ashmore commented that:

I have to assume an element of propaganda in this, but I also say that I believe the Colonel meant what he said, and was consciously reflecting the considered judgment of the North Vietnamese government.

Harry Ashmore, "Pacem in Terris II: Mission to North Viet Nam," *Center Diary*, March–April 1967, 17

[22] Korea is not truly an example of Type I, but of Type IV, because the United States' role was authorized by the United Nations; see pp. 80–81 above for explanation of Type IV. Nevertheless, to point up the relationship between Korea and Viet Nam it is possible to pierce the cosmopolitan veil, emphasize Soviet opposition and question the propriety of an authorization obtained in the Security Council during the Soviet boycott, and thereby view the response in Korea *as if* it proceeded without benefit of United Nations approval. In that case, Korea would appear to be an instance of Type I authorizing whatever military action is needed to restore the *status quo ante* the armed attack. On this basis I believe that the defensive armies should not have proceeded beyond the 38th Parallel, although it would have been permissible to commit war acts against North Korean territory so as to restore the *status quo ante*.

[23] The Legal Adviser, Leonard Meeker, finds no difficulty in reconciling my categories of analysis with United States policy in Viet Nam: "The evidence does not allow for the conclusion that the war in Viet-Nam was ever a simple category-one situation. It was probably, for quite some period of time, a category-two situation. By the end of 1964, however, it had become very clearly a category-three situation" (Meeker, "Viet-Nam and the International Law of Self-Defense," *Department of State Bulletin*, 56 (1967), 59). Mr. Meeker merely characterizes the facts to support the American legal position, including the shift of the war into the third category (Type I). By the end of 1964, mainly over a period of four years, about 40,000 are reported to have infiltrated from North Viet Nam according to official United States statistics. Most of those infiltrated during this period were ethnic Southerners that joined up with Vietcong units. There are several factors that militate against Mr. Meeker's inference of "armed attack" (that is category three): First, the insurgency preexisted North Vietnamese infiltration; as Fall notes, "there had been a fairly strong anti-Diem insurgent current of non-Communist origins even before the 1956 deadline on elections between the two zones went by" (Fall, *The Two Viet-Nams* (2d rev. ed., 1967), 356 (*cf.* map showing pattern of insurgent control as of 1962–63,

There is also some uncertainty as to whether a particular conflict belongs in one category rather than another. So long as the organized international community is unable to determine the limits on authorized violence, thereby placing the conflict within Type IV (see next paragraph) it remains necessary to rely upon national discretion. The objective of articulating Types I–III is to enable a more rational exercise of national discretion through the clarification of the relationship between factual patterns and legal expectations. If states would adhere in practice to these limits, *ex parte* interpretations of fact and of law on claims to use violence in international society would decline in importance.

Professor Moore's world order position, as presently stated, ignores the relevance of international institutions and of a supranational perspective to an assessment of the legal status of a controverted use of military power. To emphasize the problem of curtailing national discretion in a world of political conflict I would now add Type IV to the previous three types.[24] Type

---

p. 354); second, the Saigon regime was enabled to resist the NLF in the years before 1961 only because it was given such large amounts of economic support by the United States in the years after 1954; as the first Mansfield Report observes, "in matters of defense, internal stability and economic support, the Vietnamese Government has come to depend almost wholly on the United States for outside assistance. In terms of aid the assumption of this preponderant responsibility has meant US outlays of $1.4 billion for economic assistance during the period of 1955–62. This economic aid has had some effect on Vietnamese development, but its primary purpose has been to sustain the Vietnamese economy so that it, in turn, could maintain the burden of a military establishment which has been upward of 150,000 men for the past half-decade. On top of the economic aid, there has also been provided large amounts of military equipment and supplies and training for the Vietnamese Army, Navy, and Air Force and for other defense purposes. For the period 1955–62 the total of aid of all kinds in Viet Nam stands at more than $2 billion" (Mansfield Report, app. II, 19). For tables on the degree of United States involvement since 1954, see G. Kahin and J. Lewis, *The United States in Vietnam* (New York: Delta, 1967), 73, 185.

The point is that North Vietnamese military assistance to an ongoing insurgency was a proportionate response at all stages to the extent of United States involvement on behalf of Saigon. And when one considers that North Viet Nam had a reasonable (if not absolutely assured) expectation that the Geneva settlement would lead to unification under their control after a period of transition enabling the French to depart, then the American interposition of a powerful non-Vietnamese "presence" must also enter into an appraisal of North Viet Nam's pre-1965 role. In such a context it seems unreasonable and without legal foundation to construe North Viet Nam's military assistance to the Vietcong as becoming an attack by one country on another. Without such a premise of attack, the United States response against North Vietnamese territory would be "unprovoked aggression." Recourse to self-defense implies a prior armed attack, and that is why United States position depends on "the armed attack" taking place before bombing the North began in February 1965.

24   In my earlier article, then, Korea and Suez are not properly examples of Type I after there was authorization of defensive action by the United Nations. Type I becomes Type IV as soon as the United Nations itself acts or authorizes action. The description, then, of Type I, in Falk, "International Law and the United States Role in the Viet Nam War," 1126, should be amended accordingly. Types II and III can also be transferred into Type IV, although the

IV conflict exists whenever a competent international organization of global (IVa) or regional (IVb) dimensions authorizes the use of force.[25] Type IVa can be illustrated by reference to United Nations actions in Korea (1950), Suez (1956), Cyprus, and the Congo (1960). The authorization or prohibition of violence by the United Nations resolves the issue of legality, even though a particular decision may be arbitrary or unjust in any given set of circumstances.[26]

The point here is that Type IV entails an authoritative consensus that may be absent in Types I–III.[27] Thus, the context of my first *Yale* article and of this

---

conjectural nature of the facts and the less direct connection to international peace and security make such a transfer less likely to take place. The Indian attack upon Goa and the Chinese attack upon Tibet are examples of Type I provided the victim entities are entitled to the status of "states." Goa's defensive prerogatives are also qualified by the limited legitimacy of colonial title to territory as of 1961.

[25] The legal status of Type IVb is more problematical than that of Type IVa. For one thing, regional organizations are themselves subject to regulation by the Security Council (Article 53(1) says that "no enforcement action shall be taken under regional arrangements or by regional agencies without the authorization of the Security Council"). For another, the opposition of the Arab League to Israel, of the Organization of African Unity to South Africa, and of the Organization of American States to Castro's Cuba points to the danger of "aggression" under the legitimizing aegis of supranationalism. At the same time, the existence of regional support for recourse to coercion is a factor that alters the legal status of a controversial use of military power. It is important to distinguish a regional actor – such as the OAS – from an *ex parte* defensive alliance – such as SEATO. Authorization by SEATO would not move the conflict into Type IVb, although the absence of such authorization might cast light on claims to respond within the framework of Type I.

[26] This possibility leads Julius Stone, among others, to deny almost altogether the restrictive impact of the Charter system of controls upon the discretion of sovereign states: J. Stone, *Aggression and World Order* (Berkeley: University of California Press, 1958), 1–3, 78–103.

[27] In the absence of an authoritative consensus on a global level that embodies divergent perspectives, the construction of second-order constraints upon adversary perspectives is the essential task of international law. Types I–III provide quasi-objective guidelines that tend to confine an international conflict. Departures from these guidelines could be justified legally by exceptional circumstances and for specific objectives. But the second-order system of constraint depends on a fair correlation of the conflict with the system of graduated categories. The United States insistence on viewing North Viet Nam's role as warranting a Type I response is destructive of second-order constraints as the basic categorization does not command respect from many uncommitted observers. The generalized bombing of North Viet Nam could not be easily justified as an exception to Type II. Specific attacks upon extra-territorial guerrilla sanctuaries might be justified if the conflict was otherwise contained within Type II limits. But the objectives of bombing North Viet Nam seem primarily connected with an overall effort to secure their acquiescence to our conception of the war in South Viet Nam. President Johnson's letter of March 1, 1967, to Senator Jackson gives the Government's rationale for bombing North Viet Nam in fairly complete terms; significantly, this letter ends by saying "we shall persist with our operations in the North – until those who launched this aggression are prepared to move seriously to reinstall the agreements whose violations have brought the scourge of war to Southeast Asia." Earlier the letter says that bombing will end when the other side "*is willing to take equivalent action*" (emphasis added). See "President Reviews US Position on Bombing of North Viet-Nam," *Department of State Bulletin*, 56 (1967), 516. What is equivalent

reply to Moore is provided by the conflict in Viet Nam, a conflict in which the United Nations has not been able to act collectively through its main political organs.[28] This context is in the range of Types I–III.[29]

Having set forth the factors that shape my world order position, I will turn now to Professor Moore's specific criticisms of my approach. He has three main objectives:

(1) I have construed the Viet Nam facts in a one-sided manner;
(2) My system of categorization imposes arbitrary limits on a state using force for defensive purposes;

---

action if it is conceded that extra-territorial violence is, at best, an extraordinary incident of a Type II conflict? Supplying and sending troops to aid the NLF is a normal incident of Type II conflict. To demand, as seems implied by the official United States position, the elimination of a normal claim by a third-party state in exchange for the termination of an *extraordinary* claim (and in Viet Nam the extraordinary nature of the claim is aggravated by its assertion in extravagant, unspecific, and accelerating form) by its third-party opponent seems highly unreasonable. It is worth recalling that the United States' original justification for bombing North Viet Nam in February 1965 was formulated in the restrictive and exception-explaining logic of Type II as a reprisal for Vietcong attacks on United States airfields in South Viet Nam; it is worth noting that the legal reflex in February 1965 was in the manner of Type II, not Type I. This is worth noting because of the subsequent official explanations that the Viet Nam war clearly belonged to Type I by the end of 1964. *Cf.* n. 23 above; see also "The Legality of United States Participation in the Defense of Viet-Nam," Office of the Legal Adviser, Department of State, 112 *Congressional Record* 5274 (daily ed. March 10, 1966). For original reliance on a reprisal theory, see Falk, "International Law and the United States Role in the Viet Nam War," 1145; for legal criticism of even the attempt to rely on a reprisal theory, see Lawyers Committee, *Vietnam and International Law*, 53–57.

[28] But the United States bears a heavy burden of responsibility for the inaction of the United Nations as a consequence of the following considerations:

(1) Non-compliance with the proposals of the Secretary General, U Thant;
(2) Non-submission of the claim to act in self-defense to the Security Council or General Assembly for serious community review;
(3) Refusal in early stages of conflict to seek a peaceful settlement through negotiations;
(4) Alienation of China from the United Nations by its continuing exclusion from the activities of the Organization;
(5) Ambiguity as to the sincerity of United States offers to negotiate, as a consequence of coupling peace moves with steps up the escalation ladder.

For scholarly documentation, see Schurmann, Scott, and Zelnik, *The Politics of Escalation in Vietnam*.

[29] The important distinction is between the sort of legal order that exists for Types I–III and for Type IV:

Types I–III are governed by second-order constraints self-imposed by sovereign states and based upon such quasi-objective sources of guidance and limitations as past practice, public opinion, recommendation of impartial third-party actors such as the Secretary General and the Pope, and well-defined international boundaries.

Type IV conflicts are governed by first-order constraints consisting of the determinations of international institutions. First-order constraints are procedural outcomes on a supranational level, whereas second-order constraints are substantive outcomes on a national level.

(3) My system really declares my views as to what international law *ought to be* although it pretends to be a statement of present legal obligations binding upon a state.

Professor Moore's first principal criticism pertains primarily to my argument that it would have been appropriate to regard the conflict in Viet Nam as an example of a Type III conflict, that is, as an example of civil strife internal to one country. The second and third criticisms pertain primarily to my chief argument that the conflict in Viet Nam, whatever its early history, has become an example of Type II conflict, that is, an example of civil strife in South Viet Nam with substantial intervention on behalf of the two contending factions, the Saigon regime and the National Liberation Front (NLF) (these criticisms are discussed below in Section II).

I THE RATIONALE RESTATED IN SUPPORT OF A TYPE III CLASSIFICATION OF THE VIET NAM WAR

Let me state clearly that when large-scale military participation by the United States in the war began to take place – say 1963 – it became appropriate to treat the conflict as Type II. North Vietnamese large-scale military participation on behalf of the NLF accentuates this classification of the war. My principal contention denies that the *factual* basis exists to warrant treating the Viet Nam war as belonging in Type I (which would authorize extra-territorial defensive measures) and, as a correlate, denies that there exists a *legal* basis for extra-territorial violence if the war is classified as Type II. However, it remains important to consider the conflict in Viet Nam also as belonging originally in Type III so as to appreciate the principal role of the United States in converting the war into Type II, such a conversion involving conduct itself seriously at variance with my conception of the requirements of world order.[30]

---

[30] The transformation from Type III to Type II is a matter of policy rather than law in any normal sense; "In sum, international law has never been equipped to intervene in civil war situations": W. Friedmann, "Intervention, Civil War and the Role of International Law," *Proceedings of the American Society of International Law*, 59 (1965), 74. There are no criteria that are usefully available to identify prohibited interventions, although some efforts have been recently made to prohibit overt and direct military participation. See T. Farer, "Intervention in Civil Wars: A Modest Proposal," *Columbia Law Review*, 67 (1967), 266–79. The real issues of policy confronting the United States are the degree to which it reacts to revolutionary events in the Afro-Asian and Latin American countries as properly hostile to its interests. For critical accounts of this aspect of foreign policy, see E. Stillman and W. Pfaff, *Power and Impotence* (New York: Random House, 1966), 15–59, 184–226; H. Zinn, *Vietnam: The Logic of Withdrawal* (Boston: Beacon Press, 1967), 37–50; and see Hanh, *Vietnam*, 60–68, for the entangling of nationalism and communism in the Viet Nam setting. For a pro-Administration judgment of the American

It is also important to acknowledge that the expectations of North Viet Nam and of the NLF were likely formed prior to the overt, large-scale intervention by the United States – that is, when the conflict still belonged in the Type III category. Clarifying the factual and legal reasons for regarding the early stages of the war as Type III is very centrally related, in my view, to the North Vietnamese perception of what would constitute a reasonable outcome of the Viet Nam war (regardless of its subsequent Type II history).

In considering the war in Viet Nam as belonging in Type III, especially in its early (pre-1963) phases, I intended a two-pronged argument: first, a civil war between the two factions in the South and, second, a civil war between the Northern and Southern Zones. My argument was essentially that in either case such a conflict should be determined by the domestic balance of forces and that, in the setting of Viet Nam under either interpretation, the anti-Saigon "entity" would have prevailed but for American (that is, non-Vietnamese) military intervention. My reasoning is essentially as follows: South Viet Nam had evolved, despite the contrary intentions of the Geneva Settlement, as a separate *de facto* political entity, and the NLF emerged as a sufficiently indigenous opposition movement to be deemed South Vietnamese in character rather than as an "agent" or "puppet" of North Viet Nam.[31] In this circumstance

---

response to foreign revolutionary activity, see W. Rostow, "The Great Transition: Tasks of the First and Second Postwar Generations," *Department of State Bulletin*, 56 (1967), 491–504.

The transformation from Type II to Type I is regulated by international law as it implies violent conflict between sovereign states rather than within a sovereign state. Initiating recourse to international violence, as distinct from interventionary violence, requires the prior occurrence of an armed attack.

The consequences of this difference between shifting from III to II and from III or II to I are to make different kinds of legal arguments appropriate in each context. At the same time the difference in argument can be over-stated. A successful claim by a state to act in a manner not previously regarded as legal may itself constitute authoritative state practice that can be relied upon in the future by others, thereby transforming what had once been regarded as prohibited into what comes to be regarded as permissible. In a context where legal expectations have been regarded as well-fixed policy, considerations may incline an actor to posit a legislative claim, which if effectively asserted and accepted by the wider community, tends to reshape legal expectations. In both contexts, therefore, there is an unavoidable discretionary role played by the state with the capability to act in different ways, but in the interventionary axis of decision (III–II) there is less disposition to regard the decision to intervene as a weakening of legal order than in the armed attack–self-defense axis of decision wherein legal expectation of fairly settled character had been thought to exist, especially in view of the coordinated United States–Soviet opposition to the French-British-Israeli recourse to overt violence in the Suez campaign of 1956.

31   To take seriously the issue of the autonomy of the NLF it would be necessary to compare its dependence on Hanoi with Saigon's dependence on Washington at the various phases of the war. See J. Lacouture, *Viet Nam: Between Two Truces*, 61–119 (New York: Random House, 1966); Kahin and Lewis, *The United States in Vietnam*, esp. "Americanization of the War," 151–80. The autonomy of Saigon's discretion to terminate the war on *its own terms*, as distinct

the outcome of the NLF–Saigon struggle would have been an NLF victory if both the United States and North Viet Nam had remained out of the conflict, and the quantum and phasing of United States and North Vietnamese aid to the contending factions were imbalanced in favor of Saigon at every stage subsequent to 1954. This interpretation of the early stages of the Vietnamese conflict seems to enjoy the support of almost all disinterested analysts.[32]

The second prong of the Type III analysis conceives of the war in Viet Nam as a civil war between South Viet Nam and North Viet Nam waged for control of the state of Viet Nam. According to Professor Moore, such a characterization of the war overlooks the separateness as of 1960 of these two political entities, as well as the essential ambiguity of the Geneva settlement, especially with regard to reunification. Professor Moore, although sensitive to the particularities of the division of Viet Nam in 1954, closely associates the status of Viet Nam with such other divided countries as Korea, Germany, and China. Force across a partition boundary is, as he properly points out, dangerous to world peace since the *de facto* divisions express major unresolved conflicts between the Communist and non-Communist worlds. I challenge Professor Moore's analysis on two principal grounds:

(1) The division in Viet Nam is not usefully comparable on policy grounds to that of other divided countries;

(2) The defeat of the French by the Viet Minh as embodied in the Geneva Settlement of 1954, the attitude of Saigon toward the Geneva Accords, the Southern locus of the uprising, the small magnitude of Northern interference as compared to the direct and indirect military contributions of the United States Government to Saigon, the non-viability of the regime in the South, and the national popularity of Ho Chi Minh are factors that when taken into joint account make it misleading to talk of "the aggression" of the North.

---

from those insisted upon by Washington, is certainly as doubtful as is the autonomy of the NLF to terminate the war on conditions at variance with those insisted upon by Hanoi.

As to the extent of the American role at earlier preinsurgency stages of South Viet Nam's history, see E. Hammer, *The Struggle for Indo-China 1940–1955* (Stanford: Stanford University Press, 1955), 346–64; "However much American officials may have wished to regard southern Viet Nam as independent, the fact and the promise of substantial American aid to the Nationalist regime gave them such influence that in the fall of 1954 it was the United States, not the Vietnamese people, who decided that Ngo Dinh Diem would continue to be Prime Minister of southern Viet Nam" (*ibid.*, 356).

[32] Lacouture, *Vietnam: Between Two Truces*, 186–90; Kahin and Lewis, *The United States in Vietnam*, 127–206; Mansfield Report, 11–12.

The Geneva Settlement: Face-Saving or Partition

Sir Anthony Eden, introducing his discussion of the Geneva Accords of 1954 and his ideas for settling the present war in Viet Nam, has said that

> No agreement can be so drawn as to be proof against every malevolent intention. That is why the observance of international engagements is the first condition of any peaceful society. Once allow treaties to be torn up with impunity and the world is headed for trouble; violators soon have imitators.[33]

It seems to me that Professor Moore is somewhat cavalier in explaining away the United States' insistence on non-implementation of the election provision in the Final Declaration by setting it off against a Western preference for "partition" that was consistently denied both by the language of the Agreement on the Cessation of Hostilities in Viet Nam and of the Final Declaration.[34]

Ignoring the relevance of formal international engagements, Professor Moore also supports the double standard whereby North Viet Nam's alleged export of coercion through the NLF is viewed as a material breach of the Geneva Accords, whereas the United States' provision of military aid to Saigon, even though it admittedly preceded North Vietnamese coercion, is approved of as a "permitted defensive response." Moore facilely circumvents the determination by the International Control Commission that both sides were guilty of violations of the Geneva Accords which were not weighted as to relative seriousness by asserting that "this neutral reporting proves little."[35] In fact, for Professor Moore the determination of the ICC proves less than does the unsupported balancing of these two violations by an interested party – namely, the United States Government. As elsewhere in his analysis Professor Moore seems to endorse the discretionary competence of sovereign states at the expense either of binding international arrangements or of the determinations of impartial machinery set up to implement these arrangements. If the United States was so convinced that its aid to Saigon was a permissible defensive response, then why did it not have this conclusion confirmed by the ICC or by a reconvened Geneva Conference in the course of the years since 1954? There

[33] A. Eden, *Toward Peace in Indochina* (London: Oxford University Press, 1966), 31.
[34] See especially Articles 1–9, 11–15, and 27 of Agreement on the Cessation of Hostilities in Viet-Nam, July 20, 1954, and Articles 6 and 7 of the Final Declaration of Geneva Conference, July 21, 1954, Senate Foreign Relations Comm., 89th Cong. 1st Sess., *Background Information Relating to Southeast Asia and Vietnam* (rev. ed. June 16, 1965), 28–42, 58–60 (hereinafter cited as *Background Information*).
[35] For example, paragraph 84 of the Sixth Interim Report of the ICC, December 11, 1955–July 10, 1956, reads as follows: "While the Commission has experienced difficulties in North Vietnam, the major part of its difficulties has arisen in South Vietnam." See 33 Parliamentary Sessional Papers, Cmd. 31, at 30 (1956–57).

is little doubt that from the time when the meetings were going on in Geneva in 1954 the United States was determined to use its unilateral military power to avoid the translation of the Viet Minh's military victory over the French in the First Indochina War into a corresponding political victory. Once again it is worth quoting Anthony Eden, partly because he was a principal participant at Geneva and partly because his Tory credentials are so impeccable:

> [Dulles] reiterated his fears that, in the event, France would be compelled to depart from the seven points, and the United States would then have to disassociate herself from the resulting agreement. He said that even if the settlement adhered to the seven points faithfully, the United States still could not guarantee it.[36]
>
> I had already been warned by Bedell Smith that the United States Government could not associate themselves with the final declaration. The most they could do was to issue a declaration taking note of what had been decided and undertaking not to disturb the settlement. Since Dulles had been at least as responsible as ourselves for calling the Geneva Conference, this did not seem to me reasonable.[37]

There are two points to note. First, the United States' determination from the outset not to be fully associated with the Geneva Settlement. Why is this so if Professor Moore's view of its essential understanding is correct? To answer this by saying that the United States wanted to avoid ratifying the Communist acquisition of North Viet Nam is hardly a sufficient explanation (even if it is a part of the story) in light of Dulles' overall insistence upon preserving a free hand for American action in the future. The second point, one that strikes me as legally pertinent, is why it matters whether the United States approved of the Geneva Accords or not. The parties to the conflict had full power to settle it by agreement. It is rather far-fetched to contend that the United States assent is needed to secure a formally binding arrangement reached to end a war in which the United States was not itself a direct participant.

Not everything complex is ambiguous. Professor Moore's argument that the Geneva Settlement was ambiguous on the issue of unification is unconvincing on several grounds:

(1) The election provisions of the Geneva Accords are explicit as to date, auspices and preconditions;[38]

---

[36] A. Eden, *Full Circle* (London: Cassell, 1960), 156.
[37] *Ibid.*, 159–60.
[38] Falk, "International Law and the United States Role in the Viet Nam War," (and authorities cited in n. 31 above); Lawyers Committee, *Vietnam and International Law*, 43–48; Kahin and Lewis, *The United States in Vietnam*, 52–55, 80–87; Buttinger, *Vietnam*, Vol. II, 839–40; the

(2) The fact that the Geneva Declaration was unsigned does not seriously detract from its character as a binding legal instrument;[39]

(3) The refusal of the Saigon regime to accept the Geneva Accords does not relieve it of the obligation to comply as France had the capacity that it explicitly sought to exercise, to bind its "successor";[40]

(4) Experienced and impartial observers generally agree that (a) unification by means of elections was part of the Geneva Settlement and (b)

---

most detailed support for regarding the failure to hold the elections promised by Article 7 of the Final Declaration for July 1956 as frustrating Hanoi's sincere understanding of the Geneva Settlement is contained in a well-researched monograph, F. Weinstein, "Vietnam's Unheld Elections" (Data Paper No. 60, Southeast Asia Program, Cornell Univ., 1966); *cf.* Lacouture, "The 'Face' of the Viet Cong," *War/Peace Report*, May 1966, 7, 8: "One cannot say . . . that the North resigned itself, with only *pro forma* protestations, to Diem's refusal to hold the elections that had been legally set for July, 1956. During his trip to New Delhi in 1955 as well as in three separate attempts at the end of 1955 and at the beginning of 1956, Pham Van Dong, the present premier of North Vietnam, attempted to implement the provisions of the Geneva agreement. He even offered to delay the elections on condition that Saigon pledge to allow them. It was the great powers – the USSR and Peking included – who forgot the Geneva recommendations, not Hanoi, which found itself for the second time 'cheated.'" For a full account of the first time Hanoi was "cheated," see Hammer, *The Struggle for Indo-China*, 148–202; a briefer account is contained in Kahin and Lewis, *The United States in Vietnam*, 25–28.

[39] *See* Kahin and Lewis, *The United States in Vietnam*, 51 (and citations contained in n. 7 therein), including reference to Article 3(b) and commentary thereto as contained in U.N. Doc. A/16309 (1966). The fact that the United States withheld its oral assent from the Final Declaration and attached a Declaration somewhat at variance with Article 7 does not alter the legal expectations created among the real parties in interest – the French and the Viet Minh. For text of the United States Declaration, see *Background Information*, 61: "In connection with the statement in the declaration concerning free elections in Viet-Nam my Government wishes to make clear its position which it has expressed in a declaration made in Washington on June 29, 1954, as follows:

> In the case of nations now divided against their will, we shall continue to seek to achieve unity through free elections supervised by the United Nations to insure that they are conducted fairly.

With respect to the statement made by the representative of the State of Viet-Nam [Bao Dai], the United States reiterates its traditional position that peoples are entitled to determine their own future and that it will not join in an arrangement which would hinder this. Nothing in its declaration just made is intended to or does indicate any departure from its traditional position."
It is obvious that the United States alters the terms of Article 7 by the conspicuous omission of a definite date upon which elections should be held in Viet Nam and by the call for United Nations supervision. It is also clear that the refusal to give oral assent to the Final Declaration and the reference in the United States Statement to its refusal "to join in an arrangement" which "would hinder" its election policy indicates the serious intention of the other participants to take seriously the terms of Article 7. It is one thing for the United States and the Bao Dai regime to disassociate themselves from the Final Declaration, it is quite another to contend that the enforceability and centrality of the election provision were in any respect reduced thereby.

[40] This conclusion appears to be persuasively established in D. Partan, "Legal Aspects of the Vietnam Conflict," *Boston University Law Review*, 46 (1966), 289–92.

elections, if held, would have resulted in the consolidation of Viet Nam under the control of Hanoi;[41]

(5) The United States was from the beginning manifestly discontented with the Geneva solution, refused to endorse the outcome as a party, and set about almost immediately thereafter to undo the fulfillment of its terms.[42]

Moore advises analysts to consider the total context of Geneva and yet he neglects these critical factors. He is correct in pointing to a certain aura of ambiguity connected with securing the compliance of Saigon with a settlement that was expected to extinguish its sphere of influence. It is also appropriate, as Moore suggests, to acknowledge the subsequent *de facto* sovereignty of both North and South Viet Nam, regardless of the intentions at Geneva in 1954.[43]

It would consume too much space to refute Moore's interpretation of the Geneva Accords on a point-to-point basis especially as this task has already been done effectively by other authors.[44] I would, however, suggest the weakness of Moore's position by reference to the long passage he approvingly quotes from a book by Victor Bator. In this passage Bator argues that the Geneva Accords really intended "partition" and that this position is borne out by "the detailed accounts of Bernard B. Fall, Jean Lacouture, and Philippe Devillers."[45] Here is what Devillers actually thought about the Geneva Settlement:

The demarcation line was to be purely provisional; the principle of Vietnamese unity was not questioned, and the idea of partition was officially rejected with indignation by both sides ...

[41] See the authorities cited in n. 38 above for relevant references, especially Weinstein, "Vietnam's Unheld Elections." A typical comment is in Fall, *The Two Viet-Nams* (2d rev. ed., 1967), 231, who writes that "On the grounds of its nonsignature, South Viet-Nam refused to hold elections by July 1956, since this would have meant handing over control of the South to Ho Chi Minh."

[42] *Cf.* Fall, *The Two Viet-Nams* (2d rev. ed., 1967), 229–33; Kahin and Lewis, *The United States in Vietnam*, 57–63; Buttinger, *Vietnam*, Vol. II, 834–42.

[43] The expectations created as of 1954 remain relevant to the perception by North Viet Nam of what constitutes a reasonable outcome of the Second Indochina War, and influences the formulation of minimum negotiating demands.

[44] See Kahin and Lewis, *The United States in Vietnam*, 43–65; also relevant on many points is D. Lancaster, *The Emancipation of French Indochina* (New York: Oxford University Press, 1961), 313–58.

[45] In a long and significant scholarly review article, itself not hostile to the United States' role in Viet Nam, John T. McAlister says of Bator's longer interpretation of the Geneva Conference in V. Bator, *Viet Nam: A Diplomatic Tragedy* (New York: Oceana, 1965), that it "is an emotional and polemical book making no claims to be a scholarly work": McAlister, "The Possibilities for Diplomacy in Southeast Asia," World Politics, 19 (1967), 269; Bator's article from *The Reporter* has been reprinted along with a series of other strongly pro-Administration articles drawn from the magazine and reflecting its partisan editorial slant in Viet Nam: *Vietnam: Why – A Collection Of Reports and Comments from The Reporter* (New York: Reporter Magazine Co., 1966). It is, hence, strange to rely upon an occasional piece by Bator, were it not the case that the more trustworthy commentators in the Geneva Conference all cast doubt upon "the partition" hypothesis.

The disproportion between the monolithic power of the Vietminh, armed and with the halo of victory, and the almost derisory weakness of the so-called Nationalist Viet Nam was such that in the summer of 1954 almost no one thought that the two years' delay won by M. Mendes-France at Geneva could be anything but a respite in which to salvage as much as possible from the wreck. *At the end of the period unity would certainly be restored this time to the benefit of the Vietminh, the basic hypothesis then acknowledged by all being that the Geneva Agreements would definitely be implemented* [emphasis supplied].[46]

Devillers' position has recently been reaffirmed by Professors Kahin and Lewis in their careful and fully documented account of the Geneva Conference. These authors describe Geneva as the event that "officially registered France's defeat by the Vietminh and provided her with a face-saving means of disengagement."[47] In this regard Kahin and Lewis aver that it was the "promise of elections that constituted an essential condition insisted upon by the Vietminh at Geneva." Their reasoning is well worth quoting:

France was prepared to pay the political price of that condition in order to get the armistice that she so urgently wanted. Her successor [in Saigon] would be obliged to abide by that condition or face the certain resumption of hostilities. The reason for this is patent: when a military struggle for power ends on the agreed condition that the competition will be transferred to the political plane, the side that violates the agreed condition cannot legitimately expect that the military struggle will not be resumed.[48]

Professor Moore relies upon the memoirs of Anthony Eden to establish "that the real core of the settlement, at least from a Western standpoint, was partition of Viet Nam" (1059). These memoirs are too imprecise to clarify legal analysis and are internally inconsistent,[49] although they do provide considerable

---

[46]   P. Devillers, "The Struggle for Unification of Vietnam," *China Quarterly*, Jan.– Mar. 1962, 2–3.
[47]   Kahin and Lewis, *The United States in Vietnam*, 43.
[48]   *Ibid.*, 57.
[49]   Anthony Eden seems primarily concerned with obtaining a Western negotiating consensus that would enable the war in Indochina to be brought to an end. There is no detailed interpretation given by the terms of the Geneva settlement and there is every indication that Eden thought that the election provisions would be carried out, despite the intra-Allied discussion in terms of "partition." See Eden, *Full Circle*, 158–59. It is very strange to argue that the negotiating hopes of the United States, which were not to any degree reflected in the language or terms of the Accords themselves, should be given any weight in construing treaty-type obligations that are unambiguous on their face. It is an elementary rule of treaty interpretation that one consults the context of the agreement only to the extent that the provisions themselves are unclear. Even if the Accords do not qualify as treaties in the strict sense, their content was affirmed in a solemn and formal manner. In any event, although the rhetoric of partition does imply a permanent separation of Viet Nam into two separate states, it is quite consistent with a temporary period

insight into the divergence of the American position from that of the other Western powers at Geneva in 1954. Eden, who holds very intense anti-Communist views, is especially convincing in his account of the effort that he made to discourage the United States from undermining the whole project of a conference to end the First Indochina War.[50] The United States was lobbying at Geneva in support of a collective Western intervention in support of the French, support that the French no longer desired. Eden indicates that he was distressed to learn from a French diplomat about an official document in which the United States secretly proposed to the French that military intervention in Indochina occur "either after the failure of Geneva, *or earlier if the French so desired, and he emphasized that the American preference had been clearly expressed for the earlier date*" (emphasis supplied).[51] It seems to me that a fair-minded reading of the Eden memoirs would emphasize the degree to which talk of "partition" may have been designed to mollify the United States apprehensions about the Conference. In any event, if "partition" was the bargain, it was nowhere reflected in the Geneva Accords that resulted from the Conference. Why not?

The partition hypothesis also does not reconcile easily with Eden's evident feeling that the election provision in the Final Declaration was to be taken seriously:

> The Communists insisted that elections should be held during 1955 in Viet Nam, whereas the French maintained, I thought rightly, that it would take at least two years for the country to be restored to a condition in which elections would be possible.[52]

I conclude that (1) partition was not written into the Geneva Accords and that (2) unification by elections in July 1956 was the essential political bargain struck at Geneva in exchange for a regroupment of the fighting forces into two zones and the withdrawal to the North of the Viet Minh armies. This interpretation of the Geneva Accords is crucial for an interpretation of the relevance of the post-1954 events, especially of the extent to which one emphasizes or disregards the non-implementation of the election provision.

---

of partition followed by elections seeking reunification. Only such an interpretation brings consistency into the Eden accounting. For the most persuasive skeptical view of the Geneva Accords – one that puts a curse on both houses – see Buttinger, *Vietnam*, Vol. II, 978–81.

[50] Eden, *Full Circle*, 120–63.

[51] *Ibid.*, 134; *cf. ibid.*, 93, 103, 117, 126–27 (for a sense of Eden's perception of American attitudes toward the Geneva Conference). Buttinger's account of the American attempts to rally support for military intervention is one of the most complete and accurate: Buttinger, *Vietnam*, Vol. II, 797–844; he writes that "the moves that Radford, Dulles, and Nixon made during April 1954, to stop Communism in Indochina are among the saddest chapters of U.S. diplomacy" (*ibid.*, 819).

[52] Eden, *Full Circle*, 158, 159; see also Eden, *Toward Peace in Indochina*, 38.

My principal contention is that, once it became clear that the election provision would not be carried out, recourse to coercion by Hanoi was both
predictable and permissible in either of the two Type III variants – the NLF
versus Saigon or North Viet Nam versus South Viet Nam. On this basis I find
it highly misleading and false to analogize the evidence of North Vietnamese
support for the insurgency in the South with the massive attack by North
Korea on South Korea in 1950. It is false even if (which is hardly possible)
one accepts the State Department's "white papers" as accurate descriptions
of the North Vietnamese role in the early stage of the conflict in South Viet
Nam. Among other considerations distinguishing Korea are the following:
The effort of Hanoi proceeded against a quite opposite political background,
it was based on much more ambiguous evidence of coercion, and the coercion was of a such small scale that it could not have resulted in any substantial
disturbance had not a revolutionary potential preexisted in South Viet Nam.[53]

Viet Nam cannot be regarded as relevantly similar to the other divided
countries of China,[54] Korea, or Germany. Although Korea and Germany
differ significantly from one another as divided countries, the political "settlement" in each case consisted of a reciprocal acceptance of partition, at
least until a more satisfactory political settlement could be agreed upon as
to reunification. Until such a second or new political settlement emerges, if
ever, the use of coercion in any form to achieve a favorable military settlement
of the reunification issue is, as Professor Moore properly indicates, a dangerous disturbance of world order, a disturbance that entitles the victim entity
to claim full defensive rights and one that entails the gravest consequences;
the Korean War illustrates and vindicates the principle that frontiers within
divided states enjoy at least the same sanctity as frontiers between undivided
states. The Saigon regime cannot invoke the sanctity of the seventeenth parallel in the same persuasive manner as the Seoul regime invoked the sanctity
of the thirty-eighth parallel. The political settlement at Geneva in 1954 provided a formula for the nullification (rather than one for the maintenance) of
the division. In Viet Nam, Saigon's establishment, rather than the subsequent

[53] E.g., A. S. Feldman, "Violence and Volatility: The Likelihood of Revolution," in H. Eckstein,
ed., *Internal War* (Glencoe, IL: Free Press, 1964), 111–29.

[54] It can be persuasively argued, I think, that Formosa is wrongly conceived of as an integral
part of China. Therefore, China is not "a divided country" at all, but there are two countries each of which is entitled to sovereign status. For a complete argument to this effect, see
L. Chen and H. Lasswell, *Formosa, China, and the United Nations: Formosa's Place in the World
Community* (New York: St. Martin's Press, 1967).

attempt at its removal, of a political frontier at the seventeenth parallel represented the coercive challenge to world order.[55]

In this spirit it is worth reexamining Professor Moore's central policy test in the Viet Nam setting – namely, the prohibition by international law of coercion as a strategy of major change. On one level such a policy is an essential ingredient of minimum world order in the nuclear age. But peace cannot be divorced from minimum expectations of fair play on related matters. The Geneva Conference confirmed the results of a long anti-colonial war won at great cost to Vietnamese society by the armies of Ho Chi Minh.[56] The achievement of national independence is a goal of such importance in the Afro-Asian world that it clearly takes precedence for these countries over generalized prohibitions on force or rules about non-intervention.[57] The Geneva Accords are not just an international agreement about which a dispute arose, but a formalized acknowledgment of a political outcome that it is reasonable to suppose could have been attained legitimately by the Viet Minh in 1954 through military means.[58] In effect, the Accords were a political bargain struck by the French as an alternative to continuing the appalling destruction of lives and property. To cast aside this political bargain is to undermine severely the security of solemn international agreements and to put in jeopardy collective procedures for pacific settlement.[59]

---

[55] See Fall, *The Two Viet-Nams* (2d rev. ed., 1967), 231–32; the effort to build up the military strength of the Saigon regime was coupled with its refusal to allow the election provision of the Geneva settlement to be carried out. To defend the seventeenth parallel as if it were an international boundary was itself tantamount to an illegal effort at splitting a state into two parts, an effort frequently productive of severe civil strife. It is only necessary to recall the American Civil War or the post-1960 efforts of Katanga to split off from the Congo.

[56] See Hammer, *The Struggle for Indo-China.*

[57] For example, the African states overtly proclaim their intention to resort to force against the countries of Southern Africa to end colonialism and racism. The legal status of this claim is considered in Richard Falk, "The New States and International Order," *Recueil des Cours*, 118 (1966), 1–103.

[58] After Dien Bien Phu the only way to prevent a total Viet Minh victory would have been a massive United States military intervention, one that included combat troops; as it was, even Anthony Eden points out that the French were the recipients of at least nine times as much foreign support from the United States as the Viet Minh received from China: Eden, *Full Circle*, 126–27.

[59] The refusal of the United States to take the Geneva Accords of 1954 more seriously as the terms of settlement may help partly to account for the reluctance of Hanoi to negotiate with the United States. Of course, there are independent reasons to suppose that the United States may not be sincere about its various offers to negotiate an end to the Viet Nam war. See T. Draper, "Vietnam: How Not to Negotiate," *New York Review of Books*, May 4, 1967, 17; Draper's criticism of the Government is so impressive because of his earlier support of the United States' anti-Castro foreign policy: T. Draper, *Castroism: Theory and Practice* (London: Pall Mall Press, 1965). *Cf.* Kahin and Lewis, *The United States in Vietnam*, 207–37.

My conclusion, then, is that Professor Moore has not persuasively demonstrated that the use of coercion across the seventeenth parallel by North Viet Nam should have been regarded as coercion across an international boundary. I wish to argue only that it was reasonable for Hanoi, given the stakes and outcome of the First Indochina War, to regard Saigon's intransigence on the issue of elections as a material breach of the Accords allowing it to act on the basis of the *status quo ante* 1954. In my terms choosing this option would result in an example of Type III conflict, a situation of internal conflict for control of all of Viet Nam in which outside participation on behalf of either faction is "intervention," at least in the sense of interfering with the process of self-determination.[60]

Despite its plausibility from the perspective of law, there are three problems with this interpretation:

(1) Hanoi has not really contended that the action of Saigon nullifies the Geneva Accords; on the contrary, Hanoi continues to urge implementation and compliance;

(2) South Viet Nam has existed as a separate political entity for more than twelve years and has been accorded diplomatic recognition by many foreign governments; the consequence is a condition of statehood with all of the normal defensive prerogatives;

(3) During the last five years third powers have become increasingly involved on both sides in the Viet Nam war; South Korea, Thailand, Australia, New Zealand, the Philippines, the Soviet Union, and China are the principal third-party participants as of April 1967.

As I have indicated at the outset of this section, the war in Viet Nam now belongs in Type II; the functions of clarifying the argument that it was originally an example of Type III and that the United States should have left it that way are to indicate the reasonable basis of a settlement and to emphasize the unilateral role of the United States in shifting the war to an internationally more serious category of conflict.[61]

[60] Quincy Wright has been a consistent advocate of this position. See Q. Wright, "Legal Aspects of the Viet-Nam Situation," *American Journal of International Law*, 60 (1966), 750–69; Q. Wright, "United States Intervention in the Lebanon," *American Journal of International Law*, 53 (1959), 112–25.

[61] As a conflict moves from Type III toward Type II it tends to become more dangerous to international peace and security; as it proceeds from Type II to Type I it tends to become even more dangerous, other things being equal. Therefore, the United States' role in transforming the conflict from Type III to Type I without seriously attempting at a Type IV classification is to follow a path destructive of world order in relation to the civil strife–revolution phenomena occurring throughout the Afro-Asian world.

II THE RATIONALE RESTATED IN SUPPORT OF A TYPE II
CLASSIFICATION OF THE VIET NAM WAR

To classify the Viet Nam war as a Type II conflict implies considering the war as a variety of civil strife in which two domestic factions, each of which receives substantial assistance from foreign states, are struggling for control of a sovereign state. I maintain that international law then requires that belligerent conduct remain within the territorial limits of South Viet Nam. The United States Government officially repudiates this interpretation of the war and insists that the violent conflict is properly viewed as "an armed attack" by North Viet Nam upon South Viet Nam. South Viet Nam is thus entitled to act in self-defense, including, to the extent necessary, the commission of acts of war in North Viet Nam. In my terms, the United States Government has inappropriately characterized "the facts" as vindicating a Type I classification.[62]

Professor Moore agrees with the Government that the war in Viet Nam belongs in Type I, but he goes further by arguing that even if the facts warrant a Type II classification there are no legal restrictions that necessarily confine the war to territorial boundaries and that, in the context of Viet Nam, the air and sea strikes against North Vietnamese territory have been legally reasonable. There are thus two broad sets of questions to which Professor Moore and I give different answers:

(1) Is North Viet Nam "intervening" in "civil strife" going on in South Viet Nam or is North Viet Nam "attacking" South Viet Nam? Who decides, by what criteria, and subject to what conditions?

(2) If North Viet Nam is regarded as merely "intervening" in civil strife, does international law prohibit South Viet Nam and states allied with her from committing war acts against the territory of North Viet Nam?

As Professor Moore effectively argues, South Viet Nam's *de facto* sovereignty makes it important to analyze the legal rights of the Saigon regime on the assumption that South Viet Nam is a sovereign state, as entitled as any other to act in self-defense and to receive military assistance. Moore's interpretation

---

[62] The objective of establishing two categories of international conflict, Type I and Type II, is to underline the importance in policy and in law to distinguish between the Korea-type situation and the Viet Nam-type situation. Analytic categories are ideal types; there is no comparable clarity in real-world situations. Nevertheless, the ambiguities and antagonistic misperceptions that are likely to accompany a conflict of the Viet Nam variety make it very important for states to limit their involvement to the boundaries of the society wherein the violence is located.

of North Viet Nam's role depends on two sets of assertions, neither of which I accept as to fact or law:

(1) The nature of North Viet Nam's military assistance to the NLF and the political objectives motivating it constitute "an armed attack" upon South Viet Nam;

(2) The United States assistance to the Saigon regime, including bombing North Viet Nam, is a reasonable and lawful exercise of the right of self-defense.

My argument as formulated in the first article is that the conflict in South Viet Nam closely resembles other instances of prolonged civil strife in which substantial intervention by foreign countries on behalf of both the insurgent and the incumbent faction has taken place. I regard two assertions as legally determinative of the argument being made by Professor Moore:

(1) Covert assistance, even of a substantial nature, to an insurgent faction does not constitute an armed attack;

(2) Counter-intervention on behalf of an incumbent faction may not extend the conflict beyond its existing territorial boundaries.

This reasoning seemed directly applicable to the situation in Viet Nam with the consequence that the extension of the war to the territory of North Viet Nam by the United States is deemed to be a violation of international law.

Professor Moore, if I understand him correctly, argues:

(1) My Type II paradigm confuses what the rules of international law ought to be with what the rules actually are;

(2) The weight of legal authority supports Saigon's discretion to treat North Viet Nam's aid to the NLF as an armed attack and thereby authorizes defensive measures undertaken against North Vietnamese territory;

(3) Bombing North Viet Nam has been a reasonable defensive measure for the United States to undertake on behalf of South Viet Nam in view of the facts of attack and the law authorizing a proportionate response to it;

(4) The policy interests at stake are more consistent with such discretion than with the territorial limitations embodied in the Type II paradigm. Thus Professor Moore concludes there is "greater reason [than not] to believe both as a matter of the is and the ought that the bombing of the North is a permissible defensive response."

The Distinction Between "Is" and "Ought" in the Context
of Viet Nam: The Doctrinal Level of Discourse

I find it peculiar that Professor Moore argues, on the one hand, that the ambiguity of the legal and factual setting in Viet Nam makes it essential to assess the respective rights and duties of the parties by reference to the world order policies at stake, and on the other that my major line of legal analysis confuses what the law ought to be with what the law is. It is peculiar that Professor Moore should rely on Hans Kelsen, an arch-positivist, to support a critique that is explicitly couched in terms of the sociological jurisprudence of Myres McDougal, especially when Kelsen is invoked to show what is meant by the phrase "armed attack" as it appears in Article 51 of the Charter. Of course, Kelsen stresses the dichotomy between the "is" and the "ought," but it is this stress that seems quite contrary to Moore's assertion, one that I share, that international law is above all a process whereby actors clarify through their conduct the world order policies that each deems decisive in a particular context. For sake of clarity of discussion I shall try, despite this jurisprudential ambivalence that I detect in Professor Moore's critique, to respond directly to his analysis.

Does Type II Embody a Preference About
What International Law Ought to Be

Type II acknowledges the indeterminacy of international law with respect to intervention and counter-intervention. There is no weight of legal authority that can be crystallized in terms of rules commanding universal, or even widespread, respect. In fact, respectable and responsible international jurists disagree as to whether international law:

(1) allows discrimination in favor of the incumbent;[63]
(2) requires impartiality as between the incumbent and the insurgent;[64]
(3) allows discrimination in favor of the just side.[65]

---

[63] E.g., Professor Moore (1080–93), and J. Garner, "Questions of International Law in the Spanish Civil War," *American Journal of International Law*, 31 (1937), 66–73; see also E. Borchard, "'Neutrality' and Civil Wars," *American Journal of International Law*, 31 (1937), 304–06.

[64] E.g., Wright, "Legal Aspects of the Viet-Nam Situation" and "United States Intervention in the Lebanon"; and W. Hall, *A Treatise of International Law* (8th ed.; Oxford: Clarendon Press, 1924), 347.

[65] This position has been enunciated in its classical form by E. Vattel, *The Law of Nations* (Washington, DC: Carnegie Institution of Washington, 1916), Bk. II, 56, 131. Although positive international law promotes either discrimination in favor of the incumbent or impartiality, the practice of states increasingly vindicates giving help to the side deemed "just." From the

In face of this indeterminacy it seems useful to acknowledge the extent of sovereign discretion as to participating in a foreign civil war. International law does not provide authoritative rules of restraint or, stated more accurately, it provides contradictory rules of restraint of approximately equal standing. To invoke international law in this international setting, then, is to argue about desirable policy or to communicate in precise form what a particular state intends to claim; international law does not, however, postulate rules of order the transgression of which is illegal.

One of the authorities relied upon by Moore, Ian Brownlie, an international lawyer in the strict positivist sense, gives the following support to insisting upon the applicability of territorial restriction in a Type II situation:

> When foreign assistance is given to the rebels, aid to the government threatened is now generally assumed to be legal. Whether this is permitted in relation to minor disturbances caused by foreign propaganda or other forms of interference is an open question. It is also uncertain as to whether the foreign assistance must be a decisive element in the imminent and serious threat to the existing government or whether it is sufficient if foreign assistance is a contributory cause. Finally, *foreign assistance to the government will be confined to measures on the territory of the requesting state unless the foreign aid to the rebels amounts in fact and law to an "armed attack"* [emphasis supplied].[66]

It is worth noticing that Brownlie attributes uncertainty to the positive law in this area but, more immediately, it is important to take account of his reliance upon territoriality as a limiting criterion. Brownlie reinforces the quoted

---

perspective of world order it is crucial to develop community procedures to identify which side is "just." Such procedures seem to work for those situations in which the principal rival states have apparently converging interests, as with the unresolved problems of bringing independence and racial equality to Rhodesia, South West Africa, Angola, Mozambique, and South Africa. But where rival principal states disagree, as when civil strife between "radical" and "conservative" elites occurs in the developing countries, then the determination of which side is "just" is likely to generate competitive interventions if the contradictory perceptions are acted upon. The Communist ideas of support for wars of national liberation are in conflict with American thinking on the legitimacy of helping any anti-Communist regime sustain itself against Communist opposition. In a world of antagonistic ideologies it is dangerous to maintain complete discretion on the national level to identify which faction is "just"; but, equally, in a world of insistent legislative demands it is dangerous to preclude discrimination in favor of an insurgency that is deemed just by the overwhelming consensus of international society. One approach for cold war issues and another for Southern African issues seems imperative at this point.

66 I. Brownlie, *International Law and the Use of Force by States* (Oxford: Clarendon Press, 1963), 327. See also R. Pinto, "Les règles du droit international concernant la guerre civile," *Recueil des Cours*, 114 (1965), 544–48.

passage in the course of his discussion of claims to use force in self-defense against alleged aggression:

> It is suggested that so far as possible defensive measures should be confined to the territory of the defending state and the hostile forces themselves unless there is clear evidence of a major invasion across a frontier which calls for extensive military operations which may not be confined merely to protecting the frontier line. The precise difficulty in the case of indirect aggression is to avoid major breaches of the peace of wide territorial extent arising from defensive measures based on vague evidence of foreign complicity.[67]

It seems reasonable to regard Brownlie's discussion as a generalization of past state practice that reflects international law. My Type II boundary rule places an outer limit on the discretion of the sovereign state and is precisely the kind of quasi-objective limit that is so crucial for the maintenance of world order.

It is correct, as Professor Moore argues, that if the insurgent faction is the "agent" of the outside state then it is permissible for the victim state to respond at the source by regarding the apparent insurgency as an armed attack. But such a response requires a real demonstration of instigation and control, as distinct from either a mere allegation or evidence of some assistance to a faction that appears to possess an independent character and objectives.

International law is not really indefinite on this subject. A state is not permitted to use sustained military force against a foreign country unless the justification is overwhelmingly clear.[68] It is difficult to establish unilaterally that covert uses of force by an external enemy can ever constitute an ample

---

[67] Brownlie, *International Law and the Use of Force by States*, 373; "Indirect aggression and the incursions of armed bands can be countered by measures of defense which do not involve military operations across frontiers" (*ibid.*, 279). A recent Western visitor to North Viet Nam confirms the distinction between intervention in the South and bombing of the North as vital to the North Vietnamese perception of themselves as victims of United States aggression:

> Their [North Viet Nam] position is that the bombing of the North is a separate act of aggression from fighting in the South. While they might understand and tolerate, although disapprove, American intervention in the South on behalf of the Saigon government, they regard the bombing of the North as an unconscionable act of aggression against a sovereign nation.
>
> Ashmore, "Pacem in Terris II," 17, 12, 14

[68] Action and reaction sequences involving "incidents" have not been regulated in any very clear and definite way by international law. States interact by claim and counter-claim and the degree of legality is very largely dependent on the general impression of the reasonableness of the action undertaken by the contending states. The Gulf of Tonkin incident was a characteristic illustration of this process. The legality of the United States response depends primarily on (a) the reality of the provocation and (b) the proportionality of the response. For useful background as to practice, policy, and law in this kind of setting of sporadic violence, see

justification. It is difficult to distinguish a pretext from a justification, especially as the status of assistance to either side in an ongoing civil war seems legally equivalent. That is, one side may discriminate in favor of the incumbent, whereas the other side may discriminate in favor of "the just" faction, and both possess an equal legal basis.[69] In such a situation any serious concern with the policies of conflict minimization would insist, at least, that neither side has the discretion to extend the war to foreign territory.

The dynamics of internal war are such that both sides must, as the war progresses, almost certainly seek increasing external support to maintain their position in the struggle; if the scene of the internal war is a minor country then it is increasingly likely that both factions will become dependent for their political leadership upon a larger external ally.[70] Insurgent dependence on external support is not by itself proof of an aggressive design on the part of the supporter state. This dependence on an external ally is normally only an expression of the changing ratios of influence between the benefactor and recipient of military assistance on both sides as the conflict progresses to higher magnitudes. It would be detrimental to world order to treat such ratios as equivalent to an armed attack by one state on another and prior to the war in Viet Nam there had been neither serious juridical support nor diplomatic practice that would justify treating assistance to an insurgent as an armed attack. In fact, for world order purposes, bombing North Viet Nam has to be appraised as if it were seeking to establish a new legal precedent upon which other states could and should subsequently rely.[71]

F. Grob, *The Relativity of War and Peace: A Study in Law, History, and Politics* (New Haven: Yale University Press, 1949).

[69] This flexibility of international law is confirmed by the discretion states possess to accord or withhold recognition from a partially successful insurgency: L. Chen, *The International Law of Recognition*, ed. L. C. Green (London: Stevens & Sons, 1951). It is not necessary for recognition to be accorded in an express or formal manner. De facto recognition arising out of intercourse between the third-party state and the anti-government faction is sufficient provided the facts of the civil war justify the inference of dual sovereignty; i.e., each faction governs a portion of the society and this situation is likely to continue for a considerable period of time. As Lauterpacht concludes, "It is not contrary to international law to recognize the insurgents as a government exercising *de facto* authority over the territory under its control": H. Lauterpacht, *Recognition in International Law* (Cambridge: Cambridge University Press, 1957), 294. See generally *ibid.*, 279–94.

[70] The process by which an internal war is internationalized is well depicted in G. Modelski, "The International Relations of Internal War," in J. Rosenau, ed., *International Aspects of Civil Strife* (Princeton: Princeton University Press, 1964), 14–44.

[71] The international law applicable to Type II situations is subject to "legislative" modification by principal states asserting new claims in an effective fashion and defending their assertion by an appeal to international law. It would be very difficult for the United States to oppose the legal argument it has developed to support its claim to bomb North Viet Nam. In this respect, my criticism of the Meeker legal rationale for "self-defense" in Viet Nam is more that it constitutes bad "legislation" than that it is "a violation." But *cf.* Meeker, "Viet-Nam

Professor Moore regards as "mysterious" my assertion that bombing North Viet Nam is simultaneously both

(1) a violation of international law and
(2) a law-creating precedent.

It may be mysterious, but it is a mystery locked into the international legal process. As a consequence of the absence of a legislature in international society, the assertion of a claim by a state to act in a certain way, if supported by an appeal to the policies and rules of law and if effectively asserted in practice, is both a violation of law as measured by prior expectations about what was permissible in a given situation and a precedent that can be subsequently invoked to legitimate future conduct of a similar sort. This can be stated more concretely by asking about whether *prior* to the war in Viet Nam a response against the territory of the state assisting an insurgent faction was regarded to be as permissible as it might be in some *subsequent* war of the Viet Nam variety.[72] Certainly, the precedent of Viet Nam will provide valuable support for any victim state that attacks foreign territory on the ground that it was substantially assisting the insurgent. Other international settings in which a legally dubious claim was converted by its successful assertion into a legally authoritative precedent can be mentioned – for instance, testing nuclear weapons on the high seas, orbiting reconnaissance satellites, and imposing criminal responsibility upon individuals who lead their country in an aggressive war. Professor Moore once again appears hesitant to accept the full jurisprudential implications of the McDougalian orientation that he advocates: If there is a process of law-creation at work in international society, then the distinction between a violation and a law-creating precedent is one of perspective and prediction, but not logic.[73]

---

and the International Law of Self-Defense." Often a precedent established for one context can be successfully invoked for different objectives in a series of subsequent contexts. This general process is very ably depicted in connection with the activities of the International Labor Organization by Ernst Haas. See E. Haas, *Beyond the Nation-State* (Stanford: Stanford University Press, 1964), esp. 381–425 (describing precedent-creation in a cold war context later being invoked in anti-colonial and anti-racist contexts with regard to "freedom of association").

[72] The United States has not even restricted bombing to certain specific objectives related directly to the Vietcong war effort – for instance, the specific interdiction of supplies and infiltrators or destruction of staging areas. President Johnson explicitly includes punishment as one of three principal objectives of bombing North Viet Nam: "[W]e sought to impose on North Viet Nam a cost for violating its international agreements" ("President Reviews US Position on Bombing of North Viet-Nam," 515). For a description of the impact of bombing on North Viet Nam, see H. Salisbury, *Behind the Lines – Hanoi December 23–January 7* (New York: Bantam Books, 1967).

[73] This process is summarized in part by the maxim *ex factis jus oritur*; without legislative organs and without a general conference procedure, the growth of international law reflects the process by which claims and counter-claims interact, especially if principal states are participants.

Is North Viet Nam's Assistance to the NLF "an
Armed Attack"? The Factual Level of Discourse

Only if North Viet Nam's assistance to the NLF can be considered an armed attack is proportionate self-defense available to Saigon and its allies.

Professor Moore argues that North Viet Nam is guilty of an armed attack on South Viet Nam for the following principal reasons:

(1) A substantial body of scholarly opinion holds that Hanoi actually *initiated*, as well as *assisted*, the insurgency;

(2) Hanoi exercises control over the activities of the NLF;

(3) Hanoi's principal objective is to reunify Viet Nam under its control; therefore, its assistance is, in effect, a project for the territorial expansion of North Viet Nam at the expense of South Viet Nam.

These issues concern the quality, quantity, and phasing of Hanoi's role. Reasonable men disagree about the facts. Many observers, especially in the United States, regard the resolution of these factual questions as critical to their assessment of whether the United States has responded in a lawful manner. For purposes of my own analysis I would argue that *even if* the facts are accepted in the form that Professor Moore presents them the conflict in Viet Nam is appropriately treated as Type II. I would additionally argue, however, that Professor Moore's construction of the facts relies on the reporting of biased observers. Furthermore, I would contend that it is inappropriate to appraise Hanoi's connection with the NLF without taking into account Washington's connection with the Saigon regime, especially after the insurgency had succeeded in establishing itself as the government for many areas of South Viet Nam.

Construing the Controverted Facts

The ambiguity of the facts in a situation in which civil strife has been allegedly abetted by external assistance is one reason why it is important to regulate the scope of conflict by objective limits. It is obviously easy for any interested state to manipulate the evidence to vindicate any response. The gradual emergence of a serious struggle for the control of South Viet Nam gave the Saigon regime and the United States an adequate opportunity to establish the facts by

---

It is, of course, possible to distinguish an arbitrary recommendation of a particular author as to preferred regulatory schemes from a reasoned application of preexisting community legal policies to a controversial fact situation. In the former case one is dealing with a criticism of the legal order, whereas in the latter one is concerned with an application of law, albeit an application that interprets obligations in light of policy preference.

impartial procedures and to have recourse to international institutions to vindicate the legal inferences of "aggression," and later "armed attack," that were drawn from the facts. It is important to realize that the United States made very little effort to secure wider community support for its preferred course of action in the decade after the Geneva settlement of 1954.[74]

Furthermore, recourse to self-defense was not prompted by any sudden necessity. It was decided upon in February 1965, with considerable deliberateness after consideration over a period of months, if not years.[75] In this circumstance, the burden of justification seems to fall heavily on the United States for the following reasons:

(1) the essential ambiguity of the alleged aggression, especially in view of the refusal of the Saigon regime to implement the election provisions and its suppression of all political opposition;

(2) the non-recourse to the organs of the United Nations, despite the time available and the refusal to adopt the war-terminating suggestions of the Secretary General;[76]

(3) the absence of a clear showing of necessity and justification required in contemporary international law to validate the exercise of the right of self-defense;

(4) the consistent previous international practice of confining civil strife, even in cases where the insurgent faction was aided and abetted by outside powers, to territorial limits;

(5) the locus of conflict being outside the immediate security sphere of the United States, thereby distinguishing the protective role exhibited by United States diplomacy in Latin America.[77]

---

[74] Lawyers Committee, *Vietnam and International Law*, 71–76.

[75] See the original official explanations for bombing North Viet Nam in *Background Information*, 148–52, and the more recent explanation in "President Reviews US Position on Bombing of North Viet-Nam."

[76] Compare Falk, "International Law and the United States Role in the Viet Nam War," 1140–43, with text of Goldberg's Letter to the Secretary General on December 19, 1966, *New York Times*, Dec. 20, 1966, 6, col. 4, and excerpts from U Thant's introduction to the annual report on the work of the United Nations, Sep. 19, 1966, 18, col. 5.

[77] There are broad deferences accorded to principal sovereign states to prevent hostile political changes in countries located within a traditional sphere of influence; these interferences, although vigorously controversial, do not generally endanger international peace and security because a principal state is reluctant to use force in a rival sphere of influence. Such geopolitical toleration is not intended to serve as a juridical vindication for unilateral interventionary practices that have been solemnly renounced. For a legal critique of intervention carried on within a sphere of influence, see Richard Falk, "American Intervention in Cuba and the Rule of Law," *Ohio State Law Journal*, 22 (1961), 546–85; this analysis applies *a fortiori* to the 1965 intervention in the Dominican Republic.

These factors in the Viet Nam context are mentioned to indicate the legal background. Such a background seems to require, at minimum, a clear demonstration that the facts are as the United States contends. The so-called "white papers" issued by the State Department[78] are considered to be too one-sided even for Professor Moore. Instead he relies heavily upon Douglas Pike, author of a detailed study entitled *Viet Cong*, written at the MIT Center for International Studies, during a one-year leave of absence from his role as an official of the United States Information Agency;[79] Mr. Pike had spent the preceding six years serving in Viet Nam, during which period the research was done. One need not be an editor of *Ramparts* to note that MIT's Center has long been subsidized by the CIA and has given consistent guidance and support for United States foreign policy, especially with regard to the containment of communism; a list of Center publications indicates a consistent pro-Administration outlook. Mr. Pike's analysis certainly deserves careful reading, and is to some degree endorsed by Bernard Fall's interpretations, but the prospects of bias must be noted and his conclusions must be carefully tested against those reached by neutral observers.[80] In responding to Professor Moore, I would argue that by relying as heavily on Mr. Pike (without taking serious account of the significantly different interpretations of Jean Lacouture, George Kahin and John Lewis, and Bernard Fall) he bases his conclusions of fact on *ex parte*

---

[78] US Department of State, A Threat to the Peace: North Viet-Nam's Effort to Conquer South Viet-Nam (Washington, DC: US Government Printing Office, 1961); US Department of State, Aggression from the North: The Record of North Viet-Nam's Campaign to Conquer South Viet-Nam (Washington, DC: US Government Printing Office, 1965) (both reprinted in *Department of State Bulletin*, 52).

[79] D. Pike, *Vietcong: The Organization and Techniques of the National Liberation Front of South Vietnam* (Cambridge, MA: MIT Press, 1966); see also the apparent deception in an earlier attempt to show that Hanoi dominated the NLF, wherein the author's CIA affiliation was disguised by presenting him as "a student of political theory and Asian affairs . . . former officer in US AID Mission in Saigon; author of 'Aesthetics and the Problem of Meaning'": G. Carver, Jr., "The Faceless Vietcong," *Foreign Affairs*, 44 (1966), 347–72.

[80] Among other unintended conclusions that emerge from Pike's study is the clear sense that the National Liberation Front possesses the organizational efficiency, cohesion, and talent to govern South Viet Nam in a manner never achieved by the Saigon regime. From the perspective of international order, the capacity to govern is certainly an element in claiming political legitimacy. A second unintended conclusion is the extent to which Hanoi's increasing influence upon the NLF has been a direct consequence of the American entry into combat operations. This increase in influence has, according to Mr. Pike, temporarily at least submerged real differences in outlook and objectives between the NLF and Hanoi, differences that belie the more general hypothesis that the NLF is a creation and creature of Hanoi's conjuring.

presentations which, due to an appearance of academic impartiality, are more misleading than "the white papers" he dismissed as "one-sided." [81]

Space permits me only to give two illustrations of why, aside from his vested vocational outlook, I find it difficult to regard Mr. Pike as a trustworthy guide to the facts in Viet Nam. The Preface ends with this rather emotional statement of Pike's personal commitment to the United States role in Viet Nam:

> The plight of the Vietnamese people is not an abstraction to me, and I have no patience with those who treat it as such. Victory by the Communists would mean consigning thousands of Vietnamese, many of them of course my friends, to death, prison, or permanent exile . . . My heart goes out to the Vietnamese people – who have been sold out again and again, whose long history could be written in terms of betrayal and who, based on this long and bitter experience, can only expect that eventually America too will sell them out. If America betrays the Vietnamese people by abandoning them, she betrays her own heritage.[82]

What is striking about this passage is its identification of "the Vietnamese people" with the American support of the Saigon regime. Does not Mr. Pike think that if Marshal Ky prevails "thousands of Vietnamese" would be consigned "to death, prison, or permanent exile"?[83] This is what happened to the anti-Diem opposition in the South after 1954 (and, incidentally, to the anti-Ho opposition in the North), and it is a common, if tragic, sequel to a bitter civil war. To associate the prospect of such oppression exclusively with an NLF victory, as Pike does, is to endorse the most naive and sentimental American propaganda. Also Pike's passage indicates the emotional character of his commitment to "the American mission," a commitment that is unqualified by any reference to the doubtful claims to rulership possessed by the present Saigon leadership.[84]

---

[81] See, e.g., Max F. Millikan's Foreword in which he stresses the academic and disinterested character of the Center for International Studies and its sponsorship of Mr. Pike's inquiry: Pike, *Vietcong*, v–vi.

[82] *Ibid.*, xi–xii.

[83] *Cf.* R. W. Apple, Jr., *New York Times*, May 17, 1967, 3, col. 2, describing the activities of Miss Cao Ngoc Phuong in organizing a non-Communist, Buddhist opposition to the Saigon regime's war policy and the harassment to which she has been subjected by Premier Ky's police officials while trying to carry on her activities.

[84] Consider, for instance, the inconsistency between the claims of a democratic society in South Viet Nam and the Constitution approved by the Constituent Assembly in 1967. See, e.g., Article 5: "1. The Republic of Viet-Nam opposes communism in every form. 2. Every activity designed to propagandize or carry out communism is prohibited"; Article 81(2): "The Supreme Court is empowered to decide on the dissolution of a political party whose policy and activities oppose the republican regime." For the text of the Constitution, see the *Congressional Record* (daily ed.) for June 6, 1967, S 7733–37. For a full account of the terror that commenced in 1954, see Buttinger, *Vietnam*, Vol. II, 893–916.

When Pike explains the creation of the NLF his bias appears in the form of the following undocumented conjecture:

> The creation of the NLF was an accomplishment of such skill, precision, and refinement that when one thinks of who the master planner must be, only one name comes to mind: Viet Nam's organizational genius, Ho Chi Minh.[85]

Even Pike suggests that prior to the emergence of the NLF in 1960 there had been sustained resistance to the Diem government by "Communists, the religious sects, and other groups."[86] The point is that even a biased accounting of the facts is compelled to take account of the pre-Communist and non-Communist role in the early years of the insurgency.[87]

---

[85] Pike, *Vietcong*, 76.

[86] *Ibid.*, 75. This non-Communist resistance to Saigon has also been emphasized by Bernard Fall's accounts of the early phases of the insurgency. And as recently as May 1967, Miss Cao Ngoc Phuong, who, according to R. W. Apple, Jr., of the *New York Times*, "is regarded as a heroine by peace-oriented intellectuals in South Vietnam," is quoted as saying:

> Many of my friends seem to have joined the Vietcong. We are losing the elite of our country. These people know the National Liberation Front is closely allied with the Communists and we don't like Communism. But they see no future in this [the Ky] Government.

> *New York Times*, May 17, 1967, 3, col. 2

[87] Buttinger, *Vietnam*, Vol. II, 972–92, contains a very balanced account (but one written from an anti-Communist perspective) of the origins of the Second Indochina War during the Diem regime. Buttinger writes that, "The Diem Government itself created the conditions that pushed the population to the brink of open rebellion, and this convinced the Communist leadership that the South could be conquered by force" (*ibid.*, 977). Buttinger believes the

> concerted effort to overthrow the Diem regime and its successor by force was organized by the Communists, and while it would have made little headway without wide popular support, neither would it have had its amazing success without guidance and assistance from the North.

> But the Saigon–Washington version of these events, which had been reduced to the flat assertion that "the Vietnam war is the result of external aggression," strays even farther from historical truth. Neither the strenuous efforts of Saigon nor those of Washington have produced evidence that anti-Diem terror and guerrilla warfare started as a result of infiltration of combatants and weapons from the North. No significant infiltration occurred before 1960, and very little during the next three years.

> *ibid.*, 981–82

Even according the North as substantial a role as Buttinger does, great doubt is still cast on the American inference of "external aggression," without which Professor Moore's entire legal edifice is without proper foundation.

But if one turns to disinterested observers the situation looks significantly less supportive of the official American factual account. Jean Lacouture[88] wrote in May 1966:

> In the beginning most people in the National Liberation Front (NLF) were not Communist, although more are becoming Communist day by day . . . Until 1963, at least, the Communists were a minority in the NLF, and if they found it necessary one year before to create the People's Revolutionary Party (PRP) within the heart of the NLF, it was precisely to bolster their inadequate influence.[89]

Lacouture also shows that the evidence of Hanoi's influence on the NLF is very tenuous as a consequence of differences in the style and contents of its texts relevant to the war.[90]

It would appear, then, that impartial interpretations of the role of Hanoi in aiding the NLF do not significantly support Professor Moore's factual inferences.[91] At best, the factual situation in Viet Nam is ambiguous with respect to the relations between North Viet Nam and the NLF.[92] Each side resolves the ambiguity to suit the image of the war that it seeks to rely upon. I am convinced that the facts, although ambiguous in some particulars, do not support equally convincing interpretations by the supporters of Saigon and by the supporters of Hanoi; I am convinced that the weight of the evidence and the burden of impartial commentary lends far closer support to Hanoi's version of "the facts" than it does to Saigon's version. But, for sake of analysis, let's assume that the ambiguity supports equally convincing, if mutually inconsistent, accounts of the role of Hanoi in the creation, control, and outlook of the NLF. Even so, neither legal precedent, nor legal commentary, nor sound policy analysis, supports the United States' contention, as of February 1965, that North Viet Nam

---

[88] Jean Lacouture is a distinguished correspondent for *Le Monde* who has written extensively on Viet Nam for more than a decade, and holds a strongly anti-Communist position.

[89] Lacouture, "The 'Face' of the Viet Cong," 7 (written as a reply to Mr. Carver's article in *Foreign Affairs*, "The Faceless Vietcong"); *cf.* Kahin and Lewis, *The United States in Vietnam*, 109–16, especially at 109: "When the deadline for the promised election passed in July 1956, Hanoi Radio continued to counsel moderation and peaceful tactics to its Southern-based supporters. For the next two years revolts against Diem emanated primarily from non-Vietminh quarters."

[90] Lacouture, "The 'Face' of the Viet Cong," 8.

[91] Kahin and Lewis, *The United States in Vietnam*, 110–16.

[92] It is not only the facts as such, but their interpretation that is subject to disagreement. The interpretation of the Vietcong's character depends on the orientation of the interpreter toward such related matters in the Viet Nam setting as Afro-Asian nationalism, the Saigon regime, the effects of American involvement, and the kind of society that would evolve from the various alternative lines of development open to South Viet Nam (including reunification with the North).

had committed "an armed attack." Such a claim to strike back virtually elimi-
nates all legal restraint upon the discretion of a state or its allies to transform an
internal war into an international war. As such, it repudiates the entire effort of
twentieth-century international law to fetter discretionary recourse to force by a
sovereign state. In addition, in a situation of ambiguity the burden of asserting
the right to use military power against the territory of a foreign country should
be placed upon the claimant state. This burden is especially difficult to sustain
when the claim to use force is generalized rather than being justified as a proportionate response to some specific provocation or being directed at some specific
external target relevant to the internal war, such as a sanctuary or infiltration
route. The United States has increasingly claimed for itself the right to bomb
whatever it deems appropriate without restraint as to time, target, or magnitude.

Oppression by Saigon as a Causative Agent

Professor Moore's contextual account is strangely devoid of any reference to
the effects of Premier Ngo Dinh Diem's reign of terror in the 1956–57 period
in South Viet Nam. Bernard Fall, among others, points out that the uprising of peasants against Saigon arose as a consequence of Diem's policies that
preexisted the formation of the Vietcong and was accomplished without any
interference on the part of Hanoi.[93] It is difficult to establish causal connec-
tions in the Viet Nam setting, but any account of how the violence started in
South Viet Nam should call attention to the priority in time, as well as to the
oppressiveness and social backwardness of the Diem regime.

It seems worth considering the account given by Joseph Buttinger, an ardent
anti-Communist and the most knowledgeable narrator of the relevant historical period (World War II to the assassination of Diem in 1963).[94] Buttinger
calls "[t]he manhunt against the Vietminh [the coalition of Vietnamese forces
that had fought against French colonialism] an almost incomprehensible violation of common sense, and one of the major contributions to the success
of the later Communist-led insurrection."[95] In addition to spreading terror
throughout South Viet Nam there was "an unending series of sermons about
the evils of Communism, delivered in compulsory meetings by officials whom
the peasants had every reason to despise."[96] The victims of Diem's oppression

---

[93] B. Fall, *The Two Viet-Nams* (1st ed.; New York: Praeger, 1963), 272: "the countryside largely
went Communist in 1958–60," i.e., before the Vietcong came into existence (quoted in
Buttinger, *Vietnam*, Vol. II, 977).
[94] Buttinger, *Vietnam*, Vol. II, 974–81.
[95] *Ibid.*, 975.
[96] *Ibid.*

included many non-Communists; "[e]fficiency took the form of brutality and a total disregard for the difference between determined foes and potential friends."[97] Death, preceded by torture, was the form of governmental action in this pre-Vietcong period in the South when there was only an apprehension about a Communist-led insurrection, but no action. Buttinger gives an explanation of why Diem's reign of terror did not provoke official American protest that exposes the root of the Viet Nam tragedy: "The American public, which a little later was told of the many Diem officials murdered by the so-called Vietcong, learned nothing at all about these earlier events, not so much because of Saigon's censorship but rather because of *the West's reluctance openly to condemn crimes committed in the name of anti-Communism.*"[98] It is this ideological biasing of perception that has led the United States Government and its supporters to believe in the rationalization of the war in Viet Nam as defense against aggression. To give Diem and his successors the kind of backing that we have given him can only be explained as part of a global crusade against the spread of Communist influence.[99]

The Relevance of United States Aid to the Incumbent Regime

The inference of "armed attack" must include an examination of the overall relevant context. But Professor Moore ignores altogether the relevance of the United States connection with the Saigon regime to an appraisal of Hanoi's role. The assistance to the NLF given by Hanoi takes on a very different character if interpreted as neutralizing the assistance given by the United States to the other side in an ongoing civil struggle.[100] International law does not

---

[97] *Ibid.*, 976.

[98] *Ibid.* (emphasis added).

[99] This understanding of the American commitment must have prompted U Thant in the Introduction to the Annual Report on the work of the United Nations in 1966 to say: "I see nothing but danger in this idea, so assiduously fostered outside Vietnam, that the conflict is a kind of holy war between two powerful political ideologies" (*New York Times*, Sep. 19, 1966, 18, col. 5). Stillman and Pfaff write in a similar vein in the course of a major analysis of US foreign policy: "Our dominating impulse in Vietnam is ideological; the conventional political and strategic justifications for the American involvement in Vietnam seem peripheral, and even doubtful" (Stillman and Pfaff, *Power and Impotence*, 171).

[100] Consider the relevance of these words of John Stuart Mill:

But the case of a people struggling against a foreign yoke, or *against a native tyranny upheld by foreign arms*, illustrates the reasons for non-intervention in an opposite way; for in this case the reasons themselves do not exist ... To assist a people thus kept down, is not to disturb the balance of forces on which the permanent maintenance of freedom in a country depends, but to redress that balance when it is already unfairly

prohibit discrimination in favor of an insurgent, especially one that has already enjoyed a degree of success, who is deemed to be "just" nor does it prohibit counter-interventionary efforts designed to offset intervention on behalf of the incumbent.[101] The policies of self-determination at stake are best served by an attitude of impartiality. The coercive apparatus of the modern state is able to suppress even very widely based popular uprisings; the evolution of social control increasingly favors the government in a domestic struggle. The advantages of the domestic government are accentuated by its normal intercourse with foreign states, including its option to continue to receive foreign aid. If peaceful domestic opposition is disallowed and a coercive government is aided by a powerful external ally, then the sole possibility of approximating the ideas of self-determination is to accord equivalent rights to insurgent or anti-incumbent groups that solicit aid from foreign countries.

If the insurgency succeeds in establishing itself as the *de facto* government of a substantial portion of the territory in controversy, then foreign states are legally as entitled to deal with the insurgent faction as with the constituted government. Such discretion, expressed in traditional international law by the shifting of insurgent status from "rebellion" to "insurgency" to "belligerency," embodies a sound compromise between according respect to the constituted government as the source of domestic stability and avoiding interferences with the way in which contending groups in a national society work out a domestic balance of forces. This reasoning is applicable to the situation in South Viet Nam. As of 1961, at the latest, the National Liberation Front was in effective control of a substantial portion of South Viet Nam and often was exercising its authority in areas under its control with more success than was the constituted regime in Saigon.[102] At such a stage in civil strife, international law fully allows third parties to treat the society in question as exhibiting a condition of *dual sovereignty*. In these circumstances North Viet Nam's assistance to the NLF

---

and violently disturbed . . . Intervention to enforce non-intervention is always rightful, always moral, if not always prudent [emphasis added].

J. S. Mill, Essays on Politics and Culture , ed. G. Himmelfarb
(Garden City, NY: Doubleday, 1962), 412

[101] See nn. 62–64 and pp. 96–99 above.

[102] *Cf.*, e.g., W. Burchett, *Vietnam: Inside Story of the Guerilla War* (New York: International Publishers, 1965). No friend of the NLF, Bernard Fall nevertheless writes that "on the local level, American sources have privately stated matter-of-factly that the local NLF administration clearly outperformed the GVN's on every count until the heavy bombardments of 1965–66 made orderly government impossible. It was an established fact that in most areas the NLF did proceed with local elections that were by and large unfettered – Communist control would exist in the form of a *can-bo* (a cadre) detached to the village chief for his paperwork – and produced more effective and more popularly supported local government than the country had enjoyed since its loss of independence in the 1860's": Fall, *The Two Viet-Nams* (2d rev. ed., 1967), 365.

enjoys the same legal status as does the United States' assistance to the Saigon regime.[103] Such an interpretation bears centrally on any contention that North Viet Nam committed an armed attack on South Viet Nam subsequent to whatever critical date is chosen to affirm substantial *de facto* sovereignty by the NLF.[104] The argument of the State Department, then, that the level of support given to the NLF up through 1965 establishes "aggression" of such magnitude as to be "an armed attack" is unresponsive to the basic legal issues at stake. Even accepting as accurate the conclusion that, "by the end of 1964, North Viet Nam might well have moved over 40,000 armed and unarmed guerrillas into South Viet Nam," there is no consideration given to the critical fact that as of 1962 the NLF enjoyed enough *de facto* sovereignty in South Viet Nam to allow North Viet Nam to furnish military assistance on the same legal premises as relied upon by the United States vis-à-vis Saigon.[105] The whole legal tradition of third-party relationships to contending factions in a civil war is to distinguish the degrees to which a revolutionary struggle has succeeded in establishing itself as a partial "government." Neither the State Department nor Professor Moore take this essential contextual factor into account to any extent in characterizing North Viet Nam's role as "an armed attack."

Given a post-1962 assumption of *de facto* dual sovereignty in South Viet Nam, third powers are entitled to neutralize and offset external assistance to the other side. Certainly, then, North Viet Nam's military assistance to

---

[103] See generally A. Thomas and A. J. Thomas, Jr., *Non-Intervention: The Law and Its Import in the Americas* (Dallas: Southern Methodist University Press, 1956), 215–21; Richard Falk, "The International Regulation of Internal Violence in the Developing Countries," *Proceedings of the American Society of International Law at Its Annual Meeting (1921–1969)*, 60 (1966), 58; for the reality and extent of NLF control as of mid-1965, see Fall, *The Two Viet Nams* (2d rev. ed., 1967), 381, 388.

[104] See especially the basis of argument in the State Department's Memorandum of Law in its opening section vindicating recourse to collective self-defense because of a prior armed attack: Lawyers Committee, *Vietnam and International Law*, 113–14. There is obviously no "armed attack" if the foreign assistance is being given lawfully to one governmental unit in a situation of civil strife in which the adversary unit is receiving a much larger quantity of foreign assistance.

[105] That is, the notion of neutrality was supposed to guide third powers in the event of an ongoing civil war. See, e.g., Thomas and Thomas, *Non-Intervention*, 219:

> A neutral power is always at liberty to decide whether it will permit or will prohibit aid to the disrupted state; its main duty as a neutral is that it must treat both sides equally.

> An obvious corollary of this norm is that when a neutral favors one side, then this advantage can be offset by discrimination in favor of the other side. Depending on the phasing of intervention with the existence of a conflict pronounced enough to qualify as a civil war, both the United States and North Viet Nam could reasonably perceive their roles to be one of offsetting or neutralizing the intervention or non-neutrality of the other side. *Cf.* White, "Misperception of Aggression in Viet Nam."

the NLF seems proportionate to the United States' military assistance to the Saigon regime. Even more certainly, it is unreasonable to characterize North Viet Nam's role after 1962 as "an armed attack" and the United States' role as "lawful assistance." It is also relevant to note that no American official contended that the pre-1962 role of North Viet Nam deserved to be regarded as "an armed attack"; even during the debates on the American claims of "reprisal" arising out of the Gulf of Tonkin incident in August 1964, there was no intimation that North Viet Nam's role in South Viet Nam was of the extraordinary character justifying recourse to "self-defense." It seems clear and significant to conclude that the post-1965 contention of "armed attack" besides being unconvincing on its merits is also an example of arguing *post hoc, ergo propter hoc.*

In the months immediately after the Geneva Conference in 1954 it was widely believed that the Diem regime would collapse from its own dead weight because of its unpopularity and inefficiency. The United States gave substantial economic and indirect military support to the Saigon government from the beginning of its existence. This support included training, guiding, and paying the main units of Saigon's military establishment.[106] The United States also played an increasingly significant role in influencing the composition and outlook of Saigon's government, so significant that by the time serious civil strife broke out there was hardly any prospect of resolution being reached by the domestic balance of forces.

As the American military participation on the side of Saigon grew more overt and massive, it became clearer that it was Washington and not Saigon that was the main adversary of the NLF.[107] As Hanoi acted to offset this American military presence in South Viet Nam it was naturally drawn into ever more substantial and overt military participation on the side of the NLF.[108] And certainly since 1963 the United States' control of Saigon's war effort and war aims appears to be much more explicit and decisive than does Hanoi's control over the NLF's war effort and war aims. Given the ratio of external participation on the two sides of the Viet Nam war it seems contrary both to the perceptions of common sense and to the dictates of international law to regard North Viet Nam as guilty of an armed attack. The total context suggests that the phasing

[106] Kahin and Lewis, *The United States in Vietnam,* 77–80; Mansfield Report, 20.
[107] Increasingly, it became clear that the United States, and not South Viet Nam, was determining the course of the war and the conditions for its settlement.
[108] But can one imagine a conference of the NLF allies summoned under the auspices of North Viet Nam in the manner of the 1965–66 conferences at Honolulu, Manila, and Guam? For comparative statistics on foreign involvement in the war in Viet Nam, see Kahin and Lewis, *The United States in Vietnam,* 185; Fall, *The Two Viet-Nams* (2d rev. ed., 1967), 358.

and extent of the United States participation in the war has had a much greater impact upon its course than has the North Vietnamese participation, and that neither side enjoys a privileged legal status so far as the principles of either self-defense or non-intervention are concerned, at least once it became clear that the insurgent challenge was a serious and prolonged one. In fact, the legal status of Hanoi's role in assisting the insurgency is according to conventional approaches of international law dependent upon the extent to which it is reasonable to regard the insurgent faction as a counter-government in effective political control over portions of the contested territory.[109] If Professor Moore stresses the *de facto* sovereignty of South Viet Nam (regardless of the terms at Geneva), then it seems essential to acknowledge all relevant *de facto* circumstances including those that benefit the legal contentions of North Viet Nam. In the first Mansfield Report it was acknowledged that "[b]y 1961 it was apparent that the prospects for a total collapse in South Viet Nam had begun to come dangerously close."[110]

In the context of Viet Nam, however, the normal legal situation is even less favorable to the incumbent regime than it might otherwise be. Chapter III of the Cease-Fire Agreement contains a series of provisions that disallows the incumbent regime its normal freedom to receive military assistance.[111] Article 4 of the Final Declaration "takes note of the clauses in the agreement on the cessation of hostilities in Viet Nam prohibiting the introduction into Viet Nam of foreign troops and military personnel as well as of all kinds of arms and munitions."[112]

Therefore, it is arguable that without the authorization of the International Control Commission it was illegal to give any direct military assistance to the Saigon regime; it is also arguable that the United States immediately fostered the violation of the spirit of the Accords by the extension of SEATO to cover South Viet Nam and by the extension of economic aid of such a character that freed Saigon to develop and modernize its military capability as directed by a growing number of United States military advisers. It is difficult to read the Geneva Accords without receiving the strong impression that one of the principal purposes was to prohibit post-1954 Great Power intervention in Vietnamese affairs, and given the United States' attempt to mobilize support

---

[109]   *Cf.* n. 102 and p. 110 above.
[110]   Mansfield Report, 21.
[111]   Articles 16–18; convenient text of Final Declaration, Lawyers Committee, *Vietnam and International Law*, 148–50; Further Documents Relating to the Discussion of Indochina at the Geneva Conference (Misc. No. 20) CMD. No. 9239 (1954).
[112]   Convenient text of Final Declaration can be found in Lawyers Committee, *Vietnam and International Law*, 148.

for a Great Power intervention as an alternative to the Geneva Settlement it is difficult to avoid the conclusion that the provisions on foreign military intervention were directed, above all, at the United States.

Professor Moore suggests that the belligerent objective of North Viet Nam is reunification under Hanoi's control, and he contends that this objective is the functional equivalent of territorial conquest. Such reasoning leads Moore to conclude that Hanoi's assistance to the NLF is more suitably treated as equivalent to North Korea's attack on South Korea than it is to Germany's aid to the Franco insurgency during the Spanish Civil War. I find Professor Moore's conclusion on this point, also, to rest upon a selective interpretation of the relevant context for the following reasons:

(1) Hanoi's pursuit of unification by limited, low-order coercion needs to be understood in light of the outcome of the First Indochina War and the terms of the Geneva Settlement; from the perspective of law North Viet Nam must be accorded a reciprocal discretion in interpreting post-1954 events as is claimed for South Viet Nam;

(2) The evidence advanced by Professor Moore to show that North Viet Nam is seeking reunification is largely hypothetical and speculative;

(3) Both Hanoi and the NLF disavow reunification as an objective of their war effort.[113]

On this basis it seems unconvincing to equate North Korea's sudden and massive overt attack upon South Korea with North Viet Nam's slow build-up of support for the NLF through covert assistance to an insurgent effort against a hostile neighboring regime allied with a hostile superpower. The United States' ill-fated support for the Bay of Pigs venture in 1961 was not so long ago.[114] We went to considerable lengths to disguise our sponsorship of the Cuban exiles intent on overthrowing Castro. Why? Precisely because different world order consequences attach to covert rather than to overt sponsorship of insurrectionary activity in a foreign country.[115] And what of the role of the CIA in the overthrow of an allegedly pro-Communist regime in Guatemala in 1954?[116]

---

[113] *Both* sides evidently avow peaceful reunification. South Viet Nam goes so far as to incorporate the following two provisions into its new Constitution: Article 1(1): "Viet-Nam is a territorially, indivisible, unified and independent republic"; Article 107: "Article 1 of the constitution and this Article may not be amended or deleted." May not North Viet Nam espouse a comparable objective? See generally Draper, "Vietnam: How Not to Negotiate."

[114] See Falk, "American Intervention in Cuba and the Rule of Law."

[115] See Falk, "International Law and the United States Role in the Viet Nam War," 1126, n. 18.

[116] D. Wise and T. Ross, *The Invisible Government* (New York: Random House, 1964). For a relevant account of Guatemala events, see D. Horowitz, *From Yalta to Vietnam* (Harmondsworth: Penguin, 1965), 160–61.

I mention these examples of covert interference not to defend this pattern of practice, but to suggest that when the United States has been an active party in support of insurrection a great effort has been made to keep its role as covert as possible for as long as possible. Likewise it was the overtness of our interference with domestic events in the Dominican Republic in 1965 that provoked such intense criticism of our action; it was probably less interventionary than the covert role in Guatemala.[117] Thus it is not accurate to analogize the covert pursuit of an interventionary policy in a foreign society with its overt pursuit in terms either of its perceived or actual world order consequences, even assuming for the sake of argument that the two modes of interference are equally effective. And therefore, and this is critical for my approach, a unilateral defensive extra-territorial response to covert coercion cannot possibly acquire the same legitimacy as would such a response if made to overt coercion. For these reasons I find it inappropriate to rely upon the Korea analogy; the Spanish Civil War I continue to regard as a helpful precedent because there was no counter-intervention undertaken against the territory of intervening states despite substantial foreign assistance to the insurgent faction.

Type II Geographical Restrictions upon "Defensive" Measures Promotes World Order: The Normative Level of Discourse

Professor Moore argues that the restrictions imposed upon the incumbent regime in a Type II situation are arbitrary and that in a particular situation defensive measures against the territory of a state supporting an insurgent *ought* to be permitted. I would agree with Professor Moore that in a *particular* war it can be argued that extra-territorial military measures may minimize the extent and duration of destruction. Relevant rules of restraint, however, must be devised with a generality of instances in mind. In the context of a Viet Nam-type war I would maintain that Type II restrictions are, *in general*, desirable. First of all, the appreciation of whether a measure is "defensive" or "offensive" cannot be reliably achieved by interested parties. Second, to the extent that extra-territorial "defensive" measures are justified by the specific characteristics of foreign support, then a precise claim to use extra-territorial force should be explained in terms of particular military necessities. For example, an air strike directed against extra-territorial insurgent sanctuaries would be more easily justifiable in the context of normal Type II restraints

---

[117] For an account critical of the United States intervention in the Dominican Republic, see J. Fulbright, *The Arrogance of Power* (New York: Random House, 1966).

if these sanctuaries bore a significant specific relationship to the conduct of the war. But bombing North Viet Nam has not been justified in terms of specific, limited military objectives requiring exceptional action; in fact, the American rationale for bombing North Viet Nam has changed character from time to time and the scope and intensity of the bombing action appear disproportionate to the military justification. In addition, independent, non-Communist world public opinion almost universally condemns the continuation of bombing by the United States and the Secretary General of the United Nations has repeatedly called upon the United States to stop bombing on a unilateral and unconditional basis. Hanoi, too, has insisted that the unconditional termination of bombing is the essential precondition for peace talks. The United States' effort to negotiate a reciprocal deescalation by North Viet Nam in exchange for a halt in bombing overlooks both the general attitude in opposition of the bombing and the inequality in bargaining power that exists between the greatest military colossus in world history and a tiny war-torn and unmodernized state.

Third, the frequency of patterns of intervention and counter-intervention in civil strife throughout international society underlines the danger of spreading violence beyond its original national locus. Greece and Turkey in Cyprus and the United Arab Republic and Saudi Arabia in the Yemen are two examples of civil struggles that could grow much worse if the external sponsor of the incumbent regime felt entitled and did, in fact, attack the territory of the insurgent's external sponsor.[118] It does not require much knowledge of fire-fighting to conclude that confining the spatial scope of a fire is one way to restrict its damaging impact.

If the coercion is sustained and substantial then the prospects of dealing with it by community procedures are improved. Because of the ambiguity of the facts and the tendency to interpret them in a self-justifying fashion in the Viet Nam setting, it is important to restrict responses to the limits of Type II unless a sufficient consensus can be mobilized to shift the conflict into the Type IV category. If it qualifies as a Type IV conflict, then the organized international community authorizes the response that is deemed appropriate. *Community authorization* takes the place of overtness as the key factor

[118]   In fact, one would imagine a serious regional war emerging if either side transgressed the limits that I argue are embodied in a Type II conflict. Only the mutual forbearance of both sides, despite their recriminations about each other's aggression, keeps the conflict at its present level. It is only because the United States is a superpower and North Viet Nam a minor state that the war in Viet Nam has not escalated to much higher levels; it is the power differential that encouraged the United States to transgress Type II restrictions in the spirit of relative prudence.

vindicating a defensive response against foreign territory. I have already indicated why covert forms of coercion are so difficult to construe, especially in a mixed-up political setting. It follows from this assessment that the resources of world order should be built up to facilitate the authoritative community identification of covert coercion as "aggression." For this reason it would be desirable to establish border-control, fact-finding machinery, and peace observation groups in those sectors of the world containing target societies that are highly vulnerable to covert coercion. The objective of these devices is to make covert forms of coercion more *visible* to impartial observers, facilitating a consensus, legitimating a decisive defensive response, and discouraging recourse to such coercion as a means to resolve international disputes.

My overall approach to Viet Nam-type conflicts has been altered in response to Professor Moore's criticisms in several important respects:

(1) The creation of Type IV to establish an analytic contrast with Types I–III and to permit "self-defence" in the Viet Nam-type setting provided a suitable prior community authorization has been given.[119]

(2) The realization that aggressive designs can be effectively carried out at present by covert forms of international coercion and that it would be desirable to discourage such coercion by making it more *visible*; the eventual world order goal would be to treat *covert* coercion as we now treat *overt* coercion. The effect would be to make Type II conflicts more easily transferable into the Type IV category or more susceptible to Type I treatment. However, in international society as now constituted it seems clearly preferable to deny the victim state unilateral discretion to treat what it perceives to be "aggression" by covert means as justifying its recourse to "self-defense."[120] In a sense this legal conclusion merely restates the adverse judgment rendered by the international community on several occasions when Israel has had recourse to overt military force in retaliation for damage that it has suffered from semi-covert coercion. The rejection of Israel's claim is impressive because Israel has a much more convincing security rationale than does South Viet Nam for striking back overtly and because the Arab states surrounding Israel

---

[119] A defensive alliance, such as SEATO, only multi-lateralizes decisions to use force to a very slight degree; "the community" must be defined in wide enough terms to include principal divergent elements.

[120] This denial is especially justifiable since (a) legitimate defensive interests can be upheld within the terms of Type II, and special exceptions thereto; and (b) shift to Type I tends both to increase the obstruction of international peace and to increase the role of military power differentials in achieving a settlement of an international dispute.

are avowedly committed to its destruction.[121] One may argue against the fairness of such constraints upon Israel's discretion in these circumstances, but it is essentially an extra-legal appeal as the organs of the United Nations have the procedural capacity to authorize or prohibit specific uses of force, and it is the exercise of this capacity that most clearly distinguishes what is "legal" from what is "illegal" with regard to the use of force in international society. Legality depends more upon the *identity* of the authorizing decision-maker than upon the *facts of the coercion*. With respect to Viet Nam, if a principal organ of the United Nations authorized the United States' bombing of North Viet Nam, then it would be legal (unless an argument could be successfully made that the decision was "unconstitutional").[122]

Professor Moore also usefully singles out "divided" country problems for separate treatments. He is correct in pointing out that world order is especially endangered by attempts to alter coercively the *status quo* prevailing in a divided country. In this respect the tragic consequences in Viet Nam can be understood as foredestined as soon as Saigon, with the backing of the United States, acted to locate Viet Nam in the divided country category.[123] The uncertainty as to whether Viet Nam is properly classified as "divided" in Professor Moore's sense involves an interpretation of the Geneva Accords. The classification of Viet Nam as a divided country also appears to have been imprudent in view of the logistic difficulties of securing South Viet Nam against attack and in view of the inability to evolve a tolerable regime in Saigon that could provide South Viet Nam with effective government without a huge American military and economic commitment.[124] Even without a hostile North Viet Nam embittered by a sense of being cheated by the non-implementation of the Geneva Accords, there is reason to suspect that without American backing the Saigon regime would have been unable to govern South Viet Nam with any success.

---

[121] Israel's responses have seemed to conform much more closely to the requirements of proportionality than has the United States–South Viet Nam response, even if its allegations of coercion are taken at face value.

[122] To be legal in the last analysis is to be authorized by the appropriate decision-maker; one can seek to correct "the mistake" attributed to the decision-maker, but the capacity to confer legality persists so long as the legal order is a valid one.

[123] The seeds of conflict seem to have been sown by the contradictory interpretations of what was "settled" at Geneva in 1954 with regard to the terms and timing of reunification; although there is room for some misunderstanding, my orientation is heavily influenced by regarding Hanoi's interpretation of the settlement as far more reasonable than Saigon's or Washington's.

[124] See the critique advanced by Stillman and Pfaff, *Power and Impotence*, 169–74. The opportunity costs of the Viet Nam war are enormous both with respect to the pursuit of international security goals and with regard to domestic welfare goals.

Predictions of imminent collapse were widespread until the American military presence assumed major proportions in 1965.[125] In addition, there was only minimal and grudging alliance support, much less community support, for regarding South Viet Nam as an inviolable sovereign entity of the same sort as West Germany or South Korea, or even Formosa. For these reasons I do not find it convincing, independent of the issue of ambiguous facts, to analogize Viet Nam to other divided country problems.

III COMMENTS ON PROFESSOR MOORE'S POLICY INQUIRY VIS-À-VIS TYPE III CONFLICT

Professor Moore's perceptive discussion of the considerations that bear on the international management of intra-state conflict deserves careful study. His stress in the setting of Type III upon the policies of self-determination and minimum world public order points up the difficulty that results from the sort of over-generalization that is implicit in the kind of categorization of international conflict situations that I have proposed. I accept his criticism that my original formulation of Type III rules is "simplistic" if applied mechanically to a large variety of greatly varying international contexts. A complete response to Professor Moore's critique cannot be undertaken within the compass of this article, but will be attempted on another occasion.[126] I will restrict myself here to a few general comments on Professor Moore's approach to suggest wherein my policy emphasis differs from his with regard to the regulation of third-party participation in intra-state conflict.

Let me say in my own intellectual defense that the division of international conflict situations into three broad categories (now four)[127] was intended primarily to facilitate and organize thought about the management of all forms of international violence through a preliminary sorting out of relevant contexts and by explicating the decisive legal consequences of each. Once this preliminary task of classification has been accomplished, then it is appropriate to

---

[125] Kahin and Lewis, *The United States in Vietnam*, 66–87.
[126] For instance, Types I–IV should be appropriately sub-divided to take account of recurrent contexts that can be grouped together within each broader category. Thus in Type III there is a difference between the legislative contexts relevant to uprisings in the five countries of southern Africa, the humanitarian context of slaughter that followed after the generals' counter-coup in Indonesia (1965–66), the anarchy that has been threatened from time to time in the Congo and Nigeria from prolonged civil strife, and the hegemonial context that exists when one superpower has claimed over time special geo-political prerogatives, acquiesced in by other states, in relation to a region.
[127] See 80–82 for explanation.

question whether there need to be more specific subcategories and whether rules stating exceptions should not also be included.[128] On this level, then, my response to Professor Moore is to accept his criticism, but to suggest that the attempt to categorize international conflict appears to add greater focus to policy inquiry than is possible by either an *ad hoc* response to a specific conflict (Viet Nam) or by a generalized description of the policies bearing most heavily on the legal regulation of recourse to international violence.

On a more fundamental level of policy Professor Moore, as the result of a very sophisticated analysis, appears to conclude that given the conditions of the modern world it is more desirable to endorse an approach to civil strife that authorizes discrimination in favor of the incumbent faction, especially in cold war settings, and prohibits assistance to the insurgent faction.

I am persuaded by Professor Moore's analysis to modify my original formulations to a certain extent. A neutral rule of impartiality does not preclude the continuation of (or even the moderate increase in) the level of assistance furnished a constituted government prior to the outbreak of civil strife. There are, however, restraints upon the scope and form of discriminatory external participation.[129] For one thing, foreign assistance should not include direct participation in combat operations. For another, it should not attempt to bear more than a fairly small percentage, certainly under 50 percent, of the increased military requirements created by the domestic uprising. And, finally, the external assistance should not be conditioned upon increased influences in the process of decision-making within the recipient country. In the event that the restraints sketched above are ignored, then the conflict is shifted from Type III into the Type II category, the shift itself reflecting "the violation" committed by a third-party state. If the restraints are respected with respect to aid furnished to the incumbent, then substantial aid to instigate or sustain an insurgency is a violation of Type III restraints that shifts the conflict into the Type II category as a consequence of the illegal conduct of the third party.

In the event, however, that the uprising succeeds in establishing control over a substantial portion of the area and population of the country, then a condition of *de facto* dual sovereignty exists such that third parties can furnish assistance to the insurgent on the same basis as to the incumbent. If substantial assistance is accorded to one or both sides subsequent to *de facto* dual sovereignty, the

---

[128] Note the development of international law governing the use of the oceans as depicted by M. McDougal and W. Burke in *The Public Order of the Oceans* (New Haven: Yale University Press, 1962).

[129] For a creative effort at emphasizing limits on the character of intervention rather than upon its occurrence, see Farer, "Intervention in Civil Wars: A Modest Proposal."

conflict is necessarily shifted into Type II, but there is no violation of international law committed by third powers. The internal situation generated a shift from Type III to Type II, as distinct from a shift coming about through interventionary roles by foreign states on either side of a Type III conflict.

If the United States had chosen to give military assistance to the Batista regime in its struggle against the Castro insurgency in Cuba, then this would be permissible unless the United States entered Cuba in the last stages of the war with its independent military capability so as to foreclose the outcome that would have resulted from the domestic balance of forces. The Soviet intervention in Hungary (1956) definitely succeeded in reversing the outcome of a domestic struggle, and was appropriately condemned by the political organs of the United Nations; the United States intervention in the Dominican Republic in 1965 designed to displace the incumbent regime was given presumably an even more objectionable form of decisive external assistance as it was directed against the incumbent faction.[130]

Professor Moore is also correct to suggest that in cold war contexts rules supporting the stability of existing regimes are probably desirable. It may be helpful to restrict pure Type III analysis to the Afro-Asian world wherein the geo-political context is of different order. In effect, Professor Moore is pointing out that the rival superpowers – the United States and the Soviet Union – provide their own form of conflict management within those segments of international society regarded as belonging to their respective spheres of influence or adhering to their respective security communities. In this regard it may be helpful to consider that concentric security zones surround each superpower and affect the actual treatment of Type III conflicts to a considerable degree:

I. *Primary Security Zone*: The United States, the Soviet Union, and possibly mainland China and the principal states of Western Europe, as sovereign states in relation to their own national security;

II. *Secondary Security Zones*: Groups of countries that are traditionally subject to the influence of one superpower or the other and whose security interests are governed by the political preference of the superpower;[131]

III. *Tertiary Security Zones*: The Afro-Asian world of recently independent states in which policies of non-alignment and non-intervention are affirmed.

---

[130] For a sympathetic account of the legal basis of the Dominican intervention, see Thomas and Thomas, *Non-Intervention*.

[131] E.g., Latin America, East Europe; one might argue that the problems in Asian affairs arise out of China's attempt to establish a Secondary Security Zone on its periphery and the United States resistance to this attempt.

These security zones describe the geo-political condition in the world as of 1967. It is a complex world order issue to interrelate these political realities with the role of law in establishing common standards of restraint and interaction. It is generally true that in the Secondary Security Zones the dominant actor is able to exercise control over the outcome of Type III conflicts, although Hungary in 1956 and the Dominican Republic in 1965 were governed by interventions that did not accord generally with permissible uses of military power, at least as understood by general community expectations.[132]

Viet Nam has become such a sustained and major war because the United States has converted a Type III conflict into Type I conflict without the legitimizing benefit of an overt armed attack and without the geo-political tolerance accorded to superpower diplomacy that is confined within its own Secondary Zone. Therefore, the extra-legal categorization of security zones may help to identify those situations in which external military assistance that is carried beyond a certain threshold is likely to trigger a major off-setting military action by a principal adversary. It is now commonplace to note that the most severe forms of international violence since World War II have been the result of competing superpower interferences in the Tertiary Security Zone, especially in those circumstances, such as Viet Nam, where it is unclear whether the territory in dispute belongs in the Secondary Zone, and if so on which side, or in the Tertiary Zone.

Professor Moore's discussion is strangely devoid of any reference to the role of international institutions or to the relevance of the will of the organized international community with respect to the relative merits of contending factions in a Type III situation.[133] It seems to me that many of the problems that Professor Moore points out, that arise in discriminating between various Type III contexts, can be resolved by according regional and global international institutions the competence to identify which faction is entitled to benefit from external assistance. Thus in the context of Southern Africa the decisive expression of the will of the international community would appear to legitimize discrimination in favor of the insurgent faction in the event that a Type III situation should arise at some future occasion;[134] such discrimination has been stridently endorsed in the African context by the Organization of African

---

[132] I.e., there is a geo-political level of practice that exists in a state of tension with a moral-legal level of commitment; both levels converge in the policy-making process relevant to international decisions.

[133] Cf. Falk, "The New States and International Order."

[134] On jurisprudential basis, see Falk, "On the Quasi-Legislative Competence of the General Assembly."

Unity.[135] Types I–III are residual categories that exist only when there is no consensus formally reached by a competent international institution.

A residual rule of impartiality does seem to minimize the role of both extra-national and domestic violence in situations where no international consensus exists. The absence of consensus is itself indicative of a potentiality for major conflict, disclosing seriously opposed interpretations of the appropriate external attitude toward the intra-state conflict. Therefore, in a Type III situation it would seem generally desirable to promote adherence to Hall's view that neither incumbent nor insurgent should be the beneficiary of discrimination.[136] What level of support for the incumbent constitutes "discrimination" and at what point a civil disturbance is properly regarded as belonging in Type III are complex determinations of fact and law for which no definite answer can here be provided.

Professor Moore, in my judgment, underrates once again the detrimental consequences of affirming the discretion of sovereign states to project their military power into foreign political conflicts. It is true that covert forms of coercion can subject a society to an "attack" that jeopardizes its political independence and territorial sovereignty, but it is also true that "the defense" of that society may involve its destruction and manipulation. To allow discrimination in favor of the incumbent to increase without limit in a situation of civil strife is to defeat altogether the ideals of self-determination without promoting the kind of world order premised upon the ordering capacities of territorially based sovereign states. To insulate Type III conflicts it is as important to restrict discrimination in favor of the incumbent as it is to improve the process of detecting covert assistance to the insurgent by making it more visible. To do one without the other is to invite Viet Nam-type confrontations throughout the Tertiary Security Zone. I would espouse a foreign policy of Cosmopolitan Isolationism as most suited to the attainment of world order in the Tertiary Security Zone: National military power should be brought to bear, if at all, only after formal authorization by the organized international community.[137] In my revised system of categorization, then, external assistance beyond *status quo* levels is only permissible if the intra-state conflict can be shifted from Type III to Type IV.

---

[135] For some consideration of the difficulties that attend regional authorization of the use of force, see Richard Falk, "Janus Tormented: The International Law of Internal War," in Rosenau, ed., *International Aspects of Civil Strife*, 242–46.

[136] On the assumption, of course, of some *de facto* control and some substantial prospect of eventual success, and subject to the geo-political qualifications of the three-zone analysis.

[137] I have developed this viewpoint in an essay to appear in *Adept*, a literary journal published in Houston, Texas. [Note from the editor: I have not managed to locate this article.]

IV THE STATE DEPARTMENT BRIEF: A FURTHER COMMENT

Professor Moore explains that the State Department Memorandum of Law was written mainly to deal with the public debate initiated by a widely circulated (and now redrafted) brief of the Lawyers' Committee on American Policy Toward Viet Nam.[138] As such, it should not be appraised as the full statement of the Government's position. This is undoubtedly true, but it is nevertheless disappointing that when the Department's Legal Adviser enters the public debate, he does so in such an unconvincing manner. Certainly, it does not clarify the discussion to over-clarify the facts or to make complex legal questions appear self-evident. A citizens' white paper in opposition to Government policy is primarily a call for an impartial accounting, it is intentionally and appropriately one-sided; especially in the security area it is impossible to proffer criticism in effective form unless the issues are somewhat overstated.[139] It is true, as Professor Moore writes, that the Lawyers' Committee first Memorandum emphasized many of the "wrong" issues or stated the "right" issues in the "wrong" way, but it did provoke the Government after a decade of involvement in Viet Nam to make its first serious effort to reconcile United States foreign policy in Viet Nam with our proclaimed commitment to a law-ordered international society. That serious effort was impaired, in my judgment, by defining the issues and maintaining the adversary spirit of the Lawyers' Committee document. In a second round of public debate, the Lawyers' Committee has prepared under the auspices of a Consultative Council composed of academicians a reply to the Government's Memorandum. This reply does focus more directly on the world order issues at stake and does provide the Government with a new intellectual context within which to respond. It is a sign of health for a democratic polity to engage in this sort of a dialogue during the course of a major war; it may be almost unprecedented for citizens to call their own government to account by an appeal to the constraints and institutional procedures of international law. The outcome of this dialogue, as well as its more scholarly analogues, may well shape our perceptions of the requirements of world order so as either to endorse or to inhibit American involvements in a series of Viet Nam-type wars in the decades ahead.

---

[138] Lawyers Committee, *Vietnam and International Law*, 19–111.

[139] Citizens do not have access to classified information, national news coverage is slanted toward affirming foreign policy in periods of crisis, and only clear conclusions will receive attention in press or government; the more balanced scholarly critique will be ignored except, perhaps, by other scholars, but it will not influence the public debate.

V ON THE CONSTITUTIONALITY OF VIOLATING
INTERNATIONAL LAW

Professor Moore suggests that there is no legal authority to support a view that the Executive has a Constitutional obligation to obey international law. What is more, he accuses me of advancing a "somewhat monistic argument." I acknowledge my guilt. It appears to me that the Constitution embodies the legal framework within which the Government is entitled to act. The condemnation of aggressive war and the United States' endorsement of the Principles of the Nuremberg Judgment seem to make adherence to international law a matter of Constitutional necessity. True, there is no established legal doctrine to this effect, but the question is open enough that it seems reasonable to contend that this is the way the Constitution ought to be authoritatively construed. As in domestic affairs, so in foreign affairs, we should remember that it is a Constitution that we are expounding; as the organic law of the society it must be constantly readapted to the needs of nation and its citizenry. No need is more paramount at the present time than to develop a Constitutional tradition of restraint upon the Executive's virtually discretionary power to commit the nation to war of any scope and duration. To insist on Constitutional sources of legal restraint is a part of the wider global need to erode the prerogatives of the sovereign state in the area of war and peace. So long as international society remains decentralized, the most effective legal restraints are likely to be self-restraints, those that are applied from *within* rather than from *without* the sovereign state. For this reason we cannot neglect the Constitutional dimension of an allegedly illegal participation by the United States in the Viet Nam war. And for this reason it seems appropriate for domestic courts to pronounce upon, rather than to evade, such legal challenges as have been presented in the selective service context.[140]

VI A COMMENT ON PROFESSOR MOORE'S CONCLUSION

Professor Moore concludes his article by affirming "that the conflict cannot be meaningfully generalized in black and white terms" and yet proceeds to do so. He acknowledges that "[i]f because of Viet Nam Americans must ask themselves hard questions about the use of national power and the proper goals of foreign policy, the North Viet Namese must ask themselves equally

[140] See the important dissenting opinion of Mr. Justice Douglas in the decision by the Supreme Court to deny a petition for a writ of certiorari in Mitchell v. United States, 35 U.S.L.W. 3330 (1967).

hard questions about the use of force as an instrument of major international change." These two sets of questions as formulated by Professor Moore are not equally hard, nor are they, it is well to add, impartial in tone or content. As expressed throughout Professor Moore's article the United States' failure, in his view, may at most involve errors of judgment and lapses of prudence, whereas North Viet Nam's failure consists of committing the most serious possible international delinquency – waging a war of aggression. Such a construction of the adversary positions greatly falsifies, in my judgment, the true situation. An objective interpretation of the war, as sympathetic with the United States contentions as the facts seem to permit, would acknowledge that the conflict in Viet Nam is one in which both sides sincerely, and even reasonably, perceive the other side as the aggressor. Most disinterested interpretations would, in all probability, tend to regard the United States as the sole aggressor, at least with regard to carrying the war into North Vietnamese territory.

The way in which responsibility for the war is distributed is vitally connected with what sorts of steps taken by which side are reasonable preconditions to achieve a negotiated settlement. In this regard when Professor Moore invokes U Thant to support the conclusion that "the Viet Nam war [is] basically a political problem that can only be solved by a political settlement," it seems only reasonable to add that the Secretary General has laid most of the blame upon the United States for prolonging and intensifying the war. In fact, U Thant's preconditions for a negotiated settlement include the prior termination of war acts by the United States against North Vietnamese territory.

A second point of disagreement. Professor Moore writes as if the United States and North Viet Nam are in a position of bargaining parity. Such a predisposition not only overlooks the enormous disparity in scale between the two countries, but also overlooks the fact that the United States is fighting the war at a safe distance from its own society, whereas the destructive impact of the conflict is now focused directly upon the North Vietnamese homeland. This bargaining inequality is directly relevant to Professor Moore's comments about the "hard line from Hanoi." To advise the United States that it "must continue to emphasize a negotiated settlement" is to write as if no credibility gap existed as to the sincerity and diligence of prior American peace efforts. Such a statement also ignores the extent to which the American emphasis on negotiations has been expressed more through threatened and actual escalations than by realistic offers to end the war on some basis that preserves Hanoi's stake in the outcome to the same extent as it preserves Washington's stake.

It is not possible to consider here the basis for a negotiated settlement. I share Professor Moore's emphasis upon search for compromise in Viet Nam and for a way eventually to give effect to the principle of self-determination for the forsaken Vietnamese population. There are, however, very serious problems with a negotiated settlement that explain, perhaps, why neither side can envision any middle ground between surrender and victory. Among these serious problems the following can be mentioned:

(1) A coalition government in South Viet Nam seems unworkable that either (a) excludes both Premier Ky and the NLF, (b) includes Premier Ky but excludes the NLF, (c) includes the NLF but excludes Premier Ky, or (d) includes both Premier Ky and the NLF. These four alternative patterns exhaust the logical possibilities, and yet no one of them seems to be a plausible basis for a stable South Viet Nam if the war is ended without prior victory by either side;

(2) The negotiating dialogue has stressed bargaining between North Viet Nam and the United States without any close attention being accorded to the more immediately concerned adversaries, namely, the NLF and Saigon. There is no strong basis to believe either that the two external actors can completely impose their will upon the two internal factions or that the two external actors espouse views identical with those held by the two internal factors. Therefore, bargaining toward peace should be broadened at least conceptually to examine the positions and leverage of all four major participants in the Viet Nam conflict. An obstacle to this position is the United States' insistence, contrary to widespread neutral and expert interpretation, that the NLF has no identity separate from Hanoi;

(3) The administration of a peaceful settlement in South Viet Nam must find a way to define what constitutes "infiltration" and what constitutes foreign military intervention. These conceptions are hard to define and even harder to administer effectively. Is an ethnic "Southerner" an infiltrator when he returns unarmed from North to South Viet Nam? By what criteria? Can the regime in Saigon purchase or receive military equipment from outside states as it wishes? Can the government in Hanoi? What criteria can be developed to limit foreign participation in a post-cease-fire environment in Viet Nam? Can a means be found to apply these criteria on a non-political basis? The Geneva machinery of 1954, with its International Control Commission, operates on a troika principle (Poland, Canada, and India) with each rival ideological orientation holding a veto. Would either side be willing to eliminate its own veto or to allow a veto to its adversary? If not, can a mutually acceptable basis for impartial administration be agreed upon?

These are some of the tough questions that beset the search for a negotiated settlement. Their answer is obviously worth seeking. A solution may rely upon substituting an all-Asian presence, possibly under Japanese initiative, for the Western presence that has dominated Vietnamese society since the nineteenth century (except for the equally tragic interlude during World War II).

VII A CONCLUDING UNSCIENTIFIC POSTSCRIPT

The extra-legal setting of the United States involvement in Viet Nam is essential if a serious attempt is to be made to rethink the foreign policy premises that have led to this long and painful involvement. If it is correct that we have been led into a costly and unjust war in Viet Nam by ignoring our real interests in world affairs, then it is important to explain how this came about. In the context of a discussion of the relevance of international law, the main contention is that a fair-minded attention to the restraints and procedures of the international legal order would have served and continue to serve the real interests of the United States to a far greater extent than do policies arrived at by calculating short-term national advantage purely in terms of maximizing national power, wealth, and prestige. In Viet Nam, the American attempt to control the political outcome to accord with its geo-political preferences (regardless of world order consequences) requires an altogether disproportionate commitment even if one approves of the objective sought.

Such a disproportionality suggests that our policy-making process is not being rationally focused upon our "real national interests" in world affairs. This lack of focus seems to arise from a sort of rigidity that comes from endorsing an ideological interpretation of contemporary international conflict. This endorsement takes precedence over world order considerations in American foreign policy and is likely to lead us into future Viet Nams unless it is repudiated. Ideological opposition to Communism and Communist influence as the main premise for military commitment is more dangerous than discredited foreign policies based on the pursuit of wealth and power. At least the policies of conquest left the victor with tangible gains and the prospect of tangible gain allowed for a rational calculation of the proportionality of means and ends. But in the circumstances of a Viet Nam, precisely because the putative gains are intangible – even sacrificial – there is no way to conclude that it costs too much. To question this reasoning it is necessary to be explicit about its relevance. Therefore, to convey my own sense about bringing United States foreign policy into a closer appreciation of its real interests, including a greater deference to the constraints and procedures of international law, it seems useful to carry the legal analysis beyond the boundaries of law and world order. Hence, an unscientific postscript that is at once an explication of the wider orientation of United States foreign policy and a plea for its reorientation.

The United States Government contends that it has no selfish motives in Viet Nam. As President Johnson explained:

> We're not trying to wipe out North Viet Nam. We're not trying to change their government. We're not trying to establish permanent bases in South Viet Nam. And we're not trying to gain one inch of new territory for America.[141]

This absence of selfish motives does not establish the beneficial quality of the American involvement in Viet Nam. The United States pursues its military course in Viet Nam because it is determined to defeat a Communist-led insurgency that sprung up years ago in South Viet Nam as a consequence of many domestic and international factors, only one of which was encouragement from and support by North Viet Nam. The United States acts *as if* the war in South Viet Nam was a consequence solely of aggression from the North.

In actuality, the war in South Viet Nam is being waged in a complex post-colonial setting wherein pressures for national self-assertion interact with ideological movements. Many Vietnamese are concerned with attaining their nationhood unencumbered by foreign domination. The United States is opposing revolutionary nationalism, as well as Communism, in South Viet Nam. And the United States is fighting on behalf of a native regime dominated by a reactionary military elite; Premier Ky was a mercenary pilot for the French in both the Algerian War of Independence and the First Indochina War and identifies himself with the politics of military dictatorship.

To wage war for or against an idea is no less destructive than to embark upon conquest for territory or for treasure. Over a century ago John Stuart Mill warned about the use of military power in the service of an idea:

> We have heard something lately about being willing to go to war for an idea. To go to war for an idea, if the war is aggressive, not defensive, is as criminal as to go to war for territory or revenue.[142]

Ideological motivation may indeed be intense. Its roots are often hidden in the past. We embarked upon a program to resist Communism in 1947 with

---

[141] President Johnson's Address to the American Alumni Council, *New York Times*, July 13, 1966, 2, col. 3.
[142] Mill, *Essays on Politics and Culture*, ed. Himmelfarb, 405.

the formulation of the Truman Doctrine.[143] Such a program, at that time, was closely and sensibly related to certain geo-political realities. The Soviet Union was ruled by a military dictator and it maintained tight control over Communist states and parties elsewhere. Western Europe was still weak from World War II. The colonial system was in its early stages of disintegration. Global Communism was a reality to be resisted and feared, although the Communist adversary was cautious, itself badly stunned and damaged by World War II. Since 1947 many changes have taken place, not least of which is the development of nuclear weapons and their deployment in a posture of mutual deterrence. The Soviet Union has followed an increasingly conservative foreign policy and its domestic society has been the scene of progressive liberalization. The Communist group of states has fallen into conflict, and many rather disjoined national varieties of Communism have emerged. Communism is today often a species of nationalism, not internationalism. Western Europe has recovered fully. Its main states are prosperous and stable.

Despite these changes in the international setting, the United States has not significantly altered its dogmatic opposition to Communism. In Viet Nam President Johnson is carrying forward the basic policies of prior Administrations.[144] These policies center upon the assumption that it is always adverse to United States interests to allow a society to become identified as "Communist." To call a movement "Communist" that can also draw upon the revolutionary nationalism of a society, as both the Vietcong and Hanoi can, is to overlook one real base of political potency. Viet Nam, unlike other Asian states, is a country where Communist leadership under Ho Chi Minh has for several decades commanded almost all of the forces of anti-colonialism and nationalism. To resist these forces is to become allied with reactionary elements in the society. Unaided, these reactionary elements would have no prospect of prevailing over a popularly based nationalist movement, whether or not it is Communist-led. To defeat such a nationalist movement,

---

[143] For a persuasive comprehensive analysis of the evolution of the United States foreign policy response to Communism, see Horowitz, *From Yalta to Vietnam*.

[144] "There *is* an American consensus on foreign affairs, and the Johnson Administration may legitimately argue that its programs carry out in action what the country demands in principle . . . Mr. Johnson escalated the war in Vietnam, but so did Mr. Kennedy when he altered the American commitment in that country from one of assistance and counsel to the South Vietnamese government to direct, if still limited, military engagement with the Vietnamese insurgents. So did Mr. Eisenhower 'escalate,' or more properly inaugurate, the American involvement when, in 1954, he stepped into the role the exhausted French abandoned and chose to sponsor and sustain a noncommunist government in Saigon that would prevent the country's unification under the communist Viet Minh movement which had led the war to expel the French": Stillman and Pfaff, *Power and Impotence*, 4.

if at all, presupposes an enormous foreign effort on behalf of the reactionary faction, an effort of the sort the United States has been making on behalf of successive reactionary regimes in Saigon. The result for South Viet Nam is, at best, a dependence that entails a new subservience to an alien Western power. Certainly the United States has introduced more military might into Viet Nam than the French ever used to dominate the country during the colonial period. To have allowed a Vietcong victory and a possible subsequent reunification of Viet Nam under Hanoi's auspices would have merely ratified the process of self-determination internal to Viet Nam that evolved since the early efforts against the French. Such a nationalist solution even if Communist in form would not have posed any serious danger to Western interests and certainly not to direct United States security interests. Viet Nam has a long tradition of fearing and resisting Chinese domination, and there is every reason to suppose that this tradition would persist in a Communist era. The non-Communist neighbors of Viet Nam have, with the possible exception of Laos, stable governments and strong capabilities to maintain internal security.

The United States has made an utterly unconvincing appeal to principles of world order; it purports to be resisting aggression in South Viet Nam. Such a contention is without any firm factual base, but its allegation in a circumstance of ambiguity allows the United States Government to maintain its war effort without admitting its true motivation, thereby confusing its supporters and angering its opponents. As Ralph K. White, an American psychologist who has made an unemotional study of the basis for perceiving aggression in Viet Nam, writes: "There has been no aggression on either side – at least not in the sense of a cold-blooded, Hitler-like act of conquest. The analogies of Hitler's march into Prague, Stalin's takeover of Eastern Europe, and the North Korean attack on South Korea are false analogies." White also documents his conclusion that "aggression by us seems as obvious to them as aggression by them seems to us."[145]

One trouble with fighting for an idea is that there is no way to measure how much sacrifice its defense is worth. An absolutism sets in. The image of the enemy that justifies his destruction is held secure against prudence, reason, and morality. Only clear inferences of Communism, of aggression, and of good intentions vindicate the death and destruction inflicted upon Viet Nam. The United States can maintain these clear inferences only by denying reality or by testing reality in the same primitive way that the Aztecs justified their belief that the corn on which their civilization depended would not grow

---

[145] White, "Misperception of Aggression in Vietnam," 125.

unless there were human sacrifices. "The fact that the corn did grow was probably considered solid evidence for such a view; and in those years when the
harvest was bad, it was doubtless argued that the gods were angry because the
sacrifices had been insufficient. A little greater military effort would result, a
few more hearts would be torn from their quivering bodies, and the following
year it was highly probable that the harvest would be better and the image
consequently confirmed."[146] Kenneth Boulding regards primitive reasoning of
this kind as the way we sustain our commitment in Viet Nam – that is "by
appeals to analogy, self-evidence, and to the principle that if at first you don't
succeed try more of the same until you do."[147] We are entrapped in a dangerous, self-destructive myth in Viet Nam, the elimination of which can only be
sought after the relief of peace, if then. Now we can only justify the sacrifices
we have already made by increasing them to the point where we hope its
objective will be reached, regardless of the cost to ourselves and to Viet Nam.

Finally, there is "the credibility gap." Not only is the inference of aggression needed to enable the use of a rhetoric of legitimacy in describing the
American efforts in Viet Nam, but the objective of these efforts is disguised.
We proclaim over and over again our search for a negotiated settlement, the
sincerity of which Professor Moore endorses, and yet we accompany this
search by ever-higher escalation and by preconditions that by mid-1967 must
be interpreted to entail surrender by the adversary. President Johnson writes
to Ho Chi Minh that he is "prepared to order a cessation of bombing against
your country and the further augmentation of United States forces in South
Viet Nam as soon as I am assured that infiltration into South Viet Nam by
land and by sea has stopped."[148] How could the Vietcong maintain itself at this
stage without supplies and equipment from the North? The effect of Johnson's
proposal is to suggest that United States military effort in the South cannot be
matched by Northern aid to the NLF: it is to compel the other side to act as
if it had been the aggressor. Ho Chi Minh's rejection of such an offer had to
be expected. Only a combined disposition by Hanoi and the NLF to call off
the insurgency would seem acceptable, only a victory for American power
and a defeat for its adversary made militarily possible, if at all, because we are
not fighting against Communism, but only against the relatively beleaguered
small Communist state of North Viet Nam.

[146] Kenneth Boulding, "The Learning and Reality-Testing Process in the International System,"
Journal of International Affairs, 21 (1967), 1–15.
[147] *Ibid.*, 2.
[148] For the texts of President Johnson's letter (dated Feb. 2, 1967) and President Ho Chi Minh's
reply (dated Feb. 15, 1967), see *New York Times*, Mar. 22, 1966, 10, col. 2.

This note in conclusion is an attempt to provide a political setting for the world order claims that the United States has made on behalf of its action in Viet Nam. Without a sense of this setting, any appraisal of the legal issues at stake is ultimately without its proper context. Since it is "we" who are perceiving the aggression in Viet Nam, it is essential to know why our understanding of the war is not shared by people elsewhere. Only after making an ideological jail-break and thereafter rediscovering our real values and our interests at home and abroad can we avoid future Viet Nams. I am convinced that we will look back upon the war in Viet Nam as the greatest tragedy ever in American foreign policy, as a deviation from American political traditions that will appear comprehensible in retrospect only because, in Mill's phrase, we were "willing to go to war for an idea."

5

The Six Legal Dimensions of the Vietnam War

This monograph deals with the legal status of the United States involvement in the Vietnam war. It tries to move beyond the existing legal literature in two principal respects:

(1) By developing arguments for bringing international law to bear more effectively on the foreign policy-making process in the future than has been evident through the course of the Vietnam war;

(2) By expanding legal inquiry to include questions of war crimes, constitutional procedure, and war-related litigation; this second undertaking is carried out through the device of briefly considering the six major legal dimensions of the United States involvement in the Vietnam war.

It is important to make clear that I do not attempt a balanced, fully documented argument on "the grand question" of aggression and self-defense in Vietnam. There is an abundant literature on this question that reflects a variety of normative perspectives.[1] My objective is to develop a coherent position that builds upon, rather than duplicates, my previous writing on the subject.[2] In this respect, the monograph proceeds from the presupposition that international law forbids both the underlying involvement and the battlefield practices being relied upon in Vietnam by the United States government.[3]

---

[1] Most of the more significant legal writing up through 1967 has been collected by the Civil War Panel of the American Society of International Law in Richard Falk, ed., *The Vietnam War and International Law*, Princeton, Princeton University Press, 1968.

[2] See especially Falk, ed., *The Vietnam War*, pp. 362–400, 445–508.

[3] As such, I make no effort to consider and respond to the legal arguments that have been made on behalf of the position taken by the United States. My purpose is to delimit the contours of inquiry in as comprehensive a fashion as possible rather than to argue the merits of the various legal conclusions. The most effective presentation of the government position on the central legal questions is that of Professor John Norton Moore to be found in Falk, ed., *The Vietnam*

At the same time, my purpose is not to engage in polemics; it is rather to argue for a constructive reconsideration of the governmental procedures and practice that enable an American President to involve the country in the internal affairs of a foreign society, especially through policies designed to influence the outcome of struggle for control of governmental machinery. The need for reconsideration extends far beyond the power that commits United States armed forces to battle without any prior legislative authorization. It extends to the discretionary use of the CIA to effectuate desired political changes in foreign countries, if necessary, by means that violate the legal order of the target state. The need for reconsideration extends, as well, to the provision of military aid and advice to regimes that govern in a manner violating the liberal democratic creed that our government is pledged to uphold within the United States.

In my judgment, there has been a persistent failure by the United States throughout the Vietnam war to adhere to the specific rules of international law governing recourse to and conduct of war. This failure also characterizes the behavior of other principal sovereign states. Therefore, the criticism directed against the decision-process that operates in the United States government is applicable to other states within international society, although the power of the United States and the severity of its apparent violations of international law make the focus on the American situation logical at this point.[4]

It may also be wondered why attention is not given to violations of international law that might be attributed to North Vietnam or the National Liberation Front in the Vietnam war. Would it not, it might be asked, be more persuasive to examine critically the legal status of each side's involvement in the Vietnam war?[5] Such an examination might be an appropriate supplemental task, but it

---

War, pp. 237–70, 303–17, 401–45; a rather comprehensive study generally supportive of the United States position is Roger H. Hull and John C. Novograd, *Law and Vietnam*, Dobbs Ferry, N.Y., Oceana, 1968.

[4]   The prominent role of the United States throughout international society gives its conduct a particular influence in shaping patterns of diplomatic practice. There are other prominent states, of course, whose use of force may also exert a considerable influence, but it is the United States that has made the most frequent sustained uses of its military power in recent decades. Soviet military intervention in East European countries is also of great importance, both because of the formidable character of Soviet power and because it exerts so much influence upon the American image of conflict in international affairs. In this latter respect, it is impossible to overestimate the damage done to the cause of world order by the Soviet military interventions in Hungary in 1956 and in Czechoslovakia in 1968.

[5]   Note that the arguments for and against the legality of the basic American claims to be defending South Vietnam against "aggression" are different from, although in some sense interconnected with, the arguments concerning the comparative legality of United States and North Vietnamese participation in the Vietnam war.

is clearly supplemental, as the emphasis here is upon the role of international law in future foreign policy-making by principal sovereign states. It is the principal states that establish the patterns that dominate international society, and it is their acceptance or rejection of legal restraint and of the entire habit of law that vitally shapes the system of order that prevails at any given time. North Vietnam is not such a principal state; its conformity to or violation of international law does little to influence the shape of the overall system.

Besides, the weight of evidence suggests a great disproportion between the violations of international law by North Vietnam and by the United States – the American violations involve the reliance upon hyper-modern modes of warfare to devastate on an indiscriminate basis a relatively undeveloped and undefended society. There is a David-and-Goliath category of international conflict in which it is a mockery to ask whether the weaker side is also guilty of illegal behavior. It is revealingly rhetorical to consider whether it is necessary to determine whether Ethiopia in 1935, Finland in 1939, or Czechoslovakia in 1968 violated international law in their effort to defend their national autonomy against encroachment by much more powerful states. It is absurd to suppose that the small state might have been the aggressor rather than the victim of aggression. The struggle in Vietnam is more complex in many ways than those mentioned two sentences ago, but the essential structure of conflict is the same – a powerful state, here the United States, is seeking by means of its superior military power to thwart the expression of the domestic balance of political forces in Vietnam. The many phases of the struggle for Vietnam since the late 1940s have all exhibited this characteristic of foreign intervention, first principally in the form of a French colonial intervention progressively displaced in the 1950s by the United States. This underlying political interpretation makes it casuistic to look seriously upon the contention that the Saigon regime is representative of South Vietnam or that this regime enjoys sufficient sociopolitical autonomy to be capable of "inviting" assistance from the United States.

The comparative merits of argument strike me as so unequal with respect to the underlying issue of justification in Vietnam that it does not appear worthwhile to examine the legal arguments against North Vietnam and the NLF in the same spirit as one examines the arguments against the United States. Of course, this assertion of disparity rests upon the earlier proposition that the American case on the grand issue of aggression and self-defense is unpersuasive. It also rests on the inequality in size between the United States and North Vietnam. The idea that the greatest military power in world history is the victim of the illegal conduct of a third-rank Asian country is hardly very persuasive, especially in circumstances where the United States homeland is completely free from military countermeasures by North Vietnam.

I THE POLICY FRAMEWORK

Insisting on the relevance of international law to the American role in the Vietnam war is significant for one overriding reason: To conduct foreign policy in conformity with international law tends to discourage those choices and acts most likely to produce or intensify political disorder and human suffering. This faith in law presupposes that patterns of adherence generally, but not always, are more compatible with human welfare than are patterns of violation. Otherwise, the anarchist's plea might well be heeded.

The case for law in international affairs is strengthened by the awesome fragility of the nuclear age. Despite such circumstance, the relevance of international law to the use of violence by national governments cannot be posited as a ground rule without considerable explication. The exercise of sovereign discretion to wage war remains deeply rooted in political consciousness and evident in the patterns of statecraft. As a consequence, it remains incumbent upon an analyst to persuade his audience of the importance of using law to erode the tradition of sovereign discretion as rapidly as is feasible, as part of the struggle to evolve a stronger system of world legal order.

Such an endorsement of the ideals of respect for law implies only that the rules, procedures, and institutions needed for an effective legal order should be established and sustained; there is no implication of such legal absolutism that it is never justifiable to act outside or against the law. The position being urged is only the more modest one that the burden of legal justification is upon the state that uses or escalates the use of force in international relations, and that every effort should be made to assure that decisions are reached in such a way as to reflect an appreciation of the legal status of proposed courses of action. In international law, the special precedent-setting role of principal sovereign states creates a distinctive responsibility for decision-makers not nearly so evident in nongovernmental settings.

It is this kind of jurisprudential basis that causes distress about the failure to heed the claims of law in relation to the initiation and prosecution of the Vietnam war. The United States government has paid little attention to the legality of its involvement in Vietnam. This inattentiveness is evident whether principal concern is with the rules, procedures, and institutions applicable to the day-to-day conduct of the war or to the use of law to shape foreign policy through the incorporation into the decision-process of a set of authoritative world-order goals (such as are embodied in the Charter of the United Nations). I am mindful, in making these assertions, of the difficulty that attaches to any effort to pass legal judgment in a situation of controversy about the facts and the content of many of the applicable rules; there exists a situation of considerable legal indeterminacy in relation to the international law of internal war. Nevertheless, judgment can be passed on the diligence and sincerity of the effort of officials in the United States government to apply inherited legal doctrine or to evolve policy in such a way as to establish a body of precedent that might guide other governments confronted by future circumstances of a comparable character.

It is not correct, of course, to suggest that the United States government has neglected international law altogether throughout the Vietnam war. Government officials have used legal arguments to vindicate the US involvement, but these arguments have been advanced only after the commitment to defend the Saigon regime had been widely proclaimed. These legal arguments also appear to have been shaped to answer domestic critics of the war who first gave prominence to questions of legality.[6]

Coupled with the tardiness of their enlistment, the tenuousness at times apparent in their advocacy suggests that reliance on international law argumentation at a post-commitment stage is little more than a rationalization of conduct determined by non-legal factors.[7] It is thus important to distinguish

---

[6] It was not until after the Lawyers Committee on American Policy Towards Vietnam had prepared a Memorandum of Law in 1965, questioning the legality of United States involvement in Vietnam (reproduced in *Cong. Rec.* of September 23, 1965), that the State Department issued an official legal justification of US actions. On March 4, 1966, a second, more detailed State Department memorandum, entitled "The Legality of the United States Participation in the Defense of Vietnam," was issued: *US State Department Bulletin*, Vol. 54, No. 1396, March 28, 1966. The Lawyers Committee challenged each of the State Department's conclusions and allegations in full in *Vietnam and International Law*, Flanders, N.J., O'Hare, 1967.

[7] In addition to the lateness of their invocation, the legal arguments supporting US involvement in Vietnam have throughout the war been involved with uncertainty by administration officials. Until late 1965 the US military involvement in Vietnam had been based largely on the moral basis of reputed promises or pledges of former presidents to Saigon. In the Senate Foreign Relations Committee Hearings of February 1966, Secretary Rusk did make passing reference to communiques from both Eisenhower and Kennedy to the Diem government, but the Secretary's main approach was to stress our "obligations" under SEATO. In his testimony, however, there was reason to believe that Rusk was willing to admit that the "obligations" under which we acted in Vietnam referred not necessarily to our legal duties under the treaty, but to our moral duties or commitments that we believed implicit in the pact:

> THE CHAIRMAN.   But in this case do you maintain that we had an obligation under the Southeast Asia Treaty to come to the assistance, an all-out assistance, of South Vietnam? Is that very clear?
> SECRETARY RUSK. It seems clear to me, sir, that this was an obligation –
> THE CHAIRMAN.   Unilateral.
> SECRETARY RUSK. An obligation of policy. It is rooted in the policy of the treaty. I am not now saying if we had decided we would not lift a finger

between the relevance of law as a source of constraint and guidance, capable of establishing a framework for foreign policy, and legal argumentation that merely seeks to justify foreign policy positions by translating them into a rhetoric oriented toward law or world order.[8]

In assessing United States involvement in the Vietnam war it is useful to distinguish among considerations of prudence, morality, and law.[9] For instance, it is quite possible to conclude that the United States role in the war has been imprudent in the sense that a disproportionate cost has been incurred given the end in view, as formulated over time by the administration. The future of Vietnam (or its relation to a South Asian balance of power) may very well not be of sufficient significance in the perspective of United States national

---

about Southeast Asia that we could be sued in a court and be convicted of breaking a treaty. This is not the point I want to talk about.

US Congress, Senate, Committee on Foreign Relations, *Supplemental Foreign Assistance, Fiscal Year 1966 – Vietnam,* 89th Cong., 2nd sess., 1966, S. Doc. 2793, Washington, D.C.: Government Printing Office, 1966, p. 45

Finding it difficult to obtain the basis of a clear-cut legal obligation for our actions in Vietnam from the SEATO Treaty, the terms of obligation in Vietnam have in the last year or two again relied more heavily on moral commitment and the jargon of credibility – in terms of both the credibility of the US commitment to Vietnam and the credibility of US power in general – to stop the expansion of Communist-led wars of liberation wherever they arise. See n. 11 in this chapter.

[8] The distinction drawn in this sentence is crucial to the basic line of argument and is subject to empirical investigation. It is the distinction between bringing law to bear on the shape and shaping of government policy and bringing legal language to bear so as to make as persuasive a case for government policy as possible. My argument rests on the proposition that we need to restructure both the bureaucracy and expectations about governmental behavior so that the role of law will be significant in the first sense as well as the second. It is well to appreciate that in more routine areas of governmental conduct the bureaucratic machinery does accord a significant guidance role to international law. The area of war and peace is one in which normal bureaucratic procedures are suspended and decisions reached and implemented with the direct participation of the top political officers in government. It is for political decision-making that the need exists for constitutional reform to assure a greater relevance for considerations of international law.

[9] It is of course obvious that there is considerable interplay among these three considerations. For instance, a deep moral feeling dictating certain minimal humanitarian standards of conduct is at the foundation of much of the law of war. And one can always argue that prudence is also a factor in obedience to this law, since disobedience may bring damaging reprisal from the enemy. But, while such interplay is important to recognize, it seems necessary also to distinguish among these three categories as far as possible in order to understand more fully our actions in Vietnam in terms of justifications and results with varying connotations of gravity in both our international and our domestic relations, such results hinging in part on the conflict between the official line and the conclusions as to legality that one must draw from our conduct in Vietnam.

interests to justify the expenditure of blood and money,[10] especially in view of the failure of even disproportionate means to realize or even to approximate the obscure and shifting ends of policy there.[11] Geopolitical considerations can also be invoked to suggest that the United States course in Vietnam is imprudent in terms of our national interest in upholding viable states, in promoting a regional balance of power, in containing the expansion of a Chinese sphere of influence, or in buying time for the present states of South Asia to evolve more stable governments. Perhaps, despite the ghastly irony entailed by the great effort to produce a victory for the Saigon regime, these interests would be served better by a united and stable Vietnam under the leadership of a Hanoi regime or a regime including Communist elements indigenous to South Vietnam than by a divided Vietnam, each half of which is hostile to and afraid of the other. The point is that concern about the *prudence* of the United States involvement raises a different order of issues than does an assessment of its legal quality, although there are notable areas of overlap.

[10]   The war in Vietnam became the longest war in US history in June 1968. Among US forces alone, over 26,000 soldiers had been killed in action and over a half million men were committed to the conflict, not including air and naval support forces located outside the territory of Vietnam. The cost of the war has been reflected in the observation that the US was spending $300,000 to kill a single Viet Cong. See "The War in Vietnam," prepared by the Staff of the Senate Republican Policy Committee, Washington, D.C., Public Affairs Press, 1967, p. 9. These figures reflect none of the suffering of the "enemy" – the Viet Cong or "regular" North Vietnamese forces – or of the peasant caught in between the forces of war to face both the terror of the Viet Cong and the awesome firepower of the United States while living off land that has become pockmarked by bombs and defoliated by sprays. See n. 39 below.

[11]   Just as the United States has based its "commitment" to defend South Vietnam on uncertain and shifting moral and legal grounds, so too have the reasons for our presence in Vietnam in terms of national interest undergone subtle changes, often in parallel with the changes in popular support of the war efforts. In the early years of the war, the apparently limited objectives of helping South Vietnam rid itself of the aggressive threat from North Vietnam and make the country safe for democracy, as it were, received wide public support in this country, a support that perhaps reached its high point after the Tonkin incidents of August 1964. As the war shifted to the North after February 1965, and more US soldiers were injected into the struggle without immediate and favorable results, the American public's patience with events in Southeast Asia seemed to diminish. The situation was not helped by continued reports of corruption in the Saigon government, alleged violations of the law of war, and persistent claims that the United States had repeatedly failed to take advantage of reported peace overtures from Hanoi. Increasing emphasis was placed on containing China and on regarding South Vietnam as the dike that kept the Communist flood from overrunning Southeast Asia. Perhaps to maintain at least a semblance of public support for the war in the United States, the reasons officially given for the US presence in Vietnam were slowly framed in new terms. Thus, the very security of the US has been increasingly said to be at stake, a logical extension of the argument that if the United States does not fight Communism in Vietnam it may in the foreseeable future have to fight it in California. See also Franz Schurmann and others, *The Politics of Escalation in Vietnam*, Boston, Beacon Press, 1966.

Similarly, a moral assessment raises distinct issues. It is quite possible to conclude that the destruction of Vietnamese society, measured in terms of both devastation and human suffering, mainly inflicted by a great power whose own society is beyond the reach of its adversary, places an enormous moral burden of justification upon those who would defend the United States involvement. It should be noted, however, that these *moral* costs of involvement would not be necessarily reduced if the basis of United States involvement were found to be fully compatible with requirements of international law.

It is thus important to acknowledge that the prudential and moral status of the United States involvement is quite separable from its legal status. To be more concrete, the prudential and moral basis of the United States role in the Korean war is, and certainly was, subject to question, but few doubts were ever seriously expressed about the legality of the United States role in defending South Korea under the auspices of the United Nations in response to the massive (if somewhat provoked) attack by North Korea in June of 1950.[12]

---

[12] The legality of US action in Korea was enhanced by at least three conditions absent in the Vietnam situation. First, the North Korean attack, whatever the underlying reasons for it, was an open and large-scale attack across the border of South Korea, an act that with no difficulty could be labeled "aggression" even by nations which had no empathy with the South Korean government. By contrast, North Vietnam's intervention into South Vietnam has been far less open and on a far smaller scale. Indeed there is considerable opinion that North Vietnamese intervention was not on the scale of an "armed attack" under international law, until large United States forces had been deployed in the South under the justification that they were assisting Saigon in meeting such an attack.

Second, the aura of legality surrounding US actions in Korea was greatly enhanced by the fact that they were undertaken within the international auspices of the United Nations. While the United States certainly played the major role by far in the Korean war, its participation under the cloak of the UN gave it a generally persuasive defense against any charges of unilateral action solely in the name of its own national interest. In Vietnam, on the other hand, such charges are far more difficult to meet. Not only has the UN not given its blessing to the US effort, but its principal officer, U Thant, has been steady in his condemnation of that effort. In addition, while the United States enjoys token support in Vietnam from some of its Asian allies, it is significant that the two principal parties, other than the United States, to the SEATO Treaty – France and Pakistan – have openly disavowed US actions in Vietnam. And South Korea, with the largest contingent of allied troops in Vietnam, is able and willing to offer that assistance only because the US has made a similar number of its own troops available in South Korea and has agreed to equip most of the South Korean troops as a precondition to their presence in Vietnam, besides agreeing to rely to the extent possible on Korean sources of supplies for war-related need.

And, third, South Korea possessed a reasonably stable government with a demonstrated capacity to govern its own society without external military support. In contrast, the South Vietnamese leaders have never appeared to enjoy a sufficiently wide base of public support to maintain governmental control unless the United States maintained a strong military presence in the country. Also Vietnam, unlike Korea, had experienced an anti-colonial war fought for control of the entire country and lost by those elements in South Vietnam that have been given support by the United States. Therefore, in Vietnam the military cause of the United States

It seems desirable to make explicit the various arguments that counsel a serious consideration of international law in a war/peace context such as is presented by the Vietnam war.[13]

First, it would appear that the welfare of domestic society would be better served at this historical time by strengthening the framework of legal restraint relevant to the formation and execution of foreign policy, thereby limiting the scope of executive discretion. The Vietnam war has made it clear to many Americans that the public requires protection from its own government just as surely in external arenas of action as it does in domestic affairs. We have reached a point at which public interest demands the structuring of certain legal constraints to regulate governments of democratic society whenever they propose long-term reliance on military forces to carry out their foreign policies. Some might say that a government cannot afford the luxury of adhering to a framework of constraint, that the imperatives of national security are so compelling as to require full trust in the wisdom of the President. In earlier periods of history, especially in times of stress, such arguments in favor of unrestraint were often made with respect to the execution of domestic policy. The vitality of a law-ordered society has been often demonstrated by the non-erosion of legal procedures in periods of domestic stress. The overall balance and welfare of the society have seemed better served by endorsing the capacity of the Supreme Court to confine executive discretion than by allowing those pragmatic arguments advanced on behalf of unrestricted executive power to prevail. With regard to international policy, the necessity of quick action under threat of atomic war has also tended toward unrestraint on executive decision-making. Under conditions in which planned nuclear attack constitutes far less of a danger than does escalation from sub-nuclear to nuclear conflict over an extended period, the need for renewed restraints on executive action have become more obvious. Let the United States involvement in Vietnam serve as a learning experience to demonstrate that the welfare of the country would benefit from building a tradition whereby foreign policy is carried out with due regard for the restraints of law.

---

runs counter to the political drift of revolutionary nationalism, whereas in Korea the conflict was between two rather autonomous political entities, each of which sought to subject the other to an alien ideology. North Korea was the aggressor mainly because it struck first across an international boundary. In South Vietnam the early phases of warfare were largely initiated and managed by southern opponents to the Saigon regime and, therefore, the charge of "aggression" against North Vietnam seems far too tenuous to sustain, even if these charges are approached on the basis of evidence gathered by employees of the US government. E.g., see Douglas Pike, *Viet Cong*, Cambridge, Mass., MIT Press, 1966.

[13] On the need for such explicitness critics and supporters of United States policy agree. See, in particular, Professor Moore's various presentations cited in n. 3, esp. at pp. 430–44.

Second, to achieve this kind of framework of restraint, two kinds of structural reform appear necessary. The first is the creation of the post of the Attorney General for International Affairs, securing at cabinet level a person who would have a vested vocational interest in bringing to bear the legal dimension of proposed policy throughout the decision-making process.[14] The present structure of government is such that no official expert on matters of international law has direct access to the policy-forming process except for the very diluted and generally belated access enjoyed by the Legal Adviser to the Secretary of State. This indirect access tends to exclude legal considerations until after policy has been shaped and a public commitment made. The role, then, of the Legal Adviser in critical cases often becomes one of rationalizing policy in such a way as to offset criticism of a legally controversial policy.[15] In contrast, an Attorney General for International Affairs might be expected and even encouraged to insist that the policy options considered by

[14] An individual trained principally in the law and somewhat independent of the internal political power struggles in decision-making circles in Washington could be expected to be persistent in his injection of legal consideration into any policy-forming process and, it is to be hoped, would be able to make his conclusions and recommendations felt at the highest level and at a pre-"commitment" stage. He might in addition, although this is by no means his principal intended role, be a rallying point for dissenters among top advisers, whose disagreement with imprudent or immoral policy could gain weight by its expression in legal as well as political terms.

A certain added importance could be given to the office by making its occupant a member of the highest official decision-making groups such as the National Security Council. At the same time it is to be hoped that an Attorney General for International Affairs would, because he spoke – or would speak – for no interest group but that favoring world order, eventually become a trusted adviser outside official circles as well.

The methods by which an Attorney General for International Affairs should be selected or dismissed pose no special problem. As with other cabinet members, the President would be expected to choose a competent individual to fill the office. In the case of the Attorney General the President might, however, be expected to select a man of neutral convictions on legal issues, rather than one who sided with the Chief Executive on certain important matters. Only in the event of such apolitical traditions of selection would the office fulfill its purposes.

One would also tend to minimize the possibility that the Attorney General could be intimidated in any way by the threat of removal from office. Perhaps more than for any other officer in government, dismissal of the AGIA because of disagreement over basic issues in controversial situations like Vietnam would be an excellent indication that US policy was not being formulated in consideration of the law of nations.

The entire proposal for an AGIA would be very much influenced by the context in which the office was created, the kind of considerations relied upon by its proponents, and the sorts of functions such an officer would be expected to perform. The initial selection of a candidate for the office would naturally have a considerable additional capacity to define the role. It seems essential to stress the responsibility of the AGIA to introduce legal considerations into foreign policy-making (and not to serve as a buffer against domestic criticism). Such a stress requires a professionalization of the proposed government post and a sense that its occupant would have the same kind of duty to abstain from partisan politics as does, say, a member of the Joint Chiefs of Staff.

[15] This was so, for instance, with the March 4, 1966, memorandum on Vietnam. See n. 1 above.

the government reflect the limits set by international law. Such expectations might appropriately accompany any effort to establish the office.

Leadership groups appear to be experiencing the infiltration of their political consciousness by world-order ideals. This process of infiltration takes place at an uneven rate and some leaders are more susceptible than others.[16] An important point seems to be, however, that this development has gradually made it more acceptable to appeal to legal restraint even in the setting of foreign policy-making. This appeal may be weak on occasion and it may be eventually overridden by other considerations of national interest: Quite possibly legal consideration may be allowed to condition the execution of foreign policy to some extent, even after these considerations have been largely excluded from the selection of the ends of foreign policy. The Bay of Pigs Expedition of 1961 offers an excellent example of a compromise between deference to world-order prohibitions on the use of force and the adoption of a course of action in foreign policy that flouted these prohibitions. The results, as we know, were disastrous, but perhaps not so irreversible as they would have been if no deference to world-order expectations had been expressed, representing both a defeat for law-ordered foreign policy and a setback for a purely geopolitically determined foreign policy. Failures in action of this type are characteristic of periods of normative ambiguity and compromise, periods of transition from one belief-system to another. Blanket acceptance of the limits of international law decision-making in crises cannot realistically be expected. However, the hope is that over time an exposure to the value of legal considerations in the planning and execution of short- and long-term policy formulation would lead the government toward becoming a government of laws, not men, in international affairs.

The second structural reform that the Vietnam war suggests as essential is a redefinition of the role of Congress in authorizing and sustaining policies that entail the use of military force. It seems clear that the present dichotomy between according Congress virtually no role and an insistence on a declaration of war is far too rigid to provide for meaningful legislative participation in the policy-forming process relevant to war–peace problems. In general, there exists a need to evolve a procedure of legislative participation that results in diluting the present degree of executive control over this subject matter.

---

[16] For some very suggestive discussion of these issues, see Harold D. Lasswell, "The Social and Political Framework of War and Peace," in Carmine D. Clemente and Donald B. Lindsley, eds., *Aggression and Defense: Neural Mechanisms and Social Patterns*, Vol. V, *Brain Function* (Berkeley: University of California Press, 1967), pp. 317–35, esp. pp. 317–24.

The practicalities of restraining recourses to military force appear to take precedence over the arguments for unrestrained executive discretion.

In searching for a new understanding of separation of powers between the principal branches of government, it is also important to consider carefully the role of domestic courts. Domestic courts have taken the position that a private litigant cannot question the legal status of the United States involvement in a war. The legality of the United States involvement is treated as a "political question" not susceptible to adjudication. If the general position urged here is correct – namely, that it is highly desirable to establish framework of legal restraint relevant to foreign policy – then the protection of rights of individual redress through judicial action appears essential. If, as the Constitution and the Supreme Court have affirmed, the obligations of international law constitute part of the "supreme law of the land" then it seems inappropriate to hold that individuals are unable to rely upon this area of governmental restraint in resisting calls to perform government service, especially when these calls may entail risk to their lives, infringements of their consciences, or participation in internationally criminal behavior.

It is well to appreciate that the concentration of legal authority in the executive branch was accomplished at a time when international law made little pretense of regulating the discretion of a sovereign state to wage war. Only after the Kellogg–Briand Pact of 1928 was widely ratified by many states, including the United States, could it be persuasively argued that recourse to aggressive war was illegal.[17] This trend toward the legal prohibition of nondefensive uses of force in international affairs is carried strongly forward in the Charter of the United Nations. But prior to 1928 there was no occasion for judicial review, as there were no relevant legal criteria, by which to appraise a challenge directed at a given war policy. Similarly, the role of legislative participation was purely one of confirming a direction of national policy. There was no basis for a charge that the President was acting illegally by going to war, unless possibly in an unlikely circumstance in which the adversary state was joined to the United States by a treaty of alliance. The main conclusion on this issue is that international law has evolved so significantly in the area of war and peace as to make traditional notions about the separation of powers appropriate for this subject matter now seem dangerously obsolete.[18]

---

[17] For a convenient account of the legal steps taken to prohibit aggressive warfare, see Quincy Wright, *The Role of International Law in the Elimination of War*, Dobbs Ferry, N.Y., Oceana, 1961.

[18] This subject has been explored recently in preliminary hearings on the President's power of deployment and use of United States forces in Vietnam and related testimony on the Gulf of

Third, it also now appears clear that the ideology of world order professed by the United States government in common with the governments of many other countries has influenced the attitudes of a significant portion of our domestic population. The class of the government's professed views with its actions in Vietnam has engendered a rising level of legal awareness among attentive members of the American public. This awareness has grown out of the atmosphere created by the controversy surrounding numerous legal points concerning United States intervention in Vietnam and, more recently, concerning the tactics of war there. In all probability, this trend toward awareness is not a temporary aberration of opinion provoked by an unpopular and unsuccessful war. The permanence of this growth of awareness is at least partly assured by the realization that major power confrontations of the future will, because of military technology, continue to be characterized by third-party intervention – initially carefully regulated, but almost inevitably tending to increase – in support of one or another faction within the borders of single, strife-torn states. This intervention will not often carry with it the aura of legality that would accompany a response to open aggression across state boundaries. Neither is it likely to involve methods of warfare that distinguish between the populace and the enemy.[19]

Tonkin Resolution. See United States Senate Foreign Relations Committee Hearings on S. Res. 151 relating to US commitments to foreign powers, S. Res. 151, 90th Cong., 1st Sess.:

> Whereas accurate definition of the term "national commitment" in recent years has become obscured:
> Now, therefore, be it
> *Resolved*, that it is the sense of the Senate that a national commitment by the United States to a foreign power necessarily and exclusively results from affirmative actions taken by the executive and legislative branches of the United States Government through means of a treaty, convention, or other legislative instrumentality specifically intended to give effect to such a commitment.

See also "Congressional Inquiry into Military Affairs," Senate Foreign Relations Committee, Memorandum of Legislative Reference Service of Library of Congress, March 1968.

[19] One of the great tragedies of the Vietnam war is that the United States has employed as anti-personnel weapons napalm, phosphorus, cluster bomb units (CBUs), and gases that can cause horrible and unnecessary suffering. But this tragedy is enlarged by the fact that the traditional anti-guerrilla concept of the necessity of separating the guerrilla from the population that may hide and support him has been applied in a most devastating way in Vietnam. The futility of attempts to separate the guerrilla from a population that gives him increasing assistance has led to tactics that apply massive firepower indiscriminately to "suspected" enemy areas in the form of blanket bombing or search-and-destroy operations. In addition, "Operation Ranch Hand" has sprayed millions of gallons of defoliants over South Vietnam to deprive the Viet Cong of both cover and food, particularly rice, in the area. The choice left to the "neutral" peasants in those areas bombed, burned, and sprayed is simple. Stay and be killed or move to "resettlement areas" under the control of the US and allied forces. Separation of the fish from

The American legal consciousness is sufficiently great at this time to suggest that a decision by the national government to carry out a foreign policy in apparent violation of the United Nations Charter and other standards of international law will predictably precipitate serious domestic opposition. A portion of the citizenry of democratic states now gives preference to the dictates of their sense of legal requirements even when these dictates contradict imperatives of national loyalty in the old sense of "my country right or wrong, my country." This shift in public sentiment is a dramatic one and suggests the importance of taking seriously the restraining claims imposed on national discretion by international law. It is not now (nor has it ever been) accurate to presume that the population of a domestic society will blindly follow the flag into battle. As a consequence, a governmental decision to pursue a foreign policy regarded by a sizable segment of public opinion as illegal is likely to generate sizable domestic opposition.[20] The existence of this loyal opposition will imperil both the war effort and the maintenance of democratic traditions at home. The continuation of such a war for any length of time will place increasing pressure on a government to choose between upholding war commitments and maintaining domestic liberties.

Fourth, I think that it isn't possible to separate governmental attitudes toward international law from public adherence to ideals of respect for law in domestic society. It is very artificial to inculcate respect for law in our cities and practice lawlessness in Vietnam. As the more militant leaders of ghetto communities have made clear, the domestic order of our society is continuous with the sort of international order that prevails. In addition, it becomes more difficult to socialize citizens in the direction of respect for law in relation to the pursuit of personal goals if the government does not set an example of using comparable restraint in the pursuit of national goals.[21] Socialization is

---

the water in which they swim has thus taken on a new and ugly meaning in Vietnam. For some documentation of these charges, see the newspaper extracts collected in Clergy and Laymen Concerned About Vietnam, *In the Name of America*, Annandale, Va., Turnpike Press, 1968. For material on North Vietnam, see John Gerassi, *North Vietnam: A Documentary*, New York, Bobbs Merrill, 1968. See n. 39 below.

[20] This opposition has persisted during the Vietnam War despite the warnings of administration spokesmen like Vice President Humphrey who told a group of business executives in late 1967: "I have not forgotten the lessons of the '30s when men cried 'peace' and failed a generation. I, for one, would not want to be responsible for a policy which deferred today's manageable troubles until they became unmanageable . . . a policy of Armageddon on the installment plan" ("Dissenting from the Dissenters," *Newsweek*, November 6, 1967). In August of 1968 it became evident that the President of the United States was deterred from attending the political convention of his own party because he was told of the unpopularity of his war policies.

[21] Disrespect for the law of nations by the US can certainly be expected to promote an increasing disrespect for its domestic law among US citizens, particularly minority groups that have for years been counseled to pursue their goals within the law and now see their country act on the

especially difficult in these circumstances for groups such as the blacks who are being urged to pursue their grievance against white America within the limits and through the procedures of law.

Fifth, the standards of law provide a yardstick that is relied upon by responsible groups in our society who seek to express their opposition to a line of policy. For instance, the Clergy Concerned About American Policy in Vietnam issued a strong moral condemnation of the American involvement in Vietnam documented by reference to instances of United States departure from the traditional standards of behavior embodied in the laws of war.[22] This was an instance in which legal norms provided an aura of objectivity that served to anchor moral judgment.

Sixth, principal sovereign states by their behavior establish global patterns that influence the behavior of all states in international society. Given a decentralized international system lacking a legislative organization, the most powerful sovereign states necessarily play a quasi-legislative role. Their acts set precedents upon which other states rely. At stake in the Vietnam war is the United States claim that substantial covert assistance to an insurgency is tantamount to an armed attack by one country upon another. Given the pervasiveness of insurgent behavior and given the allusiveness of the factual relations between insurgent groups and foreign governments, the United States has set an important precedent by its unilateral determination to engage in virtually unrestricted bombing of North Vietnam in response to North Vietnamese support of the NLF.[23] The experience of atmospheric nuclear testing illustrates

---

international plane with very limited consideration of that law. This very real problem, when connected with the other domestic difficulties the Vietnam war represents, are well worth noting. Vietnam is a place where many Negroes find themselves fighting a war allegedly to protect democratic ideals that many of them have never fully enjoyed at home. It is for some a white man's war fought in disproportionate numbers by black men against yellow people with much of the same savagery of method that allowed the United States to decimate Hiroshima and Nagasaki during World War II. It is a war that has channeled billions of dollars away from long-promised domestic programs to improve the position of the black communities of America. And finally, and most important for the United States as a nation, it is a war in which many thousands of black men who have been badly disappointed by the lack of domestic progress return to the United States with a training in the tactics and strategy of guerrilla warfare that can very well be used by those seeking radical change in America.

[22] *In the Name of America*, pp. 1–15.

[23] The decision to bomb North Vietnam in February of 1965 was initially justified as a reprisal for the attacks on the large American air base at Pleiku; subsequently it was vindicated as an effort to interdict infiltration and, finally, as a means of "hurting" North Vietnam sufficiently to induce a settlement on terms acceptable to the United States government. Neither the claim of reprisal, nor the claim of interdiction, nor the claim of generalized belligerency rests, in my judgment, on firm legal foundation. Gerassi, in *North Vietnam: A Documentary*, accumulates considerable material on the additional issue of whether, independent of the legal theory used to vindicate the bombing, the specific selection of targets discloses wilful violation of the most minimum humanitarian laws of war.

how difficult it may be for even powerful states to repudiate the precedents they have created when these precedents are invoked by other states engaged in comparable activity. The United States and the Soviet Union are immobilized by their own prior records of atmospheric testing in relation to positing objections to French and Chinese nuclear weapons tests. A kind of reciprocity operates in international relations, underscoring the importance of conditioning unilateral national action by a full awareness and acknowledgment of its legal consequences. One legal consequence of this common-law social process is to lend a presumption of legality to behavior by other states that falls within the province of national claims.

Seventh, reference to legal norms and procedures provides insight into the reasonableness or unreasonableness of a particular diplomatic posture. For instance, war-terminating proposals can be assessed for their reasonableness by reference to the degree to which they rest upon a mutual and symmetrical acceptance of the relevant restraints of law. This kind of insight into the character of reasonableness suggests a way of cutting through diplomatic impasses that result from each country's selectively perceiving and interpreting facts so as to conform to its preferences and failing to appreciate the contradictory perceptions and interpretations of its adversary.[24] Especially in a situation of the Vietnam type, potentialities for mutual misinterpretation are great. Each side sees facts that confirm only its claims and thereby feels vindicated in intensifying its response and its reliance on coercion. The only way to inhibit this process is to establish objective limitations, such as international boundary lines or third-party procedures, that assure reference to authoritative organs of conciliation and settlement.[25]

II THE SIX CATEGORIES OF LEGAL ISSUES RELEVANT TO AN APPRAISAL OF THE UNITED STATES INVOLVEMENT IN THE VIETNAM WAR

Because of the incredible complexity of the legal issues generated by the Vietnam war, it seems useful to group these issues into a series of categories. These groupings are intended to assist understanding and should not be taken as rigid and mechanical separations.

[24] See Ralph K. White, *Nobody Wanted War*, Garden City, N.Y., Doubleday and Co., Inc., 1968.
[25] Legal order evolves in a social setting that lacks a government in two principal ways: (1) substantive standards of limitation on behavior that are sufficiently self-defining to be self-enforcing; an international boundary line or a prohibition on nuclear weapons is such a clear standard; (2) procedural requirements of reference that allow either party to a dispute as to fact or law to solicit and obtain an impartial determination that will be accepted as binding by the losing side. Both of these ordering strategies can operate successfully in a society that exhibits little institutional centralization.

1. *The Geneva Agreements:* There is a series of legal issues that pertain to the origin of the Vietnam war. These issues concern primarily the interpretation of the Geneva Accords, a series of international agreements reached in 1954 at the end of the first Indo-China war that had been fought between the French and the Vietminh.[26] The Vietminh was the organization presided over by Ho Chi Minh and represented a coalition of anti-colonial forces that prevailed against the French in the first Indo-China war. The basic diplomatic context at Geneva has remained very obscure. Many of the misunderstandings subsequent to 1954 appear to stem from doubt as to whether the Geneva Accords sought to ratify the battlefield victory of the Vietminh over the French or sought to reach a compromise whereby the country of Vietnam would be partitioned into a Communist North Vietnam and an anti-Communist South Vietnam. If the Geneva Accords are looked upon as ratifying the French defeat in much the manner that the Evian Accords of 1962 ratified the French defeat in the Algerian war, then the remainder of the issues tend to be resolved along the lines alleged by North Vietnam. If, on the other hand, the Geneva Accords are seen as producing a divided country of the Korean variety, then the interpretive issues are much more difficult to resolve. The Soviet Union acted as co-chairman with the United Kingdom at the Geneva Conference and yet urged in 1957, after the date for election on reunification had passed, that both North and South Vietnam be separately admitted to the United Nations. The Soviet effort was opposed by the United States although it now gives some support to the contention that Vietnam was converted into a divided country in 1954.[27]

Further dispute surrounding the Geneva Accords has dealt with the extent to which the Saigon regime was bound by the terms of the Geneva settlement, most specifically the extent to which it was bound to the obligation to hold elections in July of 1956. The Diem government never acknowledged its obligations to abide by the Geneva arrangements and persistently refused to enter pre-election consultations with North Vietnam despite the frequent requests that it do so by the Hanoi

---

[26] For convenient copies of the text of these Accords, see Falk, ed., *The Vietnam War*, pp. 543–64.

[27] The United States was pressing for the admission of the Republic of Vietnam, as the sole representative in the State of Vietnam, to the United Nations. For a summary account, see John Norton Moore and James L. Underwood, with the collaboration of Myres S. McDougal, "The Lawfulness of United States Assistance to the Republic of Viet Nam," privately published, May 1966, pp. 23–28.

government.[28] It is also problematic as to what the full legal significance is of a failure to hold elections and how this failure relates to the responsibility of North Vietnam for instigating and supplying the NLF uprising in South Vietnam. In essence, then, the legal questions that center on the Geneva Accords concern the binding nature of those Accords and the apportionment of blame for their violation.[29] I think that we are forced to conclude that the Geneva settlement was extremely ambiguous on its face, that the Hanoi government was to some extent a victim of great-power diplomacy, and that the non-participation and non-assent of the Saigon regime prompted, if it did not altogether assure, a misunderstanding about the terms of settlement emerging subsequent to 1954. The North Vietnamese might have given tacit acquiescence to the existence of a divided Vietnam had the Saigon regime either collapsed on its own or displayed reasonable competence to govern South Vietnam in a tolerable fashion. However, the repressive policies of the Diem regime produced a revolutionary situation in South Vietnam such that a combination of indigenous insurgency and external support coalesced in the insurgency of the National Liberation Front.[30]

2. *The Charter Arguments*: Most of the legal debate about the United States involvement in Vietnam has raised the question of whether North Vietnam's assistance to the National Liberation Front has been equivalent to an "armed attack" against a sovereign state. The issue has been debated generally in terms of the United Nations Charter, and the question has been asked in terms of whether North Vietnam's support of the NLF constituted an "armed attack" of a sort that justified action in "self-defense" by South Vietnam and the United States, as these two legal terms are employed in Article 51 of the Charter. This issue raises

---

[28] One of the fullest accounts of this period is to be found in Joseph Buttinger, *Vietnam: A Dragon Embattled*, New York: Praeger, 1967, Vol. II, pp. 845–1010. An able short analysis is contained in George McT. Kahin and John W. Lewis, *The United States in Vietnam*, New York, Delta, 1967, pp. 66–126.

[29] One of the fullest studies of the Geneva Conference has been done as a Ph.D. thesis by an aide to Prince Bua Loe, who was the Prime Minister of the Saigon regime at the time of the Geneva Conference. See Ngo Ton Dat, "The Geneva Partition of Vietnam and the Question of Reunification During the First Two Years (August 1954 to July 1956)," unpublished Ph.D. dissertation, Cornell University, Ithaca, N.Y., 1963. See also John S. Hannon, Jr., "A Political Settlement for Vietnam: The 1954 Geneva Conference and Its Current Implications," *Virginia Journal of International Law*, 8 (1968), pp. 4–93.

[30] See Jean Lacouture, *Vietnam: Between Two Truces*, New York, Random House, 1966, pp. 51–60, for a short analysis of the emergence of the Front. See also Bernard B. Fall, *The Two Viet-Nams*, New York, Praeger, rev. ed., 1964, pp. 203–384.

the general questions as to whether assistance given to an insurgent faction is covered within Article 51 at all and, if so, what degree of assistance is equivalent to an armed attack on a foreign society. In Vietnam
each side accuses the other of committing aggression and alleges its
own use of only defensive force. The problem of aggression and armed
attack under the Charter has several main elements: First, how do we
evaluate legally North Vietnamese assistance to the NLF; second, how
do we evaluate legally United States assistance to the Saigon regime;
third, how do we assess the extension of the air war to North Vietnam
after the Tonkin incidents in August of 1964 and then permanently after
the Pleiku incident of February of 1965? In Charter terms, we are dealing with contentions that the principal belligerent states are violating
Article 2, Paragraph 4, and are not acting within the scope of Article 51
defining self-defense.

There is a subsidiary argument made by the United States that its
action on behalf of South Vietnam is a fulfillment of its obligations under
the SEATO treaty. In my judgment, the SEATO treaty neither adds to
nor detracts from the Charter Arguments and, if the United States possesses grounds for proceeding against North Vietnam, it possesses them
on a Charter basis. There is, finally, the much-controverted question in
this context as to whether the United States discharged its procedural
duty, under Article 33 of the Charter, to submit the Vietnam conflict to
the United Nations for peaceful settlement before having recourse to
military force. The United States appears only to have sought a nominal
involvement for the United Nations in the Vietnam conflict until after
it had become evident that a military solution could not be achieved
successfully at a tolerable cost.[31]

3. *The Westphalia–Budapest Arguments*: The basic structure of international society was constituted in 1648 at the Peace of Westphalia.[32] This
structure rests on the coordinated principles of sovereign independence,
territorial jurisdiction, the equality of states, sovereign immunity, and the
doctrine of nonintervention. These Westphalia principles were formally

---

[31] For a fairly complete account up through October 1967, see "Submission of the Vietnam
Conflict to the United Nations," Hearings, Senate Committee on Foreign Relations, 19th
Cong., 1st sess., October 26, 27, and November 2, 1967.

[32] This Westphalia conception of the basis of international order is more fully discussed in
Richard Falk, "The Interplay of Westphalia and Charter Conceptions of International Legal
Order: Past, Present, and Near Future," in Richard Falk and Cyril E. Black, eds., *The Future
of the International Legal Order*, Princeton, Princeton University Press, 1969, Vol. I, ch. 2,
pp. 32–70.

evolved in the course of settling the bloody ideological conflict known to students of history as the Thirty Years' War. The basic idea at Westphalia was to rest international peace and security upon the capacity and prerogative of national governments to maintain order within their national boundaries, and upon the endorsement of their exclusive authority to do so. The national government whose existence is internationally certified through the conception of diplomatic recognition, and more recently through access to international institutions, is the exclusive political authority able and entitled to act on behalf of a nation. The capacity of the constituted government includes its right to receive foreign aid, including military assistance, and in periods of emergency to request foreign military assistance to help repel external attack or to sustain internal order. In the Vietnam context, the Westphalia Argument has been strongly relied upon by the United States government. In essence, the argument of the United States government has been that the Saigon regime is the constituted government of South Vietnam, as legitimized by widespread diplomatic recognition.[33] This Saigon regime requested the United States government to provide military assistance to enable it to deal with an emergency created by the combined challenge of indigenous uprising and foreign aggression. The United States position, then, is that its military role in Vietnam is sanctioned by the view that it is coming to the rescue of a beleaguered incumbent government.

There are two fundamental difficulties with the application of the Westphalia Argument to the Vietnam situation. The first difficulty is that it is oriented toward the status quo. In certain circumstances, support of the constituted government may frustrate the realization of self-determination for the people and the society involved. In the event that a particular state is ruled by an oppressive government, then outside support of that government tends to reinforce regressive structures of domination. In effect, the Westphalia Argument needs to be correlated with certain internal considerations that bear on the capacity to govern and the degree to which fundamental human rights are protected by the government. To take extreme examples, it would be possible to contend that Germany under Hitler, like South Africa since 1946, lost its political legitimacy to such an extent that it was no longer entitled to receive external support of a military character. The Westphalia conception of world order, if taken too literally, appears to give no protection whatsoever to

---

[33] See, e.g., Moore and Underwood, "The Lawfulness of United States Assistance to the Republic of Viet Nam," pp. 28–29.

a right of revolution enjoyed by suppressed populations. When the ratio between the magnitude of external support and the contribution of the incumbent government grows so great that the former overshadows the latter, then the external involvement appears incompatible with the values of self-determination.[34] These considerations support the conclusion that the Westphalia Argument provides only provisional justification for external military assistance in a situation of the Vietnam type. In essence, the consent of the incumbent regime is only one of several complementary considerations that enter into an appraisal of legality.

In the specific context created by the Vietnam war, a further set of difficulties is apparent. These difficulties are suggested by the argument made in support of the Soviet intervention in Hungary to suppress the uprising of 1956 (the Budapest Argument) or, even more flagrantly, the contention that the Soviet-led military intervention in Czech affairs was at the invitation of Prague leaders. It will be recalled that the Soviet government legitimized its military intervention in Hungary by according the symbols of political legitimacy to the Kadar elite. The Soviet intervention in Hungarian affairs could then subsequently be justified as the provision of support in response to an invitation by the constituted government. The Budapest Argument emphasizes the degree to which states can self-legitimize the conditions of their participation in foreign civil wars. This issue further suggests the need for some kind of centralized international procedure to identify which elite, if any, is entitled to act on behalf of a particular national society. In Vietnam it has now become common knowledge that the United States government, through the CIA and other official activities, participated in the selection, maintenance, and transformation of the various Saigon regimes that have been in existence since 1954. Therefore, the contention that the legitimacy of the United States role rests on the legitimacy of Saigon's request for assistance is a seriously circular argument. It is the United States prior intervention that itself provided successive Saigon regimes with the political orientation that would assure an invitation for United States assistance. Such a veil of legitimacy should be lifted in an inquiry into the legal basis for using military force in a foreign country.[35]

---

[34] There are some interesting implications to this effect in an essay by Karl W. Deutsch titled "External Involvement in Internal War," in Harry Eckstein, ed., *Internal War*, Glencoe, Ill., Free Press, 1964, pp. 100–10.

[35] The point here is that an invitation from a constituted government is only one factor in the appraisal of legality that should be made when one state uses its military power within the territory of another. The legitimizing value of this invitation is diluted to the extent that the constituted government is subject to a serious internal challenge from a counter-elite and it is

These circumstances are accentuated in Vietnam by the evident incapacity of the Saigon regime to administer its national society in either an effective or a reasonably consensual manner. The problem is further complicated by the plausibility of treating the Vietnam war as a secessionist struggle initiated by the southern zone of Vietnam.[36] In this connection, it is worth noting that even the South Vietnamese Constitution proclaims the unity of all of Vietnam as a single sovereign entity.[37] The removal of United States and North Vietnamese external assistance from South Vietnam would have led, it seems highly likely, to victory by the NLF at any relevant stage of the struggle for control of South Vietnam. Furthermore, the effective control exercised by the NLF over portions of South Vietnam suggests that there is a dual government prevailing in large sectors of the country. In a situation of dual government, outside states are entitled to treat either of the two contending elites as legitimate.[38] This set of circumstances existed during the Spanish civil war. In a situation of dual government, then, the United States might be entitled to aid the Saigon regime, but it could hardly contend that North

rendered worthless if "the government" is constituted through the prior intervention of the foreign state that is then the recipient of an invitation. The Soviet intervention in Czechoslovakia in August 1968 was a particularly crass example of invasion beneath a transparently false claim to be responding to an earlier invitation.

[36] That is, at minimum North Vietnam cannot be looked upon as an outsider in the setting of South Vietnamese development. There is considerable support for suggesting that the Geneva solution looked toward a unified Vietnam under Hanoi's control and that post-1954 efforts to prevent that expectation from being fulfilled were tantamount to secession by South Vietnam from the single country of Vietnam. In this light, the effort resembles the effort of Katanga to break away from the Congo with the United States playing the role supportive of secession in Vietnam that Belgium played in the Congo. In any event, North Vietnam's efforts to frustrate the division of its country in violation of a major international agreement gives its military participation in the struggle some legal and geopolitical foundation.

[37] Even the South Vietnamese Constitution of 1967 proclaims in Article 1 (1): "Vietnam is a territorially indivisible, unified and independent republic." And Article 107 states: "Article 1 of the Constitution and this Article may not be amended or deleted." See "Background Information Relating to Southeast Asia and Vietnam," Senate Committee on Foreign Relations, 3rd rev. ed., 1967, pp. 287–304.

[38] For fuller consideration and some documentation of the dual-sovereignty argument, see Falk, ed., *The Vietnam War*, pp. 484–90. As of September 1968 the NLF has made no claim to be the legitimate government of South Vietnam, although its missions in over twenty countries are accorded diplomatic status normally reserved for foreign states. The failure to proclaim a government may reflect the continuing search for a political compromise such that a coalition of South Vietnamese interest, ethnic, and ideological groups might join in the governance of the country. The relevant point in the text is merely that the NLF exercises enough effective political control over enough of the country to allow third states to accord it governmental status equivalent to that enjoyed by the Saigon regime.

Vietnamese assistance to the NLF amounted to aggression. All external participation would be placed on an equivalent legal level.

It is exceedingly difficult to resolve the legal issues that emerge in connection with the Westphalia Argument. These issues are extremely important, however, because so often the outcome of a civil war depends on which faction receives assistance at which stage and in what form. Given the frequency of civil warfare, it appears to be a most unfortunate precedent for the United States to assert not only that it was entitled to provide unlimited military support for a government elite it had helped to create, but that North Vietnamese military assistance to a counter-elite amounts to aggression of such a severe nature that it constituted an armed attack justifying action in self-defense.

4. *The Hague Arguments*: The legal issues presented under this heading are very diverse, but they may be grouped in two main categories. First of all, there are the various issues raised by the contention that the United States is conducting the war in multiple violation of minimal standards of legal restraint embodied in treaties of long standing. These treaties are principally the Hague Conventions of 1907 and the four Geneva Conventions of 1949. The rules of warfare contained in these treaties are made applicable to the armed forces by the field manuals issued to all servicemen, and have been accepted as binding upon the war policies of all countries. The range of apparent violative activity occurring in the course of the Vietnam war has now been rather fully documented in a series of persuasive publications.[39] The main kinds of violations involve the mistreatment of civilians, bombing of nonmilitary targets, the use of prohibited weapons, and the destruction of villages and other settlements of Vietnamese people. The legal consequence of the disparity between American battlefield practices and the laws of war suggests either that these laws are obsolete under conditions of modern guerrilla warfare, or that the United States is engaged in a massive and

---

[39] See books cited in n. 19 and also Harrison Salisbury, *Hanoi – A View From the North*, New York, Harper and Row, 1967, and David Schoenbrun, *Vietnam: How We Got in It, How to Get out*, New York, Atheneum, 1968, particularly pp. 3–78, for narrative accounts of the war, particularly in North Vietnam, see also Lawrence C. Petrowski, "Law and the Conduct of the Vietnam War," prepared for the Civil War Panel of the American Society of International Law, Washington, D.C., December 1967. See also Jean J. S. Salmon, "Violations du droit de la guerre par les Etats-Unis d'Amérique," a paper prepared for the Conference of the International Council of Jurists, Grenoble, 1968, and Henri Meyrowitz, "Le droit de la guerre dans le conflit vietnamien," *Annuaire Français de Droit International* (1967), 153–201. See also *Crimes de guerre Américains au Vietnam*, Institut des Sciences Juridiques, Hanoi, n.d.

systematic violation of the most elementary humanitarian rules evolved to restrain governments in periods of war. These rules were not formulated by idealistic reformers. The content of the laws of war, on the contrary, represents the hard-core, basic wisdom of practical men of affairs and statesmen trained to uphold the best interests of their particular countries. Therefore it seems to be a serious cause of concern that the United States government has been led to conduct the war in Vietnam in such flagrant and comprehensive disregard of these rules of restraint. The role of international law in this area is very much connected with giving legal authority to fundamental principles of decency.

The second main category of issues arises directly from the conclusion that a counter-guerrilla strategy rests on the sustained violation of the rules of warfare. It goes beyond the assertion that counter-guerrilla tactics produce a series of specific violations of particular rules of war. The contention is that the only combat strategy available to the counter-guerrilla faction, if the war is popularly based and has grown to a certain scale of magnitude, is to destroy large sections of the population of the society wherein the struggle is taking place. That is, the roots of insurgency sink so deeply into the society experiencing the struggle that they can be torn out of that society only through its substantial destruction. This view of the cumulative legal effect of the United States role in the Vietnam war, especially its role after 1965, suggests a conclusion of an entirely new legal magnitude. That is that the cumulative effect of counter-guerrilla warfare is necessarily barbaric and inhumane to such an extent as to taint the entire effort with a genocidal quality. [40]

This line of argument does not ignore the fact that the NLF at early stages of the Vietnam war engaged in terrorist tactics often directed against civilian targets. I would suggest, however, that the insurgent faction in an underdeveloped country has, at the beginning of its struggle for power, no alternative other than terror to mobilize an effective operation. Wherever there is insurgency there is likely to be terror of this sort, whether it be South Africa or South Vietnam. An important element of differentiation is that insurgent terror tends to be discriminating in its application and to involve relatively small numbers of victims. In contrast, the terroristic tactics of the regime and its supporters

---

[40] For a clarification of the conception of genocide in the Vietnam setting, see n. 51 below. The most complete accusation of genocide available is contained in the proceedings of the Russell Tribunal. See *Tribunal Russell*, Paris, Gallimard, 1968, Vol. II, pp. 312–39, 349–68; see also the separate declaration of Stokely Carmichael, pp. 370–71.

tend, as the conflict increases, to become increasingly indiscriminate and to affect larger and larger numbers of victims, most of whom must be presumed innocent of belligerent participation. A relatively isolated incumbent regime is gradually forced into the position of waging war against its own population, the weakness of the regime being disguised by the receipt of external military assistance. The foreign state becomes the critical adversary of the revolutionary faction, and the war takes on the character of a war of national defense, enlisting all patriotic energies against foreign domination. Such a sequence has been manifest in the Vietnam war, and has been most recently dramatized by the formation in April 1968 of the Alliance of National, Democratic, and Peace Forces whose leadership is drawn from conservative, upper-middle-class circles in the cities of Saigon and Hué.[41] The April Manifesto of the Alliance disclosed the agreement of this non-Communist coalition group with many of the objectives of the NLF, and most especially with the effort to secure the withdrawal of foreign armed forces from Vietnam.

We are faced, then, with the general question of the extent to which a major counter-guerrilla effort can be generated in opposition to a well-organized insurgency without violating the minimal rules of legal and moral restraint. The necessity of excluding these minimal rules is bound to have a brutalizing impact upon those who conduct such a war. It is also bound to result in domestic spillovers, especially to the extent that those who are conscripted into the counter-guerrilla effort are themselves aggrieved members of a minority in their own society. It is worth recalling that the Algerian war of independence was initiated shortly after conscripts returned to Algeria from periods of service on behalf of the French in the first Indo-China war. It seems clear that learning how to fight against an insurgency also involves learning how to create and sustain a successful insurgency. Therefore, to send a conscripted army from the United States to fight in Vietnam poses something of a threat to our own domestic tranquility. It is no accident, I suppose, that various escalations of United States participation in the Vietnam war have been accompanied by parallel escalations of militancy on the part of ghetto leaders in the United States. The opponents of the established order in the United States, whether black militants or the New Left, have increasingly seen themselves as domestic homologues to the NLF; hence

---

[41] For some discussion of the Alliance, see Richard Falk, "A Vietnam Settlement: The View from Hanoi," Center of International Studies, Princeton University, Policy Memorandum No. 34, 1968 (Chapter 1 in this volume).

the symbolic act of carrying the NLF flag and the cult of admiration for the efforts of the NLF.

5. *The Tonkin Arguments*: There has been a growing debate about the degree to which the executive branch has complied with constitutional procedures in the course of making and increasing the commitment to use armed forces in Vietnam.[42] We are dealing here with a fundamental question about the separation-of-powers idea in the setting of war and peace. There has been a legislative tendency to defer to the executive branch whenever matters of foreign policy seemed to be involved. Courts, in particular, have used language suggesting that the making and conduct of foreign policy are a matter of executive discretion and therefore not susceptible to legal appreciation. The Congress, on the other hand, has tended to feel that the executive branch is in a better position to appreciate the national security requirements of the United States in periods of emergency and has deferred to the President as Commander-in-Chief of the armed forces, especially in time of war. We have grown accustomed to the idea that the President exercises extraordinary powers during a period of war.

The Vietnam war illustrates, I think, that we need to rethink very fundamentally the whole conception of separation of powers in the context of legislative and executive responsibilities for the waging and authorizing of force in foreign lands. It is one thing to give the President the authority to respond to emergency situations in which there is no time available for useful consultation with the legislative branch. In this respect, it might seem desirable to affirm the sort of executive authority, extreme though it was, exercised in the context of the Cuban missile crisis in 1962.[43] The Cuban missile crisis demanded an immediate response based on a very close appreciation of a mass of factual information, much of it secret and technical. However, in the setting of the Vietnam war, the Senate has been effectively excluded from meaningful participation

[42] The most complete analysis of these issues presently available is Lawrence R. Velvel, "The War in Vietnam: Unconstitutional, Justiciable, and Jurisdictionally Attackable," *Kansas Law Review*, 16 (1968), 449–503(e); see also I. F. Stone, "International Law and the Tonkin Bay Incidents," in Marcus G. Raskin and Bernard B. Fall, eds., *The Viet-Nam Reader*, New York, Vintage, 1965, pp. 307–15; I. F. Stone, "McNamara and Tonkin Bay: The Unanswered Questions," *New York Review of Books*, March 28, 1968, 5–12.

[43] See Elie Abel, *The Missile Crisis*, New York, J. B. Lippincott Co., 1966; Albert and Roberta Wohlstetter, "Controlling the Risks in Cuba," in Linda B. Miller, ed., *Dynamics of World Politics*, Englewood Cliffs, N.J., Prentice Hall, 1968, pp. 62–95. From a more juridical perspective, see Neill H. Alford, Jr., "The Cuban Quarantine of 1962: An Inquiry into Paradox and Persuasion," *Virginia Journal of International Law*, 4 (1964), 35–72.

in the policy-forming process. The choice between a declaration of war and doing nothing appears too rigid in view of the policy consequences of either established alternative. There is, it seems clear, a need to find procedures that enable effective legislative participation in the evolution of executive policy that involves the waging of war in a foreign country. The present level of legislative participation involving mainly the power to disapprove budgetary recommendations and withhold appropriations from the executive is very inadequate. The typical congressional perception of this choice is one of withholding support from Americans on the battlefield confronted with threats directed at their lives. There is in this sense no real determination as to whether the waging of the war is itself in the interests of the United States. In addition, the role of Congress, especially the Senate, has been confined to debating with the executive branch through the device of widely publicized Senate Hearings, most particularly those conducted by Senator Fulbright as Chairman of the Senate Foreign Relations Committee.[44] Even this role, small as it is, has had a significant bearing on establishing a climate of opinion about the war in the United States: the depth and generality of opposition have become more and more pronounced and have solicited the participation of very responsible elements of the community. This kind of role for the Senate was largely a consequence of the fact that Senator Fulbright, with his enormous prestige, happened to be a strong opponent of the war. Such a fortuitous legislative circumstance does not seem adequately to preserve the possibility of establishing constructive legislative participation in the development of a war policy on behalf of the country. Therefore, it would seem that there does exist a need for a significant constitutional modification that aims to make the role of Congress, particularly the Senate, meaningful at early stages of a national commitment to use forces in foreign lands.

It would seem clear that a first step in this direction would be to establish some kind of Presidential commission of the sort that has investigated other major unresolved problems of the society. This commission, perhaps modeled on the National Advisory Commission on Civil Disorders,[45] could study this question of legislative–executive relations in a period of war and come forth with a set of recommendations as to how these relations might be reconstituted for the future.

---

[44] "US Commitments to Foreign Powers," Senate Foreign Relations Committee Hearings, 90th Cong., 1st sess. (1967); see also references cited in n. 42 above.

[45] See *Report of the National Advisory Commission on Civil Disorders*, New York, Bantam, 1968.

There should also be parallel investigation of the relationships between the courts and the executive and the courts and legislature with respect to problems of war and peace. In this latter context, it would also be necessary to reappraise the political-question doctrine that has so far insulated from judicial appraisal most executive action in the area of foreign policy. Again, it is important to note that most of the thinking underlying the grant of broad discretion to the President in matters of foreign policy antedated serious efforts to outlaw non-defensive warfare.

This call for a reexamination of the conception of separation of powers in the war–peace area is prompted by the conviction that we need more effective procedures for regulating national policy. Such a need flows from the urgency of bringing law to bear on governmental behavior in the nuclear age when the margin of error tolerable by even a powerful country has grown very small.[46] There is also, it seems to me, a need demonstrated by the Vietnam war to make law a more significant strategy for the assertion of restraint within domestic structure whenever the government, or a part of it, has made commitments to use force abroad in a manner that arouses large-scale opposition, including moral and legal objection, in American society. The broad constitutional issue at stake involves the extent to which the United States can make democratic ideology meaningful for the real issues of the age by providing machinery and procedures whereby Americans can register legal objection in matters affecting their vital interests. It may not be possible or even desirable to determine foreign policy by the results of public-opinion polls, but it does seem desirable, except in situations of true emergency, to erode the tradition of executive discretion that has grown up over the years. There is, accordingly, a need to promote effective legislative and judicial review of executive policies involving the use of force in international society. The weight of persuasion suggests that these executive policies should be subjected to far greater constitutional restraint in the future than they have been in the past.

---

[46] The consequences of miscalculation in the area of war and peace have become so great that any additional source of restraint on governmental discretion seems constructive. Such a position runs contrary to the thought underlying deterrence theory, which seeks to discourage extreme provocation by credibly threatening unrestrained response. Given the terrible consequence of nuclear devastation, it seems persuasive to me that the need to demonstrate a credible deterrence posture has been greatly exaggerated. In contrast, the dangers associated with unrestraint have been greatly understated. The effort to strengthen the world legal order by containing foreign policy within a legal framework is an effort to reduce somewhat these dangers of unrestraint.

The Vietnam war has itself, of course, given rise to extended arguments about the constitutionality of the American involvement and the legal basis upon which it rests. First, it has been contended that the United States is involved in an undeclared war and that the failure of the executive branch to secure a declaration of war is itself a violation of constitutional expectations. The argument here rests on the notion that the Gulf of Tonkin resolution does not amount either to a declaration of war or to a legislative authorization for a war of the magnitude waged after August 1964, when the resolution was initially adopted. The executive failure, in other words, to obtain a declaration of war is the allegedly unconstitutional act. In opposition to this claim, it can be contended with considerable persuasiveness that a declaration of war might have expanded the war without putting a brake on executive discretion. The presupposition of this argument is that if the executive had sought and received congressional authority to wage war against North Vietnam, then the theretofore limited character of objectives, and means used to obtain those objectives, would have been almost impossible to maintain. A domestic-war psychology would have taken hold in the country transforming dissent into treason or quasi-treason. The President might well have sought and received emergency powers. The war aims of the United States would probably have been expanded. A declaration of war probably would have ended the search for a negotiating settlement on reasonably favorable terms and replaced this search with a determination to win the war by obtaining the collapse or surrender of the National Liberation Front and North Vietnam. An official declaration of war against North Vietnam might also have activated whatever tacit or secret collective security arrangements exist between Communist countries, with the consequence of widening the war to include either or both the Soviet Union and China as active belligerents.[47] Therefore, it is plausible to argue that a declaration of war by the United States might have risked the initiation of World War III without even having established any legislative power of restraint over the exercise of Presidential powers. The President did, it seems plain, have sufficient legislative backing for the Vietnam policies to obtain a declaration of war at virtually any stage of the Vietnam war, at least up to the Presidential reversal of stance on

---

[47] In continuing compliance with the Geneva Accords of 1954, North Vietnam is not, so far as is known, a party to any formal arrangement of collective security with foreign states. See especially Article 19 of the Agreement on the Cessation of Hostilities in Vietnam, in Falk, ed., *The Vietnam War*, p. 550.

March 31, 1968. The power of Congress to declare war would not, it is evident, provide the restraining check on the exercise of executive power that this monograph contends to be necessary.

It does not seem very prudent, in view of this analysis, to argue strongly that the war is unconstitutional simply because there has been a failure to declare war against North Vietnam. And the law has evolved a broad acquiescence in the power of the President to commit the country to the use of force in time of peace. This power, however, has never been tested in circumstances in which it has been alleged that the use of force violates international treaties to which the United States is a party. It is one thing to affirm the power of the President to order the use of force without a declaration of war; it is quite another thing to suggest that this power can be exercised in violation of international law. The former problem needs to be dealt with by the invention of procedures for legislative participation other than a declaration of war, whereas the latter is a more general issue of bringing international law to bear on the policies of government.

There is a second line of argument contending that the Gulf of Tonkin resolution was obtained by deception and that, at most, it indicated congressional authorization of the executive policy in Vietnam up through 1964. The Tonkin setting was a limited one created by the alleged attack by North Vietnamese patrol boats on two American destroyers that were officially described as operating in a peaceful and normal manner on the high seas. The reprisal raids directed against the ports in North Vietnam used by the torpedo boats seemed to be a limited, if disproportionate, act. The setting and language used in the Tonkin resolution do not vindicate the major war effort against North Vietnam that was initiated in February 1965, an effort that has eventually expanded to involve upward of 550,000 American soldiers in Vietnam and to include persistent, widespread bombing of North Vietnam. The Vietnam war since 1965 seems so different from the Tonkin context that there is no real ground for drawing the conclusion that legislative authorization was given in the Tonkin resolution for subsequent war policies of the executive in Vietnam.

The point here is that the Senate did not by the Tonkin resolution authorize subsequent executive policy. This point is rather important because of the effort of the executive to rely on the Tonkin resolution in response to critics in the Senate, especially those who alleged a failure to secure adequate legislative authorization for carrying the Vietnam war to its later stages. I would think that it would have been possible to draw up a presentment of impeachment against the President that relied upon the misuse of the Tonkin resolution, including the impropriety of using the resolution to satisfy the requirements for the balance of power between coordinate branches of government within the United States.

The third and final aspect of the Tonkin argument concerns deception that appears to have surrounded the reporting of the Tonkin incident itself and its presentation to the Senate. There is evidence, originally brought to public attention largely by the columnist I. F. Stone, and later confirmed in Senate hearings held during February 1968, that suggests that the executive branch distorted the Tonkin incident to secure from the Senate the authorization it received for a war buildup.[48] In particular, the aggressiveness of the North Vietnamese torpedo boats was exaggerated, the innocence of the American naval vessels was asserted in a manner that obscured their military role, and there was a failure to disclose the rising executive branch intention, independent of the Tonkin incident, to extend the war to North Vietnam. There was some indication that the executive branch sought an incident of this kind, maybe even to the extent of provoking it, to secure an adequate political pretext that might serve to justify an expansion of the war to North Vietnamese territory. In this context, then, the main argument bears on the misleading way the executive dealt with the Senate. The effect of this alleged deception was substantially to discredit whatever authorization was given the executive by the Tonkin resolution, as well as to establish some basis for charging the executive branch with a separate abuse of its relations with Congress. Here, too, in any strong indictment of the executive management of the war a heavy stress might be expected to be made upon the ways in which Congress was misled, either by an intentional desire to mislead or by a negligent failure to disclose. The emphasis on this level of insufficient communication between the executive and the legislature is justified to some degree by the failure of the executive to clarify the misunderstandings that appear to have emerged in the Tonkin context. It was only as a result of the probing criticism belabored over a period of years by certain Senate and other critics of the war that a reexamination of the facts and explanations underlying the Tonkin grant of legislative authorization took place.

The Tonkin arguments form part of the domestic legal context. These arguments are concerned with the extent to which the executive branch respected constitutional procedures in evolving national

---

[48] See references cited in n. 42, especially Velvel, "The War in Vietnam," n, 38, p. 454.

policies throughout the period of United States involvement in the Vietnam war. The deeper question raised at the outset of this section was whether the constitution itself needs to be reformed to provide for more constructive forms of legislative participation in American foreign policy-making than is presently possible in the area of war and peace. It does not appear desirable to confront the executive branch with the polar options of either declaring war or being completely at liberty to wage war at any level of violence without securing any direct legislative authorization. The policy issue is a broad and deep one and extends to the whole problem of defining legislative responsibility as well as legislative authority in the war–peace area. This kind of definition – or redefinition – would help strengthen domestic pressures growing in support of a more law-ordered foreign policy. Much of the concern with the legal dimension of the Vietnam war involves demonstrating the extent to which war policies affecting the security of the nation and its people are now evolved in a manner that did not assure much attention to counterbalancing forces implicit in the separation-of-powers doctrine that lies at the foundation of the American system of constitutional government.

There is also the question as to whether the President of the United States and, less directly, the coordinate branches of the government are constitutionally empowered to pursue foreign policy in violation of international legal obligations. It should be remembered that the treaty rules to which the United States is subject form part of the supreme law of the land. It should also be remembered that domestic courts are normally expected to apply international law whenever it is relevant to domestic litigation, although if a federal statute is found in conflict with an international treaty, courts have held it to be their duty to apply the more recently incurred obligation. The broad constitutional point here is that it would seem that the President and his leaders are acting unconstitutionally to the extent that they are guilty of a foreign policy that violates the legal obligations to which the United States has given its formal assent. It may be quite reasonable to confer considerable discretion on the executive with respect to interpreting these legal obligations, especially in periods of emergency and urgency, but there seems very little justification in either policy or more formal terms for exempting the executive altogether from this framework of restraint. It is true that any framework of restraint may tend to hamper the discretion and flexibility of executive policy. But restraint is the purpose of all law, and it is certainly the cornerstone of any government that prides itself on being "a government of laws, not men." Legal order is a failure to the extent that it doesn't hamper flexibility. The underlying argument for establishing an effective system of world law is convincing precisely because unhampered national flexibility does not sufficiently assure the survival or welfare of the human race, nor does it give other societies the security they need. The argument that legal restraint is an encumbrance on the discharge of executive functions is always advanced in times of crisis and tension. During the Great Depression of the 1930s in the United States, the argument was often made on behalf of the New Deal administration that the Supreme Court was a serious inconvenience to the country in a period of dire emergency. It seems clear that the Supreme Court was an obstacle in the way of increasingly popular executive responses to the problems of national economic crisis. Efforts were made to undermine the authority of the Supreme Court so as to nullify legislative acts. The notorious court-packing plan of the 1930s was conceived to assure that a majority of New Deal judges would be appointed to the Court, and was narrowly defeated in Congress. In retrospect, it appears that the strength of the constitutional system was demonstrated by the very inconvenience the executive and the public endured as a consequence of judicial obstruction. This affirmation of an experience of constitutional restraint is particularly impressive because the New Deal experiment is looked back upon as very successful, whereas the Court's role is understood as largely reactionary and negative.

In the setting of the Vietnam war, by contrast, the executive is widely held responsible for fostering a regressive kind of policy orientation. In this setting the case is even more persuasive that action by legislative and judicial organs to inconvenience the executive might have worked out to national advantage. For the future, therefore, it seems clear that there is a need to establish a strong basis for implementing this international framework of restraint within the structure of national society; to reach this goal we need to bring the claims asserted on behalf of international law effectively to bear on executive action. This requires, as I have said, new modes of legislative participation that establish new conceptions of legislative authority and responsibility; such a revision also demands a repudiation of the political-questions doctrine that has traditionally insulated executive policy in the war–peace area from judicial review. It now seems desirable to allow questions of executive policy to come before the courts as part of a wider effort to bring law effectively to bear on a government's action with regard to war–peace issues.[49]

---

[49] The right of a citizen to obtain a judicial determination would be an important additional basis for securing governmental compliance with the rules and standards of international law. Such a right would complement other recommended steps to assure an increased role for international law in the foreign policy-making process.

6. *The Nuremberg Arguments:* These legal issues arise from the experience after World War II, at which time leaders of Germany and Japan were held individually accountable for inciting and waging an aggressive war and for specific war crimes. These determinations by duly constituted tribunals were significant because they clearly depended on an acceptance of the legal principle that an individual is not excused from complying with obligations under international law because he is acting in response to superior orders given him by his national government. The war-crimes tribunals, most notably the Nuremberg Tribunal, were exclusively concerned with defendants who occupied positions of leadership and responsibility in the state apparatus. However, the wider logic of Nuremberg extends to embrace all those who knowingly, at any rate, participate in a war effort they have reason to believe violates the restraints of international law. The degree of complicity with such an aggressive war effort needed to establish criminal responsibility has never been established authoritatively. On the other hand, there is no denial of the potential criminal responsibility of individuals other than leaders who participate in an aggressive war. This whole web of connection joining individual responsibility, national citizenship, and responsibility to impose the legal restraints on the use of force on nation-states enjoys a confused and indefinite status at the present time. It is for this reason essential that both scholars and tribunals attempt to clarify the effect of international law on individual responsibility with respect to participating in a war that is or is believed to be in violation of minimum constraints on the use of force.

Two central branches of the Nuremberg Argument can be briefly mentioned. The first branch of the Argument refers to the prosecution of governmental leaders for war crimes. By war crimes in this context, I have in mind three different categories of potential offenses that appear relevant to the Vietnam context. First, what are called "crimes against the peace": namely, the contention that leaders in the United States and South Vietnam are responsible for the commission of aggression against North Vietnam subsequent to February 1965. This argument rests on the assumption that prior support given by the North Vietnamese to the National Liberation Front did not amount to an armed attack that might have legally justified recourse to action in self-defense against North Vietnam. As a consequence, the United States attack upon North Vietnam amounted to an armed attack on that territory of such magnitude that it should be viewed as aggressive war, of the most serious variety. Second, what are called "war crimes": namely, the allegation that some of the battlefield tactics relied upon by the American,

South Vietnamese, and other allied forces involve the systematic commission of specific war crimes. The very existence of a pattern of battlefield behavior incompatible with legal restraint establishes a kind of
responsibility that could be imposed on either the military or civilian
leadership of the country. Search-and-destroy missions, free bombing
zones, forcible transfer of the civilian population, and mistreatment of
prisoners would all appear to provide bases for criminal prosecution
of the political and military leadership of counter-guerrilla forces and
their allies.

The third sort of criminal charge that could be made against the
leadership of the United States and South Vietnam would fall into
the category called "crimes against humanity" and would involve the
contention that the specific violations of the law of war have a cumulative impact that can fairly add up to genocide. That is, systematic
counter-guerrilla tactics that must separate the enemy from the population to achieve military victory require the devastation of territory
where the guerrilla faction exerts influence, as well as the removal of
the population by transfer or death. The accounts of the Vietnam war
increasingly suggest that where the guerrilla efforts of the National
Liberation Front have taken hold the response of the Saigon–United
States forces has been to create a kind of scorched-earth atmosphere
to eliminate the guerrilla efforts. This kind of combat tactics has been
partly responsible for producing over 4,000,000 South Vietnamese
refugees by the beginning of 1968, in a country with a population of
under 16,000,000. This drastic dislocation of the people of the country
has not even led to military success. Therefore, whatever weight might
be given the argument that these tactics are justified by considerations
of military necessity has to be reduced by their failure to facilitate
the attainment of military objectives, and by the overall failure of the
United States military effort in Vietnam. This argument that waging counter-guerrilla warfare beyond a certain threshold of violence
amounts to genocide[50] has been forcefully made by Jean-Paul Sartre.[51]

---

[50] See *Tribunal Russell*, Vol. II, n. 40, pp. 349–68.
[51] There is a common preconception that the crime of genocide occurs only when there is an
effort to kill off an entire race or ethnic group in the manner of "the final solution" devised by
the Nazis to eliminate the Jews. But the definition incorporated in the Genocide Convention,
as approved by the United Nations General Assembly on December 9, 1948, in GA Res. 260
(III) is considerably broader, extending to the pursuit of policies that destroy part of that ethnic
group. Article II of the Convention provides:

Sartre argues that for the regime and its supporters there is no alternative to the destruction of the society and its population where the guerrilla effort enjoys considerable popular support. Although the Russell Tribunal operated on the basis of one-sided adjudicative machinery and procedure, nevertheless it did turn up a good deal of evidence about the manner in which the war was conducted and developed persuasively some of the legal implications it seems reasonable to draw from that war.[52]

The second branch of the Nuremberg Argument involves the defensive appeal to the principles of the Nuremberg judgment to avoid cooperating with the United States government so far as participating in the war effort is concerned. There are many bases for this non-cooperation that rest on rather unaugmented moral arguments that the war is wrong and therefore it is wrong to participate in the war. There are also, however, some legal arguments that seem to be increasingly seriously offered to domestic courts in the United States in various contexts. These arguments suggest various ways in which the Nuremberg judgment becomes relevant. First of all, the defendants may suggest that the legal standards governing the use of force with respect to both the recourse to war and the conduct of it provide an objective and externally verifiable correlative to their moral consciences. Such an attitude seems to accord with the whole tradition of just and unjust wars that has evolved over several centuries of western civilization. This tradition rests on the assumption that neither pacifism nor unqualified deference to the sovereign will follow

---

In the present Convention genocide means any of the following acts committed with intent to destroy, in whole or in part, a national, ethnical, racial or religious group, as such:

(a) Killing members of the group;
(b) Causing serious bodily or mental harm to members of the group;
(c) Deliberately inflicting on the group conditions of life calculated to bring about its physical destruction in whole or in part;
(d) Imposing measures intended to prevent births within the group;
(e) Forcibly transferring children of the group to another group.

For further elaboration of the Convention, see Raphael Lemkin, "Genocide as a Crime Under International Law," *American Journal of International Law*, 41 (1947), 145–51.

In the Vietnam War the use of bombing tactics and cruel weapons against the civilian population appears to me to establish a *prima facie* case of genocide against the United States. By the Convention, genocide can be committed in a condition of either war or peace.

52 The full record of proceedings is now available in a convenient French edition and warrants careful study. See *Tribunal Russell*.

from Christian morality. Some wars are just and other wars are unjust, and in cases of confusion it is up to the conscience of the individual to try to mediate between these two moral categories. The role of a domestic court should be to assess whether a particular assertion of individual conscience is in good faith, and whether, if it is, there exists some reasonably objective standard that can be verified by evidence external to the beliefs of the individual upon which to rest assertions of conscience. International law provides such a useful yardstick by which to measure claims of conscience. The Nuremberg conception reinforces this legal dimension of the problem by its stress on the need for individuals to find a way of determining which of two conflicting sources of obligation they are bound to uphold: obligations emanating from national governments, or obligations emanating from the perceived requirements of international law. The different ways in which the arguments about the individual's right to establish that the US role in the Vietnam war is illegal have come up in domestic courts are illustrated in recent litigation: Eminente, Mitchell, Luftig, Mora, Berrigan, and Spock.[53] These cases all involve individuals who in one way or another regarded the United States involvement in the Vietnam war as unjust and felt that their individual obligations as human beings took precedence over their duty to obey the government or to respect its laws. Many of these cases arise when individuals refuse to be drafted. Cases may also arise when an individual, subsequent to induction, refuses to obey his military commander either by declining to train soldiers for activity or duty in Vietnam or by not following an order to report for duty in Vietnam. Analogous cases furthermore can arise if someone such as Dr. Spock or Rev. William Sloane Coffin counsels individuals not to cooperate with the draft – when, in the language of the selective service statute, an individual aids and abets draft avoidance. The Spock prosecution was based on a conspiracy theory – cooperation among the defendants to counsel draft avoidance.

In these cases that have come before the domestic courts of the United States, there has been a consistent refusal to adjudicate the substantive issues posed by arguments of international law. The courts have held, with the partial exception of the Levy case, that the legality of

[53] Eminente v. Johnson, 361 F. 2d 73 (D.C. Cir. 1966), cert. den., 385 U.S. 929 (1966); Luftig v. McNamara, 373 F. 2d 664 (D.C. Cir. 1967), cert. den., sub. nom. Mora v. McNamara, 389 U.S. 934 (1967); Mitchell v. McNamara, 386 U.S. 972 (1967). See, in general, briefs submitted on behalf of Dr. Benjamin Spock and Michael Farber in U.S. v. Coffin and others, Criminal No. 68-1-F., US District Court, Boston, Mass., 1968.

the war and its conduct are matters beyond judicial appreciation, that these issues are embedded in foreign policy and must be taken up, if at all, within the executive branch. The Levy case, in the context of a court-martial, did permit the nominal presentation of evidence designed to show that *the conduct* of the war is illegal, although it did not consider the legality of the underlying involvement of the United States in the Vietnam war (see the Geneva and Charter Arguments). The military court rejected Levy's contention of illegality and went on to find him guilty, and has sentenced him to three years in prison.

As I have observed earlier, the reassertion of an active judicial role in this area would appear to be a creative contribution to the doctrine of separation of powers in the war–peace context. It appears increasingly unfair and unfortunate to require individuals to participate in a war that by reason of conscience they object to. In addition, those who seek access to the courts in order to test the legality of the war – for instance, by refusing to pay all or part of their income taxes – are also, it would seem, entitled to a substantive determination of the issue. These citizens are, in effect, seeking to enforce the wider claims of the international community against their own government. It remains extremely important to try to reinforce this link between the individual and world society by allowing, and even requiring, domestic courts to assume an active role in the process of confining the scope of governmental action to those limits that are internationally permissible. Such a willingness to adjudicate these questions would not doom the domestic legal and political system. On the contrary, the availability of procedures to test the legality of governmental conduct is essential to the health of a system that claims to rest upon the exercise of political power within the limits set by law. The only convincing reason to refuse adjudication of such substantive issues is in order to insulate the exercise of power, however arbitrary, from serious legal challenge. To disrupt an "illegal" war, if that would be the consequence of judicial inquiry, would be to serve the national interest if adherence to law is itself to be preferred over the arbitrary assertion of power. Such a result is unlikely to occur unless there were many other social, moral, and political forces opposing the course of involvement in a war. Of course, it is likely that there would be military and industrial leaders and others who would bitterly oppose any judicial pronouncement that might inhibit the continuation of an "illegal" war, but there would always be groups unwilling to govern in accordance with a framework of legal restraint. This monograph is essentially a proposal that the risks of law and order be taken in world affairs as surely as they are taken for granted in domestic affairs.

III CONCLUSION

The Vietnam war has demonstrated the vulnerability of the United States political system to a prolonged involvement in a foreign conflict perceived as illegal by a significant segment of the population. It seems important to learn from this experience and to discourage its repetition. The constitutional process needs reform and reorientation in the area of war and peace. In the executive branch, it appears important, as we have suggested, to introduce the guidance of law earlier in the policy-forming process and from a position higher in the bureaucratic structure.

The underlying integrity of the constitutional system of the United States depends on the continuous implementation of the idea of a separation of powers among the three principal branches of government. The Vietnam war has demonstrated persuasively that this balancing process of government, resting on the notion of separated and divided powers, is no longer operating successfully in the area of war and peace. For this reason it seems very important to reconsider ways in which the legislative branch can participate more fully in the evolution and authorization of foreign policy involving the use of force. It would not contribute to a solution of this problem to define more rigorously the conditions under which the use of force by the government must be preceded by or accompanied by a declaration of war. There may be a need for joint commissions of inquiry and periodic authorizations and review procedures that would raise questions about the continuation of any particular use of force when the international community had not itself provided the nation with either a prohibition or an authorization. Part of the position taken in this monograph is that individuals need to be provided with legal procedures to uphold dictates of conscience when these dictates collide with the will of the government. For this reason there should exist some opportunity to challenge various obligations to participate in a war deemed unjust and illegal, through recourse to courts. Additionally, it is important that judges become persuaded of their competence and responsibility to restrain the execution of government policy by either executive or legislative institutions if such policy is found to exceed the boundaries set by international law.[54] The Vietnam war has given rise to an expression of widespread cosmopolitan attachments in the sense that many American citizens have felt it more important to uphold international

---

[54] Such a view is endorsed by the most conservative elements of the legal community when the question in controversy is whether the foreign expropriation of alien property conforms with international law. See any of the extensive literature associated with the Sabbatino controversy, e.g., Eugene F. Mooney, *Foreign Seizures – Sabbatino and the Act of State Doctrine*, Lexington, University of Kentucky Press, 1967; see esp. Bibliography, pp. 161–64.

obligations involving restraints on the use of force than to support their own national government in its pursuit of policy.[55] In effect, we may be witnessing a redefinition of the meaning of citizenship in the contemporary world, a redefinition in which the priorities of a citizen are reshaped in such a way as to ensure popular insistence upon the maintenance of a framework of restraint for his own government.[56] Such a development would be very encouraging. It would provide a way in which the sovereign state might be curbed, or at least inhibited, in the use of its military power by action taken within its own political structure. Such efforts, leading to restraint imposed from within, might create the sort of climate that would support transfers of sovereign authority from the national level to the regional and global levels and help the international community build more centralized structures of control over the affairs of state.

In moving toward the end of the Vietnam war, it seems important to reorient American foreign policy in a direction that avoids either the pseudo-globalism of neo-Wilsonism or the qualified isolationism of neo-Kennanism.[57] By neo-Wilsonism I intend to refer to the policies that have been associated especially with Dean Rusk and W. W. Rostow throughout the Vietnam war.[58] These policies suggest that the United States has a unilateral responsibility and prerogative to establish ideologically self-serving global rules of order as part of its mission to bring into being a peaceful world. It is the unilateral quality of the partisan political use of force that appears to be the most objectionable formal feature of neo-Wilsonism. It is also somewhat doubtful whether the United States is in any position to exercise moral leadership within an international setting so long as its own society is subject to such great discord and distress. Therefore, it does not seem appropriate for the United States to act against what it perceives to be aggression except in situations where there has been a direct military attack mounted across an international boundary of the Korean type or in situations where international institutions have genuinely authorized the use of defensive force.

---

[55] These attachments are "cosmopolitan" in the sense that they reflect the acceptance of universal standards and procedures impartially construed. At the same time such attachments are "nationalistic" in the sense of favoring a course of action that is in the best interest of the state given the belief that national adherence to law in foreign affairs promotes national security in the nuclear age.

[56] For fuller discussion, see Chapter 23 in Richard Falk, *The Status of Law in International Society*, Princeton, Princeton University Press, 1970.

[57] For a fuller discussion, see *ibid.*, Chapter 22.

[58] For the specification of the Wilsonian ideas of national self-interest in world affairs, see Arno J. Mayer, *Wilson v. Lenin – Political Origins of the New Diplomacy 1917–1918*, New Haven, Yale University Press, 1959; N. Gordon Levin, Jr., *Woodrow Wilson and World Politics*, New York, Oxford University Press, 1968.

Neo-Kennanism, in contrast, is a reaction against moralistic and legalistic rhetoric that one often finds associated with the neo-Wilsonian position. A neo-Kennanist argues that it is important to remove self-serving rationalizations of foreign policy and examine in each situation the real national interest of the United States in a more detached fashion. It would seem clear that when this neo-Kennanist perspective is allowed to operate, the United States has very few interests of the traditional sovereign sort that would warrant the use of military force outside the western hemisphere or in the defense of Europe. Therefore, neo-Kennanism leads to or implies a partial withdrawal from participation in world affairs. Senator Fulbright has been the most prominent advocate of a neo-Kennanist position, along with George Kennan himself.[59]

The inadequacy I find with the neo-Kennanist position – although I find much of it persuasive in its role as a criticism of the neo-Wilsonist pretensions – is that the quality of international society at present is such that it would be undesirable for the United States to withdraw to a position of defending only its immediate and generally perceivable interests. In fact, there is a need for American foreign policy to find a new normative foundation for the assertion of influence and military power throughout the world to replace the present combination of ideological resistance to Communism and geopolitical resistance to the expansion of the Soviet and Chinese spheres of influence. The Vietnam war represents, it seems to me, the culmination and the termination of a tradition of foreign policy based on these considerations of ideology and geopolitics. This normative foundation should embody a world-order orientation – one that is sensitive to regional and world-community procedures for authorizing collective measures and that defines permissible recourse to international force by reference to treaty standards of prohibition directed at intervention in internal affairs and at non-defensive recourses to military action. I think that it is probably possible to conclude that direct military aggression of the type used in Korea is unlikely to be repeated in the context of east–west relations in the foreseeable future. However, it is equally plausible to anticipate considerable revolutionary violence throughout Asia and Africa that will bear on the relative degree of influence possessed by these competing centers of world power and guidance. The United States has played a largely counterrevolutionary role in world society since World War II, beginning in Greece and Turkey with the Truman Doctrine and culminating in its major involvement in the Vietnam war. The original basis for a counterrevolutionary posture was created by a very expansionist mood on the part of Stalinist

---

[59]   E.g., J. William Fulbright, *The Arrogance of Power*, New York, Vintage, 1966.

Russia immediately after World War II, a mood that caused concern because of the weakness of the western European countries during that period. This weakness was made more serious both because of the apparent unity of the world Communist parties and because of large internal Communist parties in France and Italy. The Soviet Union's relation to eastern Europe is also counterrevolutionary, reaching a new highwater mark through its leadership of the anti-Dubcek intervention in Czechoslovakia in August of 1968.

The United States needs a new foreign policy to deal with revolutionary violence, a foreign policy that avoids unilateral military commitments to the constituted governments of other countries, especially when those governments are themselves imposed by external political forces on a society that is not susceptible to governance by such a regime. These sorts of conflicts should be left alone by the United States. The exception should involve occasions on which the host government appeals through an international institution for external military support and that appeal is endorsed by that institution. Even this kind of procedure is not secure against abuse. It is quite possible for the political vagaries of international organizations to produce legitimacy on behalf of a government that is oppressing its population by terroristic means. Despite this danger, however, it seems clearly preferable to risk the uncertainties of supranational consensus than to rest world order upon the claim of special imperial prerogatives by the United States or any other sovereign state.[60] It has become evident, in any event, that the domestic political system of the United States is not able to sustain support for such a foreign policy without forfeiting both order and liberty within its domestic setting.[61] It should also be clear that the United States military capability is not suited to waging successfully this kind of counter-guerrilla struggle when the scale of the undertaking is substantial. International lawyers could have a major role to play by clarifying the consequences to the world of the choices that can be made with respect to foreign policy in the future. These choices can be highlighted by a careful analysis of the policy implications of the opposing sets of legal arguments that have been

---

[60] For some consideration, see George Liska, *Imperial America – The International Politics of Primacy*, Baltimore, Johns Hopkins University Press, 1967; Ronald Steel, *Pax Americana*, New York, Viking Press, 1967.

[61] It is worth noting that Soviet citizens are reported to have demonstrated in Moscow against the Soviet military intervention in Czechoslovakia during August 1968. Although the demonstration is reported to have been quickly suppressed, the principal participants made defiant statements after their release. Domestic pressures against the excesses of one's own government appear to be growing throughout those national societies that have been modernized, although the right of opposition continues to be severely curtailed in many principal states of the world. For a brief account of the Soviet demonstration, see *New York Times*, September 1, 1968, Sec. IV, 3.

raised in the Vietnam war. These arguments suggest some of the problems
that exist as a result of a legal superstructure's being designed for a world that
had neither nuclear weapons nor large-scale and widespread revolutionary
violence. It seems important in light of these developments in military technology and in the pursuit of domestic political objectives to rethink the legal
basis for controlling violence in situations such as the Vietnam war. A central
function of law is to help structure the expectations of national governments
and their populations. This is a time when it is important to try to restructure expectations about what is permissible and impermissible in the context
of a category of conflict of which the Vietnam war is the most prominent
instance to date. Such a restructuring of legal expectations demands not only
the assessment of the legal standards governing national behavior, but – even
more importantly – a sense of how the procedures of national governments
and international institutions may bring these standards to bear more effectively both throughout such a conflict and at pre-violent stages of conflict.

PART II

WAR AND WAR CRIMES

"Appropriating Tet," *Massachusetts Review*, 29, 3 (Fall 1988), 391–420.

"Son My: War Crimes and Individual Responsibility," *Toledo Law Review* (Fall–Winter 1971), 21–41.

"The Cambodian Operation and International Law," *American Journal of International Law*, 65, 1 (Jan. 1971), 1–25.

6

Appropriating Tet

I guess information ricochet is getting more rapid.

Tom Wolfe[1]

In Vietnam there was a war inside a country in which one side, not the other, was entirely paid, recruited, etc.

Daniel Ellsberg[2]

The Tet Offensive more than twenty years ago was, most agree, a decisive moment in the American involvement in the Vietnam War. But the interpretation of that decisiveness remains murky, obscure, contested. In this essay, my attempt is to explore Tet as a symbolic event, to describe varying interpretations of its military and political impact upon the Vietnam War, and to suggest its legacy for United States Government policy and practice with regard to armed intervention in the Third World.

I POINTS OF DEPARTURE

No one has yet addressed the life history of international symbolic events that resonate in the public mind: Munich, Pearl Harbor, Yalta, Auschwitz, Hiroshima. Each name conjures up its own images. The appropriation of the name to impart a particular lesson of history can sometimes shape, even deform, public debate, as well as help establish the societal boundaries of acceptable belief. Relying on symbolic utterance to form policy in place of argument and analysis is a way of closing off the mind to the complexity

Prepared for "Tet Plus Twenty: The Legacy of the Vietnam War" Conference, Five, College Program in Peace and World Security Studies, Hampshire College, February 19–21, 1988.
[1] Interview, *Rolling Stone*, 20th Anniversary Issue, 1987, p. 219.
[2] Interview, *Rolling Stone*, 20th Anniversary Issue, 1987, p. 221.

of reality, including the exclusion of possibly more constructive alternative courses of action.

The Tet Offensive – or simply Tet – is one such symbolic and paradoxical event. But, unlike most of the others, its meaning remains as obscure and controverted as the war of which it was a part. Revealingly, Norman Podhoretz and Noam Chomsky, in the course of comments on the occasion of the tenth anniversary of the fall of Saigon, invoked Tet for their own contradictory reconstructions of what the Vietnam War signified. For Podhoretz, Tet was the moment when the public, Congress, and the media gave up on the war ("Only after the 1968 Tet offensive did that support begin to ebb as people felt the war was being lost, or simply not winnable").[3] For Chomsky, Tet is invoked not for the event itself, but as a disclosure of American reliance on unrestrained violence in the aftermath of the surprise attack upon US positions ("After the murderous post-Tet pacification campaigns and other atrocities in Laos and Cambodia").[4] And so it goes, to recall Vonnegut's world-weary refrain in *Slaughterhouse Five*.

In the symbolic landscape of Tet, the secondary related symbolic presence is Dienbienphu, the decisive Vietminh victory in 1954 that led directly to defeat for French colonial rule in Indochina. There is an initial disposition to seek the equivalent of Dienbienphu in the second Indochina war to signal the American defeat. Certainly, Tet, especially at the time of its occurrence, was commonly and insistently linked up with Dienbienphu in the political imagination, and as insistently de-linked by those who wanted the war to go on. Also, there was a literalism about Dienbienphu that preoccupied and misled war planners and seems to have been exploited brilliantly by the Vietnamese adversary, setting up the siege of Khe Sanh weeks earlier as an apparent decisive testing-ground, diverting American troops from other war zones, preoccupying the policy-makers with the prospect of a literal repetition (the siege of an American stronghold leading to surrender and a loss of commitment to the war) and thereby adding to the surprise and lack of preparation for the actuality of the Tet Offensive. Weeks after Tet, American air power broke the siege at Khe Sanh. There is no indication that the North Vietnamese ever attached much strategic significance to this isolated garrison town in the northwestern part of South Vietnam, but the Americans did!

And, then, there are other symbolic and sometimes romanticized military events that invite comparison. The Battle of Algiers is an obvious one, as it shared with Tet the sense of the diehards, that the French political leadership

[3] Norman Podhoretz, "Impotence," *Granta*, 15 (1985), 125.
[4] Noam Chomsky, "Dominoes," *Granta*, 15 (1985), 131.

misunderstood their own success.[5] John Talbott assesses a relevant handwritten memorandum on Algeria composed by General Charles de Gaulle in 1959 on the day after Christmas:

> He reviewed the advantages the French held over the revolutionaries: crushing military superiority; officers and noncommissioned officers "incomparably better trained than the illiterates of the insurrection"; a much lower casualty rate; a vastly superior propaganda apparatus; an influence in world politics beyond comparison with that of the FLN. "It is perfectly true," he went on, "that our crushing military superiority is putting an end to the greater part of the [guerrilla] bands. But, morally and politically, it is less than ever toward us that Algerian Muslims are turning. To claim that they are French, or that they want to be, is a dreadful mockery . . . It is simply mad to believe that our forced domination has any future whatsoever."[6]

This excerpt from De Gaulle's reflections helps set the stage for an exploration of the American presence in Vietnam, and for a rendering of who won what at Tet, as well as for a broader realization of the cruel fatuousness of the view that by military means the United States (or France or the Soviet Union) can always work its bloody will against the weight of nationalist tendencies in the Third World.

There is also the elusive connection between a battle and a war that Tolstoy depicts memorably in *War and Peace*. In defending one's own sacred territory, losing battles may be the gateway to victory. Tolstoy in one of his excursions into the philosophy of history notes this:

> But then, in 1812, the French gain a victory near Moscow. Moscow is taken and after that, with no further battles, it is not Russia that ceases to exist, but the French army of six hundred thousand, and then Napoleonic France itself . . . The period of the campaign of 1812 from the Battle of Borodino to the expulsion of the French proved that the winning of a battle does not produce a conquest and is not even an invariable indication of conquest, it proved that the force which decides the fate of peoples lies not in the conquerors, not even in armies or battles, *but in something else.*

In examining Tet, the search to identify this "something else" may help us gain insight into its significance or, in a more totalist or Tolstoyan spirit, its significance.

---

[5] Cf. John Talbott, *The War Without a Name: France in Algeria 1954–1962* (New York: Knopf, 1980), esp. pp. 78–89.

[6] *Ibid.*, p. 153 (emphasis added).

As events in Central America, southern Africa, and Asia suggest, revolutionary nationalist movements and imperial interventions are very much part of our world. In certain respects the Iran–contra disclosures added yet another chapter in the unfinished, written, and rewritten story of Vietnam, as much fictionalized in the annals of foreign policy as in the stream of films and novels that seek to transmit the experience of Vietnam in the form of a particular message to Americans, for America. The reality of Vietnam, of course, transcends and eludes these many interpretive forays, but at their best insights and some greater appreciation can emerge.

My outlook is sympathetic with Gloria Emerson's important insistence that the essential failure of the American presence in Vietnam was its total impotence, regardless of motive: "[E]ven the most well-meaning plans and gestures did not help the Vietnamese, since, nearly always, it was we who had injured them and made them helpless." As she put it, at once, clearly and eloquently, "But so huge, so rich, so powerful were the foreigners, their presence became a poison in the Vietnamese blood."[7] The armed resistance movement was one way of expelling this poison from the body politic of Vietnam. It was not quick or pretty but, in time, it got the job done.

"With 1968, a new phase is now starting. We have reached an important point when the end begins to come into view." These words were spoken by General William C. Westmoreland, then commander of US forces in Vietnam, in an address back in the United States on November 21, 1967. Following the expected completion of the current phase Westmoreland went on with his notorious prediction that victory would ensue. According to Westmoreland, we would shortly "see the conclusion of our plan to weaken the enemy and strengthen our friends until we become progressively superfluous. The object will be to show the world that guerrilla war and invasion do not pay as a new means of Communist aggression."[8]

Against this background of American optimism and official reassurance, the extreme shock of the Tet Offensive was registered as political trauma. In the mainstream literature this attitude is expressed by the phrase "then came Tet" that one finds repeated over and over again in textbook discussions of the Vietnam War to express an assault on expectations and attitudes that was as harsh as that on battlefield positions.[9] Frequently quoted, also, as an indication

[7] Gloria Emerson, *Winners and Losers* (New York: Random House, 1976), p. 242.
[8] In G. Porter, ed., *Vietnam: A History in Documents* (Pine Plains, NY: Earl M. Coleman Enterprises, 1979), pp. 352–53.
[9] E.g. Stephen F. Ambrose, *Rise to Globalism*, 4th ed. (New York: Penguin, 1985), p. 228; Loven Baritz, *Backfire: A History of How American Culture Led Us into Vietnam and Made Us Fight the Way We Did* (New York: Morrow, 1985), p. 179.

of the impact of Tet, was the reaction of CBS anchorman Walter Cronkite, who exclaimed, "What the hell is going on? I thought we were winning the war." Lyndon Johnson recognized Cronkite as a barometer of public opinion, saying privately at the time, "Well, if I've lost Walter, I've lost middle America."[10]

Often left out of account is the degree to which the waning of popular support for the war in 1967 encouraged a campaign orchestrated from the Oval Office to rebuild public confidence designed to convince citizens and Congress that the war policies were, despite appearances, moving toward success at an impressive rate. And here Lyndon Johnson's sense of American political culture was on target, as America can be made to swallow an ugly war with promises of "victory," especially if the process does not intrude too greatly on the normalcy of domestic life. And so the need to build confidence on the home front by exaggerating battlefield prospects also created a vulnerability of the sort exposed by the Tet Offensive, whether knowingly or fortuitously by the timing of the Vietcong/DRV attacks. The dynamics of hopes raised can quickly shift to the dynamics of hopes crushed.

II THE IMPACT OF TET: CONTENDING IMAGES

What, then, was Tet? As decisive, spectacular battles go, it was not very impressive by the criterion of battlefield numbers. Fewer than 100,000 troops of the National Liberation Front and North Vietnam participated; no permanent shift of territorial control was achieved, not even the retention by the attacking forces of any position captured. And yet in its way it was a spectacular moment in military history. In a 48-hour period starting on January 29, 1968, Communist forces launched military attacks on five of South Vietnam's six major cities, on 36 of its 44 provincial capitals, on at least 64 district capitals, and on more than 50 villages.[11] A surprise, coordinated attack on this scale by an enemy supposedly on the ropes was by its very character an extraordinary logistical feat without precedent in the history of revolutionary warfare. Much of the visual damage to the American war effort was done in Saigon, especially by a group of NLF fighters who entered US Embassy grounds, where they remained in partial control for more than six hours, until they were killed. Tan Son Nhut Airport, the presidential palace, and the staff headquarters of South Vietnamese military forces were other prominent targets in Saigon. The ancient city of Hue was invaded and held by 7,500 troops for over three

---

[10]   As quoted in Barbara Tuchman, *The March of Folly* (New York: Ballantine, 1984), p. 35.
[11]   George C. Herring, *America's Longest War*, 2nd ed. (New York: Knopf, 1986), p. 189.

weeks. In the end all Communist forces were dislodged. Losses during the Tet Offensive were definitely heavy, although estimates of Communist casualties may have been inflated. Western experts accept these figures for the period: 3,895 US soldiers killed, plus 214 Australian, New Zealand, South Korean, and Thais killed, 4,954 Republic of Vietnam killed, and 58,373 forces of the NLF/DRV (Democratic Republic of Vietnam) killed.[12] In addition, at least 14,300 Vietnamese civilians were killed. In the military encounter, then, the attacking side suffered seven times as many fatalities, including a large proportion of its overall strength and many of its most experienced cadres, especially in the southern, agriculturally rich part of the country. And to begin with the NLF/DRV were greatly outnumbered in the war. At the time of Tet there were 492,000 American soldiers in the country, augmented by 626,000 South Vietnamese and another 61,000 troops belonging to the armed forces of Asian allies.[13] As well, during Tet the South Vietnamese military units generally fought well, better than expected, and the civilian population revealed no disposition to rise up and welcome the attackers as liberators. In fact, mounting the offensive during the Tet holidays might have had an alienating effect on overall Vietnamese attitudes in the South, as did, most certainly, the mass execution in Hue of alleged civilian collaborators with the Saigon government. I shall return to these dimensions of Tet later.

It remains intriguing to speculate about why such a defeat as Tet could have been transmuted into a decisive victory for NLF/DRV forces, what is described in the literature on the war as "the Johnson administration's Dienbienphu." Recalling Dienbienphu even in this restricted sense is, at once, unavoidable and misleading. Unavoidable because the French, like the Americans, had been officially presented as "winning" the war until General Giap in 1954 laid siege on a French garrison trapped in the relatively unimportant and geographically remote town of Dienbienphu. Also, the Americans, who were by then paying most of the costs of the French war, resisted, but barely, a French midnight appeal in 1954 to enter their war directly by mounting air strikes, possibly with atomic bombs to be used against the entrenched Viet Minh forces in the surrounding area. But the comparison between Dienbienphu and Tet is misleading, as well. The French were outnumbered and outgunned at Dienbienphu, and the siege led to a surrender. And the surrender led to an ending of the war in a matter of weeks, culminating in negotiations that produced the Geneva Accords in June 1954. In contrast, Tet produced no

---

[12] Don Oberdorfer, *Tet* (Garden City, NY: Doubleday, 1971), figures given on unnumbered dedication page; see Herring, *America's Longest War*, pp. 190–91.

[13] Oberdorfer, *Tet*, p. 8; on military capabilities of North Vietnam, p. 53.

American surrender, and the narrow battlefield result could certainly, but not necessarily, be viewed as an American victory. True, Tet induced a change of political leadership in the United States, but arguably the shift from Johnson to Nixon included a new and stronger resolve to escalate American involvement in Vietnam and find a way to prevail; Nixon's electoral promise of "a secret plan" to end the Vietnam War was really a scenario for renewing the war effort based on a proposed shift of tactics and a concealed reassertion of maximal goals. Many commentators reject my argument, contending that everything after Tet was a wind-down, and the only issues left were matters on the pace of disengagement and the maintenance of appearance.[14] In fact, the Vietnam War went on for seven years after Tet, the negotiations subsequently initiated in Paris during 1968 were protracted and inconclusive, and it remains unclear (and perhaps indeterminate) as to whether, without the immobilizing effects of the Watergate disclosures upon Nixon's capacity for action, the war would have ended as it did in 1975. There is no reason to doubt Nixon's resolve to keep the Thieu government in power even if it meant an abrupt American reentry into the war in the form of highly punitive aerial bombardment. Few to this day realize that American casualties were greater in the period after Tet than they were in the preceding six war years.

Should we, then, call Tet the Dienbienphu of the Vietnam War? Should it even be understood as a turning-point in American involvement? Unlike most other decisive battles, the ramifications of Tet remain difficult to establish even if we consider only its effects on the character of American involvement in Vietnam. We tend to distort the Vietnam War by treating it primarily as an American experience whether we think of ourselves as hawks or doves. But this Americanization of the war's importance is itself part of the imperial mindset. Tet was and remains overwhelmingly a Vietnamese experience – as noted in the grisly statistics of war, the dying and most of the grieving were done in Vietnam and by Vietnamese, and it was their cities, their lunar new year, and their ancient buildings and traditions that were the scene and subject of the Tet Offensive.

Yes, as Americans, we are bound to emphasize the importance of Tet for us. If the imperial tendency to appropriate the event is indulged for purposes of reflection, it then becomes possible, even healthy, to learn from the experience, provided we understand that our relationship to the overall experience was necessarily marginal, partial, and of dubious legitimacy, as compared to that of the Vietnamese.

---

[14] Such analysis is well stated in Jonathan Schell, *The Real War* (New York: Pantheon, 1987), esp. pp. 30–31.

The American debate about Tet continues. It remains a mirror for restating opposed preconceptions and validating contending ideological biases. In effect we look at Tet and see various partisan images of ourselves, and yet seek to foster an impression of sorting out what happened in an objective, realistic manner that yields a coherent interpretation. And, of course, there is the further complexity of time – Tet in 1968 versus Tet as understood in 1988. Our interpretative agenda shifts, and putting Tet on the agenda is itself a kind of political statement. There has developed a tendency by those who look back on the Vietnam War as a whole to regard Tet as a milestone along the way, not as a decisive turning-point or watershed. Nevertheless, reactions by American policy-makers and others remain instructive.

Take, Robert Komer, for instance, the flamboyant head of the pacification program directed at the countryside (aptly known as "Blowtorch Bob," a nickname that well conveys his gruesome enthusiasm for "the other war," that of pacification), who gives his assessment in the following vivid language:

> What really surprised us about Tet – and boy it was a surprise, lemme tell you, I was there at Westy's elbow – was that they abandoned the time-tested Mao rural strategy where the guerrillas slowly strangle the city, and only at the end do they attack the seat of imperial power directly . . . They abandoned the countryside where they were doing very well, and boy did they get creamed in the city . . . I always felt that the Tet offensive was a desperate gamble on the part of Hanoi. We had a startling success in pacification after the Tet offensive because the enemy had sacrificed the core of his guerrilla movement. After Tet it really became an NVA war.[15]

Or consider Colonel Harry Summers' widely studied strategic analysis of the Vietnam War as a military experience:

> The North Vietnamese offensive was a resounding tactical failure. They expended what one analyst described as about half of their entire strength – over 100,000 fighting men – without any apparent gain.[16]

According to such readings, Tet presented the United States with "a golden opportunity" to gain the decisive advantage in the war. This opportunity never materialized due to "wavering" in Washington and an alleged general misconstruction of the post-Tet true correlation of forces in Vietnam.

---

[15] Komer Interview, in Kim Willenson, *The Bad War: An Oral History of the Vietnam War* (New York: New American Library, 1987), p. 95.

[16] Harry G. Summers, Jr., *On Strategy: A Critical Analysis of the Vietnam War* (Navato, CA: Presidio Press, 1982), p. 184.

Those who promote this line of interpretation are not oblivious to the strategic dimension of Tet, which is understood to center upon Washington and American public opinion. There are various ways of explaining why Washington, Johnson, the media, and the American people reacted as they did. Komer reflects a consensus among policy-makers when he makes this assessment: "Now I wasn't born yesterday, and I knew in one day that whatever had happened out there, Tet had changed absolutely everything in Washington."[17] Similarly, Colonel Summers realizes that something profound was changed by Tet: "With this disastrous tactical defeat North Vietnam struck what was to prove a fatal blow against our center of gravity – the alliance between the United States and South Vietnam." Of course, in the background is the Clausewitzian understanding of war as a form of politics. Tet induced a split in the ranks of the war-makers. It divided those who believed Tet to have been a successful blow against the American war because it provided evidence that war could not be won for an acceptable cost and those who believed Tet produced a mental breakdown in Washington by somehow confusing most political leaders, and making them incapable of realizing that Tet made it far easier than previously to reach American goals in Vietnam.

General Westmoreland has been a champion of this latter line. As he puts it in his memoirs, no one "foresaw that, in terms of public opinion, press and television would transform what was undeniably a catastrophic military defeat for the enemy into a presumed debacle for Americans and South Vietnamese." Properly perceived, Tet should have been perceived as a last-gasp desperate gamble by a defeated enemy, comparable in Westmoreland's view to Nazi Germany's effort in the Battle of the Bulge at the close of World War II, a prelude to defeat that reflected the true military outcome. But instead Tet was treated as if it were a kind of replay of Dienbienphu, an unexpectedly formidable challenge by the militarily weaker side that finally broke the political will to persist on the part of the stronger side. Westmoreland, seeking in part to justify his own pre-Tet optimism about the war, even in retrospect, berates his adversary for their foolishness: "Why would the enemy give away his major advantage," he asks, "which was his ability to be elusive and avoid heavy casualties?" Such a rhetorical question is hardly rhetorical in light of the outcome of the war. If the war was correctly analyzed as being won or lost in the minds of the Washington elite, then the Tet costs for Hanoi were in

---

[17] Willenson, *The Bad War*, p. 97. Komer's pet explanation is the mistake of using Tet as an occasion to recommend a call-up strategic reserve and an additional request for 206,000 troops: "The goddamn Chiefs of Staff. Wheeler's the evil genius of the Vietnam war in my judgment" (p. 97).

military terms modest if assessed by their dramatic effects on American attitudes. And Westmoreland explains the lack of full readiness for the Tet attacks by claiming that he never suspected that the North Vietnamese and NLF would so odiously offend the Vietnamese people by mounting their offensive in the midst of a sacred holiday that had been declared by both sides to be a time of truce.[18]

There is an element of moral absurdity here. Westmoreland, it should be remembered, was associated with heartless war-fighting tactics that tended to obliterate the distinction between civilian and combatant, between those on our side and Vietnamese society as a whole. For him to pass judgment on the moral propriety of the Tet Offensive is an instance of extreme hypocrisy. And yet Westmoreland may have unwittingly correctly identified a long-term weakness of the Tet strategy, not in his analysis of the war, but so far as its bearing on the peace that followed upon the eventual North Vietnamese victory. As we will consider later, the haunting possibility exists that the North by its tactics could have prevailed over the Americans in a heroic struggle and yet still manage to lose out as liberators with their own people.

Perhaps the most self-serving of all American readings of Tet is that of Richard Nixon. In his book *No More Vietnams* Nixon pushes the logic of the Komer/Westmoreland position to its full policy conclusions. He sees Tet not as defeating Johnson's approach to the war, but as creating a real opportunity to win the war in a manner that would be acceptable to the American people. In essence, Nixon believes that Tet created an extraordinary opportunity to move the strategy of American war-fighting from attrition to pacification. In his words, "the decisive defeat of the 1968 Tet Offensive changed the balance of power in South Vietnam."[19] With the enemy infrastructure decimated and exposed, Tet so thinned the NLF presence in the countryside as to provide a basis for successful pacification managed by American advisors. At the same time, the military campaign could be carried forward by primary reliance on modernized South Vietnamese troops supported in battle by uncontested high-tech US air and naval power. The additional Nixon tactic was to extend the war zone to hit cross-border sanctuaries and logistical supply lines. Nixon definitely believed that his approach was succeeding in the post-Tet years but, as with Westmoreland before him, that American political ineptitude managed to produce a defeat in the context of real victory. For Nixon, "Pacification had worked wonders in South Vietnam. We had won the political struggle

---

[18]   William C. Westmoreland, *A Soldier Reports* (Garden City, NY: Doubleday, 1976), pp. 422, 421, 418.

[19]   Richard Nixon, *No More Vietnams* (New York: Arbor House, 1985), p. 131.

for the allegiance of the South Vietnamese people." Tet, then, led to a defeat that was really a victory: "We won the war in Vietnam, but we lost the peace. All that we had achieved in twelve years of fighting was thrown away in a spasm: of congressional irresponsibility."[20] This outcome, then, was conceived by Nixon as a consequence of "the outcry over Watergate and the backlash against Vietnam in Congress." In effect, in Nixon's eyes, Watergate became America's Dienbienphu!

The American bureaucratic center and "the wise men" of the Eastern Establishment didn't see Tet at all the way Nixon or Westmoreland did, and this despite earlier solid backing for the war. For many of them Tet was tantamount to an American Dienbienphu, an eye-opening development that confirmed gnawing prior doubts about the war's overall viability. As the influential mainstream interpretation by Leslie Gelb and Richard Betts explains, "Tet 1968, like Dien Bien Phu 1954, was a symbol. It signified that Washington–Saigon progress toward ending the war was without foundation and could be swept away in weeks." "Tet exposed the extreme vulnerability of the GVN that lay beneath the veneer of military progress, but it also exposed the vulnerability of administration policy at home."[21] The whole concept of the Vietnam War as a military struggle against a Communist adversary who was being defeated without any huge American mobilization of resources or war fever was what had made this war in a remote Asian country politically acceptable in the first instance. The Johnson Administration had deliberately sought a blank check for escalation in the Gulf of Tonkin Resolution (in 1964), but had not wanted to declare war and put the country on a war footing.

Such ambivalence toward war has its justifications, but it also has pitfalls, especially if things don't work out. Possibly, the political leadership didn't want to go to war in the full sense in a distant country where there was no claim of self-defense. More central, undoubtedly, were the convictions of LBJ, in particular, that Vietnam was a sideshow and that his real challenges for his presidency involved race and poverty at home. It was Johnson's genuine liberalism on these issues, the ones he cared and knew most about, that made it necessary to fight overseas without diverting resources and energies from these domestic "battlefields." While understandable, succumbing to the temptation

---

[20] *Ibid.*, pp. 133, 165. Consider also this revealing passage about illusion and reality that is like walking into a hall of mirrors: "As Kissinger saw it, we were up against a paradoxical situation in which North Vietnam, which had in effect lost the war, was acting as if it had won, while South Vietnam, which had effectively won the war, was acting as if it had lost" (p. 153). Paradoxical, yes, but an alignment of mirrors is suspect if it yields such a clear image.

[21] Leslie Gelb and Richard Betts, *The Irony of Vietnam: The System Worked* (Washington, DC: Brookings Institution Press, 1979), pp. 171, 333, 172.

to engage half-heartedly in war reflects a flawed political and moral imagination, as well as dramatic underestimation of the resolve and skill of the other side. These underlying miscalculations help us understand better the bitterness of so many American combat veterans. To be asked, as a citizen, to risk life and limb for a struggle that was never removed from the backburner is to be told that one's life meant little except as one form of currency available to power-wielders for their casual practice of diplomacy of calculated gains and losses. Such an outlook also makes the war policy quite abruptly reversible if the balance sheet is read differently. A free society cannot summon its young to fight in a sustained and ambiguous war that is regarded as worthwhile only if the costs can be kept low and, for reasons of practical efficiency and domestic politics, the draft was abandoned after Vietnam as a source of American manpower. In effect, interventionary diplomacy has rested since Vietnam on a professional army, largely a mercenary undertaking. Only on an occasion of unprecedented national emergency can this supreme sacrifice be exacted over time without generating a backlash. Such an unconditional commitment was never made in relation to Vietnam, and many veterans of all political persuasions continue to feel betrayed to this day.

Johnson's restraint was not a matter of respecting popular will in the form of the restraining hand of the American people. Indeed, the Johnson presidency conceived of itself all along as moderate, resisting right-wing war fever, while prosecuting the war in a manner that was effective enough to yield victory without imposing a heavy cost on the United States. Up through Tet, and beyond, the American people generally supported a military solution in Vietnam, although the support began to weaken and splinter in mid-1967 as it became evident that the adversary was formidable and no end was in sight. More of the supporters of the war policies came to object to a leadership and an approach to Vietnam that seemed indecisive; most Americans even before Tet wanted either victory or withdrawal. The post-Tet political signals revealed a new stage of this process of polarization. By 1968 Americans increasingly felt that in retrospect the Vietnam involvement was a mistake, but even after Tet they favored an invasion of North Vietnam over withdrawal by a 5:3 ratio. What is more, Gene McCarthy's New Hampshire campaign astonishingly attracted more votes from hawks than doves, as shown by exit polls and by the later shift of his supporters after he dropped out of the race for the presidency to super-hawk candidate George Wallace in greater numbers than to Hubert Humphrey.

But the Washington establishment saw the issues differently than the public. They saw the rising tide of intense opposition of the anti-war movement as dividing the country in a dangerous way, often reaching into their own homes, creating severe tensions between fathers and sons, especially among the families of "the best and brightest" still in charge of the war at the time of Tet. Furthermore, they assessed the balance of forces in Vietnam differently. They began to appreciate that comparable battlefield casualties were of less consequence than the comparative will and capability of the leadership in Hanoi and Saigon. They realized that, whatever the losses at Tet, Hanoi retained the manpower, will, and logistical means to replenish its capabilities in the South, and could continue to do so for an indefinite future. In essence, the light at the end of the tunnel, always dim and distant, disappeared altogether. In this regard, the magnitude of Tet convinced many who had earlier been civilian hardliners that the actual American war-makers were either deceived or incompetent, or both. After Tet, the consensus of wise men was that this was no longer a war that could be won at an acceptable cost.[22]

LBJ was noncommittal to the end, stuck with these conflicting consequences of Tet and yet unable to act on their basis with any effective resolve; whereas he gave up on the war emotionally, he stuck with it tactically. As Gelb and Betts note, the choice posed by Tet for the Johnson Administration was one of either "decisive escalation" or "moderate deescalation." Earlier in the war, Johnson had actually seemed to welcome far lesser challenges to American primacy in the Indochina region as pretexts for dramatic escalation of military involvement. In the Gulf of Tonkin in August 1964 North Vietnamese torpedo boats were charged with attacks upon American warships that had been gathering intelligence for air operations against the North; these charges exaggerated the North Vietnamese attack and suppressed the military mission of the ships, and may well have fabricated part of the event.[23] This incident became the occasion for a major US military response by way of heavy bombardment of the torpedo bases in the North and for rallying the US Senate to give Johnson a virtually unanimous congressional mandate by way of resolution to use whatever force he deemed necessary to safeguard American interests in the area. Later, in February 1965, an NLF attack on American barracks in Pleiku was seized upon by Washington as an occasion to initiate Rolling Thunder, the sustained, massive, and overt extension of the air war to North Vietnam, which was correctly perceived at the time as a massive

[22] Ably recounted in Walter Isaacson and Evan Thomas, *The Wise Men: Six Friends and the World They Made* (New York: Simon & Schuster, 1986), pp. 696–713; cf. also the account in Herbert Y. Schandler, *The Unmaking of a President: Lyndon Johnson and Vietnam* (Princeton, NJ: Princeton University Press, 1977), esp. pp. 74–176, 256–65.

[23] See Joseph C. Gouldsen, *Truth Is the First Casualty – The Gulf of Tonkin Affair: Illusion and Reality* (Chicago: Rand McNally, 1969); Anthony Austin, *The President's War* (Philadelphia: J. B. Lippincott, 1971).

escalation of American involvement. In both instances, DRV/NLF actions directed at blunting the American combat role in their own country were treated in Washington as if they were malicious and outrageous provocations directed at the legitimate imperial role of the United States.

Why, then, was Tet treated so differently? Tet was, indeed, by this same imperial logic a far more malicious provocation – it was a massive military attack initiated during an official period of truce that inflicted heavy casualties and humiliated the United States by penetrating even its embassy compound. In light of the past US pattern of response, why such a wimpy response to Tet? Of course, timing and confidence are the answer. If Tet had occurred two years earlier, it seems reasonable to assume it would have produced a massive escalatory response by the United States almost as a matter of strategic reflex – conceivably, the aerial and naval bombardment of an equivalent number of cities and towns in the North. Franz Schurmann notes that "Johnson's restraint was indeed remarkable. But seen in terms of available policy options his restraint appears more as a paralysis in the face of choices all of which were bad."[24] If the war was being won, how could Tet have occurred? By 1968 the American investment in the war had peaked for the leadership in Washington. If it couldn't be won at that level then it certainly wasn't worth getting in deeper. It was, instead, time to get out. This latter attitude was what made the post-Tet request by Westmoreland and Earle Wheeler, then Chairman of the Joint Chiefs of Staff, for a 206,000 increase in troop deployment such a colossal bureaucratic blunder on the part of those who continued to believe in the Vietnam policy, as it significantly hardened the impression among those on the fence in Washington that Tet was a massive, unacknowledged American defeat and that the war if it went on would be an even greater drain than it already was, and this the United States could not long afford either politically or economically.[25] Already the dollar strain of the war was beginning to be felt, and the financial community was becoming worried about inflationary deficits

---

[24] Franz Schurmann, *The Logic of World Power* (New York: Pantheon, 1974), p. 524.

[25] Those who interpret Tet as a suppressed victory for the American side hold Wheeler responsible for making it impossible to recover political momentum after Tet. Robert Komer's rage has not subsided with the passage of time; in an interview in the mid-1980s he burst forth with invective: "The goddamn Chiefs of Staff. Wheeler's the evil genius of the Vietnam war in my judgment" (Willenson, *The Bad War*, p. 97). Komer believed that Wheeler discounted Westmoreland's confident assessment of the post-Tet situation and believed that additional American troops were needed in Vietnam to stave off defeat (and also used the occasion to obtain additional forces for assignment at other overseas locations). Such a tactic inflated the size of the troop increase at the very worst time and shook decisively what little faith American policy-makers and opinion-makers had in the course of American involvement. Well-narrated in Schandler, *The Unmaking of a President*, pp. 105–76.

at home, which it started to associate with the added outflows of currency caused by the war. In Paul Johnson's words, "It was a significant turning-point in American history: the first time the Great Republic, the richest nation on earth, came up against the limits on its financial resources."[26] Additionally, Atlanticists, who were still preeminent in the counsels of government, increasingly believed that Vietnam was pulling America away from its proper emphasis on the Euro-American alliance.

These considerations help us understand the way Tet was perceived by a preponderance among policy-makers: Relative costs are the Achilles Heel of imperial war. Vietnam was not a struggle for the defense of territory, or even of close allies, neighbors, or traditional spheres of influence. Of course, it was sold at home by a series of arguments put forth in sequence: as a "crusade" against Communism, as a way to avoid falling dominoes in the region, as a challenge to containment diplomacy, as a test of American credibility, as a test of Southeastern Asian regionalism, as a parallel to the defense of South Korea, as a test response to the challenge of wars of liberation. But these were abstract claims that were, in part, ideological and, in part, geopolitical, and were never fully endorsed or widely accepted. The wearying succession of primary reasons for the Vietnam War itself suggested a lack of clear conviction and purpose, and undermined the rationale for its continuation.

These imperial bureaucrats with their mental slide rules can pull the switch at any point without any loss of sleep. Tet was such a point, but probably not as definitively as apparent at the time, because Nixon did successfully, if deceptively, revive the war once elected in 1968. An imperial mentality based on calculations of gains and losses, including the balance sheet on the home front, collided with the crusader mentality characteristic of his extreme right and given credence in war propaganda, resurfacing in the form of a fictive superhero named Rambo, a dedicated warrior ready to die for the cause of anti-Communism on behalf of his beloved country, but betrayed again and again by passionless civilian bureaucrats. The fury of this rightist disenchantment with Washington is also at the center of Oliver North's saga, both his vision of purity on the battlefields of anti-Communist resistance and his contempt for inhibiting constitutional arrangements and the confining routines of standard governmental practices. Col. North epitomizes a contradictory attitude toward authority: willing to stand on his head, as he put it, to show obedience to presidential wishes while simultaneously upholding a discretion to disobey the law, lie, cheat, and work with organized crime to carry

---

[26] Paul Johnson, *A History of the Modern World* (London: Weidenfeld & Nicolson, 1983), p. 637. A significant gloss by such an avid anti-Communist, anti-left observer.

out his self-construed mission to sustain the contras. Tet was a time when many rational bureaucrats reassessed the Vietnam commitment, and wanted to end it. As Richard Holbrooke notes, it was Johnson's personal ambivalence that might have cost Humphrey the election in 1968 and made it necessary years later for Nixon to experience his own version of Tet – the Great Spring Offensive of 1975, the final shattering of South Vietnam's military resistance.[27] But there is a big difference between getting out of Vietnam and renouncing the counterrevolutionary mission of imperial geopolitics. The Vietnam diehards in the Washington bureaucracy might have lost out in Indochina, but their "wisdom" has persisted and, during the Reagan years, has been reasserted, most spectacularly in the campaign to reverse the outcomes of the Nicaraguan Revolution by reliance on the contras, but more widely through the adoption of the Reagan Doctrine. In this long view, Tet remains not a defeat, but a victory misunderstood!

The Vietnamese attitude toward the Tet Offensive is unclear. The official writing on all aspects of the war is self-serving, uncritical, and hence, in the end, unilluminating. Every single encounter during the long course of the warfare is presented as an instance of a smashing Communist victory. Losses are never acknowledged, claims of damage to the other side are wildly exaggerated. Despite this, some elements of the DRV attitude toward Tet can be inferred, and are an important part of the story. Tet is presented in Vietnamese Communist interpretations as a key stage in the process of achieving victory rather than as a turning-point in the war, but it is not highlighted. For instance, in the *History of the Communist Party of Vietnam* the Tet experience is discussed in a few pages under the rather bland title, "Frustrating the US Strategy in Limited War in the South and Foiling the First War of Destruction While Continuing to Build Socialism in the North (1965–1968)." In contrast, the end of the French war is described in a lengthy chapter entitled "Strategic Offensive in 1953–1954 – The Dien Bien Phu Victory," and the end of the second war in a chapter of its own under the title, "The Spring 1975 General Offensive – The Complete Liberation of the South (Feb. 1973–April 1975)."[28]

In discussing Tet, the official history attributes the undertaking to a plan launched at the 14th plenum of the Party Central Committee in January 1968 "to deal a stunning blow to American aggressors." The account reports that any one of three results was expected to flow from the offensive: total victory at once; some specific successes, but the war would go on; the United States

---

[27] Willenson, *The Bad War*, p. 151.
[28] For an account by the Chief of Staff, Vietnam People's Army, see General Van Dien Dung, *Our Great Spring Victory* (New York: Monthly Review Press, 1977), p. 5.

would feel challenged and would respond by augmenting "its forces and expanding the war to North Vietnam, Laos, and Kampuchea." The official assessment concluded that "the Tet 1968 offensive and uprising had a great and all-embracing significance; it upset the enemy's strategic position, shook the US aggressive will, foiled the strategy of limited war in the South and compelled him to end the war of destruction against North Vietnam and to accept negotiation with us." A more measured assessment of Tet was made by the Lao Dong (Communist) Party Headquarters in the South in a document dated March 1968 in which "great and unprecedented successes" were claimed, but also disappointments acknowledged, including a failure to destroy "much of the enemy's live force" or to create "favorable conditions for motivating the masses to arise in towns and cities."[29] The essence of Tet's combat success was the recapture of control over the countryside by disrupting pacification efforts, thereby forcing the South Vietnamese armed forces to retreat temporarily to the towns and cities. As Le Duan indicates, *the orientation for our offensive and uprising is aimed at towns but we should bear in mind that the greatest and most important result is to conquer and keep the countryside.*[30]

With the shift in US tactics after Tet, including Johnson's replacement by Nixon and Westmoreland's by Abrams, the Vietnam War remained unresolved. From the perspective of 1975 and later, the Vietnamese definitely did not look back on Tet as decisive in the manner of Dienbienphu. It shifted the course of the war, but didn't end it. Le Duan, the important party leader, writing in 1970, said that Tet "forced the US imperialists to deescalate the war, and then, by default, to expand it to Kampuchea," which produced "the offensive and uprisings in Kampuchea" leading to a revolutionary process there that "was beyond our calculations."[31]

All in all, then, Tet was more like Johnson's personal Dienbienphu than it was a decisive battle for the overall war effort. As Nixon makes clear, his plan was packaged for domestic political reasons as one to end the war, but in actuality it represented a renewed effort to prevail in the war. Even if Nixon had not been elected, it remains ambiguous whether Humphrey would have pursued a very different course in the war.[32] After rejecting Westmoreland's request for more troops and announcing a partial bombing halt, the Johnson strategy in the remaining months of his presidency was to seek negotiations

[29] Porter, *Vietnam: A History in Documents*, pp. 201, 202, 363.
[30] Le Duan, *Letters to the South* (Hanoi: Foreign Language Press, 1986), p. 99.
[31] *Ibid.*, p. 123.
[32] See e.g. telegram from Nicholas Katzenbach to US ambassadors on US post-Tet war policies, in Porter, *Vietnam: A History in Documents*, pp. 365–66.

on more favorable terms than Nixon/Kissinger agreed upon in the 1973 Paris Agreements, and to shift the burden of the ground war to the greatly strengthened South Vietnamese military forces. These were surely postures unacceptable to Hanoi. They were correctly perceived in Hanoi as a search in Washington for new ways to gain leverage in the war by fighting.

But if Tet wasn't Dienbienphu neither was it the Battle of the Bulge. It was not a desperate last-ditch gamble by an otherwise defeated adversary. Bernard Brodie, in one of the more balanced and illuminating interpretations of Tet, concludes that the Communist planners of Tet knew what they were doing, and that their plan was to shock Washington into a change of heart on the war so as to hasten American withdrawal from the ground war, such withdrawal being the necessary and sufficient condition for victory in the South.[33] Conservative interpreters of the period have tried to suggest that the shock-effect of Tet on the Johnson administration was a windfall result that compensated the North Vietnamese for their battlefield miscalculations, that it was not, in other words, part of their plan.

Stanley Karnow's influential PBS series on the Vietnam War and subsequent book lend support to the view that the North Vietnamese were disappointed by the results of Tet in the combat zones and never considered or expected overseas impacts. He and others who adhere to this line of interpretation rely on material based upon interviews with North Vietnamese military participants, especially General Tran Do, who was Deputy Commander of the forces of North Vietnam operating in the South. General Tran Do has said of Tet, "In all honesty, we didn't achieve our main objective, which was to spur uprisings in the South. Still, we inflicted heavy casualties on the Americans and their puppets, and that was a big gain for us. As for making an impact in the United States, it had not been our intention – but it turned out to be a fortunate result."[34] I don't find such commentary persuasive. The perspective of a theater commander may be confined to the battlefield context, but the overall planners of Tet in Hanoi were quite likely to have a broader conception of belligerent objectives than those in the field. The timing of the offensive in an election year after a period of intense US government propaganda to show that it was winning the war, as well as the prior history of the Vietnamese approach to revolutionary warfare – including spectacular success on an earlier occasion by resorting to the device of the decisive battle – makes it more plausible to follow Brodie than Karnow with respect to our identification of

[33] See B. Brodie, "The Tet Offensive," in Noble Frankland and Christopher Dowling, eds., *Decisive Battles* (New York: David McKay, 1976), pp. 321–34.
[34] Quoted in Stanley Karnow, *Vietnam: A History* (New York: Viking Press, 1983), p. 523.

the general orbit of North Vietnamese intentions. General Vo Nguyen Giap who, along with Ho Chi Minh, was the architect of Hanoi's strategy, has been both praised and criticized for his reliance on high-risk tactical maneuvers that are intended to have a decisive impact on the conflict.[35] He was the guiding force behind Dienbienphu, as well as Tet. Such drastic challenges directed at a militarily stronger overall adversary do accept the danger of provoking a punishing escalation. For instance, had the United States intervened at the time of Dienbienphu with an atomic bomb, or had a massive escalation of the war against the North occurred after Tet, our perception of these events and General Giap would be quite different. But these responses did not occur, and we must, I think, credit Giap with an understanding that the knockout blow cannot be attempted until the imperial power's resolve to go on with the war has been very much weakened. Even so, the North Vietnamese can be criticized for Tet – for its disastrous, disabling effects on the NLF in the South and because it didn't knock the Americans altogether out of the war. The Vietnamese political leadership seemed always acutely conscious of outside public opinion and the American peace movement as dimensions of the war, and realized clearly in their struggle against the French that raising the direct and indirect costs to the colonial power was alone what made the war eventually winnable, that is, reversing the locus of attrition, and thereby striking a dagger into the Achilles Heel of the basic imperial undertaking.

The historical actuality of Tet remains mystifying twenty years later. Only two sets of results seem clear beyond controversy:

– The shock of Tet pushed Johnson from the White House, Westmoreland from his command post; with this push went an abandonment of reliance on a ground war fought by American troops; also clear was the post-Tet effort to change the color of the bodies by invigorating Saigon's will and capability, as well as some need to reassure the American public and most of its leadership that the post-Tet emphasis would be on "honorable" disengagement by way of negotiations rather than a continuing quest for victory or endless stalemate; in actuality, this reassurance may itself have been a deception, buying time to find some means by which to impose upon Vietnam a diplomatic solution that left the South in anti-Communist hands, permanently perpetuating the temporary partition originally accepted by Hanoi as a short-term expedient in 1954 to enable the French to save face. (Indeed, the most tragic consequence

---

[35] See, e.g., Chalmers Johnson, *Autopsy on People's War* (Berkeley: University of California Press, 1973), p. 50.

of Tet may have been registered in Kampuchea. The determination by
the Nixon Administration to compensate for the gradual loss of US firepower on the ground by expanding the theater of operations to include
Kampuchea (and Laos), contributed directly to the conditions that led to
the establishment of the Pol Pot regime and its reign of terror.)[36]
– The battlefield and political consequences of Tet also decisively shifted
  control over subsequent conduct of the war to Hanoi, and removed the
  NLF from its former prominence, in the countryside of the South, and
  altered the situation in the Mekong Delta; after Tet the war ironically
  became what the Americans had claimed it was from the outset, when
  indeed it wasn't, namely, a war by the North to conquer the South.

Beyond these agreed developments, there is confusion, controversy, and
indeterminacy. It seems as if pacification was successful, if brutal, in rural
South Vietnam after Tet, mainly because the NLF was weakened and exposed
by the Tet Offensive. In the end, this didn't alter the overall outcome because
the war came to be decided in the northern provinces of South Vietnam by
combat between unequally matched main forces units of North and South in
the 1972–75 period.

III TWO TALES OF CRIMINALITY

Except in passing references, little attention is devoted by scholarly interpreters to the conduct of the two adversaries during and after Tet. In my view,
although much more research and analysis need to be done, troublesome
questions are posed by the ways in which both sides treated the Vietnamese
people and the cultural reality within which the struggle for the future was
unfolding. Tet disclosed, in my view, acute alienation of the sort that destroys
the very things that make struggle meaningful, and scarred badly the whole
sense of what the war was about for either side.

Further, it seems as if both sides alienated the civilian population in the
Vietnamese cities and countryside through their behavior during and after
Tet. The Communist side violated a truce and encroached violently upon
a sacred holiday. It is difficult to tell whether this issue of timing and shock
was disturbing at the time to Vietnamese civilian sentiment. Westmoreland
claimed so, but he is hardly a credible witness on matters of Vietnamese

---

[36] This story is best told by William Shawcross in *Sideshow: Kissinger, Nixon and the Destruction
of Cambodia* (New York: Simon & Schuster, 1979). How history would have otherwise
unfolded cannot, of course, be known, but conditions for a Kampuchean bloodbath were
certainly created by America's way of continuing the Vietnam War in the post-Tet years.

cultural sensitivity. There is also some testimony collected by Al Santoli, supporter of the American effort in Vietnam, that must be received skeptically. Tran Van Luu, a student in Saigon, evidently spoke to Santoli as follows:

> Tet has always been a very sacred time for Vietnamese families. People got very angry at the Viet Cong attack during this time . . . Everybody was shocked and surprised. Because the holiday ceasefire was first suggested by the VC. So the Viet Cong played a trick by asking for a longer ceasefire than in previous years. And they used this to launch the attack on the cities.[37]

And yet the issue of civilian hearts and minds cannot be ignored. The DRV/NLF claimed the mantle of nationalist authenticity for their war of liberation and condemned the GVN/US coalition as a mixture of domestic puppets and residues of colonialism. To sustain these claims, a deep show of respect for cultural symbols seems indispensable.

More serious in this regard were the overall effects of civilian executions carried out by the invading troops who arrived in Hue with death lists of those who collaborated with Saigon or the Americans. Of course, collaboration in a bitter internal war has often been treated as a crime by those who resist alien rule, and yet the civilians executed in Hue seemed to include "innocent" minor functionaries, including schoolteachers and minor civic officials. Perhaps, the harshness of this conduct was designed to convey a message to all Vietnamese that they must side with authentic nationalist forces at a time of critical struggle. Even if this was the motive for such brutality, it nevertheless discloses a criminal mentality in the guise of military necessity, and must have been deeply frightening to Buddhists and those in the middle, as well as to those who were overtly siding with the Americans.

The subsequent history of Vietnam makes one wonder whether the shadow cast by Tet did not add significantly to the fear and hostility of Southerners toward the North, to the mass exodus after liberation, and even to the phenomenon of "the boat people" that undercut the basic claim of national liberation and reunification. Undoubtedly, also, a vicious circle extended the cycle of fear and suspicion, each round validating the hostile outlook of the other side. Of course, there were other factors at work. The Catholics who had fled south after 1954 were inclined to flee again in the face of a Marxist-Leninist prospect, and then there were hordes of war profiteers in the South who could not imagine life without the Americans. In terrifying the population of Hue and, by extension, giving credibility to fears of a post-war bloodbath throughout South Vietnam, did not the victorious side in the war years later make

---

[37] Al Santoli, *To Bear Any Burden* (New York: Dutton, 1985), pp. 172–73.

itself exceedingly vulnerable to propaganda that besmirches its image, perhaps unfairly, to this day? In this regard, the Hue executions – about which there is still no significant interpretation – remain an important. if only dimly understood, aspect of the legacy of Tet.

But there is another complementary story of human abuse, also largely untold. The response to Tet by Saigon and by US forces showed a total disregard for life and for Vietnamese tradition. To drive the invading Vietnamese out of the cities and towns, firepower and bombing were used as if the war was still located primarily in the jungle. The ancient sections of Hue city were devastated from the air, and numerous civilian casualties resulted. Civilians caught in the crossfire of Tet were assimilated to enemy forces and indiscriminately attacked, destroying entire towns and large sections of cities in the name of freeing them. No account of post-Tet is complete without that spontaneous insight of a marine major asked about the destruction of Ben Tre: "It became necessary to destroy the town to save it." For opponents of the American involvement, and even for some of those undecided, detached media voices, these few words said it all. In assessing the devastation of Tet it is almost impossible to apportion blame and responsibility between the adversaries. Both sides were substantially, perhaps irreparably discredited as responsible constructive actors to Vietnamese political development by their behavior during and after Tet.

But it was not merely the bloody character of American/GVN (Government of South Vietnam) effort to dislodge the Vietnamese fighters from entrenched positions in these cities and towns, it was the quality of the pacification campaign that was put into operation in the countryside in the months after Tet. The United States relied heavily on a tactic of widespread civilian assassination, supposedly to decimate the NLF infrastructure that survived the Tet Offensive. David MacMichael, a former CIA analyst who split with the government on the issue of disinformation relating to Sandinista support for revolutionary activity in El Salvador, has estimated that 40,000 Vietnamese were killed in this assassination program.[38] The "success" claimed for these post-Tet tactics has been influential in recasting subsequent counterinsurgency theory and practice, to be considered in the next section.

Yet there is one comparison that seems to challenge the temptation to conclude that both sides showed their true colors at Tet. The attacking NLF cadres invariably fought with courage and resolve unmatched by their

---

[38] Others have used even higher figures, but the magnitude of the Phoenix Program or its essential tactic is not in serious doubt. Cf. Richard Ryan, "Christie Institute Attacked by Right and Not-So-Right," *In These Times*, Feb. 24–Mar. 8, 1988, p. 5.

adversaries. Whatever the basis of this extraordinary display of commitment, and it could not be explained as entirely a matter of indoctrination, the attackers acted as if their cause was sacred and worth dying for, and the defenders, at most, did their professional duty as soldiers. Such an asymmetry of motivation and commitment often expresses a historical judgment by the participants about the relative degree of legitimacy that two opposed sides in a conflict possess, and prefigures, as a consequence, the outcome of the struggle itself, even if long deferred, especially if there exists an offsetting inequality of military capabilities. When the Americans partially disengaged after Tet, it was evident that Saigon, even with vast assistance in every form, could not mobilize the people of the South to anything like a comparable degree to that achieved by both Hanoi and the NLF. It was not surprising that the Thieu government was opposed at every stage to any further US disengagement and seemed mortally afraid of negotiations or coalition arrangements despite access to superior weaponry and its possession of far greater financial resources than its adversary.

IV FROM POST-TET TO LOW-INTENSITY CONFLICT

Refighting the Vietnam War remains a preoccupation in Washington. Neither Tet, nor the subsequent failures of Vietnamization, did much to convince the Komer/Nixon pacification school of thought. Looking backward they viewed Vietnam (and Tet) as pseudo-defeats that generated the occasion for learning better how to protect US interests in the Third World, while looking ahead they established doctrinal redesign as a foreign policy priority in their concern to avoid repeating the Vietnam outcome. In Nixon's words, "In Vietnam, we tried and failed in a just cause. 'No more Vietnams' can mean we will not *try* again. It *should* mean that we will not *fail* again."[39]

In an important speech on the tenth anniversary of the American defeat in Vietnam, the Secretary of State, George P. Shultz, echoes these sentiments: "[T]he President has called our effort a noble cause, and he was right. Whatever mistakes in how the war was fought, whatever one's view of the strategic rationale for our intervention, the *morality* of our effort must now be clear."[40] In effect, the moral case for intervention is sanctified, opening the way for two elements in subsequent instances of interventionary practice: a sufficient strategic rationale by way of national interests and a mastery of the tactics of struggle that will assure a reasonable prospect of victory (and

[39] Nixon, *No More Vietnams*, p. 237.
[40] From "The Meaning of Vietnam," delivered April 25, 1985, *US Department of State Bulletin*, Vol. 85, Nos. 2094–99, 1985, pp. 13–16.

that takes into account the vulnerability of sustained imperial interventions to domestic backlash). In his speech Secretary Shultz explicitly linked Vietnam to the latest testing ground for American policy: Nicaragua. In the background was the notion that "the ordeal of Indochina . . . should teach us something"; "the larger lesson of the past decade is that when America lost faith in itself, world stability suffered and freedom lost ground." Underneath this call for activism was the realization that it was desirable to apply the post-Tet approach to Nicaragua and other conflict zones in the Third World – that is, avoid battlefield deaths for Americans and keep the American combat role as low-profile as possible, while using covert action to go after the civilian infrastructure of the revolutionary side (the Phoenix approach). It is precisely this set of inferences from the Vietnam era – both the supposed nobility of the cause and the unnecessary failure – that helped produce the pathological excesses of the Casey/Poindexter/North approach to interventionary diplomacy.[41]

The persisting vitality of this commitment to interventionary diplomacy in the Third World is evident in a recent government-sponsored study: the Report of the Commission on Integrated Long-Range Strategy chaired by Fred Ikle and Albert Wohlstetter, and including such national security stalwarts as Kissinger, Brzezinski, and Samuel Huntington. The report, released in January 1988, was signed by all its members without even any dissenting comments, and published under the title "Discriminate Deterrence." Although it includes a discussion of nuclear strategy, a surprisingly strong emphasis is accorded to rehabilitating interventionary diplomacy in the Third World: "Our failure in Vietnam still casts a shadow over US intervention anywhere . . . and ha[s] left some predisposed to pessimism about our ability to promote US interests in the Third World." The report sets out to overcome this pessimism and proposes a cluster of policies that is put forward to gain this result. The stakes are high, the text argues, nothing less than the global position of the United States. The report contends that unless the United States adopts an activist role in the Third World it "will have an adverse cumulative affect on US access to critical regions, on American credibility among allies and friends, and on American self-confidence." It goes on, "If this cumulative effect cannot be checked or reversed in the future, it will gradually undermine America's ability to defend its interests in the most vital regions, such as the Persian Gulf, the Mediterranean and the Western Pacific." Note, especially, the geopolitical logic prominent here. This report is not a Cold War tract

---

[41] For an instructive early account, see Jonathan Marshall, Peter Dale Scott, and Jane Hunter, *The Iran–Contra Connection: Secret Teams and Covert Operations in the Reagan* Era (Boston; South End Press, 1987).

(although it relies on some anti-Communist suppositions to depict US interests) as much as it is a primer by the national security elite on what must be done with the military instrument to sustain America's global preeminence or, more precisely, to avoid the consequence of what is now widely regarded as a period of imperial decline. It associates this new activism with a grasp of the character of low-intensity conflict, which it describes as the brunt of the challenge to US interests, and it suggests that the approach advocated "could be funded with about 4 percent of the defense budget, requiring annual outlays of perhaps $12 billion." These amounts, the report suggests, could be provided by reallocations within the frame of current defense appropriations "without significantly impairing our ability to prosecute higher-intensity wars."[42]

The approach advocated for low-intensity conflict is based on "six basic propositions"[43] that can be briefly set forth here:

1 *"US forces will not in general be combatants,"* i.e. sustain Vietnamization if at all possible by limiting the US role to security assistance programs, including "military training, technical training and intelligence and logistical support."

2 *"The United States should support anti-Communist insurgencies."* This broad mandate, in effect, endorses the Reagan Doctrine, although it is limited in application to "carefully selected situations, where important US objectives would be served and US support might favorably affect outcomes." A flexible approach is recommended, one that includes many varieties of support, including provision for its non-acknowledgment by way of covert action, whenever a distancing seems desirable. It is important, the report notes, to provide the government with an option to "maintain official silence." Herein the rationale for secret government based on lies and deception directed toward the American people and their selected representatives.

3 *"Security assistance requires new legislation and more resources."* In effect, the report suggests more resources be made available to friendly regimes and appropriate insurgencies, and that the current proportion of assistance given Israel and Egypt is too high, given the global array of US interests. It seeks legislative cooperation, including the elimination of current inhibiting constraints (for instance, "Legislation from the post-Vietnam era unwisely continues to bar US training for police forces").

---

[42] *Discriminate Deterrence* (Report of the Commission on Integrated Long-Term Strategy), Department of Defense, Jan. 1988, pp. 13, 16.

[43] *Ibid.*, pp. 16–22.

4 *"The United States needs to work with its Third World allies at developing 'cooperative forces.'"* This proposal extends the notion of not involving the United States in protracted combat roles, but also laments that the United States is acting on the basis of "competitive disadvantages" vis-à-vis the Soviet Union in these matters. The Soviet Union is better placed "both in minimizing its own risks of confrontation with the West and in making available troops that blend readily into the environment." What seems noteworthy here, as compared to earlier documents on US strategic interests, for instance, NSC-68, is the absence of any kind of moral or legal censure of Soviet practices. On the contrary, the United States Government is goaded to find appropriate equivalent means to project its power to Third World settings. We have definitely entered a period of imperialist coexistence, possibly at the expense of the Third World.

5 *"In the Third World, no less than in developed countries, US strategy should seek to maximize our technological advantages."* In effect, the government is instructed to fine-tune high-tech capabilities to fit the specific features of various low-intensity conflict arenas. Illustrative technological emphases are specified, including "advanced information-processing systems," "low-cost space systems, long-endurance aircraft and robotic reconnaissance vehicles," "networks of sensors and other microelectronic equipment," "bio- and micromechanical sensors," and "vivid digital graphics of dangerous areas." There is a caveat attached that compulsive reliance on high tech is ill-advised in some situations – "Providing canned field rations and a means of manufacturing boot soles may be more important to the mobility of a Third World army than advanced aircraft."

6 *"The United States must develop alternatives to overseas bases."* Here is a realization that access to Third World countries has in the post-1945 era often depended on foreign bases, and that these facilities are coming under a rising tide of nationalist pressures. The report recommends that high tech can again provide a fix by way of replacement facilities: using space more for monitoring purposes, developing "impressive naval options," as well as "the use of standard merchant container ships to support specially configured units, with the containers carrying all military equipment needed."

It is notable that the revival of this line of thinking, so well depicted over the years in the work of Michael Klare, is virtually uncontested in its current form.[44] To be sure, there are persisting anxieties about being drawn into

---

[44] For his recent interpretation of these matters, see Michael T. Klare and Peter Kornbluh, eds., *Low Intensity Warfare* (New York: Pantheon, 1988).

losing efforts even along the lines proposed above, accounting for some of
the reluctance by some low-intensity enthusiasts to side fully with Reagan
on the contras. But, in general, there is an acceptance of what is essentially
the pre-Vietnam view that American interests and Third World revolutionary
nationalism are on a permanent collision course such that the United States
must do its best to crush the latter by reliance on its ever new and superior
technologies of destruction to control political outcomes. Except for some
adjustments based on a wider geopolitical screen, the new thinking on Third
World issues is indistinguishable from either Komer's approach to pacification or Nixon's general call for successful Vietnam-style interventions. Daniel
Ellsberg's insistence that we shift our sense of role from being *on* the wrong
side to *being* the wrong side, quoted as an inscription to this essay, pertains
here. He extends his observation by saying, "And the US is the wrong side
again today – in Central America."[45] The continuity of policy also relies on
this delusion that we are taking sides in a civil war rather than understanding
our action as one of intervening imperially against revolutionary nationalist
movements, using some compromised and antagonized elements of the target
society as protective cover.[46]

V A CONCLUDING COMMENT

On this twentieth anniversary of Tet we seem still caught up in the Vietnam
maelstrom of deadly illusion, being reenacted in a series of Third World
countries. History has placed a thick jungle canopy over the whole Tet phenomenon, depriving us of the satisfaction of clear imagery, and yet this very
obscurity invites wider meditation and reflection. We cannot any longer plausibly dismiss Tet with some literal designation such as, "The battle that turned
the war around for the Vietnamese," or "The battle that the Americans really
won even though they acted as if they lost it."

Tolstoy's reflections can help us attain moral focus: "On the twelfth of
June, 1812, the forces of Western Europe crossed the Russian frontier and war
began, that is, an event took place opposed to human reason and to human
nature. Millions of men perpetrated against one another such innumerable
crimes, frauds, treacheries, thefts, forgeries, issues of false money, burglaries,
incendiarisms, and murders as in whole centuries are not recorded in the
annals of all the law courts of the world, but which those who committed

---

[45] "Interview," *Rolling Stone*, 20th Anniversary Issue, 1987, p. 221.
[46] For a mainstream critique along similar lines, see Robert A. Pastor, *Condemned to Repetition: The United States and Nicaragua* (Princeton, NJ: Princeton University Press, 1987).

them did not at the time regard as being crimes." It is, in the end, the sheer criminality of these imperial interventions and the human suffering that they entail which must be the basis of reassessment. As long as analysis is limited to a pragmatic debate on tactics and prospects for victory, the inevitable tendency will be to repeat the pattern, each time vindicating intervention by a particular contextual rationale and hoping against hope that this time military superiority can be translated into a positive political outcome, which is not, of course, inherently precluded. Intervention can succeed but, in the overwhelming generality of cases, it shouldn't.

A final point of assessment is this. The Tet Offensive both broke the psychological resistance by the political leadership to anti-war sentiments in the United States during the latter stages of the Vietnam War *and* provided a text for war planners who could look back at the violent encounter and its bloody aftermath to show how revolutionary nationalism can indeed be crushed by military and paramilitary means. The reality of Tet is more a point of intense light and of persisting mystery than it is an event whose significance can be elucidated once and forever.

7

Son My: War Crimes and Individual Responsibility

No voice has been more passionate and persuasive in its call for a renewal of the laws of war than that of Josef Kunz. Especially in the period since the end of World War II Professor Kunz wrote against the prevailing tendency to regard the idea of law-in-war as little more than a relic from the pre-nuclear age.[1] The Vietnam War has emphasized, although the Korean War, the three Middle Eastern wars, and the many lesser wars throughout the world since 1945 should have made it plain, that the development of nuclear weapons did not mark the end of so-called conventional warfare, nor assure us that there would be either peace or catastrophe in world society. The massacre at Son My was, I suppose, the most macabre possible demonstration that the law of war remains relevant, and that its effective enforcement would mitigate the horrifying experience of warfare for a society torn apart by struggling armies.

But there is a danger of misunderstanding. The most minimal reading of customary rules of international law prohibits the acts that took place at Son My, and yet they happened. Rules of international law do not assure conforming conduct unless the military and civilian leadership of the armed forces gives these rules active and genuine respect and unless the official tactics of the war are themselves sensitive to the basic principles of limitation on warfare embodied in the rules of customary and treaty international law.

The spelling Son My follows the Vietnamese practice. As Richard Hammer has pointed out, Son My (and not Song My or Songmy) is what appears "On all Vietnamese maps, in all Vietnamese writings": R. Hammer, *One Morning in the War: The Tragedy at Son My* (New York: Coward-McCann, 1970), xiii. In an earlier version I used the mistaken spelling in my title "Songmy: War Crimes and Individual Responsibility," *Trans-Action* 7, 3 (Jan. 1970), 33–40; republished, in somewhat modified form, under the title "War Crimes: The Circle of Responsibility," *The Nation*, Jan. 26, 1970, 77–82.

[1] J. Kunz, *The Changing Law of Nations* (Columbus: Ohio State University Press, 1968), 831–68.

Thus, new rules more responsive to the actualities of contemporary warfare would offer no assurance of their respect. An entire political climate of support for such rules must be brought into being. In working, then, for the reform and revitalization of the laws of war – the essence of Professor Kunz's eloquent plea – it is essential to work for a new political climate, as well as to urge the adoption of new rules and procedures for interpretation and enforcement.[2] The Vietnam War has amply demonstrated how easily modern man and the modern state – with all its claim of civility[3] – relapse into barbarism in the course of pursuing belligerent objectives in a distant land where neither national territory nor national security is tangibly at stake.

I SON MY IN CONTEXT

The dramatic disclosure of the Son My massacre produced a flurry of public concern over the commission of war crimes in Vietnam by American military personnel. Such a concern is certainly appropriate, but insufficient if limited to inquiry and prosecution of the individual servicemen involved in the monstrous events that apparently took the lives of upwards of 400 civilians in the My Lai No. 4 hamlet of Son My village on March 16, 1968.[4] The Son My massacre itself raises a serious basis for inquiry into the military and civilian command structure that was in charge of battlefield behavior at the time.

The evidence now available suggests that the armed forces have made efforts throughout the Vietnam War to suppress, rather than investigate and punish, the commission of war crimes by American personnel. The evidence also suggests a failure to protest or prevent the manifest and systematic

---

[2]   Concern with rules, procedures, and institutions alone can lead to banal forms of legalism; it is essential to be concerned also about the politics of a legal order so that ideas of justice do not collide with the actualities of the law. In a somewhat different setting I have explored these issues in Richard Falk, "Law, Lawyers, and the Conduct of American Foreign Relations," *Yale Law Journal*, 78 (1970). See Section V for specific proposals along these lines.

[3]   Future students of the American scene will be struck, no doubt, by the fervent appeals for civility at home while the war rages on in Vietnam. One such prominent appeal, of late, has come from Chief Justice Warren E. Burger, who, in addressing the American Bar Association, contended that "unseemly, outrageous episodes" in courtrooms were undermining public confidence in the judicial process. The Chief Justice did not note that one of the reasons for these episodes is that anti-war defendants have not been allowed by courts to make their arguments about the illegality and criminality of the war and of war policies. For an account of Chief Justice Burger's speech, see *New York Times*, Aug. 9, 1970, 1, 34.

[4]   For principal accounts, see Hammer, *One Morning in the War*; S. Hersh, *My Lai 4: A Report on the Massacre and Its Aftermath* (New York: Random House, 1970); see also *The Son My Mass Slaying* (South Viet Nam: Giai Phong Editions, 1969); N. Chomsky, "After Pinkville," *New York Review of Books*, Jan. 1, 1970, 3–14.

commission of war crimes by the armed forces of the Saigon regime in South Vietnam.[5]

The scope of proper inquiry is even broader than the prior paragraph suggests. The official policies developed for the pursuit of belligerent objectives in Vietnam appear to violate the same basic and minimum constraints on the conduct of war as were violated at Son My. B-52 pattern raids against undefended villages and populated areas, "free bomb zones," forcible removal of civilian populations, defoliation and crop destruction, and "search-and-destroy" missions have been sanctioned as official tactical policies of the United States government. Each of these tactical policies appears to violate the international laws of war binding upon the United States by international treaties ratified by the US government with the advice and consent of the Senate. The overall conduct of the war in Vietnam by the US armed forces involves a refusal to differentiate between combatants and noncombatants and between military and nonmilitary targets. Detailed presentation of the acts of war in relation to the laws of war is available in a volume bearing the title *In the Name of America* published under the auspices of the Clergy and Laymen Concerned About Vietnam, in January 1968, or several months before the Son My massacre took place.[6]

Ample evidence of war crimes has been presented to the public and to its officials for some time without producing an official reaction or rectifying action. A comparable description of the acts of war that were involved in the bombardment of North Vietnam by American planes and naval vessels between February 1965 and October 1968 appears in a book by John Gerassi.[7]

The broad point, then, is that the United States government has officially endorsed a series of battlefield activities that appear to constitute war crimes.

---

[5] This point is made by Alfred P. Rubin, "Legal Aspects of the My Lai Incident," *Oregon Law Review*, 49 (1970), 267–68.

[6] Clergy and Laymen Concerned About Vietnam, *In the Name of America* (Annandale, Va.: Turnpike Press, 1968). An introduction to the volume by such distinguished religious leaders as Rev. Martin Luther King, Rev. William Sloan Coffin, John Bennett, and Rev. Richard Fernandez was totally ignored by the media and thus the volume made no impact outside already sensitized anti-war groups. Other early publications – pre-Son My – on the war crimes aspects of the war include J. Duffett, ed., *Against the Crime of Silence: Proceedings of the Russell International War Crimes Tribunal, Stockholm–Copenhagen* (New York: Bertrand Russell Peace Foundation and O'Hare Books, 1968); F. Harvey, *Air War – Vietnam* (New York: Bantam, 1967); see "Kill Anything That Moves," an essay review of the Harvey book in P. Slater, *The Pursuit of Loneliness: American Culture at the Breaking Point* (Boston: Beacon Press, 1970), 29–52; another sensitive reaction to Harvey's book is R. Crichton, "Our Air War," *New York Review of Books*, Jan. 4, 1968, 3–5; E. Norden, "American Atrocities in Vietnam," *Liberation*, Feb. 1966, 1–19 (reprint).

[7] See J. Gerassi, *North Vietnam: A Documentary* (London: Allen & Unwin, 1968).

It would, therefore, be misleading to isolate the awful happening at Son My from the overall conduct of the war. It is certainly true that the perpetrators of the massacre at Son My are, if the allegations prove correct, guilty of the commission of war crimes, but it is also true that their responsibility is mitigated to the extent that they were executing superior orders or were even carrying out the general line of official policy that established a moral climate in which the welfare of Vietnamese civilians is totally disregarded.[8]

II PERSONAL RESPONSIBILITY: SOME BASIC PROPOSITIONS

The US prosecutor at Nuremberg, Robert Jackson, emphasized that war crimes are war crimes no matter which country is guilty of them.[9] The United States more than any other sovereign state took the lead in the movement to generalize the principles underlying the Nuremberg Judgment that was delivered against German war criminals after the end of World War II.[10]

At the initiative of the United States, in 1945, the General Assembly of the United Nations unanimously affirmed "the principles of international law recognized by the Charter of the Nuremberg Tribunal" in Resolution 95(1). This Resolution was an official action of governments. At the direction of the membership of the United Nations, the International Law Commission, an expert body containing international law experts from all of the principal legal systems in the world, formulated the Principles of Nuremberg in 1950.[11] These

---

[8]   One of the most revealing inquiries in this regard accompanied the prosecution and defense of Lt. John Duffey, who was accused of killing a Vietnamese prisoner under his control. The court martial proceedings, especially several witnesses for the defense, made it evident that "the body count philosophy" was the proximate cause of Lt. Duffey's action even though there was no specific superior order given to kill "enemy" prisoners. For an account of the Duffey trial and some accompanying documents, see *Tan Am Base Vietnam – Feb. 12 – 1000 Hrs.*, *Scanlan's*, Apr. 1970, 1–11. See *New York Times*, Mar. 28, 1970, 1, 13; Apr. 5, 1970, 6.

[9]   Indeed, this was a principal theme in the Opening Statement of Robert H. Jackson at Nuremberg. See R. Jackson, *The Case Against the Nazi War Criminals* (New York: Knopf, 1946), 8–11, 70–78, 86–91.

[10] For documentary record, see Report of Robert H. Jackson to the International Conference on Military Trials, London, 1945 (Dept. of State Publ. 3080, released Feb. 1949). For a fully researched inquiry into prevailing attitudes toward Nuremberg, see W. Bosch, *Judgment on Nuremberg: American Attitudes Toward the Major German War-Crimes Trials* (Chapel Hill: University of North Carolina Press, 1970).

[11] For official text, see 5 UN GAOR Supp. 17 (A/1316), II. The seven Principles are as follows:

       Principle I: Any person who commits an act which constitutes a crime under international law is responsible therefor and liable to punishment.
       Principle II: The fact that internal law does not impose a penalty for an act which constitutes a crime under international law does not relieve the person who committed the act from responsibility under international law.

Principles offer the most complete set of guidelines currently available on the legal relationship between personal responsibility and war crimes.[12]

Neither the Nuremberg Judgment nor the Nuremberg Principles fixes definite boundaries on personal responsibility. These boundaries will have to be drawn in the future as the circumstances of alleged violations of international law are tested by competent domestic and international tribunals. However, Principle IV makes it clear that superior orders are no defense in a prosecution for war crimes, provided the individual accused of criminal behavior had a moral choice available to him.[13]

Principle III: The fact that a person who committed an act which constitutes a crime under international law acted as Head of State or responsible Government official does not relieve him from responsibility under international law.

Principle IV: The fact that a person acted pursuant to order of his Government or of a superior does not relieve him from responsibility under international law, provided a moral choice was in fact possible to him.

Principle V: Any person charged with a crime under international law has the right to a fair trial on the facts and law.

Principle VI: The crimes hereinafter set out are punishable as crimes under international law:

    a. *Crimes against peace*: (i) Planning, preparation, initiation or waging of a war of aggression or a war in violation of international treaties, agreements or assurances; (ii) Participation in a common plan or conspiracy for the accomplishment of any of the acts mentioned under (i).

    b. War crimes: Violations of the laws or customs of war which include, but are not limited to, murder, ill-treatment or deportation to slave-labour or for any other purpose of civilian population of or in occupied territory, murder or ill-treatment of prisoners of war, of persons on the seas, killing of hostages, plunder of public or private property, wanton destruction of cities, towns, or villages, or devastation not justified by military necessity.

    c. Crimes against humanity: Murder, extermination, enslavement, deportation and other inhuman acts done against any civilian population, or persecutions on political, racial or religious grounds, when such acts are done or such persecutions are carried on in execution of or in connexion with any crime against peace or any war crime.

Principle VII: Complicity in the commission against peace, a war crime, or a crime against humanity as set forth in Principle VI is a crime under international law.

[12] For a cautious, but helpful analysis, see J. O'Brien, "The Nuremberg Principles," in J. Finn, ed., *A Conflict of Loyalties* (New York: Pegasus, 1968), 140–94.

[13] One of the most significant repudiations of the superior orders defense is contained in *United States v. Wilhelm List, et al.* (The Hostage Case), reprinted in *Trials of War Criminals Before the Nuremberg Military Tribunals*, Vol. XI (Washington, D.C.: United States Government Printing Office, 1950), 757–1319.

The Supreme Court upheld in *The Matter of Yamashita* a sentence of
death against General Yamashita imposed at the end of World War II for acts
committed by troops under his command.[14] The determination of responsibility rested upon the obligation of General Yamashita for the maintenance
of discipline by troops under his command, which discipline included the
enforcement of the prohibition against the commission of war crimes. Thus
General Yamashita was convicted even though he had no specific knowledge
of the alleged war crimes, which mainly involved forbidden acts of violence
against the civilian population of the Philippines in the closing days of World
War II. Commentators have criticized the conviction of General Yamashita
because it was difficult to maintain discipline under the conditions of defeat
during which the war crimes were committed, but the imposition of responsibility sets a precedent for holding principal military and political officials
responsible for acts committed under their command, especially when no
diligent effort was made to inquire, punish, and prevent repetition.[15] *The
Matter of Yamashita* has an extraordinary relevance to the failure of the US
military command to secure adherence to minimum rules of international
law by troops serving under their command. The following sentences from
the majority opinion of Chief Justice Stone in *The Matter of Yamashita* have
a particular bearing:

> It is evident that the conduct of military operations by troops whose excesses
> are unrestrained by the orders or efforts of their commander would almost
> certainly result in violations which it is the purpose of the law of war to
> prevent. Its purpose to protect civilian populations and prisoners of war from
> brutality would largely be defeated if the commander of an invading army
> could with impunity neglect to take reasonable measures for their protection.
> Hence the law of war presupposes that its violation is to be avoided through
> the control of the operations of war by commanders who are to some extent
> responsible for their subordinates.[16]

The Field Manual of the Department of the Army, FM 27-10, adequately develops the principles of responsibility governing members of the
armed forces. Section 3(b) makes it clear that "the law of war is binding
not only upon States as such but also upon individuals and, in particular,

[14] For a full account and critical interpretation of General Yamashita's conviction and execution
      written by a member of the prosecution staff, see A. Reel, *The Case of General Yamashita*
      (Chicago: University of Chicago Press, 1949).
[15] See Reel's recent reassessment of his earlier analysis in A. Reel, "Must We Hang Nixon Too?,"
      The Progressive, Mar. 1970, 26–29.
[16] 327 U.S. 1, 15 (1945).

the members of their armed forces." The entire manual is based upon the acceptance by the United States of the obligation to conduct warfare in accordance with the international law of war. The substantive content of international law is contained in a series of international treaties that have been properly ratified by the United States. These include twelve Hague and Geneva Conventions.

These international treaties are listed in the Field Manual and are, in any event, part of "the supreme law of the land" by virtue of Article VI of the US Constitution. Customary rules of international law governing warfare are also made explicitly applicable to the obligation of American servicemen in the manuals issued to the armed forces. The extent of legal obligation is established by very broad norms of customary international law, especially the prohibition upon inflicting unnecessary suffering and destruction as measured by the criterion of military necessity. A competent tribunal would have to apply this general norm – certainly no more general, however, than basic constitutional norms involving "due process," "equal protection," and "privileges and immunities." It is important to realize that not every viola-tion of law needs to be discovered in a treaty rule although where a treaty rule applies to a specific issue – such as the identification of prohibited targets – then it takes precedence over more abstract norms of customary international law.

It has sometimes been maintained that the laws of war do not apply to a civil war, which is a war within a state and thus outside the scope of international law. Some observers have argued that the Vietnam War represents a civil war between factions contending for political control of South Vietnam. Such an argument may accurately portray the principal basis of the conflict, but surely the extension of the combat theater to include North Vietnam, Laos, Thailand, Cambodia, and Okinawa removes any doubt about the international character of the war from a military and legal point of view.[17] Nevertheless, even assuming for the sake of analysis that the war should be treated as a civil war, the laws of war are applicable to a limited extent, an extent great enough to cover the events at Son My and the commission of many other alleged war crimes in Vietnam. Section II of the Field Manual recites Article 3, common

[17]   Also the international character of the conflict has been the cause of protests against the treat-ment of American prisoners of war held in North Vietnam. For legal discussion of this issue, see my debate with Professor John Norton Moore, reprinted in Richard Falk, ed., *The Vietnam War and International Law* (Princeton: Princeton University Press, 1968), Vol. I, 362–508; see esp. 362–73, 403–38, 470–90; see Ch. 4 in this book.

to all four Geneva Conventions on the Law of War (1949), and establishes a minimum set of obligations for civil war situations:

> In the case of armed conflict not of an international character occurring in the territory of one of the High Contracting Parties, each Party to the conflict shall be bound to apply, as a minimum, the following provisions:
>
> (1) Persons taking no active part in the hostilities, including members of armed forces who have laid down their arms and those placed *hors de combat* by sickness, wounds, detention or any other cause, shall in all circumstances be treated humanely, without any adverse distinction founded on race, color, religion or faith, sex, birth or wealth, or any other similar criteria.
>
> To this end, the following acts are and shall remain prohibited at any time and in any place whatsoever with respect to the above-mentioned persons:
>
> (a) violence to life and person, in particular, murder of all kinds, mutilation, cruel treatment and torture;
>
> (b) taking of hostages;
>
> (c) outrages upon personal dignity, in particular, humiliating and degrading treatment;
>
> (d) the passing of sentences and the carrying out of executions without previous judgment pronounced by a regularly constituted court, affording all the judicial guarantees which are recognized as indispensable by civilized peoples.
>
> (2) The wounded and sick shall be collected and cared for. An impartial humanitarian body, such as the International Committee of the Red Cross, may offer its services to the Parties to the conflict.
>
> The Parties to the conflict should further endeavor to bring into force, by means of special agreements, all or part of the other provisions of the present Convention.[18]

Such a limited applicability of the laws of war to the Vietnam War flies in the face of the official American contention that South Vietnam is a sovereign state that has been attacked by a foreign state, North Vietnam. This standard

---

[18] Geneva Convention for the Amelioration of the Condition of the Wounded and Sick in Armed Forces in the Field, Aug. 12, 1949, [1955] 3 UST 3114, TIAS No 3362, 75 UNTS 31; Geneva Convention for the Amelioration of the Condition of Wounded, Sick and Shipwrecked Members of Armed Forces at Sea, Aug. 12, 1949, [1955] 3 UST 3217, TIAS No. 3363, 75 UNTS 85; Geneva Convention Relative to the Treatment of Prisoners of War, Aug. 12, 1949, [1955] 3 UST 3316 TIAS No. 3364, 75 UNTS 135; Geneva Convention Relative to the Protection of Civilian Persons in Time of War, Aug. 12, 1949, [1955] 3 UST 3516, TIAS No. 3365, 75 UNTS 287. For a consideration of the application of the laws of war to a Vietnam-type conflict, see Falk, ed., *The Vietnam War and International Law* (1968), Vol. II, 361–571.

American contention, repeated in President Nixon's speech of November 3, 1969, would suggest that the United States government is obliged to treat the Vietnam conflict as a war of international character to which the entire law of war applies.

Several provisions of the Army Field Manual clearly establish the obligation of the United States to apprehend and punish the commission of war crimes.[19]

These provisions make it amply clear that war crimes are to be prosecuted and punished and that responsibility is acknowledged to extend far beyond the level of the individuals who performed the physical acts that inflicted harm. In fact, the effectiveness of the law of war depends, above all else, on holding those in command and in policymaking positions responsible for the behavior of the rank-and-file soldiers on the field of battle. The reports of neuropsychiatrists, trained in combat therapy, have suggested that unrestrained behavior by troops is an expression almost always of tacit authorization, at least, on the part of commanding officers, a form of authorization that conveys to the rank-and-file soldier the absence of any prospect of punishment for the outrageous behavior.[20] It would thus be a deception to punish the triggermen at Son My without also looking further up the chain of command to identify the truer locus of responsibility.[21]

III COMMENTS ON THE SON MY MASSACRE

The events took place on March 16, 1968. The Secretary of Defense admitted knowledge of these events eight months before their public disclosure. The disclosure resulted from the publication in the *Cleveland Plain Dealer* in November 1969 of a photograph of the massacre taken by Ronald Haeberle. The lapse of time, the existence of photographs, the report of the helicopter pilot, the large number of American personnel (approximately eighty men

---

[19] "The Law of Land Warfare," Department of the Army Field Manual, FM 27-10, July 1956 §§ 506–11, 181–83.

[20] See Edward M. Opton, Jr., and Robert Duckles, "Mental Gymnastics on Mylai," *New Republic*, Feb. 21, 1970, 14–16.

[21] It might also be a deception to punish the civilian and military leaders as war criminals, the opposite kind of deception from that which results from punishing the men on the battlefield. By punishing the leaders, the public is able to distance itself from events which are largely acquiesced in at the time of their occurrence. The enterprise of criminal punishment has not yet demonstrated that the punishment of criminals reduces the prospects for crime even in domestic society, much less in international society. At the same time, the identification of crime is essential for the establishment of limits on permissible behavior and to encourage the formation of clear lines of moral consciousness that might condition and guide future leaders and their followers.

of Company C, First Battalion, 20th Infantry Division) involved in the incident, create a deep suspicion that news of the massacre was suppressed at various levels of command and that its disclosure was delayed at the highest levels of military and civilian government. The numerous other reports of atrocities connected with the war have also not been generally investigated or punished with seriousness. In fact, other evidence of atrocities has been ignored or deliberately suppressed by military authorities at all levels of the US command structure.

The massacre at Son My exhibits a bestiality toward the sanctity of civilian lives that exceeds earlier atrocities that took place at Lidice or Guernica. At Lidice, Czechoslovakia, on June 10, 1942, the male population of the town was shot, women were taken off to concentration camps, and the children sent off to schools and families.[22] At Son My women and children were not spared. At Guernica bombs were dropped on an undefended Spanish village, terrorizing and killing the inhabitants, a scene made universal by Picasso's mural commemorating the horrifying events. Such military tactics are daily employed by American forces in Vietnam. At Son My civilians were systematically chosen; they were the intended victims of the act, not the uncertain, random victims of an air attack.

The Son My massacre is the culmination of the policies of counterinsurgency warfare in South Vietnam. It is not, however, an isolated atrocity, as many other occurrences in South Vietnam have revealed a brutal disregard of Vietnamese civilians and have disclosed little or no effort by military commanders to punish and prevent this behavior. In addition, the Son My massacre is consistent with the overall effort of "denying" the National Liberation Front its base of support among the civilian population of Vietnam, whether by the assassination of civilians alleged to be NLF cadres (from December 1967 to December 1968 several thousand civilians were killed in the Phoenix Operation), by fire-bomb zone attacks against villages in NLF-held territory, defoliation and crop destruction, and by search-and-destroy missions that involved the destruction of the homes and villages of many thousand Vietnamese civilians. It is estimated by the US Senate Subcommittee on Refugees, chaired by Senator Edward Kennedy, that over 300,000 South Vietnamese civilians have been killed since the beginning of the war, mainly by US air strikes and artillery. Such a figure represents a number six times as great as American war dead, and suggests the indiscriminate use of weapons

---

[22] For an account of the Lidice massacre, see J. Hutak, *With Blood and with Iron: The Lidice Story* (London: R. Hale, 1957). It is true that Son My was not an occurrence that was ordered by the United States military command in Vietnam in any explicit fashion.

against the very people that the US government contends it is fighting the war to protect.[23]

The massacre at Son My stands out as a landmark atrocity in the history of warfare, and its occurrence represents a moral challenge to American society. This challenge was summarized by Mrs. Anthony Meadlow, the mother of David Paul Meadlow, one of the soldiers at Son My, in a simple sentence: "I sent them a good boy, and they made him a murderer."[24] Another characteristic statement about the general character of the war was attributed to an army staff sergeant: "We are at war with the ten-year-old children. It may not be humanitarian, but that's what it's like."[25]

IV PERSONAL RESPONSIBILITY IN LIGHT OF SON MY

The massacre at Son My raises two broad sets of issues about personal responsibility for the commission of war crimes:

First, the legal scope of personal responsibility for a specific act or pattern of belligerent conduct;

Second, the extralegal scope of personal responsibility of citizens in relation to war crimes and to varying degrees of participation in an illegal war.

A *The War Criminal: Scope of Responsibility*

We have already suggested that evidence exists that many official battlefield policies relied upon by the United States in Vietnam amount to war crimes. These official policies should be investigated in light of the legal obligations of the United States and, if found to be "illegal," then these policies should be ceased forthwith and those responsible for the policy and its execution should be removed and barred from positions of leadership.[26] These remarks definitely apply to the following war policies, and very likely to others: (1) the Phoenix Program, (2) aerial and naval bombardment of undefended villages, (3) destruction of crops and forests, (4) "search-and-destroy" missions, (5) "harassment and interdiction" fire, (6) forcible removal of civilian

---

[23] For a full presentation of United States war crimes in Vietnam, see E. Herman, *Atrocities in Vietnam: Myths and Realities* (Philadelphia: Pilgrim Press, 1970). A slightly fictionalized report of one war crime reveals the overall moral depravity of the American conduct in Vietnam: D. Lang, *Casualties of War* (New York: McGraw-Hill, 1969).

[24] *New York Times*, Nov. 30, 1969, 1.

[25] *New York Times*, Dec. 1, 1969, 12.

[26] The purpose of such action would be to confirm the limits of official discretion and to assert criteria for responsible leadership. Punishment would not be an objective.

population, (7) reliance on a variety of weapons prohibited by treaty. In addition, allegations of all war atrocities should be investigated and reported upon.[27] These atrocities – committed in defiance of declared official policy – should be punished. Responsibility should be imposed upon those who inflicted the harm, upon those who gave direct orders, and upon those who were in a position of command entrusted with overall battlefield decorum and with the prompt detection and punishment of war crimes committed within the scope of their authority.

Finally, political leaders who authorized illegal battlefield practices and policies, or who had knowledge of these practices and policies and failed to act, are similarly responsible for the commission of war crimes. The following paragraph from the Majority Judgment of the Tokyo War Crimes Tribunal is relevant:

> A member of a Cabinet which collectively, as one of the principal organs of the Government, is responsible for the care of prisoners is not absolved from responsibility if, having knowledge of the commission of the crimes in the sense already discussed, and omitting or failing to secure the taking of measures to prevent the commission of such crimes in the future, he elects to continue as a member of the Cabinet. This is the position even though the Department of which he has the charge is not directly concerned with the care of prisoners. A Cabinet member may resign. If he has knowledge of ill-treatment of prisoners, is powerless to prevent future ill-treatment, but elects to remain in the Cabinet thereby continuing to participate in its collective responsibility for protection of prisoners he willingly assumes responsibility for any ill-treatment in the future.
>
> Army or Navy commanders can, by order, secure proper treatment and prevent ill-treatment of prisoners. So can Ministers of War and of the Navy. If crimes are committed against prisoners under their control, of the likely occurrence of which they had, or should have had, knowledge in advance, they are responsible for those crimes. If, for example, it be shown that within the units under his command conventional war crimes have been committed of which he knew or should have known, a commander who takes no adequate steps to prevent the occurrence of such crimes in the future will be responsible for such future crimes.[28]

The United States government was directly associated with the development of a broad conception of criminal responsibility for the leadership of a

---

[27] Modest efforts along these lines have been undertaken by a group of courageous young Americans who have been working with returning veterans of the Vietnam War: National Committee for a Citizens' Commission of Inquiry on US War Crimes in Vietnam.

[28] See L. Sohn, ed., *Cases on United Nations Law* (London: Stevens, 1956), quoted in excerpt from Judgment of the International Military Tribunal for the Far East, Nov. 4–12, 1948, 909.

state during war. A leader must take affirmative acts to prevent war crimes or dissociate himself from the government. If he fails to do one or the other, then, by the very act of remaining in a government of a state guilty of war crimes, he becomes a war criminal.[29]

Finally, as both the Nuremberg and the Tokyo Judgments emphasize, a government official is a war criminal if he has participated in the initiation or execution of an illegal war of aggression. There are considerable grounds for regarding the United States involvement in the Vietnam War – wholly apart from the conduct of the war – as involving the violation of the United Nations Charter and other treaty obligations of the United States.[30] If US participation in the war is found illegal, then the policymakers responsible for the war during its various stages are theoretically subject to prosecution as alleged war criminals.

B *Responsibility as a Citizen*

The idea of prosecuting war criminals involves using international law as a sword against violators in the military and civilian hierarchy of government. But the Nuremberg Principles imply a broader human responsibility to oppose an illegal war and illegal methods of warfare. There is nothing to suggest that the ordinary citizen, whether within or outside the armed forces, is potentially guilty of a war crime merely as a consequence of such a status. But there are grounds to maintain that anyone who believes or has reason to believe that a war is being waged in violation of minimal canons of law and morality has an obligation of conscience to resist participation in and support of that war effort by every means at his disposal. In this respect, the Nuremberg Principles provide guidelines for citizens' conscience and a shield that can and should be used in the domestic legal system to interpose obligations under international law between the government and the society. Such a doctrine of interposition has been asserted in a large number of selective service cases by individuals

---

[29] For various perspectives on the scope and extent of criminal responsibility in relation to the Vietnam War, see G. Wald, "Corporate Responsibility for War Crimes," *New York Review of Books*, Jul. 2, 1970, 4–6; T. Hoopes II, "The Nuremberg Suggestion," *Washington Monthly*, Jan. 1970, 18–21; J. Reston, Jr., "Is Nuremberg Coming Back to Haunt Us?," *Saturday Review*, Jul, 18, 1970, 14–17, 61.

[30] For succinct argument along these lines, see Q. Wright, "Legal Aspects of the Viet Nam Situation," in Falk, ed., *The Vietnam War and International Law*, Vol. I, 271–91; a more extended legal analysis reaching these conclusions has been prepared by the Consultative Council of the Lawyers Committee on American Policy Toward Vietnam, published under the title *Vietnam and International Law* (J. Fried, rapporteur, 2d ed., 1967).

refusing to enter the armed forces. This assertion has already enjoyed a limited success.[31]

The issue of personal conscience is raised for everyone in the United States. It is raised more directly for anyone called upon to serve in the armed forces. It is raised in a special way for parents of minor children who are conscripted into the armed forces. It is raised for all taxpayers whose payments are used to support the cost of the war effort. It is raised for all citizens who in various ways endorse the war policies of the government. The circle of responsibility is drawn around all who have or should have knowledge of the illegal and immoral character of the war. The Son My massacre put every American on notice as to the character of the war.

And the circle of responsibility does not end at the border. Foreign governments and their populations are pledged by the Charter of the United Nations to oppose aggression and to take steps to punish the commission of war crimes. The cause of peace is indivisible, and all those governments and people concerned with Charter obligations have a legal and moral duty to oppose the continuation of the American involvement in Vietnam and to support the effort to identify, prohibit, and punish the commission of war crimes. The conscience of the entire world community is implicated by inaction, as well as by more explicit forms of support for US policy.

V SOME STANDARD OBJECTIONS

Several objections to the position that I have taken are frequently made. The purpose of this section is to consider these objections briefly.

All War Is Hell. This objection emphasizes that war is the basic evil and that the effort to prohibit certain acts of conduct is futile (all prohibitions yield to military necessity) or, worse yet, deceptive (fostering the belief that war can somehow be reconciled with the dictates of conscience, provided only that the rules of the game are upheld). There is an undeniable element of validity in both grounds of this objection but, in my view, there is a far larger element of misapprehension and nihilism present. First of all, the minimum objective of the laws of war is to deter military behavior that causes death, suffering,

---

[31] United States v. Sisson, 297 F. Supp. 902 (D. Mass. 1969). For some insight into the reasoning of war resisters, see N. Woodstone, *Up Against the War* (New York: Tower Publications, 1970); W. Gaylin, *In the Service of Their Country/War Resisters in Prison* (New York: Grosset & Dunlap, 1970); see also P. Berrigan, *Prison Journals of a Priest Revolutionary* (New York: Ballantine Books, 1970).

and destruction, but which is not related to the rational pursuit of belligerent objectives – that is, which is not consistent with a reasonable interpretation of military necessity. The events at Son My appear to be of such a character as to work *against* rather than *for* the military objectives of the American involvement in Vietnam. In any event, the safeguarding of noncombatants, of prisoners of war, of sacred cultural and religious sites, of the sick and wounded and the prohibition of certain weapons and tactics of warfare have had the effect of sparing a certain finite number of people – especially the aged, the infirm, and the young – from the full horror of warfare in which plunder, pillage, and wanton destruction were regarded as unavoidable aspects of warfare. The modern history of international law, beginning with the work of Grotius in the early seventeenth century, proceeded from the perception that it is desirable and possible to reduce the suffering associated with war even if it is impossible to eliminate the institution of war itself from the experience of mankind. Recent warfare in Vietnam, Korea, Nigeria, and the Congo suggests the importance of strengthening, rather than abandoning, the long tradition of the law of war.

The Crimes of the Other Side. A second principal objection to the position in my text is that it is not even-handed, that it imposes responsibility for war crimes on one side and ignores (or worse, overlooks) the war crimes of the other side. In this view, the National Liberation Front and North Vietnam are guilty of a variety of atrocities including systematic recourse to wanton terror against the civilian population of South Vietnam. My response to this contention is partly a logical one, namely, that the commission of war crimes by the other side is irrelevant (or at least must be shown to be relevant) to the commission of war crimes by the United States in Vietnam. In this vein, I find no connection whatsoever between allegations of "enemy" war crimes and the American reliance on concentrated firepower, napalm, B-52 raids, and chemical poisons; in both instances, the principal victims are Vietnamese civilians. Furthermore, the high-technology military machine used by the United States inflicts the great proportion of civilian casualties and results in the destruction of most villages. Such a comparison of effects is a natural consequence of a 500:1 edge in relative firepower and expresses the character of a war between a high-technology political system and a low-technology political system. Finally, my best information suggests that the alleged atrocities attributed to the other side have either been exaggerated or have involved recourse to discriminating tactics of violence such as satisfy the military necessity test in this kind of military struggle for political control (for instance, the selective assassination of village officials loyal to the Saigon regime).

Laws of War Are Obsolete in Counterinsurgency Situations. The objection here is that in counterinsurgency warfare of the Vietnam variety the traditional bases of the laws of war are undermined. There are no discernible lines of battle, no military targets, no uniforms by which to differentiate "the guerrilla fighter" from the rest of the population. A successful insurgency, it is true, works to blur, and eventually to eliminate, the distinction between the insurgent and the general civilian population. How can the incumbent fight against such an enemy without using tactics that suspend deference to the civilian population or to nonmilitary targets? Furthermore, in a primitive country, there are very few military targets. Reliance on airpower as a continuing weapon leads to destroying anything that stands or moves in territory where the insurgent holds sway. Ideas of "free bomb zones," search-and-destroy missions, and incidents such as took place at Son My are the logical sequel of such a doctrine of counterinsurgency warfare. At such a point, the continuation of the war by relying on modern weaponry does take on a genocidal character.

In a more technical vein, to the extent that the Hague and Geneva treaty rules are obsolete, then it is appropriate, without awaiting new treaties, to attempt new applications of the basic customary rules at stake; the avoidance of unnecessary suffering and destruction; the maintenance of the distinction between civilian and military targets and personnel, at least to the extent possible; and the avoidance altogether of the inherently cruel.

Some may say that war crimes have been committed by both sides in Vietnam and, therefore, prosecution should be even-handed, and that North Vietnam and the Provisional Revolutionary Government of South Vietnam should be called upon to prosecute their officials guilty of war crimes. Such a contention needs to be understood, however, in the overall context of the war, especially in relation to the identification of which side is the victim of aggression and which side is the aggressor. More narrowly, the allegation of war crimes by the other side does not operate as a legal defense against a war crimes indictment. This question was clearly litigated and decided at Nuremberg.

Others have argued that there can be no war crimes in Vietnam because war has never been "declared" by the US government. The failure to declare war under these circumstances raises a substantial constitutional question, but it has no bearing upon the rights and duties of the United States under international law. A declaration of war is a matter of internal law, but the existence of combat circumstances is a condition of war that brings into play the full range of obligations under international law governing the conduct of a war.

VI PROPOSALS

The evidence suggests that the current condition of the laws of warfare is inadequate for several principal reasons:

First, the rules were evolved long ago under conditions that seem remote from the nature of modern warfare;

Second, such remoteness in time and tactics tends to obscure the persisting relevance of underlying policies – the prohibition of cruel and unnecessary suffering not clearly related to the legitimate pursuit of belligerent objectives.

Hence, the rules need to be restated and the climate for their effective implementation needs to be created. Technicians need to prepare new draft treaties, and statesmen have to be persuaded to sign and adhere. The widespread revulsion with the persistence of war creates the basis for such constructive developments.

I would propose three concrete steps at the present time:

(1) A *Second Series of Hague Conferences* to agree upon a new code of warfare. Such conferences should be regarded as political occasions (as contrasted to the 1949 series of meetings of experts in Geneva) on which a new moral and legal consensus is formed such as emerged, quite unexpectedly, from the Hague Conferences of 1899 and 1907. It would be difficult, of course, to reach agreement on many matters, partly for reasons of ideology, partly for reasons of technology and military doctrine, but it would clearly be worth the effort. The process of proposing, discussing, and responding would heighten the awareness of government officials and would help revive a clearer appreciation of the basic policies to be served by the laws of war. This appreciation would, I think, without being too optimistic or naive, be likely to influence the decision processes of governments during a period of war and would make the international community more likely to repudiate departures from these policies.

(2) A *National Board of Legal Experts* appointed, perhaps, by a legal society such as the American Bar Association, to undertake an inquiry into the extent to which the laws of war were violated during the course of the Vietnam War.[32] Such a Board should be empowered to subpoena military and civilian officials and to hear testimony from soldiers and from

---

[32] This suggestion closely resembles the recommendation of Leonard B. Boudin in a paper given at the 1970 Annual Meeting of the American Bar Association in St. Louis under the title "Nuremberg and the Indochinese War" (mimeographed draft dated Aug. 12, 1970).

civilian complainants. The purpose of the inquiry would be to facilitate a process of moral and legal clarification about the manner in which the Vietnam War was waged. The Board could be entrusted with the capacity to recommend the preparation of criminal indictments against any individual whom it had reason – after a due process inquiry – to believe committed war crimes, but such an authority is probably not desirable. First of all, it would be impractical to discharge such a mandate given the likely number of individuals who might become implicated. Second, there is no clear evidence that criminal punishment deters crime or rehabilitates the criminal. Third, the Vietnam War depended for support on so many aspects of societal cooperation that it seems to be scapegoating whether one selects the triggermen or the prominent leaders; in the one case, the leadership attempts to isolate itself from the crime, whereas in the other the populace attempts to relinquish its own responsibility. The National Board should issue a report containing its findings and recommendations. The objective should be educational in the broad sense of raising the national level of consciousness about the issue of war crimes.

(3) A *National Proclamation of Amnesty.* Part of the process of moral clarification should involve amnesty for those who refused to participate in a war deemed unjust. The criminality of the official policies accounted for much of the opposition to the war, and it seems almost a continuation of those war policies to punish as criminals those who refused to take part. Indeed, the use of criminal law and of prison to punish war resisters has eroded respect for law in general and has created in the minds of many young Americans a dangerous tension between legality and legitimacy. It will be difficult to relax this tension without a grant of amnesty for those in jail or exile because of war resistance.

VII CONCLUSION

This article has examined some of the wider implications of the Son My disclosures. These disclosures suggest the existence of a far wider net of responsibility than is implicit in the criminal prosecution of the perpetrators of the massacre. These individuals – many of whom have been described as men of good character and spotless records – were caught up in a brutalizing climate of warfare in which disregard for the lives and welfare of the Vietnamese civilian population was the essence of fighting the war. Their acts were merely an extreme enactment of official policy. In repudiating official policy it is necessary to move beyond ideas of crime and punishment. The need is for self-education and for a moral and legal renewal, epitomized by a new code of laws and by a belated realization that war resistance was behavior in the nation's service. By proceeding along these lines it may be possible to gain something even from the massacre at Son My.

8

The Cambodian Operation and International Law

I believe the United States has a strong interest in developing rules of international law that limit claimed rights to use armed force and encourage the peaceful resolution of disputes.

John R. Stevenson, Legal Adviser, "United States Military
Actions in Cambodia: Questions of International Law,"
Department of State Bulletin 62 (1970), 766

[P]ublic, Congressional and international support also depends on a prompt and convincing demonstration of the legality of our actions; we cannot afford to wait until action is taken to start preparing our case.

William P. Rogers, Secretary of State, Memorandum dated June 13, 1970,
reported in *New York Times*, June 24, 1970, p. 3

The invasion of Cambodian territory by the armed forces of the United States and South Viet-Nam in the spring of 1970 raises serious questions of international law. The development of international law since the end of World War I exhibits a consistent effort to prohibit recourse to force by governments in international society. The Nuremberg Judgment called aggression against a foreign country "the supreme crime" against mankind. The United Nations Charter is built around the notion that the only occasions on which it is legal to use force are in response to an armed attack and as authorized by an organ of the United Nations. The Cambodian operation was obviously neither a response to a prior armed attack upon South Viet-Nam nor an action authorized or ratified by the United Nations. In announcing the decision to the American public on April 30, 1970, President Nixon made no effort to justify the invasion under international law. Such a failure of explanation illustrates the extreme unilateralism that has been exhibited by the United States Government throughout the Viet-Nam War. This failure lends credence to the contention that the

United States is conducting an imperial war of repression in Indochina and that it owes explanations for its policy, if at all, only to the American public and, even then, mainly to provide reassurance about the relevance of a challenged policy to the welfare of American troops. Perhaps the most remarkable passage in Mr. Nixon's April 30th address is the arrogant assertion that an American invasion of an Asian country is of no international concern:

> These actions [in Cambodia] are in no way directed at the security interests of any nation. Any government that chooses to use these actions as a pretext for harming relations with the United States will be doing so on its own responsibility and on its own initiative, and we will draw the appropriate conclusions.[1]

The United States Government had been on record over and over again in support of the position that when a border-crossing armed attack occurs, it is a matter of grave concern for the entire community of nations, and that it is a matter of collective determination whether or not a challenged action is disruptive of world order and its fundamental norms of prohibition.[2]

---

[1] Text of Address reprinted in *Department of State Bulletin*, 62 (1970). President Nixon's attitude toward international law as revealed in the Cambodian operation was foreshadowed in a significant passage in his book, *Six Crises* (rev. ed.; New York: Pyramid Books, 1968). In analyzing the 1960 campaign for the presidency Mr. Nixon acknowledges that Kennedy outmaneuvered him by advocating a hard line against Castro's Cuba. To differentiate his position from that of Kennedy and to shield the Bay of Pigs operation, then in a planning stage, from premature disclosure, Nixon felt obliged in 1960 to "go to the other extreme" and "attack the Kennedy proposal of such aid as wrong and irresponsible because it would violate our treaty commitments." Reflecting on his presentation, Nixon writes "that the position I had taken on Cuba hurt rather than helped me. The average voter is not interested in the technicalities of treaty obligations. He thinks, quite properly, that Castro is a menace, and he favors the candidate who wants to do something about it – something positive and dramatic and forceful – and not the one who takes the 'statesmanlike' and 'legalistic' view": Nixon, *Six Crises*, 382, 384. President Nixon's handling of the Cambodian invasion embodied the same scornful disregard for legal restraint, urging a bold course of action on the basis of sovereign prerogative that seemed designed to appeal to patriotic rather than to world-order impulses of the citizenry.

[2] One prominent example of the American attitude toward the Charter prohibition upon recourse to force was the initial statement by the US delegate, Adlai Stevenson, in the Security Council debate occasioned by India's invasion of Goa on December 18, 1961: Security Council, Official Records, 987th meeting, Dec. 18, 1961. Two portions of Ambassador Stevenson's statement are of particular relevance to the relationship between the Cambodian operation and the UN Charter, the fundamental legal document governing recourse to force in international affairs. The first, near the beginning of his presentation, is:

> When acts of violence take place between nations in this dangerous world, no matter where they occur or for what cause, there is reason for alarm. The news from Goa tells of such acts of violence. It is alarming news, and, in our judgment, the Security Council has an urgent duty to act in the interests of international peace and security.

(p. 66)

What made Mr. Nixon's statement especially troublesome – and it was not qualified or balanced by other statements – is the refusal to acknowledge the possible relevance of any external source of authority with respect to American claims to use force across an international boundary. The sovereign word is endorsed as the final word, and critical reactions by other countries are to be regarded, it would seem, as unwarranted and unacceptable interference in our affairs. Would the United States want the same rules of non-accountability to govern the behavior of China or the Soviet Union, or even small countries like Cuba or Israel? What if Cuba had attacked the exile base areas in Florida and Central America where planning was going forward for the Bay of Pigs operation that was to occur in April 1961? Would the United States have indulged Cuban claims that such action was not directed at "security interests" of other nations? And not only security interests are at issue; more importantly, the concern is with the existence of minimum standards of international behavior applicable to all governments on a basis of mutuality. The United States made this very clear in 1956 when it refused to acquiesce in the limited invasion of Egyptian territory by its own allies. Such a refusal to overlook these actions at the height of the Cold War, during a period when the Soviet Union was so brutally intervening in Hungarian internal affairs, suggests how strongly the United States Government at one time supported a strict interpretation of UN Charter prohibitions on the use of force.

It is true that on May 5, 1970, Ambassador Charles Yost reported by letter to the President of the Security Council that the United States had acted in "collective self-defense" because of the intensification of North Vietnamese activity in Cambodian base areas.[3] It is also true that the Legal Adviser to the Secretary of State, John R. Stevenson, fully developed an international law argument in support of the Cambodian operation in an address delivered at the Hammarskjöld Forum of the Association of the Bar of the City of New York, which was subsequently published in the *Department of State*

Ambassador Stevenson made it clear that the Charter prohibition, aside from circumstances of self-defense, is not properly susceptible to self-serving interpretation:

> Let it be perfectly clear what is at stake here; it is the question of the use of armed force by one State against another and against its will, an act clearly forbidden by the Charter. We have opposed such action in the past by our closest friends as well as by others. We opposed it in Korea in 1950, in Suez and in Hungary in 1956 and in the Congo in 1960.

(p. 72)

[3]   UN Doc. S/9781, May 5, 1970; *Department of State Bulletin*, 62 (1970); *American Journal of International Law*, 64 (1970). The reasoning of Ambassador Yost's letter will be found in n. 47 below.

Bulletin as an official document.[4] But Mr. Stevenson spoke primarily to a domestic audience (and then not until May 28 and the publication date was not until June 22). Although his formulation constitutes the most authoritative legal argument put forth by the Administration, it hardly qualifies, because of its domestic setting and its timing, as compliance with the requirement that a government give an accounting to the world community of its decision to use military force in a foreign society. President Nixon's formulation has to be treated as the prime datum for assessing the merit of the Administration's contention that the invasion of Cambodia was consistent with the rules and standards of international law. Aggressors normally disguise their action by making claims of legal right. The Soviet Union claimed an invitation from the "legitimate" government as the basis for its action in Hungary in 1956 and again in Czechoslovakia in 1968, although in the latter case it relied more heavily upon an alleged right of collective intervention to maintain the integrity of the Socialist community.[5] It is always possible to put together a legal argument in support of any partisan position. The whole idea of legal order is based on the possibility of fair and reliable procedures to assess which of several competing legal arguments best fits the facts and governing legal rules. The purpose of this article is to demonstrate that the American invasion of Cambodia was a violation of international law, given the facts, the law, past practice, public policy, and the weight of expert opinion.

I THE ADMINISTRATION ARGUMENT

It seems necessary, first of all, to clarify to the extent possible the scope of the claim being asserted by the United States in relation to Cambodia. The shifting line of official explanation is ambiguous about the real objective. On April 30 President Nixon repeated several times in different formulations that the purpose of the invasion was to destroy North Vietnamese sanctuaries along the Cambodian border and thereby to protect American lives. In Mr. Nixon's words, "attacks are being launched this week to clean out major enemy

---

4   John R. Stevenson, "United States Military Actions in Cambodia: Questions of International Law," *Department of State Bulletin*, 62 (1970); reprinted in *American Journal of International Law*, 64 (1970).

5   The so-called Brezhnev doctrine rests on the subordination of individual Socialist countries to the interests of world Socialism as these interests are construed by "the camp of Socialism" as a whole. For some interpretation see Richard Falk, "The Legitimacy of Zone II as a Structure of Domination," in H. Sprout, M. Sprout, J. Rosenau, V. Davis, and M. East (eds.), *The Analysis of International Politics* (New York: Free Press, 1972), and E. Firmage, "Summary and Interpretation," in Richard Falk (ed.), *The International Law of Civil War* (Baltimore: Johns Hopkins University Press, 1971), 405–28.

sanctuaries on the Cambodia–Vietnam border." The timing of the attack was justified by reference to two separate circumstances:

(1) "the enemy in the past 2 weeks has stepped up his guerrilla actions, and he is concentrating his main forces in these sanctuaries . . . where they are building up to launch massive attacks on our forces and those of South Viet-Nam."

(2) "North Viet-Nam in the last 2 weeks has stripped away all pretense of respecting the sovereignty or the neutrality of Cambodia. Thousands of their soldiers are invading the country from the sanctuaries; they are encircling the Capital Phnom Penh . . . [I]f this enemy effort succeeds, Cambodia would become a vast enemy staging area and a springboard for attacks on South Viet-Nam along 600 miles of frontier, a refuge where enemy troops could return from combat without fear of retaliation."

President Nixon seemed to suggest that the invasion was responsive to both of these occurrences, given the parallel American decision to provide the Lon Nol régime with arms assistance and to pay for Thai "volunteers." In essence, then, alleged North Vietnamese actions within Cambodia were given as the sole basis for initiating a military attack across the boundary. Mr. Nixon seemed to emphasize *future* danger rather than any *immediate* threat to the safety of American lives – "Unless we indulge in wishful thinking, the lives of Americans in Vietnam after our next withdrawal of 150,000 would be gravely threatened." And in the course of a news conference on the evening of May 8, Mr. Nixon made even clearer that the focus of his concern was the rather distant set of circumstances existing after the scheduled withdrawal of 150,000 American soldiers has been completed in April 1971.[6]

The invasion claim was limited in mission, scope, and duration, although in *execution* villages were destroyed that were neither sanctuaries nor weapons depots, and vast quantities of rice belonging to Cambodian peasants were either confiscated or destroyed. The mission was confined to the destruction of sanctuaries which were supposed to have included, according to Mr. Nixon, "the headquarters for the entire Communist military operation in South

---

[6] Mr. Nixon was asked how he could have announced on April 20th that Vietnamization was going so well that 150,000 Americans could be withdrawn by the spring of 1971 and then on April 30th that the Cambodian operation was necessary to protect the Vietnamization program from disruption. The President's response included these two sentences: "I found that the action that the enemy had taken in Cambodia would leave 240,000 Americans who would be there a year from now without many combat troops to help defend them, would leave them in an untenable position. That is why I had to act" (*Department of State Bulletin*, 62 (1970), 642).

Viet-Nam." The scope of the invasion, at least for American ground forces, was confined to a 21.7-mile strip of Cambodian territory along the border, and the invasion, again at least for American troops, was to be terminated by the end of June 1970.[7] In reporting on the invasion, Mr. Nixon said on June 3 that

> The success of these operations to date has guaranteed that the June 30 deadline I set for withdrawal of all American forces from Cambodia will be met . . . This includes all American air support, logistics, and military advisory personnel.
> The only remaining American activity in Cambodia after July 1 will be air missions to interdict the movement of enemy troops and material where I find that is necessary to protect the lives and security of our men in South Viet-Nam.

Initially the main official response to the legal challenges directed at the President's decision consisted of an effort to show that the Cambodian operation was a valid exercise of Mr. Nixon's powers as Commander-in-Chief of the armed forces.[8] At his May 8th news conference, Mr. Nixon said: "As Commander in Chief, I alone am responsible for the lives of 425 or 430,000 Americans in Viet-Nam. That's what I've been thinking about and the decision that I made on Cambodia will save those lives." Such an assertion of responsibility – presumably a responsibility shared in common with all Heads of State – is hardly relevant to a discussion of the status of the invasion in international law. Surely, the lives of the North Vietnamese armed forces are deeply endangered by the use of air fields in Thailand, Guam, and Okinawa. The point here is that such an explanation is at best responsive to the line of criticism that has contended that the initiation of the Cambodian invasion by Presidential decision amounted to an act of Executive usurpation in violation of the United States Constitution.[9]

---

[7]   The failure by the Government to disclose additional American activity in Cambodia makes it difficult to describe the claim with accuracy. Only on June 21, 1970, was it reported that American air strikes were regularly penetrating far beyond the announced 21.7-mile limit. These raids were initiated at the same time as the invasion, but have not been officially acknowledged or defended as yet. The report also indicated doubt as to whether the raids would end with the June 30th pull-out of American troops. The purpose of these raids is to prevent the North Vietnamese from establishing a new supply route into South Viet-Nam: *New York Times*, June 22, 1970, 1, 20. It has become subsequently clear, of course, that the United States regularly provides close air support to Cambodian ground operations.

[8]   The validity of such executive authority has been largely supported even in the US Senate, which affirmed by a vote of 79–5 the power of the President as Commander-in-Chief to take military action in Cambodia to protect the welfare of American troops in South Viet-Nam. The vote was taken in relation to an amendment offered to modify the Cooper–Church amendment: *New York Times*, June 23, 1970, 1, 3.

[9]   See W. D. Rogers, "The Constitutionality of the Cambodian Incursion," *American Journal of International Law*, 65 (1971), 26–37; *New Yorker*, May 16, 1970, 31–33.

Subsequently, as has already been indicated, the Legal Adviser did indeed develop a full-dress international law argument consisting of the following main elements: (1) a contention of clear and present danger to American and South Vietnamese troops arising out of the expansion of sanctuary activity in Cambodia by North Viet-Nam and the National Liberation Front; (2) a limited claim by the United States to use force in Cambodia proportional and responsive to this danger; (3) a claim that the inability of the Cambodian Government to prevent its neutral territory from being used as a sanctuary for armed forces engaged in the Viet-Nam War amounts to an abrogation, in part, at least, of Cambodia's neutral status, and justifies belligerent action of limited self-help; (4) a claim that Cambodia has been primarily invaded by North Viet-Nam and is a victim of North Vietnamese aggression; (5) the absence of any formal complaint by the Cambodian Government concerning the invasion suggests that there has been no victim of aggression and hence no aggression; and (6) the contention that North Viet-Nam is guilty of aggression against South Viet-Nam and that the United States and South Viet-Nam are entitled to take whatever steps are necessary to assure the success of their action in collective self-defense.

The Legal Adviser's argument deserves the most careful consideration so far as an analysis of the facts, rules of law, and legal expectations is concerned. As Mr. Stevenson himself says,

> It is important for the United States to explain the legal basis for its actions not merely to pay proper respect to the law but also because the precedent created by the use of armed forces in Cambodia by the United States can be affected significantly by our legal rationale.[10]

However, even if this line of argument is persuasive, which I do not believe it is, nevertheless the President's failure to reconcile a national decision to invade a foreign country with the rules of international law constitutes a major negative precedent that cannot be undone by any subsequent legal explanation. There are, in essence, two separate precedents both of which, in my judgment, violate international law: (1) the manner in which the claim was put forward; and (2) the substance of the claim. These are both serious world-order issues. Issue (1) bears upon the rôle of international law as providing a basis for governments to communicate claims and counterclaims in situations of conflict, while issue (2) concerns the framework of restraint that should be operative in the conduct of international relations. My argument is that the timing and

---

[10]   Stevenson, "United States Military Actions in Cambodia," 766.

location of Mr. Stevenson's legal presentation make it virtually irrelevant to issue (1), but important to an assessment of issue (2).

II SOME DIFFICULTIES OF LEGAL ANALYSIS

There are several special factors complicating the analysis of the Cambodian operation:

(1) *The extent of United States responsibility for South Vietnamese actions in excess of limitations of space, time, and mission imposed by the United States Government.* The underlying claim of the United States Government rests on a theory of collective self-defense. From a legal point of view, it is the victim of attack, not its external ally, that defines the necessities of action in self-defense. Of course, the realities of United States control do not change the legal situation, except to give evidence of the non-independence and illegitimacy of the Saigon régime. With respect to the Cambodian operation, it does not seem legally acceptable to confine United States responsibility to the actions of its troops. The undertaking is a joint one, and the American claim is derivative from the alleged South Vietnamese right of self-defense; furthermore, American advisers are operating in conjunction with the Saigon régime at every level of military and political operations. Thieu and Ky have repeatedly stated their Cambodian objectives in broader terms than the United States, and South Vietnamese troops have penetrated Cambodian territory beyond the 21.7-mile limit. In my judgment, the United States, from a legal perspective, is a co-venturer, responsible for the full extent of claim being made by the Saigon régime. Indeed, Secretary of Defense Laird confirmed on June 23, 1970, that the armed forces of South Viet-Nam will have a free rein to act in Cambodia after the June 30th deadline, thereby making explicit American complicity with the wider and vaguer South Vietnamese invasion claim.[11]

    When the United Kingdom, France, and Israel initiated the Suez War in 1956 as a joint venture, there was no effort to assess relative degrees of legal responsibility for the event. It seems reasonable, then, to resolve this initial complication by measuring United States responsibility by the full extent of the South Vietnamese claim and conduct in Cambodia.

(2) *The Cambodian operation represented only a battlefield decision to protect troops in the field and did not constitute an expansion of the*

---

[11] For an extensive account, see *New York Times*, June 24, 1970, 1, 7.

United States rôle in Indochina. The argument has been made by supporters of the Administration's decision that the Cambodian operation
has only tactical significance in relation to the Viet-Nam War. In this
spirit, the strike against the Cambodian sanctuaries is not different in
legal character from the decision to attack and capture Hamburger Hill.
Such matters of battlefield tactics may be criticized as ill-conceived or
ill executed, but they are not appropriately challenged on legal grounds.
    This position is defective in a fundamental respect. If a battlefield tac-
tic involves a separate issue of legality, then it is subject to legal scrutiny;
sustained border-crossing by armies is always a separate legal event of
first-order magnitude in international affairs. The main effort of modern
international law is to moderate warfare, and this effort depends greatly on
maintaining respect for boundaries. Besides, since July 1, 1970, the United
States has engaged in a series of air strikes inside Cambodian territory that
are designed to provide close support for troops of the Lon Nol régime.[12]
(3) *The failure of the United Nations to pass judgment.* The political organs of the
    United Nations system have been singularly ineffective throughout the long
    course of the Viet-Nam War. This ineffectiveness is a result of several fac-
    tors. First, the United States possesses sufficient political influence within
    the Organization to prevent an adverse judgment against it. Second, the
    non-membership of China and North Viet-Nam in the Organization makes
    these governments opposed to any United Nations rôle; in their eyes, the
    United Nations, at least as presently constituted – with Formosa continuing
    to represent China in the Security Council – is itself an illegitimate actor
    and is in no position to act on behalf of the world community. Third, the
    United Nations has been totally ineffective whenever the two super-Powers
    were deeply and directly involved in a political conflict. Fourth, the Lon
    Nol Government has not complained to the United Nations about the inva-
    sion of its territory or the destruction of its villages either by United States
    and South Vietnamese forces or by North Vietnamese and NLF forces.
    In these circumstances, it is impossible for the United Nations to
play any positive rôle, even to the extent of interpreting the requirements of its own Charter.[13] The Secretary General, U Thant, has tried to

---

[12] See J. Sterba, "Cambodia: Fact and Fable of US Air Missions," *New York Times*, Aug. 16, 1970,
    §4, p. 6.
[13] Mr. Stevenson came close to acknowledging that an American complaint before the invasion
    about North Vietnamese violations of Cambodian neutrality would not have resulted in a
    positive response: "Soundings in the Security Council indicated very little interest in taking up
    the North Vietnamese violations of Cambodian territorial integrity and neutrality" (Stevenson,
    "United States Military Actions in Cambodia," 770).

undertake peace initiatives at various points during the long course of the war, but his efforts have been resented by the governments of both sides, particularly by the United States during the Johnson Administration.

Although the United Nations has been unable to act as an Organization, the Charter continues to provide governing legal standards for a case like this one. The Charter is itself *declaratory* of prior legal standards embodied in the Kellogg–Briand Pact of 1928 and provides the most authoritative guidelines for identifying the outer limits of permissible state behavior. And surely the United States Government has not yet claimed the discretion to act in violation of the Charter. Indeed, the Charter is a treaty that has been ratified with the advice and consent of the Senate, and is, according to the US Constitution, part of "the supreme law of the land."

(4) *The failure of the Cambodian Government to condemn the invasion.* The Cambodian operation has an ambiguous character. The claim to eliminate the sanctuaries was explicitly linked by President Nixon in his April 30th speech with the struggle for political control of Cambodia. The United States, South Viet-Nam, and North Viet-Nam have intervened in this struggle in a variety of ways. The overthrow on March 18, 1970, of Prince Sihanouk as Head of State and his subsequent efforts to organize a counter-movement to regain power have been deeply destabilizing occurrences for Cambodia.[14] The Lon Nol régime almost immediately, and somewhat inexplicably, unleashed a campaign against ethnic Vietnamese who were living in Cambodia, resulting in several reported massacres, large-scale forced resettlement, and the creation of a large number of refugees.[15]

This régime was evidently unable to rule its population without strong external support. The campaign against ethnic Vietnamese and the insistence that North Viet-Nam abandon its Cambodian base areas were part of a larger effort by a weak régime to create a political climate appropriate for foreign help.

Cambodia has now become the scene of increasing foreign intervention. The Thieu–Ky régime of South Viet-Nam, despite Lon Nol's anti-Vietnamese policies, is seeking to maintain Lon Nol in power. Thailand has mobilized forces along the western boundary of Cambodia and is reported to have sent contingents of ethnic Khmers to Cambodia to fight on behalf of the Lon Nol

[14] For background, see M. Leifer, *Cambodia: The Search for Security* (London: Pall Mall Press, 1967).

[15] *New York Times*, April 19, 1970, §1, p. 28, §4, p. 3.

régime. The United States tried to persuade Thailand to send 5,000 troops to Cambodia by agreeing to finance the entire military operation.[16]

Under these circumstances it is difficult to accord any serious respect to the Lon Nol régime as a government of Cambodia. This régime does not seem able to represent the interests of its people. Its failure to protest the invasion, pillage, and occupation of its territory bears witness to its own illegitimacy, just as the willingness of the Saigon régime to enter into a friendship pact with a governing group that had so recently initiated ruthless anti-Vietnamese policies, exhibits its illegitimacy in relation to the Vietnamese people. These régimes are struggling at all costs to maintain power in the face of a highly unfavorable domestic balance of power. In this setting, their invitations to foreign governments to send in armies are of only slight legal consequence.[17] The failure of the Cambodian Government to protest the invasion of its territory by foreign forces does not, under these circumstances, amount to a valid legal authorization. Cambodia may be the victim of aggression even if its governing élite does not choose to regard it as such, especially if, as is the case, a counter-government exists that has protested the invasion. Unless such a position is taken, outside forces could intervene to place a régime in power and then use its invitation to validate its later plans of domination. There is a need to move beyond a pretense of legitimacy whenever a government demonstrates both its dependence on foreign sources of authority for its own existence and its willingness to jeopardize the independence of its country, the welfare of its people, and the inviolability of its territory on behalf of some foreign Power whose support is needed to keep the régime in control.

George McT. Kahin, an outstanding specialist on Asian affairs, pointed out the following defects of the argument that the decision to invade Cambodia did not provoke protest from the Lon Nol régime:

> It must be noted that Cambodia renounced the SEATO protocol providing protection for the former Indochina states. In point of fact, Sihanouk formally requested SEATO powers in May 1965 to amend Article IV to *exclude* Cambodia

[16] *Ibid.*, 1, 9; *ibid.*, April 26, 1970, 1; *Christian Science Monitor*, April 23, 1970, 2.

[17] The German reliance during the Nazi period upon Fifth-Column tactics to undermine the governing process in countries which were the targets of aggression should be recalled in the Cambodian context. A "Quisling" régime is one that operates in the name of a nation, but serves as agent of its dismemberment and destruction. Vidkun Quisling was the head of the Nationalist Party of Norway, a pro-Nazi group with no parliamentary representatives and little popular following. In April 1940, when Hitler invaded Norway, Quisling welcomed the German occupation of Norway and eventually obtained dictatorial powers in Norway from the Germans. The Quisling experience is an extreme case, but it usefully illustrates the undesirability of accepting a constituted régime as automatically empowered to act as the legitimate government of a country.

from SEATO's perimeter of intervention. His request was ignored but he was advised that the language of the treaty provided that intervention would not be undertaken without the request and consent of the Cambodian government.[18]

It is clearly evident that, whatever took place *subsequent* to the invasion, there is no evidence or even claim that the Cambodian Government requested or authorized the invasion, or participated in any way to define its limits.[19] In the post-invasion context, a weak, tottering régime could not be expected to protest an invasion of its territory by its principal "friend." Without American support, the Lon Nol régime would have no prospect whatsoever of maintaining power.

III THE FUNDAMENTAL LEGAL ANALYSIS: AGGRESSION OR COLLECTIVE SELF-DEFENSE

Under modern international law an invasion of a foreign country that is not authorized by a competent international institution is either an act of aggression or an exercise of self-defense. Under most circumstances, states that initiate large-scale, overt violence across an international boundary have been identified as "the aggressor." It is almost impossible for the invading government to make out a persuasive case of self-defense. Possibly the only recent counter-example was the Israeli initiation of the June War in 1967 under conditions of evident and imminent provocation and danger.

In reporting the invasion to the Security Council, the United States seemed to rest its legal case on a claim of collective self-defense. This case was later developed into a serious legal argument in Mr. Stevenson's address at the Hammarskjöld Forum.[20] The obligations of international law can be divided

[18] The Congressional Record, memorandum prepared by George McT. Kahin, "Cambodia: The Administration's Version and the Historical Record," 57431.
[19] For Administration interpretation on this point, see Stevenson, "United States Military Actions in Cambodia," 766, especially n, 9.
[20] There is a curious inconsistency in Mr. Stevenson's presentation. At the outset of his address he refers to the legal controversy over whether South Viet-Nam and the United States had a good legal basis for asserting a claim of collective self-defense, and contends that "Many of the differences rested on disputed questions of fact which could not be proved conclusively." He goes on to say that "this administration, however, has no desire to reargue those issues or the legality of those actions, which are now history" (*ibid.*, 765). But, then, throughout the address, he asserts the position of the prior Administration; for instance: "Since 1965 we and the Republic of Viet-Nam have been engaged in collective measures of self-defense against an armed attack from North Viet-Nam" (*ibid.*, 770). The Cambodian invasion is justified as a temporary extension of the underlying claim to be exercising rights of collective self-defense. By forswearing argument on whether a case for self-defense exists in Viet-Nam, Mr. Stevenson must be understood as saying either that it makes no difference or that, once troops are engaged in battle, then, whether their cause is legal or illegal, it is proper to carry out their

into two categories: *substantive norms that restrain behavior of governments,* and *procedural norms applicable to situations of alleged violation of substantive norms.* In the area of war and peace, the procedural norms are as important as the substantive norms.

Substantive Norms. The United Nations Charter provides a convenient starting point for an analysis of the norms governing recourse to force in international affairs. Article 2 of the Charter has the following key paragraph:

> (4) All Members shall refrain in their international relations from the threat or use of force against the territorial integrity or political independence of any state, or in any other manner inconsistent with the Purposes of the United Nations.

Article 51 qualifies this prohibition upon force by its limited authorization of self-defense:

> Nothing in the present Charter shall impair the inherent right of . . . self-defense if an armed attack occurs against a Member of the United Nations, until the Security Council has taken the measures necessary to maintain international peace and security . . .

The prohibition and the exception have not been defined, despite numerous international efforts, in any more specific way.

The Charter law is fairly clear: It is not permissible to use force against a foreign territory except in response to an armed attack.[21] This Charter conception expresses general international law, except that a literal reading of its language might be taken to prevent non-Members of the United Nations from claiming self-defense. North Viet-Nam and South Viet-Nam are not Members of the Organization, but this analysis will proceed on the assumption that any *state* is legally entitled to act in self-defense, whether or not a Member of the United Nations. Although there are some difficulties associated with treating South Viet-Nam as a *state*, given the language and proclaimed intentions of the Geneva Accords of 1954 to create a unified Viet-Nam no later than July 1956, nevertheless, for purposes of this article, South Viet-Nam will be treated as a sovereign state entitled to exercise rights of self-defense.[22]

---

mission. The extension of such reasoning to other settings exposes its absurdity. Should the burglar be exonerated merely because he has persisted? Or should the notion of burglary be abandoned once the burglar finds himself engaged in an encounter with the homeowner or the police?

[21] For one persuasive analysis along these lines, see Louis Henkin, "Force, Intervention, and Neutrality in Contemporary International Law," *Proceedings, American Society of International Law* (1963), 147–62.

[22] But see *Vietnam and International Law*, Legal Memorandum prepared by the Consultative Council of the Lawyers Committee on American Policy Towards Vietnam (2nd rev. ed., 1967), 34–41.

Especially, so far as the United States is concerned, the invasion of Cambodia rests on a claim of *collective* self-defense. Such a claim places a heavier burden of demonstration on the claimant, as its own territory and political independence are not at stake. Some experts even argue that under no circumstances can a state satisfy the requirements of self-defense merely by associating its action with a state that is acting in valid individual self-defense: *alliance relations* are not sufficient to vindicate the claim of the non-attacked state to participate in the exercise of rights of collective self-defense. The infringement of some more direct legal interest must serve as the basis of the claim to join in the defense of an attacked state.[23] The United States has no such distinct legal interest in relation to the defense of South Viet-Nam – neither regional, cultural, historical, nor even ideological – such as would justify its participation in the Cambodian invasion, even if South Viet-Nam could validly claim to be acting in self-defense. Dr. Bowett, who argues in favor of this restrictive view of collective self-defense, emphasizes the distinction between self-defense and the enforcement of international law:

> our contention is simply that a state resorting to force not in defense of its own rights, but in the defense of another state, must justify its action as being in the nature of a sanction and not as self-defense, individual or collective. The aim is to redress the violation of international law, not to protect its own rights.[24]

Such a view takes seriously the idea of "self" embodied in the concept of self-defense. Bowett concludes that

> The requirements of the right of collective self-defense are two in number; firstly that each participating state has an individual right of self-defense, and secondly that there exists an agreement between the participating states to exercise their rights collectively.[25]

In the context of the Cambodian operation it is clear that the first requirement of collective self-defense has not been met. Since the Charter fails to authorize states to uphold international law as a separate justification for the use of force, then it seems clear that the United States could not, under any circumstances, associate itself with a South Vietnamese claim of self-defense unless the

[23] D. W. Bowett, *Self-Defense in International Law* (New York: Bowett, 1958), 206, 216–17.
[24] *Ibid.*, 207.
[25] *Ibid.*; see also J. Stone, *Legal Controls of International Conflict* (New York: Rinehart, 1954), 245, especially the assertion that "under general international law, a State has no right of 'self-defense' in respect of an armed attack upon a third State."

exercise of the right of self-defense were converted into a United Nations action, as happened, of course, in relation to the defense of South Korea in 1950.

Such a conception of self-defense has been criticized as unduly restrictive and unrealistic, given the evolution of collective security arrangements. For instance, Myres S. McDougal and Florentino P. Feliciano, in a major work on the modern international law of force, contend that collective self-defense can be validly claimed "whenever a number of traditional bodies-politic asserting certain common demands for security as well as common expectations that such security can be achieved only by larger cooperative efforts . . . present themselves to the rest of the general community as one unified group or collectivity for purposes of security and defense."[26] This broader conception of collective self-defense underlies the various regional security pacts that the United States organized during the Dulles era as part of its containment policy directed at what was conceived to be a monolithic Communist movement intent upon world conquest.[27] Under this broader view of collective self-defense, which is probably more descriptive of practice and is generally accepted as being compatible with modern international law, the United States would be entitled to join in the Cambodian operation *provided* the facts validated the underlying claim by South Viet-Nam. Even McDougal and Feliciano place a *higher* burden of demonstration for claims of collective than for individual self-defense:

> it may be appropriate to require a higher imminence of attack and more exacting evidence of compelling necessity for coercive response by the group as such than would be reasonably demanded if the responding participant were a single state.[28]

As it is, "the traditional requirements imposed upon resort to self-defense" are most exacting: "a realistic expectation of instant, imminent military attack and carefully calculated proportionality in response."[29] There was nothing about the events in Cambodia that could qualify as establishing "a realistic

---

[26] M. McDougal and F. Feliciano, *Law and Minimum World Public Order* (New Haven: Yale University Press, 1962), 248 and, generally, 244–53.

[27] Stanley Hoffmann has recently written that "Professor McDougal's theory . . . will remain an astounding testimony to the grip of the Cold War on American thought and practice": Hoffmann, "Henkin and Falk: Mild Reformist and Mild Revolutionary," *Journal of International Affairs*, 24 (1970), 120.

[28] McDougal and Feliciano, *Law and Minimum World Public Order*, 251.

[29] *Ibid.*, 67; the most widely relied-upon description of conditions appropriate for a claim of self-defense was given by Daniel Webster on April 24, 1841, in a diplomatic note to Canada. Mr. Webster, in his capacity as US Secretary of State, wrote that there must be shown by the claimant government a "necessity of self-defense, instant, overwhelming, leaving no choice of means, and no moment for deliberation." See *British and Foreign State Papers*, 29 (1840–41), 1138.

expectation" of "instant, imminent military attack" such as could justify a claim of individual self-defense under these circumstances. Since it is more difficult to establish a claim of collective self-defense than individual self-defense, the demonstration that no basis for individual self-defense exists entails a rejection of the official United States argument.

Prior to May 1, 1970, the invasion date, there was no report of increased fighting along the border, and there were no indications of increased South Vietnamese or American casualties as a result of harassment from across the Cambodian border. Mr. Nixon never claimed more than that the expansion of the Cambodian base area might place American troops in great jeopardy by April 1971 (or almost a year after the invasion). Such a contention overlooks the prospects for interim changes either by way of negotiated settlement or successful Vietnamization of the war. The Cambodian base areas were sanctuaries used to provide logistic support to the anti-régime side in the war to control South Viet-Nam.[30] In this sense, and to a far greater extent, the United States has relied upon external base areas in Japan, South Korea, Thailand, Okinawa, Guam, and elsewhere, to conduct its belligerent operations in South Viet-Nam. Would the United States regard a Soviet air strike against these base areas as a legitimate exercise of the right of collective self-defense by North Viet-Nam or by the Provisional Revolutionary Government of South Viet-Nam? Consideration of a hypothetical reciprocal claim helps to expose the unreasonableness of the United States position and the utter absurdity of the Administration contention that expanding the combat area across the Cambodian border is not a major escalation of the war. Note also that this same unreasonableness pertains to the South Vietnamese claim of self-defense which is put forward in more extravagant terms, relating itself to the internal Cambodian struggle for control, to the treatment of Vietnamese inhabitants by the Cambodian régime, and to the presence of North Vietnamese military personnel in any part of Cambodia. Any objective reading of the facts amply demonstrates that there was no instant necessity that might lend legal support to the Cambodian operation as an exercise of the right of individual or collective self-defense.

There is, in addition, no relationship of proportionality between the claim to invade Cambodia and the alleged impact on the struggle taking place in South Viet-Nam. Indeed, it was the build-up of pressure by the Lon Nol régime to

[30] A learned and instructive discussion of the status of sanctuaries in international law is present in John H. E. Fried, "United States Military Intervention in Cambodia in the Light of International Law," paper presented to the International Conference of Lawyers on Vietnam, Laos, and Cambodia, Toronto, Canada (May 22–24, 1970), 7–25.

alter the long persisting status quo in the base areas that appeared to be the initial unsettling force. The Lon Nol régime insisted that the North Vietnamese cease to use these base areas altogether, and, as we have already mentioned, also brought provocative pressure to bear on Vietnamese residents living in Cambodia. Such tactics, presumably a dual consequence of the weakness and reactionary orientation of the régime and the strength of American pressure, were part of the effort by the Lon Nol régime to mobilize support in the building struggle against the forces supporting the deposed Prince Sihanouk, who has in recent months joined dynastic with revolutionary legitimacy, a potent political linkage in any developing country. Therefore, the main precipitating event seems to be the consequence of changes in the political situation in Cambodia, rather than any *imminent* threat to South Viet-Nam; these changes were supported, not resisted, by American action. The American claim to destroy base area camps within the 21.7-mile border strip had the predictable consequence of pushing North Vietnamese and NFL troops back toward the center of Cambodia, intensifying the struggle for political control of Cambodia, and utterly destroying any prospect for the resumption of the delicate, if stable, condition of relative neutrality that Cambodia had managed to maintain under Sihanouk's rule. Therefore, the Cambodian operation seemed ill-conceived in relation to the principal alleged danger, the collapse of a pro-Western régime in Phnom Penh and its replacement by a radical anti-Western régime.

Mr. Nixon's report to the nation on June 3, 1970, stated that "all of our major military objectives have been achieved" in the Cambodian operation.[31] These objectives were described on that occasion mainly in terms of the capture of war matériel. Reports from military officers in the field indicated that probably no more than half of the war matériel stored in the base areas was discovered and captured by the withdrawal date of June 30, 1970.[32] In that event, the alleged success of the operation would seem virtually unrelated to the level of future

---

[31] *Department of State Bulletin*, 62 (1970), 762. The legal status of the invasion is not, of course, determined by the military success or failure of the operation. However, the reasonableness of a limited claim of self-defense depends on the proportionality of means and ends, and an assessment of military success or failure may give some insight into whether the force used was proportional to the end sought.

[32] *New York Times*, June 9, 1970, 1, 5. Vice President Agnew described American objectives in more grandiose (and possibly more criminal) terms in the following statement: "The purpose of the strikes into the sanctuaries is not to go into Cambodia but to take and reduce these supply depots, *the hospital complexes*, the command network, the communications, the weapons and munitions factories and maintenance facilities that are there" (emphasis added). Hospitals as a military objective of the invasion were mentioned a second time in Mr. Agnew's remarks. See transcript of CBS TV broadcast, "Face the Nation," May 3, 1970, 3; the second reference is to be found on p. 6.

military activity in South Viet-Nam. There is no evidence that equipment shortages are likely to result for North Viet-Nam or the NLF if as much as one-half or more of the war matériel captured will still remain in the Cambodian base areas. In addition, the North Vietnamese, especially during the heavy bombardment of North Viet-Nam between February 1965 and October 1968, demonstrated great resourcefulness in circumventing efforts to interdict their supply routes.

The element of proportionality seems absent from the claim of self-defense, whether the claim is considered from the angle of the United States or from the perspective of the Saigon régime. Indeed, the invasion seems to have aggravated the very conditions it was designed to cure. Even long-time supporters of American military action have criticized the invasion as lacking any rational relationship to its proclaimed goals.[33] Certainly, Mr. Nixon's assertion that the Cambodian operation would shorten the war seems without any foundation. The arena of violence has been widened, a new country has become a theater of military operations and its people a victim of invasion,[34] and, taken in conjunction with the stepped-up American military operations in Laos, an all-Indochina war has emerged in place of the Viet-Nam War. Such an enlargement of the arena of violence and an expansion of principal actors involved in combat appear greatly to complicate the search for a negotiated settlement, which remains the proclaimed end of United States policy.

The Cambodian operation is properly compared to the earlier American extension of the war to North Viet-Nam, and much of the legal analysis of self-defense claims in the earlier setting fits the Cambodian operation as well.[35] From the point of view of legal doctrine, the assertion of a claim of self-defense against Cambodia has even less merit than did the earlier assertion against North Viet-Nam. To cross the Cambodian boundary with large armies and supporting air-force bombardments is to make a unilateral decision to attack the territory of a foreign country under circumstances where an armed attack on

[33] See Letter to the Editor, *New York Times*, May 25, 1970, 32, signed by five men, including Bernard Brodie, Morton H. Halperin, and Thomas Schelling, who write of themselves and of the Cambodian operation as follows: "We, the undersigned, have spent our professional lives in the study of strategy and American foreign policy . . . the move into Cambodia simply does not make sense." See also Les Gelb and Morton H. Halperin, "Only a Timetable Can Extricate Nixon," *Washington Post*, May 24, 1970, B1–B2.

[34] After the South Vietnamese armed forces captured the Cambodian city of Kompong Speu, extensive pillage took place. One of the Cambodian military officers on the scene, Major Soering Kimsea, reacted by saying that "the population now has more fear of the South Vietnamese than of the Vietcong. They took everything – furniture, radios, money . . . What they didn't take, they broke . . . Monks were robbed too." See *New York Times*, June 23, 1970, 2.

[35] I have written a legal analysis of this earlier phase of the conflict. See Richard Falk, ed., *The Vietnam War and International Law* (Princeton: Princeton University Press, 1968), Vol. I, 362–400, 445–508; see Vols. I and II for main legal positions in relation to the war.

South Viet-Nam was neither imminent nor probable. The most that can be said is that political changes taking place in Cambodia were jeopardizing its neutrality from both sides. This kind of circumstance may involve competing claims of limited intervention, but it certainly does not support a claim of self-defense.

Such a conclusion must be understood in relation to the entire effort of international law to remove from national governments the discretion to initiate or expand warfare across boundaries on the basis of a calculation of national advantage. Central to this endeavor is the restriction of occasions upon which it is permissible to cross openly the boundary of a foreign country with armed force. The United States, until the Viet-Nam War, had played a central rôle in using international law to build slowly an external framework of restraint based on widely shared normative conceptions.[36] Although it is true that no agreed definitions of self-defense exist, there has been a general acknowledgment that the core meaning of self-defense relates to responses against either an *actual armed attack* or a credible impression of *imminent armed attack*.[37] The diplomatic practice of the United States Government lends support to this interpretation – the United States Government has condemned as aggression the attacks by North Korea on South Korea in 1950, by Israel on Egypt in 1956, and by Belgium on the Congo in 1960, in which instances there was considerable provocation by the target countries. Egypt, for instance, was being used as a base area for persistent and officially sanctioned attacks by paramilitary forces upon Israeli territory, with the scale and frequency of attacks mounting in the months before the invasion. Nevertheless, the United States interpreted the Suez operation as a violation of the Charter and of general international law. In other words, the mere use of foreign territory as a base area has not been previously claimed by the United States to constitute such a violation of rights as to validate a claim of self-defense.[38] Under these

---

[36] There has been a steady erosion of this rôle under the pressure of geo-political and ideological considerations. Among the instances where this pressure has been resolved at the expense of legal restraints are Guatemala (1954), Lebanon (1958), Bay of Pigs (1961), the Stanleyville operation (1964), and the Dominican Republic (1965), as well as a number of less visible interventions in the affairs of foreign countries through the activities of the CIA. See n. 2 above.

[37] There are certain special circumstances of imminence, especially in relation to nuclear weapons, that make it unreasonable to limit the right of self-defense to the victim of the first act of violence. The Cuban missile crisis of 1962 and the Middle East War of 1967 are cases where it is plausible to argue that the "victim" state was also the one that struck first.

[38] The precedents relied upon by Mr. Stevenson to establish a basis for the invasion are not very convincing, as they consisted either of brief "incidents" or involved extensions of claims of "hot pursuit." See Stevenson, "United States Military Actions in Cambodia," 768–69. The United States has, indeed, denied such precedents to other countries claiming the right to strike across boundaries against external base areas. Such strikes, because of their short duration, small magnitude, and generally light casualties, represent a far less serious use of force than the Cambodian invasion.

circumstances the assertion of such a claim is itself an illegal act of aggression that may amount, if on a sufficient scale, to an armed attack upon Cambodia giving rise to a right of self-defense on the part of the state of Cambodia (even if this right is not claimed by the presently constituted régime).

In summary, then, the American contention that the Cambodia operation is a valid exercise of the right of collective self-defense seems without foundation in international law for *reasons of doctrine, diplomatic practice,* and *public policy.*

A *Special Limited Claim.* The American legal position has also been asserted in the form of a special limited claim to eliminate the base areas on Cambodian territory. This position has not been developed in a serious fashion by the United States Government. The Deputy Secretary of Defense, David Packard, did allude to this line of justification in the course of a virtually unreported speech given to the Rotary Club in Fort Worth, Texas. On that occasion Mr. Packard did say:

> Under international law we had every right to strike the enemy in areas put to such uses. The inability of Cambodia over a period of years to live up to its legal obligations as a neutral state freed us from the obligation to stay out of these areas. They were not under Cambodian control. They were not neutral.

Interestingly, Mr. Packard attributed the timing of the invasion to the changed political situation: "Our failure to disrupt the Cambodian bases earlier was dictated by political considerations which, as long as Prince Sihanouk remained in power, it was felt overrode military considerations." Mr. Packard went on to say: "With the downfall of Sihanouk, there was no longer any reason to believe that the action by South Vietnam or the United States in the occupied border areas would be objectionable to the government of Cambodia."[39] Note that Mr. Packard does not rest the case on any imminent threat to the security of American forces or on any building up of North Vietnamese capabilities. He did, in passing, mention the expansion of base area operations by "occupying enemy forces" as increasing the potential danger faced by American forces. What is important here is that, in the context of arguing on behalf of the alternate theory of enforcing Cambodia's neutral duties, Mr. Packard undercuts any assertion that conditions of imminent attack created an emergency justifying recourse to self-defense.

On its own grounds, however, the claimed right to make a limited use of force to remedy the failure by Cambodia to uphold its neutral duties vis-à-vis North

---

[39] Address by David Packard, Department of Defense News Release, May 15, 1970, 5.

Viet-Nam faces formidable difficulties.[40] First of all, the South Vietnamese claim is clearly not limited to the enforcement of neutral duties; it takes precedence over the American definition of the mission and provides the primary legal measure of what is being claimed. Secondly, sustained uses of overt force against foreign territory by governments for purposes other than self-defense are not compatible with the language of the Charter or the practice of the United Nations.[41] Thirdly, the United States has consistently condemned as illegal much more modest claims to use force against base areas across boundaries.

During the Algerian war of independence, French forces in 1957 attacked Sakret-Sidi-Youssef, a town in Tunisia being used as a sanctuary and staging area by Algerian insurgents. The United States rejected the French claim that it was permissible to destroy external base areas and supply depots on the Tunisian side of the Algerian border and expressed its public displeasure, even though France was an American ally at the time. Similarly, Adlai Stevenson, as United States Representative in the Security Council, condemned in 1964 a British raid against Habir in Yemen, which was in reprisal for the use of the town as a base for operations against the British colonial occupation of the Protectorate of Aden. Finally the United States has on numerous occasions joined in criticizing and censuring Israel for attacking external base areas. The expansion of the theater of violent acts across a boundary by overt and official action has been consistently regarded as illegal under modern international law.

Mr. Packard's assertion that the Lon Nol Government would probably not find an invasion objectionable is also a very fragile basis upon which to launch a large-scale invasion that caused the death and displacement of many Cambodians, subjected the country to civil war conditions, and has entailed widespread destruction of Cambodian villages, forests, and croplands. No United States official even contends that Cambodia requested or even authorized the invasion, nor was there evident any attempt to secure consent in advance.[42]

---

[40] See Note from *Columbia Law Review*, "International Law and Military Operations Against Insurgents in Neutral Territory," reprinted in Falk, ed., *The Vietnam War and International Law*, Vol. II, 572–93.

[41] For an analysis of the compatibility between special claims to use force and international law (including the UN Charter), see Richard Falk, "The Beirut Raid and the International Law of Retaliation," *American Journal of International Law*, 63 (1969), 415–43. Note that the Beirut raid conducted by Israeli military units on December 28, 1968, was far more limited in scope, duration, and effects than has been the Cambodian operation. It seems questionable whether a use of armed forces on the scale of the Cambodian operation can be ever considered as a special claim falling outside the Charter, but must be justified, if at all, as an exercise of the right of self-defense. Cf. Stevenson, "United States Military Actions in Cambodia," 768–69.

[42] See above, p. 236 and n. 19.

Furthermore, contrary to Mr. Nixon's contention on April 30th that "American policy" since 1954 has been "to scrupulously respect the neutrality of the Cambodian people," the number of border-crossing and airspace violations has been extensive ever since the intensification of the Viet-Nam War in 1964.[43] Prince Sihanouk complained frequently about American violations of Cambodian neutrality, prominently displayed in Phnom Penh captured American equipment, complained to the International Control Commission, and invited American citizens to visit Cambodia and inspect for themselves evidence of US raids against border areas. These American incursions, although more disruptive for Cambodians than the North Vietnamese use of Cambodian territory as a sanctuary, did not draw Cambodia into the war, and were generally consistent with the maintenance of Cambodian peace and security and the confinement of the war to the territory of South Viet-Nam.

Furthermore, there seems to be something peculiarly perverse about widening the war at a time when the official claim is that American involvement is being diminished. Casualties have been far lower during the withdrawal process initiated by Nixon than at other times during the war. If these base areas could be tolerated for so many years – even when American objectives were being set forth in more ambitious terms – then what was the reason to assert suddenly a claim based on Cambodia's failure to uphold neutral duties? The only partially satisfactory explanation of the timing of the Cambodian operation has to do with the fear that the Lon Nol régime was on the verge of collapse.[44] Such explanation lacks much plausibility because the invasion has had the primary effect of pushing the régime closer to either foreign dependence or collapse and may encourage the virtual partition of the country between South Viet-Nam, North Viet-Nam, Laos, and Thailand. Such an outcome has nothing to do with the enforcement of neutral rights, or, for that matter, with self-defense.

As with the claim of self-defense, there is no support in doctrine, practice, or policy to vindicate an American claim of the proportions of the Cambodian operation. In the past, the organs of the world community have consistently condemned lesser claims – single raids lasting a few hours – to attack or

---

[43] For summary of US and South Vietnamese violations of Cambodian neutrality prior to April 30, 1970, see Kahin, "Cambodia: The Administration's Version and the Historical Record," 57429; *cf.* also Chomsky, "Cambodia," *New York Review of Books* (June 4, 1970), 40; Fried, "United States Military Intervention in Cambodia in the Light of International Law," Appendix 1, "Protests by Cambodia About Violations of Its Territory," 1–9.

[44] For speculation on motivation, see F. Schurmann, "Cambodia: Nixon's Trap," *The Nation* (Jun. 1, 1970), 651–56; P. Scott, "Cambodia: Why the Generals Won," *New York Review of Books* (Jun. 18, 1970), 28–34.

destroy external base areas relied upon by the insurgent side in an internal war. Here, the limits are not narrow – a 21.7-mile territorial belt and a period of two months, besides less restrictive time and space zones for air attacks.[45] Mr. Packard reports that even these limits were imposed on the operation by the President "because he wants the American people to understand that this is a temporary and limited operation."[46] What about respect for norms prohibiting border-crossing uses of force? What about the welfare and autonomy of the Cambodian people who are the most permanent victims of the claim? Again, we are left with an *imperial* impression, the President giving an *internal* account, without any sense of obligation to respect world standards. Such a peremptory claim to enforce neutral rights is the essence of unilateralism which it has been the overriding purpose of modern international law to discourage and moderate in the area of war and peace.

Procedural Norms. One of the most disturbing features of the American rôle in the Cambodian operation is the evidence that the US Government has acted without any sense of respect for the rules and procedures of law and order on an international level. The minimum legal burden imposed on a Head of State is to provide a legal justification to the international community for undertaking action that raises fundamental issues of international law as manifestly as does the invasion of a foreign country.

Yet the American claim to undertake the Cambodian operation was made in peremptory form. American policy was put forward as an exhibition of sovereign discretion, moderated by some sense of limits, but not subject to review or challenge. In this spirit it is necessary to recall Mr. Nixon's assertion forewarning foreign governments that any effort to regard our invasion of Cambodia as a serious breach of international order – or as a flagrant violation of the Charter – would be entirely unacceptable to us. Even the outrageous invasion of Czechoslovakia in 1968 was accompanied by some Soviet effort to give an international accounting, admittedly a flimsy one. I am comparing the American assertions vis-à-vis Cambodia with a sub-legal standard of comparison by citing the Czech occupation, and not in any sense intimating that the Soviet contention was consistent with the obligations of international law just

---

[45] The air strikes have continued on a regular basis since the July 1 withdrawal deadline. President Nixon has made no effort to change his earlier pledge on this point. It also is clear that these air strikes are intended to influence the military struggle in Cambodia, as well as to interdict supplies and troops that might be used against Americans in South Viet-Nam. A new "credibility gap" has arisen as a result of the discrepancy between the actual bombing patterns in Cambodia and the official statements on the subject. A useful summary of this situation is to be found in a newspaper article by Sterba, "Cambodia."

[46] Address by David Packard, Department of Defense News Release, May 15, 1970, 6.

because there was some effort to provide an international justification for the action. The provision of an explanation in such a setting is a necessary, but hardly *sufficient* condition of legality.

The United States did make certain gestures of compliance with Charter norms after the Cambodian operation was under way. Ambassador Yost made a short report on behalf of the United States to the President of the Security Council on May 5, 1970, explaining that the Cambodian operation was an exercise of the right of collective self-defense.[47] Administration officials have subsequently developed a variety of legal arguments in response to objections raised in the domestic arena. To put forward legal arguments is not, of course, to be confused with the overall persuasiveness of a legal position which must depend on weighing an argument against the facts, norms, and policies at stake, as well as against arguments developed in support of contrary legal positions. For reasons already discussed, the United Nations cannot provide a suitable forum for legal appraisal in the Indochina context. In any event, the United States since the beginning of its involvement in the Viet-Nam War has displayed only a nominal willingness to operate within a Charter context.[48]

Beyond the obligation to justify recourse to international force to the Security Council is the obligation to seek a peaceful settlement of an international dispute. Articles 2 (3) and 33 of the Charter express this obligation in clear form. The Cambodian operation is only the latest instance of a continuing American refusal to seek a peaceful settlement of the conflicts that exist in Indochina. It is not possible here to make a detailed analysis of the failure by the United States to respond to the NLF proposal of May 1969, for a settlement of the Viet-Nam War, the American failure to offer any counterproposal, and the failure to appoint a negotiator of prestige and stature from November 1969, when Henry Cabot Lodge resigned, until June 1970, when David Bruce was designated as his successor. The Thieu–Ky Government has never made

---

[47] UN Doc. S/9781, n. 3 above. Ambassador Yost's legal position was developed as follows: "The measures of collective self-defense being taken by US and South Vietnamese forces are restricted in extent, purpose and time. They are confined to the border areas over which the Cambodian Government has ceased to exercise any effective control and which ha[ve] been completely occupied by North Vietnamese and Viet Cong forces. Their purpose is to destroy the stocks and communications equipment that are being used in aggression against the Republic of Viet-Nam. When that is accomplished, our forces and those of the Republic of Viet-Nam will promptly withdraw. These measures are limited and proportionate to the aggressive military operations of the North Vietnamese forces and the threat they pose."

[48] For more detailed appraisals of the UN rôle in relation to the Viet-Nam War, see articles by L. Bloomfield, "The UN and Vietnam," and M. Gordon, "Vietnam, the United States and the United Nations," in Falk, ed., *The Vietnam War and International Law*, Vol. II, 281–320 and 321–57.

a secret of its opposition to a negotiated end to the war; its presence in Paris is a result of American pressure. Indeed, President Nixon's initial appointment of Mr. Lodge, known as an ardent supporter of the Saigon régime, and his subsequent non-replacement of a chief delegate for more than seven months after Mr. Lodge's resignation seemed designed to *reassure* the Thieu–Ky group that the United States has no intention of encouraging serious negotiations in Paris, rather than to convince North Viet-Nam and the Provisional Revolutionary Government of South Viet-Nam that we are interested in serious negotiations.[49] Such an American posture is made even more cynical by the frequent reiteration to the American public of our eagerness for serious negotiations, and by the allegation that negotiations are being blocked by the stubborn refusal of the other side to discuss anything other than the terms of its "victory." The effort to convey contradictory messages to the Saigon régime and to the American public places an overwhelming burden upon the credibility and sincerity of our negotiating posture and represents a serious failure to carry out the procedural norms relating to peaceful settlement.

The Cambodian operation, then, illustrates a refusal on the part of the United States to comply with minimum procedural norms of international law:

(1) There has been no indication of any willingness to submit to community review the claim to attack a foreign state.

(2) There has been no official effort to reconcile the invasion with the requirements of international law beyond the nominal letter of report to the Security Council. This failure to provide an external explanation of recourse to force against a foreign country violates Charter norms, at least as these norms have been interpreted on past occasions by the United States in relation to foreign states.

(3) There has been a failure to comply with the legal duty to seek a peaceful solution to the conflicts taking place in Indochina.

(4) South Viet-Nam has also provided no accounting for its more extensive claims to occupy Cambodian territory, and the United States seems legally responsible to the full extent of these wider claims – claims which even its own legal arguments, developed since April 30th, have not tried to justify.

---

[49] For the text of the ten-point proposal setting that was supported by North Viet-Nam and the National Liberation Front and put forward in the Paris negotiations, see G. Kolko (ed.), *Three Documents of the National Liberation Front* (Boston: Beacon Press, 1970), 15–23. This proposal represents a serious basis for negotiations. It has never drawn either a response or a counterproposal of comparable detail from the US–South Vietnamese delegations.

IV SOME CONCLUDING WORLD-ORDER COMMENTS

The development of international law is very much a consequence of the effective assertion of claims by principal states. Such claims create legal precedents that can be relied upon on subsequent occasions by other states. The Cambodian operation, in this sense, represents both a violation of existing procedural and substantive rules of international law and a very unfortunate legislative claim for the future. It will now be possible for states to rely on the Cambodian operation in carrying out raids against external base areas or even when invading a foreign country allegedly being used as a sanctuary. It will no longer be possible for the United States Government to make credible objections to such claims. The consequences of such a precedent for the Middle East and southern Africa seem to be highly destabilizing.

In this case, the precedent was established without any effort to justify the claim from the point of view of international public policy. One of the important thresholds of restraint had involved respect for international boundaries, especially with regard to the initiation of full-scale armed attacks. International law has relied on second-order restraints to limit the combat area, even when the wider prohibition on recourse to violence has failed. The precedent set by the Cambodian operation seriously erodes this second-order restraint and appears to increase the discretion of national governments as to the permissible limits of force in international affairs.

Covert and sporadic uses of force across international boundaries have been part of the way in which a balance has been reached between the use of external sanctuaries by insurgent groups and the security of the target state. Peremptory strikes against these external base areas have been generally condemned, but the short duration of these claims and the direct response to provocative actions by groups operating from the target state have usually meant that such retaliatory force has not greatly nor indefinitely expanded the theater of combat operations. The Cambodian operation was a campaign that included at its height more than 74,000 men (31,000 Americans, 43,000 South Vietnamese), heavy air support, the occupation of a large area of foreign territory for a long period of time, and the prospect of future incursions by land and air. As such, it widens considerably the prior understanding of the limits of retaliatory force. Such widening is of serious consequence for at least three reasons:

(1) There are many conflict situations in which one or both contending factions can claim the need to attack external base areas.

(2) The claim to destroy the external base areas of the insurgent will undoubtedly generate counter-claims to destroy the external base areas of incumbent factions.

(3) The unilateral character of a determination as to when it is appropriate to attack external base areas is very subjective, tends to be self-serving, and is difficult to appraise.

In essence, then, the Cambodian operation represents a step backward in the struggle to impose restraints on the use of force in the conduct of foreign relations. In the specific setting of the Viet-Nam War, the Cambodian operation is a further extension of the United States' illegal involvement in Indochina. It has widened the theater of combat, complicated the task of negotiating a settlement, brought additional governments into positions of active co-belligerency, and has been convincingly justified by neither a demonstration of military necessity nor a claim of legal prerogative.

The Cambodian operation is, perhaps, the most blatant violation of international law by the United States Government since World War II, but it represents only the most recent instance in a series of illegal uses of force to intervene in the internal affairs of a sovereign society. Until Cambodia, the United States Government either disguised its interventions, as in Guatemala in 1954, or made a serious effort to justify them, as in relation to the Dominican intervention of 1965. The Cambodian operation represents a peremptory claim to take military action; such action violates the letter and spirit of general international law and the Charter of the United Nations, and seems to vindicate the allegation that the United States is acting in Southeast Asia with imperial pretensions rather than as one among many states subject to a common framework of minimum restraint in its international conduct.

Within the present world setting, the United States is contributing to the deterioration of the quality of international order rather than to its improvement. Such a rôle is particularly tragic at this juncture of world history, a crossroads in human destiny at which the converging dangers of population pressure, ecological decay, and the possibility of nuclear war create the first crisis of world order that threatens the survival of man as a species and the habitability of the planet.[50] The prospects for creative response are vitally linked with the orientations toward issues of international order that prevail in the principal national centers of power and authority in the world. Unless constructive changes are sought by national governments, there is no way to meet the threats posed, in part, by the present fragmented political organization of world society. One precondition for change is a greater reluctance by powerful

[50] A depiction of this crisis and some proposals for overcoming it are the subject of my forthcoming book, *This Endangered Planet: Prospects and Proposals for Human Survival,* to be published in 1971 by Random House.

governments to rely on military capabilities to promote their foreign policy goals. Recent actions by the Soviet Union and by the United States have displayed, above all, a return to the political consciousness associated with pre-World War I attitudes of sovereign prerogative and *raison d'état*, and a total abandonment of the serious search for a new system of world order responsive to the needs of our time, except to be prudent about provocative acts in a crisis situation in which the nuclear contingency appears relevant. It is in this sense that the Cambodian operation bears witness to the persistence of the war system and to the strength and vitality of the most destructive attitudes and forces active in our world.

There is, perhaps, some reason for encouragement in the report that the Secretary of State, William P. Rogers, circulated a memorandum addressed to the Assistant Secretary of State, dated June 13, 1970, in which the following language appears:

> When crises occur in any area of the world those in the department who are most directly involved should be careful to insure that the legal implications are not overlooked.[51]

Imagine, if such sentiments began to shape the choice of policy, as well as to influence the process of its rationalization!

---

[51] *New York Times*, June 24, 1970, p. 3.

PART III

THE VIETNAM WAR AND THE NUREMBERG PRINCIPLES

"The Nuremberg Defense in the Pentagon Papers Case," *Columbia Journal of Transnational Law*, 13, 2 (1974), 208–38.

"A Nuremberg Perspective on the Trial of Karl Armstrong," in Richard A. Falk, *A Global Approach To National Policy*, Cambridge, Mass.: Harvard University Press, Copyright © 1975 by the President and Fellows of Harvard College, as chapter 8: 133–45.

"Telford Taylor and the Legacy of Nuremberg," *Columbia Journal of Transnational Law*, 37, 3 (1999), 693–723.

9

The Nuremberg Defense in the Pentagon Papers Case

I INTRODUCTION

The most celebrated case brought by the United States Government against domestic opponents of the Vietnam War arose out of the release in 1971 of major portions of the so-called Pentagon Papers by Daniel Ellsberg and Anthony Russo. As is generally known, the Government's misconduct in *United States v. Russo*[1] eventually led to the dismissal of the charges. As a consequence, important questions concerning the application of international criminal law embedded in the litigation were never resolved, although interim rulings by Judge Matthew Byrne suggested their disposition at the trial level.[2] In particular, the defendants Ellsberg and Russo tried to argue that the disclosure of the Pentagon Papers was a reasonable and effective method of terminating their complicity with a war conducted in violation of international law.

International law imposes criminal liability for complicity in crimes against the peace. It is arguable that this potential liability of Americans has been officially recognized as part of the American law. Hence, fairness to potential defendants makes it essential that they be allowed to rely upon any defense that arises out of their accountability under international law standards. In addition, the substantive merits of international criminal law make it desirable to encourage national implementation, including a recognition that individual action undertaken to prevent the consummation of international crimes should be accorded precedence over conflicting dictates of national law.

---

[1] Criminal No. 9373 (C.D. Cal., dismissed Dec. 29, 1971).
[2] The rulings in the trial generally precluded the defendants from introducing testimony in the presence of the jury pertaining to the illegality of the American role in the Vietnam War and the bearing of this alleged illegality on the actions taken by the defendants.

This article will examine these issues in the context of *United States v. Russo*. I shall show that the released portion of the Pentagon Papers contained strong evidence supporting a reasonable belief that the United States had pursued and was continuing to pursue a Vietnam policy which violated international law; and that the defendants, Ellsberg and Russo, could reasonably infer that they were accessories to the commission and execution of public policies in violation of international law. Furthermore, I will argue that the defendants could have been internationally indicted for these acts in accordance with precedents established by the Allied prosecutions of German citizens following World War II.[3] Therefore, by partially disclosing the contents of the Pentagon Papers the defendants, I would contend, were making a reasonable effort to terminate their complicity in such illegal acts.[4] Furthermore, the "superior orders" dictated by domestic law to prohibit the disclosure of such information would not act as a bar against international prosecution or conviction based on alleged violations of international criminal law. Consequently, a national prosecution should allow defendants to demonstrate that their actions, which might appear illegal if viewed exclusively under national standards, were undertaken to discharge their obligations under a higher applicable law, namely, international criminal law. To disallow such a demonstration in an American court seems to deny defendants a very fundamental ingredient of due process.

Beyond these considerations of procedural fairness in criminal cases lies a fundamental issue of public policy. I would argue that it serves the national and global interest to encourage *non-violent acts of conscience based on reasonable belief* of the sort taken by the defendants in the Pentagon Papers case. That is, there is more at stake here than fairness to the defendants; what is really at issue is whether civilians should be any more beholden to "superior orders" (in this case taking the form of classification restrictions) than soldiers confronted by unlawful battlefield commands. Accepting the Nuremberg defense

---

[3] It should be noted that the hypothetical character of the defendants' liability under international criminal law should make no difference as to the availability of the defense under domestic law.

[4] It is important to appreciate that Daniel Ellsberg deliberately withheld the four volumes of the Pentagon Papers which dealt with international negotiations concerning Vietnam. He explained that these volumes were withheld because they contained information pertaining to United States relations with foreign governments that might be viewed as falling within the ambit of legitimate national security. Whether or not one agrees with Ellsberg's judgment, this does support the view that he was trying to minimize the disruptive effects of his disclosure initiative. Note that, from the prosecution standpoint, Ellsberg was not entitled to possess copies of these documents; therefore, the negotiating volumes were covered in the conversion counts of the indictment.

in a national trial setting is one way of rejecting any such dichotomy. Note, too, that to accept the defense as permissible is not to vindicate whatever a particular defendant might be accused of doing in a specific case. A defendant's reliance on the claim that he was acting to oppose the commission of an international crime would be subject to an appraisal of reasonableness. To succeed with the Nuremberg defense a defendant must show two things:

- first, that he acted on the basis of a reasonable belief that an international crime had been committed;
- second, that his action was a reasonable and prudent way of either terminating his own complicity with the criminal conduct or of seeking to terminate the criminal conduct itself.

In other words, the Nuremberg defense is not theoretically restricted to those who, like Ellsberg and Russo, had been participants at some stage of the allegedly criminal enterprise. It could be invoked by any citizen who had a reasonable belief that an international crime had been or was being committed. However, the fact of complicity should be considered in determining whether there were sufficient objective and subjective bases for such a reasonable belief.

The recent case involving Karleton Armstrong is an apt example. Armstrong participated, by his own admission, in exploding a bomb in the Army Mathematics Research Center at the University of Wisconsin on August 24, 1970. Despite precautions taken by the defendant to assure that the building would be unoccupied at the hour planned for the explosion, the bomb accidentally killed Robert Fassnacht, a research physicist who was in the building. Armstrong pleaded guilty in a Wisconsin state court to charges of second degree homicide but was allowed to raise the Nuremberg defense during an extensive hearing held to determine the proper sentence.[5] A very complete record on the Nuremberg defense was made in the Armstrong case, but Armstrong's sentence was reduced from the maximum only by the time he had been held in jail pending disposition of the case. The point of this reference to the Armstrong case is to illustrate the relevance of the Nuremberg defense in a *non*-complicity context – and to indicate that allowing the Nuremberg defense to be made does not by itself assure its influence upon the outcome of a trial proceeding or even upon the extent of punishment imposed on a criminal defendant.

---

[5] See Richard Falk, "The Claim of Violent Resistance and the Nuremberg Obligation," *Contact*, 4 (1973), 3–8.

II THE APPLICABILITY OF INTERNATIONAL
CRIMINAL LAW TO THE INSTANT CASE

Article VI, paragraph 2, of the United States Constitution provides that rules of international law embodied in treaties made under the authority of the United States are part of the "supreme Law of the Land." Mr. Justice Gray, in the case of *The Paquete Habana*, concluded that even in non-treaty contexts:

> International law is part of our law, and must be ascertained and administered by the courts of justice of appropriate jurisdiction, as often as questions of right depending upon it are duly presented.[6]

The application of treaty international law by domestic courts has never been seriously challenged, although there are complexities arising out of the question of whether the treaty is non-self-executing or has been superseded by subsequent inconsistent acts of Congress. That this procedure extends to the non-treaty norms associated with the Nuremberg Principles seems equally clear. Even the Assistant General Counsel for International Affairs of the Department of Defense, Benjamin Forman, has acknowledged that

> from an international criminal law point of view . . . the Nuremberg norms are part of our municipal law and may be enforced by our courts.[7]

In recent years the Nuremberg defense has been asserted in domestic courts in a variety of contexts, principally tax and selective service cases arising from the Vietnam conflict. The courts have relied upon several legal doctrines in an effort to avoid inquiry into the applicability of international criminal law in these cases. None of these doctrines, which are discussed below, was entirely applicable to the special claims put forward by the defendants in *United States v. Russo*.

---

[6]   175 U.S. 677, 700 (1900).

[7]   B. Forman, "The Nuremberg Trials and Conscientious Objection to War: Justiciability Under United States Municipal Law," in Richard Falk (ed.), *The Vietnam War and International Law* (Princeton: Princeton University Press, 1972), Vol. III, 399, 403. Mr. Forman does add that from an enforcement perspective these norms are not enforceable against American nationals except "to the extent that provision has been made therefor in our criminal laws" (*ibid.*). But the relevant point is that if the United States could, even without implementing legislation, enforce Nuremberg norms – by means of military commissions – against foreign nationals, then a comparable claim could be lodged by foreign military commissions against American nationals such as Ellsberg and Russo. Thus, their claim of hypothetical criminal liability acquires technical, if indirect, support from the leading Pentagon spokesman on the question.

The first of these doctrines is the assertion made in many cases that the defendant lacks standing to assert the international law argument.[8] But surely, where the legal argument, as here, is that the defendants were accessories to violations of international law such that it was necessary for them to take steps to dissociate themselves from the circle of complicity, it seems clear that the legal interest asserted is direct and concrete, and not hypothetical (as when the argument is advanced by a draftee seeking to avoid future complicity in an illegal act) or indirect (as in the case of a taxpayer seeking to withhold that portion of his taxes which would be used to finance the illegal actions). Ellsberg and Russo clearly had a personal stake in the controversy over the applicability of international law.[9]

The second of these doctrines arises over the issue of justiciability. In particular, is there a sufficiently close causal connection between the actions which the defendants have taken and the alleged violation of international law which they assert? D'Amato, Gould and Woods have stated that:

> An American soldier who refuses to obey an order to torture a prisoner of war would face no difficulties defending himself before a court-martial. Clearly he would have a valid "Nuremberg Defense" based on the argument that the international law of war crimes on this matter is part of American law, that his military obligation is only to obey "lawful" orders, that the order given him is unlawful, and the so-called defense of superior order is not available to him. He would face no serious procedural hurdles nor any questions of justiciability.[10]

Ellsberg and Russo have claimed that their actions were analogous to that of an American combat soldier who has refused to obey an illegal order. Civilians subjected to criminal prosecution for illegal behavior should be able

---

[8] The most pertinent criteria on standing to present a claim are those set forth by the United States Supreme Court in *Flast v. Cohen*, 392 U.S. 83, 99–101 (1968). Domestic courts thus far have refused even to consider whether the application of the *Flast* test of standing can be satisfied by a claimant who relies upon a Nuremberg defense.

[9] On standing issue, see L. Velvel, "The War in Vietnam: Unconstitutional, Justiciable, and Jurisdictionally Attachable," in Falk, ed., *The Vietnam War and International Law*, Vol. II, 651; see also A. D'Amato, H. Gould and L. Woods, "War Crimes and Vietnam: The 'Nuremberg Defense' and the Military Service Resister," *ibid.*, Vol. III, 407. On aspects of these questions, see *Youngstown Sheet and Tube v. Sawyer*, 343 U.S. 579 (1952); D'Amato et al., "War Crimes and Vietnam," 460–61; M. Tigar, "Judicial Power, the 'Political Question Doctrine,' and Foreign Relations," in Falk, ed., *The Vietnam War and International Law*, Vol. III, 654; and W. Schwartz and W. McCormack, "The Justiciability of Legal Objections to the American Military Effort in Vietnam," *ibid.*, Vol. III, 699.

[10] D'Amato et al., "War Crimes and Vietnam," 457; see *ibid.*, n. 302, for citation to the major cases in US courts.

to demonstrate the reasonableness of their contention that, under the circumstances in which they acted, the domestic claims (or regulations) amounted to "illegal" superior orders.

It should also be noted that, in *United States v. Russo*, it was unnecessary for the court to determine whether violations of international law by the United States Government *actually* took place. Rather, it only had to determine whether the defendants reasonably believed that such violations had occurred, and whether partial disclosure of the Pentagon Papers by the defendants was a reasonable act in light of that belief. In this sense, in the Ellsberg–Russo situation, the causal connection between the acts done by the defendants and the alleged violation of international law was much closer than in the context of withholding war-related taxes or destroying selective service records.[11] There was reason to believe, for instance, that disclosure of the Pentagon Papers would erode congressional and public support for the Vietnam War more effectively than would isolated acts of individual resistance. A case raising the justiciability of such limited issues, focusing on the attitude and perception of the defendant vis-à-vis the allegedly unlawful governmental conduct, would create far less difficulty and embarrassment to the courts than would a case seeking to have the court pass on the legality of the conduct itself. Consequently, in a case such as *United States v. Russo* judicial abstention on the ground of non-justiciability of the issue would be inapposite.

The third device employed by courts to avoid the application of international law in the Vietnam War context has been premised on the view that the "political question" doctrine precludes that application.[12] However, even the most orthodox view of this doctrine would not require its application to the specific facts of *United States v. Russo*. Here, the defendants were seeking their day in court with respect to a criminal indictment charging them with violation of domestic laws in releasing the classified Pentagon Papers. Surely, it would have been reasonable – and indeed necessary – to determine whether such laws as relied upon in the indictment were, as applied to the facts of the case, "illegal superior orders," especially given the defendants' credible contention of acting to end complicity in the underlying violations of international law. There was nothing about this defense that touched upon the allocation of powers or upon the Executive's prerogatives in foreign affairs.[13]

---

[11]   See, e.g., *United States v. Berrigan*, 283 F. Supp. 336 (D. Md. 1968).

[12]   The rationale for the "political question" approach is supported and some major Vietnam-related judicial applications are cited by Professor Louis Henkin in "Viet-Nam in the Courts of the United States: 'Political Questions,'" in Falk, ed., *The Vietnam War and International Law*, Vol. III, 625.

[13]   See text accompanying nn. 10 and 11 above.

Indeed, as Judge Wyzanski has indicated in *United States v. Sisson*, it would violate a defendant's right to due process if the court excluded basic issues relevant to his defense merely by invoking the political question doctrine.[14]

On a more fundamental level, the propriety of judicial deference to Executive policy in the area of war and peace is subject to serious question. This pattern of deference is premised upon cases decided in the pre-Nuremberg context, in which special circumstances existed and in which no clear legal standards of limitations upon governmental conduct existed. However, since World War II there has developed a reasonably definite set of legal criteria by which to appraise challenges to Executive action.[15]

There is no longer any justification for the political question doctrine, which rests on the notion that the judiciary cannot displace Executive discretion. Now that international law has constrained Executive discretion, it seems appropriate for courts to administer these constraints and, indeed, inappropriate to act as if no such constraints exist – which is the effect of applying the political question doctrine to a given situation. At a minimum, a court should reconsider the applicability of the political question doctrine to the war–peace area in light of the post-World War II international legal developments. To date, however, courts have been hiding beneath the political question cloak without even addressing themselves to the substantial question as to whether, in light of shifts in international law, this mode of deference is any longer appropriate.

III THE PENTAGON PAPERS AS EVIDENCE OF THE ILLEGALITY OF US INVOLVEMENT IN VIETNAM

That portion of the Pentagon Papers which was covered in the indictment of Ellsberg and Russo contained evidence which supported at least an inference that the United States Government was guilty of several major violations of the international law that applied to its conduct throughout the course of its

---

[14] *United States v. Sisson*, 297 F. Supp. 902, 912 (D. Mass. 1969).

[15] The best statement of support for continued deference is to be found in L. Henkin, *Foreign Affairs and the Constitution* (Mineola, NY: Foundation Press, 1972), 208–16. In my view, the rationale for deference contained in *United States v. Curtiss-Wright Export Corp.*, 299 U.S. 304 (1936), is ripe for reconsideration; the facts of that case provided a very limited context in which to enunciate the broad questions of policy at stake. Not only has international law developed criteria for appraisal of challenged state conduct since 1936 and imposed liability on state officials for its violation, but the Supreme Court has set forth more precise criteria by which to identify "a political question" in *Baker v. Carr*, 369 U.S. 186 (1962). Professor Velvel argues that Vietnam-related issues are justiciable by reference to these criteria; see Velvel, "The War in Vietnam," 681–87.

Vietnam involvement after 1954. This evidence was relevant to the defendants' arguments because it formed the basis of their belief that they were both
entitled and obligated to act to dissociate themselves from the continued prosecution of such policy. Furthermore, the disclosure of this evidence to the
public and to Congress could be reasonably calculated to increase and sub-
stantiate opposition to the continued prosecution of the war.

The Pentagon Papers disclosed established patterns of activity by the United
States Government that appear inconsistent with fundamental obligations
which are embodied in international law and, hence, are binding on national
governments. The United States violated international law in at least three
respects: by failing to accord respect for international agreements seeking to
secure international peace; by failing to seek peaceful settlement of international disputes; and by intervening in the internal affairs of a foreign state. In
each of these legal contexts, there exists extensive support for the contention
that the United States Government is subject to the relevant obligations of
international law.

A Failure to Accord Respect for International Agreements Seeking to Establish International Peace

There is a legal duty to accord respect to international agreements seeking to
establish peace. It is an aspect of the wider legal duty to refrain from the use of
force in international relations except in self-defense or under the authority of
the United Nations. It is also a special case of the general legal duty to respect
valid international agreements.[16]

The General Treaty for the Renunciation of War, known as the Treaty of
Paris or the Kellogg–Briand Pact, signed on August 27, 1928, is a fundamental
assertion of these legal duties and is a treaty that has been validly ratified by
the United States. Article 1 reads as follows:

> The High Contracting Parties solemnly declare in the names of their
> respective peoples that they condemn recourse to war for the solution of
> international controversies, and renounce it as an instrument of national
> policy in their relations with one another.[17]

The character of this obligation was specified in the international agreement
signed August 8, 1945, governing Prosecution and Punishment of Major War

---

[16]   These norms are set forth in authoritative treaty form in UN Charter, arts. 1, 2 and 51.
[17]   For a convenient text, see L. Friedman, ed., *The Law of War: A Documentary History*
(New York: Random House, 1972), Vol. I, 468.

Criminals of European Axis, the so-called London Agreement.[18] Article VI(a) of the London Agreement defines Crimes against the Peace as:

[P]lanning, preparation, initiation or waging of a war of aggression, or a war *in violation of international treaties, agreements or assurances* [emphasis supplied].[19]

This same definition of crimes against peace was incorporated in Control Council Law No. 10, signed in Berlin by the four Allied commanders, December 20, 1945, and used as the basis for prosecuting persons below the highest levels of the German leadership.[20]

Several of the volumes of the Pentagon Papers cited in the indictment of Russo and Ellsberg reveal an intention by policy-makers in the United States Government to wage war in violation of the Geneva Accords, a set of validly concluded international agreements ending the French war in Indochina in July 1954.[21] The United States filed a Declaration at Geneva stating that "it will refrain from the threat or use of force to disturb" the Geneva Accords and "would view any renewal of the aggression in violation of the aforesaid agreements with grave concern."[22] Even without such a Declaration, the United States, along with all governments, would be legally obligated not to disturb a peace agreement. As a Member of the United Nations, the United States has a legal obligation to respect its Charter, especially the principles as to international peace set forth in general terms in Article 2.

However, the Pentagon Papers Task Force Summary characterizes the United States response to the Geneva Accords as follows:

It is charged that the US tried to sabotage the Geneva Conference, first by maneuvering to prevent the conference from taking place, then by attempting to subvert a settlement, and finally, by refusing to guarantee the resulting agreements of the conference. The documentation on this charge is complete, but by no means unambiguous. While "sabotage" may be a strong word, it is evident that the US by its actions and statements during this period did seek to down-play the conference, dissociate itself from the results, and thereby did cast doubt on the stability of the Accords.[23]

---

[18] For the text, see *ibid.*, 883 *passim.*
[19] *Ibid.*, 886–87.
[20] *Ibid.*, 908.
[21] The Geneva Accords are reprinted in Falk,ed., *The Vietnam War and International Law*, Vol. I, 543 *passim.*
[22] *Ibid.*, 559.
[23] US Department of Defense, *United States–Vietnam Relations 1945–1967* (Washington, D.C.: US Government Printing Office, 1971) (hereinafter cited as Pentagon Papers), Vol. I, Part III.A, A-1.

As is well known, the Geneva Accords were not implemented in the years following 1954, and their collapse led to the renewal of warfare in Indochina. The United States, by its support of Ngo Dinh Diem, the Prime Minister of South Vietnam, who refused to implement the critical provision of the Accords relating to general elections of a government for a reunified Vietnam, played a major role in assuring the collapse of the Geneva arrangements. Article 7 of the Final Declaration at the Geneva Conference called for general elections in July 1956, preceded by consultations between the representatives of the two zones of Vietnam commencing on July 20, 1955.[24] The Pentagon Papers confirm that "[b]acked by the United States, Diem refused to open consultation with the North Vietnamese concerning general elections when the date for these fell due in July, 1955."[25] It is also clear that France and Britain realized that the collapse of the Accords would lead to a renewal of war:

> [T]he French Government urgently sought to persuade Diem to accept consultations about the elections scheduled to begin in July 1955 . . . Britain wanted to prevent any public repudiation of the Accords and joined France in urging Diem to talk to the Vietminh. But Diem had not changed his view of the Accords: he had refused to sign them and continued to insist he was not bound by them.[26]

In a sense, the elections issue was used by Diem and the United States as a symbolic demonstration of their refusal to implement the Geneva arrangement beyond the very minimal extent of a partition of Vietnam into two separate states, one Communist, one anti-Communist. Even the minimal acceptance of the Geneva solution cannot be understood as a tactical position responsive to geopolitical realities. There are indications that Saigon, as well as Hanoi, nurtured dreams of reunification, and the post-1954 paramilitary penetration of North Vietnam gives tangible evidence of these dreams at a time *prior* to any claim by Saigon or Washington of North Vietnamese activity in the South.

[24] For the text of art. 7 of the Final Declaration, see Falk, ed., *The Vietnam War and International Law*, Vol. I, 558.
[25] Pentagon Papers, Vol. I, Part IV.A.3, v. This essential violation is reiterated frequently in the Papers. For example:

> France was never able to meet Geneva obligations concerning the elections of 1956, for Diem matched his refusal to consult with the Vietnamese about elections with an adamant refusal to ever hold them. Neither Britain nor the Soviet Union pressed the matter; the United States backed Diem's position.

[26] Pentagon Papers, Vol. I, Part IV.A.3, vi.

The United States position of support for Diem was a natural sequel to its opposition to a negotiated settlement of the war between the French and the Viet Minh, and its evident belief until the 1970s that the battlefield served its interests in the conflict better than peace talks. Such a policy objective must be understood in a context where "substantial military gains" could not be anticipated. Even where military gains had been achieved or claimed, the main orientation of policy-makers was that, in view of the favorable military situation, peace talks were less necessary than ever.[27] The Pentagon Papers quote from President Eisenhower's personal message to Winston Churchill to demonstrate the attitude of the United States government toward peaceful settlement:

> I can understand the very natural desire of the French to seek an end to this war which has been bleeding them for eight years. But our painstaking search for a way out of this impasse has reluctantly forced us to the conclusion that there is no negotiated solution of the Indochina problem which in its essence would not be either a face-saving device to cover a French surrender or a face-saving device to cover a Communist retirement.[28]

It is also important to note that the Pentagon Papers reported that North Vietnam adhered to the Geneva Accords and was prepared to allow the future to be governed by their terms.[29]

Even more revealing of official intentions is NSC 5429/2 of August 20, 1954, which set forth United States policy toward Vietnam and openly planned a campaign of paramilitary disruption of the recently concluded peace agreements. "Covert operations on a large and effective scale" were urged so as to make "more difficult the control by the Viet Minh of North Vietnam."[30] This document provides other clear indications of US policy to

---

[27] See discussion in Sec. III.B.

[28] Pentagon Papers, Vol. I, Part II.B.2, B-21. A Pentagon analyst went so far as to conclude that "French insistence on strict legal interpretation of the Geneva Accords was one example of accommodation thinking": Pentagon Papers (edited by Sen. Mike Gravel; Boston: Beacon Press, 1971), Vol. I, 221.

[29] In the immediate aftermath of Geneva, the Democratic Republic of Vietnam (DRV) deferred to the Geneva Accords for the reunification, and turned inward: Pentagon Papers, Vol. II, Part III.A.5, 27. The DRV repeatedly tried to engage the Geneva machinery, forwarding messages to the Government of South Vietnam (GVN) in July 1955, May and June 1956, March 1958, July 1959, and July 1960, proposing consultations to negotiate "free elections by secret ballot" and to liberalize North–South relations in general. Each time the GVN replied with disdain, or with silence: *ibid.*, Part IV.A.5, 7.

[30] *Ibid.*, Vol. X, Part IV.B.c, 737.

pursue its objectives in Vietnam without exhibiting any regard for the basic peace-restoring provisions and intentions of the Geneva Accords.[31]

Even though it was not a combatant in the Indochina war between France and the Viet Minh, the United States Government opposed the Geneva negotiations from the outset and disapproved of their outcome. Subsequently, it supported the policies of Diem which were avowedly in defiance of the Geneva Accords, and it proposed and undertook covert paramilitary actions designed to disrupt Viet Minh control in North Vietnam, as well as to invite retaliatory actions by North Vietnam which could then serve as a pretext for further escalation and militarization of the conflict. These various actions led to a collapse of the Geneva Accords and a renewal of large-scale and prolonged warfare.

The United States Government, then, seems clearly implicated in a pattern of behavior that involved a failure to show respect for a validly negotiated agreement restoring international peace. As the Task Force Summary makes clear,

> Geneva might have wrought an enduring peace for Vietnam if France had remained a major power in Indochina, if Ngo Dinh Diem had cooperated with the terms of the settlement, [and] if the US had abstained from further influencing the outcome.[32]

It was also evident that the United States blocked the French desire to adhere to the Geneva Accords. "The GVN remained adamantly opposed to elections, and neither the US nor any other western power was disposed to support France's fulfillment of its responsibility to the DRV."[33]

B *Failure to Seek Peaceful Settlement of International Disputes*

In addition to its obligation to respect international peace agreements, the United States is obligated to seek a peaceful settlement of any international dispute likely to endanger international peace, and to seek a peaceful settlement of any ongoing conflict involving the use of force. Article II of the Pact of Paris recites the agreement of the contracting parties

> that the settlement or solution of all disputes or conflicts of whatever nature or of whatever origin they may be, which may arise among them, shall never be sought except by pacific means.[34]

---

[31] *Ibid.*
[32] *Ibid.*, Vol. II, Part IV.A.5, 3.
[33] *Ibid.*, Tab. I, 5.
[34] Friedman, *The Law of War*, Vol. I, 469.

The obligation of pacific settlement is an integral aspect of the underlying obligation to renounce war as an instrument of national policy and was so understood by the Nuremberg and Tokyo War Crimes Tribunals.

In addition, the United Nations Charter is a duly ratified treaty of the United States and, as such, forms part of the supreme law of the land. The Charter imposes the obligation on its Member states to pursue pacific means of settlement,[35] and imposes the complementary obligation to renounce the use or threat of force as an ingredient of diplomatic persuasion.[36] These obligations were more recently reaffirmed by the United States Government in its formal endorsement of the Declaration of Principles of International Law concerning Friendly Relations and Co-operation among States.[37]

It is my judgment, based on an analysis of the volumes of the Pentagon Papers covered by the indictment, that this legal obligation to seek a peaceful solution to an international dispute was persistently violated by the United States Government. The Pentagon Papers exhibit both an official American preference for military as opposed to pacific settlement methods in Vietnam and a tendency to use negotiating contexts either to create an illusion of respect for pacific settlement or to act as a useful channel for the delivery of threats to use force in the event that a settlement was not reached in terms satisfactory to the United States. In both respects the Pentagon Papers provide an authoritative basis for assessing, and most reasonably rejecting, the United States Government's contention that it was negotiating in good faith and that it at all times sought a peaceful settlement of the Vietnam War.

The papers disclose that the opposition of the United States Government to pacific settlement dates back to the immediate post-World War II period. Ho Chi Minh's several appeals by letter to the United States Government to play

---

[35] See art. 2(3), which reads: "All Members shall settle their international disputes by peaceful means in such a manner that international peace and security, and justice, are not endangered." See also art. 33(1), which reads:

> The parties to any dispute, the continuance of which is likely to endanger the maintenance of international peace and security, shall, first of all, seek a solution by negotiation, enquiry, mediation, conciliation, arbitration, judicial settlement, resort to regional agencies or arrangement, or other peaceful means of their own choice.

[36] Art. 2(4) states:

> All Members shall refrain in their international relations from the threat or use of force against the territorial integrity or political independence of any State, or in any other manner inconsistent with the Purposes of the United Nations.

[37] GA Res. 2625 (and Annex), 25 UN GAOR Supp. 28, at 121, UN Doc. A/8028 (1970). Among other relevant provisions, the Declaration proclaims that "[t]he parties to a dispute have the duty, in the event of failure to reach a solution by any one of the above peaceful means, to continue to seek a settlement of the dispute by other peaceful means agreed upon by them."

a diplomatic role that would avoid a war of independence were ignored.[38] In 1954, during the closing months of the French war in Indochina, the official American position, as summarized in the Task Force Study, was

> to attempt to steer the French clear of the negotiating table pending substantial military gains on the battlefield . . . In general, the US sought to convince the French that military victory was the only guarantee of diplomatic success.[39]

The support of the United States Government for Diem when he refused to open consultations with the North Vietnamese concerning general elections as required by the Geneva Accords has already been noted.[40]

The "negotiating volumes" of the Pentagon Papers also make clear that the United States often used negotiations either to relay threats or to create a public expression of interest in peaceful settlement, thereby evidencing a failure to negotiate in good faith. When the Canadian emissary, Seaborn, was preparing to leave on a negotiating mission to Hanoi, the US Ambassador to France, Douglas Dillon, conveyed a number of threats to the French Finance Minister that were to be included in Seaborn's message to North Vietnam. These threats included "the devastation of the DRV" unless the US succeeded in confining the "DRV to the territory allocated to it" and "in securing GVN's writ throughout SVN."[41] In fact, it was clearly stated that,

> Seaborn should get across to Ho and his colleagues the full measure of US determination to see this thing through. He should draw upon examples in other parts of the world to convince them that if it becomes necessary to enlarge the military action, this is the most probable course that the US would follow.[42]

Cable 2212, dated May 15, 1964, from the US Ambassador to South Vietnam, Henry Cabot Lodge, to President Johnson, underscored the intimidation aspects of Seaborn's mission by suggesting that,

> If prior to the Canadian's trip to Hanoi there had been a terroristic [sic] act of proper magnitude, then I suggest that a specific target in North Vietnam be considered as a prelude to his arrival.[43]

---

[38] Pentagon Papers, Vol. V, Part I.C.2, C-76 *passim.*
[39] *Ibid.*, Vol. I, Part II.B.2, B-18. This attitude was evidenced in many passages of the Pentagon Papers. For example, NSC 64 stated that: "Unless the situation throughout the world generally, and Indochina specifically, changes materially, the United States should seek to dissuade the French from referring the Indochina question to the United Nations" (*ibid.*, Part IV.A.2, 14).
[40] *Ibid.*, Part IV.A.3, v; see also text accompanying n. 25 above.
[41] Pentagon Papers, Vol. VI, Part C.I, 1.
[42] *Ibid.*, 2.
[43] *Ibid.*

Lodge went on to suggest a "selective use" of Vietnamese air power to accomplish this effect, so as to avoid provoking Chinese or Soviet responses. He also noted, as a way of supporting limited air strikes, that "if you lay the whole of the country to waste, it is quite likely that you will induce a mood of fatalism in the Viet Cong." The purpose of the "negotiations" was not to search for mutually satisfactory solutions, but to change the behavior of the North Vietnamese by the threat of intensified application of force unless American war aims were realized.[44] As Ambassador Lodge put it,

> it is . . . a relatively simple concept to go out and destroy North Vietnam. What is complicated but really effective is to bring our power to bear in a precise way so as to get specific results.[45]

Secretary of State Dean Rusk indirectly confirmed the coercive intent of the diplomatic mission when, in Cable 2049, May 22, 1964, he acknowledged the Canadian reluctance to deliver messages to Hanoi "that they will be punished."[46] Although Rusk informed Lodge that air attacks on the DRV as proposed would "simply not be feasible," he accepted Lodge's approach to negotiations as an occasion to intimidate rather than to come to terms. In Rusk's words, "We recognize that something a little stronger than the present OPLAN 34-A might be carried out on the basis you propose."[47] (OPLAN 34-A was the covert armed missions carried out in North Vietnamese territory by GVN forces under specific US direction.) Seaborn's final negotiating instructions were to tell Hanoi that unless it stopped military activity within a week, including that of the Viet Cong, "the US will initiate action by air and naval means against North Vietnam."[48]

The same kind of reasoning underlay the bombing pauses between 1965 and 1968 that allegedly were made to encourage a settlement of the conflict. The Pentagon Papers show that these pauses were viewed partly as public relations efforts to quiet public opinion and partly as a new means of conveying threats of further escalation.[49] In fact, the conclusion evidently was reached by some policy-makers in Washington that the war would be ended by this threat

---

[44] "We are not interested in destroying Ho Chi Minh (as his successor would probably be worse than he is) but getting him to change his behavior": *ibid.*
[45] *Ibid.*
[46] Pentagon Papers, Vol. VI, Part C.1.
[47] *Ibid.*
[48] *Ibid.*
[49] [The] US Mission [in Saigon] was hard at work trying to clarify its own thinking – and that of Washington – on the persuasive, or rather coercive, possibilities of bombing pauses . . . In particular the Mission was hoping to link the intensity of US bombing after the resumption closely to the level of VC activity during the pause. The purpose would be to make it clear to Hanoi that what we were trying to accomplish with our bombing was to get the DRV to cease

strategy without ever having to enter formal negotiations.[50] Thus, the supposed negotiating contexts were really alternative means by which to convey battlefield objectives coupled with threats of further escalation in the event that these military objectives were not accepted by the North Vietnamese.

The missions of Chester Ronning to North Vietnam also were viewed as an opportunity to provide a public relations foundation for a planned course of escalation of the air war.[51] Canadian officials expressed concern that it "would appear the US used Ronning as a means of obtaining a negative readout on negotiations that would justify escalation."[52] This was indeed the case. Secretary of State Rusk already had informed Secretary of Defense McNamara that:

> If he [Ronning] had a negative report, as we expect, that provides a firmer base for the action we contemplate and would make a difference to people like [the United Kingdom's Prime Minister Harold] Wilson and [the Canadian Prime Minister Lester] Pearson.[53]

In relation to the so-called Marigold initiative the subordination of the negotiating prospect to the bombing effort was made explicit in United States Government correspondence. Attorney General Nicholas deB. Katzenbach cabled the United States Ambassador in Warsaw, John A. Gronouski, that the "[p]resent bombing pattern has been authorized for some time and we do not wish to withdraw this authorization at this time."[54] Katzenbach also conceded that the bombing pattern "may well involve targets which Rapacki [the Polish Foreign Minister] will insist represent further escalation."[55] According to Gronouski, the Polish negotiating intermediaries accused the United States of deliberately provoking breakdowns of the negotiating contacts.[56] In his cable of December 15, 1966, Gronouski stated that if the escalated bombing produced a breakdown, the Soviet Union, Poland, and North Vietnam "will

---

directing and supporting the VC and to get VC units to cease their military activities in the South (*ibid.*, 55).

[50]   *Ibid.*

[51]   The persistent reliance on the bombardment of North Vietnam as a negotiating tool after February 1965 has been frequently attacked as an illegal use of force because it was initiated in circumstances other than as a response to an armed attack. See Falk, "International Law and the United States Role in the Viet Nam War," in Falk, ed., *The Vietnam War and International Law*, Vol. I, 373–91; and Falk, "International Law and the United States Role in the Viet Nam War: A Response to Professor Moore," *ibid.*, 490–94.

[52]   Pentagon Papers, Vol. VI, Part C.I, 152.

[53]   *Ibid.*, 178.

[54]   *Ibid.*, Vol. II, 83.

[55]   *Ibid.*

[56]   *Ibid.*, 88.

have no trouble convincing leadership in every capital of the world that our stated desire for peace negotiations is insincere."[57]

C *Intervention in the Internal Affairs of a Sovereign State*

An important development in international law since World War II has been to acknowledge a right of national self-determination and to emphasize, as a legal duty, the prohibition against a state intervening in the internal affairs of foreign states. This emphasis has found expression in a series of documents which are declaratory of customary international law.

The Declaration on the Inadmissibility of Intervention in the Domestic Affairs of States and the Protection of their Independence and Sovereignty was adopted as a United Nations General Assembly Resolution on December 21, 1965, by a unanimous vote, including the vote of the United States.[58] Among its other provisions the Declaration proclaimed that

> no State has the right to intervene, directly or indirectly, for any reason whatever, in the internal or external affairs of any other State. Consequently, armed intervention and all other forms of interference or attempted threats against the personality of the State or against its political, economic and cultural elements, are condemned.[59]

In 1970, the General Assembly adopted without vote the Declaration of Principles of International Law concerning Friendly Relations, which elaborated the duty of non-intervention and the related right of self-determination.[60] In light of the developing Vietnam experience, this Declaration amended the Declaration on the Inadmissability of Intervention to declare intervention a violation of international law and to extend the scope of the prohibition to include groups of states.[61] This prohibition against intervention is undoubtedly

---

[57] *Ibid.*, 91.
[58] GA Res. 2131, 20 UN GAOR Supp. 14, 11, UN Doc. A/6014 (1965).
[59] *Ibid.*, art. 1.
[60] GA Res. 2625 (see n. 37 above).
[61] The principle concerning the duty not to intervene in matters within the domestic jurisdiction of any State, in accordance with the Charter:

> No State or group of States has the right to intervene, directly or indirectly, for any reason whatever, in the internal or external affairs of any other State. Consequently, armed intervention and all other forms of interference or attempted threats against the personality of the State or against its political, economic and cultural elements, are in violation of international law.

See GA Res. 2625 (n. 37 above), 123.

vague at the edges and has been manipulated by governments to serve their political preferences in a wide series of global situations. Nevertheless, the basic non-intervention norm clearly seems to form part of customary international law, the conception of which has been given a rather authoritative statement in the widely endorsed United Nations resolutions. This basic norm has two elements: first, no military intervention in foreign societies; second, the invitation of one party in a civil strife does not suspend the non-intervention norm unless it has also been endorsed by a consensus of Members in a formal act of the United Nations.

In Vietnam, then, it would seem that the United States action violated a most minimal conception of the non-intervention norm. The Pentagon Papers exhibit throughout an American commitment to frustrate national self-determination: first, by helping France to prevail in its war against the Viet Minh; and then by taking over the French role in South Vietnam. Indeed, at first, the United States tried to persuade France not to relinquish its presence in Vietnam and sought to organize a pro-colonialist collective intervention on behalf of France even while the Geneva talks were underway in 1954.[62] Subsequently, on numerous occasions the United States has intervened in a variety of ways in Vietnamese internal affairs, both in relation to an ongoing civil war and in disregard of the sovereign rights of the government in Saigon that it was supporting.

The United Nations Declaration of Principles explicitly taints intervention on behalf of a colonial government as an interference with the rights of national self-determination.[63] Military intervention in a foreign country, absent the justification of individual or collective self-defense permitted by the United Nations Charter or absent a specific act of endorsement by the Security Council or General Assembly, also violates the more general Charter prohibitions against the use of force. Article 2(7) of the Charter even prohibits intervention by the United Nations itself "in matters which are essentially

---

[62] See Sec. 3.1 above.

[63] Every State has the duty to promote, through joint and separate action, realization of the principle of equal rights and self-determination of peoples, in accordance with the provisions of the Charter, and to render assistance to the United Nations in carrying out the responsibilities entrusted to it by the Charter regarding the implementation of the principle, in order:

. . .

(b) To bring a speedy end to colonialism, having due regard to the freely expressed will of the peoples concerned; and bearing in mind that subjection of peoples to alien subjugation, domination and exploitation constitutes a violation of the principle, as well as a denial of fundamental human rights, and is contrary to the Charter.

See GA Res. 2625 (n. 37 above), 123–24.

within the domestic jurisdiction of any state" except under the carefully speci-fied conditions involving United Nations "enforcement measures" authorized by the Security Council.[64]

The indictment volumes of the Pentagon Papers contain considerable doc-umentary and interpretative evidence supporting an inference of an illegal United States military intervention in South Vietnamese affairs in violation of the non-intervention principles of international law. The entire pattern of military involvement in the ground war in South Vietnam from 1965 onwards clearly substantiates the allegation of United States military intervention in an ongoing civil war in South Vietnam.

Beyond this, even if we only consider relations between Saigon and Washington, there is much evidence that the United States Government deprived South Vietnam of its legal right of political independence. For instance, as early as 1954, American officials acted as if they were entitled to select the leadership of South Vietnam's government. The Task Force noted that during the Diem regime in 1954–55, "Secretary [of State] Dulles and the Department of State in general seemed disposed to consider favorably suggestions that an alternative leader for the Vietnamese be placed in power."[65] General Lawton Collins, while acting as special American envoy to Vietnam charged with overseeing all United States operations, persistently urged Washington to accomplish Diem's removal from power. For a short period in the spring of 1955, Collins succeeded in persuading his superiors in Washington to consider shifting support to other potential leaders.[66]

The Pentagon Papers also indicate that American military involvement during this immediate post-Geneva settlement period included playing an interventionary role in various internal struggles in South Vietnam.[67] This role contradicts the claim that American policy was concerned with protect-ing the Saigon Administration against external attacks. The Task Force Study also confirms the contention that the establishment of SEATO and its later invocation to support American involvement were regarded as little more than cosmetic ways of disguising the unilateral pursuit of American interests by military means in Vietnam.[68]

---

[64]   See art. 2(7) in relation to Chap. VIII of the UN Charter.

[65]   Pentagon Papers, Vol. I, Part IV.A.3, iv.

[66]   *Ibid.*, 29, 31.

[67]   "[A]t this stage MAAG was charged solely with the task of assisting the Vietnamese to develop a force capable of establishing and maintaining internal security": *ibid.*, Vol. II, Part ill.A.4, 18.

[68]   "As is well known, the SEATO treaty was pressured into existence by the United States": *ibid.*, Part IV.A.4, 11.

The indictment volumes of the Pentagon Papers disclose further American interventionary pressure on the Diem regime in its later years. United States Ambassador Elbridge Dubrow proposed to Washington that alternatives to Diem be considered to assure attainment of the overriding objective of securing a "strongly anti-Communist Vietnamese government" in South Vietnam.[69] Such an American objective was in direct violation of the non-intervention and self-determination legal norms. The choosing of its own government by a state is the essence of its political independence.

In 1963, as a result of the American participation in the overthrow and assassination of Diem, the interventionary role became a matter of complicit *deed*, as well as *wish*. "The US . . . was asking Diem to forego independence by accepting the wisdom of American recommendations for reform."[70]

By mid-1963 the United States Government had chosen to support anti-government efforts in South Vietnam that led to the coup by a group of generals in December 1963.[71] The Task Force concluded that "by virtue of its interference in internal Vietnamese affairs, the US had assumed a significant responsibility for the new regime."[72] In the period leading up to the coup American pressure for reform of the Diem regime continued. For example, "Diem was . . . warned that Nhu must go."[73] The Task Force summarized its assessment of the American role in the coup of Diem as follows:

> For the military coup d'etat against Ngo Dinh Diem, the United States must accept its full share of responsibility. Beginning in August of 1963 we variously authorized, sanctioned and encouraged the coup efforts of the Vietnamese generals and offered full support for a successor government. In October we cut off aid to Diem in a direct rebuff, giving a green light to the generals. We maintained clandestine contact with them throughout the planning and execution of the coup and sought to review their operational plans and proposed new government. Thus, as the nine-year rule of Diem came to a bloody end, our complicity in his overthrow heightened our responsibilities and our commitment in an essentially leaderless Vietnam.[74]

[69] *Ibid.*, Part IV.A.5, Tab 4, 57.
[70] *Ibid.*, Vol. III, Part IV.B.2, 19.
[71] *Ibid.*, Part IV.B.5, i.
[72] *Ibid.*
[73] *Ibid.*, iv. Ngo Dinh Nhu was an important official, as well as Diem's brother and confidant, in the legitimate government of South Vietnam with which the United States claimed to be allied at the time.
[74] *Ibid.*, viii.

Taken alone, the sections of the Pentagon Papers which formed the basis for the indictment in *United States v. Russo* clearly supported an inference that the United States conducted its Vietnam policy in violation of international law. This view was reinforced by other evidence contained in portions of the Pentagon Papers not included in the indictment but which formed the essential legal context in which Daniel Ellsberg's decision to release portions of the Papers was made: the decision to initiate the bombardment of North Vietnam ("Rolling Thunder"); the reprisal claims associated with the Tonkin raids in August 1964, and the first bombardment of North Vietnam in February 1965; and the United States' role in the use of covert force in North Vietnam and Laos, especially in the period 1963 to 1965.

IV THE PERCEIVED AND POTENTIAL CONSEQUENCES OF
THE DEFENDANTS' INVOLVEMENT IN THE VIOLATIONS OF
INTERNATIONAL LAW OUTLINED IN THE PENTAGON PAPERS

Having argued that the Pentagon Papers evidenced the violation of international law by the United States Government, it is now appropriate to show that such violations could have led to the indictment and conviction of individuals, civilian as well as military, for criminal acts arising out of their connection with the United States involvement in Vietnam. It is also relevant to establish that both defendants in *United States v. Russo*, Daniel Ellsberg and Anthony Russo, occupied positions for which a presumption of legal jeopardy was not unreasonable if one were to assume an American willingness or an international capability to implement relevant portions of international criminal law.

In addition, it is relevant throughout that the defendants, independent of their jeopardy, may also have had a legally protected right to disclose information that they might reasonably calculate would bring an illegal war to a close. In this context, the prudence of Ellsberg in seeking the most effective means of disclosure compatible with preserving American interests at stake (e.g., withholding the negotiating volumes) is relevant to a determination of reasonableness. Proceeding by way of emphasizing their right of exculpation is really taking a *minimalist* position on the Nuremberg Obligation. A *maximalist* position would extend inquiry in the direction of occasions other than those arising out of prior complicity, in which individuals might be justified in violating domestic law so as to oppose an illegal war or illegal conduct in the course of conducting a war.

A *The United States and the Imposition of Criminal Liability on
Individuals for the Violation of International Law During World War II
and the Subsequent Endorsement of These Principles of International Law*

The United States recognized the principle of individual responsibility for violations of international law with respect to the initiation and waging of war during World War II. The Moscow Declaration of 1943, signed by Roosevelt, Churchill, and Stalin, declared the intention of the Allied Powers to prosecute Germans for violations of international law in initiating and waging World War II.[75] This intention was implemented by the London Agreement of August 8, 1945, which specified the Charter which was to govern the International Military Tribunal (IMT) convened at Nuremberg.[76] The Allied Commanders in Berlin issued Control Council No. 10 on December 20, 1945, to provide a framework governing the prosecution of individuals charged with criminal violations of international law.[77] This document defined "crimes against the Peace" as the "planning, preparation, initiation or waging of a *war of aggression, or war in violation of international treaties agreement or assurances*" [emphasis supplied].[78]

Control Council No. 10 also sought to identify the range of individuals who could be held responsible for criminal violations of international law:

> Any person without regard to nationality or the capacity in which he acted, is deemed to have committed a crime as defined in paragraph I of this Article, if he was (a) a principal or (b) was an accessory to the commission of any such crime or ordered or abetted the same or (c) took a consenting part therein or (d) was connected with plans or enterprises involving its commission or (e) was a member of any organization or group connected with the commission of any such crime or (f) with reference to paragraph I(a), if he held a high *political, civil* or military (including General Staff) position in Germany or in one of its allies, co-belligerents or satellites or held high position in the financial, industrial, or economic life of any such country [emphasis supplied].[79]

---

[75] For the text, see R. Falk, G. Kolko and R. Lifton, eds., *Crimes of War* (New York: Random House, 1971), 73–75.

[76] Friedman, *The Law of War*, Vol. I, 883–93.

[77] *Ibid.*, 908–12.

[78] Art. II(1)(a), *ibid.*, 908. The Nuremberg Judgment concluded: "To initiate a war of aggression, therefore, is not only an international crime; it is the supreme international crime differing only from other war crimes in that it contains within itself the accumulated evil of the whole" (*ibid.*, Vol. II, 925).

[79] Art. II(2), in Friedman, *The Law of War*, Vol. I, 909.

The fact that an individual "acted pursuant to the orders of his government or of a superior" could not free him of culpability, although it could be considered in mitigation.[80]

Similarly, with reference to a Japanese cabinet minister, the Tokyo War Crimes Judgment held that persons in high political positions would not be held responsible for violations of international law that occurred outside the scope of their official function *unless*:

> (1) They had knowledge that such crimes were being committed and having such knowledge they failed to take such steps as were within their power to prevent the commission of such crimes in the future, or (2) they are at fault in having failed to acquire such knowledge . . . [and] if such a person had, or should, but for negligence or supineness, have had such knowledge he is not excused for inaction if his Office required or permitted him to take any action to prevent such crimes.[81]

It follows logically and as a matter of policy implication that anyone with knowledge of illegal activity and an opportunity to do something about it is a potential criminal defendant unless he takes affirmative steps to "prevent the commission of such crimes in the future."

The case law developed in the War Crimes Trials after World War II established that the zone of individual responsibility for crimes against the peace extended well beyond principal policy-makers and state leaders.[82] The responsibility of secondary figures for war crimes generally turned upon whether they had voluntarily aided and abetted illegal acts in a situation in which they had or should have had adequate knowledge of their character. The basis of potential legal responsibility rested on the extent of complicity as reflected in actions and knowledge. Many of the war crimes cases support the conclusion that a defense of necessity was only admissible in cases where the defendant had no practicable way to dissociate himself from criminal features of German or Japanese war policy.

Furthermore, it was established that the legal duty to comply with international law was not confined to public officials or political and military leaders. *The Flick Case* involved indictments brought against German

---

[80] Art. II(4)(b).
[81] Tokyo War Crimes Trial Decision, quoted in Falk, Kolko and Lifton, eds., *Crimes of War*, 113. The opinion is substantially reprinted in Friedman, *The Law of War*, Vol. II, 1029 *passim*.
[82] See, e.g., the Ministries Case, *Trials of War Criminals* (Washington, DC: US Government Printing Office, 1952), Vols. XII–XIV, reprinted in part in Friedman, *The Law of War*, Vol. II, 1373 *passim*.

industrialists;[83] the Tribunal had to face squarely the issue of civilian responsibility for violations of international criminal law:

> [I]t is urged that individuals holding no public offices and not representing the state, do not, and should not, come within the class of persons criminally responsible for a breach of international law. It is asserted that *international law is a matter wholly outside the work, interest, and knowledge of private individuals*. The distinction is unsound. International law, as such, binds every citizen just as does ordinary municipal law. Acts adjudged criminal when done by an officer of the government are criminal when done by a private individual. The guilt differs only in magnitude, not in quality. The offender in either case is charged with personal wrong and punishment falls on the offender *in propria persona*. *The application of international law to individuals is no novelty* [emphasis added].[84]

Different issues of civilian responsibility were presented in the *Zyklon B Case*[85] in which the civilian defendants were charged with supplying Zyklon B, prussic acid, for use in concentration camps. The defendants argued that Zyklon B could be used in beneficial as well as harmful ways and that they had no specific knowledge that the supplies which were being sent to the government were being used to administer lethal poison to inmates of concentration camps. The judgment in the case dealt explicitly with the application of liability for criminal complicity to civilian defendants:

> [T]he present case is a clear example of the application of the rule that the provisions of the laws and customs of war are addressed not only to combatants and to members of state and other public authorities, but *to anybody who is in a position to assist in their violation.*
>
> The activities with which the accused in the present case were charged were commercial transactions conducted by civilians. The military court acted on the principle *that any civilian who is an accessory to a violation of the laws and customs of war is himself also liable as a war criminal* [emphasis supplied].[86]

The adaption of the principles established by the Nuremberg and Tokyo War Crimes Trials into the permanent corpus of international law was considered a priority item in the post-war world. President Truman, in an address to the United Nations General Assembly, affirmed the Nuremberg Principles

---

[83] *Trials of War Criminals*, Vol. VI, reprinted in part in Friedman, *The Law of War*, Vol. II, 1281 *passim*.
[84] Quoted in Friedman, *The Law of War*, Vol. II, 1284.
[85] *Ibid.*, 1487–98.
[86] *Ibid.*, 1498.

and declared that they pointed "the path along which [international] agreement might be sought, with hope of success."[87] Accordingly, the United States delegation introduced a Resolution before the General Assembly to make the Principles a permanent part of international law. The Resolution, which "Affirm[s] the Principles of International Law recognized by the Charter of the Nuremberg Tribunal," was adopted unanimously on December 11, 1946.[88]

These principles of international law were restated by the International Law Commission. Principle II states:

> The fact that internal law does not impose a penalty for an act which constitutes a crime under international law does not relieve the person who committed the act from responsibility under international law.[89]

Principle IV recognizes that superior orders are no defense against complicity in violations of international law. The scope of actions for which individual responsibility attaches is defined by Principle VI.[90] Principle VII notes that complicity in the commission of these crimes constitutes a violation of international

---

[87] The first Secretary General of the United Nations, Trygve Lie, asserted that:

> In the interests of peace and in order to protect mankind against wars, it will be of decisive significance to have the principles which were implied in the Nuremberg trials . . . made a permanent part of the body of international law as quickly as possible.

Both quotations are reprinted in Friedman, *The Law of War*, Vol. II, 1028.

[88] GA Res. 95(1), UN Doc. Af64fAdd.1, 188 (1947).

[89] The text of the Nuremberg Principles, as formulated by the International Law Commission in 1950, is reprinted in Falk, Kolko and Lifton, eds., *Crimes of War*, 107–08.

[90] The text of Principle VI states:
The crimes hereinafter set out are punishable as crimes under international law:

a. Crimes against peace:
(i) Planning, preparation, initiation or waging of a war of aggression or a war in violation of international treaties, agreements or assurances;
(ii) Participation in a common plan or conspiracy for the accomplishment of any of the acts mentioned under (i).

b. War crimes:
Violations of the laws or customs of war which include, but are not limited to, murder, ill-treatment or deportation to slave-labour or for any other purpose of civilian population of or in occupied territory, murder or ill-treatment of prisoners of war or persons on the seas, killing of hostages, plunder of public or private property, wanton destruction of cities, towns, or villages, or devastation not justified by military necessity.

c. Crimes against humanity:
Murder, extermination, enslavement, deportation and other inhuman acts done against any civilian population, or persecutions on political, racial or religious grounds, when such acts are done or such persecutions are carried on in execution of or in connexion with any crime against peace or any war crime.

criminal law.[91] These principles, if they have become part of international law, are by virtue of such development a valid part of the domestic law of the United States. In a due process sense, whether or not international law has developed to supersede domestic law, it may be enough if defendants in a criminal prosecution (such as *United States v. Russo*) have adequate reason to believe that the domestic legal norms under which they had been charged with illegal acts had been superseded by international legal norms.

B *The Reasonableness of the Defendants Regarding Themselves as Subject to Prosecution and Conviction for Their Roles as Accessories to the Violation of International Law*

Given the premise of potential individual liability for violations of international law, and in light of the evidence contained in the indictment volumes of the Pentagon Papers that such violations took place, it was not unreasonable for the defendants in *United States v. Russo* to regard themselves as implicated in a criminal enterprise from which they had a responsibility to dissociate themselves. If one were to imagine a procedure of accountability in the United States for the Vietnam War comparable to that which was used after World War II, establishing individual responsibility for violations of international law, then the defendants in this case, especially defendant Daniel Ellsberg, could have been indicted. Both defendants occupied positions for which a presumption of legal jeopardy was not unreasonable if one were to assume an American willingness to implement relevant portions of international criminal law.

Ellsberg, as a prominent policy adviser to the Assistant Secretary of Defense and as a Senior Analyst with the RAND Corporation, exerted a direct role on the formation of American military policy in Vietnam. His role in policy formation included work relating to the implementation of "Rolling Thunder," the bombardment of North Vietnam which was carried out in direct violation of international law.

Defendant Anthony Russo, as a staff employee of RAND, was entrusted with specific studies related to battlefield operations, including the crop destruction program practiced by the United States in South Vietnam during the 1960s. This program of crop destruction involved, as he came to appreciate, a war tactic whose principal impact was to deprive Vietnamese civilians, especially women, children, and the aged, of food; the purported target of such a program, the National Liberation Front, enjoyed priority access to available food

---

[91] "Complicity in the commission of a crime against peace, a war crime, or a crime against humanity as set forth in Principle VI is a crime under international law."

supplies. Russo was aware that the crop destruction program continued to be maintained even after the United States Government had ample evidence that its impact was primarily on civilians.

It should be noted that the defendants' affiliation with the RAND Corporation is in many respects similar in character to that of the defendants in the *Zyklon B Case*,[92] who were civilian employees of a private company supplying their government with products which allowed it to commit violations of international criminal law. In the instant case, the RAND Corporation was a quasi-public entity closely linked to United States Government war policies. The products it supplied were policy analysis and information rather than prussic acid. The critical point is that Ellsberg and Russo were "in a position" to assist in the violation of international law with respect to the initiation and conduct of war.

V THE OBLIGATION TO TERMINATE COMPLICITY IN THE VIOLATION OF INTERNATIONAL CRIMINAL LAW AND "SUPERIOR ORDERS"

It has been argued above that the United States Government violated international law in the conduct of its Vietnam policy; that international law assesses individual responsibility for the commission of such crimes against the peace; and that the professional roles of the defendants in the instant case as defense policy specialists supported their belief that they were implicated in a criminal enterprise and thus subject to a hypothetically plausible indictment and conviction. Under these circumstances, international law imposed an obligation on the defendants to take such action as was available to them to terminate their complicity in the illegal activity and to attempt to prevent the continued commission of such crimes. "If such a person [in a high political or civilian position] . . . had such knowledge [of crimes against the peace] he is not excused for inaction if his office required or permitted him to take any action to prevent such crimes."[93]

Ellsberg and Russo determined that the release of the Pentagon Papers was the one action available to them which would likely eliminate, or substantially diminish, their potential liability. The Pentagon Papers contained official government documentation of the illegality of the war and evidence that the violations of international law were causally linked to their own roles in

---

[92] See text accompanying nn. 86 and 87 above.
[93] Tokyo War Crimes Judgment, quoted in Falk, Kolko and Lifton, eds., *Crimes of War*, 118. See also text accompanying nn. 80 and 81 above.

the war effort. The evidence contained in the Papers also had contributed to the formation of their belief that they had to take action to dissociate themselves from the continued prosecution of the war. Most important of all, the disclosure of the Pentagon Papers to the Congress and the public could be calculated to establish the illegality of the war and secure support for efforts to insure its speedy conclusion.

In a more general sense, the defendants acted in the spirit of the message sent by President Roosevelt to the German people in 1944:

> I ask every German and every man everywhere under Nazi domination to show the world by his action that in his heart he does not share these insane criminal desires . . . I ask him to keep watch, and to record the evidence that will one day be used to convict the guilty.[94]

As citizens of a country with a democratic tradition we should welcome a doctrine that confers on citizens a responsibility and a duty to take steps to terminate an illegal war or illegal war tactics; at a minimum we should allow individuals to make available information to the public that confirms the illegal character of the war so that the elected members of Congress can properly exercise their functions, including an obligation to respect the international law as part of the law of the land.

The prosecution in *United States v. Russo* relied upon statutes, regulations, and classification procedures which allegedly prohibited the disclosure of the Pentagon Papers. To the extent that these statutes and regulations applied to the Papers, the defendants were seemingly caught between contradictory legal duties. On the one hand, they were obligated to respect the secrecy status accorded the Pentagon Papers. On the other, they were compelled to terminate their complicity in the illegal war and to attempt to speed its conclusion by releasing the Papers. The contradiction, of course, was resolved by one of the most fundamental Nuremberg Principles, namely, that continued complicity in international crimes is not excused by a continued deference to the requirements of municipal law. The so-called "defense of superior orders" is not available to defendants accused of war crimes. The International Law Commission has provided guidance in this area in its restatement of the principles of law recognized at Nuremberg.[95] The release of the Pentagon

---

[94] Falk, Kolko and Lifton, eds., *Crimes of War*, 76.

[95] See *ibid.*, 107-08. Principle II posits the related principle that the absence of a municipal law imposing sanctions for the commission of acts which constitute crimes under international law does not relieve the person who commits such acts from responsibility under international law. See text at n. 89 above. Even Professor John Norton Moore, in his discussion of selective service cases which raised the Nuremberg defense, has argued:

Papers by Ellsberg and Russo, regardless of administrative or municipal legal inhibitions, was a reasonable interpretation of their primary legal duty.

Courts presume, as a matter of law, that domestic legislation must be construed in conformity with relevant rules of international law, wherever such a construction is possible. It would violate the fundamental principles of fairness and due process of law guaranteed by the Fifth Amendment of the United States Constitution to subject the defendants to contradictory legal claims on their behavior. To interpret those claims protecting governmental secrecy as precluding the disclosure of information where such disclosure is justified under relevant principles of international law would have been to deny the defendants due process of law. Administrative regulations, such as the classification procedures, are of course subordinate to international law under the Supremacy Clause of the Constitution and *a fortiori* could not have been construed as prohibiting the defendants' actions. In addition, inhibitions on public disclosures of information are themselves devalued to the extent that they involve placing unnecessary burdens on First Amendment freedoms.

VI CONCLUSION

At stake in the case of *United States v. Russo* were several significant and related lines of development. First, there is the question as to whether the basic provisions of international criminal law are incorporated into national law in such a way as to be operative in domestic courts. Secondly, there is the constitutional question of due process, or more generally of fairness, as to whether civilian defendants are to be denied a Nuremberg defense in situations wherein they regarded themselves as being confronted by illegal "superior orders" (in the instant case, in the form of secrecy regulations). Thirdly, there is the broad question as to the extent to which governmental control over the use of force in international affairs can be penetrated by according legal status to opposing claims of individual conscience.

I believe that one legacy of the Vietnam War should be to vindicate the argument that national security is helped, not hindered, by heeding the

---

To the extent that an action would entail personal responsibility under the Nuremberg Principles, the Uniform Code of Military Justice, or any other valid international standard, certainly the criminality of the action should be a valid defense to state compulsion to engage in it. The sense of justice boggles at the thought that a man may be legally compelled to perform an act entailing criminal liability.

See Moore, "The Justiciability of Challenges to the Use of Military Force Abroad," in Falk, ed., *The Vietnam War and International Law*, Vol. III, 650.

conscience of the citizenry. In large, depersonalized bureaucracies it is difficult for individuals to act responsibly or to be held accountable in the complex settings of war-making. The locus of action is too diffuse and dispersed. It
is particularly necessary, then, that we encourage and protect individuals who
do make responsible claims on behalf of individual conscience. If these claims
take the form of resistance actions, then a domestic court should examine the
reasonableness of such a claim in context and not dismiss it out of hand by
invoking mechanically applied labels such as lack of standing, non-justiciability, or the political question doctrine. Such an inquiry into the reasonableness
of the claim should be conducted to include the following guidelines:

- the extent to which international law experts had written or spoken as to
  the illegal character of a war;
- the degree to which individuals were familiar with such an international
  law analysis;
- the extent to which the action by the individuals was reasonably calculated to bring the official illegality to an end;
- the extent to which the individuals tried to rectify the official illegality by
  peaceful and acceptable means before resorting to resistance activity;
- the extent to which the resistance claim was developed to minimize the
  disruption of domestic "law and order," given the situation and opportunities available to the claimant;
- the extent to which resistance activity avoided physical violence and
  damage to property, and especially the extent to which it avoided threat
  or harm to third parties.

Such a checklist of factors, had it been used, would in my judgment have
vindicated the decision by Daniel Ellsberg and Anthony Russo to release the
Pentagon Papers, regardless of prohibitions on the disclosure of classified materials
and national security information.

10

A Nuremberg Perspective on the Trial
of Karl Armstrong

There is considerable disagreement over the extent of the Nuremberg obligation, especially when it is used to justify opposing an illegal war, as was attempted on a number of occasions by Americans resisting the United States involvement in Indochina. At issue in particular is the claim of an ordinary citizen to engage in violent acts of resistance, illegal under domestic law, in opposition to a war that can reasonably be considered to violate international treaties and to defy basic moral precepts. The broader question is whether a movement for global reform, which includes among its goals the elimination of the war system, should, as one of its operative principles, renounce reliance on violent tactics.

In the years since the Nuremberg judgment of 1945, no official attempt has been made to apply the Nuremberg Principles to the concrete circumstances of violent conflict. An unofficial and symbolic application of the Nuremberg idea underlay the proceedings of the Bertrand Russell War Crimes Tribunal held in 1967 in two Scandinavian countries. The proceedings of the tribunal depict accurately the basic pattern of combat violations of the laws of war characteristic of the early years of heavy American involvement in Vietnam.[1] Aside from this single controversial incident, there has been no effort by governments, international institutions, or public opinion to take seriously the justly celebrated American pledge at Nuremberg of the chief prosecutor for the United States, Justice Robert H. Jackson: "If certain acts in violation of treaties are crimes, they are crimes whether the United States does them or whether Germany does them, and we are not prepared to lay down a rule

[1] John Duffett, ed., *Against the Crime of Silence: Proceedings of the International War Crimes Tribunal* (New York: Simon & Schuster, 1968); Frank Browning and Dorothy Forman, eds., *The Wasted Nations: Report of the International Commission of Enquiry into United States Crimes in Indochina, June 20–25, 1971* (New York: Harper & Row, 1972).

of criminal conduct against others which we would not be willing to have invoked against us."

Even as Justice Jackson uttered these sentiments on behalf of the United States, there were grounds for suspicion. After all, the Allied powers after World War II did not allow inquiry into the legal status of their own war policies, even though their obliteration bombing of cities in Germany and Japan and the atomic bombing of Hiroshima and Nagasaki could not easily be reconciled with prevailing views of the restraints embodied in rules of international law applicable at the time. The long dissent by the Indian jurist Radhabinod Pal to the majority opinion in the Tokyo war crimes trials argues that the whole judicial exercise of prosecution and conviction was a kind of pompous farce.[2] Indeed, a Japanese domestic court some years later did conclude, after an exhaustive and soul-searching inquiry, that the atomic bombings violated international law.[3] In an apparent effort to avoid any impression of self-righteousness, the Japanese court released this decision on December 7, the anniversary of Japan's surprise attack on Pearl Harbor.

Furthermore, the governments that initiated the Nuremberg experiment have exhibited no disposition to implement standards of accountability in subsequent contexts. Even in bitter warfare, where evidence of atrocities exists, there is little support for a war crimes approach. After the Indo-Pakistan War of 1971, there was some demand from Indian and Bangladeshi leaders for war crimes trials.[4] However, it is doubtful whether any trials will ever be held, despite the capture of many of those who had played an active part in the genocidal repression of East Pakistan in the period prior to the war. In general, then, the Nuremberg Principles seem neither to have had a deterrent impact on leaders nor to have motivated any community insistence on the formal prosecution of those who violate such principles.[5]

---

[2]   Justice Pal's dissenting opinion is published separately under the title *International Military Tribunal for the Far East: Dissentient Judgment* (Calcutta: Sanyal, 1953). For an assessment of the work of the Tokyo War Crimes Tribunal, see Richard H. Minear, *Victor's Justice: The Tokyo War Crimes Trial* (Princeton: Princeton University Press, 1971).

[3]   The Shimoda case decided on December 7, 1963, by the Tokyo District Court. See the *Japanese Annual of International Law* for 1964, 212–52; Richard A. Falk and Saul Mendlovitz, *The Strategy of World Order* (New York: World Law Fund, 1966), Vol. I, 314–54.

[4]   See e.g. Subrata Roy Chowdhury, *The Genesis of Bangladesh: A Study in International Legal Norms and Permissive Conscience* (New York: Asia Publishing House, 1972), 76–148.

[5]   See Eugene Davidson, *The Nuremberg Fallacy: Wars and War Crimes Since World War II* (New York: Macmillan, 1973). However, I do not share Davidson's view that, because the Nuremberg idea has not prevented war or war crimes, it has failed. My position is that the Nuremberg idea needs to be transformed from an intergovernmental tool and criterion of judgment into an instrument of global populism that opposes the domestic and international manifestations of the war system, however embellished with the trappings of state power.

Is it appropriate, then, to repudiate the Nuremberg Principles and to write off the Nuremberg and Tokyo experiments as little more than a pretentious form of "victors' justice"? Not in my view. In a series of conflicts, but especially during the American involvement in Indochina, the Nuremberg idea has provided conscientious citizens with a legal and moral foundation for condemning official policy, and has facilitated citizen demonstrations of governmental lawlessness. As such, the Nuremberg orientation provided certain elements of the American antiwar movement with a legal rationale for their rage, a rationale that could be conveyed with increasing credibility to the general population and to a wide spectrum of leaders. The My Lai disclosures in late 1969 helped to dramatize the criminal side of America's combat role in Vietnam, and also gave war critics a larger audience for their view that My Lai was only the tip of the atrocity iceberg. That is, My Lai was only one of many massacres, and was only a more spontaneous assault on the civilian population than such premeditated official counterinsurgency policies as crop denial, the Phoenix Program, free-fire zones, herbicidal destruction, area bombing, the massive use of antipersonnel weaponry, and the forcible removal of civilians from their homes.[6] It is difficult to calculate the extent to which reliance on the Nuremberg idea lent strength to a variety of antiwar stands. Mainstream opposition to the war was developed on a far more pragmatic basis, with the war being generally characterized as a mistake; liberals shied away from the drastic implications of concluding that national leaders were indictable as war criminals by Nuremberg standards. More radical postures toward the war did generally embody an acceptance of the central Nuremberg postulate that wrongful resort to military power was a criminal act for which the responsible officials were accountable. After the release of the Pentagon Papers in June 1971, it became difficult for an even broader segment of public opinion to resist the conclusion that American policy-makers directly and illegally intended to carry the violence in South Vietnam across international boundaries. Perhaps the prima facie criminality of America's war policies did eventually firm up liberal opposition to the war and finally undergird a belated congressional willingness to impose the August 15, 1973, cutoff on Cambodian bombing. But such a supposition is highly speculative and probably far too charitable.[7]

---

[6] See Edward S. Herman, *Atrocities in Vietnam: Myths and Realities* (Philadelphia: Pilgrim Press, 1970); Committee of Concerned Asian Scholars, *The Indochina Story* (New York: Bantam, 1970).

[7] For evidence of continuing American paramilitary involvement in Indochina, see *Indochina Chronicle*, published by the Indochina Resource Center, PO Box 4000D, Berkeley, California, 94704, issues that have appeared since the Paris Agreements and the August 15 cutoff of bombing.

The most direct significance of Nuremberg thinking involved its impact on resistance activity. In a wide variety of contexts, antiwar groups premised their actions, especially their defiance of enacted law, on an acceptance of the right or even the duty of citizens to resist an illegal and criminal war. Draft resisters, tax resisters, and other militant opponents of the war justified their position in this way. The members of Redress, a loosely organized group of professionals in the arts and letters, based their willingness to confront Congress and go to jail for a symbolic interval on this principle. More significantly, Daniel Ellsberg and Anthony Russo so justified their release of the Pentagon Papers, as did various religiously oriented groups intent on stopping the flow of munitions by obstructing rail and ship passages. In other words, the plausibility of the Nuremberg obligation in the context of resistance activities became crystallized as the Vietnam War proceeded, providing a moral and legal thread that ran through a wide variety of such activities.

Such a norm-related concept of resistance seems highly relevant for any serious global reform movement. Drastic and progressive global reform will come about, if at all, only when coalitions of progressive or change-oriented individuals in the highly industrialized countries (plus perhaps an occasional government) work together along parallel political lines with the more militant governmental and nongovernmental elements in the Third World. Such populist tendencies need to anchor their opposition to prevailing policies and structures through an association with widely shared and potentially planetary community principles of decency. The Nuremberg Principles enjoy such a stature, as well as the nominal adherence of virtually every government in the world.[8]

THE RESISTANCE CLAIM

The circumstances that condition the effectiveness of acts of resistance vary greatly: What is an effective act of resistance in one national setting may be meaningless or worse in others. Norman Morrison's martyrdom when he set fire to himself on the steps of the Pentagon in 1967 is virtually unknown among Americans, but it had a surprisingly strong resonance for the Vietnamese, inspiring songs, poems, and postage stamps.

Did Morrison's act of suicide overstep the limits of effective resistance? Can we identify such limits? It is a complicated matter to characterize an act of political suicide. Most generally it is viewed as a self-destructive action

---

[8] The principles of international law recognized in the Charter and in the judgment of the Nuremberg Tribunal were unanimously affirmed by the General Assembly of the United Nations on December 11, 1946.

designed to bear witness in an extreme form. But sometimes its intention is to provoke others of similar persuasion to undertake action, even violent action, to rectify the perceived wrong. In any case, although suicide is not itself an act of violence against another person or even against property, its very extremity provokes the most serious thought and inquiry on the question of whether violent acts of resistance can effectively be justified in contexts like the Vietnam antiwar movement. The elemental character of this issue emerged during the course of Karl Armstrong's trial in Madison, Wisconsin, for his admitted participation in the bombing of the Army Mathematics Research Center at the University of Wisconsin on August 24, 1970. The 3:00 A.M. bombing accidentally caused the death of Robert Fassnacht, a research physicist whose work was totally unrelated to the war. Armstrong pleaded guilty to charges of second-degree homicide, carrying a maximum punishment of twenty-five years, in exchange for an assurance that a full-scale hearing on motivation would be permitted and taken into account by the sentencing judge. At this hearing the war was put on trial by a variety of witnesses – including antiwar veterans and such well-known opponents of the war as Robert Jay Lifton, Gabriel Kolko, Senator Ernest Gruening, Howard Zinn, Daniel Ellsberg, and Philip Berrigan – who were not constrained by the rules of evidence which had largely kept such testimony out of earlier antiwar trials around the country.

The deeper question presented by the trial was whether Armstrong had transgressed the limits of resistance and ought to be held accountable, despite the fact that he was motivated by antiwar sentiments and had reason to believe that the building was unoccupied when the bomb exploded. It may seem as though Armstrong's motivation, whatever its moral status, has no relationship to the application of the criminal law. In one narrow sense such a view is correct. In the course of appraising guilt or innocence, a judge or jury is not supposed to go behind the intended consequences of a criminal defendant's actions. In other words, motivation is irrelevant. But on this, as on many other legal issues, the quick answer is not always very helpful, especially in illuminating the choices posed by a difficult case. For one thing, as the legal philosopher Ronald Dworkin argued in another context, the prosecutor enjoys a large measure of discretion over whether to prosecute and, if so, at what level of criminality. As Dworkin suggested with regard to the related area of draft resistance, the moral features of a technical violation of enacted law ought properly to enter into a prosecutor's decision.[9] Furthermore, the issue of motivation is properly taken into account in affixing the level of punishment; indeed, it

[9] Ronald Dworkin, "On Not Prosecuting Civil Disobedience," *New York Review of Books*, Jun. 6, 1968, 14–21.

is one of the principal justifications for the considerable judicial discretion that is allowed at the sentencing stage. Finally, it is at least arguable that juries do in fact take such considerations into account in reaching verdicts, and that such tempering of the letter of the law is not only desirable but is even encouraged by the fact that juries are not asked to disclose the reasoning by which they have arrived at their verdicts. These elements of discretion all operated in the antiwar contexts created by draft resistance. As the motivation of antiwar defendants on wider approval in the community, there was a tendency for the courts to defer or avoid criminal prosecutions, or to proceed halfheartedly or even apologetically, and there was a corresponding tendency toward greater judicial leniency at the sentencing stage than had been true in similar cases earlier in the war. In sum, then, "the law" encompasses a far wider set of issues than whether given acts violate the statute in question.

In cases of resistance there is a further complication that has not been adequately identified in most discussions of this subject. Resistance claims have been generally treated as examples of civil disobedience. Consequently, there is a disposition to evaluate particular acts of resistance in relation to certain criteria that have come to be widely, though not universally, accepted in the civil disobedience tradition. For instance, the philosopher John Rawls defines civil disobedience "as a public, nonviolent, conscientious yet political act contrary to law usually done with the aim of bringing about a change in the law or policies of the government."[10] In contrast, the political historian Howard Zinn, extending civil disobedience to the antiwar context that evolved during the period of United States involvement in Vietnam, contends that it is "a fallacy" to condition the legitimacy of a claim of civil disobedience by an absolute requirement of nonviolence. Zinn argues that the validity of an act of resistance depends on a variety of contextual factors, including the harm being perpetrated by the policies which have occasioned the resistance and the prospects for mounting effective opposition to these same policies.[11] However, even Zinn's broader concept of the civil disobedience tradition allows room for Armstrong's act to be variously interpreted as valid or invalid.

A clearer and more appropriate approach to the Armstrong case is provided by the Nuremberg tradition, where the context of resistance is characterized by conflicting sets of obligations, at least if one grants Armstrong's basic contentions that the Nuremberg Principles are part of international law, that international law is part of the law of the land, and that he, Armstrong, reasonably believed that the United State government's prosecution of the Vietnam

---

[10]   John Rawls, *A Theory of Justice* (Cambridge, Mass.: Harvard University Press, 1971), 364.
[11]   Howard Zinn, *Disobedience and Democracy* (New York: Random House, 1968), 39–53.

War was in flagrant violation of international law. If one accepts these asser-tions, then the reasonableness of Armstrong's resistance claim depends on whether he acted or believed he was acting in accordance with an applica-ble law, namely, the legal duty of individuals to oppose wars believed to be wars of aggression. Unlike the traditional practitioner of civil disobedience, who deliberately oversteps the bounds of legal conduct because he intends his behavior as a symbolic form of resistance to alleged injustices, but whose acts involve no harm to other persons or to property and are carried out with full acceptance of the anticipated legal consequences, the resister may be opposing in a substantive rather than a symbolic way those policies that he considers abhorrent. Americans applauded this form of substantive opposi-tion when citizens of many foreign countries engaged in violent resistance to Nazi rule during World War II. Indeed, most Americans would have been morally offended if those resisters had been apprehended after the war and subjected to prosecution, even though their actions clearly violated domestic statutes of criminal law and in some instances resulted in injuries to innocent third parties.

I believe it is within this tradition of resistance that Armstrong's action should be evaluated. Because resistance can properly be substantive rather than symbolic, it does pose grave threats to the security of the community; and certainly there are many potential claims of resistance that we would not want to endorse as legitimate extensions of the Nuremberg tradition. Stringent tests of reasonableness must be developed, especially when the claimant acts violently against people or property. But to argue in favor of such tests is to acknowledge that under certain circumstances the Nuremberg tradition does provide a legal basis for giving legal protection to acts of resistance even as extreme as Armstrong's, or at least justifies a more lenient approach at the sen-tencing stage. Admittedly this argument is speculative, but it warrants serious consideration as part of an effort both to make effective the rules of interna-tional law in the area of war and peace and to restore a measure of balance into the relationship between a citizen and his government. At a minimum, such a tradition of resistance might encourage the courts to pronounce upon the constitutional and international legal status of a controversial war that exacts a heavy toll in human casualties, imposes serious financial burdens, and may even risk the stability of world society. In effect, the Nuremberg argu-ment can be thought of as a technique to extend the doctrine of "checks and balances" to the relationship between citizen and government in the critical area of war and peace. Even if the province of a valid claim of resistance is kept very small, the resister can exercise a populist "check" on the powers and pretensions of the government.

Finally, the growing interdependence of the contemporary world makes the territoriality of a particular claim seem much less relevant. Thus, although the antiwar movement was attempting to change policies which emanated from Washington but whose direct effects of death and destruction were felt only in Vietnam, the movement's attempt was no less valid than if these same effects had been felt within the United States itself. The hard question to ask is whether an act of resistance which is reasonable in other respects is plausibly linked to opposing or changing the policies it seeks to repudiate.

On one level it is easy to argue, as many defense witnesses did, that Karl Armstrong's rage against the criminality of the war had no effective nonviolent outlets of the sort available to intellectuals, officials, or even soldiers; this would help us understand and perhaps even excuse his act, but not necessarily accord it our approval. More relevant from a legal angle is the argument that the prosecution in this case was so tainted by its own criminality arising from the war that it was in no position whatsoever to arrange for the punishment of any resister.[12] Certainly this view would justify the decision to testify on behalf of Armstrong, but it still does not clarify the moral and political status of his kind of act. On this point it can be argued persuasively that as of September 1970, Armstrong could have no reasonable expectation that nonviolent modes of antiwar activity would be effective, nor that Congress, the courts, or even the media were effectively available to someone with his views about the war. Furthermore, the harm inflicted on the Indochinese during that period was of such a magnitude that exceptional actions of resistance were appropriate. This position is not refuted by the suggestion that such random violence was or might reasonably have been thought to be "counterproductive," in the sense of vindicating government repression and turning public opinion against resisters rather than against the war. Less drastic means had been tried with no apparent success, and it is at least possible now to contend that one source of pressure to end the war, although difficult to calculate and never officially acknowledged, was a sense that the fabric of American society was unraveling, a sense created largely by resistance actions at the extreme.[13]

---

[12]   An editorial on the case put the issue well: "Without condoning in the least the violence he was guilty of, it must be said that Karleton Armstrong was one more casualty of the war in Vietnam, along with Robert Fassnacht and 50,000 Americans and countless Indochinese killed over the past dozen years by the policies of US leaders. The bitter irony that remains is that these leaders have yet to face a judge or jury for the numberless and horrifying war crimes they have committed" (*Progressive*, Dec. 1973, 103). David Wagner expresses the point more aggressively: "Those who take a moral position on the death [of Fassnacht] have the onus to weigh against it the calculated colonial barbarism which it negatively reflects. To do any less is not morality but evasion and cowardice" (Wagner, "Free Karl," *Liberation*, May 1973, 43).

[13]   The effectiveness of such obstruction of orderly government will always be denied by rulers.

A more provocative and less equivocal kind of support came from Van Ba, a representative of the Provisional Revolutionary Government of South Vietnam, who lauded Armstrong's deeds at an August 1972 rally against the war: "The bombing of the Army Math Research Center was a heroic act, not on the fringes of North American left extremism, but in the center of a world-wide revolutionary struggle."[14] This contention is forceful. Armstrong's act was an expression of deep conviction, involving risk-taking of the sort that is characteristic of genuine revolutionary struggle. Armstrong was thus in close solidarity with the National Liberation Front, which itself might not hesitate to bomb civilian buildings if such acts could be related to its war aims. In Vietnam these aims included disrupting the tranquility of urban populations in South Vietnam, who sought to remain uninvolved in the struggle. Furthermore, the extremity of Armstrong's act created the kind of transnational bond with Indochinese victims of the war that more restrained forms of resistance could never achieve. In this regard, Armstrong to some extent transcended his national identity as an American by acting as if he had as much at stake as a Vietnamese patriot. It is difficult to know whether these considerations dominated Armstrong's state of mind at the time of his controversial act, but Armstrong's own explanations are consistent with this possibility, and wide-ranging testimony from many sources supports his exceptional sincerity. Armstrong's father, a factory worker in the Madison area, was moved by his son's sincerity to the point of being able to comprehend sympathetically an act that he had previously viewed with abhorrence.[15] Of course, Van Ba's enthusiasm for Armstrong's act arises from its objective quality as an extreme form of opposition to the war and as an acceptance by the actor of risks somewhat comparable to those taken by participants in the struggle within Vietnam.

But even if Armstrong's act can be explained on moral grounds and from certain political perspectives morally endorsed, that does not resolve the question of whether it can also provide a general precept for resistance or radical reformist action. This issue is fundamentally the question of whether the best strategy for a movement of resistance and drastic global reform is to be found within a framework of violent or nonviolent action. Richard Goldensohn, an editor of *Liberation* magazine, argues that the Armstrong bombing should be viewed as a case of terror – "We understand terror to be a political tactic which relies upon instilling fear of personal harm in part or all of a population in order to motivate it to act in a particular way. Ultimately it is a

---

[14] Quoted from Mabel Dodge Brigade, "On the Road to New Nation," *Liberation*, Sep.–Oct. 1973, 2, 6.
[15] Conversation with author.

threat." Goldensohn distinguished such terror from "revolutionary violence, which – so it can be argued anyway – can at least be directed toward a 'particular enemy' or object with the purpose of destroying a specific obstacle to the success of a movement."[16] He maintained that the bombing of the research center was, in effect, "a symbolic warning that, if the war did not end, yet another installation might be next, and so on"; it was terror rather than revolutionary violence, because it sought to frighten the American people into opposing the war, rather than to destroy the war machine itself. This distinction is not persuasive. Van Ba's enthusiasm for the bombing seems credible precisely because he viewed it as a pure instance of revolutionary violence. The research center was a war-related facility, contributing research designs and models relevant to the electronic battlefield,[17] and the death of Robert Fassnacht was an unintended as well as highly unlikely side-effect. The main question, therefore, is whether violence can be considered the best resistance tactic, when all relevant factors are taken into account.

I think not. I am increasingly convinced that, from a global perspective, violence creates at least as many problems as it solves, that it sets in motion and feeds destructive processes over which we have less and less control. Because violence almost always begets violence, its use initiates a vicious circle that deprives a progressive movement of one of its principal strengths, its moral superiority over opponents. Furthermore, in military contexts the use of violence is increasingly indiscriminate, whether considered from the nuclear or from the insurgency/counterinsurgency end of the violence spectrum, and tends to inflict so much damage and suffering as to negate any possible advantage.

We must distinguish the moral quality of an act of resistance that is motivated by a reasonable belief in its necessity and proportionality from its political quality as an act likely to elicit wider support or to bring about increased pressure on policy-makers. In the American context, it is important for political reasons to repudiate Armstrong's act, while it is important for moral reasons to protest his punishment and imprisonment. My reasons for politically repudiating this act stem in part from an adverse appraisal of the relation of forces between revolutionary and repressive constituencies in American society. That is, violence which is endorsed and encouraged on the Left provides the government with a more plausible case for employing repressive tactics of its own, and nurtures an indulgence for violence emanating from

---

[16]　Richard Goldensohn and others, *Liberation*, Sep.–Oct. 1973, 2, 6.

[17]　For documentation, see "The AMRC Papers: An Indictment of the Army Mathematics Research Center" (pamphlet, Science for the People Collective, 306 North Brooks Street, Madison, Wis., 1973).

the extreme Right. In effect, then, if we vindicate violent claims of resistance even within the Nuremberg framework, we are also creating a climate for other forms of violence that are likely to have greater wellsprings of support in American society, at least at the present time.

This appraisal of Armstrong's defense of violent resistance leads to several conclusions. First, the state itself was sufficiently discredited that Armstrong's prosecutors lacked legitimacy. This dubious status of the prosecution is legally relevant to the controversial procedure of trying to determine what the law should have been if correctly applied to the war policies in Vietnam (although less relevant to the conventional procedure of accepting what authoritative interpreters of the law, such as the Supreme Court, declare the law to be).

Second, the violent element of the action was less deserving of punishment because the premeditated target was property rather than life; the death which resulted in this case was an unforeseeable and completely accidental side-effect. While it is generally true that criminal accountability is extended to the harm that actually results from illegal acts of violence, it is also true that the intent to avoid inflicting personal harm is relevant at the sentencing stage. Admittedly, to be relevant is not necessarily to be decisive. Surely, a judge who must weigh various legal factors and social priorities might reasonably conclude that a heavy sentence is required in cases like that of Armstrong because the kind of violence involved has implicit within it a risk to life as well as to property. Again, however, if the Nuremberg concept of legitimated resistance is to be accorded any status, acts of resistance must be appraised in context. It is worth recalling once more the anti-Nazi resistance claims in order to underscore the contention that even violent claims may win general approval if the political and moral climate is supportive.

Third, although Armstrong's specific acts are potentially justifiable within the Nuremberg tradition, any grant of actual support, to whatever extent and from whatever source (including private observers like myself or the sentencing judge), necessarily depends on an overall evaluation of the reasonableness of the acts undertaken. Such an evaluation could lead to an eventual rejection of the claim altogether or to various degrees of acceptance, including mitigation of the sentence. Since Armstrong pleaded guilty to second-degree homicide, in a technical sense the only issue before the court was whether the judge should be more lenient when passing sentence because the actions in question reasonably fit the Nuremberg tradition. Moreover, the Armstrong action seemed, for those who identified with the revolutionary claims of the National Liberation Front, like an appropriate extension of the arena of revolutionary struggle beyond the territory of South Vietnam. The action had a depressant impact, however, on progressive politics and militancy in the

United States, and thereby contributed unwittingly to official designs to pacify America. The ultimate moral status accorded to Armstrong's action depends on one's overall views as to the role of violence or its renunciation with regard to progressive politics. Yet in the wider setting of global reform, it seems desirable at the present time to orient opponents of the war system around a nonviolent ethos, for several reasons: to gain an audience in a war-weary world, to avoid becoming sucked into the war-making cult even while opposing it, to take comparative advantage of moral assets, and to expose the reliance of most rulers on violence and cruelty.

A distinction should be drawn between Armstrong's plight as a political prisoner and the moral, legal, and political status of his role in detonating bombs at the Army Mathematics Research Center in 1970. Regardless of one's appraisal of the latter, Armstrong seems to have been victimized on a number of grounds that qualify him as a political prisoner. For one thing, Armstrong was found in Canada and returned to the United States following a request for extradition. Political crimes are explicitly categorized as nonextraditable in the relevant treaty, yet the Canadian judge concluded that Armstrong was subject to extradition because the acts with which he was charged did not qualify as political crimes. This conclusion seems arbitrary and unfortunate. I doubt that many Americans would advocate that violent resisters from other countries who have found sanctuary in the United States should be turned over by the United States authorities for prosecution by their respective governments. In other words, the capacity to prosecute Armstrong was itself based on a dubious interpretation of an extradition treaty that contained a provision expressly exempting politically motivated behavior from procedures designed to facilitate transnational cooperation for enforcing domestic criminal law.

Even more fundamental than jurisdictional competence, however, is the question of legitimacy presented by a governmental and prosecutorial system that was itself tainted through its involvement in violent crimes of war. The judicial system, too, by its failure to pass judgment on issues of legality and criminality raised with respect to the Vietnam War, was not likely to provide a fair context for considering the kind of claim that Armstrong was trying to make. This particular claim could be fairly appraised only in a tribunal not tied to the American governmental system, unless Congress had previously directed American courts to consider the Nuremberg Principles as part of the law of the land whose relevance must be taken into account. As it was, Armstrong was judged by the ordinary rules of law applicable to any incendiary incident, and the claim that acts of resistance might, under certain exceptional circumstances, be entitled to legal protection was completely put aside.

The Armstrong case raises important, difficult, and controversial questions about which reasonable people might disagree. Above all, it raises questions of how we really feel about the Nuremberg precedent as operative law when its teachings are turned inward. These questions go to the essence of global reform, for what is at stake is whether the nonviolent processes of the law will at least give a hearing to individuals engaged in conscientious acts of resistance designed to curb the war-waging propensities of a sovereign state. It is true that Armstrong's violent act has anarchic potential and that violence always poses threats to bystanders, but this does not dispose of the underlying contention that we are legally required by the Nuremberg Principles to look beyond the confines of domestic criminal law, however circumspectly, whenever an appropriate claim of resistance is reasonably made. If the state system is ultimately to be eroded, it will be partly as a consequence of reinvigorating the individual citizen as an actor whose perspectives have legitimacy and relevance in the delicate process of balancing justice and order in world affairs.

Nevertheless, although the Nuremberg argument should be taken into consideration in determining a fair sentence for Armstrong, I believe that his act of exploding bombs should not be granted legal exoneration in toto. That is, the Nuremberg argument is persuasive enough for leniency, but not for complete exoneration. My conclusion rests on two principal reasons. First, the burden on the claimant to show that violent resistance was both warranted and effective was not adequately sustained by Armstrong. Second, a resistance claim of the Armstrong sort should be reserved for a situation of objective desperation where all legal paths of opposition are blocked off. These legal paths were certainly obstructed at the time Armstrong acted in 1970, but it is not reasonable to conclude that a situation of objective desperation existed.

Despite my acceptance of these lines of objection to Armstrong's action, I can envisage an altered historical and moral setting in which violent tactics would be efficacious for resistance purpose or reformist ends, and in which the ethical ambiguities of renouncing violence might be so great as to tip the scale in the other direction. At this stage in world history, however, nothing could be more revolutionary than a militant nonviolent movement for drastic global reform in which adherents exhibited discipline, courage, and tactical ingenuity.

11

Telford Taylor and the Legacy of Nuremberg

Today, "Nuremberg" is both what actually happened there and what people think happened, and the second is more important than the first . . . it is not the bare record but the ethos of Nuremberg that we must reckon today.

Telford Taylor[1]

We must never forget that the record on which we judge these defendants is the record on which history will judge us tomorrow. To pass these defendants a poisoned chalice is to put it to our lips as well.

Justice Robert H. Jackson[2]

In keeping with Telford Taylor's admonition, the focus of this article is upon "the ethos of Nuremberg" rather than on a reconstruction of the historical record yet again.[3] And this ethos is itself shaped by the unfolding historical setting. The interpretation of the Nuremberg ethos is at the present juncture very much caught up in the global atmosphere brought about by the end of the Cold War. It has been especially shaped by the decision of the United Nations Security Council in 1993 to convene an ad hoc tribunal at The Hague to indict and prosecute individuals accused of war crimes arising out of the breakup of the former Yugoslavia, especially in relation to the war in Bosnia, as well as those associated with the genocidal events occurring in Rwanda during 1994.

---

[1] Telford Taylor, *Nuremberg and Vietnam: An American Tragedy* (Chicago: Quadrangle Books, 1970), 13–14.
[2] Opening Statement, Nuremberg Trials (1945), reprinted in Robert H. Jackson, *The Case Against the Nazi War Criminals* (New York: Knopf, 1946), 7.
[3] With a certain irony, it is Taylor himself who gave us the most compelling historical account. See Telford Taylor, *The Anatomy of the Nuremberg Trials* (New York: Macmillan, 1970). But there is, as well, an enormous secondary literature. One useful overview is Joseph E. Conot, *Justice at Nuremberg* (New York: Harper & Row, 1983).

Almost fifty years passed between the establishment of the Nuremberg Tribunal and the ad hoc arrangements occasioned by the events in the former Yugoslavia and Rwanda. In the intervening period there were many atrocities assuming the form of "crimes against humanity" and even "genocide," yet no intergovernmental or United Nations initiative ensued. It would seem that the East/West divide precluded the convening of a war crimes tribunal throughout the Cold War, while the absence of strategic conflict in the 1990s has allowed such initiatives. The idea of an international criminal process has even been relied upon as a kind of compensatory undertaking expected to reduce the heat from the public for the failure to mount effective humanitarian interventions to protect the peoples of Bosnia and Rwanda, who were at extreme risk.

Our current interest in Nuremberg is also fueled by the recent push to establish an international criminal court that would function as part of a structure of global governance for international society – a process that tabled a treaty open for signature and ratification at Rome in June 1998.[4]

From the outset, the Nuremberg enterprise has been controversial, as has each major occasion of its reenactment. For some, including Taylor, it was a great step forward in the struggle for justice in international relations. For others, it was and will always remain an exercise in hypocrisy that cannot be otherwise given the character of international society.[5]

There exists another matter of fundamental interpretation. Until quite recently it has been natural to view the narrative of international law as an expression of the optimistic Western idea of linear history. In this sense, Nuremberg is both an event and a process. This process is often interpreted teleologically as containing an assured promise of future justice – one dimension of which will be the accountability of leaders for severe violations of international law. It is merely a matter of patience, allowing political evolution to run its course. A useful contribution of the critical side of postmodernism has been to cast severe doubt upon any and all such "meta-narratives," suggesting that what purports to be an objective account is more properly understood as a self-serving rationale of power by the powerful. The West has been particularly

---

[4]   See Leila Sada Twexler and S. Richard Carden, *A First Look at the 1998 Rome Statute for a Permanent International Criminal Court: Jurisdiction, Definition of Crimes, Structure, and Referrals to the Court* (Washington University School of Law Working Paper No. 98-10-1, 1998).

[5]   See, e.g., Istvan Deak, "Misjudgment at Nuremberg," *New York Review of Books*, Oct. 7, 1993, 46–53 (reviewing Taylor, *The Anatomy*); Eugene Davidson, *The Trial of the Germans* (New York: Macmillan, 1966); Hedley Bull, "The Grotian Conception of International Society," in M. Wight et al., eds., *Diplomatic Investigations: Essays in the Theory of International Politics* (Cambridge, Mass.: Harvard University Press, 1966), 51–73.

proficient at mythologizing its experience as the foundation for a beneficial order for the whole of humanity.

Taking seriously this deconstructive insight clarifies the scope of this inquiry. The prospects for an effective legal framework for the accountability under international law of leaders are dependent on the outcome of a social struggle currently underway. Whatever the result, it will reflect *social construction* by prevailing political tendencies rather than historical inevitability. At the same time there are predisposing elements that are animating and shaping the struggle, including the intensifying interconnectedness of life on the planet due to technological innovation, economic integration, and global media. This dynamic also generates much speculation about the decline of the state as the only effective ordering instrument on a global level, and a growing receptivity to alternative accounts.[6] Among those alternative accounts that are being taken more seriously are those concerned with "global governance" and "cosmopolitan democracy."[7] It seems more natural than it did in a statist world to posit accountability of leaders as an essential attribute of a more globalized world order.[8]

Finally, it is important to appreciate the special role of the United States in relation to this range of concern. As with so many elements of the normative (ethical and legal) side of international relations, the standpoint of the United States is both complex, variable, and highly ambivalent. During the Vietnam era the behavior of American leaders and their refusal to accept the relevance of Nuremberg retrospectively strengthened the hand of those who had condemned the process as self-serving and opportunistic from the outset. It also affected those with more positive expectations at Nuremberg – as was certainly the case with Justice Jackson, despite the image of a poisoned chalice, and with Taylor, who in light of Nuremberg found it necessary to regard Vietnam as an

---

[6]   On the decline of the state, see Joseph A. Camilleri and Jim Falk, *The End of Sovereignty: The Politics of a Shrinking and Fragmenting World* (Aldershot: Edward Elgar, 1992); Kenichi Ohmae, *The End of the Nation State: The Rise of Regional Economies* (London: HarperCollins, 1995). See also the array of accounts in a stimulating collection of essays, Karen T. Litfin, ed., *The Greening of Sovereignty in World Politics* (Cambridge, Mass.: MIT Press, 1998).

[7]   See *Our Global Neighborhood: The Commission on Global Governance* (Oxford: Oxford University Press, 1995); Daniele Archibugi and David Held, eds., *Cosmopolitan Democracy* (Cambridge, UK: Polity Press, 1995). On the wider consequences for international relations, see James N. Rosenau, *Global Politics in a Turbulent World* (Princeton: Princeton University Press, 1990). On the sharply contested implications for citizenship and political identity, see Martha Nussbaum et al., *For Love of Country* (Boston: Beacon, 1996).

[8]   For a world order perspective on this changing reality, see Richard Falk, *Law in an Emerging Global Village* (Ardsley, N.Y.: Transnational Publishers, 1998). See also discussion in Section II.

"American Tragedy."[9] Both of these actors on the stage at Nuremberg had at the time vigorously repudiated the taunt made by the Nuremberg defendants that the whole proceeding was "a kangaroo court" and a spectacle of "victors' justice," in part because they genuinely believed that Nuremberg would be accepted as a respected precedent by the leaders and citizenry of the governments that had sat in judgment of the leaders defeated in World War II.[10] The United States is both the principal originator of the Nuremberg ethos, and also the lion that is currently blocking the path to its consistent application and evolution since 1946. And yet it is also Americans that have done the most to keep the spirit of Nuremberg alive during the last half-century, mainly as a consequence of its citizens of conscience acting vividly within the spaces of civil society. This double relationship toward normative achievement is a feature of the overall contradictory connection of the United States to virtually the entire agenda of international normative concerns – starting of course with Woodrow Wilson's extraordinary crusade to establish the League of Nations after World War I, which culminated in the Senate's refusal to ratify the Versailles Peace Treaty that established the organization.[11] Such a contradictory stance is evident today in the dual role of the United States in the UN as both leading debtor and biggest bully. Because the preoccupation of Americans with the American role is so great, the interpretative perspective of an American – regardless of her particular slant – is likely to exert a major influence on what issues need to be discussed and on how the Nuremberg experience is to be regarded.[12]

Against this background I propose to consider, first, the specific features of Telford Taylor's interpretation of the Nuremberg ethos, or in my terminology "the legacy of Nuremberg." This is followed by a short section on the main

[9]   The subtitle of Taylor's book, "An American Tragedy," is a reference to the tension between what was decided at Nuremberg and what was being done in Vietnam.
[10]   Along similar lines, see the assessment of Nuremberg by the famous philosopher Karl Jaspers from the perspective of its legitimacy for German society. See Karl Jaspers, *The Question of German War Guilt* (E. B. Ashton, trans.; Westport, Conn.: Greenwood Press, 1978); Karl Jaspers, *The Future of Mankind* (E. B. Ashton, trans.; Chicago: University of Chicago Press, 1961).
[11]   See Thomas J. Knock, *To End All Wars: Woodrow Wilson and the Quest for a New World Order* (New York: Oxford University Press, 1992).
[12]   It is helpful to recall that the Tokyo Tribunal was constituted on a broader basis than Nuremberg, and that it produced a far wider range of views on the fundamental issues of priority. The most vigorous dissent was written by an Indian judge, R. B. Pal. Pal sees the whole of World War II from an interpretative perspective located in the South and refuses to exempt the behavior of the victorious powers from critical scrutiny – including their role in pushing Japan toward "aggression" and expansionism. For a partial text of Justice Pal's dissenting judgment, see Leon Friedman, ed., *The Law of War: A Documentary History* (New York: Random House, 1972), Vol. II, 1159–83.

phases of this legacy in the period 1946–99, and then some discussion of the peculiar US role throughout the entire period. On this basis, a reassessment of Nuremberg is made as of the present, and then in relation to the future.

I TELFORD TAYLOR AND THE LEGACY OF NUREMBERG

More than any other individual, Telford Taylor's remarkably realized career has held aloft the torch for Nuremberg. It was important that Taylor's authority included a distinguished military service that culminated with his role in the trials, in which he assumed prominence both by being promoted to the rank of Brigadier General for his service to the prosecution during the main trial, and by serving as Chief Prosecutor throughout the course of the secondary series of twelve trials at Nuremberg. In these important judicial proceedings that have been understudied (as compared both to the main trial and on their own) 177 defendants were charged with Nuremberg crimes because of their roles as army officers, medical doctors, industrialists, judges, and leaders of the SS. The decisions established crucial norms of responsibility for those acting on behalf of the state in various roles and for those who serve the state as private sector actors, which is the case for large business entities. Subsequent to Nuremberg, Taylor became a widely acclaimed constitutional law professor at Columbia Law School and a widely respected historian of the World War II era.

Taylor contributed two crucial books to the appreciation and understanding of Nuremberg which remain influential to this day: *Nuremberg and Vietnam: An American Tragedy* and *The Anatomy of the Nuremberg Trials*. Also important was Taylor's willingness to discuss the relevance of Nuremberg on many university campuses during the height of the Vietnam War. Such a willingness, although tempered on all occasions by a conservative style and demeanor, lent vital credibility to those who were opposing the war on legal and moral grounds – including those Americans who were resisting participation in the military because of their belief that the war was not legally sanctioned under constitutional and international law. Taylor carried his identification with these efforts to the extent of representing Marcus Raskin in the first major anti-war trial held in Boston and by his reluctant willingness to visit Hanoi during the latter period of the war.[13]

---

[13] Among the several prominent adult defendants accused of encouraging American youth to destroy their draft cards were William Sloan Coffin and Dr. Benjamin Spock. For material on the Nuremberg defense within the context of the Vietnam War, see generally Richard Falk, ed., *The Vietnam War and International Law* (Princeton: Princeton University Press, 1968–76). See also Vol. III, 193–485; and Vol. IV, 363–475.

It seems appropriate at this point to acknowledge that I participated with Telford Taylor at several university discussions of Nuremberg and Vietnam, and that we differed significantly on the central issue of relevance. Taylor argued essentially that the tactics being employed in Vietnam were inconsistent with the laws of war, and that they constituted grounds for the investigation and possible indictment of those American political and military leaders responsible for devising and enacting such policies. In his words, "the integrity of the nation is staked on those principles,[14] and today the question is how they apply to our conduct in Vietnam, and whether the United States Government is prepared to face consequences of their application."[15]

I agreed with such an assessment, but took it a step further by proposing that the "wider logic" of Nuremberg included the legal right, and possibly the legal duty, to oppose the war by non-violent means – including a right of resistance with respect to participation by way of obligatory military service or payment of federal taxes normally due. I testified along these lines as an expert witness on international law in numerous cases brought before domestic courts that relied to varying degrees on the Nuremberg Defense. Taylor set forth his grounds for disagreement, arguing that the World War II trials did not decide that individuals could avoid "military service on the basis of an individual's personal judgment that his country's foreign and military policies are wrong."[16] In addition, Taylor regarded domestic courts as lacking the evidentiary basis to reach decisions about war crimes, especially when contrasted with the international tribunals that sat in judgment at Nuremberg and Tokyo, and that were "surrounded by virtual libraries of the defeated governments' most secret papers."[17]

Taylor has written that my advocacy overlooks these factors, but I would point out that I was not seeking to reproduce the Nuremberg process in a domestic court, but rather to address the far narrower contention that it was reasonable for an individual familiar with the Nuremberg Principles to believe that the Vietnam War was "illegal" and "criminal," and that by "the wider logic" of Nuremberg there existed a personal right, and possibly a duty, to take proportionate, non-violent, and reasonable measures of resistance – including a refusal to participate by way of military service and taxes. There are two

---

[14] That is, the Nuremberg Principles as adopted by the General Assembly in a resolution put forward by the United States Government. See Affirmation of the Principles of International Law Recognized by the Charter of Nuremberg Tribunal, GA Res. 95(1), UN GAOR, 1st Sess., UN Doc. N236 (1946).

[15] Taylor, *Nuremberg and Vietnam*, 94.

[16] *Ibid.*, 120.

[17] Taylor, *The Anatomy*, 120.

closely interrelated issues: the appropriate role of domestic courts in international law cases and the implications for ordinary citizens of the Nuremberg Principles.[18]

I have mentioned my direct experience with Telford Taylor because I think it situates his approach both jurisprudentially and politically.[19] Taylor's approach to Nuremberg was an exemplary way of viewing law, the legal vocation, and the conflicting sentiments of citizenship.

A *Telford Taylor as Exemplary Participant: Positivism, Professionalism, and Patriotism*

In my view, Taylor combined attributes that made him the ideal bearer of the Nuremberg tradition in the half-century after the Nuremberg Judgment. In addition to the credibility associated with direct participation in World War II and at Nuremberg, Taylor's view of the evolution of international law was neither stultifyingly narrow nor alarmingly broad, but was conditioned very much by adherence to the jurisprudence of legal positivism. In effect, the significance of Nuremberg as a precedent is circumscribed by the legal texts that gave rise to the process, but especially by the formal holdings of the Nuremberg Tribunal (and the associated proceedings in the Far East, and those of lesser defendants in supplementary trials). These holdings were then given an authoritative rendering by the International Law Commission in the form of the Nuremberg Principles.[20]

Taylor offered criticisms of the Nuremberg proceedings from a similar positivist perspective. He criticized specific indictments, prosecutions, convictions, and punishments as lacking in sufficient evidence. He expressed regret that the lawyers for the defense did not have access to the archival materials, and that they were expected to live and work in substandard conditions. But, overall, he approved of the whole effort as a historic step in the direction of implementing the law of war, and as a measured political response to the

---

[18] My views on domestic courts are presented in Richard Falk, *The Role of Domestic Courts in the International Legal Order* (Syracuse, N.Y.: Syracuse University Press, 1964), while those on the relevance of Nuremberg are set forth in Richard Falk, "War Crimes and Individual Responsibility," in Falk, ed., *The Vietnam War*, Vol. III, 327–45.

[19] On a personal note, I should add that Taylor's manner with me and others was almost courtly in style, a bit distant and invariably formal. I welcomed the opportunity to know him more informally – which occurred only because we discovered that we were both squash players (indeed, he had played on the Harvard team) and we "bonded" on the court – itself a very American form of "courtship."

[20] Initially a UN General Assembly Resolution, later as formulated by the International Law Commission. See n. 16 above.

passions released by the end of World War II – especially the need to come to terms with the Nazi phenomenon in a manner that acknowledged the shock and anger that were present in 1945, but that transcended the level of retributive vengeance that had served Germany and the world so badly when imposed after World War I. In this regard, Taylor both took pride in the generally professional quality of the Nuremberg proceeding, and undoubtedly did his part to bring the skills and methods of a constitutionally oriented lawyer to bear so as to professionalize the proceeding – and, within its four corners, to accord defendants full rights of due process.

At the end of *The Anatomy*, Taylor devotes only two pages in seven hundred to the structural shortcomings of Nuremberg, which he calls its "political warts."[21] According to Taylor, "[t]he biggest wart was the presence, necessary as it was, of the Soviet judges on the bench."[22] The Soviet presence was troublesome for Taylor mainly because the Soviet government had itself participated in aggressive war through its participation with Germany in the attack on Poland and its partition, and in its later attack on and partial annexation of Finland – making the allegations against Germany of Crimes Against the Peace seem less like departures from the norms of international behavior. It was also awkward for the Tribunal to allege German responsibility for the Katyn massacre of several thousand Polish military officers when there existed strong suspicions of Soviet responsibility, which were later confirmed. Taylor also alluded to the lesser failure of the British government to turn over some documentary material to the Tribunal that might have affected the prosecution conducted against the Nazi defendant Admiral Erich Raeder.

Taylor also refers very briefly to what many subsequent commentators viewed as the most serious deficiency of Nuremberg, namely, the massive and sustained aerial bombardment of German cities by the victorious Allies. He considers the question somehow to be outside the scope of his undertaking in *The Anatomy*, pausing only long enough to "remind the reader that there were no recognized laws of war pertaining to aerial bombardments during World War II and that none were formally proposed by the nations until 1977."[23] In discussing the legality of the bombing campaigns against North Vietnam in the course of the Vietnam War in *Nuremberg and Vietnam*, Taylor reaffirms the absence of a legal foundation "for war crimes charges based on the bombing of North Vietnam." He adds, "[w]hatever the laws of war in this field *ought*

---

[21] Taylor, *The Anatomy*, 638–39.
[22] *Ibid.*, 638.
[23] *Ibid.*, 640.

to be, certainly Nuremberg furnishes no basis for these accusations."[24] Those who disagreed with Taylor on this point generally relied on the customary norms framing the international humanitarian law of war on the basis of principles of necessity, proportion, discrimination, and humanity that could then be applied more concretely.[25]

Taylor does offer a secondary rationale for the basic pattern of aerial bombardment in World War II by reference to "the principle of reason and proportion" in the application of force. Perhaps too readily accepting the military rationale for strategic air warfare, Taylor suggests that "[t]o a degree this rule of proportion was observed: Oxford and Cambridge were not bombed; neither was Heidelberg, and it is a terrible memory that we did not stay our hand at Dresden, when the war was as good as won."[26] In an ambiguous assessment, Taylor concludes that "it is difficult to contest the judgment that Dresden and Nagasaki were war crimes, tolerable in retrospect only because their malignancy pales in comparison to Dachau, Auschwitz and Treblinka."[27] Part of Taylor's positivist orientation is to draw a bright line between law and morality, and to regard the war as morally suspect, and even legally so – at least at its outer limits. Part of Taylor's professionalism, particularly his combined military/legal identity, is to give the benefit of the doubt to official justifications of military tactics as provided by the US government.[28]

It is also important to appreciate the extent to which Telford Taylor continued to view himself as a patriot loyal to the American government, even while dissenting openly from its policies as they were being carried out in the midst of a war. It is noteworthy in this regard that he chooses "An American Tragedy" as the subtitle for *Nuremberg and Vietnam*. Why not "A Vietnamese Tragedy"? And, if American, why a tragedy? Taylor provides an

---

[24] Taylor, *Nuremberg and Vietnam*, 142.

[25] See Richard Falk, "Methods and Means of Warfare," in Peter D. Trooboff, ed., *Law and Responsibility in Warfare: The Vietnam Experience* (Chapel Hill: University of North Carolina Press, 1975), 37–53, 102–13.

[26] Taylor, *The Anatomy*, 143.

[27] *Ibid.* Note that with reference to Hiroshima Taylor accepts the views that "[t]he rights and wrongs of Hiroshima are debatable, but I never heard a plausible justification of Nagasaki" (*ibid.*) For most of the world, it is Hiroshima, not Nagasaki, that stands out as a moral outrage, challenging the moral imagination in a manner quite comparable to that of the Holocaust itself. Perhaps the most daring and perceptive explorations of this equivalence, and its limits, are by Robert Jay Lifton. See Robert Jay Lifton and Eric Markuson, *The Genocidal Mentality: Nazi Holocaust and Nuclear Threat* (New York: Basic Books, 1990).

[28] In this regard, see Taylor's effort to come to terms with the controversy over the bombing tactics used in the Vietnam War in Taylor, *Nuremberg and Vietnam*, 144–48.

answer of sorts in the closing pages of the book. His words there are worth quoting at length:

> One may well echo the French proverb and say all this "is worse than a crime, it is a blunder" – the most costly and tragic blunder in American history. And so it has come to this: that the anti-aggression spirit of Nuremberg and the United Nations Charter is invoked to justify our venture in Vietnam, where we have smashed the country to bits, and will not take the trouble to clean up the blood and rubble. None there will ever thank us, few elsewhere that do not see our America as a sort of Steinbeckian "Lennie," gigantic and powerful, but prone to shatter what we try to save. Somehow we failed ourselves to learn the lessons we undertook to teach at Nuremberg, and that failure is today's American tragedy.[29]

There is much in this passage that bears analysis, but only a few salient points will be made. By characterizing blunders as worse than crimes, Taylor seems to be endorsing the cynical logic of political realism and subordinating the Nuremberg experience to the margins of international relations. I doubt that such sentiment represents Taylor's own deeper views, which stress the importance of respecting the Nuremberg precedent without pausing to calculate the political gains and losses of respect in particular instances. It also conflicts with the last sentence of the passage, which regards as tragic this failure to learn the lessons of Nuremberg which were supposedly being taught by the trials in the aftermath of World War II. It is here that Taylor, as participant, may have been swayed more by the sincerity of the US government approach, and that of the other victorious nations – thereby not realizing that Nuremberg was *primarily* an exercise in victors' justice, and that it therefore was never treated as a political or moral precedent in the Vietnam setting, even by the liberal Americans who dominated the inner circle of advisors during the Kennedy/ Johnson presidencies.[30]

Nuremberg and Vietnam is dedicated "To the Flag and The Liberty and Justice For Which It Stands." On the dedication page is a large black-and-white drawing of the American flag. There is no doubt in my mind as to Taylor's sincerity in affirming such a view, and it may well have reflected his strong wish not to be misunderstood. He was not at all alienated from America and its ideals as a nation, but he was stepping forward as a critic of the government and

---

[29] *Ibid.*, 207.
[30] Along these lines, see the important criticism of the Tokyo trials in Richard H. Minear, *Victors' Justice: Tokyo War Crimes Trial* (Princeton: Princeton University Press, 1971); C. Hosoya et al., eds., *The Tokyo War Crimes Trial: An International Symposium* (Tokyo: Kodansha, 1986); B. V. A. Röling, *The Tokyo Trial and Beyond* (Antonio Cassese, ed.; Cambridge: Polity Press, 1993).

its practices in the limited setting of the Vietnam War, and even in this setting he gave the impression of being a cautious and reluctant critic. It is relevant to observe that Taylor waited to write his book until late in the war, after the Tet Offensive of 1968 and the My Lai atrocity disclosures of a year later. What may come as a surprise is that Taylor supported "American intervention in Vietnam" until 1965, not for Cold War reasons as was generally the case for Americans, but in a more legalistic vein "as an aggression-checking undertaking in the spirit of the United Nations Charter."[31]

B *The Legacy*

But there is one element of Nuremberg that seems to have had a strong impact on Taylor from the outset. It was the effort by the Chief Prosecutor, Justice Robert H. Jackson, to suggest that the legal quality of the Nuremberg proceedings would be deeply compromised if the approach taken was not made applicable in the future to the governments of the states sitting in judgment of the surviving Nazi leaders. He cites on the very first page of *Nuremberg and Vietnam* the famous Nuremberg Promise that was articulated by Jackson in his eloquent opening statement: "While the law is first applied against German aggressors, if it is to serve any useful purpose it must condemn aggression by any other nations, including those which sit here now in judgment."[32] Further to the point, Taylor ends *The Anatomy* by recounting that when it appeared as though the Korean War would end with a US victory, journalists inquired whether the US would initiate war crimes tribunals against North Korean leaders. As he put his position: "I was quite unable to predict whether or not such trials would be undertaken, but I replied that if they were to take place, the tribunal should be established on a neutral base, preferably by the United Nations, and given jurisdiction to hear charges not only against North Koreans but South Koreans and Americans (or any other participants as well)."[33] And then at the very end of that massive book, published in 1992, Taylor reiterates what for him seems to stand firm as the main legacy of Nuremberg: "I am still of that opinion. The laws of war do not apply only to the suspected criminals of vanquished nations. There is no moral or legal basis for immunizing victorious nations from scrutiny. The laws of war are not a one-way street."[34]

---

[31] Taylor, *Nuremberg and Vietnam*, 206.
[32] *Ibid.*, 11–12.
[33] Taylor, *The Anatomy*, 641.
[34] *Ibid.*

Additionally, Taylor affirms Nuremberg as the best possible way of address-ing the issue of war guilt under the specific circumstances that existed at the end of World War II – a way far better than ignoring Nazi misdeeds or than inflicting summary justice on suspects. Nuremberg was far from inevitable, as Taylor suggests in *The Anatomy*,[35] especially considering the more direct solutions favored by Soviet and British leaders.

Also, for Taylor Nuremberg was a milestone in the development of the inter-national law of war – especially due to its anti-aggression posture reinforced in the UN Charter, its imposition of responsibility on the highest echelons of authority in the state, its rejection of "superior orders" as a defense. He also credits Nuremberg with supplying the political energy to specify the human-itarian law of war to a far greater extent than in the past, leading indirectly to the four Geneva Conventions of 1949 and the two Geneva Protocols of 1977.[36] Finally, Taylor believed that, despite mistakes and imperfections, Nuremberg demonstrated that a judicial process, even if constructed by the victors, could be generally fair to those accused – as the differentiation in sentences and the three acquittals demonstrated.

Both in method and substance, then, Nuremberg is affirmed by Taylor as a positive precedent. Indeed, this sense that a beneficial model was created at Nuremberg explains Taylor's strong conviction that America's failure to heed the substantive outcome in the Vietnam setting amounted to a national tragedy.

But let us also take note of three features of Taylor's orientation that oper-ate as limitations on the interpretation of Nuremberg and its legacy: (1) the absence of a world order perspective that assesses whether, given the persisting role of sovereignty, force, and statist logic, it was ever reasonable to expect the Nuremberg idea to move beyond "victors' justice" in the future; (2) the ten-dency of legal positivism to view Nuremberg from a legal perspective makes it insensitive to the degree to which intergovernmental initiatives that encroach on state sovereignty are likely to reflect geopolitical convenience far more than principled respect for international law and its development; and (3) a positivist jurisprudence tends also to neglect the lawmaking significance of civic initiatives by individuals, especially in domains where considerations of sovereignty and geopolitical ambitions are particularly strong.[37]

[35] On the diplomacy that led to Nuremberg, see Bradley F. Smith, *The Road to Nuremberg* (London: Deutsch, 1981).
[36] For texts, see Burns H. Weston et al., eds., *Supplement of Basic Documents to International Law and World Order* (St. Paul, Minn.: West Group, 1997), 154–92, 237–60.
[37] For explication, see Section IV.

It is my claim that neither the limitations nor the persistence of the Nuremberg idea can be adequately understood without reliance either on a world order framework of analysis or on recourse to a more configurative jurisprudence.[38]

Such a contention has acquired added force in the last two decades as a result of a series of developments often discussed by reference to the rubric of "globalization," which has both diminished the influence of the state and opened a variety of political spaces within which transnational social forces act.

II THE NUREMBERG IDEA UP AGAINST WORLD ORDER

Throughout this century, mainly in reaction to the devastation caused by the two World Wars, there has been a series of reformist steps taken that challenge statist logic. These involve efforts to restrain the state legally and institutionally in relation to its discretion to use force as an instrument of policy. It is outside the scope of this article to evaluate the overall success of these various efforts, except to suggest that the record is, at best, mixed.[39] The central effort is associated with the fundamental undertaking of the UN Charter to prohibit aggressive force and to offer the collective capabilities of international society to victims of aggression. It was this commitment that was also at the heart of the Nuremberg experience, especially if considered *textually* in view of the stress placed in the Judgment on Crimes Against Peace, and if considered *contextually* in view of the Nuremberg stress on criminalizing severe abuses of people, associated with Crimes Against Humanity.[40]

---

[38] For the world order approach, see the writings of the World Order Models Project, especially Saul H. Mendlovitz, ed., *On the Creation of Just World Order* (New York: Free Press, 1975); Richard Falk, *On Humane Governance: Toward a New Global Politics* (Oxford: Polity Press, 1995). On configurative jurisprudence, see Myres S. McDougal and associates, *Studies in World Public Order* (New Haven: Yale University Press, 1960); Myres S. McDougal and Harold D. Lasswell, *A Jurisprudence for a Free Society: Studies in Law, Science and Policy* (New Haven: Yale University Press, 1992).

[39] The Nuremberg condemnation of aggressive war was only one aspect of the effort by international law to impose strict limits on the right of states to use force. For generally skeptical assessments of this undertaking, see Anthony Clark Arend and Robert J. Beck, *International Law and the Use of Force* (London: Routledge, 1993); A. Mark Weisburd, *Use of Force: The Practice of States Since World War II* (University Park, Penn.: Pennsylvania State University Press, 1997).

[40] One of the substantive contributions of the UN War Crimes Tribunal at The Hague has been to confirm that Crimes against Humanity can stand apart from a war context. See Payam Akhavan, "Justice in The Hague, Peace in Former Yugoslavia? A Commentary on the United Nations War Crimes Tribunal," *Human Rights Quarterly*, 20 (1998), 737–816.

The idea that the Nuremberg precedent would bind states in the future, including the victorious parties, is what seems in retrospect to be naïve. It is naïve because there continue to be no alternatives to self-help in order to uphold the security of the state, except in those rare situations where implementing the anti-aggression norm coincides with geopolitical interests of the main political actors. This happened in response to the 1990 attack and annexation of Kuwait by Iraq, even prompting the American president to put forward the prospect of "a new world order" in which the UN would finally fulfill its Charter commitment to make the world unsafe for aggression. But, just as with Nuremberg, once Kuwaiti sovereignty was restored and geopolitical priorities again pointed to a reliance on self-help in the form of unilateral force, the discourse of a new world order disappeared from the language of diplomacy.

It is important not to become irresponsibly cynical in light of these disappointments; but it is also equally important to take account of the prevailing ideas about security among governmental elites and the patterns of international practice in recent decades. Realism in a variety of forms tends to be the prevailing orientation toward the formation of policy by the leadership of most states. It puts state interests at the top and tends to regard respect for international law and morality as instruments of propaganda useful in relation to adversary states, rather than as providing policy guidelines that clarify national interests for one's own country. Such realism, especially as an ideological orientation of elites in the American setting since 1945, views the restraining claims on behalf of a Nuremberg world view as "legalistic" or "moralistic," and as misplaced and dangerously sentimental given the structure of international society. The complacency of liberal democracies in the face of the rise of Hitler gave the realist assessment great leverage during the last half-century in the process of learning "the lessons of Munich." American realists are a divergent lot, ranging from Henry Kissinger to George Kennan, but they share the fundamental view that interests, not rules or values, are the grounds of policy for a state in its external relations.[41]

Realist opponents of the Vietnam War invariably argued that it was imprudent due to its high costs relative to the calculus of expected gains.[42] To insinuate Nuremberg considerations into the debate over Vietnam policy was

[41] Realism is also dominant, and divergent, in academic circles. For useful surveys, see Robert O. Keohane, ed., *Neorealism and Its Critics* (New York: Columbia University Press, 1986); Michael Joseph Smith, *Realist Thought from Weber to Kissinger* (Baton Rouge: Louisiana State University Press, 1986).

[42] See George F. Kennan, *On Dealing with the Communist World* (New York: Harper & Row, 1964); George F. Kennan, *Democracy and the Student Left* (New York: Bantam Books, 1968); Hans Morgenthau, *A New Foreign Policy for the United States* (New York: Praeger, 1969).

completely alien to the realist discourse for critics and apologists alike, and it remains so to this day. Hedley Bull provided an early non-American realist set of principled arguments for not moving in a Nuremberg direction, resting on his belief that the quality of international order needed to be premised on continuing respect for the sanctity of sovereign rights and on an ethos of noninterventionism.[43] In Bull's view, international society lacked sufficient solidarity to impose on individuals acting on behalf of their states "a higher law" than that provided by their domestic political circumstances. From such a perspective, the Nuremberg idea was structurally unsound.

Such an argument is persuasive so long as the structure of world order is more or less exclusively shaped by sovereign states, with the more powerful states assuming special prerogatives. What such a realist perspective overlooks, however, is the emergence in the last several decades of a series of world order challenges, especially those associated with regionalism, globalization, and civic transnationalism. Along with such changes in world order structure, there also have been important ideological challenges mounted to realism, at least in its hardest edge forms. Among these challenges, the most subversive of all might turn out to be the internationalization of protection for human rights and the associated support for a legal entitlement to democratic governance.[44] These factors combine to produce a political climate in which the promotion of the Nuremberg idea is a feasible political project, but only to the extent that it is no longer conceived to be an inter-governmental undertaking.

In my reading of Taylor (and Jackson, for that matter), their expectations about Nuremberg are linked to tacit assumptions about the receptivity of liberal democratic governments to moral and legal pedagogy. Such assumptions lead to the view that a legal precedent can by its own force overcome contrary pressures, and it also incorporates, without being explicit, the belief that moral and legal progress in relation to international behavior is the natural course of history. Taylor, to be fair, at the end of *Nuremberg and Vietnam* is himself "a realist" when it comes to the role of domestic courts in the US with respect to the continuation of the Vietnam War. As usual, Taylor's formulation is worthy of quotation: "There is no simple way to end the Vietnam

---

[43] Bull develops such a position in "The Grotian Conception." See also Hedley Bull, *The Anarchical Society: A Study of Order in World Politics* (London: Macmillan, 1977).

[44] The emerging right to democratic governance has been given prominence by Professor Franck. See Thomas M. Franck, "The Emerging Right to Democratic Governance," *American Journal of International Law*, 86, 1 (1992), 46–91. On the subversive tendency of human rights norms, see Richard Falk, "The Quest for Human Rights in an Era of Globalization," in Michael G. Schechter, ed., *Future Multilateralism: The Political Framework* (Basingstoke: Macmillan, 1999), 153–78.

tragedy, for the Supreme Court is not a *deus ex machina*. This war, and the agony and rancor that are its product, have been the work of the President and the Congress – the people's elected agents – and the war can be ended only by action of the national will, exerted through political, not judicial, channels."[45]

But again to express a disagreement, the role of judicial action would be to embed international law in the constitutional structure of democratic govern- ance. It would thereby give civil society an instrument by which to challenge a wayward national will – a prerogative of especial importance with respect to the actions of the US government that involve protecting a wide range of global interests, the frequent recourse to force, and a range of undertakings that affect the well-being of persons with no access to the processes of decision within the United States.[46] For Taylor to accept this realist account internally, but ignore it externally, seems to invite both an underestimation of the role of civil society in implementing the Nuremberg idea and an overestimation of the willingness and capacity of governments operating in a realist mode to adhere to Nuremberg constraints if doing so runs counter to their percep- tions of vital national interest. Without a world order perspective it is almost impossible to assess either the potential or the limitations associated with the original Nuremberg experience.

III THE AGENCY OF "GEOPOLITICAL CONVENIENCE"

An essential feature of the Westphalian state system of world order that is often overlooked, or simply not discussed, concerns the managerial role played by leading or dominant states – what used to be called, in the colonial era, the "Great Powers." It is a problematic feature because it does not fit comfortably into the juridical logic of equality among states that is integral to the idea of sovereignty and to modern international law in general. If a political entity qualifies as a "state," enters into diplomatic relations with other states, and participates as a member of international institutions, then it enjoys a *juridical* equality of status with all other states (that structures most formal activities in organized international political life). The UN broke to a limited extent with this logic of equality by conferring permanent membership and veto power on five major countries that were most prominently associated with the outcome

---

[45] Taylor, *Nuremberg and Vietnam*, 121.
[46] See Richard Falk, "The Extension of Law to Foreign Policy," in Alan S. Rosenbaum, ed., *Constitutionalism: The Philosophical Dimension* (New York: Greenwood Press, 1988), 205–21.

of World War ll.[47] The Bretton Woods institutions also rest on inequality to the degree that they incorporate weighted voting based on levels of contribution into their operations.[48]

But far more important than these formal encroachments on the idea of sovereign equality are those aspects of international life that exhibit inequalities of power, size, wealth, and diplomatic ambition. Especially in relation to the war/peace agenda, these inequalities exert a decisive influence on the character of international relations and have done so since the rise of the sovereign territorial state as a political actor on the global stage. In the absence of strong central institutions of regional and global governance, dominant states have assumed leadership roles in a variety of settings with more or less approbation.[49] In this century, particularly since the end of World War I, it has been the United States more than any other country that has played this role, especially with respect to the politics of global reform. To varying degrees, this role has been shared with other states, either as alliance partners or adversaries – making a full rendering of global leadership rather complicated because of the variations over time, which are not central to this inquiry into the Nuremberg legacy.

In focusing on the relevance of inequality to Nuremberg and its legacy, it is of special importance to take note of the priorities of dominant states. It is these priorities that give coherence to the idea of "geopolitics," a shorthand for those dimensions of international relations that are primarily shaped by assertions of political power. It is only by being attentive to geopolitics that we can begin to grasp the puzzling pattern of achievements and disappointments that have flowed from the Nuremberg idea since its inception, in relation to its principal antecedents.[50]

In a fundamental sense, as with human rights, it is difficult to comprehend why sovereign states should have been ever willing to validate such a

[47]   It is also true that during the Cold War when the Security Council was generally gridlocked and attention shifted to the General Assembly, attacks were made on the legitimacy of the Assembly's recommendations because a coalition of states representing only a small percentage of either the world's population or of annual dues paid to the UN could muster a voting majority.

[48]   Such inequality has also been criticized for its failure to give sufficient weight to the views of economically disadvantaged states. Divergent views as to the *appropriate* criteria of inequality have so far prevented the selection of additional permanent members of the Security Council, despite the widespread acknowledgment that the selection that was done in 1945 needs to take account of the immense changes in world order, especially reflecting the impact of decolonization and globalization.

[49]   Bull has most influentially theorized this role in *The Anarchical Society*.

[50]   On pre-Nuremberg antecedents, see especially Taylor, *The Anatomy*, 14–20.

subversive idea as that of international criminal accountability of leaders for war crimes. It goes directly against the spirit and ideology of sovereignty. It only makes sense from a statist perspective if the imposition of accountability is understood to be a *particularly* advantageous response to a given geopolitical challenge whose wider implications can be avoided. For this reason the Nuremberg promise of Justice Jackson, later reinforced by Taylor as indicated above, is so revealing. By insisting that what was done at Nuremberg would become a general framework in the future, Jackson was implicitly advocating future limits on the use of power by states and their leaders that would, if implemented, transform the practice of geopolitics as it had developed over the centuries. Generalizing such accountability, particularly if accompanied by effective institutional mechanisms, would represent a *radical* change in the functioning of the state system, involving the elevation of law above the will of the sovereign. But without this insistence, Nuremberg would, in retrospect, certainly seem to support the most cynical appraisals to the effect that "it was nothing more than victors' justice," and, as such, would seem profoundly hypocritical – imposing selective punishment on an unfortunate group of individuals. Such a view is itself misleading as it overlooks the likely *traditional* fate of such individuals – severe punishment without any pretense of fairness.

Taylor bravely recognized that the Vietnam War was a decisive test of the Nuremberg Promise. But his intergovernmental orientation and inherent conservatism led him to view the failure of the US government to follow through on Nuremberg as an "American Tragedy."[51] The problem with such an assessment is that it does not recognize the degree to which Nuremberg was an exceptional circumstance that allowed geopolitical forces to coalesce around the idea of a criminal prosecution of surviving leaders. Among the factors that can be mentioned are the following: the claim of the victorious powers that the losing side embodied an evil ideology; the public pressure for some sort of punitive action against those believed responsible for waging such a devastating war; the consensus among leaders that Germany (and Japan) must not be held collectively responsible in the manner of the peace settlement after World War I (what might be called "the lesson of Versailles"); the closely related geopolitical idea in the West that the defeated enemy states might soon become valued allies in the next phase of geopolitical rivalry; the guilty conscience in the West that not enough had been done to protect the

---

[51] It is notable that each of the four victorious powers that sat in judgment at Nuremberg subsequently embraced policies and practices that appear to be in flagrant violation of the Nuremberg Principles. As a result there is a "British tragedy," a "French tragedy," and a "Soviet tragedy," as well as an American tragedy.

victims of Nazi persecution before and during the war itself (for example, the refusal of liberal democracies to accept Jewish refugees and the failure to bomb the railroad tracks leading to Auschwitz); and the overall sense that the reconstruction of world order around moderate lines would be helped by a dignified trial of German defendants as opposed to the impression created by a vengeful process of summary execution. In addition, there were those – such as Jackson and Taylor – who believed that Nuremberg represented a solemn commitment by the convening governments to submit to the rule of law in their international activities, and that such submission might help to prevent the recurrence of major wars in the future. And there were those who went further, viewing Nuremberg as a desirable and necessary step toward realizing a far wider program of global reform. In this latter view, only some form of world government accompanied by disarmament at the level of the state could save the human species from extinction, given the prospect of the next world war being fought with nuclear weaponry.[52]

Despite agreeing with Taylor's invocation of Nuremberg during the Vietnam War, my expectations of compliance were not disappointed. I never expected the Nuremberg Promise to be kept by leaders confronted by geopolitical challenges that could not be met within the four corners of the UN Charter, especially its anti-aggression norm.[53] To this day I disagree with the geopolitical calculus that prevails in realist circles, which accords such a low priority in the form of national interest to respect for the Rule of Law in the setting of security policy. But it seems to me impossible to deny the existence of such a realist calculus and its virtually unchallenged control over foreign policy. The consensus is so strong in the US that uses of force have been generally backed by overwhelming bipartisan citizen support – as was the case in relation to Vietnam for many years – and the role of international law is minimal, at most one of rationalization. Only when the war began to be perceived in elite circles as too costly for the interests at stake, as occurred after the Tet Offensive in early 1968, did some concerns about the restraints

[52] See Jonathan Schell, *The Fate of the Earth* (New York: Avon Books, 1982); Jonathan Schell, *The Gift of Time: The Case for Abolishing Nuclear Weapons Now* (New York: Metropolitan Books, 1998).

[53] For varying views, see Thomas M. Franck, "Who Killed Article 2(4) or: Changing Norms Governing the Use of Force by States," *American Journal of International Law*, 64 (1970), 809–37; W. Michael Reisman, "Criteria for the Lawful Use of Force in International Law," *Yale Journal of International Law*, 10 (1985), 279–85; Oscar Schachter, "The Lawful Resort to Unilateral Use of Force," *Yale Journal of International Law*, 10 (1985), 291–94; Oscar Schachter, "The Right of States to Use Armed Force," *Michigan Law Review*, 82 (1984), 1620–46. See generally Myres S. McDougal and Florentino P. Feliciano, *Law and Minimum World Public Order* (New Haven: Yale University Press, 1961); Weisburd, *Use of Force*.

of international law become evident – and then in the form of half-hearted self-enforcement at low command levels, such as that which occurred in response to media disclosures of the My Lai massacre.[54]

My point here is that Nuremberg occurred only for opportunistic reasons within the specific historical setting of the ending of World War II, and that far deeper than the normative impulses associated with imposing criminal liability on the individuals responsible were the currents of opinion that stressed the vital importance of moving toward unabashed realism in terms of American participation in the world. This outlook included warnings by such prominent figures as Dean Acheson and George Kennan to avoid taking the UN too seriously as a basis for collective security, and the corresponding importance of peacetime military vigilance at the level of the state. The main realist contention was that only countervailing power or containment and the credibility associated with a readiness to act could both keep the peace and avoid aggressive attacks on the established territorial and political order. The requirements for such security were shaped both by the existence and developments of nuclear weaponry and by the character of the expansionist threat posed by the Soviet Union. Doctrines of "containment" and "deterrence" reflected such thinking, and their implementation, as in Vietnam, was not very much affected by the relevance of legal factor. As the American debate developed, it was mainly conducted among realists, with anti-war realists such as Hans Morgenthau, George Kennan, and George Ball arguing against the war on pragmatic grounds associated with foreign policy priorities and opportunity costs, as well as the overextension and misapplication of containment.[55]

If such a reading of Nuremberg is made, how then can one explain its resurfacing in the 1990s? There are at least four lines of explanation. First, the end of the Cold War meant that allegations of criminality would not be perceived mainly as an exercise in hostile propaganda that dangerously inflamed efforts to sustain what had come to be called "peaceful coexistence," which was a necessity given the large arsenals of nuclear weapons possessed by both superpowers. Second, as discussed in the next section, to an extent not even imagined at Nuremberg, the Nuremberg Promise was taken seriously by morally engaged sectors of civil society. Third, the war in Bosnia with its genocidal features, especially "ethnic cleansing," again challenged the liberal

---

[54] See Taylor, *Nuremberg and Vietnam*, 122–53.
[55] For representative works, see George F. Kennan, *The Cloud of Danger: Current Realities of American Foreign Policy* (Boston: Little, Brown, 1977); Kennan, *Democracy and the Student Left*; Morgenthau, *A New Foreign Policy for the United States*; George Ball, *The Past Has Another Pattern: Memoirs* (New York: Norton, 1982).

democracies to show that they cared about the victims – a pressure intensified by "the CNN factor."[56] And, fourth, there was a geopolitical incentive to create some sort of international criminal tribunal to cope with the security threats to the established order posed by "rogue states," international terrorism, the drug trade, and the revival of piracy at sea. These international factors led to the reemergence of a circumstance through which the revival of Nuremberg was again, almost fifty years later, a matter of "geopolitical convenience."[57] It also generated a campaign to establish an international criminal court that has so far culminated in a draft treaty agreed upon in Rome last year, but its generality of ambition to reach perpetrators of *all* states has engaged geopolitical concerns and provoked opposition by the US government.

Despite these developments, the idea of criminal accountability remains in my view subordinate to the realist orientation toward the practice of geopolitics. This subordination is especially manifest in the American reluctance to endorse even the rather feeble proposal for an international criminal court agreed upon at Rome. It was also evident in relation to the American reluctance to support UN humanitarian peacekeeping efforts with the will and commitment of resources required for effectiveness – a pattern especially pronounced since the 1993 Somalia experience resulted in American casualties. This American reluctance was decisive in relation to the failure of the UN to provide timely protection to the Tutsi minority in Rwanda in 1994, which was confronted by a manifest Hutu genocidal assault, and its efforts a year later to block efforts to protect refugees threatened by warfare in Zaire. Given the degree of American leadership in relation to UN peacekeeping, this reluctance reinforced the view that realist geopolitics was still in command of the policy-making process, and that recourse to Nuremberg would remain confined to situations in which it was geopolitically convenient for leading states. Such a reassessment is bolstered by consideration of the American policy toward Iraq since 1991, and of its behavior generally in the Gulf region, where major strategic concerns (including nonproliferation, oil reserves, containment of

---

[56] Also in the background was the so-called "transition to democracy" problem affecting a series of important states in Latin America, as well as those in East Europe and South Africa. For representative writings, see Neil J. Kritz, ed., *Transitional Justice: How Emerging Democracies Reckon with Former Regimes* (Washington, D.C.: United States Institute of Peace Press, 1995); Naomi Roht-Arriaza, ed., *Impunity and Human Rights in International Law and Practice* (New York: Oxford University Press, 1995). See also the discussion in Section V.

[57] See the literature on the establishment of the Hague Tribunal, including Lawyers Committee for Human Rights, *Prosecuting War Criminals in the Former Yugoslavia* (New York: Lawyers Committee for Human Rights, 1995); Symposium, "A Critical Study of the International Tribunal for Former Yugoslavia," *Criminal Law Forum*, 5 (1994).

political Islam, and security for Israel) are clearly at issue. In the Gulf context, there is no reluctance to have recourse to high magnitudes of destructive force, although the objectives and approach also express an overriding effort to avoid American casualties.[58]

The geopolitical convenience that led to the Nuremberg trials arose in the setting of the defeat and occupation of the country whose individuals were being accused of criminality. It also involved taking advantage of the extensive documentary archives that had been developed by the Nazi regime and that functioned as an invaluable source of evidence for the prosecution, particularly as they contained so many admissions against interest. This setting was not available for Bosnia, and was not entirely available in relation to Rwanda. As a result, it has been difficult to obtain custody over the most prominent perpetrators of criminality in the former Yugoslavia, with two of the prime suspected culprits remaining not only unindicted, but retaining positions of formal authority (that is, Slobodan Milosevic and Franjo Tudjman).[59] Also at large are the main architects of ethnic cleansing in Bosnia – Radovan Karadzic and Ratko Mladic. Although the momentum in support of the Hague Tribunal has led to more impressive results than seemed likely at the outset, there is still the impact of geopolitical concerns that go *against* holding the maximum leaders responsible for what they have done. Part of that geopolitical pressure is aimed at stabilizing the internal situation in Bosnia and elsewhere in the former Yugoslavia so that the transition to "peace" can proceed, thereby sustaining the Dayton Agreement in the face of the many forces arrayed against it. It is in this sense that widening the arc of personal responsibility to encompass the top Serb leaders allegedly might provoke a Serbian backlash that either could lead to a resumption of war in Bosnia or, at the very least, could prompt violent efforts to disrupt the NATO presence. The other geopolitical pressure involves the incentive to work with Milosevic and Tudjman as established leaders so as to produce and sustain a diplomatic

---

[58] Comprehensive sanctions of the sort applied against such countries as Iraq and Cuba need to be subsumed under the category of force directed at civilian society. The result of such a combination of considerations is lethal destructiveness so far as the adversary is concerned, but with virtually no human risks – a one-sidedness of outcomes that raises its own problems of morality and law. When military force is used in such a one-sided way, the structure of violence resembles torture, as the torturer decides how to inflict pain in controlled conditions in which the victim is helpless to retaliate or even to defend himself. For profound reflections on the role of violence in different settings, see Elaine Scarry, *The Body in Pain: The Making and Unmaking of the World* (Oxford: Oxford University Press, 1985); John Keane, *Reflections on Violence* (New York: Verso, 1996).

[59] See the criticism of the Hague Tribunal in comparison to Nuremberg in Deak, "Misjudgment at Nuremberg," 46.

settlement. A further geopolitical pressure that emerged subsequently to Dayton concerns the Western response to claims for self-determination in the form of independent statehood for Kosovo. European and American diplomatic initiatives have proceeded on the dubious assumption that the Kosovar case for self-determination should be legally, politically, and morally rejected in favor of support for an autonomy arrangement.[60]

In summary, it can be concluded that the Nuremberg idea remains alive on an *inter-governmental* level, but that its enactment is highly selective and depends upon an international context that supports implementation due to the balance of geopolitical considerations at stake. Whether this pattern of implementation can be made less selective will be determined by two sets of other considerations: the degree to which the endorsement of the Nuremberg idea by transnational civil society can mount a successful challenge to the influence of geopolitical realists in the shaping of governmental policy, particularly in the United States; and the extent to which the application of international standards relating to the punishment of those accused of crimes of state can be addressed by judicial bodies internal to the state.

IV THE RELEVANCE OF GLOBAL CIVIL SOCIETY

Little of the vast corpus of literature on Nuremberg gives attention to the role of civil society[61] as an agency of implementation, yet it is primarily through the efforts of individuals and small groups that Nuremberg persisted as a challenge to political elites in the decades between 1946 and the convening of the Hague Tribunal. Of course, the potency of these civic initiatives is greatly enhanced in settings where the political elite finds itself divided, as was the case in the US in the latter stages of the Vietnam War and, less dramatically, with respect to forming a response to the terrible ordeal of Bosnia in the period 1992–95. At some point, the energies of civil society are sufficient to alter the international climate in a manner that places geopolitical realism on the defensive, or that isolates its adherents. Arguably, this has happened to a limited extent with respect to anti-personnel land mines, the status under international law of nuclear weapons, and the institutionalization of criminal accountability.[62] Transnational civic forces have been able to mobilize

---

[60] In 1999, this assumption is dubious given the uncontested, overwhelming wish of the people in Kosovo for secession and the lengthy record of brutal Serbian oppressive rule.

[61] On the terminology, see Richard Falk, "Global Civil Society: Perspectives, Initiatives, Movements," *Oxford Development Studies*, 26 (1998), 99–110.

[62] See generally Richard Falk, "The Nuclear Weapons Advisory Opinion and the New Jurisprudence of Global Civil Society," *Transnational Law and Contemporary Problems*, 7 (1997), 333–52.

widespread grassroots support and media interest and have enlisted many governments in the effort to shape their policy on a basis that is less responsive to geopolitical realism, and more in line with legal/moral factors and a genuine commitment to global humane governance as a long-term goal. In each instance, the US as the undisputed geopolitical leader has been able to block serious implementation and to cast a shadow over these projects, at least for the present.

It seems most important to acknowledge the unexpected, yet vital role that civil society has played in keeping the Nuremberg idea alive during the Cold War era. The two substantive concerns that contributed most explicitly to this process were opposition within the United States to the Vietnam War and concerns within Europe and the US with respect to the deployment of nuclear weaponry and the related doctrines governing use. Also closely related was the surprising emergence of human rights as an active dimension of public policy debate and as an instrument of foreign policy.[63] It becomes more evident that if governments assume the legal responsibility for upholding international standards with respect to human rights, then it is less of a leap to expect adherence to the Nuremberg Principles – especially as Crimes Against Humanity overlap to a considerable extent with the imperatives of human rights. Put differently, by formally accepting limited international accountability for severe violations of human rights, states have themselves already compromised their claims to be "sovereign."

The contributions of civil society are too numerous and scattered to be recited comprehensively here, even if the focus is limited to the Nuremberg idea. What can be mentioned in a summary form is the degree to which anti-Vietnam and anti-nuclear protesters who broke "the law" consistently relied on the Nuremberg argument to uphold their claims of legal innocence in domestic courts. Such claims were bolstered by international law specialists who testified as expert witnesses, essentially arguing that it was reasonable for individuals to believe that the war in Vietnam was a Crime Against Peace in the Nuremberg sense and that it violated the anti-aggression norm in the UN Charter.[64] Similar lines of legal defense were put forward in anti-nuclear settings, alleging either that nuclear weapons were intrinsically illegal, mounting a threat that if carried out would be necessarily a Crime Against Humanity

---

[63] For discussion on this, see Richard Falk, "A Half Century of Human Rights," *Australian Journal of International Affairs*, 52 (1998), 255–72.

[64] For the most sustained argument from a legal perspective in this direction, see Francis Boyle, *Defending Civil Resistance Under International Law* (New York: Transnational Publishers, 1987).

even if used in self-defense, or that particular weapons systems or doctrines of use were illegal (e.g., the neutron bomb, Trident submarines, cruise missiles, first-strike).

Some dramatic instances can be mentioned. Daniel and Philip Berrigan both defended their recourse to nonviolent resistance by an appeal to Nuremberg (and to religious authority), as did James Douglass. Their activities covered a range of resistance moves, such as burning and pouring blood on draft cards of young Americans, entering nuclear weapons facilities and damaging warheads, trespassing to prevent trains from carrying nuclear warheads to submarine bases, and writing eloquent accounts of the rationale for resisting state authority.[65] Another prominent instance of a civic initiative occurred when Daniel Ellsberg explained that his decision to release the Pentagon Papers (containing a vast repository of internal, classified documents under Pentagon control) was based on a reading of the Nuremberg Judgment and on his belief that, when the American people were exposed to the truth about how Vietnam War policy had been made, they would rise up to reject the war itself. As with Taylor, Ellsberg's expectations were too optimistic, underestimating the degree to which the American citizenry entrusts its fate in foreign policy to its elected leaders and bureaucratic appointees, and is not seriously committed to legality and morality beyond territorial limits. In other words, such initiatives overlook the extent to which the political identity of civil society is itself predominantly concerned with the prospects of winning and losing in its overseas involvements, and whether the strategic stakes of conflict are worth the costs being incurred. Nevertheless, the appeal to Nuremberg was important in challenging war policy, if only to ground the actions of opponents on a basis believed to be legally and morally well founded, and in keeping the Nuremberg flame at least as a flicker.

With the Cold War over and the resurfacing of Nuremberg on the intergovernmental level with a measure of geopolitical support, the transnational effort moved in a different direction. It formed a campaign to pressure governments to support the establishment of an international criminal court that could operate as an integral element in any viable scheme for global governance. This lobbying campaign was waged at the level of grassroots opinion, but mainly in relation to the official policy of governments, resulting in "a new internationalism" that consisted of a rather formidable coalition between a large number of governments and representatives of global civil society.

---

[65] See Daniel Berrigan, *The Trial of the Catonsville Nine* (Boston: Beacon Press, 1972); Francine Du Plessix, *Divine Disobedience* (London: Hamish Hamilton, 1970); James W. Douglass, *The Nonviolent Coming of God* (Maryknoll, N.Y.: Orbis Books, 1991).

V THE TRANSITION TO DEMOCRACY PROBLEM
AND THE PINOCHET INCIDENT

The collapse of militarist rule in the Southern Cone countries of Latin America revived the Nuremberg ethos in a series of distinct political settings that shared the need to solve "the transition to democracy problem" within the confines of state/society relations.[66] In essence, the problem was one of negotiating the voluntary renunciation of power by a previous authoritarian political leadership. Such a negotiation was complicated and influenced by the extent to which the former oppressive elite retained great influence in the security sectors of the state bureaucracy, namely the military, police, and intelligence sectors. It was also complicated by the anger and resentment in civil society, which in large part regarded their prior leaders as responsible for unforgivable crimes against the people. Even before power was relinquished, there was speculation that militarist rule persisted longer than otherwise because "the ghosts of Nuremberg" were lurking in the background, inhibiting beneficial political changes out of fear on the part of entrenched leaders of exposure to criminal prosecution in relation to policies pursued during the period of governmental tenure.[67]

On one side, the memory of Nuremberg served to reinforce claims in civil society for justice and the rectification and documentation of past evils, especially among those who had been directly affected and their political allies. There was a need to have some sort of closure in relation to the past, particularly for families that had experienced the loss of a close relative due to "disappearance" or through torture and execution. On the other side was the strong political will to negotiate a peaceful and irreversible transition that would emancipate a country from its earlier reign of terror, and succeed in restoring constitutional moderation and successful economic development. Such a process required some meeting of the minds between the old and new leadership and compromises on both sides, and was carried on subject to the scrutiny of global society.

This process produced what has been derisively called "the culture of impunity," as it restricted greatly the option of indicting and prosecuting individuals placed high in the former government, that is, it effectively granted immunity to individuals who were comparably culpable to the defendants at Nuremberg

---

[66] Subsequently, comparable problems have surfaced in many other regions, including other parts of Latin America, Africa, Eastern Europe, the former Soviet Union, and parts of Asia.

[67] The phrase is from a conversation at Princeton with Jacopo Timmerman, the Argentinian journalist and human rights activist, while he was living in exile in the late 1970s.

(and Tokyo). Part of the wider compromise was to establish an array of truth and reconciliation commissions at the level of the state that took on the job of documenting the crimes of the past and provided an accounting for past wrongs, but detached their findings from any application of the ethos of individual responsibility. The degree of success achieved by these commissions varied from country to country and depended on how they were perceived by the citizenry in relation to their stated objectives of "truth" and "reconciliation." It remains a matter of controversy as to whether the bargains struck were reasonable under the circumstances, or whether they were the best result that could be achieved in circumstances where the oppressive elite has not surrendered, but voluntarily gives up political power, thereby avoiding a longer period of abuse for the population and achieving a nonviolent transition to constitutional democracy.

The dramatic detention of General Augusto Pinochet in Britain in the fall of 1998 brought this issue before the court of world opinion in a vivid manner, thereby bringing to the surface the contradictory priorities at stake, including the usual exclusion of external sources of authority from the decision-making process on these matters. Pinochet was detained in response to a request for extradition from a Spanish criminal court that was prepared to hear evidence against him relating to Crimes Against Humanity (including rape, torture, disappearances, massacres, murders) of which Spanish nationals had been the victims during Pinochet's time as the Chilean head of state. The issue remains unresolved in Britain at this time, awaiting final decision by the House of Lords, and has been treated in the media as mainly posing the legal issue of whether diplomatic immunity should be given to Pinochet because he was head of state during the period when the alleged crimes were committed.

In my view, the more fundamental issue at stake is whether the immunity arrangement negotiated in Chile with Pinochet while he was still dictator should be respected at an *international* level under circumstances in which the democratic government in Chile that reached the agreement and remains in power requests his release and return to Chile.

The encounter can be understood as being between the implementation of universal standards and the encouragement and maintenance of past and future peaceful transitions to democracy. How should this encounter be resolved? By deference to the Government of Chile that currently represents the Chilean people and that presumably weighs the *pro* and *contra* arguments on the basis of its assessment of well-being in Chile (an assessment itself controversial within the country)? Or, in a judicial arena external to Chile, should the dominant consideration become the maximum possible implementation of international law enforcement – putting aside claims that holding Pinochet accountable before a Spanish court of law would hurt diplomatic relations between Chile and Spain and Chile and Britain, as well as threaten the sustainability, or at least the serenity, of the transition to democracy in Chile?[68]

It is a policy dilemma with no obvious answers. Jurisprudentially, it seems most flexibly handled by a contextual approach. Account needs to be taken of whether the government objecting to extradition is a democratic political entity, of the nature of the agreement reached with the military regime, of the severity of the crimes committed, of the degree to which a fair trial could be anticipated in the country requesting extradition, and many other considerations. Diplomatic immunity, however, does not seem relevant if the Nuremberg Principles are treated as expressive of positive international law at this point, which should be the case.[69] The difficulty arises in balancing the desirability of prosecuting someone accused of a great number of unforgivable crimes against the importance of not disrupting the fragile transition process underway in the very society that has collectively suffered from a pattern of criminality.

Also in the picture is the highly speculative impact of the outcome of either deterring future crimes of state by punishing perpetrators wherever and whenever caught or, to the contrary, of deterring dictators from giving up their power without a violent struggle since an immunity bargain is not binding beyond the borders of the country where it is struck. Without any clear empirical guidelines, the best approach would seem to support a presumption of extraditability and subsequent criminal jurisdiction that could only be overcome by a convincing showing that the implementation of international law would constitute a "clear and present danger" for the country of the objecting government. What seems clear is that Pinochet has no valid personal claim of immunity or exemption from prosecution outside Chile, regardless of the bargain struck earlier within Chile.

However the Pinochet incident is resolved, it has been a momentous event in the struggle to extend the Nuremberg Idea. It has given unprecedented salience to the question of the international accountability of a head of state for Crimes Against Humanity. It has suggested a possible major role for domestic courts in extending the reach of the Nuremberg Principles. And it has added

---

[68] For a supportive view of extradition, see Peter Kornbluh, "Prisoner Pinochet: The Dictator and the Quest for Justice," *The Nation*, Dec. 21, 1998, 11–24; Grahame Russell, "Pinochet and the Law," *Third World Network Features*, Dec. 16, 1998. For a more skeptical view of prosecution, see "Pinochet's Paradox" (editorial), *Wall Street Journal*, Dec. 9, 1998, A22; George Melloan, "Pinochet, Ocalan, and the Hypocrisy of the Left," *Wall Street Journal*, Dec. 1, 1998, A23.

[69] For the text of the Nuremberg Principles, see Weston, et al., eds., *Supplement of Basic Documents to International Law and World Order*, 193–200.

to the momentum in civil society to press forward with its campaign to establish an international criminal court along the lines agreed upon in Rome.

VI CONCLUSION

The legacy of Nuremberg remains complex and controversial, but the 1990s
have seen the revival of a serious effort on several fronts to push forward with
the central effort to hold perpetrators of crimes of state individually accountable. In this respect also, Telford Taylor's underlying commitment to treat
the Nuremberg Judgment as the foundation for future accountability seems
somewhat closer to realization than it was during the Cold War, but still with
a long path ahead littered with obstacles. One of the most formidable of these
obstacles is the reluctance of major states, especially the US and China, to
participate in this process if it includes the risk that their leaders might stand
accused at some future point – as would be the case if an international criminal court freed from the constraints of Security Council vetoes were allowed
to come into existence. International experience to date suggests that an international tribunal of the Nuremberg type will only be brought into being if
it is geopolitically convenient for the governments of the leading states, an
observation that casts some shadows across the current efforts at The Hague
and in Arusha.

There is also the possibility of empowering domestic courts to hear charges
against those accused of crimes of state. Israel initiated this possibility when
it abducted Adolf Eichmann in Argentina, and put him on trial in Israel
during 1961 for crimes committed before the country existed and outside its
territory.[70] In such circumstances – vividly evident in relation to the illegal
Turkish seizure of Kurdistan Workers' Party (PKK) leader, Abdulla Ocalan –
there is a serious concern as to whether minimal conditions of fairness to an
accused defendant can be met in the inflamed setting that prevails. As with
piracy, there exists universal jurisdiction for such crimes of state, and a large
potential implementation and enforcement role for domestic courts around
the world. The Pinochet incident and the Ocalan seizure underscore these possibilities, but also the difficulties, especially when prosecution proceeds in the
face of an earlier negotiated bargain that gave perpetrators a promise of immunity from prosecution in exchange for letting go of the reins of power, or when
it involves overseas abduction and prosecution of a revolutionary leader at war
with the prosecuting state. Whether such a bargain is entitled to extraterritorial

---

[70] For an important assessment, see Hannah Arendt, *Eichmann in Jerusalem: A Report on the
Banality of Evil* (New York: Viking Press, 1963).

application is one question that remains unresolved at this point, as does the related question of extraterritorial paramilitary seizure and trial.

It seems evident that individual accountability for crimes of state is an integral part of any adequate conception of a *just* world order.[71] But it seems equally evident that the realist gatekeepers of the international legal order will not accept comprehensive legal and moral restraints on the exercise of force as an instrument of foreign policy.[72] In this regard, Taylor's notion that America made "a tragic mistake" in Vietnam by contradicting the standards it had established at Nuremberg missed the central point that American leadership was never prepared to accept such a framework of restraint as seriously applicable to its future diplomacy. In fact, the country was led all along mainly by realists in the Machiavellian tradition that believed that the security interests of the state were paramount, especially in light of "the lessons of Munich," and found discussions of limits imposed by international law diversionary unless used as propaganda tools for castigating enemies or rationalizing contested moves in foreign policy.

For these reasons, the prospects for subordinating geopolitics to an ethos of individual responsibility subject to third-party implementation in a court of law remain remote at this point. To bring Taylor's bright hopes for the legacy of Nuremberg to fruition will depend on a major push from transnational civil society. Pinochet's detention and Ocalan's seizure suggest that this matter of accountability is "a hot issue" for many persons around the world, as does the campaign to bring the international criminal court into being. But the resistance from political elites to genuine judicial independence for this subject matter is likely to be insurmountable in the near future – although the struggle is underway, rooted in the aspirations of global civil society. It is a confusing, controversial struggle, polarizing support and opposition in relation to dramatic contexts of policy choice on both state and global levels of decision.

---

[71] See Richard Falk, "The Pursuit of International Justice: An Imagined Future and Present Dilemmas," *Journal of International Affairs*, 52 (1999), 409–41.

[72] There is an encouraging official disposition to confine recourse to force to military targets, but such disposition seems eroded by the indiscriminate nature with which sanctions are used even in the face of sustained massive suffering and death for the civilian population – as has occurred in Iraq since the ceasefire in 1991.

PART IV

THE LEGACY OF THE VIETNAM WAR

"Learning from Vietnam," in A *Global Approach to National Policy* by Richard A. Falk, Cambridge, Mass.: Harvard University Press, Copyright © 1975 by the President and Fellows of Harvard College, as chapter 4: 57–74.

"The Vietnam Syndrome: From the Gulf of Tonkin to Iraq," chap. 8 in *The Record of the Paper: How the New York Times Misreports US Foreign Policy*, by Howard Friel and Richard Falk, Verso, London, 2004: 226–50.

"'The Vietnam Syndrome': The Kerrey Revelations Raise Anew Issues of Morality and Military Power," *The Nation*, Jul. 9, 2001, pp. 18–23.

"Why the Legal Debate on the Vietnam War Still Matters: The Case for Revisiting the International Law Debate."

12

Learning from Vietnam

Since 1950, five American Presidents have supported a series of policies designed to maintain a pro-West, anticommunist government in control of South Vietnam. The persistence of such policies exhibits remarkable continuity, given the enormous difficulties encountered in pursuing this objective. There have been many efforts to explain the origins and durability of the American commitment. None has proved entirely satisfactory. It seems clear that the impetus for the policy arose from at least three principal objectives: the containment of the world communist movement, the more specific containment of mainland China, and the containment of revolutionary nationalism. But such goals can be pursued in a variety of ways, and it remains unclear why over the years the United States was prepared to make such immense sacrifices in blood, treasure, and prestige in their pursuit.

One rationale offered was the recollection that policies of appeasement – in what might be called the "lesson of Munich" – had not prevented World War II. American policy-makers prominent during the buildup of a military commitment to defend the Saigon regime seemed to believe the idea that the international communist movement was monolithic and committed to world conquest; they therefore saw the choice as one between "standing up to aggression" or provoking World War III. The notion of "containment" or "holding the line" arose as a reaction to Stalinism but persisted into the 1960s, long after Stalin's death and despite hard evidence of a deep Sino-Soviet split. This notion was accompanied by an image of "falling dominoes": If South Vietnam should fall to communism, then Thailand, Cambodia, Laos, and the Malay peninsula would also fall in inevitable succession. Therefore, although the stakes in Vietnam might appear small and remote if taken in isolation, it was argued that a large commitment was nevertheless justified because of these larger concerns – namely, the geopolitical stability of all of South Asia and the establishment as precedent of a significant prohibition against a communist aggressor.

Such reasoning is abstract and ideological and does not fit too well with the concrete facts of conflict in Asia, especially in Vietnam. When the United States made its original economic commitment to the French in 1950, the struggle for Indochina was a typical anticolonial war of independence of the sort that developed in Asia and Africa after World War II. True, the leadership of the Vietnamese independence movement had a communist background and might be suspected of bringing a liberated Indochina within the communist orbit of influence. But it was also true that the procolonial Vietnamese were politically isolated in their own country and were unlikely to govern effectively or humanely. As a result, the anticolonial movement in Vietnam developed into a broad united front effort that by the end of the first Indochina War in 1954 had attracted support from many noncommunist elements in the population. Ho Chi Minh had emerged as a national leader of extraordinary stature, commanding respect and allegiance from almost every segment of Vietnamese society.

In subsequent years the United States involvement has been shaped and facilitated by the Geneva Conference of 1954 that divided Vietnam into two zones. This division was initially provisional but with time assumed a certain permanence, as the zones of North and South Vietnam emerged as separate political entities. In this divided country setting, the United States was compelled to rely on military means to perpetuate the geographical and ideological divisions embodied in the Geneva solution, and found itself drawn increasingly into a large-scale and prolonged counterinsurgency war. The American objective since 1954, despite incredible shifts in tactical stress, has remained surprisingly constant: to maintain an anticommunist government in South Vietnam and hence to assure the continuing division of Vietnam into two sovereign states.

When Nixon assumed the presidency, the tactics of American involvement came to emphasize the replacement of American by Vietnamese combat forces – the so-called "Vietnamization of the war" – reinforced by fantastic levels of air support. At the same time the zone of violence spread to Cambodia, and the American military involvement in Laos intensified. The Vietnam War remained unresolved until 1973, the negotiations in Paris being stalled on two issues: refusal by the American government to make a commitment to total withdrawal by a definite time, and the American unwillingness to accept a provisional government for South Vietnam that represented a fair coalition of contending forces.

The Paris Agreement of 1973 represented an immense step in the direction of satisfying the two preconditions for peace. However, the political side of the agreement has not been implemented. Although the United States has now disengaged itself from the combat level, the war persists at high levels of intensity between well-armed Vietnamese antagonists. American insistence on implementing the Paris bargain would even today lead rapidly to peace in South Vietnam and to the emergence of a government in Saigon that is neutralist in foreign policy and reformist in domestic affairs, in other words, to an ideological compromise between the goals of the United States and of the Provisional Revolutionary Government (PRG) of South Vietnam, which was earlier known as the National Liberation Front (NLF). In addition, the reunification of Vietnam would be put off for a number of years and the longer-term future of South Vietnam would be allowed to reflect internal forces of national self-determination. The balance of these internal forces would and should lead during a period of several years to the emergence of a pro-PRG government, but one that governs by coalition politics and is quite autonomous in dealing with North Vietnam.

With this background it seems possible to speculate about what lessons American policy-makers should have learned from the long and anguished experience of the Vietnam involvement. Future American policy toward Asia is likely to be guided by whichever of several possibilities becomes the dominant interpretation of the Vietnamese experience, although the combination of detente and a world economic crisis may inhibit future American temptations to engage in Vietnam-type conflicts whatever the Vietnam learning experience turns out to be. Already much attention has been given in American intellectual circles to the question "beyond Vietnam," and there is a variety of competing efforts to present the most influential statement of guidelines for the future. An examination of this debate seems especially important, as all of the positions being seriously considered carry forward into the future our earlier mistakes of policy and perspective that prompted the Vietnam involvement in the first place.

TRUSTWORTHINESS OF THE OFFICIAL DEBATE

A major caveat must first be offered. Both the debate on "the lessons of Vietnam" and my analysis of it proceed on the assumption that there is a good faith connection between the persuasiveness of alternative lines of public justification and the course of governmental policy. Unfortunately, with respect to matters bearing on both interventionary diplomacy and national security, I have become increasingly skeptical about this connection.[1] In my judgment, the external debate may even function as a mystification, obscuring the real

---

[1] See Richard A. Falk, "Drifting Toward Armageddon," *Progressive*, Oct. 1970, 48–54.

bases of national policy; that is, the explication of a rationale may serve to confuse and distract, rather than to enlighten public opinion. Anyone who followed closely the evolving American official position on the deployment of an ABM system saw that the rationale was expendable, but the policy was not. The American involvement in the Vietnam War appears to have had the same quality.

This hypothesis is implausible without a fuller explanation of why the real bases of policy must remain obscure and therefore excluded, for the most part, from explicit mention. This is a complicated question, which can be only superficially discussed in this setting. It would appear that policy-makers are implementing a set of policies that contradict popularly held attitudes about why America uses military power in foreign affairs. These attitudes center around a self-righteous conception that, whereas other governments have interests, the United States only has responsibilities.[2] As a result, it is an unwritten rule that no responsible defense or criticism of United States foreign policy positions takes account of self-interested economic motivations and pressures. Only radicals of the Right or Left, who are by definition outside the policy-making elite, give attention to issues of economic self-interest or, as the Left puts it, to the dynamics of economic imperialism.[3]

Similarly, it is not considered reasonable to attribute foreign policy positions to the pressures or momentum of domestic political forces. Yet in the Vietnam setting there is considerable evidence of a bureaucratic momentum that carried the policies forward independent of any rational assessment of their merit. The extent to which the government is itself an unwitting (and perhaps unknowing) captive of the military-industrial complex is part of the problem, one that is almost always excluded from "responsible" discussions of the future of American policy in Asia. The bureaucratization and militarization of American national security policy-planning efforts are treated like intellectual ghosts.

The influence of these economic and governmental forces on policy-making may well be decisive in the years ahead. If so, the dialectics of intellectual debate are misleading, as the outcome of the debate will depend on considerations other than degrees of evidence and persuasiveness. Indeed, the actual situation may be the reverse, namely the argument that is finally appropriated may be the one which seems best calculated to uphold a

---

[2]   See Richard J. Barnet, *Intervention and Revolution* (New York: World, 1968), esp. 3–46.
[3]   See, e.g., from the Right, Hanson W. Baldwin, *Strategy for Tomorrow* (New York: Harper and Row, 1970); from the Left, William Appleman Williams, *The Roots of the Modern American Empire* (New York: Random House, 1969).

preselected policy. Surely during the Kennedy-Johnson-Nixon period of Vietnam involvement, the official search was for a plausible defense of the interventionary policy rather than for assessment of its plausibility. Thus, the various lines of explanation – such as to deter wars of national liberation, contain China, uphold the SEATO commitment, avoid a bloodbath in South Vietnam, guarantee that no solution be imposed on South Vietnam, protect the honor of the United States, uphold the credibility of its commitments, and so on – were used, dropped, and revived with no particular qualms, so long as a particular rationale met the mounting criticisms directed at earlier justifications of the war and restored public confidence for a while. When the more recent rationale was in turn undermined, then it too would be superseded by new lines of justification, again calculated to maintain enough support to enable the leadership to carry on the policy.

Thus, the policy debate is a puppet show of sorts. To challenge it on its own grounds may dangerously tend to lend credence to the seriousness of the overall inquiry by implying that evidence and reasoning are likely to shape future American policy in Asia. Nevertheless, it seems important to explicate the debate so as to demonstrate why the contending positions are inadequate, and to understand why a position heretofore excluded from serious attention provides a better guideline for future American policy in Asia.[4]

Several kinds of uncertainty could influence the course and explanation of American policy in Asia. These uncertainties may in the end make the present debate seem time-bound. First, the presentation of American foreign policy will depend heavily on the domestic and foreign stances of a number of key countries, especially Japan, China, the Soviet Union, and India. It is uncertain whether Japan will turn out to be a partner or a rival of the United States. There are already indications that Japan's continuing economic growth is beginning to hurt the American economy, and some respected analysts expect a revival of fierce economic competition and even trade wars between the United States and Japan. Similarly, the Soviet decision on whether or not to remain largely aloof from Asian politics is likely to influence United States choices in definite ways. Whether China remains preoccupied with domestic concerns, or reaches an enduring accord with either the Soviet Union or the United States, or both, or whether China pursues an avowedly expansionist foreign policy – all such factors are likely to shape the United States response. Finally, whether India is reasonably successful with a moderate government and remains nonaligned is likely to be important. These kinds of uncertainty are accentuated by their

---

[4] I intend to develop this link between domestic political forces and the course of foreign policy in subsequent writing.

interactive character: China's response to Japan may influence the Soviet relationship to India, and so on. Also, these uncertainties and complications will be affected by what goes on in other regions of the world. A revolutionary surge in Latin America or Soviet pressure in Europe or the Middle East may lead to a total American withdrawal from Asia, especially if Japan assumes the American role as surety for the political status quo on the Asian rimland.

Even more important than these external contingencies are the uncertainties of the future course of domestic politics in the United States. It now appears that domestic social and economic forces are likely to determine the overall orientation of American government, including its foreign policy. In other words, imperialists, isolationists, or advocates of world order are likely to be swept into power by reference to issues of employment, inflation, crime control, and even pornography. The substance of foreign policy positions has little independent salience for the American voter at present. This situation may change, but probably not very soon despite the salience of international economic issues.

It is even more difficult to assess the consequences for American foreign policy of the increasing significance of ecological strains. Serious forms of environmental decay, population pressure, and resource shortages are almost certain to emerge. But it is not clear whether this deepening ecological crisis will lead to more moderate forms of political competition, or will instead induce recourse to desperate political strategies by those governments under the greatest pressure from overpopulation, poverty, urban crowding, or mass unemployment. The recent upsurge of interest in environmental matters in the United States may lead in the years ahead to a lessening of national concern about maintaining influence in Asia and may even induce a partial reversion to isolationism, especially if the costs of maintaining clean air and clean water are mostly deducted from the defense budget rather than from the welfare budget.

Although their impact cannot now be anticipated in any useful way, these kinds of uncertainty with respect to foreign alignments, internal stresses, and ecological strains are of great potential significance. They underscore the speculative character of any assessment of American propensities to intervene militarily, and they may also make Americans more likely, even anxious, to revise their sense of the future.

A QUALIFIED SUCCESS

Despite these imponderables, in the concluding phases of American military involvement, three different interpretations dominated the debate over the consequences of the Vietnam conflict. According to the first position, which can be associated with the liberal internationalist who fully endorsed the cold war ideology, the war was a qualified success. This was the view taken by most professional military men and the American Right. They saw American involvement in Vietnam as a proper exercise of military power, but felt that the effort was compromised by presidential insistence on pursuing limited ends by limited means. They criticized Washington for seeking "settlement" rather than "victory," and joined the Left in condemning President Johnson for his failure to declare war on North Vietnam. They argued that the armed forces had to fight the war with one hand tied behind their backs, pointing as examples to the refusal to authorize unrestricted bombing of the dikes in North Vietnam, the early restrictions on targets in the Hanoi and Haiphong area, and the failure to impose a blockade on shipping to North Vietnam early in the war.

Even though victory was not pursued by all means at our disposal, this view does not regard the Vietnam War as a failure. In a characteristic statement, Colonel William C. Moore of Bolling Air Force Base, writing in the *Air University Review*, argued: "There is reason to believe that Ho Chi Minh would never have initiated action in Vietnam had he vaguely suspected that US determination would escalate the war to its current magnitude. There is also reason to believe that this lesson has not been lost on other would-be aggressors."[5] This interpretation of the lesson of Vietnam relied on two assumptions: first, that the Vietnam War was similar to the Korean War because in each case the United States shrank back from the complete execution of its mission, but did at least display its willingness to defend a noncommunist society against attack by a communist aggressor. Proponents of this view held that the Vietnam War was not a civil war but a war of conquest by one country against another: The NLF was a mere agent of Hanoi, whose role was to pretend that this was a civil war and thereby discourage any effective response in defense. Thus, they accepted fully the image of the war developed by Dean Rusk and Walt Rostow during the Johnson presidency. The implication for the future is that the United States should not be fooled into treating communist-led insurgencies any differently from outright communist aggression against a friendly state.

The second assumption behind Moore's assessment of the Vietnam War had an even greater implication for the future, because it perceived the Vietnam experience as a demonstration that deterrence works in the counterinsurgency setting as well as it has worked in the nuclear setting. In Moore's words,

[5]   Col. William C. Moore, "History, Vietnam, and the Concept of Deterrence," *Air University Review*, 20 (September–October 1969), 58–63.

"This willingness to escalate is the key to deterring future aggressions at the lower end of the spectrum of war. This, I think, is why history will be kind to President Johnson and Secretary of State Rusk because if we continue to stand firm in Vietnam, as they advocate, then the world will have made incalculable progress toward eliminating war as the curse of mankind."[6] Thus, the key to the future was America's willingness to escalate the conflict to high levels of destructivity – so high, in fact, that when confronted by such a prospect, no right-minded revolutionary would ever initiate a war. Those who supported this position were critical of Johnson's war diplomacy only insofar as it failed to carry the logic of escalation to even higher levels on the battlefield and at home.

This interpretation also claimed that the American decision to fight in Vietnam gained time for other anticommunist regimes in Asia to build up their capacities for internal security and national defense, assuming that the American effort in Vietnam created a shield that held back the flow of revolutionary forces across the continent of Asia. More extravagant exponents of this liberal internationalist line of interpretation even contended, on the most slender evidence, that the Indonesian generals would not have reacted so boldly and successfully to the communist bid for power in Djakarta in October 1965 had not the American presence in Vietnam stiffened their resolve.

Advocates of this position tended to admire the Dominican intervention of 1965, where massive force was used and results quickly achieved with little loss of life. The domestic furor over the Dominican intervention disappeared quickly, mainly as a consequence of the undertaking's "success" and brevity. Sophisticated adherents of this position also privately admired the Soviet intervention of August 1968 in Czechoslovakia for similar reasons. That model of overwhelming capability, rather than the slow escalation of capability as in Vietnam, is likely to influence the doctrine and future proposals of those who favor interventionary diplomacy.

A FAILURE OF PROPORTION

The second principal position taken in the debate over the Vietnam War, associated with the espousal of Machiavellian notions or state interest, adopted an increasingly critical stance toward the American involvement, regarding it as a failure of a sense of geopolitical proportion. This second view was widely held among moderate and influential Americans, especially among civilians of a less ideological and more geopolitical cast of mind. They felt that the Vietnam War had become a mistake, often isolating as the threshold of error

---

[6]   *Ibid.*, 63.

President Johnson's decisions in 1965 to bomb North Vietnam and to introduce large numbers of American ground combat forces. This position also by
and large rejected the notion that the war was caused by the aggression of one
state against another, viewing it instead as an internal civil war with both sides
receiving considerable outside support. A leading proponent of this position
was Townsend Hoopes, who served in the Pentagon from January 1965 to
February 1969, first as deputy assistant secretary of defense for international
security affairs and then as undersecretary of the Air Force. Hoopes explained
the failure of Vietnam as the result of a loss of a sense of proportion by the
men at the top. He built a convincing insider's case that Johnson and his
principal advisers were locked into a rigid and ideological view of the war,
and hence were unable to moderate the objective to conform with the costs in
blood, dollars, and domestic cohesion. Writing of the situation that prevailed
in Washington late in 1967, just a few months before Johnson's withdrawal
speech of March 31, 1968, Hoopes stated: "The incredible disparity between
the outpouring of national blood and treasure and the intrinsic US interests
at stake in Vietnam was by this time widely understood and deplored at levels
just below the top of the government. But the President and the tight group of
advisers around him gave no sign of having achieved a sense of proportion."[7]

This view of the lesson of Vietnam had no quarrel with the effort to defend
Saigon or to defeat the NLF, but urged that the effort be abandoned if it could
not be made to succeed within a reasonable time and at a reasonable cost.
Many Kennedy officials who originally supported the United States role in
Vietnam came later to hold similar views, concluding either that the war was
weakening our ability to uphold more significant interests in Europe and the
Middle East, or that the disproportionate costs resulting from the Vietnam
War deprived the country of the energies and resources that were desperately
needed to solve our own domestic problems.

Former Ambassador Edwin O. Reischauer, a respected figure among establishment groups, carried this kind of analysis to a more general level of interpretation:

> The "central lesson" of Vietnam – at least as the American public perceives
> it – is already quite obvious . . . the limited ability of the United States to
> control at a reasonable cost the course of events in a nationally-aroused less-
> developed nation . . . I believe that we are moving away from the application
> to Asia of the "balance of power" and "power vacuum" concepts of the cold
> war, and in the process we no doubt will greatly downgrade our strategic
> interest in most of the less-developed world.[8]

---

7   Townsend Hoopes, *The Limits of Intervention* (New York: McKay, 1970), 58.
8   Richard N. Pfeffer, ed., *No More Vietnams?* (New York: Harper & Row, 1968), 267–68.

According to Reischauer, the means used in Vietnam were disproportionate to the end pursued, and, in general, a country like the United States cannot effectively use its military power to control the outcome of Vietnam-type struggles.

David Mozingo, an Asian specialist, took this argument one step further, recognizing the need for a perspective on Asia that was suited to the special historical and political conditions prevailing there, a perspective that foresaw the end of a rigid policy of containment of China: "Since the Korean War . . . United States policy in Asia has been modeled after the containment doctrine so successfully applied in Europe after 1947 . . . Washington has seen the problem of Chinese power in Asia in much the same light as that posed by Soviet power in Europe and has behaved as if both threats could be contained by basically the same kind of responses." Mozingo argued that there were essential differences between Asia and Europe: "In Asia the containment doctrine has been applied in an area where a nation-state system is only beginning to emerge amidst unpredictable upheavals of a kind that characterized Europe three centuries earlier . . . The kinds of American technical and economic power that could help restore the historic vitality of the European systems would seem at best to have only partial relevance to the Asian situation."[9] Such a view of the Vietnam experience supported a policy shift in a nonmilitary direction with respect to particular struggles for control in various Asian countries.

Among the lessons to be learned from Vietnam, according to the school that called it a failure of proportion, was the futility – perhaps more than futility – of aiding a foreign regime that lacked the capacity to govern its own society: In fact, certain types of intervention, if carried too far, can become counterproductive. Thus, the American failure in Vietnam was laid partly to ignorance about Vietnamese realities and partly to exaggerated confidence in the ability of massive military intervention to fulfill political objectives. This was essentially the view of Stanley Hoffmann, a respected academic critic of Washington's approach to Vietnam. Again, as with Hoopes, Hoffmann's concern was to delimit an effective foreign policy, imbued with a sense of proportion and an awareness of the inherent limits imposed on American capabilities. But, like Moore's interpretation, his Machiavellian critique did not repudiate American objectives in Vietnam. According to Samuel Huntington, another influential advocate of this approach and the head of Hubert Humphrey's Vietnam task force during the 1968 presidential campaign, the

[9]   David P. Mozingo, *The United States in Asia: Evolution and Containment* (New York: Council on Religion and International Affairs, 1967), 7–8.

main guidelines for the future should be to keep Vietnam-type involvements "reasonable, limited, discreet, and covert."[10]

A QUALIFIED FAILURE OF TACTICS

The third main position taken in the debate over the Vietnam War was that it represented a qualified failure of tactics. This view combines a general approach of the outcome and effort, regarding the war as a qualified success, with a judgment that such results could have been achieved in more acceptable ways by an early adoption of the approach introduced in the final years of American combat involvement. This third interpretation was the one favored by President Nixon and important foreign advisers such as Henry Kissinger, William Rogers, and Melvin Laird. The Nixon Doctrine, announced at Guam on July 25, 1969, was an explicit effort to avoid repeating the mistakes of Vietnam, as these leaders understood them, without renouncing the basic mission of American policy. The Nixon Administration was critical of the Vietnam effort to the extent that it believed that the same ends could have been achieved at less cost in American blood and treasure and, as a result, with less strain on American society. In his November 3, 1969, address to the nation on Vietnam, President Nixon explained the Nixon Doctrine as embodying "three principles as guidelines for future American policy toward Asia":

> First, the United States will keep all of its treaty commitments;
> Second, we shall provide a shield if a nuclear power threatens the freedom of a nation allied with us or of a nation whose survival we consider vital to our security;
> Third, in cases involving other types of aggression, we shall furnish military and economic assistance when requested in accordance with our treaty commitments. But we shall look to the nation directly threatened to assume the primary responsibility of providing the manpower for its defense.[11]

The "central thesis" of this doctrine, according to the President, was "that the United States will participate in the defense and development of allies and friends, but that America cannot – and will not – conceive *all* the plans, design *all* the programs, execute *all* the decisions and undertake *all* the defense of the free nations of the world. We will help where it makes a real difference

---

[10]   Stanley Hoffman, in Pfeffer, ed., *No More Vietnams?*, 193–203, 255.
[11]   Pres. Richard M. Nixon, "The Pursuit of Peace in Vietnam," *Department of State Bulletin*, 61, 1587, Nov. 24, 1969, 440.

and is considered in our interest."[12] Thus, the Nixon Doctrine backed a step away from the global absolutism of Johnsonian diplomacy. Instead, it advocated specific assessments of each potential interventionary situation in terms of its strategic importance to the United States, and of this country's ability to control the outcome.[13] It remains difficult, however, to extract concrete policy implications from Nixon's rhetorical statements regarding his doctrine, for example, that, "The fostering of self-reliance is the new purpose and direction of American involvement in Asia."[14]

In practical terms this position remained ill defined but seemed to fall midway between those of Moore and Hoopes: Uphold all treaty commitments, give all allied regimes our help and advice, but get fully involved in a direct military way only when vital interests are at stake and when the military instrument can be used effectively, which means successfully, quickly, and without losing too many American lives. One expression of the Nixon Doctrine, Vietnamization, for several years left the main burden of ground combat to Saigon's armed forces, without any reduction in American logistic support from the air via B-52 strikes and long-distance artillery support. Ambassador Ellsworth Bunker was reported to have said that adopting Vietnamization as a policy involved only changing the color of the bodies. Another expression of the Nixon Doctrine was the escalation of American involvement in Laos prior to the Paris Agreement, increasing our covert role in training and financing government forces and engaging in saturation bombing of contested areas, thereby causing a new flow of Asian refugees while depriving the Pathet Lao of its population base.

These three positions defined the boundaries of the main political debate involving the relevance of the Vietnam experience for the future of American foreign policy. This debate has now lost some of its relevance because the combined effects of the pricing policy on oil supplies of the Organization of Petroleum Exporting Countries (OPEC) and of the related Arab–Israeli conflict have so overwhelmed the political imagination of the foreign policy establishment. Nevertheless, the interpretation of the Vietnam War lies just below the surface and is likely to have a bearing on the approach taken toward these new challenges directed at American interests. We may yet see a struggle for ascendancy, possibly worked out in relation to Middle East

---

[12] Pres. Richard M. Nixon, "United States Foreign Policy for the 1970s: A New Strategy for Peace," A Report to Congress, *New York Times*, Feb. 19, 1970.

[13] See Henry A. Kissinger, "Central Issues of American Foreign Policy," in Kermit Gordon, ed., *Agenda for the Nation* (Washington, D.C.: Brookings Institution Press, 1968), 585–614.

[14] Nixon, Report to Congress.

policy, between the more ideological advocates of a liberal internationalism on the one hand, and the neo-Nixonians on the other, those who contest only the means of interventionary diplomacy but fully accept the basic geopolitical mission implied by such tactics. Such a controversy over tactics for the future would ignore the claim that the Vietnam War successfully extended the deterrence doctrine to counterinsurgency situations. This view, associated above with the military judgment of Vietnam as a qualified success, might be revived if important revolutionary movements emerge in noncommunist countries and if the political forces behind George Wallace and Barry Goldwater gain greater influence as a "third force" in American politics.

The first position accepted "victory" as the proper goal of the American involvement in Vietnam and regarded the means used as appropriate to the end of defeating the insurgency in South Vietnam, whether that insurgency was viewed as a species of civil war or as an agency of North Vietnamese aggression. In contrast, the second position shifted away from victory as a goal, once it became evident that the means required for this goal were too costly in lives, dollars, and domestic support. This position moved instead toward advocating some kind of mutual withdrawal of foreign forces, in conjunction with an effort to reach a settlement by nonmilitary means. The third position specified its goal as establishing conditions of self-determination for South Vietnam and its present governing regime, a position that implied an outcome of the war that was close to total victory. However, there was some ambiguity as to whether the real goals were not more modest than the proclaimed goals. In any event, this position regarded the means used as having been unnecessarily costly, given the goals of the involvement. At least in theory, it accepted the desirability of a nonmilitary outcome through a negotiated settlement of the war.

The first position seems to have interpreted Vietnam as a qualified success and to have favored, if anything, a less constrained military effort to defeat any future communist-led insurgencies that might erupt on the Asian mainland or elsewhere in the Third World. As with the strategic doctrine, the deterrence of insurgent challenges rests on possessing a credible capability and on indicating a willingness to respond with overwhelming military force to any relevant challenge.

The second position was much less tied to an overall doctrine, viewed the post-Kennedy phases of the Vietnam involvement as a clear mistake, and argued for a greater emphasis on nonmilitary responses to insurgent challenges. This position also sought to restrict overt intervention to situations in which its impact could be swift and effective. The position depends, therefore, on having a fairly secure regime in power in the country that is the scene of the struggle. It also emphasizes the need to keep a sense of proportion throughout such an involvement, either by explicitly limiting the magnitude of the commitment or by liquidating an unsuccessful commitment.

The third position was midway between the first two positions in tone and apparent emphasis. It developed a more globalist strategy, emphasizing that the United States had far-flung treaty relations with Asian countries, and urging that these commitments be honored for the sake of the overall preeminence of the United States in world affairs and the continuing need to resist communist pressures everywhere in the world. The merits of the particular case were thus tied to a global strategy, but an effort was made to shift more of the burden of response to the local government. But what does this mean in cases where the government cannot meet these burdens, as was surely the case in Vietnam all along? What happens when self-reliance fails? The prevailing response to this question may well determine the central line of American foreign policy in Asia throughout the coming decades. Both this position and the previous one look toward Japan as a more active partner in the development of a common Asian policy. President Nixon's decision to return Okinawa to Japan by 1972 arose out of this hope for sharing the geopolitical burdens of the region with Japan.

What was most surprising about these three positions was the extent to which they all accepted the premise that an American counterrevolutionary doctrine was applicable only in situations that appeared to be revolutionary. Where there was no formidable radical challenge on the domestic scene, as in India or Japan, the American preference was clearly for moderate democracy, the kind of political orientation that the United States imposed on Japan during the military occupation after World War II. However, where an Asian society was beset by struggle between a rightist incumbent regime and a leftist insurgent challenger, then American policy threw its support, sometimes strongly, to the counterrevolutionary side. As a result there was virtually no disposition to question the American decision to support the repressive and reactionary Saigon regime, provided that support could lead to victory at a reasonable cost. In fact, the four American Presidents from Eisenhower to Nixon were in agreement on the political wisdom of the decision to help Saigon prevail in its effort to create a strong anticommunist state in South Vietnam, even though this decision defied both the military results of the first Indochina War and the explicit provisions on the reunification of Vietnam embodied in the Geneva Accords of 1954. All three positions also shared an acceptance, although to varying degrees, of the basic postulates of the "domino theory." The second position was least inclined to endorse the image of falling dominoes; indeed, some of its adherents, such as the Asian political analyst Donald Zagoria, argued that the prospects for communism needed to be assessed on a country-by-country basis because the success or failure of communism in Vietnam or Laos would not necessarily have much impact on the prospect for revolution in other Asian countries.

McGeorge Bundy, a belated convert to the second position after an earlier allegiance to a moderate form of the first position, gave up on the war because its burden was too great on American society. Nevertheless, he took pains to reaffirm the wisdom of the original undertaking. "I remind you also, if you stand on the other side, that my argument against escalation and against an indefinite continuation of our present course has been based not on moral outrage or political hostility to the objective, but rather on the simple and practical ground that escalation will not work and that a continuation of our present course is unacceptable."[15]

Arthur Schlesinger, Jr., has said: "The tragedy of Vietnam is the tragedy of the overextension and misapplication of valid principles. The original insights of collective security and liberal evangelicalism were generous and wise." Actually, adherents of the second position, while sharply dissenting from the Vietnam policies of both Johnson and Nixon, still maintained the spirit of an earlier statement by McGeorge Bundy, made at a time when he was rallying support for Johnson's air war against North Vietnam: "There are wild men in the wings, but on the main stage even the argument on Vietnam turns on tactics, not fundamentals."[16]

Unfortunately, all three positions affirmed the continuing wisdom of two American objections in Asia. The first objection was to prevent Chinese expansion, if necessary by military means. The second was to prevent any anticommunist regime, however repressive, reactionary, or isolated from popular support, from being toppled by internal revolutionary forces, whether or not such forces were receiving outside help.

THE EXCLUDED FOURTH POSITION

There is another interpretation that has been largely excluded from the public dialogue on the war. It repudiates United States objectives in Vietnam on moral and political grounds. It holds, first, that there is no reason to believe that China has expansive military aims in Asia; second, that even if China were militarily expansive it would still not be desirable or necessary for the

---

[15] McGeorge Bundy, "DePauw Address," in Richard A. Falk, ed., *The Vietnam War and International Law* (Princeton: Princeton University Press, 1969), Vol. II, 964–75.

[16] Arthur Schlesinger, Jr., "Vietnam and the End of the Age of Superpowers," *Harper's*, Mar. 1969, 41–49.

United States to contain China by armed force; and, third, that there is neither occasion nor justification for aiding repressive governments merely because they follow anticommunist policies. I favor this fourth position for several reasons. There is no evidence that China needed containing by an American military presence in Asia. Of course, small countries in the shadow of a dominant state tend to fall under the influence of that state whenever it is effectively governed. This process is almost universal and has deep historical roots in Asia. But there are important countervailing forces that qualify even this expectation.

First, China is preoccupied with its own domestic politics and with its principal foreign struggles against the Soviet Union and Formosa. Second, many of the countries surrounding China had struggled at great sacrifice to achieve independence, could count on Soviet support if Chinese pressure mounted, and treated their national search for domestic autonomy as more significant than common ideological sentiments. And, third, China's foreign policy may often have been crude and ill conceived, but it rarely exhibited any intention to rely on military force to expand its influence beyond its boundaries; its use of force against India, Tibet, and the Soviet Union was to support its claims to disputed territory, and its entry into the Korean War in 1950 seemed mainly motivated by a reasonable concern about danger to its industrial heartland.

The evidence thus suggests that the American effort to contain China in Asia was a determination to contend with a paper tiger. More significantly, the multifaceted conflicts in Asia and elsewhere in the Third World cannot be comprehended in abstract or ideological terms. Asia is undergoing a two-phase revolution that began as a struggle against colonialism and will continue for at least another decade. The first phase has been concerned with reacquiring national control over the apparatus of government by defeating foreign rule. This aspect of the struggle is now largely completed. In most parts of Asia the colonial system has finally collapsed and foreigners have been removed from power.

But in most Asian countries, including South Vietnam, the native groups allied with the colonial system have held onto political power, stifling social progress and economic reform. Thailand too, although never formally a colony, continues to be governed by a traditional elite that is ill inclined to initiate the reform vitally needed by the mass of its population. The residues of the colonial system include the more informal patterns of domination that result from large American donations of military equipment, foreign aid, covert "presence" (the CIA), and political and economic advice. Most governments in Asia today are composed of conservative forces that maintain their dominance with the aid of such donations and advice, usually at the expense of their own people. Therefore, the second, postindependence phase of the revolutionary struggle involves wresting political control from traditional ruling classes and instituting a mass-based program of land reform, education, public hygiene, social equality, radical consciousness, and economic development. In most of Asia, aside from India, the United States is allied with regimes that are trying to hold back this second surge of the revolutionary energy that has swept across the Third World to crush the colonial system.

The fourth position accepts this analysis of political conflict in Asia and seeks to adjust American policy accordingly. First of all, it seeks to proceed rapidly with an accommodation with China through a flexible compromise of outstanding issues, including the future of Formosa. What is implied here is the removal of the American military presence from the area, especially the withdrawal of the Seventh Fleet and the elimination of American military bases on Taiwan. Such a course would leave the outcome of the Chinese civil war, which has not yet been fully resolved, to the contending forces on both sides. It would encourage the possibility of negotiations between Peking and Taipei regarding the governance of Formosa, perhaps allowing for semi-autonomous status within the Chinese People's Republic, with guarantees of a measure of economic and political independence for the island.

An American accommodation with China would help the United States handle an increasingly competitive economic relationship with Japan and give Washington more bargaining power in relation to the Soviet Union. More importantly, accommodation with China could make it possible to proceed more rapidly with arms control and disarmament, to denuclearize world politics, and to resist pressures to proliferate weapons of mass destruction to additional countries.

The fourth position entails the total abandonment of America's counterrevolutionary foreign policy in Asia. This would mean renouncing all treaty relations with governments that are repressing their own populations and holding back the forces of self-determination. Clearly such a revision of policy would require the renunciation or at least the reinterpretation of American treaty obligations to promote the security of the regimes now governing South Vietnam, Cambodia, Laos, South Korea, Formosa, Thailand, and the Philippines. The only commitment that should be reaffirmed is the United States obligation under the United Nations Charter to resist large-scale overt military attacks across internationally recognized boundaries. Civil strife is likely to eventually displace the current governments of several Asian countries. But to the extent that such conflict tends to reflect the true balance of political forces within these national societies, it would be in general beneficial for the welfare of the population and for the stability of the country and the region. At present, several regimes are being maintained in power only through a combination of domestic oppression and American support.

There seems virtually no prospect that this position will be adopted or even seriously considered unless major shifts occur within American political life. Only extraordinary domestic pressure, fueled perhaps by economic troubles at home and foreign policy setbacks abroad, is likely to produce a change of leadership and a change of world outlook in America.

Yet, in historical retrospect, it is important to appreciate the fact that this position once came close to being our foreign policy. Its rejection by today's American leaders was not the inevitable outcome of America's Asia policy after World War II. Franklin D. Roosevelt was opposed to restoring the French colonial administration in Indochina at the end of the war. If Indochina had been allowed to become independent after the Japanese left, then Ho Chi Minh would clearly have emerged as the leader of a united Vietnam, and perhaps of a united Indochina. In his initial Proclamation of Independence of September 25, 1945, Ho Chi Minh explicitly referred to the French and American Revolutions as the main sources of inspiration for the Vietnamese struggle for national independence. The communist response to Ho in the West was not altogether enthusiastic: The Soviet Union withheld recognition from Ho Chi Minh's Republic of Vietnam; and in 1947, Maurice Thorez, the French communist leader who was then Vice-Premier of France, actually countersigned the order for French military action against the newly proclaimed Republic. As O. Edmund Clubb, an area expert, pointed out: "In 1945 and 1946 the Ho Chi Minh government looked mainly to the United States and Nationalist China for foreign political support."[17] In the period since World War II, anticolonialism would surely have been a better guideline for American foreign policy in Asia than anticommunism. And even now it makes better sense. Anticolonialism would work better because it accords more closely with historic trends in Asia and with the dynamics of national self-determination in most noncommunist Asian countries, and because it flows more naturally out of the United States' own heritage and proudest tradition. But the whole debate may well be irrelevant, or virtually so. Existing policy may merely represent the continuing potency of economic and bureaucratic pressures. If so, those who wield power and are sensitive to the parameters of acceptable variation are correct to ignore lines of argument that would have to be rejected. But also correct are those who say that no amount of working within the system can secure a humane and rational foreign policy for the

---

[17] O. Edmund Clubb, Jr., *The United States and the Sino-Soviet Bloc in Southeast Asia* (Washington, D.C.: Brookings Institution Press, 1962), 15.

United States if its basic orientation is set by those who would maintain an empire abroad for the benefit of its rulers at home. And, indeed, those who stand outside the debate – the adherents of the fourth position – do in fact appear to be dissociated from any political base that might be used to gain lawful access to power in the near future. It is their dissociation from power, and not the poverty of their analysis, that explains the irrelevance of their plea for an end to empire and the diplomacy of counterrevolution. It is possible, of course, that economic pressures will so constrain America's foreign policy options in the near future as to lead this fourth position to prevail by default. Thus, America will not be in a position to respond militarily to revolutionary challenges directed at anticommunist governments, unless those challenges are directly perceived as bearing upon the overriding imperative of shoring up the Western position in a deteriorating world economic situation.

13

The Vietnam Syndrome:
From the Gulf of Tonkin to Iraq

At 11:37 p.m. on August 4, 1964, President Lyndon Johnson announced on national television that US air attacks against North Vietnam were underway in response to "open aggression on the high seas against the United States of America" in the Gulf of Tonkin. The president was referring to North Vietnamese PT-boat attacks on two American destroyers – the USS *Maddox* and USS *Turner Joy* – that he said had occurred earlier that day, and to his decision to order a reprisal bombing of North Vietnam.[1] Minutes later, Secretary of Defense Robert S. McNamara reported that the US military reprisal was an "appropriate action in view of the unprovoked attack in international waters on United States naval vessels."[2]

The next day, August 5, the eight-column headline on the front page of the *New York Times* reported:

US PLANES ATTACK NORTH VIETNAM BASES; PRESIDENT ORDERS "LIMITED" RETALIATION AFTER COMMUNISTS' PT BOATS RENEW RAIDS.[3]

The lead front-page story on the incident said that the president's order to bomb North Vietnam "followed a naval battle in which a number of North Vietnamese PT boats attacked two United States destroyers with torpedoes."[4]

A second front-page story reported that McNamara "said that the [US air] attacks had been directed against the bases used by the North Vietnamese PT

---

[1] "The President's Address," *New York Times*, August 5, 1964.

[2] "2 Carriers Used: McNamara Reports on Aerial Strikes and Reinforcements," *New York Times*, August 5, 1964.

[3] *New York Times*, August 5, 1964. (Note: While today the front page of the *New York Times* has six columns across the front page, in 1964 it had eight columns.)

[4] "Forces Enlarged: Stevenson to Appeal for Action by UN on 'Open Aggression,'" *New York Times*, August 4, 1964.

boats that attacked two United States destroyers in international waters yesterday."[5]

In a third front-page story that day on the Tonkin Gulf incident, the *Times* reported that "the Defense Department announced tonight that North Vietnamese PT Boats made a 'deliberate attack' today on two United States destroyers patrolling international waters in the Gulf of Tonkin off North Vietnam."[6] Throughout its news coverage of the Tonkin incident that day and the days that followed, the *Times* reported the North Vietnamese attacks on the *Maddox* and *Turner Joy* on August 4 as established events as claimed by top Johnson administration officials. The *Times* editorial page, on August 5, in effect confirmed those events, arguing that President Johnson had presented "the American people last night with the somber facts." The editorial, referring also to the first attack on the *Maddox* on August 2 in the Tonkin Gulf, also gave its support to the reprisal bombing of North Vietnam:

> The attack on one of our warships that at first seemed, and was hoped to be, an isolated incident is now seen in ominous perspective to have been the beginning of a mad adventure by the North Vietnamese Communists. After offensive action against more vessels of our Navy the President has backed up with retaliatory fire the warnings that North Vietnam chose frequently to ignore.[7]

The editorial also echoed President Johnson's claim that he sought "no wider war," though the decision to bomb targets inside North Vietnam clearly signaled a major US military escalation in Vietnam.[8]

We know today that the charges issued by Johnson and McNamara – that North Vietnamese boats had attacked the *Maddox* and *Turner Joy* on August 4 – were almost certainly not accurate. We also know that the *Times* headlines, news reports, and editorial on August 5 about an August 4 Tonkin incident – tied as they all were to official claims made by the Johnson administration – also were not accurate. We also know that, rather than seeking "no wider war" in its reprisal bombing of North Vietnam, the Johnson administration had already authorized secret military and paramilitary actions inside North Vietnam with the aim of provoking an incident that the administration could exploit as a pretext for escalating US military involvement in Vietnam.

[5] "2 Carriers Used: McNamara Reports on Aerial Strikes and Reinforcements."
[6] "Reds Driven Off: Two Torpedo Vessels Believed Sunk in Gulf of Tonkin," *New York Times*, August 4, 1964.
[7] "The President Acts," *New York Times*, August 5, 1964.
[8] *Ibid.*

We know these things in part because, nearly seven years after the Tonkin Gulf affair, the *New York Times* published on June 13, 1971, the first article in its series on the Pentagon Papers, the Defense Department's 43-volume classified study "of how and why the United States had become so deeply involved in Vietnam."[9] When he was defense secretary, McNamara had ordered Pentagon analysts to conduct a classified history of the Vietnam War; only a few copies of the massive study were ever printed, all of which were kept in secret locations.[10]

With regard to the Johnson administration's clandestine military and para-military campaign against North Vietnam, the *Times* reported:

> What the Pentagon papers call "an elaborate program of covert military operations against the state of North Vietnam" began on Feb. 1, 1964, under the code name Operation Plan 34A . . . Through 1964, the 34A operations ranged from flights over North Vietnam by U-2 spy planes and kidnapping of North Vietnamese citizens for intelligence information, to parachuting sabotage and psychological warfare teams into the North, commando raids from the sea to blow up rail and highway bridges and the bombardment of North Vietnamese coastal installations by PT boats.[11]

With regard to the two US destroyers that supposedly were attacked without provocation by North Vietnamese PT boats in early August 1964, the *Times* reported:

> The [US] destroyer patrols in the Gulf of Tonkin, code-named De Soto patrols, were the third element in the covert military pressures against North Vietnam. While the purpose of the patrols was mainly psychological, as a show of force, the destroyers collected the kind of intelligence on North Vietnamese warning radars and coastal defenses that would be useful to 34A raiding parties or, in the event of a bombing campaign, to pilots . . .
>
> But the [Pentagon] study makes it clear that the physical presence of the destroyers provided the elements for the Tonkin clash. And immediately after the reprisal air strikes, the Joint Chiefs of Staff and Assistant Secretary of Defense [John T.] McNaughton put forward a "provocation strategy" proposing to repeat the clash as a pretext for bombing the North.[12]

---

[9] "Vast Review of War Took a Year," *New York Times*, June 13, 1971.

[10] See Daniel Ellsberg, *Secrets: A Memoir of Vietnam and the Pentagon Papers* (New York: Viking, 2002); David Rudenstine, *The Day the Presses Stopped: A History of the Pentagon Papers Case* (Berkeley: University of California Press, 1996).

[11] "Vietnam Archive: Pentagon Study Traces 3 Decades of Growing US Involvement," *New York Times*, June 13, 1971.

[12] *Ibid.*

This information from the Pentagon Papers, reported by the *Times* in June 1971, not only contradicted what the Johnson administration had claimed in August 1964, it, ironically, exposed serious problems in the *Times'* August 1964 coverage of the Tonkin incident and its aftermath, given that the *Times* reported that North Vietnam's attacks on the *Maddox* and *Turner Joy* were unprovoked and, for this reason, the US reprisal bombing of North Vietnam was justified. Furthermore, the *Times* reported without question the Johnson administration's assertions that it sought no wider war in Vietnam, despite the *prima facie* escalation of the bombing itself.

Embracing these assumptions not only infected news reports and editorials in its coverage of the Tonkin incident, it also exposed serious flaws in the editorial policy of the *Times*. For example, how should the *Times* mediate competing factual claims between designated enemies of the United States and its own government in the midst of serious conflict or war? In this case, President Johnson announced that North Vietnam had attacked US ships without provocation in the Gulf of Tonkin on August 4. Hanoi denied that it had attacked the ships at all. Hanoi was right. Forty years later, Saddam Hussein denied having WMD, and apparently he was right too. Yet in both cases the *Times* reported and supported misleading US charges that led the United States to catastrophic wars in Vietnam and Iraq.

What, if anything, could the *Times* have done to expose US government deception prior to full-scale war in Vietnam and Iraq? And how can it modify its editorial policy to expose government deception prior to the onset of other such unwarranted wars in the future? In this chapter we propose changes to editorial policy at the *New York Times* that would improve the quality of its journalism, align its editorial mission with its constitutional mandate "to expose government deception"[13] and "enlighten the citizenry"[14] in its coverage of US foreign policy, and allow it to adopt international law as a standard to assess the legality of future threats of force and recourse to war by the United States.

So what could the *Times* have done differently in its news and editorial pages that would have allowed it to cover the late-night August 4 announcements from President Johnson and Defense Secretary McNamara with journalistic independence and integrity? There were, after all, no independent observers

---

[13] Separate Opinion of Justice Hugo Black, *New York Times Co. v. United States*, 403 U.S. 713 (1971).

[14] Separate Opinion of Justice Potter Stewart, *New York Times Co. v. United States*, 403 U.S. 713 (1971).

in the Tonkin Gulf or aboard the *Maddox* or *Turner Joy* on August 4 that could
have confirmed or denied the administration's claim of an attack. And North
Vietnamese PT boats apparently had attacked the *Maddox* two days earlier –
though with no casualties to the crew or damage to the American ship.
Furthermore, on August 7, the US House of Representatives voted 416–0 and
the US Senate voted 88–2 to support President Johnson's decision to bomb
targets inside North Vietnam in response to the reported August 4 attacks on
the *Maddox* and *Turner Joy*, and to authorize the "Commander in Chief, to
take all necessary measures to repel any armed attack against the forces of the
United States and to prevent further aggression."[15] Thus, at the time, a near
unanimous consensus existed in the US government that the *Maddox* and
Turner Joy had been attacked on August 4 and that the US military reprisal
against North Vietnam was justified.

In contrast, the government of North Vietnam had denounced the American
claim that two US destroyers had been attacked by North Vietnamese boats
on August 4 as "a sheer fabrication by the United States imperialists,"[16] and
the governments of the People's Republic of China and the Soviet Union
denounced the US bombing of North Vietnam as "deliberate armed aggression"[17] and "armed aggression."[18] In short, given the absence of any evidence
to contest the Johnson administration's claim that US ships had been attacked
on August 4, the preponderance of American opinion that the *Maddox* and
Turner Joy had been attacked on August 4, and that the reprisal bombing of
North Vietnam was justified, there were few evidentiary opportunities or political incentives for the *Times* to oppose the consensus view of its government
with respect to the Tonkin incident without appearing to position itself (without evidence) with North Vietnam's claim that the incident was fabricated by
American imperialists.

Variations on this clash between not wanting to support the claims of US
enemies in opposition to official US claims would present themselves to the
Times and its editors for decades to come after August 1964. Whether the clash
involved US assertions with respect to Iraqi WMD possession and Saddam
Hussein's denials, US claims of a Sandinista arms flow and Sandinista denials,
or implausible US claims of non-involvement in the attempted overthrow of
Hugo Chavez in Venezuela and Chavez's claims to the contrary, or any of the

---

[15] Gulf of Tonkin Resolution, Joint Resolution of Congress, HJ RES 1145 August 7, 1964.
[16] Associated Press report, untitled, *New York Times*, August 5, 1964.
[17] "Peking Condemns US 'Aggression,'" *New York Times*, August 6, 1964.
[18] "Texts of Addresses by Stephenson and Morozov Before UN Security Council," *New York Times*, August 6, 1964.

many other such clashes, the *Times* has never resolved or acknowledged this longtime vulnerability of its editorial policy.

This journalistic point between a rock and hard place – between on the one hand not wanting to be seen giving aid and comfort to the real or fictitious enemies of the United States and on the other fulfilling the paper's mission to "enlighten the citizens" and "expose government deception" – identifies a major challenge not just to the *Times* but to the US news media in general. This particular dilemma also identifies a major defect in the modern scheme of US constitutionalism. Namely, editorial policy is essentially undifferentiated throughout the US news industry, although derivative to a large extent of the gold standard of objectivity supposedly embodied by the *Times*. Because this flaw in editorial policy is common throughout the industry, the *Times* and the press in general have ceded an excess of constitutional power to the president to initiate illegal and costly military adventures that the authors of the Constitution did not intend and that the Constitution itself clearly prohibits.

So how might the *Times* address this defect, assuming any interest or desire to do so? To answer this question, it is helpful to revisit the events of August 4, 1964, and the *Times*' coverage of those events the following day.

Most critics of the Johnson–McNamara announcements near midnight on August 4 have focused their attention on the likelihood that the *Maddox* and *Turner Joy* had not been attacked that day by North Vietnamese boats. One of the best accounts is by Daniel Ellsberg, who begins his excellent book on the Pentagon Papers affair by describing his own involvement with events that day:

> On Tuesday morning, August 4, 1964, my first full day on my new job in the Pentagon, a courier came into the outer office with an urgent cable for my boss. He'd been running. The secretaries told him Assistant Secretary John McNaughton was out of the office; he was down the hall with Secretary of Defense Robert McNamara. They pointed him to me, his new special assistant. The courier handed me the cable and left. It was easy to see, as I read it, why he had been running.[19]

Although most people know Daniel Ellsberg as the former Pentagon official who leaked the Pentagon Papers to the *New York Times*, he is less well known for being the person at the Pentagon on August 4, 1964, who first read the cables that Captain John J. Herrick – the commanding officer of the *Maddox* and *Turner Joy* mission in the Tonkin Gulf – had frantically sent as the *Maddox* was being attacked by North Vietnamese PT boats. Or so Herrick thought.

[19] Ellsberg, *Secrets*, 7.

Ten minutes after receiving the first cable, Ellsberg read a second cable from Herrick. "Am under continuous torpedo attack," Herrick wrote. The cables from Herrick kept coming. "The messages were vivid," wrote Ellsberg:

> Herrick must have been dictating them from the bridge in between giving orders, as his two ships swerved to avoid torpedoes picked up on the sonar of the *Maddox* and fired in the darkness at targets shown on the radar of the *Turner Joy*. "Torpedoes missed. Another fired at us. Four torpedoes in water. And five torpedoes in water . . . Have . . . successfully avoided at least six torpedoes." Nine torpedoes had been fired at his ships, fourteen, twenty-six. More attacking boats had been hit; at least one sunk. This action wasn't ending after forty minutes or an hour. It was going on, ships dodging and firing in choppy seas, planes overhead firing rockets at locations given them by the *Turner Joy*'s radar, for an incredible two hours before the stream of continuous combat updates finally ended. Then, suddenly, an hour later, full stop. A message arrived that took back not quite all of it, but enough to put everything earlier in question.[20]

That message from Herrick said:

> Review of action makes many reported contacts and torpedoes fired appear doubtful. Freak weather effects on radar and overeager sonar men may have accounted for many reports. No actual visual sightings by *Maddox*. Suggest complete evaluation before any further action taken.[21]

In later cables that day, Herrick expressed doubts that a prolonged confrontation with hostile boats and torpedoes had taken place, "except for apparent attempted ambush at beginning."[22] Ellsberg concluded that afternoon, "along with everyone else I spoke to, that there probably had been an attack of some sort" on the *Maddox* and *Turner Joy*,[23] though he also wrote: "As negative evidence accumulated, within a few days it came to seem less likely that any attack had occurred on August 4; by 1967 it seemed almost certain there had been no second attack, and by 1971 I was convinced of that beyond a reasonable doubt."[24]

It is generally accepted today that no second attack in the Gulf of Tonkin on August 4, 1964, had occurred, and that confusion on board the *Maddox* and *Turner Joy* was due to the misinterpretation of radar effects by crewmen.[25]

---

[20]   *Ibid.*, 9.
[21]   *Ibid.*, 9–10.
[22]   *Ibid.*, 10.
[23]   *Ibid.*
[24]   *Ibid.*
[25]   *Ibid.*

However, for our purposes, we need to focus on another question regarding the events of August 4, "one that went unasked in Washington in August 1964"[26] and in the *New York Times* as well: "Whether there were one or two attacks by North Vietnamese boats [between August 2 and August 4], was the US reprisal strike justified"?[27] In his memoirs, published in 1995, McNamara answered, "Probably."[28] However, after his memoirs were published, McNamara initiated and participated in a series of conferences with former North Vietnamese government officials "to review the decision-making of both sides" throughout the war in Vietnam.[29] The book that was the product of those conferences, coauthored by McNamara, and that analyzed the significance of the meetings and recorded exchanges among the participants, concluded "the reprisal, in retrospect, was clearly a mistake as originally conceived."[30] This is because of two major findings that resulted from the McNamara-sponsored conferences.

With regard to the first finding, McNamara relates how General Vo Nguyen Giap, North Vietnam's defense minister during the US war in Vietnam, told McNamara that the August 4 attack did not occur, to which McNamara responded, "I have no reason to believe he is in error."[31] Regarding the second finding, McNamara relates how General Nguyen Dinh Uoc, director of North Vietnam's Institute of Military History, confirmed that the August 2 attack on the *Maddox* had occurred in response to Operation Plan 34A attacks on North Vietnam. Furthermore, McNamara learned that the decision to attack the *Maddox* on August 2 "was not ordered by the central authority in Hanoi but rather by the commander of the torpedo boat squadron in the Tonkin Gulf" and that, therefore, "Hanoi could not read the signal" that McNamara intended to send with the US reprisal bombing "because it did not order the attack."[32]

Thus, one of McNamara's objectives in convening the meetings with former North Vietnamese officials – to determine whether the US military reprisal had contributed to the "misperceptions, misjudgments, and misunderstandings" that led to "the spiral of escalation toward a US–Vietnam war – had been achieved.[33] He concluded that bombing North Vietnam in

---

[26] Robert S. McNamara, James G. Blight, and Robert K. Brigham, *Argument Without End: In Search of Answers to the Vietnam Tragedy* (New York: Public Affairs, 1999), 202.

[27] *Ibid.*

[28] Robert S. McNamara with Brian Van DeMark, *In Retrospect: The Tragedy and Lessons of Vietnam* (New York: Times Books, 1995), 128.

[29] McNamara et al., *Argument Without End*, xi.

[30] *Ibid.*, 202–03.

[31] *Ibid.*, 215.

[32] *Ibid.*, 202–03.

[33] *Ibid.*, 158.

response to the Tonkin incident was an unnecessary escalation toward a wider war in Vietnam.[34]

Though McNamara, in our view, identifies the key question with respect to the events that occurred in early August 1964 – that is, whether the US reprisal bombing of North Vietnam was justified – and though we also conclude that it was not, we cite different reasons. We argue that, even if the North Vietnamese had attacked US ships in the Gulf of Tonkin on August 2 and August 4, and even if North Vietnam had ordered the attacks, under international law the US reprisal bombing nevertheless would have been illegal and unjustifiable.

A military reprisal involves a unilateral use of force by one state against a second state in response to a prior infliction of injury by the second state. In the context of the Tonkin incident, the United States bombed targets inside North Vietnam in response to a presumptive North Vietnamese attack on US ships on August 2 and 4. However, as the US Lawyers Committee on Vietnam argued in 1967, "in the present system of world order, injured states may take actions short of violence, but a general consensus prohibits the use of force in reprisal in view of the categorical prohibitions of the United Nations Charter."[35]

The Lawyers Committee cited a number of authoritative commentators, with a few cited here, showing a legal consensus with respect to the illegality of military reprisals. A study issued under the auspices of the British Royal Institute of International Affairs concluded: "It is now generally considered that reprisals involving the use or threat of force are illegal."[36] In April 1964, a UN Security Council resolution, in reference to British raids against Yemen in reprisal to Yemen's attacks on the British Protectorate of Aden, condemned "reprisals as incompatible with the purposes and principles of the United Nations."[37] In its decision on the merits in the *Corfu Channel Case* (1949), the International Court of Justice unanimously determined that a British mine-sweeping operation in Albanian territorial waters (after mines exploded there had caused the death of forty-seven British seamen) was an illegal military response by the British government, despite the fact that the Court found the mines had been illegally emplaced by Albania. The Court argued that military reprisal is impermissible because "from the nature of things, it would

[34] *Ibid.*
[35] The Consultative Council of the Lawyers Committee on American Policy Toward Vietnam, Richard Falk, Chair, John H. E. Fried, Rapporteur, *Vietnam and International Law* (Northampton: Aletheia Press, 1990), 57.
[36] Quoted *ibid.*
[37] *Ibid.*, 57–58.

be reserved for the most powerful states, and might easily lead to perverting the administration of international justice itself."[38]

In the extended debate in the UN Security Council on April 6, 1964, prior to the Council's resolution on the British–Yemen incident cited above, US Ambassador to the United Nations Adlai Stevenson stated: "My government has repeatedly expressed its emphatic disapproval of provocative acts and retaliatory raids, wherever they occur and by whomever they are committed."[39] Given the date and context of Ambassador Stevenson's statement, recall that Operation Plan 34A was already underway and that the US reprisal bombing of North Vietnam would be launched exactly four months later. Thus, the "repeatedly expressed emphatic" position of the US government recognized, in principle, the illegality of its own provocative Operation Plan 34A actions inside North Vietnam in addition to its reprisal bombings against North Vietnam.

With respect to the *New York Times'* coverage of the Tonkin incidents, its editors and reporters did not have until 1967 and 1971, as in the case of Daniel Ellsberg, or more than thirty years, as in the case of Robert McNamara, to determine for the purposes of its August 5, 1964, edition whether the *Maddox* and *Turner Joy* had been attacked on August 4 or not. However, as the most important newspaper in the most important democracy and most powerful nation in the world, and given the major significance of the US reprisal attack inside North Vietnam, the *Times* should have elevated its coverage to a higher level of scrutiny to consider whether the reprisal bombing of North Vietnam was or was not consistent with international law. Furthermore, any decision to resort to force by the United States – given its immense military power, its standing in the international community as the world's premier democratic state, and its official, repeated, announced commitment over two centuries to the rule of law – clearly merits the strictest scrutiny by the leading newspaper in the United States as an expression, affirmation, and symbol of that commitment. This highest level of journalistic scrutiny would include an analysis of whether a use of force by the United States was consistent with international law or not.

Instead of raising its level of journalistic review to match the seriousness of the occasion, however, the *Times* neglected on August 5, 1964, to report the *prima facie* illegality of the US reprisal bombing of North Vietnam, or to raise any questions at all with respect to legality. This negligence was due then, as today, to the *Times'* refusal to incorporate international law into its editorial policy. Without international law as a component of editorial policy

[38]   *Ibid.*, 58.
[39]   *Ibid.*, 119.

in any major US news outlet, the Johnson administration was completely free
to operate illegally toward Vietnam. Given that the US Congress had also
disregarded international law in its consensus support for the Tonkin Gulf
resolution, the constitutional system of checks and balances had completely
broken down, as it would in the future under similar conditions. Had the
press and the Congress invoked international law at that critical moment, a
debate about the legality of the president's decision to bomb North Vietnam
might have ensued, the Constitution might have been strengthened (rather
than weakened), the world might have been spared the full catastrophe of the
Vietnam War that followed, and a journalistic precedent might have been
established as a check against any future president's inclination to launch illegal military attacks based on faultily asserted factual claims.

One irony with respect to the *Times*' coverage of the Tonkin incident in
August 1964 is that it reflected the *Times*' standards of non-crusading journalism, including an excessive deference to a deployment of executive power
beyond the Constitution's limits, while its series on the Pentagon Papers,
which in effect corrected the record of the Tonkin incident as reported by the
Times, was a departure from those standards. Furthermore, even though the
Times' series on the Pentagon Papers exposed retroactively a major weakness
in its editorial policy, evident in its earlier rubber-stamping of official facts and
conduct during the Vietnam War, the *Times* apparently never reviewed its
coverage of the Tonkin incident and the reprisal bombing of August 1964 in
light of its Pentagon Papers revelations. Not only is there no public evidence
of such a review, but the *Times* proceeded for the next four decades to apply
the same uncorrected standards of editorial policy to what became a repetitive characteristic of US foreign policy – the use and threat of force, often
in flagrant violation of international law and with official justifications citing
unverifiable or inaccurate representations of fact.

In the wake of the Tonkin Gulf incident, the Johnson administration
increased its troop commitment, and by February 1965 there were 23,000
US soldiers in Vietnam.[40] Since at least 1961, the United States had been
waging a major counterinsurgency campaign in South Vietnam against guerrillas of the South Vietnamese National Liberation Front (NLF), dubbed
"Vietcong" by the United States. According to a *New York Times* report, by
February 1965, 376 Americans had been killed (263 in combat and 113 in
accidents) in Vietnam since January 1, 1961.[41] In comparison, by early 1965,

---

[40] "376 Americans Killed in Vietnam Since 1961," *New York Times*, February 8, 1965.
[41] *Ibid.*

the US counterinsurgency war in South Vietnam had killed more than 150,000 Vietnamese.[42]

This was the war context of a February 7, 1965, early-morning NLF attack on the US airbase at Pleiku in northern South Vietnam, and on a US helicopter base a short distance away. The attacks were reported on the front page of the *Times* later that day: "Communist guerrillas killed at least seven United States soldiers and wounded 80 others, two of these critically, this morning in two swift attacks on major Vietnamese Army installations in the central highlands."[43] The next day, the *Times* reported "United States aircraft struck at North Vietnam early today" in reprisal for the attacks on the American airbases.[44] In a statement issued by the White House, President Johnson said:

> Today's action by the US and South Vietnamese Governments was in response to provocations ordered and directed by the Hanoi regime . . . To meet these attacks the Government of South Vietnam and the US Government agreed to appropriate reprisal actions against North Vietnamese targets.[45]

In its report, the *Times* observed that the NLF attack at Pleiku and the US reprisal bombing represented "the most threatening crisis in Southeast Asia since the Gulf of Tonkin clash last August."[46] Indeed, the US response to the Pleiku attack, like the US response to the Tonkin incident, not only fatefully escalated US military involvement in Vietnam, but the official factual assertions justifying the US response to the Pleiku attack were nearly as flawed as those asserted to justify the US response to the Tonkin incident. While President Johnson announced at the time that the NLF attacks at Pleiku were "ordered and directed by the Hanoi regime," McNamara wrote

[42] Noam Chomsky and Edward S. Herman, *The Political Economy of Human Rights*, Volume II, *After the Cataclysm: Postwar Indochina and the Reconstruction of Imperial Ideology* (Boston: South End Press, 1979), 13. Chomsky and Herman report "the slaughter of over 150,000 South Vietnamese by 1965" (*ibid.*). Furthermore, A. J. Langguth reports that in a meeting with "an array of military advisers" on July 22, 1965, President Johnson, while distinguishing between "Vietcong" and "South Vietnamese," itemized the number of casualties in South Vietnam up to that point: "The Vietcong dead is running at a rate of 25,000 a year. At least 15,000 have been killed by air – half of those are not part of what we call Vietcong. Since 1961, a total of 89,000 have been killed. The South Vietnamese are being killed at a rate of 12,000 a year." This accounting appears to indicate that the US had been killing people in South Vietnam at a rate of 37,000 a year by 1965: A. J. Langguth, *Our Vietnam: The War, 1954–1975* (New York: Simon & Schuster, 2000), 380.
[43] "Seven GIs Slain in Vietcong Raid; 80 Are Wounded," *New York Times*, February 7, 1965.
[44] "Capital Is Tense: But President Asserts Nation Still Opposes Widening of War," *New York Times*, February 8, 1965.
[45] *Ibid.*
[46] *Ibid.*

more than thirty years later that the Pleiku attack "was not ordered by Hanoi."[47] Moreover, the US military reprisal against North Vietnam in response to the Pleiku attacks would have violated international law even if Hanoi had ordered and directed those attacks.

Like its coverage of the Tonkin incident, the *Times'* coverage of the Pleiku attacks published, featured, and supported the factual assertions of President Johnson while neglecting to address the legality of the US reprisal bombing of North Vietnam. In its editorial on the Pleiku incident, titled "Reprisal in Vietnam," the *Times* editorial page, arguing in clear disregard of international law, said "that when the other side strikes in the way that it did, there is no alternative for the United States but to strike back in reprisal," and that "the strike at North Vietnam was understandable and justifiable as a tactical response in a war situation."[48]

For one thing, these remarks apparently regard North Vietnam and the NLF as synonymous and interchangeable entities, given the conflated reference here to "the other side" that consumes at once the NLF (the entity that attacked the airbase at Pleiku) and North Vietnam (the entity that was attacked in retaliation). Furthermore, the editorial does not explain how a South Vietnamese attack on the airplanes and helicopters that at the time were the principal instruments used in killing over 150,000 South Vietnamese is less "understandable and justifiable [as a] tactical response in a war situation" than a US military reprisal that is viewed as illegal under international law.

This logic reflects the insidious influence of excluding international law as a criterion of review in an assessment of war situations and claims, evident also in the *Times'* coverage of the Tonkin incident. The *Maddox* and *Turner Joy* were powerful US destroyers belonging to the US Seventh Fleet, a 100-ship flotilla based in the western Pacific Ocean, and including up to thirty destroyers and three US aircraft-carrier groups – the USS *Ticonderoga*, the USS *Constellation*, and the USS *Yorktown* – which together carried hundreds of attack planes and bombers, including F-4 Phantoms, A-4 bombers, and A-3 heavy attack bombers.[49] In contrast, the North Vietnamese navy in 1964 was "understood to have consisted of about fifty patrol boats of various types, including modernized junks."[50] The US air strikes on August 4 and August 5 destroyed with ease twenty-five of these boats, "about half of the North

---

[47] McNamara et al., *Argument Without End*, 173.
[48] "Reprisal in Vietnam," *New York Times*, February 8, 1965.
[49] "2 Carriers Used: McNamara Reports on Aerial Strikes and Reinforcements."
[50] "4 Bases Bombed: Oil Depot Also Target of 5-Hour Attack – 2 Planes Lost," *New York Times*, August 6, 1964.

Vietnamese navy."[51] And given that neither the *Maddox* nor the *Turner Joy* sustained any damage or casualties on either August 2 or August 4, that by August 1964 "the United States ha[d] sent [Seventh Fleet] warships into the Gulf of Tonkin from time to time for nearly two years,"[52] and that the Gulf of Tonkin borders the entire coastline of North Vietnam (which is 10,000 miles from the United States), the North Vietnamese had very little capability and few opportunities to militarily injure the United States even as an initial provocation.

Thus, not only did international law escape the *Times'* attention in its coverage of the Tonkin incident, the evident logic of the situation did as well; as it did even in the following instance when the *Times* editorial page, while citing the presence of overwhelming US military power in the Tonkin Gulf, nevertheless offered little more than a senseless warning to Hanoi:

> North Vietnam's capability of injuring the Seventh Fleet is small. The power of the Seventh Fleet to damage North Vietnam is incalculable. Since this must be evident, nothing is more vital than for Hanoi to be left in no doubt about the American intention to remain in the Tonkin Gulf and to continue supporting South Vietnam's effort. The President's action should convey this message clearly.[53]

Though the legal arguments against the US reprisal attacks in response to the Tonkin Gulf and Pleiku incidents were compelling, they required *a fortiori* some ability to independently assess the basic military parameters of the situation. With respect to the NLF attacks at Pleiku, both the Johnson administration and the *Times* appeared to assume that the NLF had no right to attack US positions in South Vietnam, and that the United States, by bombing North Vietnam in a reprisal attack, had a right to retaliate against whomever it wished. In this regard, the Lawyers Committee on Vietnam argued:

> To begin with, no explanation [from the Johnson administration] was offered why the guerrilla attack at Pleiku on February 7, 1965, constituted a "provocation," or in what manner it differed, in law or fact, from previous skirmishes in South Vietnam. "Deliberate surprise" is a normal aspect of hostilities, and the United States had, for years prior to that incident, planned and otherwise participated in "deliberate surprise attacks" on a much larger scale against the [NLF] guerrillas. It is, therefore, not possible that the United States suffered a legal wrong by the attack on Pleiku.[54]

---

[51] *Ibid.*
[52] "Patrol Ended Sunday," *New York Times*, August 14, 1964.
[53] "Warning to Hanoi," *New York Times*, August 4, 1964.
[54] Lawyers Committee, *Vietnam and International Law*, 59.

Henry Steele Commager made a similar point in a letter that the *Times* published but did not heed:

> We are already falling into the pattern of a two-level vocabulary so familiar in Communist dispatches, and in "1984."
>
> Secretary McNamara spoke of the first Vietcong attack as a "sneak" attack; the President's statement of Feb. 11 characterized Vietcong warfare as "murder" and "assassination"; even your own correspondent speaks of "terrorist" attacks.
>
> Are we to suppose that our own attacks on the Vietcong are announced in advance, that they are not designed to spread terror or to kill?
>
> Surely it is not so much guerrilla attacks on military installations which deserve these terms as air bombardment which kills civilian and combatant alike. If we are to have the agony of war may we at least be spared the humiliation of double-talk.[55]

Because an editorial policy that incorporated international law would require some ability to fairly assess facts and context, and apply them logically to government conduct, the *Times* would also need to begin reporting and processing facts independently of what US government officials say, while also evaluating them within the framework of international law.

By early February 1965, the *Times* was referring to the US air strikes against North Vietnam in response to the Pleiku and Tonkin incidents as a "a policy of retaliation." By February 10, however, the Johnson administration had already transitioned to "a policy of greater flexibility," which removed even the pretext of retaliation as a rationale for bombing North Vietnam. "Greater flexibility" was simply a broad, open-ended assertion of an American entitlement to bomb North Vietnam. The *Times* duly noted the administration's transition, but neglected to note the escalating conflict between US policy and international law. For example, in the beginning paragraphs of a front-page article on February 10, *Times* reporter Tad Szulc wrote:

> The United States has adopted a policy of greater flexibility in any further retaliatory strikes against North Vietnam, officials reported today.
>
> Future [US] counterstrikes, they said, would not necessarily be limited to those in response to attack on United States forces, as in the Gulf of Tonkin and Pleiku incidents.
>
> Air retaliation might be ordered in response to Vietcong or North Vietnamese assaults upon South Vietnam's troops or installations, even if no United States men or facilities are involved, the officials said.

---

[55] "Comments on US Action in Vietnam," *New York Times*, February 17, 1965.

"There is nothing fixed or absolute about this policy," an official said. "We may strike again whenever it is justified in our view."[56]

The Johnson administration had no legal claim under international law to bomb North Vietnam "whenever it is justified" in its view. North Vietnam had not engaged in an armed attack against South Vietnam – the only possible legal justification at the time for the United States to bomb North Vietnam – nor had the Johnson administration argued that it had. The administration implicitly conceded this point shortly before February 10 when it justified bombing North Vietnam on February 7 as a "reprisal" to the Pleiku incident, not as "collective self-defense" with South Vietnam. Nor had the Johnson administration, prior to February 10, 1965, attempted to justify any US military actions in Vietnam as "collective self-defense" with South Vietnam. Furthermore, by February 1965, the United States had reported no North Vietnamese troops south of the 17th parallel – the temporary demarcation line separating the north and south zones of Vietnam – thus making any claim of collective self-defense with South Vietnam nearly impossible, given also the absence of a North Vietnamese air force or navy to speak of. In short, the Johnson administration made virtually no attempt by February 10 to justify under international law a "policy of greater flexibility" to bomb North Vietnam. And the *Times* made no attempt to evaluate within the context of international law the US claim of a discretionary option to bomb North Vietnam.

Meanwhile, by February 1965, uneasiness about the administration's Vietnam policy began to set in, and the see-saw, centrist template of editorial-page commentary – recognizable nearly forty years later in the *Times* editorials on Iraq – commenced in earnest. Thus, in an editorial on February 10, the *Times* on the one hand championed a principled American right to wage and escalate a war in Vietnam while questioning whether the "exemplary" US war mission in Vietnam was achievable:

> There is no cause to quarrel with the sentiments of President Johnson in commenting to his Boy Scout visitors on the American reprisals against North Vietnam:
> "We love peace," he said, " . . . but we love liberty the more and we shall take up any threat, we shall pay any price to make certain that freedom shall not perish from this earth."
> The people of the United States do love peace; they love freedom; they will fight for it. Mr. Johnson was on completely safe ground, even to a little forgivable plagiarism from Abraham Lincoln.

[56] "US Widens Basis For Retaliation: Aides Say Strikes at Saigon Forces May Bring Raids," *New York Times*, February 10, 1965.

Having expressed its support for President Johnson's statement of principles, the editorial page then questioned whether the president's principled
goals were attainable:

> The motives [for the US war in Vietnam] are exemplary and every American
> can be proud of them, but the crucial questions are: Can it be done? Is the
> price too high? Was the military decision in the Kennedy Administration to
> increase American forces in Vietnam mistaken? Are the dangers of escalation
> too great? Is this a good battleground of the cold war on which to fight? Is the
> United States losing more than it is gaining? All lead up to the basic question
> that some Senators are asking: Is this war necessary?[57]

Although it was already evident at the time that the US war in Vietnam
was not about "peace, freedom, and liberty" as President Johnson told the
Boy Scouts, other motives were revealed a few years later. In the first installment of the Pentagon Papers series published on June 13, 1971, the *Times'*
Neil Sheehan reported that the Pentagon study "reveals a deeper perception
among the President and his aides that the United States was now the most
powerful nation in the world and that the outcome in South Vietnam would
demonstrate the will and the ability of the United States to have its way in
world affairs."[58] Sheehan also unearthed a memo written by Assistant Defense
Secretary John McNaughton to Defense Secretary McNamara that "cap-
sulized" US war aims in Vietnam as follows (the words in parentheses are
McNaughton's):

> 70 pct. – To avoid a humiliating US defeat (to our reputation as a guarantor).
> 20 pct. – To keep SVN (and then adjacent) territory from Chinese hands.
> 10 pct. – To permit the people of SVN to enjoy a better, freer way of life.
> Also – To emerge from crisis without unacceptable taint from methods used.[59]

The memo then asserted that the US mission in Vietnam was "NOT – to
help a friend," that is South Vietnam, further undermining any notion that
bombing North Vietnam had anything to do with the collective self-defense
of South Vietnam.

Even if we were to exclude consideration of the consistently hawkish reporting and commentary on Vietnam by Hanson Baldwin and Arthur Krock, and
feature only well-articulated criticism of the war to the extent that the *Times*

[57] "What Price Vietnam," *New York Times*, February 10, 1965.
[58] "Vietnam Archive: Pentagon Study Traces 3 Decades of Growing US Involvement," *New York Times*, June 13, 1971.
[59] *Ibid.*

published such criticism, the *Times'* coverage would still be weighted toward an unwarranted principled support of US war aims in Vietnam.

In an important opinion piece on February 14, 1965, the *Times'* Washington bureau chief, James Reston, wrote that "very few people here" in Washington "question the necessity for a limited expansion of the war by US bombers into Communist territory," given that "the American and South Vietnamese position was crumbling fast, and the political and strategic consequences of defeat would have been serious for the free world all over Asia." Thus, by his own count and by implication, Reston and nearly everyone else in Washington overlooked the obvious illegality involved in bombing North Vietnam. Reston went on, however, to criticize the war effort, arguing that "nobody has made [US goals in Vietnam] clear to the American people"; "President Johnson has not made a major speech on the details of this war since he entered the White House"; and "we are in a war that is not only undeclared and unexpired, but that has not been widely debated in the Congress or the country."

In addition, Reston underscored the potential dire consequences should the US bombing campaign eventually engage "Red Chinese MIG fighters" and bases near the Chinese border. He was also concerned that bombing North Vietnam might prompt the North Vietnamese government to send its armed forces into South Vietnam:

> This is a delicate and highly dangerous situation. The United States has the air and naval power to wipe out North Vietnam and the Chinese Air Force, if it comes into the battle. But the North Vietnamese have a quarter of a million men under arms who have never been committed to the battle at all, and few observers in Washington believe this force could be stopped without the intervention of a very large American army on the ground.

Reston concludes by appealing to the consensus position in Washington to reconsider its indifference toward the war:

> Somebody, however, has to make a move to reverse the trend and stop the present crooked course. For the moment, we seem to be standing mute in Washington, paralyzed before a great issue, and merely digging our thought deeper into the accustomed military rut.[60]

Some of these criticisms were important. However, by accepting in principle the administration's right to bomb North Vietnam – a concession that Reston blandly gives the administration even in the context of its "undeclared and unexplained war" – Reston and other such critics failed to offer for

---

[60] "Washington: The Undeclared and Unexplained War," *New York Times*, February 14, 1965.

consideration the strong legal and rational case against the bombing and further US escalation, thus relieving the administration of the burden of showing that its war actions in Vietnam were legal or rational. With little opposition to its threats to bomb North Vietnam with "greater flexibility," the Johnson administration initiated in late February 1965 the "Rolling Thunder" US bombing campaign against North Vietnam, which would "remain in effect for the next three and a half years," according to former Defense Secretary McNamara. McNamara also wrote that on February 26, 1965, "the president approved the dispatch of two US Marine battalions to Danang as a security force to protect the US airbase there" and that "those Marines would be only the first installment of what would become approximately 2 million US combat personnel who would serve, at one time or another, in South Vietnam during the next decade."[61]

Although the uncontested US bombings of North Vietnam in 1964 and 1965 began the major escalation of US military involvement, the origins of direct US military involvement in Vietnam date back at least to 1954. The signing ceremony of the Geneva Accords on Vietnam in the early morning hours of July 21, 1954, marked the official end of the French colonial war in Vietnam. During that war, more than 300,000 Vietnamese were killed by the French from 1946 to 1954, with $2 billion of assistance from the United States, which accounted for most of the French costs of the war in its final years.

The Geneva Accords of 1954 consisted of three agreements on the cessation of hostilities in Vietnam, Laos, and Cambodia, five unilateral declarations issued by the governments of Laos, Cambodia, and France, and a "Final Declaration of the Geneva Conference" that, in the words of the declaration, "takes note of the agreements ending hostilities in Cambodia, Laos, and Vietnam and organiz[es] international control and the supervision of the provisions of these agreements."[62] The Final Declaration was signed by representatives of the United Kingdom, France, the Soviet Union, and the People's Republic of China. Though the United States participated in the conference, it did not sign the Final Declaration.

At the closing session of the Geneva Conference, the United Kingdom's Anthony Eden, who served as the conference chairman, asked his colleagues to vote on the Final Declaration, which would bind each of the participants to the requirements of the agreements. The representatives of France, the

---

[61]   McNamara et al., *Argument Without End*, 173.
[62]   Final Declaration of the Geneva Conference, July 21, 1954.

People's Republic of China, the United Kingdom, and the Soviet Union signed the Final Declaration with the following pronouncements:

> Mr. Mendes-France (France): "Mr. Chairman, the French delegation approves the terms of the Declaration."
> Mr. Chou En'lai (China): "We agree."
> Mr. Eden (United Kingdom): "On behalf of Her Majesty's Government in the United Kingdom, I associate myself with the Final Declaration of this conference."
> Mr. Molotov (Soviet Union): "The Soviet Delegation agrees."[63]

With respect to the legal status of the 1954 Geneva Accords, the Lawyers Committee on Vietnam wrote:

> While the Charter of the United Nations, as the most comprehensive basis of world legal order, is of course applicable to the Vietnam situation, the particular situation in Vietnam is governed by a series of compacts, namely, the Geneva Accords of 1954. Under a general principle of international law, special compacts prevail over general rules, insofar as they do not violate them in letter or spirit. The Geneva Accords, carefully designed to restore peace to a war-torn area, fulfill the highest aim of the Charter.[64]

In contrast to this assessment, *New York Times* reporter Hanson Baldwin, in describing the Geneva Accords as a "national defeat" for the French, wrote that "the Geneva peace also represented a defeat for the United States, for despite massive aid to the French our policies were ineffective." Baldwin continued: "If the Allied nations had formed a Southeast Asia alliance, if Britain and the United States had been willing to pay the high price of military intervention in Indochina, if France had given her expeditionary force wholehearted support, if the Allies had stuck together, the answer might have been different."

Referring to US and European colonial interests, Baldwin lamented further that "widespread repercussions are to be anticipated, unfavorable to the United States point of view in Asia and Africa," including "increased Nationalist and Communist-sponsored agitation in French North Africa, important to the French economy and French military strength, and to the United States for air bases." With respect to the specific terms of the treaty, Baldwin wrote: "the military problem is further sharpened by the provision that would require the withdrawal of all 'foreign troops.' About 75,000 Frenchmen, 18,000 French Legionnaires, and 50,000 to 60,000 Africans [who] have been the

---

[63] Quoted in Lawyers Committee, *Vietnam and International Law*, 167.
[64] *Ibid.*, 41.

heart and soul of the Vietnamese defense." "Moreover," Baldwin wrote, "the provision for a general election to reunite Vietnam may mean political com-munization of the whole area." In short, given the Geneva Accords and the Final Declaration, "the Communists have scored another major victory in the struggle for the world with a cease-fire attained in the Indochinese War."[65]

The *Times* editorial page was more tactful than Baldwin – for example, neglecting to mention that 50,000 to 60,000 Africans had been fighting in Vietnam on behalf of the French, with US support – but it reached similar conclusions. While it noted that "the Geneva conference reached agreement last night on an armistice ending more than seven years of armed conflict in Indochina," for which "the whole world can give grateful thanks," the editorial page also argued that the Geneva settlement "in many respects runs contrary to the principles for which we stand," and supported the American decision to disassociate itself from the Accords by refusing to sign the Final Declaration.

The editorial criticized the terms of the Accords on the grounds that they would "turn over more than half of [Vietnam's] 22 million people to Communist rule," would "give the Communist sector a great advantage in the elections scheduled to be held two years hence," which could "end in Vietnam's 'unification' under Communist domination," and that Vietnam could not "express its real choice" in the elections because of "the presence . . . of a Communist member with veto power"[66] in the International Control Commission (ICC), the independent commission charged with monitoring compliance to the accords.

However, the Pentagon Papers, which "reviewed US policy toward Indochina during and immediately following World War II," also reviewed "the refusal by the United States to extend assistance to Ho Chi Minh" after the war "despite his requests." They also "make clear the fact that Ho was acknowledged to be a genuine nationalist, as well as a communist, who was intent on maintaining his independence from the Soviet Union and China."[67] Also, "as is generally recognized, the two-year transition period [toward uni-fication elections] and the obligation to withdraw behind the 17th parallel was accepted by the Viet Minh under Soviet and Chinese pressure and con-stituted a considerable concession" to the French, British, and Americans by the Viet Minh.[68] Furthermore, Article 6 of the Final Declaration stipulated "that the military demarcation line is provisional" pending the unification

[65] "New Victory For Reds," *New York Times*, July 21, 1954.
[66] "Truce in Indochina," *New York Times*, July 21, 1954.
[67] Rudenstine, *The Day the Presses Stopped*, 28.
[68] Lawyers Committee, *Vietnam and International Law*, 43.

elections "and should not in any way be interpreted as constituting a political or territorial boundary."[69]

In any event, while "both the French and the Vietnam People's Republic [North Vietnam] properly withdrew to their respective sides of the 17th parallel, as attested to by the ICC," as the required prelude to unification elections, "the refusal of South Vietnam, with United States backing, to hold the elections for unification, violated the provisions of the Geneva Accords that had made them acceptable to the Viet Minh."[70] The US-supported refusal by South Vietnam to participate in or even discuss the unification elections – which would have been won by Ho Chi Minh with "possibly 80 percent" of the vote according to President Dwight Eisenhower,[71] and which denied the Vietnamese people their fundamental right of self-determination under international law – led to the development of the NLF insurgency in South Vietnam, and to the interventionary spiral of US involvement.

In addition to sponsoring South Vietnam's refusal to comply with the most salient feature of the Geneva Accords on Vietnam – that is, the unification elections – the United States systematically violated the second most important feature of the Accords, which prohibited any foreign military buildup in Vietnam. The Lawyers Committee on Vietnam wrote "it is common knowledge that ever since 1954 the United States engaged in a systematic and ever-increasing modernization and military build-up in South Vietnam" and that "the reports of the ICC are filled with statements about the clandestine character of those operations and describe some of the subterfuges used."[72] The contents of ICC reports from August 1955 to April 1957, which itemized US violations of the Geneva agreement, were summarized by the Lawyers Committee as follows:

- Failure to request previous ICC authorization for introduction of "replacements" of foreign personnel or war materials; "facing the Commission with a *fait accompli*," to which "the Commission takes exception," by introducing 290 United States Army service corps personnel called TERM (Temporary Equipment Recovery Mission) before the ICC had acted on the application;
- Failure to submit manifests and other documents to the ICC;

[69] Final Declaration of the Geneva Conference, July 20, 1954, Article 6.
[70] Lawyers Committee, *Vietnam and International Law*, 43, 47.
[71] Dwight D. Eisenhower, *The White House Years: Mandate For Change, 1953–1956* (New York: Doubleday & Company, 1963), 372.
[72] Lawyers Committee, *Vietnam and International Law*, 49.

- Failure to furnish advance notification to the ICC (for example, regarding United States Navy planes that "were visiting Saigon airport regularly");
- Failure to reply to ICC inquiries, for example, with regard to the establishment of two new United States military missions – TRIM (Training Reorganization Inspection Mission) in March 1955, and CATO (Combat Arms Training Organization) in May 1956;
- Claims "in many instances" that incoming war materials and military personnel were "in transit"; but failure to notify the ICC "about their exit, if any";
- Preventing the ICC from physical access to incoming United States military planes and their cargo, by having them taxi directly to the military part of the Saigon airport, from which, contrary to the Accords, the ICC teams were excluded; or by claiming that certain United States "military and other planes" are "United States Embassy planes"; . . . or preventing the ICC's reconnaissance of eight areas where, contrary to the Accords, new military airfields were allegedly being constructed.[73]

By disavowing the 1954 Geneva Accords through withholding its signature from the Final Declaration, and then proceeding systematically to violate the two most important features of the Accords, the United States tragically reignited war in Vietnam. By bombing North Vietnam, beginning in 1964 and 1965, in violation of the international law prohibition against the international use of force, the United States unnecessarily escalated its already illegal involvement in Vietnam. Thus, from at least 1954 (when the United States violated the Geneva Accords on Vietnam) to 2004 (when American armed forces in Iraq were found to have violated the Geneva Conventions with respect to detainees and civilians in Iraq), the United States has persistently violated vital and essential rules of international law in the conduct of its foreign affairs, with virtually no journalistic oversight exercised by the *New York Times* with respect to these violations. This absence of oversight and serious debate, including the failure to recognize the relevance of international law to its editorial policy, combined with its repetitive record of unwarranted deference to executive claims of an extraordinary and extra-legal right to wage war and overthrow governments, has in our minds profoundly damaged the credibility of the *Times*' coverage of US foreign policy. It has also contributed to a downward spiral of insult and injury to the US Constitution and the foundational commitment to the rule of law in the United States, especially in the setting of foreign policy.

[73] *Ibid.*, 49–50.

In an attempt to bring about the end of the Vietnam War, Daniel Ellsberg gave most of the Pentagon's 43-volume secret history of the war to Neil Sheehan, a reporter at the *Times* with whom Ellsberg was acquainted. People involved in the Pentagon Papers project at the *Times* soon realized that the contents of the classified papers "established that the US government had systematically deceived the American people during several administrations about the purpose of American involvement in South Vietnam, the risks of involvement, and the likely duration, destruction, and costs of the war."[74]

A heated debate ensued among top corporate and editorial personnel at the *Times* about whether it should publish an analysis of the documents and even portions of the secret documents themselves. Despite being counseled by a prominent New York City law firm that the *Times'* publisher and the paper's top editors might be imprisoned for violating the espionage laws, the publisher, Punch Sulzberger, and the *Times'* top editor, Abe Rosenthal, decided to publish a ten-part series on the secret papers and to publish portions of key documents. Although the *Times* made a very significant effort to avoid publishing information that might damage US national security, President Nixon's attorney general, John Mitchell, sent Punch Sulzberger a telegram on June 14 that read:

> I have been advised by the Secretary of Defense that the material published in the *New York Times* on June 13, 14 1971 captioned "key texts from Pentagon Vietnam Study" contains information relating to the national defense of the United States and bears a top secret classification.
>
> As such, publication of this information is directly prohibited by the provisions of the Espionage law, Title 18, United States Code, Section 793.
>
> Moreover, further publication of information of this character will cause irreparable injury to the defense interests of the United States.
>
> Accordingly, I respectfully request that you publish no further information of this character and advise me that you have made arrangements for the return of these documents to the Department of Defense.[75]

Also on June 14, Assistant Attorney General Robert Mardian telephoned Harding Bancroft, the *Times'* executive vice-president, to say that the government would sue the *Times* if it published other installments on the Pentagon Papers.

Most of the newspaper's reporters and editors supported the newspaper's decision to publish the series, given the importance to the country of what the documents revealed about the conduct of the war in Vietnam. But the

---

[74] Rudenstine, *The Day the Presses Stopped*, 55.
[75] *Ibid.*, 99.

publisher – along with Bancroft and Sydney Gruson, the publisher's executive assistant, as well as Abe Rosenthal and James Goodale, the *Times'* in-house attorney – had to decide how to respond to the government's threat. When these four without Sulzberger, who was in London, "got together in the *Times* executive offices on the fourteenth floor they disagreed over how to reply to the government's request." Rosenthal and Goodale "argued that the *Times* had to publish the series," while Bancroft and Gruson wanted to "suspend publication."[76] David Rudenstine describes what happened:

> Bancroft telephoned Sulzberger, who was asleep in his London hotel, and summarized the telegram Attorney General John Mitchell had sent the newspaper that evening and the position taken by Mardian during Bancroft's call with him. Bancroft also told Sulzberger that [Louis] Loeb [a prominent attorney in New York close to the *Times*] opposed further publication. Rosenthal could contain himself no longer. He shouted into the speaker phone: "Punch, this is Abe. I think you should talk to Goodale." Goodale strongly urged that the *Times* continue to publish the series as planned. Sulzberger asked Goodale if further publication would increase the newspaper's legal liability, and Goodale answered, "Not by five percent." The publisher told them to "go ahead" with the next installment.
>
> Rosenthal went to the city room on the third floor. Over 150 people were waiting to learn whether the *Times* would publish the next installment. Rosenthal announced, "Go ahead," and the crowd cheered.[77]

The Nixon administration's suit against the *New York Times* in the Pentagon Papers case quickly made it to the US Supreme Court. On June 30, 1971, the Court voted 6–3 to permit the *Times* (and the *Washington Post*) to continue publishing their respective series on the Pentagon Papers. The majority, finding no violations of the espionage laws and no threat to US national security, argued in an unsigned opinion that "any system of prior restraints of expression comes to this Court bearing a heavy presumption against its constitutional validity" and that the Government "thus carries a heavy burden of showing justification for the imposition of such a restraint."[78]

In a separate opinion, Justice Hugo Black, a 34-year veteran of the Court and in poor health, who had "worked intensely, even feverishly, on his opinion over the four days between the oral argument and the announcement of the Court's judgment," and who "may have sensed that this might be his last opinion," wrote the "most passionate and uncompromising" opinion in favor

[76] *Ibid.*
[77] *Ibid.*, 99–100.
[78] *New York Times Company v. United States*, 403 U.S. 713 (1971).

of the *Times*.[79] The night before the decisions by the justices were due, Black wrote till 4 a.m., in part to overcome a criticism of an earlier draft from his wife. Three months later, Black suffered a stroke, and six days after that, on September 25, he died.[80]

In a separate opinion (quoted earlier, but it bears repeating), his last as a Supreme Court justice, Black wrote:

> In the First Amendment the Founding Fathers gave the free press the protection it must have to fulfill its essential role in our democracy. The press was to serve the governed, not the governors. The Government's power to censor the press was abolished so that the press would remain forever free to censure the Government. The press was protected so that it could bare the secrets of government and inform the people. Only a free and unrestrained press can effectively expose deception in government. And paramount among the responsibilities of a free press is the duty to prevent any part of the government from deceiving the people and sending them off to distant lands to die of foreign fevers and foreign shot and shell.[81]

When we read the *New York Times*, especially today, we don't see the spirit of the Pentagon Papers project at the *Times*, or that of Hugo Black, in its news and editorial pages. Instead, the *Times* seems content to serve the governors more and the governed less, often simply repeating what the president says, and publishing his picture in staged settings, as front-page news. It bares few government secrets and exposes little government deception. However, even assuming that the *Times*, one day, would decide to honor Black's mandate, it would need to incorporate international law into its coverage of US foreign policy, while also ending its reliance, to the extent that it cites international law at all, on the right-wing and pro-government international law experts that have dominated even that small space of coverage in recent years.

The fifty-year habit at the *Times* of undermining or ignoring international law in its coverage of US foreign policy not only can be marked by its coverage of the 1954 Geneva Accords on Vietnam and the reprisal bombings of North Vietnam in 1964–65, but also can be seen today as a syndrome that affects not only the *Times* but, by extension and in no small part, the nation and its Constitution, the world and its legal Charter, and quite possibly the future of global civilization and life on earth.

---

[79] Rudenstine, *The Day the Presses Stopped*, 302–04.
[80] *Ibid.*, 305.
[81] Separate Opinion of Justice Hugo Black, with Justice Douglas Concurring, *New York Times Co. v. United States*, 403 U.S. 713 (1971).

14

"The Vietnam Syndrome": The Kerrey Revelations Raise Anew Issues of Morality and Military Power

The Kerrey disclosures have surfaced an array of both laudable and lamentable sentiments, but perhaps none worse than those associated with William Safire's April 30 tirade directed at the so-called Vietnam Syndrome. Safire defines the syndrome as "that revulsion at the use of military power that afflicted our national psyche for decades after our defeat." At least we can be grateful that Safire nowhere makes clear what the wars since Vietnam were that America was prevented from entering because of what he calls the "national affliction" that accompanied the syndrome. It is this alleged inhibition on warmaking that has now resurfaced in the debate about Bob Kerrey's degree of guilt and accountability, vividly presented in these pages by Christopher Hitchens[1] and Jonathan Schell.[2] Overall, Safire wants to affirm Ronald Reagan's embrace of illusion by regarding the Vietnam War as an occasion of national heroism and honor. Safire ends his column plaintively: "Are there no voices left, after that costly loss of life, to reject the Syndrome's humiliating accusation of national arrogance – and to recall a noble motive?"

Alas, there are plenty such voices, most strident among them perhaps that of Senator John McCain, who writes with the authority of a former POW who was tortured during a long period of captivity in Vietnam. For McCain, despite the disclosure of the deliberate killing of civilians in the village hamlet of Thanh Phong back in February 1969, Kerrey remains "a war hero" who should be understood as having done what needed to be done in the sort of war being fought in Vietnam. Most disturbing, McCain argues that Vietnam was the kind of war that required its participants to hate the enemy, and he una-bashedly makes a combat virtue out of hate. In his words: "I hated my enemies even before they held me captive because hate sustained me in my devotion

---

[1] "Minority Report," *The Nation*, May 28, 2001.
[2] "War and Accountability," *The Nation*, May 21, 2001.

to their complete destruction and helped me overcome the virtuous human impulse to recoil in disgust from what had to be done by my hand."[3] It is bad enough when a pilot holds such views but, when hatred informs the spirit of a ground war carried on in the midst of a densely inhabited civilian society, it is worse. It should not be surprising that atrocities became indistinguishable from normal battlefield practice, and not some anomaly that occurred on a single occasion at My Lai, or perhaps twice, counting Thanh Phong.

Kerrey's own efforts at explaining and validating are not nearly as reprehensible as McCain's, and they contain significant redeeming features, but in the end their instructional message is not much different. (I am leaving to one side Kerrey's questionable version of the narrative of the fateful night at Thanh Phong, disputed by Gerhard Klann, the most experienced member of the SEAL squad, and Vietnamese eyewitnesses.)

Let me mention first the positive sides of what Kerrey has been saying, mainly in the course of public appearances and TV interviews. He is very upfront about the shocking fact that the soldiers in Vietnam were never trained in the laws of war and that he himself only learned about the US Army's Field Manual prohibition on killing civilians long after the war. The central message of Field Manual 27-10, "The Law of Land Warfare," was clear and pertinent: "Every violation of the law of war is a war crime . . ." This fundamental failure of training is a dreadful comment on command responsibility in a war of the sort waged in Vietnam.

Proper training would have contradicted the main lines of counterinsurgency warfare, which rested on a criminal premise: that as a matter of military doctrine, in those parts of the country where the revolutionary side had societal support, the entire civilian population – including women, children, the infirm and the wounded – should be treated as "the enemy." In designating large portions of the Vietnamese countryside as "free-fire" zones, US officials authorized pilots and soldiers to kill whatever moved, even farm animals. The most fundamental idea embedded in the law of war, requiring a belligerent to distinguish civilian from military targets, was completely abandoned. It should be kept in mind that Thanh Phong was in such a zone and that Kerrey commanded a small unit of Navy SEALs, who were especially assigned to carry out assassination missions as a part of what came to be known (and decried by critics of the war) as the Phoenix Program.

In Kerrey's individual defense, he was sent on an atrocity-generating mission without proper training as to his responsibility as a professional soldier,

[3] *Wall Street Journal*, April 27, 2001.

but that does not alter the character of the incident as an atrocity. It may mitigate his individual responsibility, while at the same time intensifying that of
political and military leaders in control of the war.

In a long, friendly TV interview with CNBC's Tim Russert,[4] Kerrey made
the obvious, yet necessary, point that is almost never made in mainstream
discussion, namely, that the war "was much worse for the Vietnamese" than
it was for the Americans. Typically, the Vietnamese are treated as an alien
and cruel backdrop for an essentially American encounter with death and
dying. A concern about misrepresentation of the war was vividly expressed
by W. D. Ehrhart, a Vietnam veteran who was in the Marines, discussing the
Kerrey incident on NPR's *Talk of the Nation*: "You know, the Vietnam War,
we imagine it's this thing that happened to us when, in fact, the Vietnam War
is this thing we did to them."[5]

But there is also much that is troublesome about Kerrey's comments. Kerrey
says that he only turned against the war when he reached the conclusion that
it was unwinnable, and even more so when he realized that Americans back
home no longer supported the war effort. There is no sense that the whole
enterprise was flawed, an interference in the internal nationalist struggle of an
ex-French colony by a US military undertaking that rested on criminal modes
of warfare.

Kerrey may be correct in counseling against rearguing the merits of the war
in America, but it is necessary for the country to perceive the nature of the
conflict accurately so as to avoid stumbling into comparable disasters in the
future. Such a concern is not fanciful, and definitely persists after the end of
the cold war. The temptation of America to rely on its mastery of high-tech
weaponry to overwhelm low-tech adversaries is actually far greater these days
than during the cold war era. The success of such tactics in the Gulf War,
and especially in the casualty-free (for NATO) Kosovo War, puts the peoples
of Asia, Africa and Latin America at continuous potential risk in the current
world order. And, unlike Vietnam, there is now often no sobering reality of
American casualties to make leaders and citizens ponder the costs of war.

It is important to understand that even this much clarity about Vietnam's
moral legacy arises only because an attractive public figure was involved,
engaging media interest because of the glamorous story line of a dramatic fall
from grace. The personal drama was enriched by Kerrey's recent designation
as the president of New School University, an institution whose initial role
was as a safe haven for outstanding refugee scholars fleeing Nazi criminality.

---

[4]   *Meet the Press*, January 19, 1992.
[5]   May 2, 2001.

We should not allow the melodrama of this cover story to obscure the realization that there were many atrocity stories reported by reliable witnesses and war veterans starting in the late 1960s. I remember listening in my living room on several occasions to tear-filled stories told by returning GIs about their role in military operations that involved the deliberate killing of Vietnamese peasant women and children. But their efforts to gain a wider hearing were generally spurned by the mainstream media. Even earlier, a distinguished group of US religious leaders, including Martin Luther King, Jr., John Bennett, a prominent Protestant theologian, and Abraham Joshua Heschel, who formed Clergy and Layman Concerned About Vietnam to protest the war, endorsed the devastating findings of a privately published volume that gathered journalistic accounts of crimes associated with US military operations in Vietnam. Except among hard-core antiwar activists, this book, aptly titled *In the Name of America*,[6] attracted no notice whatsoever.

There were other peace movement efforts to detail the criminal dimensions of the war policies being relentlessly pursued in Vietnam, most notoriously the 1967 sessions of the Bertrand Russell International War Crimes Tribunals held in Stockholm and Roskilde just outside the Danish capital. Much valuable evidence and testimony was presented to a prominent international panel of jurors that included such luminaries as Jean-Paul Sartre, Simone de Beauvoir, James Baldwin, David Dellinger, the playwright Peter Weiss and others. The whole proceeding was barely noticed in America at the time, except for an occasional broadside attacking the undertaking as partisan, one-sided, a mockery of due process. Unfortunately, much of this criticism was warranted, but much more deserved would have been a serious response to the evidence presented of a war that exceeded all the bounds set by the minimal standards incorporated into the laws of war. Such standards were unhesitatingly relied upon by the US government after World War II to assess the criminal responsibility of enemy soldiers and politicians. This framework for accountability was set forth early with self-righteous legal and moral authority as the historic basis for holding German and Japanese leaders individually responsible at Nuremberg and Tokyo after World War II. The US government, back in 1945, was the most ardent champion of the Nuremberg approach among the nations. The chief prosecutor, former Supreme Court Justice Robert Jackson, famously promised at the time that the principles being relied upon to convict the Germans at Nuremberg would be used in the future to assess the behavior

---

[6] Clergy and Laymen Concerned About Vietnam, *In the Name of America*, director of research, Seymour Melman (Annandale, VA: Turnpike Press, 1968).

of those sitting in judgment. For several decades, neither the United States nor its allies in World War II made any effort to fulfill this Nuremberg pledge.

If war as such were illegal from start to finish, then there would be no point to the regulation of conduct during war. The basis of laws of war – what are now generally called international humanitarian laws – is the nonpacifist idea that, even though some wars, like World War II and armed struggles by brutally oppressed peoples, are just and necessary, their conduct needs to be regulated. And since each belligerent insists that its side is pursuing a just cause, international law has drawn the distinction for centuries between rules governing recourse to war and rules regulating its conduct. This distinction was relied upon at Nuremberg to distinguish between "an illegal war," which was regarded as a "crime against peace," and illegal combat operations, which were treated as "war crimes." A third category, "crimes against humanity," involved severe abuse of civilian populations, including one's own people, which are committed outside the war zone. The central idea of international humanitarian law, as codified in a series of widely ratified international treaties, has been to reduce the human suffering in war as much as possible and to separate this task from the prevention of war itself. For this reason, both sides are equally bound by the rules governing combat even if one side is later found by an international body to have been the aggressor.

In the period since the collapse of the Berlin wall, significant and numerous developments on the accountability front have taken place. After decades of frustration, there has been a series of successful major efforts to compensate surviving victims of the Holocaust, and a series of comparable efforts are under way involving analogous Japanese responsibility for atrocities, including the scandal of the "comfort women."

Additionally, the struggles of indigenous peoples to seek redress of grievances arising from their dispossession from their historic lands has produced a variety of surprising victories, although mainly of a symbolic character. These range from gaining access to the United Nations to draft their own Declaration on the Rights of Indigenous Peoples to the receipt of apologies and the establishment by several Commonwealth countries of trust funds devoted to the well-being of these peoples. Among these, Australia, New Zealand and Canada have been the scene of strong movements by indigenous peoples that have led governments to admit past wrongdoing and to make (so far) mostly symbolic amends.

Such developments have lent an unprecedented weight to African-American initiatives to demand reparations for the suffering and denial of rights associated with the institution of slavery. Previously such demands were dismissed as frivolous or worse, but no longer. Now, these claims are matters of controversy that engage respected voices on both sides of the issue. There is a widespread and growing agreement that past injustices leave enduring wounds unless the wrongs inflicted are repudiated and some effort at redress attempted. It need not be material or mercenary. Often the main relief sought is some sincere expression of symbolic acknowledgment.

These moves to obtain redress for past grievances are a new development in international political life and have made the question of global justice and its limits of growing interest in academic circles and among activists. It is not clear how far this process will lead, but it bears on issues of accountability for war crimes, especially to the victimized society and its citizens. The focus on victims' justice is part of this new reality.

The developments relating to matters of accountability have been particularly momentous, and undoubtedly form the unconscious backdrop for rethinking US wrongdoing in Vietnam – or, more appropriately, in the whole of Indochina. For complex ethical and geopolitical reasons, the Balkan wars of the 1990s created a new receptivity to the idea of criminal accountability, which led the UN Security Council to establish the International Criminal Tribunal for the former Yugoslavia. And then, in the aftermath of the 1994 genocide taking the lives of about 800,000 – mostly Tutsi – Rwandans, a parallel tribunal for Rwanda was set up. These initiatives in turn gave rise to an innovative collaboration between a series of moderate governments and a coalition of several hundred civil society organizations (also known as nongovernmental organizations), which produced the Rome Treaty in 1998 to establish a permanent International Criminal Court. More than 100 countries signed the Rome Treaty, and it is expected that the court will come into existence within the next year or two, when it receives the necessary sixty treaty ratifications. As is so often the case, the United States' enthusiasm for the project dimmed dramatically when it began to realize that its citizens and leaders could be among the accused, as well as being the accusers. Under domestic pressure, Bill Clinton added an American signature in his closing days as President, but the prospect of treaty ratification, which requires a two-thirds vote in the Senate, is near zero even with Democratic control during the Bush years.

There are additional international moves relating to accountability that have captured the political imagination in recent years. The most startling was the 1998 indictment in Spain and detention in Britain of the former Chilean dictator Augusto Pinochet. In the end Pinochet was sent back to Chile for medical reasons, and now Chilean courts are wrestling with a myriad of civil and criminal charges against him. The Pinochet litigation opened the way for national courts around the world to begin implementing international law in comparable circumstances, and much activity has already ensued. It has been reported that such vulnerable figures as Henry Kissinger and Ariel Sharon have altered travel plans to avoid the risk of enduring Pinochet's fate.

There is a delicious irony associated with Kissinger's publication of an article in the current issue of *Foreign Affairs* under the title "The Pitfalls of Universal Jurisdiction."[7] It is universal jurisdiction that allowed the criminal pursuit of Pinochet in Spain and Britain, and it is universal jurisdiction that would potentially allow a national court anywhere in the world to indict Kissinger for well-evidenced allegations of criminality in various countries.

In my view, this background should inform the US response to the Kerrey disclosures, but not mechanically, and not in a personal, vindictive spirit. What America needs to put in focus are those distinctive aspects of collective accountability and war that reveal the blind spots of US political culture, specifically in relation to the Vietnam War. I would highlight two such blind spots with fundamental significance to the sort of warfare likely to ensue in the near future. These corrective measures are necessary to lessen the likelihood of war crimes even in wars fought under the formal auspices of the UN and presented as "peacekeeping." The first step is an unconditional acceptance at the highest levels of civilian and military leadership of the laws of war as a framework for the conduct of belligerent operations. And the second is the appropriate training of combat personnel so that they fully understand this framework and their professional obligations to uphold the laws of war and to resist orders that defy it. It is also of great importance in recollecting the Vietnam War that Americans understand that it was a war between unequals, with most of the victims of illegal methods being on the Vietnamese side. To advance in terms of accountability, the stress has to shift from "victors' justice" (as at Nuremberg) to "victims' justice" (as in the 1990s Balkan wars).

Of course, this latter distinction should be drawn contextually, as the identity of victims depends on the circumstances of the war. In this regard, a contrast can be drawn between World War II and the Vietnam War. Also, there are important gradations of victimhood that need to be taken into account.

Such priorities can be briefly clarified. The laws of war, as set forth in international treaties and international customary law, have been drafted over the decades on the basis of input from the military and with the outlook of sovereign states intent on having the least possible interference in their pursuit of national security policy. In other words, these are minimum constraints on combat operations designed to take the fullest account of legitimate claims of "military necessity." The laws of war, or international humanitarian law, are

---

[7]   *Foreign Affairs*, 80, 4 (Jul.–Aug. 2001).

not the work of pacifists or even antimilitarists, and are designed on the basis
of mutual benefit, like the rules governing the treatment accorded POWs.
They represent the judgments of seasoned statesmen and diplomats who have
been seeking pragmatic as well as moral reasons to avoid excessive human suffering and to subject combat operations to some sort of professional discipline.
The essence of this professionalism is that civilians are not legitimate targets
under any conditions. Aryeh Neier, in his fine book *War Crimes: Brutality,
Genocide, Terror and the Struggle for Justice*, quotes to powerful effect from
Gen. Douglas MacArthur on this theme of military professionalism:

> The soldier, be he friend or foe, is charged with the protection of the weak
> and unarmed. It is the very essence and reason for his being. When he
> violates this sacred trust he not only profanes his entire culture but threatens
> the very fabric of international society. The traditions of fighting men are
> long and honorable, based upon the noblest of human traits – sacrifice.[8]

What is striking is that the attitudes expressed by McCain and Kerrey are so
at variance with these sentiments. How can McCain's emphasis on the need
to hate or Kerrey's indication of having no training in the laws of war be reconciled with MacArthur's injunction? Doesn't it point to a dangerous disconnect
between rhetoric and practice that needs to be addressed?

Looking back at Vietnam, it is evident that once such policies as free-fire
zones and assassination programs were adopted at command levels, this sort
of professionalism was effectively disowned. In this sense, the locus of responsibility should not be associated with the perpetrators of war crimes but with
their leaders, who established a rogue conception of military necessity that is
reconcilable neither with MacArthur's professionalism nor with the minimum
restraints of the laws of war. This does not exonerate the perpetrators, but
regards the Calleys (Lieut. William Calley, the main perpetrator of the My Lai
massacre) and Kerreys themselves partly as "victims" of a deformed command
structure, and partly as scapegoats for leaders hypocritically backed into the
position of opposing the violence against civilians that their policies mandate.
It is precisely these twisted circumstances that made the prosecution of Calley
such an ambiguous moral occasion, with the grotesque fallout of making him
into a temporary folk hero in Georgia.

This broad-brush treatment of an anguished background suggests the importance of not allowing the Kerrey incident to die in peace. As citizens we need
to exert greater vigilance to insure that what is done "in the name of America"

[8] Aryeh Neier, *War Crimes: Brutality, Genocide, Terror, and the Struggle for Justice* (New York:
Times Books, 1998), 230.

does not bring shame to the country and to those young Americans who bear the brunt of risk and loss. The ideal solution, mentioned by Hitchens, would be the establishment of a credible commission of inquiry into the broad issues raised, with a brief to put forward detailed recommendations. The focus should be less on individual accountability and more on reinforcing support for adherence to the laws of war, military professionalism and victims' justice. The ideal solution would involve some sort of acknowledgment of collective responsibility by the United States to Vietnam, starting with honoring the commitment Kissinger made in the Paris peace negotiations to provide Vietnam with several billion dollars of reconstruction assistance. Of course, recognition of the criminality of the war policies in Vietnam cannot bring the victims back to life, but US moves toward accepting responsibility would help heal remaining wounds and enable the United States to accept its own subjection to the rule of law in relation to uses of force and foreign policy generally. It would imply an entirely new and more mature style of global leadership.

But to wait for an ideal solution is to wait for Godot! Official America continues to be resistant to the sort of initiative being proposed here, and public opinion is not much more receptive. Recall that even an exhibition of the suffering caused by the Hiroshima bombing, scheduled to be shown at the Smithsonian Institution on the fiftieth anniversary back in 1995, caused a ferocious backlash and reduced the presentation to almost nothing. And much of the response to what Kerrey has had to say – and much of his own catechism of atonement – indicates that America is not ready to receive such messages.

If action is to be taken, it has to emerge from civil society, and it has to be primarily educational, rather than punitive or even accusatory, in intent. There has been a great deal of evolving sophistication in the way peoples' tribunals operate since the Russell experiment of the late 1960s. The Permanent Peoples' Tribunal in Rome has held many sessions over the past twenty years, dealing with issues as disparate as the Armenian genocide of 1915, self-determination for Puerto Rico, the dispossession of the Amerindians from Amazonia and the predatory lending practices of the IMF and World Bank. I think that one could obtain the participation of distinguished moral authority figures in the United States and elsewhere who would participate in a National Committee to Promote Justice and Reconciliation with the Peoples of Indochina. If well done, the process and outcome would raise consciousness of the difficult, persistent issues raised by what Kerrey did back in 1969 and what people are saying about it in 2001.

Such an initiative would also be a way of increasing civic responsibility in participatory democracy, and be a further expression of the conviction that sovereignty resides with the citizenry rather than with the government. With

party politics occasioning such justifiable disillusionment these days, especially among the young, now is the time to revitalize democratic practice and
confidence through creative undertakings that address the human wrongs
governmental institutions neglect. We have, happily, moved far beyond the
kind of sentiment that French President Charles de Gaulle expressed in his
response to Sartre's request that the Russell Tribunal be allowed to operate in
France: "I have no need to tell you that justice of any sort, in principle as
in execution, emanates from the state."[9]
Whatever else, statism can no longer claim – indeed, it never could – a
monopoly on the dispensation of justice, and most particularly not global
justice. And especially not to the victims of an unjust war who live in a distant
state. We are all challenged to make use of our democratic possibilities to
forge a constructive response that will transform Kerrey handwringing into a
process of national healing. Such an effort requires that we evolve a culture
of empathy that embraces, first of all, the people of Vietnam, and that leads to
a stronger engagement with human solidarity. Such solidarity is the only real
antidote to pathological forms of nationalism, and the only reliable repudiation of a total-war mentality.
One of the wisest voices on these troubling matters is that of Harvard law professor Martha Minow, eloquently accessible in her book *Between Vengeance
and Forgiveness*. She reminds us that "to seek a path between vengeance
and forgiveness is also to seek a route between too much memory and too
much forgetting."[10] This is a crucial message for the most agitated adversaries
engaged in the ongoing debate about criminality during the Vietnam War.
It should be neither an American Syndrome of too much forgetting nor a
supposed Vietnam Syndrome of too much remembering. Both proximity and
distance need to be respected as the more sensitive and compassionate discussions of the Kerrey experience have managed to do. Finally, Minow reminds
us that we are all responsible: Even those of us who are bystanders have a
capacity to know and to act, and, if we fail to do so, we become a form of
victim, and perpetrator.

[9] "Letter from de Gaulle to Sartre," Paris, April 19, 1967, in John Duffett, ed., *Against the Crime
of Silence: Proceedings of the International War Crimes Tribunal* (New York: O'Hare Books,
1968), 28; quoted in Robert Cover, *Narrative, Violence and the Law*, eds. Martha Minow,
Michael Ryan, and Austin Sarat (Ann Arbor: University of Michigan Press, 1995).
[10] (Boston: Beacon Press, 1998), 118.

15

Why the Legal Debate on the Vietnam War Still Matters: The Case for Revisiting the International Law Debate

This volume rests on a simple proposition: The legal arguments against military intervention in Vietnam were wrongly rejected by the US government and, until these are reconsidered and reversed, failure abroad and deterioration at home are the likely results.

It may seem, with the passage of more than fifty years since the American military engagement in Vietnam became a serious commitment of national policy, that the legal controversy that accompanied the involvement should be forgotten, and that the most reasonable recommendation would be to move on. The world has changed drastically in this past half-century, as has – especially – the context in which force is used, creating a drastically different relationship between international law and recourse to force beyond the borders of a sovereign state.

Actually, the passage of time and the preoccupation with present security challenges have led to an unfortunate neglect of the Vietnam precedent, which retains an extraordinary relevance, especially for the development of American thought and practice relative to military intervention in foreign societies. As this collection of writings attempts to show, unlike more recent legally dubious interventions, especially associated with the attack on Iraq in 2003, there has been no high-profile government attempt to provide a convincing legal rationale for its recourse to force.[1]

Until Vietnam, with some important exceptions relating to covert intervention as in Iran (1953) and Guatemala (1954), the United States was associated

---

[1] See Philippe Sands, *Lawless World: America and the Making and Breaking of Global Rules from FDR's Atlantic Charter to George W. Bush's Illegal War* (New York: Viking, 2005); Marjorie Cohn, *Cowboy Republic: Six Ways the Bush Gang Has Defied the Law* (Sausalito, CA: PoliPoint Press, 2007); Jens David Ohlin, *The Assault on International Law* (New York: Oxford University Press, 2015).

with the promotion of the rule of law in international political life and an attitude of respect toward the constraints on the use of force set forth, largely at the urging of Washington, in the Charter of the United Nations. Constructing a global legal order was a vital ingredient of its leadership role assumed at the end of World War II, and reinforced by the backing of the UN in the Korean War and the stand against recourse to war and acquisition of territory through force by its European allies and Israel in the 1956 Suez War.

Because Vietnam lasted as long as it did, and turned out to be the most important bipartisan failure of foreign policy in the Cold War era that agitated American civil society in ways that worried the guardians of the established order, it created a fork in the policy road. Either the United States would accept the historical verdict of the Vietnam War, renouncing unlawful options relating to the use of nondefensive force and resuming its constructive role as the architect of a peaceful world order, or it could treat the Vietnam experience as essentially a failure of military planning and political leadership that could and should be corrected. It chose the latter course, a triumph for the military-industrial complex and an internationalist foreign policy, which also reflected a domestic backlash against the feared radicalism of the anti-war movement.

The argument of this volume is that this was the wrong choice, and a crucial misinterpretation of the tragic lessons of the Vietnam War that has contributed to subsequent failures of security policy, which has further weakened international law and the United Nations.[2] It was wrong normatively, as a matter of legal and ethical principle, and it was wrong pragmatically, generating costly future foreign policy failures. This pattern also contributed to a gradual, cumulative weakening of democratic institutions in the United States. The explanation I would offer at this time is that the American way of responding to the Vietnam outcome, after a pause to restore confidence in its global ambitions, was to militarize the security discourse in ways that have virtually excluded international law from serious consideration in shaping national policy. This has not only resulted in an excessive and dysfunctional reliance on military options, but it has also militarized the bureaucratic machinery of the state in ways that have badly misdiagnosed the security threats of the twenty-first century.

Resubmitting the argument for adherence to the rule of law in Vietnam is deemed relevant as it illuminates "what might have been" and "still could be."

---

[2] Richard Falk, *The Costs of War: International Law, the UN, and World Order After Iraq* (New York: Routledge, 2008).

The main contention underlying the international law positions urged unsuc-
cessfully during the Vietnam War debate is that superior military force used
in aggressive modes such as intervention in a foreign society caused widespread suffering and devastation but still prove unable to control the political
outcomes. As the UN Charter clearly attempted to establish, recourse to war
by sovereign states should be limited to genuine cases of self-defense and,
even then, treated as a last resort. To avoid security challenges other than
responses to aggression, nonmilitary approaches were likely to be more effective, far less expensive, and much less prone to generate widespread violent
conflict. In addition, the Charter authorizes the Security Council to mandate
the use of force as it did in the Gulf War of 1991 and again in Libya (2011).
Both instances suggest that the UN as well as states may engage in militaristic
undertakings responsive to geopolitical pressures, and thereby refuse to abide
by the anti-war spirit of the UN Charter.

In effect, losing the international law debate in the course of the Vietnam
War also resulted in evading the relevance of international law in the most
influential postwar assessments of what went wrong in Vietnam. It is this
evasion that continues to produce negative outcomes in a variety of conflict situations, as well as making the United States susceptible to dema-
gogic populism positing a militarist agenda, most recently articulated in
relation to the threats posed by ISIS. By revisiting the Vietnam debate on
international law we have the opportunity to reconsider the road not taken
in an atmosphere of relative detachment from the passions unleashed by
the 9/11 attacks. By so doing we can better grasp the decline in world order
that has occurred during the five decades that followed upon intervention
in Vietnam.

WHY IT REMAINS RELEVANT TO REVIVE THE
ARGUMENTS OF THE VIETNAM WAR

To make the case for the continuing relevance of the Vietnam international
law debate, it is first necessary to acknowledge the current global setting.
After all, there are fresher controversies involving a variety of subsequent
military interventions, direct and indirect, large and small, of more recent
origin throughout the Middle East. There is even arguably a post-Vietnam
context involving new norms (responsibility to protect, or R2P), new weapons (drones), and new thinking (approaching counterinsurgency warfare with
greater respect for national sensitivities). Although these innovations are significant, and partly reflect attempted adjustments to the Vietnam failure, they

do not undermine the case for revisiting the rejection of international law arguments generated by the Vietnam War.

One of the unfortunate consequences of the American reaction to the Vietnam experience was to make international law almost irrelevant to its future decisions regarding international uses of force. At least, in the Vietnam context the government made determined, if rather unconvincing efforts to respond to international law criticisms, there were frequent scholarly debates, and Congress held several hearings on the international law dimensions of the war.[3] In contrast, the United States mounted its attack on Afghanistan in 2001 without establishing any substantial link between the Kabul government and the 9/11 attacks, and against Iraq in 2003 when there was no credible international law justifications put forward, but only a lame effort by the American secretary of state, Colin Powell, to convince the UN Security Council that the Baghdad government had weapons of mass destruction in its possession. In other words, after Vietnam the United States used international force whenever motivated to do so by its geopolitical strategy, with attention only to matters of the feasibility and anticipated costs of the operation, and thus without worrying, in public at least, about attempting to satisfy the niceties of international law.

What was lost in the aftermath of Vietnam was a reevaluation of the role that international law might have played, if appropriately respected, in saving the United States from a dreadful foreign policy blunder and, more humanly important, in saving the Vietnamese people from a terrible ordeal in which several million lives were lost and much of the country devastated. The American foreign policy establishment avoided any serious consideration of the potential pragmatic and humanitarian benefits that would have flowed from adhering to international law, and instead focused on overcoming the inhibitions placed on recourse to force as a result of the defeat in Vietnam. As if by a magician's necessary craft of shifting the gaze of the audience so that the manipulations of reality go unnoticed, Americans were led to reject the wisdom of "the Vietnam Syndrome," the supposed unhealthy timidity dominating American foreign policy presented by the political leadership in Washington as an overreaction to the failure in Vietnam.

---

[3] *The Legality of United States Participation in the Defense of Viet-Nam*, Memorandum of Law, Office of the Legal Advisor, US Department of State, 54 *Department of State Bulletin*, 54 (1966), 474; Congressional Record, March 10, 1966, 4274; for response, see Lawyers Committee on American Policy Towards Vietnam, *Vietnam and International Law: An Analysis of the Legality of U.S. Military Involvement*, (Flanders, NJ: O'Hare, 1967).

Except for rightwing revisionists who continue to insist that the war was lost "in American living rooms" rather than in Vietnam itself, there is a sullen realization by the American policy community that the war was indeed lost. Rather than ponder what might have been had the United States respected the constraints of international law as generally understood, the majority of policy thinkers inside and outside the government have tried to figure out what went wrong on the battlefield and on the home front. Quite influentially, a new counterinsurgency manual was drafted by David Petraeus, who later rose through the ranks in appreciation of his efforts to make military intervention an attractive policy option in the future. Petraeus essentially argued that future interventions should devote resources and energies to avoid alienating the territorial population that is the scene of the intervention.[4] This approach was given a major test, and found woefully insufficient pragmatically, in the context of Iraqi resistance to American intervention subsequent to the 2003 attack. Another adjustment was to "embed" media with combat units so as to coopt the outlook of independent journalists and discourage critical commentary.

On the home front, various efforts were made. Above all, the draft was abolished, reliance was placed on all-volunteer armed forces, and the professional military was upgraded in national esteem. This meant that urban middle-class constituencies that had made the anti-war movement potent during the latter stages of the Vietnam War would be far less likely in the future to obstruct warmakers. As important, weaponry and tactics were developed that sought to minimize American casualties in future military operations in distant lands. In effect, post-Vietnam internal wars were fought, to the extent possible, from the air, relying especially on long-range missiles, "shock-and-awe" tactics to compel quick submission, and attack drones used to destroy targets dispersed on a global battlefield, supplemented in special situations (e.g. execution of Osama bin Laden) by special forces units, small-scale transnational missions carried out on the ground. These adjustments reflected a *political* management approach to post-Vietnam uses of international force coupled with a determined, if implicit, minimization of a *legal* management approach, although reactionary criticism complains about overly restrictive rules of engagement.[5]

---

[4] See David H. Petraeus and James F. Amos, *The US Army and US Marine Corps Counterinsurgency Field Manual* (Kissimmee, FL: Signalman Publishing, 2009).
[5] Cf. John Yoo's strained interpretation of "torture" and general view of the authority of the president under the Constitution. See Yoo, *The Powers of War and Peace: The Constitution and Foreign Affairs After 9/11* (Chicago: University of Chicago Press, 2005).

As the writings collected here attempt to demonstrate, the conscientious acceptance of the discipline of international law *in the spirit of the UN Charter* would have avoided most adverse world-order effects if the American intervention in Vietnam had respected the norms prohibiting aggressive warfare. It would certainly have prevented the extension of the war to North Vietnam in 1965 and to Cambodia in 1970, probably reducing the intensity and duration of the political violence, and may have encouraged a much earlier political resolution of the conflict. International law is not pacifist, and reflects a statist and geopolitical bias, which validated the imprudent and immoral extension of military assistance to the Saigon regime in its struggle against an insurgency. The issue is more complicated as the 1954 agreement ending the French–Indochina War anticipated an election two years later to determine attitudes toward reunification. This election was blocked by the United States, which anticipated a victory for those political forces aligned with communist North Vietnam due to nationalist sentiments. Again, adherence to an international agreement would have spared the Vietnamese people and the American interveners the costly and bloody ordeal of achieving reunification twenty years later by force of arms.

THE COMPLEXITY OF INTERNATIONAL LAW

There are several points raised by this line of reasoning. First of all, although international law does prohibit *international* uses of force except in self-defense, it is much more deferential to geopolitical calculations when it comes to *intranational* uses of force. Aiding a criminal or corrupt governmental regime is legally permissible, which is arguably the case currently with regard to the Iranian and Russian support given to Assad's regime in Syria. In this regard, there is a gap in international law that should be addressed by tying military assistance of arms supplies to the observance of human rights and international humanitarian law by a recipient government. If the veto did not exist, the Security Council could be entrusted with a supervisory role of permitting or prohibiting various forms of assistance to a beleaguered government, but this is extremely unlikely given the importance attached by leading sovereign states to their freedom of action when it comes to helping friendly governments and opposing political tendencies of which they disapprove.

Secondly, for these reasons it is important to address the policy and ethical aspects of military intervention as well as the legal aspects. There is no doubt that military engagement within a country to help an ally may magnify the violence and stabilize a government that is violating international humanitarian law. Also, the insurgent side in an intranational conflict may represent a humane and democratic alternative to the political status quo, making it more in accord with an ethical foreign policy to lend such forces assistance in the interest of national liberation. Put differently, compliance with international law is not always consistent with commitments to promote global justice and human rights.

Thirdly, international law is primarily structured by and for the benefit of the most powerful and influential state actors, and has often legitimated aggressive war and economic exploitation, as well as giving governments an unrestricted mandate to abuse those resident within its sovereign domain.[6] It is only since 1945 that counterhegemonic roles for international law have been creatively explored and put to use in the practice of states.[7] In this respect, the Charter framework restraining recourse to aggression in international political life was a reaction to the carnage of World Wars I and II and anxieties about possible future major wars that could be fought with nuclear weapons in ways that would be catastrophic for all states, large or small, winners or losers. As the memory of World War II weakened, and geopolitical incentives for projecting force increased, the willingness to accept the Charter framework relative to war/peace issues was marginalized.

Fourthly, learning the lessons of defeat is different if the home country is forced to surrender, as was the case with Germany (1945) and Japan (1945), than when a powerful country experiences defeat in a distant theater of combat, as was the case with the United States in Vietnam. Rather than engage in the pedagogy of self-scrutiny, such a limited defeat acts as an occasion for geopolitical regrouping, and what tends to occur is a repetition in a new form of the old pattern. The French after their defeat in Indochina also regrouped, hoping to defend their colonial presence in North Africa, not yet realizing that the currents of history were moving strongly in favor of the dynamics of national self-determination. It took eight more years, and their humbling defeat in Algeria, to convince the French that their days as a major colonial power were essentially over. Learning from defeat depends, always, on how the geopolitical context is interpreted and internalized by the losing government.

Fifthly, because of the ways in which international law is generated, it is generally difficult to change in response to altered patterns of conflict.

[6] Ken Booth, "Human Wrongs in International Relations," *Journal of International Affairs*, 71 (1995), 103–26.
[7] See Balakrishnan Rajgopal, Richard Falk, and Jacqueline Stevens, eds., "Reshaping Justice – International Law and the Third World" (Special Issue), *Third World Quarterly*, 27(5) (2006), 707–57; see also Balakrishnan Rajgopal, *International Law from Below: Development, Social Movements, and Third World Resistance* (Cambridge: Cambridge University Press, 2003).

At present, with the tactics and doctrine of violent transnational conflict associated with terrorism and counterterrorism, the international law of war developed to address state-to-state relations is under great strain, and is in part irrelevant. This situation of challenge calls not for the abandonment of law, but for its drastic reformulation, which is unlikely to happen as the United States, in particular, does not want to have its policies subjected to legal criticisms, much less constrained. As well, its nonstate adversaries display no willingness whatsoever to conduct their violent operations within a framework of law and morality. At the same time, the United States responded to the 9/11 attacks without due diligence, immediately and thoughtlessly breaking with the tradition of treating terrorism as a law enforcement challenge rather than opting for a response within the war paradigm.[8]

Sixthly, as indicated by the debate about the relationship of international law to the US involvement in Vietnam, there are always available two legal sides to every important policy choice, and in the context of a liberal democratic society there will always be experts in international law ready to defend government policy.[9] Are we, then, to throw up our hands, and say that whether a given policy is lawful or not is undecidable until the controversy is resolved by a procedure deemed authoritative? In international society, lacking a governmental structure, such procedures are weak or nonexistent. Then what? It comes down to a question of an appeal to the marketplace of ideas in a democratic society assessing the relative merits of opposing positions as to the relevance of international law. The position argued in these essays is that international law interpreted in the spirit of world order that gave rise to the UN Charter and the formulation of norms governing recourse to international force supported the view that military intervention after 1965 – when the war was extended to North Vietnam – was a criminal enterprise.[10]

Seventhly, the balance of persuasion on policy and law shifts depending on battlefield outcomes. As long as a war is being won at what are perceived to be acceptable costs in casualties and resources, few questions are raised. Patriotism and nationalism cloud critical faculties even in democratic

---

[8] Other motivations include freedom from the remnants of "the Vietnam Syndrome" inhibiting American uses of force in pursuit of its grand global strategy, despite what George H. W. Bush said after the Gulf War of 2001.

[9] Guenter Lewy, *America in Vietnam* (New York: Oxford University Press, 1978); see also John Norton Moore and Robert F. Turner, eds., *The Real Lessons of the Vietnam War: Reflections Twenty-Five Years After the Fall of Saigon* (Durham, NC: Carolina Academic Press, 2002).

[10] See Part I of this volume.

societies, and render law a servant of power. If the war goes badly, then criticism from various perspectives, including law, begins to carry weight.

This is what happened in the Vietnam context. At first, there was very little discussion of its legally controversial character but, as the war went on and casualties mounted, criticism from an international law perspective, culminating in an argument that the perpetrators were subject to indictment for violations of international criminal law, gained mainstream political traction. It became influential in anti-war circles where moderate politicians and media gurus increasingly expressed their objections to the war by reference to international law.

Eighthly, even where there exists an authoritative decision as to the requirements of international law, enforcement is problematic, especially if a geopolitical actor is the culprit. This right of exception available to geopolitical actors is given a constitutional foundation in the form of veto power vested in the five permanent members of the UN Security Council. In effect, this right of veto legalizes a discriminatory approach to international law, especially when it comes to contested uses of international force. Beyond this constitutional provision, the dominant status of the United States in diplomatic circles gives its veto right the additional leverage provided by geopolitical muscle. Such discrimination diminishes the legitimacy of international law, allowing it to be declared that it is a legal order that imposes accountability on the weak and grants impunity to the strong. Such a generalization is only partially accurate, as there is a postcolonial pushback in a number of sectors of international law as a result of counterhegemonic successes in neutralizing some of the disparities of hard power embodied in legal rules and procedures.

Ninthly, the weakness of the international legal order with respect to controlling recourse to force by the governments of geopolitically significant sovereign states gives a crucial role to civil society. This became evident in the course of the Vietnam War. It was the anti-war movement, animated by the costs of a war with such a dubious strategic rationale, rather than by an awakening to the illegality of the war and its tactics, that exerted the greatest pressure on the political leadership of the United States and eventually led it to seek an exit strategy in Vietnam, ideally one that would disguise its defeat.[11] In important respects, it was civil society and international public opinion

---

[11] See, for instance, the insistence of Henry Kissinger and Richard Nixon that the United States achieve "peace with honor" in Vietnam, which was interpreted to mean "a decent interval" between a ceasefire and the withdrawal of American combat forces. For discussion, see Philip Zelikow, "No Peace, No Honor: Nixon, Kissinger, and Betrayal in Vietnam," *Foreign Affairs*, 80, 5 (Sep.–Oct. 2001), 156–57.

that took international law seriously as a major criterion by which to condemn the Vietnam War policies. This condemnation from a legal perspective was most clearly and influentially carried forth by the civil society tribunal convened by the British philosopher, Bertrand Russell. Although condemned at the time of the proceedings as a one-sided inquiry without any grounding in law, the authority of such undertakings has gained support over the years, and the record of the Russell proceedings provides the most comprehensive documentation of the violations of international criminal law.[12] It is still the case, despite the presence since 2002 of the International Criminal Court, that assessments of international law, where the accusing finger is pointed at a geopolitically significant actor, are more likely to be forthcoming from informal civil society proceedings than from this international institutional innovation endowed with judicial authority. At the same time, the leverage of civil society is limited, as the leadup to the Iraq War illustrates; the largest anti-war demonstrations in world history early in 2003 had no inhibiting effect on the US/UK decision to attack Iraq, nor did the Iraq War Tribunal have much of a bearing on the occupation policy, although contributing, at least regionally, to the sense of illegitimacy surrounding the American presence in Iraq.[13]

Tenthly, given this complexity associated with the distinctive character of international law, a reality maximized when the geopolitically dominant political actor uses international force in a controversial manner against a marginal national society, the effectiveness of international law constraints depends heavily on a combination of civil society activism and governmental self-restraint. The essential policy argument of my approach to the international law issues raised by the Vietnam War is that an interpretation of the legal restraints embodied in the UN Charter and customary international law reflective of their anti-war motivations serves both the national interest of the United States and the global interest of the peoples of the world. Such a view challenges those who argue that the international practice and precedents set by the United States with respect to the use of force benefit world order.[14]

---

[12] For the Russell Tribunal, see John Duffett, ed., *Against the Crime of Silence: Proceedings of the International War Crimes Tribunal* (New York: Simon & Schuster, 1968); see also Richard Falk, Irene Gendzier, and Robert Jay Lifton, eds., *Crimes of War: Iraq* (New York: Nation Books, 2006).

[13] See Müge Gürsoy Sökmen, ed., *World Tribunal on Iraq: Making the Case Against War* (Northampton, MA: Olive Branch Press, 2008).

[14] The most notorious of geopolitical apologists for the American global role is Michael Mandelbaum. Among several books see, especially, Mandelbaum, *The Case for Goliath: How America Acts as the World Government in the Twenty-First Century* (New York: Public Affairs, 2005).

Eleventh, in the end the choice of international law orientations reflects two broad underlying perceptions: What works given the historical circumstances of the past hundred years? What kind of world should we be seeking to establish over the course of the next one hundred years? The answers given here are clear. Accepting the constraints of an interpretation of law and war conforms to the new balance of forces as between international interventionary and societal resistance capacities is a world-order imperative in the present historical conjuncture. This new balance is what explains the outcome of colonial wars and of numerous other conflicts. Accepting it, rather than seeking to ignore it, avoids recourse to warfare that is destructive and in the end self-defeating. The Vietnam outcome could not have been more contrary to American goals, and yet it had no negative strategic effects, and in the long run probably accords even with national interests. Yet the war effort caused millions of casualties, destroyed many cities and villages, and introduced the ravages of environmental warfare whose toxic effects linger to this day. As we move forward in this century, facing the challenges of climate change, globalization and interdependence, disease control, and nuclear weaponry, the minimization of such warfare seems a prime unacknowledged dimension of sustainability, and compliance with and respect for international law as interpreted from a progressive world-order perspective are desirable goals.

Twelfth, given the rise of nonstate political actors capable of inflicting major harm on target societies, it seems clear that a more flexible rendering of international law is justified in relation to such provocations. This flexibility should be based on authorizations to use force provided by the United Nations and by a new framework of international humanitarian law agreed upon by governments to supplement the Geneva Conventions and the Geneva Protocols. That is, if international law designed to prohibit aggressive uses of force, as in military interventions, is overgeneralized to apply to all uses of force, then it will be overridden in practice by the urgencies of upholding national security given the nature of current mega-terrorist threats. In this regard, it is important to calibrate the role of international law with the evolving realities of state-centric world order.[15]

Thirteenth, part of the unlearned lessons of Vietnam is the relevance of root causes of conflict and violence. The American failure to comprehend the French defeat in Indochina, or suppose that it could escape the colonial stigma, reflected an inability to realize that for the Vietnamese people

---

[15] Richard Falk, *The Declining World Order: America's Imperial Geopolitics* (New York: Routledge, 2004).

"nationalism" was a primary and unconditional motivation, justifying paying high costs for resistance, and that the ideological alignment of the governing process was secondary. In relation to transnational political extremism, the provocative nature of military intervention and the perception of the United States as responsible for upholding oppressive dictators in the region should be appreciated. With such an understanding, it becomes unrealistic and self-defeating to believe and act on the view that the best line of response is via reliance on militarist tactics.[16]

CONCLUDING OBSERVATIONS

After almost seven years of deliberations, an inquiry into the United Kingdom's involvement in the Iraq War, under the chairmanship of Sir John Chilcot, issued a 6,000-page report of 2.3 million words, with a 150-page executive summary, that casts serious doubt on the integrity of then Prime Minister Tony Blair's submissions to Parliament and, although overly restrained and nationalistic in its conclusions, makes evident that recourse to war against Iraq was not legally justified.[17] There was also no compliance with the UN Charter requirement of recourse to force as a last resort. The overall impact of the Chilcot Report is hard to assess, although it did prompt some members of Parliament to suggest that the Report gives grounds for Blair's retroactive impeachment.

More significant in the context of revisiting the Vietnam War was the absence of any American initiative comparable to the Chilcot inquiry in relation to either the Vietnam or Iraq Wars. This absence of any formal public scrutiny of foreign policy disasters reflects the resistance of the American political establishment and citizenry to any objective appraisal of controversial recourse to force even after the fact and with the purpose of developing an improved governmental decision process in the future and some semblance of accountability and transparency with respect to past official behavior. The Chilcot process is a far cry from the sort of punitive judicial process relied upon to determine the culpability of German and Japanese leaders after World War II or even the tribunal set up by the UN Security Council to prosecute crimes under international law associated with the breakup of former Yugoslavia and genocidal events in Rwanda.

---

[16] For critique of militarist thinking as the basis of counterterrorist policy, see Richard Falk, "Failure of Militarism," *Perspectives of Terrorism*, 10, 4 (2016), 53–63.

[17] See John Chilcot and Lawrence Freedman, eds., *Iraq Report: The Full Chilcot Report* (Coventry, UK: Penny Press, 2016).

Nevertheless, Chilcot is an impressive display of the British wish to learn from their mistakes. As the Report itself makes clear, what went mostly wrong in committing to the Iraq War was a series of procedural errors associated with insufficient use of cabinet-level collective discussion prior to a decision to use international force, shaping such a policy on the basis of inconclusive intelligence, and insufficient planning for the postinvasion occupation phase. With an almost total disregard of the relevance of international law, the Chilcot Report leaves a reader with the following geopolitically oriented, normatively disappointing conclusion: "Above all, the lesson is that all aspects of any intervention need to be calculated, debated, and challenged with the utmost rigour."[18]

Against this background, it is particularly regrettable and discouraging that there has been a total absence of any concerted official effort in the United States to consider whether international law was violated as a result of these two major wars, Vietnam and Iraq, that have both had such severe negative consequences for the peoples affected and for the quality of world order. After such failures, it would have at least seemed prudent to determine whether American interests and values would be better served by respecting international law as interpreted in the spirit of the UN Charter in reliance on a progressive approach to world order, but the militarist grip on security policy is so strong that even gestures of evaluation are totally avoided.

The 2016 American presidential campaign did show some ad hoc recognition by several anti-establishment candidates that the kind of regime-changing interventions carried out in the Middle East were not serving American interests, and should be avoided in the future. This is a prudential step in the right direction, but it is not enough. What the writings collected here seek to demonstrate, above all, is that the indispensable missing ingredient in the policymaking process on war/peace issues is deference to international law as inscribed in the UN Charter, affirmed by the International Court of Justice, and supported widely by expert opinion and the views of the public. Unfortunately, there is no indication that such deference will be forthcoming without fundamental changes brought about by civil society activism. In this respect, it may be necessary to again convene a tribunal formed by world citizens, as was done by the Russell Tribunal in the midst of the Vietnam War, this time with the goal of insisting that foreign policy of all countries be implemented with due respect for international law and the authority of the United Nations.

---

[18] Sir John Chilcot's public statement, July 6, 2016, www.iraqinquiry.org.uk/the-inquiry/sir-john-chilcots-public-statement/.

Index

9/11, xxviii, 390, 391, 392, 395

ABM (anti-ballistic missile) system, 336
Abu Ghraib, xxviii
Acheson, Dean, 319
ad hoc tribunal at The Hague, 300
Afghanistan, xxi, xxvii, xxviii, 391
Agent Orange, xix
aggression, xv, xvi, xxi, 20, 21, 22, 23, 24, 26, 31,
    32, 42, 43, 46, 50, 51, 53, 55, 56, 58, 64,
    65, 66, 69, 70, 71, 72, 73, 75, 79, 81, 85,
    99, 103, 106, 109, 111, 116, 117, 126, 129, 131,
    132, 133, 134, 135, 136, 141, 146, 152, 153,
    156, 167, 173, 174, 182, 210, 219, 220, 222,
    226, 232, 236, 237, 244, 249, 265, 278, 281,
    293, 303, 309, 310, 311, 312, 313, 318, 323,
    333, 339, 341, 343, 345, 352, 356, 390, 394
Al Qaeda, xxviii
Algeria, xxv, xxvi, 34, 40, 47, 158, 181, 394
Alliance of National, Democratic, and Peace
    Forces, 3, 10, 11, 158
"American Tragedy," xvi, 303, 304, 308, 317
anti-personnel land mines, 322
anti-war movement, xxvii, xxxi, 190, 389,
    392, 396
April Manifesto of the Alliance, 13, 158
armed attack, 21, 22, 23, 25, 26, 29, 31, 33, 34,
    41, 43, 44, 45, 47, 48, 50, 51, 56, 57, 58,
    64, 75, 79, 83, 95, 96, 97, 98, 99, 100, 102,
    103, 108, 109, 111, 112, 122, 141, 148, 151, 156,
    167, 226, 227, 237, 238, 239, 243, 244, 272,
    356, 367
Armenian genocide of 1915, 386

Armstrong, Karl (Karleton), xix, 255, 259, 287,
    291, 292, 293, 294, 295, 296, 297, 298, 299
arrogance of power, xxvi
Arusha, 328
atmospheric nuclear testing, 148
atomic war, 142
Attorney General for International Affairs, US
    (proposed), 143
Auschwitz, 179, 308, 318

Baldwin, Hanson, 336, 368, 371, 372
Baldwin, James, 381
Basso, Lelio, xvii
Battle of Algiers, 180
Bennett, John, 209, 381
Berlin, 24, 25, 265, 278, 382
Berrigan, Daniel and Philip, 170, 262, 291, 324
Bertrand Russell Archives, ix, x, xvii
Bertrand Russell War Crimes Tribunal, 287
"best and brightest," 191
bin Laden, Osama, 392
Blair, Tony, 399
boat people, 199
Bretton Woods, 316
British Empire, xxv
Brownlie, Ian, 98, 99
Brzezinski, Zbigniew Kazimierz, 143
Budapest Argument, 154
Bull, Hedley, 301, 314, 316
Bundy, McGeorge, 347
Bunker, Ellsworth, 344
Buttinger, Joseph, 6, 14, 91, 106, 108, 151
Byrne, Matthew, 257